INFORMATION SYSTEMS
in organizations

D1402877

INFORMATION SYSTEMS
in organizations
PEOPLE, TECHNOLOGY, and PROCESSES

Patricia Wallace

Johns Hopkins University

PEARSON

Boston   Columbus   Indianapolis   New York   San Francisco   Upper Saddle River   Amsterdam
Cape Town Dubai   London   Madrid   Milan   Munich   Paris   Montreal   Toronto   Delhi   Mexico City   Sao Paulo
Sydney   Hong Kong   Seoul   Singapore   Taipei   Tokyo

Editorial Director: Sally Yagan
Executive Editor: Bob Horan
Director of Development: Steve Deitmer
Editorial Project Manager: Kelly Loftus
Editorial Assistant: Ashlee Bradbury
Director of Marketing: Maggie Moylan
Senior Marketing Manager: Anne Fahlgren
Senior Managing Editor: Judy Leale
Production Project Manager: Ann Pulido
Media Project Manager, Production: Lisa Rinaldi
Media Project Manager: Allison Longley
Senior Operations Supervisor: Arnold Vila
Operations Specialist: Maura Zaldivar
Associate Director of Design: Blair Brown
Art Director, Text and Cover Designer: Kathryn Foot
Full-Service Project Management: Sharon Anderson/Bookmasters, Inc.
Composition: Integra
Printer/Binder: Courier/Kendallville
Cover Printer: Courier/Kendallville
Text Font: 10/12 Times

Credits and acknowledgments borrowed from other sources and reproduced, with permission, in this textbook appear on the appropriate page within text.

Microsoft® and Windows® are registered trademarks of the Microsoft Corporation in the U.S.A. and other countries. Screen shots and icons reprinted with permission from the Microsoft Corporation. This book is not sponsored or endorsed by or affiliated with the Microsoft Corporation.

Copyright © 2013 by Pearson Education, Inc., publishing as Prentice Hall. All rights reserved. permission should be obtained from the publisher prior to any prohibited reproduction, storage in a retrieval system, or transmission in any form or by any means, electronic, mechanical, photocopying, recording, or likewise. To obtain permission(s) to use material from this work, please submit a written request to Pearson Education, Inc., Permissions Department, One Lake Street, Upper Saddle River, New Jersey 07458, or you may fax your request to 201-236-3290.

Many of the designations by manufacturers and sellers to distinguish their products are claimed as trademarks. Where those designations appear in this book, and the publisher was aware of a trademark claim, the designations have been printed in initial caps or all caps.

Library of Congress Cataloging-in-Publication Data
Wallace, Patricia.
  Information systems in organizations / Patricia Wallace.—1st ed.
    p. cm.
  Includes bibliographical references and index.
  ISBN 978-0-13-611562-5
    1. Organizational change. 2. Management information systems. I. Title.
  HD58.8.W345 2013
  658.4'038011—dc23

                      2011022146

10 9 8 7 6 5 4 3 2 1

ISBN 10:   0-13-611562-4
ISBN 13: 978-0-13-611562-5

To Callie, Julian, and a bright future
of human-centered computing.

About the Author

Pat Wallace is currently Senior Director for Information Technology and Online Programs at Johns Hopkins University Center for Talented Youth. Before joining JHU, she was Chief, Information Strategies, and Executive Director, Center for Knowledge Management, at the Robert H. Smith School of Business, University of Maryland, College Park. She also teaches technology management courses as Adjunct Professor in the MBA Program of the Graduate School of Management and Technology, University of Maryland University College, where she previously served as CIO for 10 years. Wallace earned her Ph.D. in psychology at the University of Texas at Austin and holds an M.S. in Computer Systems Management (databases and security track).

Brief Contents

Contents

CHAPTER **2**

Information Systems and Strategy *34*

CHAPTER **3**

Information and Communications Technologies: The Enterprise Architecture *68*

CHAPTER 4

Managing Information Resources with Databases   *104*

CHAPTER **5**

Information Systems for the Enterprise   *140*

The Web and E-Commerce *178*

Business Intelligence and Decision Support *210*

CHAPTER **8**

Collaborating with Technology *244*

CHAPTER 9

Knowledge Management and E-Learning   *276*

Ethics, Privacy, and Security *312*

Systems Development and Procurement *346*

CHAPTER 12

Project Management and Strategic Planning   *378*

Preface

Introduction

How can we engage our students in the *real* world of information systems, beyond the smartphone apps, cool web sites, and lively games they already know? To capture their attention and turn them on to this fast-moving (and well-paid) field, we need a stunningly current text with examples and topics that reach right into their lives. It should offer tips they can use *now to* gain their own competitive edge, and it should prepare them to land running when they enter a fiercely competitive job market. They should converse intelligently on their first interview, familiar with the jargon and heated debates, on topics such as business intelligence, text mining, social network analysis, e-learning, net neutrality, 4G, cloud computing, and black swans. And the text should do all of this efficiently, not in 600+ pages. For example, with the convergence of information and communications technologies, combining hardware, software, and telecom in a single chapter with enterprise architecture as the umbrella shows students the whole picture in an efficient way.

The text should also show why this field is as much about people as it is about technology. (Having been a CIO and head of an IT department much of my career, along with holding a Ph.D. in psychology and M.S. in computer systems management, I relearn this fact daily.) As for online supplements, PowerPoints and talking-head videos are helpful, but why not creatively apply some of our disruptive innovations to teaching? We should have interactive, role-playing simulations that draw students into realistic and sometimes tense situations where they make difficult choices that have consequences.

Key Features: What Makes This Text Different?

THE HUMAN ELEMENT IN INFORMATION SYSTEMS

This text takes a fresh perspective on the introductory course in information systems, one that combines comprehensive and up-to-date coverage with a stronger focus on the human element. It covers all the major topics for the course in a rigorous way, without skimping on any of the fundamentals. But it enriches those topics with probing discussions about the roles people play in building, shaping, implementing, and sometimes obstructing information systems. In the chapter that covers disaster recovery planning (12), for instance, students learn how to avoid common cognitive biases as they assess risks. In the chapter on collaborative technologies (8), readers gain insights about how different technologies and communication channels can unexpectedly alter the impression they make on others. They learn how to choose the best channel for each task to support virtual teamwork, management, negotiation, and leadership. Another chapter (9) shows how the human element can hinder attempts to capture intellectual capital because employees perceive more incentives for hoarding knowledge than for sharing it.

The processes and policies that people devise to manage information systems also receive more attention in this text. For example, students learn how organizational policies about appropriate use and ownership come about, and what impact they have on how employees use the systems (12). They find out that legal liability for workplace harassment drives employers to use surveillance, more so than qualms about "cyberslacking" (10). The book stresses how the four components of an information system—people, technology, processes, and data—are interconnected, and why an "information system" is so much more than bits, bytes, microchips, and spinning hard drives.

The grand battles over technology directions also draw in the human element. The text and case studies show why organizations around the world have a significant stake in the outcomes of debates over net neutrality, 4G standards, cloud computing, search engine optimization, behavioral targeting, and many other timely issues. These illustrate how business strategy, human motivations, and technology converge, and billions of dollars are on the line for the winners and losers. Yet most people know little about these battlegrounds because the underlying technology issues are out of reach. After reading this text, students will look at online ads, privacy policies, social networks, and their own smartphones with a new appreciation for the fierce business competitions unfolding before their eyes.

The text recognizes the growth in the number of women, minorities, international students, online students, and nontraditional students who enroll in this course, drawing on examples and settings that will resonate with them. Devon, for instance, is starting her own web design business, and students learn about relational databases by helping her build one for her small business (4). International student Prakash is the cofounder of *Leveling Up*, a smartphone app that is the centerpiece for the interactive role-playing simulation on business strategy (2). In the chapter on knowledge management and e-learning (9), Sally takes an online course in nonprofit management as she nears retirement and helps her own company build an e-learning course for the coworkers she's leaving behind.

BUSINESS, GOVERNMENT, AND NONPROFITS: BROADER COVERAGE OF DIFFERENT TYPES OF ORGANIZATIONS AND THE ROLES STUDENTS PLAY

A second objective for this new text was to broaden the coverage to include all the varied settings in which students work (or will work) and in which information systems are essential. Examples are drawn from multinational corporations, nonprofits, government agencies, midsized businesses, startups, charities, volunteer organizations, student clubs, and other settings. The text highlights how these different organizations draw on information systems to fulfill their missions, from generating profits to attracting donations.

The technologies and strategies that underlie cell-phone marketing, for instance, work as effectively for nonprofits that want to mobilize citizens as they do for businesses that tempt new customers with discount coupons. And strategic advantage is not just for business. Charities compete for volunteers and donations too, and the text underscores how CRM works for organizations such as an Australian Wildlife Rescue operation or Chicago's YMCA (2).

Just as students are gaining employment in a wide variety of organizations, they are taking on more varied roles within them. Though some will become CIOs or information systems managers, many will be engaged with information systems in other capacities—as consultants, business analysts, accountants, marketing professionals, human resources managers, volunteers, virtual team leaders, forensic specialists, legal advisors, contractors, and project managers.

Examples in the text, case studies, and simulations feature all these different roles, showing how successful information systems emerge from a broad base of stakeholders with different perspectives and specialties. Carlos, for instance, is the instructional designer on a corporate e-learning course development team, adding his knowledge of usability and accessibility for people with disabilities (9). In Chapter 11, Lily is a senior manager for an online grocery who comes up with a clever web site to capture a valuable market—busy singles who forgot to buy groceries.

THE ETHICAL FACTOR

Ethical concerns weave throughout the text, touching on very human ethical dilemmas such as the one Wikipedia founder Jimmy Wales faced when asked to delete any posts that mentioned the name of a journalist kidnapped by the Taliban. That action was directly opposed to his site's fervent commitment to free speech, and Wales raised a firestorm within the Wikipedia community when he reluctantly tried to comply.

Through a survey in Chapter 10, students learn more about how they each judge situations that involve information ethics, discovering that most people relax their call for punishment when computers and the Internet are used to violate intellectual property laws through plagiarism or copyright infringement.

A special feature in each chapter titled "*The Ethical Factor*" explores timely ethical issues such as corporate responsibility in extended supply chains or attempts to counteract flash mob violence by cutting off mobile messaging services. The privacy implications of facial recognition software that automatically tags people's faces on the public web are profound and explored in the chapter on business intelligence (7). Google's former CEO, Eric Schmidt, called that technology "even too creepy for Google." In the chapter on databases (4), ethical dilemmas come up as design questions. For instance, should ethnicity really be a 1:1 relationship for each individual? Most databases are designed that way, but studies of Medicare data suggest that design can result in misleading and biased conclusions about health outcomes.

"PRODUCTIVITY TIPS" FOR STUDENTS: PERSONAL AND PRACTICAL

A text becomes more meaningful when students can apply what they learn right away in their own lives. They will benefit from the Productivity Tips that appear in every chapter that point to ways they can improve their own productivity and gain some competitive advantage from the clever application of information systems.

In the chapter on information systems and strategy, for instance, a tip invites students to check out the software trial versions that came pre-installed on their computers to see how companies leverage this valuable product positioning, and then remove them to save space and improve the computer's performance. A tip in the section on neural nets advises students to alert their credit card companies before traveling abroad because a neural net may trigger a very ill-timed block on the card when it detects unusual purchasing behavior (7). Another tip suggests that students consider adding a second monitor to double screen real estate and reduce printing (3). Research shows solid productivity gains associated with that simple step, and students squinting at small laptop screens will cheer when they plug one in and see how helpful it is.

INTERACTIVE ROLE-PLAYING SIMULATIONS FOR EXPERIENTIAL LEARNING

Any course on information systems should tap their power for active, experiential learning. This text includes interactive role-playing simulations to dramatize the topics and challenge students to make smart decisions. They enter realistic and often tense situations, interacting with the characters via simulated smartphone or laptop, and using e-mail, text messages, web conferencing, video chat, voice mail, dashboards, ordering screens, and other applications. These online simulations are made available through MyMISLab only. Please contact your Pearson sales representative for details and access.

In *The World of Mammals* that accompanies Chapter 1, students help the harried director of a wild animal preserve interview candidates for the CIO position, after the former CIO left abruptly. Then in *Devil's Canyon* (3), entrepreneurs need the student's advice to choose the best-fitting enterprise architecture for their new mountain resort, weighing pros and cons of cloud computing, software as a service, an on-premise data center, and telecommunication services as the costs mount. Some simulations embed quantitative analysis and decision making, such as *Chocolate Lovers Unite*, in which the student settles a heated company debate over which online marketing pitch for the candy works best using weekly experiments and web analytics (7).

An important goal for these simulations is to help students learn the key terms and concepts, not just by memorizing definitions but by experiencing how they are used by real people in real conversations. The student's decisions affect the outcome and behavior of the other characters, as they draw on the chapter content and their critical thinking skills to answer questions and choose wisely. Sometimes tempers flare, as they do in *Green Wheeling*, the simulation on the software development life cycle (11). Here, the student plays the role of a volunteer fund-raiser for a college's drive to purchase a fleet of electric cars. The campaign is in total disarray, with volunteers bumping into one another and data so obsolete that embarrassed fund-raisers are soliciting deceased alums. They need a new information system badly, and the team struggles to identify priorities and make the "build or buy" decision. The computer-generated characters have strong personalities and bring their own agendas, so students experience a taste of how these situations actually unfold. Students can also answer discussion questions at the end, and they receive feedback on their choices, including points earned for any scored elements.

I've done research on games and simulations in education, and have been the principal investigator on several projects to create software that draws on the compelling features of these environments for learning. While online flash cards, Q&A games, and other interactive applications can help students memorize terms or review the chapter contents, simulations that immerse students in a relevant and authentic case can do more. Research shows they create engagement, improve learning outcomes, and build critical thinking skills through active, student-centered involvement.

Professors might use a simulation as an innovative way to deliver an interactive lecture, pausing to add comments and examples, and engaging students in debate over which decisions the class should make. If students do them independently or in teams, they can e-mail or print their results including tallies from scored choices and their responses to the discussion questions.

INTERNATIONAL EMPHASIS AND GLOBALIZATION

Information systems play a key role in globalization, especially through the Internet and all the creative destruction it unleashed. Examples abound throughout the text, highlighting how Baidu captured the search engine market in China (2) or how Ikea manages a global supply chain (5). The global financial crises underscore the important work of the International Accounting Standards Board—to promote transparent and enforceable financial reporting for companies around the world using XBRL tags— from the XML family of standards (5).

The international emphasis also unfolds in working relationships across national borders. For example, the chapter on collaboration (8) follows a team planning a campaign to launch a string of clubs in several major cities, and the team's members hail from Dallas, Texas, and Hong Kong. As they use collaborative technologies that span the Pacific, this dynamic virtual team works through differences in time zones, communication styles, and also culture.

INFORMATION SYSTEMS: A DYNAMIC AND PROMISING FUTURE CAREER

Finally, a major goal of this text and its supplements is to convey the sheer excitement and limitless potential of this field, with an eye toward inspiring students to go further. Inside are countless examples of how savvy men and women leverage information systems to transform organizations of all stripes, and even build new empires.

Some of the excitement comes from ground-breaking technological advances, such as IBM's "Watson"—the supercomputer that competed on "Jeopardy!" and soundly trounced the game's human champs in a dramatic live broadcast. The disruptive innovations that topple some industries and open star-studded paths for others are also part of the excitement. The Internet dealt crushing blows to print newspapers, for instance, as classified advertisers turned to Craigslist, and customers canceled their paid subscriptions in favor of online news sources.

The human element adds to the excitement and potential. Facebook founder Mark Zuckerberg said he created his site to empower people to share. That simple understanding of how an information system might align with human motivations led to a worldwide blockbuster with over a half-billion users. The innovative teams at Apple perform similar magic with their engineering designs that delight human beings. In each chapter, short "Did You Know?" snippets highlight a contemporary application of information systems, one that students relate to easily. In the section on artificial intelligence (7), for instance, students learn how libraries are benefiting each time someone resolves one of those annoying CAPTCHAs, because the answers help digitize very old books with those odd and blurry fonts.

If students catch some of this energy and enthusiasm, they may decide to pursue this field. With a growing shortage of information systems professionals, we need them. They will have outstanding career prospects in the private and public sectors, and they'll never be bored.

Supplements

The following supplements are available at the Online Instructor Resource Center, accessible through www.pearsonhighered.com/wallace:

INSTRUCTOR'S MANUAL

The Instructor's Manual, assembled by Jonathan Whitaker of the University of Richmond, includes a list of learning objectives and answers to all end-of-chapter questions.

TEST ITEM FILE

The Test Item File, prepared by ANSR Source, Inc., contains more than 1,300 questions, including multiple choice, true/false, and essay. Each question is followed by the correct answer, the learning objective it ties to, page reference, and difficulty rating. In addition, certain questions are tagged to the appropriate AACSB category.

POWERPOINT PRESENTATIONS

The Instructor PowerPoints, prepared by Jonathan Whitaker of the University of Richmond, highlight text learning objectives and key topics and serve as an excellent aid for classroom presentations and lectures.

IMAGE LIBRARY

This collection of the figures and tables from the text offers another aid for classroom presentations and PowerPoint slides.

TESTGEN

Pearson Education's test-generating software is available from www.pearsonhighered.com/irc. The software is PC/MAC compatible and preloaded with all of the Test Item File questions. You can manually or randomly view test questions and drag-and-drop to create a test. You can add or modify test-bank questions as needed. Our TestGens are converted for use in BlackBoard and WebCT. These conversions can be found on the Instructor's Resource Center. Conversions to Moodle, D2L, or Angel can be requested through your local Pearson Sales Representative.

MyMISLab (www.mymislab.com)

MyMISLab is an easy-to-use online tool that personalizes course content and provides robust assessment and reporting to measure individual and class performance. All of the resources you need for course success are in one place—flexible and easily adapted for your course experience. Students can purchase access to MyMISLab with a Pearson eText of all chapters or without a Pearson eText by visiting www.mymislab.com. They can also purchase an access card packaged with the text from www.pearsonhighered.com at a reduced price.

COURSESMART

CourseSmart eTextbooks were developed for students looking to save on required or recommended textbooks. Students simply select their eText by title or author and purchase immediate access to the content for the duration of the course using any major credit card. With a CourseSmart eText, students can search for specific keywords or page numbers, take notes online, print out reading assignments that incorporate lecture notes, and bookmark important passages for later review. For more information or to purchase a CourseSmart eTextbook, visit www.coursesmart.com.

Acknowledgments

Many thanks go to all the reviewers who took time to comment on early drafts and contribute their insights about what they would really like to see in a new textbook for this dynamic field. Their feedback and suggestions were invaluable, and they help ensure this text will meet the needs of faculty and students.

Dennis Adams, *University of Houston*

Joni Adkins, *Northwest Missouri State University*

Sven Aelterman, *Troy University*

Solomon Antony, *Murray State University*

John Appleman, *State University of New York College at Brockport*

Bay Arinze, *Drexel University*

Janine Aronson, *University of Georgia*

John Kirk Atkinson, *Western Kentucky University*

Robert Balicki, *Cleary University*

Cynthia Barnes, *Lamar University*

Stephen Barnes, *Regis University*

Jon Beard, *George Mason University*

Hossein Bidgoli, *California State University—Bakersfield*

Robert Bonometti, *MGB Enterprises LLC*

Ted Boone, *University of Kansas*

David Bradbard, *Winthrop University*

Jason Chen, *Gonzaga University*

Joselina Cheng, *University of Central Oklahoma*

Steve Clements, *Eastern Oregon University*

Phillip Coleman, *Western Kentucky University*

Emilio Collar Jr., *Western Connecticut State University*

Steve Corder, *Williams Baptist College*

Dave Croasdell, *University of Nevada, Reno*

Albert Cruz, *National University*

Mohammad Dadashzadeh, *Oakland University*

Don Danner, *San Francisco State University*

Dessa David, *Morgan State University*

Carolyn Dileo, *Westchester Community College*

Michael Douglas, *Millersville University*

Doris Duncan, *California State University—East Bay*

Barbara Edington, *St. Francis College*

Kurt Engemann, *Iona College*

John Erickson, *University of Nebraska at Omaha*

William Figg, *Dakota State University*

David Firth, *The University of Montana*

Saiid Ganjalizadeh, *The Catholic University of America*

Richard Glass, *Bryant University*

Tanya Goette, *Georgia College & State University*

Sandeep Goyal, *University of Southern Indiana*

Martin Grossman, *Bridgewater State University*

Bin Gu, *University of Texas at Austin*

Laura Hall, *University of Texas—El Paso*

Rosie Hauck, *Illinois State University*

Jun He, *University of Michigan—Dearborn*

Devanandham Henry, *Stevens Institute of Technology*

Michelle Hepner, *University of Central Oklahoma*

Jerry Isaacs, *Carroll University*

Jon (Sean) Jasperson, *Texas A & M University*

Brian Jones, *Tennessee Technological University*

Junghwan Kim, *Texas Tech University*

Philip Kim, *Walsh University*

Sung-kwan Kim, *University of Arkansas at Little Rock*

Charles S. Knode, *University of Maryland University College*

Brian Kovar, *Kansas State University*

Bill Kuechler, *University of Nevada at Reno*

Louis LeBlanc, *Berry College*

Albert Lederer, *University of Kentucky*

Ingyu Lee, *Troy University*

Mary Locke, *Greenville Technical College*

Sanchita Mal-Sarkar, *Cleveland State University*

Nancy Martin, *Southern Illinois University Carbondale*

Prosenjit Mazumdar, *George Mason University*

Roger McHaney, *Kansas State University*

William McMillan, *Madonna University*

Tonya Melvin-Bryant, *North Carolina Central University*

Allison Morgan, *Howard University*

Fui Hoon (Fiona) Nah, *University of Nebraska—Lincoln*

Sandra Newton, *Sonoma State University*

Ravi Paul, *East Carolina University*

Adriane Randolph, *Kennesaw State University*

Betsy Ratchford, *University of Northern Iowa*

Mandy Reininger, *Chemeketa Community College*

Nicolas Rouse, *Phoenix College*

Paula Ruby, *Arkansas State University*

Werner Schenk, *University of Rochester*

Daniel Schmidt, *Washburn University*

Aaron Schorr, *Fashion Institute of Technology*

Paul Seibert, *North Greenville University*

Narcissus Shambare, *College of St. Mary*

Larry Smith, *Charleston Southern University*

Toni Somers, *Wayne State University*

Todd Stabenow, *Hawkeye Community College*

James Stewart, *University of Maryland University College*

Joe Teng, *Troy University Troy Campus*

Evelyn Thrasher, *Western Kentucky University*

Jan Tucker, *Argosy University*

Jonathan Whitaker, *University of Richmond*

Bruce White, *Quinnipiac University*

Anita Whitehill, *Mission College*

G. W. Willis, *Baylor University*

Marie Wright, *Western Connecticut State University*

Jigish Zaveri, *Morgan State University*

Chen Zhang, *Bryant University*

Thanks also go to the excellent work of the developmental editors, Peg Monahan, Elisa Adams, and Thomas Sigel. Ann Pulido, Kelly Loftus, Steve Deitmer, Ashlee Bradbury, Allison Longley, and Ben Paris at Pearson Education, and Sharon Anderson at Bookmasters also deserve special mention. As in any organization, there are many people behind the scenes whose efforts make all the difference in a project like this, and though unnamed, they deserve recognition and thanks.

I also want to thank Jollean K. Sinclaire of Arkansas State University, and Jonathan Whitaker of the University of Richmond, who made the end-of-chapter materials and instructor's manual into the best resources I've seen for a text like this. They are filled with thoughtful questions, engaging projects, and useful material for both students and faculty.

Many thanks to Bob Horan, my editor, whose commitment to this project has continued in high gear from the start. Bob has an uncanny talent for encouragement at just the right times, recognizing how very long it actually takes to write a new book, and I appreciate his deft instincts about what will work and what won't.

And finally, thanks to Julian and Callie, and also Kita, Lili, and Marlene, a list that includes my very supportive human family and our four-footed companions.

Your Feedback Is Welcome

To all of you who are using this book, as professors, teaching assistants, and students, I welcome your thoughts and feedback. Please email your comments, questions, and suggestions, and I'll be eager to hear how your course goes.

Patricia Wallace, Ph.D.
pwallace@jhu.edu

INFORMATION
SYSTEMS
in organizations

Information Systems and *People*

Chapter Preview

ON ENTERING THE WORLD OF INFORMATION SYSTEMS, you may wonder what you need to know about that world and what is important for your success. Most of you are already superconnected with computers, cell phones, software, and Internet access, so you have a head start on understanding how systems like these are critical for every organization. What you may not know, however, is what is behind the scenes—not the electronics or program code, but the real story of how information systems spring to life, how we can leverage them, and where we can take them in the future.

This opening chapter highlights information systems in action, the nature of information itself, and the four components of every information system. You will see how the information systems (IS) discipline is evolving and why a solid understanding of this subject will give you a special edge, regardless of your major or career path. Finally, the chapter examines the promises and perils of information systems and the many ethical issues that arise with the phenomenal power within everyone's reach.

© NetPics/Alamy

Google™ Street View

Maps

...ighborhoods at stre...

CHAPTER 1

Learning Objectives

1 Describe the main roles that information systems play in organizations.

2 Compare the terms *data, information,* and *knowledge* and describe three characteristics that make information valuable.

3 Describe the four main components of an information system and the role that each plays.

4 Identify several research areas in the discipline of management information systems (MIS).

5 Provide examples of how business, nonprofit, and government managers, and information technology departments, depend on information systems knowledge.

6 Explain how information systems present both promises and perils, and pose ethical questions.

Introduction

Google's mission statement started modestly enough—"to make it easier to find high-quality information on the web." Just 7 months after its founding, however, a far bolder goal appeared on its corporate website:

"Google's mission is to organize the world's information and make it universally accessible and useful."

Is such an audacious goal possible? The world's information covers quite a lot of territory, and more is created every moment. So far, though, Google is doing an astonishing job of organizing a rising stream of text, images, videos, maps, and data, and making it accessible at lightning speeds with just a few mouse clicks. The amount of hardware alone needed to pull off such a feat is staggering. When asked how many data centers Google operated, former CEO Eric Schmidt said, "I don't actually know."

That sounded a bit coy, so he added that there were dozens, many quite immense, and the number keeps growing.

Is Google's goal desirable? The ease with which we can track down information online has transformed the way we work, how we study, what we do in our personal lives, and what we can accomplish. The search engine enables a global marketplace, where tiny shops in India, Brazil, or anyplace else can promote their services to a worldwide audience. It also empowers every individual to find sources sounding off on just about any topic imaginable, however obscure or extreme.

Nevertheless, universal accessibility is certainly not appropriate for information that should be kept private and secure, beginning with your own medical and financial records. Sensitive government documents and corporate trade secrets merit protection as well.

Easy access may also not be appropriate for information that people simply do not want googled. Cofounder Sergei Brin once remarked, "How many people do you think had embarrassing information about them disclosed yesterday because of [using Google]? Zero, it never happens." He was mistaken, of course, as thousands of people have discovered—including Eric Schmidt himself. In a 30-minute online search, a reporter found Schmidt's net worth, his political views and fund-raising history, his hobbies, his home address, and even turn-by-turn directions to his house. When she published some of this, pointing out correctly that many people might be uncomfortable that so much personal information is now universally accessible, Schmidt was appalled. As retaliation, Google refused to answer any questions from the reporter or her news outlet for a year.[1]

Unless a case can be made that the public has a right to know, perhaps because of evidence of misconduct or crime, people may legitimately protest when personal information is collected or made available, and sometimes they succeed. When a resident in a small English town spotted a car taking snapshots of his home for Google's street view mapping application, he rounded up his neighbors to block the road and chase off the intruder (Figure 1-1).[2]

Information, whether or not Google makes it accessible, and whether it appears on the balance sheet, is an organization's most important asset. Creating, capturing, organizing, storing, retrieving, analyzing, and acting on information are fundamental activities in every organization. The skill with which you carry out those tasks will be the deciding factor, not just for your company's success, but for your own as well. This book is about information and the systems that people develop and manage to perform all those tasks and more.

You will see how these systems work, why they are created, how they have become the organization's central nervous system, and why they sometimes fail. You will also learn to tap the power of information systems to help your company compete or your organization become more effective. Finally, you will become more productive yourself—working smarter, not harder—in college, in your career, at home, and throughout your life.

Like the information they manage, information systems cover a very broad scope and contribute to many different activities in an organization. What roles do they play and how do they transform work? The next section shows the enormous variety of settings in which innovative information systems play a role, well beyond the very useful Google searches.

Information Systems in Action

1 Describe the main roles that information systems play in organizations.

▶ *American Idol* launched a smash hit by engaging more than 100 million television viewers around the world in an unusual kind of decision making. Hopeful singers compete each week, and audience members cast a vote for their favorite by phoning or sending text messages to the *Idol* hotline. An information system on the back end tallies the results. Some overeager fans cast hundreds of votes using homegrown information systems that do repeat dialing.

▶ California's Department of Motor Vehicles plans to use facial recognition software to analyze the photos of its 25 million drivers. The state hopes to combat identity theft by making sure the same person shows up from one renewal to the next.

▶ Walmart, one of the world's biggest companies and worth more than $350 billion, pioneered the globe's most efficient information system to track shipments as they move from supplier factories to warehouses to retail stores. Tags attached to pallets transmit information wirelessly, so Walmart execs know exactly where merchandise is in the supply chain and can spot trouble immediately.

When those bulky computers first entered company basements in the 1970s, the term *information system* brought up images of payroll programs, general ledgers, invoice tracking, and inventory management. Those back-office functions are still critically important, but today's information systems have migrated into every facet of an organization, touching every employee from the mail clerk to the CEO. They also extend well beyond the company's boundaries, reaching out to customers, clients, suppliers, partners, citizens, and all kinds of stakeholders. Their hardware might be as vast as Google's data centers or far smaller than Walmart's pallet tags. And their connections could be the thick fiber-optic cables on the ocean floor or electromagnetic waves in the air around you.

Multinational firms, small businesses, nonprofits, governments, volunteer organizations, self-employed entrepreneurs, universities, and every other type of organization rely on information systems for a host of reasons, and they continue to adapt, expand, and interconnect them to achieve their strategic objectives. These systems play critical roles in several contexts:

▶ Operations management
▶ Customer interactions
▶ Decision making
▶ Collaboration and teamwork
▶ Strategic initiatives and competitive advantage
▶ Individual productivity

FIGURE 1-1

Google's camera-equipped vehicles pan 360 degrees to collect street view images.

© JasonDoly/istockphoto.com

MANAGING OPERATIONS

Every successful organization must excel at **operations management**, which involves the design, operation, and improvement of the systems and processes the organization uses to deliver its goods and services. Some of these deal with several very basic functions that are part of every business. Information systems are crucial for tracking employee payroll, taxes, benefits, and timesheets. Accounting information systems are essential to track accounts receivable, to process

operations management
The area of management concerned with the design, operation, and improvement of the systems and processes the organization uses to deliver its goods and services.

transactions, to procure goods and services, and to pay the suppliers. Organizations also must manage their assets and inventories, from the computers and the desks they sit on to the massive factories and equipment located in far corners of the globe. If Eric Schmidt didn't know how many data centers Google managed, his back-office information systems certainly did.

Information systems designed to handle the processes involved in these functions must also meet compliance standards set by governments and other regulatory agencies, which may change from time to time and also vary by country or state. Reports must be filed, audits must be passed, and changing regulations must be followed. Extensive regulations put into place after the global financial crisis of 2009, for example, set tighter standards for accounting practices—particularly in banking—and demanded more transparency and reporting.

Many organizations choose commercially produced information systems to handle their back-office information needs, relying on software from companies such as SAP, Oracle, NetSuite, or QuickBooks. Some organizations are moving these functions to service providers or even outsourcing them entirely. India has become known as the world's "back office" because companies there manage these applications for a growing number of multinational corporations.[3]

Depending on their missions, organizations also need information systems to manage industry specific operations, such as these:

▶ Manufacturers need systems to manage assembly lines, product quality, production schedules, and just-in-time supply deliveries (Figure 1-2).
▶ Colleges and universities need systems to manage student academic records, class scheduling, faculty assignments, and student financial aid (Figure 1-3).
▶ Transportation companies rely on information systems equipped with GPS to track their fleets, optimize routes, and conserve gas.
▶ Companies that buy products from suppliers around the globe need real-time updates on their global supply chains to manage inventories and reduce costs.

FIGURE 1-2

Manufacturing information system displaying production volumes and other metrics.

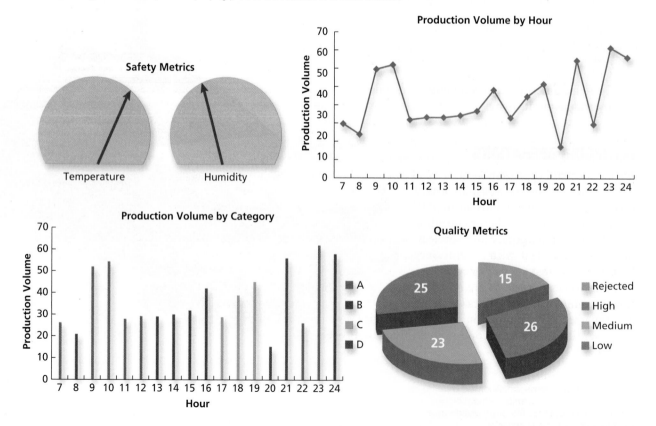

FIGURE 1-3

Student information system with online services for students and faculty.

MyCollege   MyTools   MyClasses   MyProfile

	Course	Days	Time	Location
Update contact info				
View schedules	Bus 111	MW	14:00–15:00	Macintyre
Submit request	Bus 111	MW	15:00–16:00	Doyle
View requirements	Bus 112	T-TH	9:00–10:45	Student Services
Register for courses	Bus 112	-	-	Online
	Bus 112	M	9:00–11:45	Garcia
	Bus 113	W	1:00–2:45	Doyle

Achieving excellence in operations can provide enormous cost savings and competitive advantage, as companies strive to shave every ounce of fat out of their processes without sacrificing quality. UPS drivers, for instance, know to avoid left turns on their delivery routes when possible, because they take a few seconds longer, wasting time and gas. Systems that support operations are discussed in Chapter 5.

SUPPORTING CUSTOMER INTERACTIONS

Interactions with customers, clients, students, patients, taxpayers, citizens, and others who come to your organization desiring a product or service are fundamental to success. Your customers—whether they are shoppers hunting for bargains, students hoping to graduate, retail stores buying your products to resell, or citizens applying for a visa— pay the bills. **Customer relationship management (CRM) systems**, discussed in Chapter 5, build and maintain relationships and support all the processes that underlie them.

A brick-and-mortar retail store, for example, needs a sales system that identifies each product in the shopper's basket, tallies the total, feeds the data to the inventory system, and accepts various kinds of payment. Checkout speed is paramount for shoppers, and clumsy, inefficient processes at this stage create a very bad impression. A survey of retailers found that modern point-of-sale technology was rated the most valuable element in customer satisfaction, including self-service checkout.[4] When an item lacks its bar code, impatient customers may just abandon it rather than wait for a salesclerk to track it down to confirm its price and ensure the product is properly deducted from inventory. Strategies to prevent theft, such as the check on weights added to the bag, also cause shoppers distress if they do not function properly.

Web-based front offices and online self-service applications transform an organization's relationships with its customers, freeing them from most routine direct contact. The information system processes often mimic the brick-and-mortar versions, with "shopping carts" and "checkouts" clearly labeled. Nevertheless, companies enhance their online front offices in many ways, not just to leave a good impression, but also to build stronger relationships and to better understand the motives and desires of each person who visits.

Scattered throughout Amazon.com's site, for example, are recommendations based on previous purchases, encouragements to "review this book" or "rate this item," special discounts and coupons, storage space for your wish lists and gift ideas, and many other innovative features to map out your preferences and build a stronger relationship. All of this data contributes to Amazon's customer relationship management excellence, generating an enormous capacity to understand each person, make recommendations, and predict behavior.

customer relationship management (CRM) system
An information system used to build customer relationships, enhance loyalty, and manage interactions with customers.

Infinite variations in customer interaction exist, from *American Idol*'s cell-phone voting to the Internal Revenue Service's e-file service. Organizations experiment with different strategies to improve the experience, trying to make their interactions more customer-centric and user-friendly. Developing these relationships is not just about improving sales and collecting receipts. It is about building long-term loyalty and satisfaction by listening to customers and learning what is most important to them. That also includes sensitivity to escalating concerns about privacy, as we discuss in Chapter 10.

MAKING DECISIONS

How do managers make decisions like these?

▶ Where should Starbucks open—or close—the next coffee shop?
▶ How much should Nintendo spend to develop new applications for the Wii console?
▶ Where should Hitachi build its new plant?
▶ When is the best time of year for the Red Cross to start its fund-raising campaign?
▶ Should universities require students to subscribe to the text message emergency notification system?

Managers make decisions every day, and many rely mainly on their own judgment. Indeed, researchers surveyed 250 executives and learned that 40 percent of major corporate decisions were based on gut instincts.[5] Smart managers, however, know that information systems support **data-driven decision making**, which draws on the billions of pieces of data that can be aggregated to reveal important trends and patterns. For example, historical trends will show when charitable giving peaks, and student records may reveal how many students list a cell phone as their main contact number.

Business intelligence, which collectively refers to all the information managers use to make decisions, can come from many sources beyond the organization's own operational systems. Combining Starbucks' store sales records with publicly available information about income levels by zip code, for example, could lead to smarter decisions. Tapping into the information systems of partners, suppliers, and distributors could improve Nintendo's decisions about Wii.

Decision support systems and business intelligence, discussed in Chapter 7, encompass a growing and varied category that blends rapid analysis of information sources with artificial intelligence and human knowledge. For knowledge workers, in particular, the value of knowing how to draw upon those vast mountains of information to make wise decisions is extremely high.

Did You Know?

Your online behavior is one of the most important sources of business intelligence. The sites you visit and the links you click reveal your interests and intentions, and marketers try to display ads that match. Spending for such targeted advertising may top $2.6 billion by 2014.

COLLABORATING ON TEAMS

Collaboration and teamwork have considerable support from innovative information systems that allow people to work together at any time and from any place. For example, geographically dispersed participants can hold online meetings, share documents and applications, and interact using microphones, video cameras, and whiteboards. **Social networking sites** support online communities of people who create profiles for themselves, form ties with others with whom they share interests, and make new connections based on those ties.[6] Major players such as Microsoft's Sharepoint offer tools to support project teams, with document management, forums, project updates, issue tracking, shared calendars, and varied communication capabilities.

The huge success of social networks prompts many corporations to launch experiments to see how their collaborative features could support business. Nicole Heckman, the manager of innovation research at FedEx, was astounded by how quickly the company's social networking site FaceNet took off. "We found it was much more viral than we expected. Over several months, we had 2,000 active users."[7]

Developing information systems to support collaborative human activities takes considerable ingenuity and attention to the ways in which people really do work together. The possibilities are endless, and different groups have varied preferences. In online university courses, for example, debates about whether students should turn on their webcams during virtual class sessions are common. Many prefer to keep them turned off, valuing the privacy that invisibility creates. One can doze off in a virtual class with little concern for detection.

The information systems that support virtual teamwork and collaboration, explored in Chapter 8, are in some respects still in their infancy—especially compared to the more mature operational systems. Facebook founder Mark Zuckerberg, whose social networking site attracts millions of users daily, said, "People are learning how to use the site and what's OK to share. As time goes on, people will learn what's appropriate, what's safe for them—and learn to share accordingly."[8] Expect many improvements as we learn more about what features work best for different contexts and purposes.

ACHIEVING STRATEGIC OBJECTIVES AND GAINING COMPETITIVE ADVANTAGE

Information systems potentially play their most valuable role when they are integrated closely with strategy and tied to the major initiatives that will help achieve strategic objectives—a topic we take up in Chapter 2. **Competitive advantage**, which is anything that gives a firm a lead over its rivals, can be gained through the development and application of innovative information systems. Increasingly, these systems are a core feature of a company's strategic vision. Indeed, that vision must be shaped to some extent by what information systems can achieve today and what is possible for the future.

Consider how one company achieved a competitive advantage in a crowded field of portable navigation devices from Garmin, Magellan, and others. Tiny Navigon, with just a bit above 0 percent of the market, jumped to 5 percent in a single month by including free traffic updates with its device. Widely considered a "killer application" that propels sales, the live traffic feature shows drivers updated reports on congestion, and the navigator suggests alternate routes. While Navigon's competitors charged subscribers annual fees for the service, the Navigon system taps FM radio stations from major cities that make up a central database of traffic information. Of course, competitive advantage is fleeting, and many of Navigon's competitors quickly followed suit.[9]

Strategy is equally important to nonprofit organizations and government agencies, and their information systems break considerable new ground by offering new services to the public, increasing access for all citizens, streamlining operations, reducing costs, and improving decision making. In Malaysia, for example, the government partners with Universiti Kebangsaan Malaysia in an innovative effort to identify especially talented youth, regardless of whether they reside in remote villages in Borneo or in wealthy Kuala Lumpur suburbs. University faculty designed a test that can be delivered online throughout the country's schools, which makes it accessible to students everywhere. Students who do well are tested further, and gain access to gifted education programs to nourish their special talents.

---

data-driven decision making
Decision making that draws on the billions of pieces of data that can be aggregated to reveal important trends and patterns.

competitive advantage
Anything that gives a firm a lead over its rivals; it can be gained through the development and application of innovative information systems.

business intelligence
The information managers use to make decisions, drawn from the company's own information systems or external sources.

social networking sites
Online communities of people who create profiles for themselves, form ties with others with whom they share interests, and make new connections based on those ties.

IMPROVING INDIVIDUAL PRODUCTIVITY

Tools to help people improve their own productivity on the job and in life abound, from the smartphones that combine voice calls with web browsing, contact databases, e-mail, music, and games, to the many software applications that eliminate tedious work. Even word processing has transformed work in every organization, and it offers numerous tools and add-ons that many people don't know about that can further improve individual productivity. Students, for example, can automatically create and properly format their term paper references by integrating a bibliographic manager such as EndNote or RefNote. Online libraries and reference databases offer links to export the citation in any format, so typing is unnecessary.

PRODUCTIVITY TIP

David Allen, author of the best-selling *Getting Things Done*, insists that his clients embrace information systems and technology to improve their productivity and manage their time. An example is his mandate to process your e-mail inbox to zero, performing triage with automated filtering tools as needed. An important goal is to stop wasting time on tasks that technology can do for you, and avoid becoming a slave to your e-mail.

To improve productivity at work, people can choose from a bewildering variety of computer software and electronic devices, but more is not necessarily better. It is best to select carefully, with an eye to the functions you need most, integration with your favorite applications, ease of use, and short learning curves. No one likes reading thick instruction manuals. Throughout this book, you will see productivity tips in boxes—like the ones on this page—that will help you improve your own productivity.

PRODUCTIVITY TIP

Once you leave student status behind, you'll be hard-pressed to find the academic discounts and freebies on software and hardware you can get now. Check for educational discounts offered by your college or university, or by the technology company, before you buy.

> Compare the terms *data*, *information*, and *knowledge* and describe three characteristics that make information valuable.

2

The Nature of Information

Except for words like *the, a, and, if,* and *it,* the word *information* was once one of the most common words on the Internet. No wonder people called the net an "information" storehouse. The term "information" is critical to understanding how information systems work, but it can be very slippery.

Facts, data, intelligence, knowledge, and even tips are synonyms for information, and they all touch on characteristics of the "stuff" that information systems can potentially manage. For our purposes, the term **data** refers to individual facts or pieces of information, and **information** refers to data or facts that are assembled and analyzed to add meaning and usefulness. A single high-temperature reading of an incoming patient at Patient First, a 24-hour walk-in clinic in Laurel, Maryland, is one piece of data. But entered into the patient records information system, and combined with the patient's other symptoms and previous medical records, it becomes far more valuable as a diagnostic tool.

Even more value can be obtained from this one temperature reading by aggregating it with the data from other patients entering the clinic that week. Tables and charts constructed from these data, analyzed by geographic region, may indicate a flu epidemic or the first signs of a pandemic emergency. As information from many clinics, emergency rooms, and doctors' offices pours in and public health staff at the Centers for Disease Control in Atlanta analyze maps, patient diagnoses, and many other facts, a pattern may emerge that warrants swift action.

Information can be further refined, analyzed, and combined to make it even more useful—and extremely valuable—as actionable knowledge:

Data → Information → Knowledge

Figure 1-4 shows examples of many kinds of data and how they might be aggregated and analyzed to create information and knowledge. No clear dividing lines separate these categories, and people often use the terms interchangeably. They blend together and form a continuum as more meaning and usefulness are created through analysis and skillful combination of many sources of data and human insight.

FIGURE 1-4

Examples of the continuum from data to information to knowledge, as meaning and usefulness grow.

Data	Information	Knowledge
Patient's temperature at walk-in clinic on Dec. 15 = 103.9° F.	Table showing flu diagnoses in region during month of December	Worldwide map of flu outbreaks suggesting pandemic
01010011 01001111 01010011	Binary code for SOS	HELP!!!
Microsoft (MSFT) Closing Stock Price 1/15/2009	Graph of Microsoft highs and lows for one year	Combined with analysis of other information, leads to broker's recommendation to buy, hold, or sell stock
Time spent waiting in line to vote = 5 minutes, 32 seconds	Graph of average waiting times by voting location	Pattern emerges showing waiting times related to socioeconomic levels of precinct
CWOT	Complete Waste of Time (text messaging abbreviation)	May be interpreted as an insult
GPS coordinates	Map showing location with push pin	Location of Taj Mahal in India
170 systolic 110 diastolic	Table showing blood pressure over 24 hours	May require medication and lifestyle changes to reduce risk of heart disease
Invoice #259 Total Amount = $139.23	Total Sales for Southern Region in First Quarter = $2,156,232	Fastest growing sales region; consider broader marketing campaign
(59,79) (Red = 255, Green = 0, Blue = 0)	Red pixel in a digital image (close-up)	Where's Waldo?

WHAT MAKES INFORMATION VALUABLE?

Separating useful information from the trivial is no easy task given the sheer volume of information on the planet. Three characteristics stand out, however, that contribute to making some information very valuable:

- ▶ Timeliness
- ▶ Accuracy
- ▶ Completeness

Timeliness matters a great deal in some settings, and near real-time information often costs more. For example, people pay monthly subscription fees to financial service companies to get up-to-the minute stock prices, rather than the delayed price reports shown on free stock tickers you can add to your own browser. Riswan Khalfan, CIO at TD Securities, manages the systems that analyze options trading data that pour in by the millions every second, and that can make automated decisions about what to buy or sell. His system can handle a breathtaking 5 million pieces of data per second, far more than most other banks. He points out that "if you fall behind, you're dealing with stale data and that puts you at a disadvantage." With timely, up-to-date trading data, Khalfan's systems can make quicker decisions, which he argues are better (Figure 1-5).[10]

Accuracy may seem like an obvious attribute for valuable information, but there actually are degrees of accuracy. The more accurate you want the information to be, the longer it may take to obtain, making extreme accuracy a trade-off to timeliness. A CEO who wants to know how much competitors charge for a rival product, for example, would wait quite awhile for staff to scour all the distribution channels and assemble the data. An approximate but timely answer is more valuable.

Completeness adds considerable value, particularly as a means to avoid bias or spin. A marketing survey that polls customers as they enter a store will completely miss those who shop online, for example. The survey results would be incomplete without taking greater care to assess the interests of all the customers. Striving for complete information, however, may also introduce delays that affect timeliness.

---

data
The individual facts or pieces of information.

information
Data or facts that are assembled and analyzed to add meaning and usefulness.

FIGURE 1-5

Timeliness is a critical attribute for certain kinds of information, such as stock prices. "If you fall behind, you're dealing with stale data." –Riswan Khalfan

mdd/Shutterstock

Describe the four main components of an information system and the role that each plays.

The Components of an Information System

Speeding through a red traffic light occasionally triggers a click, soon followed by the arrival of an envelope from the Department of Public Safety. Inside, you find a photo of your car in the intersection with license plate clearly visible, a speeding ticket, directions for paying online with your credit card, and a brochure with friendly tips on safe driving.

An **information system**, whether it is that speed camera network, a company's payroll system, or a social networking service, brings together four critical components to collect, process, manage, analyze, and distribute information:

▶ People
▶ Technology
▶ Processes
▶ Data

PEOPLE

The design, development, launch, and maintenance of any information system involves teams of people. They play a number of different roles—as visionaries, developers, and managers of information systems, but also as analysts, liaisons, users, customers, contributors, and sometimes opponents or roadblocks. Often underestimated, the human element plays a crucial role in the success or failure of most information systems, and you will see many examples throughout this book, marked with a palm print.

Leaders may be first to conceive the strategic objective the system will achieve and weigh the pros, cons, costs, and benefits. However, innovative ideas for such systems come from every level, provided the organization's culture openly encourages people to think about how information systems can help. Managers and staff from many departments in the organization participate on teams with technologists to design the details of a system or evaluate commercial systems that might be purchased. The information technology team, with in-depth knowledge of programming, software, servers, communications, and hardware options, works closely with staff in other functional areas to launch user-friendly, people-oriented systems.

Many systems draw from a much wider pool of people, involving users as contributors and developers, not just customers or clients. **User-generated content (UGC)**, for example, makes up most of the information in systems such as eBay, Craigslist, YouTube, Facebook, Twitter, Wikipedia, and many others. Indeed, these systems would not exist without generous contributions from the community. UGC is an important ingredient in what has come to be known as **Web 2.0**, the second generation of web development that facilitates far more interactivity, end-user contributions, collaboration, and information sharing compared to earlier models. Social networking and virtual meetings are all features of Web 2.0.

For more traditional companies, though, UGC can create considerable angst. Scott Cook, cofounder of the company that makes TurboTax software, confronted spirited opposition among his management team when he proposed involving millions of TurboTax users in online forums about tax questions. Colleagues worried that users would openly trash the software, complain about bugs and high prices, or provide incorrect answers that just made customers angry. The team eventually embedded a support forum directly into the software as a live community, so tax filers could see questions and answers related directly to the tax form they were currently working on (Figure 1-6). They could also contribute their own questions or answers.

After several months, the tension eased because the posts turned out to be remarkably accurate. They also were self-correcting in that one poster might elaborate on a tax law to clarify another's answer or point to a different reference. Some did voice complaints, but many also suggested constructive improvements, serving as a very valuable customer focus group to guide new software development. Cook insists that organizations should get users involved as contributors in this way, despite fear about what this untamed resource might do.[11]

FIGURE 1-6

A sample conversation from the TurboTax user forum showing how user-generated content is used.

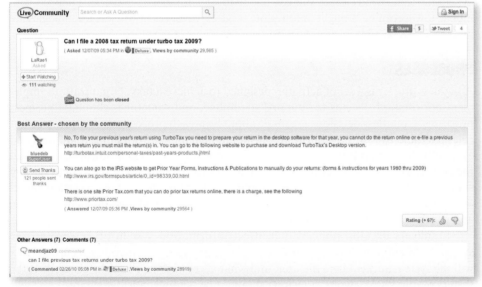

Source: TurboTax Live Community. ©Intuit Inc. All rights reserved.

information system	user-generated content (UGC)	Web 2.0
A system that brings together four critical components to collect, process, manage, analyze, and distribute information; the four components are people, technology, processes, and data.	The content contributed to a system by its users.	The second generation of web development that facilitates far more interactivity, end-user contributions, collaboration, and information sharing compared to earlier models.

TECHNOLOGY

Information technology (IT), covered in Chapter 3, includes hardware, software, and telecommunications. IT is one of the four components of an information system, though people often use the term interchangeably with "information." Rack after rack of servers in Google's windowless data centers are examples of this component, along with all the desktop computers, laptops, netbooks, cell phones, navigation devices, digital cameras, camcorders, personal digital assistants, and bar-code scanners. Anything capable of collecting, processing, storing, or displaying electronic data is potentially part of an information system. The transponder chip on your car's windshield that allows electronic toll collection is another example. The battery-powered device sends a signal to the tollbooth, and in some areas, drivers don't even need to slow down.

Software ranges widely, from the code needed to boot up a computer to programs with artificial intelligence and their own learning capabilities. The Internet and the World Wide Web unleashed an explosion of software creativity, transforming businesses around the globe. Organizations can create applications that their partners, suppliers, and customers can access wherever they are, eliminating boundaries that once existed.

Telecommunications and networks are also part of the IT component, and the term **information and communications technology (ICT)** is often used to refer to the broader collection. The main role of the telecommunications component is to move electronic signals from one place to another, properly route traffic, and provide various services to improve transmission speeds, eliminate noise, increase security, or analyze traffic patterns. Various kinds of wires appear in much of the infrastructure, including orange fiber-optic cables, the coaxial cables used by cable TV companies, and the slender copper telephone wiring common in homes.

Increasingly, wireless transmission is favored because of its flexibility and reduced cost, though speed still lags. Nevertheless, countries that are unable to build extensive wired networks because of cost or geography are transforming their communications infrastructures through wireless transmission. In much of sub-Saharan Africa, for example, copper wiring may never be deployed at all. Dr. Lil Mohan, director of an Intel program that builds wireless access for countries in the Middle East and Africa, points out the importance of broadband access for these countries because of its direct impact on economic growth. Wireless is also easier to recover after a disaster that brings down telecom facilities. When hurricane winds knock out cell-phone towers, for example, trucks equipped with mobile towers can be brought in to restore service. Advances in wireless technologies are making access possible in even the most remote corners of the globe.

PROCESSES

A **business process** is a set of activities designed to achieve a task. Organizations implement information systems to support, streamline, and sometimes eliminate business processes. Countless decisions are made about how each process should operate, what rules it should follow, how information should be handled from input to output, and especially, how the information system will support the process. For example, should the system log every change an employee makes to the data? Will the system require supervisors to electronically approve all purchases or just those above a certain value? What decisions can the information system make on its own based on incoming data, and which ones require human judgment?

Managers develop policies that affect information system processes and the systems can enforce those policies. A major policy category involves security. How will the system authenticate the user, and what access will he or she be granted? If the system requires a password, how long should it be, and when will it expire?

The nuances of many processes and all their steps are affected by thousands of decisions people make, and these are influenced by human motivations and the way people look at process improvements. For example, some organizations try to design systems that just reproduce what employees were doing, thereby reducing labor.

FIGURE 1-7

Although automatically generating letters like this one provides some process improvement, information systems offer far more potential to improve and even eliminate the process entirely.

```
NARA SELLERS
143 LA GUARDIA STREET
JACKSON, AZ

Dear Student:

We are sorry to inform you that we are unable to confirm your registration for the class
listed below for the reason checked:

FALL                        BMGT 322                        SECTION 5

☐   The class is full.

☐   Your records show you have not fulfilled the prerequisites.

☐   The class is only open to juniors or seniors.

☐   Your tuition payment has not yet been received.

☐   Other_____

Please contact the Registrations Office if you have any questions.

Sincerely,
Registrations
```

In a college registrations office, employees might send letters to students who could not enroll in a class that they selected, to explain why. One improvement might be to design a feature that automatically generates form letters to those students with their name and address, the class they selected, and a list of the most common reasons they could not register. Instead of typing the letter, the employees can check the reason, and stuff the letter into an envelope (Figure 1-7). The staff would be pleased with this handy new efficiency, though students might think the new letters are a bit mechanical.

A closer look at the process, however, might lead to far more radical changes. Moving to online registrations, for instance, could eliminate the process entirely. Classes that are full or for which the student is not eligible would not even appear as options when a student logs in to register, thus eliminating the need to send letters at all except in special cases. This new design would please students because they would get instant confirmation that their class choices were available. Also, they would no longer receive frustrating form letters by mail that thwart their academic plans. Registrations staff, however, may worry about layoffs.

Business process management (BPM) is the field that focuses on designing, optimizing, and streamlining processes, taking into account the human element. Analysts look at processes from many different angles to weigh input from all stakeholders, suggest innovative approaches that leverage the power of information systems, and propose tweaks at every step. Software is available to simulate business processes and conduct "what if" experiments to assist with the analysis. Surveys of IT leaders show that business process improvement is a very high priority (Figure 1-8).

information technology (IT)
The hardware, software, and telecommunications that comprise the technology component of information systems; the term is often used more broadly, to refer to information systems.

business process management (BPM)
Focuses on designing, optimizing, and streamlining business processes throughout the organization.

information and communications technology (ICT)
The term encompasses the broad collection of information processing and communications technologies, emphasizing that telecommunication technology is a significant feature of information systems.

business process
A set of activities designed to achieve a task; organizations implement information systems to support, streamline, and sometimes eliminate business processes.

FIGURE 1-8

The top business and technology priorities for IT leaders (chief information officers).[12]

Rank	Top Business Priorities	Top Technology Priorities
1	Business process improvement	Business intelligence applications
2	Attracting and retaining new customers	Enterprise applications
3	Creating new products and services (innovation)	Servers and storage technologies
4	Expanding into new markets or geographies	Legacy modernization, upgrade, or enhancement
5	Reducing enterprise costs	Technical infrastructure
6	Improving enterprise workforce effectiveness	Security technologies

Efforts to manage business processes also take into account the overall organizational culture and its approach to information systems. Does the organization need very tight controls over every piece of information and employees' use of it? Banks, hospitals, military units, and many other institutions bear heavy responsibilities to develop crystal clear policies. They must safeguard sensitive information, and their missions affect the way processes are designed. Free use of the Internet may not be permitted, and employees may not be able to take files home on portable USB flash drives to catch up over the weekend. Some organizations even push epoxy glue into the desktop computers' USB ports to prevent any possible temptation to copy data. In contrast, people involved in a free-wheeling start-up or a volunteer organization may not be too concerned with where or when people work, how secure their information is, or whether staff post party photos on the company servers.

Business processes and organizational policies must also be reviewed frequently because circumstances change quickly. Numerous corporate scandals, for example, have led to heightened legal requirements to retain both electronic and paper documents. If there is a pending legal case, businesses have a duty to preserve electronic documents that might be relevant, including e-mail. **E-discovery** refers to the processes by which electronic data that might be used as legal evidence are requested, secured, and searched. Because electronic documents cover such a wide scope, and since they can be quite slippery as people edit, cut and paste, and make copies, it is no surprise that most organizations are woefully behind in managing the retention process. Less than 15 percent of U.S. corporations have solid policies and procedure in place. Debra Logan, an analyst at the Gartner Group research firm, says, "In terms of a *good* electronic records system, I would say [that percentage] is closer to zero."[13]

DATA

Data are the grist for every information system, and these raw facts can present themselves in an enormous variety of shapes and forms. Figure 1-9 shows many examples of data that become part of information systems. Using a mercury thermometer, for example, a patient's temperature reading would appear as the height of the mercury bar in a glass tube. Data reflecting time intervals might appear as seconds on a stopwatch.

VoicePrism, a Chicago-based company that creates information systems to analyze vocal patterns, focuses on the streams of data contained in phone conversations between call center agents and customers. Although the words people use in these conversations reveal some information about service quality, even more can be gathered from the tone of voice, tempo, and other nonverbal data. When a customer's vocal patterns suggest emotional stress, a signal alerts a manager who can intervene to prevent any further escalation. Figure 1-10 shows an example of how voice sound waves vary.

Regardless of its initial form, incoming data is converted into digital format, which allows it to be integrated in information systems, read by computer programs, and shared across systems. Letters, numbers, money, colors, the tiny dots on an X-ray, air pollution levels, musical notes, vocal frequencies, time intervals, and much more can all be represented in digital format.

FIGURE 1-9

Examples of data. Photos: Maxim Pavlov/Alamy, D. Hurst/ Alamy, Sandra Baker/Alamy, Paul Paladin/Alamy, John Wilhelmsson/StockShot/Alamy, Roman Maerzinger/Picture Press/Alamy.

FIGURE 1-10

Voice sound waves.

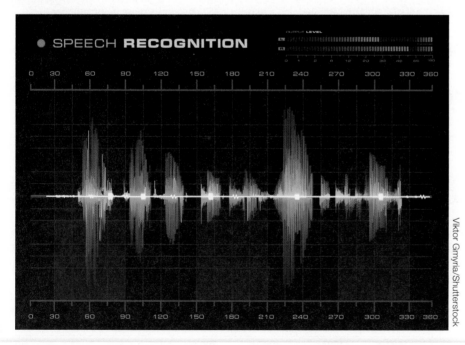

Viktor Gmyria/Shutterstock

e-discovery
The processes by which electronic data
that might be used as legal evidence are
requested, secured, and searched.

Identify several research areas in the discipline of management information systems (MIS). **4**

Information Systems, the Discipline

The study of information systems—how people, technology, processes, and data work together—is a lively discipline involving university faculty, private-sector analysts, government researchers, and more. Many refer to the field as **management information systems (MIS)**, and academic departments in colleges and universities often bear that name. (That term also is used to describe a type of information system that supports decision making at the managerial level, discussed in Chapter 7.)

The field draws researchers and practitioners from business, computer science, psychology, sociology, public administration, and many other subjects, all of whom have an interest in learning more about how we can create systems to help organizations do more with less, make companies more competitive, increase productivity, and improve the lot of people around the world. The five areas that attract much of the interest are:

▶ Development of information systems
▶ IT in organizations
▶ IT and individuals
▶ IT and groups
▶ IT and markets

It is a young discipline—barely 25 years old—and is changing rapidly. Examining the articles in the major journals since the mid-1980s, researchers found a fascinating shift in the topics (Figure 1-11).[14] Hardly anyone was investigating the impact of IT on markets in the early days, but the Internet changed that picture. The Internet offers remarkable opportunities to invent global e-marketplaces for stocks, real estate, music, used books, rare antiques, and even social encounters. How organizations build trust, protect privacy, satisfy customers, and make a profit in these worldwide e-markets are very hot topics.

Did You Know?

As of 2011, almost 2 billion people are Internet users—about 29 percent of the world's population. Asia boasts the largest number of users, topping 825 million. However, Africa has the fastest growth rate, showing a massive 2,357 percent increase in the number of users from 2000 to 2010. Visit www.internetworldstats.com for data on specific countries.

FIGURE 1-11

Trends in the discipline of information systems.

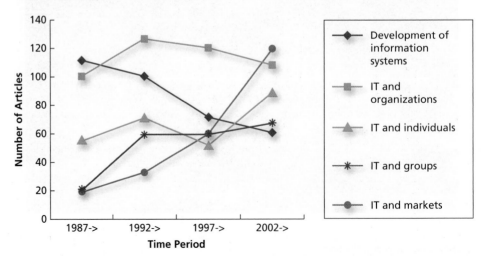

Research on group collaboration, especially when team members are dispersed around the world, is far more important now because of virtual teams and globalization. The psychology of group dynamics subtly changes when team members use online tools, and the shifts are not always positive. Investigations of successful and unsuccessful teams shed light on strategies people can use to make virtual teams more successful. Most students engage in some virtual teamwork, especially those who take some or all of their courses online. Virtual teamwork and collaboration skills are critical.

The "people" component of information systems is clearly growing in importance, and this book stresses that element. Just making technology work is not enough to create a successful information system.

Information Systems Throughout the Organization

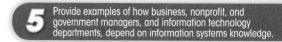

The need to learn about information systems is not always obvious. Consider these comments:

> "Why should information systems be important to me? My career is marketing, developing creative ad campaigns. Those IT folks speak their own language and I speak mine."

> "I'm in human resources—the only system we use is the one the company set up. It's really a disaster, too. We really need a way to train new people faster, before the ones who have all the knowledge here leave."

> "We're a nonprofit volunteer organization. We can't spend money on expensive overhead like IT, so what's the point? We don't need anything fancy—just e-mail and word processing."

The growing demand for people who are savvy about information systems, and how those systems can contribute to the whole organization's success, says something important about how valuable this knowledge is.

INFORMATION SYSTEMS IN BUSINESS

Information systems underlie most of the business activities and processes that thread their way through every functional business unit, from the CEO's suite to the Facilities Management Office. Just about everyone uses e-mail, cell phones, and the Internet, and most also rely on the many information systems that support the company's business processes. Strategic initiatives involving these systems can and should come from any corner of the organization to streamline processes, reduce costs, increase revenue, or launch that "killer app."

Whether your chosen career is marketing, finance, management, human resources, research, sales, law, medicine, manufacturing, or as an entrepreneur, information systems will be fundamental to your success. Consider these examples:

▶ A marketing manager who knows how to leverage social networking trends to create a viral buzz about the company's products has quite an edge over someone who still thinks the web is just a place to publish ads that also appear in print, however creative they may be. Marketing executives must also know how to analyze return on investment for their campaigns, drawing on data to make a case for their marketing strategies.

▶ A human resources professional who develops e-learning modules to reach more employees will make a significant contribution to the enterprise. In contrast, the trainer who programs many face-to-face classes with three-ring binders will reach

management information systems (MIS)
The study of information systems—how people, technology, processes, and data work together. Also used to describe a special type of information system that supports tactical decision making at the managerial level.

far fewer employees, at much higher cost. The online learning programs can also be easily updated, while information in the binders grows stale quickly.

▶ Small business owners can take advantage of rapidly dropping costs for many useful information systems if they know about them, and appreciate their potential. For instance, an entrepreneur can register a website address for a new storefront, launch the site, and then buy text ads that appear when people enter relevant search terms—all for very little money.

INFORMATION SYSTEMS IN NONPROFITS AND GOVERNMENT

If your career leads you to service in government, teaching, law enforcement, charities, or other nonprofit areas, information systems will also be critical. In some of these organizations, however, funding for IT may not be high on the priority list. Beth Kanter, who helps nonprofits adopt IT, says, "Typically, your nonprofit volunteer was a 'do-er' who simply delivered their experience face-to-face." Nevertheless, information systems can make an enormous contribution to your organization's effectiveness in innovative ways:

▶ The most successful fund-raisers know how to draw on information systems to analyze the preferences and motivations of potential donors. Linking demographic data from the U.S. Census Bureau or other sources helps fund-raisers target their audiences and develop far more effective campaigns compared to those who just blanket a community with postcards or telemarketing.

▶ UNICEF relief workers create inexpensive podcasts and "vodcasts" (podcasts with video) to relay the plight of children from war, disease, or disasters in troubled parts of the world. Rather than spending money on radio or TV broadcasts, workers freely distribute the short, timely, and compelling video messages worldwide through the net or via download to supporters' cell phones.

▶ The entrepreneurial team called the Extraordinaries creates "micro-volunteering" opportunities for people who can't dedicate many hours per week, but can spend just a few minutes of their time helping with various causes through their cell phones. While waiting in line or sitting on a bus, volunteers can use their tiny keyboards to translate a page into another language, locate potholes, or help NASA map craters on Mars.

INSIDE THE IT DEPARTMENT

The functional business unit responsible for planning, managing, and supporting information systems is often called "Information Technology," "Department of Information Systems," "Enterprise Information Systems," or something similar. Within the department are more specialized groups or individuals who oversee different areas. Figures 1-12 and 1-13 show a hypothetical department with some common subunits, but many variations exist. For instance, organizations might outsource some responsibilities, working with vendors to provide services.

Heading the department is the **chief information officer (CIO)**, Vice President of Information Systems, or similar title. The CIO might report directly to the CEO or to another vice president—often the one responsible for finance and administration.

What characteristics does a CIO need? Strong leadership abilities, excellent communication skills, and knowledge of ICT are all important, though the CIO does not need to be an expert in all technology areas. Relevant experience and an educational background in business, information systems, or a related field are also very helpful. As a senior executive, the CIO's job is not just to oversee the department, but also to help shape the organization's strategic goals and ensure that the information systems support them.

Working with the CIO, especially in larger organizations and major companies, are more staff positions with "chief" in their titles, such as those in Figure 1-14. Their roles span the activities of all the IT subunits and, indeed, the whole organization. "Chief" seems to have caught on in IT, as it did in some other business areas. Even "Chief Wisdom Officer" is turning up.

FIGURE 1-12

Hypothetical organizational chart for the Information Systems Department.

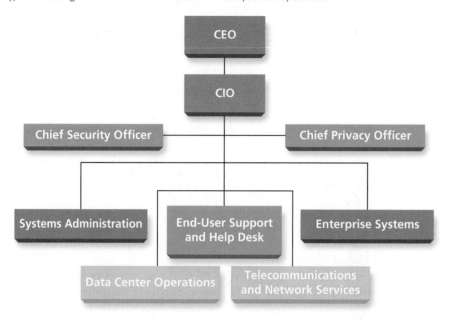

COLLABORATING ON INFORMATION SYSTEMS

Nikia Sabri, marketing director at a Los Angeles consulting firm, thought she had a brilliant idea to reduce costs and improve her department's results. Her eight-person staff was frequently shorthanded because of traffic jams, sick kids, or closed schools, but all of them had computers and Internet access at home. Her boss had rejected work-at-home proposals in the past, but she thought she could make a solid case for it—with the help of the IT department. All staff had phones and e-mail, of course, and most had accounts on a social networking site, but she wanted heightened awareness of one another's presence. Creative marketing people like to bounce ideas off each other, and she was looking for a way to simulate the easy communication that nearby office cubicles create, in which you might roll back your chair and ask your neighbor to take a quick look at your latest drawing. Surely there were web-based applications and tools that would support this.

Where should she start? Her IS department publishes only a Help Desk number to submit a trouble ticket, so she tried that first. That unit's software logged the ticket and sent out its automated message. "Thank you for your message. The Help Desk

FIGURE 1-13

Common functional areas in an information systems department.

IS Department Areas	Function
End-User Support and Help Desk	Provides services to internal and external customers on technology issues; answers the phone or e-mail "help desk" and troubleshoots problems; installs and maintains desktop equipment.
Systems Administration	Installs, manages, and updates servers.
Operations	Maintains the environmentally controlled areas in which servers and communications equipment are located; handles backups and archiving.
Enterprise Systems and Applications	Develops, installs, maintains, and oversees the organization's mission-critical software applications.
Telecommunications and Network Services	Installs and manages communications technologies and networks, including voice, cell phones, and wireless networks.

chief information officer (CIO)
The person who heads the department responsible for managing and maintaining information systems, and ensuring they support the organization's strategic goals.

FIGURE 1-14

Besides the CIO, other individuals involved in information systems play leadership roles and have "chief" in their titles.

Title	Description
Chief Information Security Officer	Oversees information security in all the systems, ensuring that all the devices and the company's confidential information are well protected from hackers, disasters, accidents, and rogue employees.
Chief Privacy Officer	Manages privacy issues and helps shape policy about how sensitive and confidential data about customers, citizens, employees, patients, and others are handled and protected.
Chief Technology Officer	Position is usually more technical compared to the CIO, overseeing technology solutions and innovative uses.
Chief Knowledge Officer	Manages efforts to improve the organization's ability to capture, nurture, and disseminate knowledge and expertise.

will respond within 24 hours. For faster service, please check the Knowledge Base to see if the answer to your question is there." Although puzzled by her request, a technician stopped by and installed a headset with microphone, wanting to be helpful and thinking that was what she needed.

Disconnects in communication between IT staff and others in the organization are not uncommon, partly because of the jargon barrier. Frustrations rise when IT doesn't respond immediately to potentially good ideas like Nikia's. Like all functional business units, IT has a full plate of ongoing projects, prioritized by the CIO working with the CEO and other top executives to ensure that resources are wisely spent with a solid return on investment. The technician had to move onto the next trouble ticket and wasn't in a position to decide whether Nikia's project was worthwhile.

Does that mean Nikia should forget her project? Absolutely not. Successful organizations rely on innovation like this from people who know their work best. Figure 1-15 lists some tips on how to improve communications between people like Nikia and the IT department, which may sometimes seem impenetrable.

FIGURE 1-15

Tips for collaborating on information systems.

For the CIO and IT Staff:

▶ *Focus on business goals.* The objective of a project is not to "upgrade all the servers," but to improve productivity, attract more customers, reduce costs, earn revenue, increase customer loyalty, reduce carbon emissions, etc.

▶ *Avoid jargon.* Learn to speak the language your colleagues in other departments understand, and reserve the technical jargon for internal IT communications.

▶ *Communicate the value of IT.* Although many focus on how much IT costs, the savings or revenue IT generates through improved productivity or added sales are captured in other departments.

▶ *Emphasize return on investment.* Evaluate projects in terms of their ultimate payoff, the same way business managers judge other kinds of initiatives.

▶ *Be proactive.* Propose and support innovative projects with clear business goals, rather than just react to problems and proposals as they arise. Ensure that people like Nikia know how to contact IT to discuss their innovative ideas.

▶ *Embrace customer service.* Strive for the highest level of customer satisfaction for your internal customers, not just the ones who buy your company's products and services.

▶ *Become a hybrid.* The most successful IT professionals have solid technology skills, but are also very well grounded in the business so they can easily communicate.

For People in Other Areas:

▶ *Describe your end goal, not the means to get there.* The more your IT colleagues understand what you want to accomplish, the better equipped they will be to help.

▶ *Learn how to contact IT for different purposes.* If you are not sure, ask.

▶ *Be familiar with how information systems are already supporting your organization.* Explore the company's intranet and review announcements about new initiatives.

▶ *Network.* Keeping in touch with your colleagues in and out of IT builds trust and creates networks of people who can share knowledge.

▶ *Do your homework.* Especially after taking this course, you will be prepared to research your ideas and the information system solutions others have attempted, so you are more familiar with what is possible.

▶ *Be an active partner.* As your project develops, keep in close touch with IT to provide timely assistance and feedback at every step. If you do not, the result may be quite different from what you expected.

A key ingredient for Nikia, as it is for you if you are not in IT, is to learn more about this crucial area. Taking this course is a major step in that direction, and you will be well prepared to interact with the IT staff on projects. In fact, information technology and strategy are so closely integrated with every aspect of business that every manager is really an "information officer."[15]

If you are in IT or aspire to be, you will probably specialize in applications development, network administration, technical support, or another field. In this course, you will gain a much broader vision of how information systems support strategic objectives and business goals, and how you can collaborate with other units on high-profile projects.

IMPROVING YOUR OWN PRODUCTIVITY

Microsoft surveyed 38,000 people in 200 countries to learn more about their productivity at work and the role that technology played.[16] The results were alarming:

▶ Though people reported working an average of 45 hours a week, they considered 17 of those hours to be unproductive.

▶ People spend about 5.6 hours a week in meetings, but more than two-thirds think meetings are not productive.

▶ Sixty percent said they don't have work–life balance.

▶ Those surveyed reported receiving an average of more than 40 e-mail messages a day. In the United States, this figure is far higher.

▶ Just 34 percent said they used computer-based scheduling and other productivity tools.

Many attributed their productivity to the technology they used and their hours of unproductive time to their inability to use software that could help them schedule their time, organize their tasks, communicate effectively, and prioritize their work.

Although learning how information systems support organizations and their missions is critical to your success, acquiring the technical skills to increase your own productivity is just as important. Do you spend too much time hunting for documents? Can you quickly find a phone number when you need it? Are you managing your e-mail inbox as effectively as you could? Do you rely on easily lost handwritten notes?

Information technology is the catalyst for building innovative information systems and achieving stunning gains in productivity for companies. It can also help you achieve a great deal more for yourself—in college, at work, and in your career. And despite jokes about the "crackberry"—the nickname for RIM's BlackBerry smartphone, whose owners feel compelled to check e-mail every few minutes—mastering certain kinds of IT for your personal productivity is essential. Used wisely, these skills will also help you distinguish yourself in college and in the workplace. They will also make it easier to maintain a healthy work–life balance, giving you more time for family, friends, and leisure.

Promises, Perils, and Ethical Issues

 Explain how information systems present both promises and perils, and pose ethical questions.

Google's eye-catching goal—organizing the world's information—stretches the imagination and promises to challenge the company's youthful achievers for decades to come. Yet information systems frequently offer promises like this, with game-changing innovations introduced every year. In 1943, former IBM Chairman Thomas Watson said, "I think there is a world market for maybe five computers." But it was his own company that introduced the IBM-PC, transforming not just the workplace itself, but the kind of work each of us is capable of performing.

In the next chapter, examples of the promise of information systems for strategic initiatives abound. Their perils, however, are not inconsiderable, particularly because of the sheer scope of their impact. Information systems are so powerful, and the data they contain so vast and personal, that everyone must appreciate the ethical issues involved in their development and use.

PRIVACY BREACHES AND AMPLIFICATION EFFECTS

Privacy breaches present major risks. In the United Kingdom, for example, just two computer discs were misplaced by government workers. The tiny platters contained personal data, including bank account information, on 25 million residents, and their black market value was estimated at US$2.5 billion. Events like this one, in which information systems play a central role, can threaten the privacy and security of millions and affect huge geographic areas. These events were once highly improbable, but because information systems have become ever more powerful and interconnected, the risks are far greater.[17] Minor mistakes are amplified and events can turn catastrophic quickly.

Reputations are also far more vulnerable, given the power individuals have to spread damaging information at lightning speed. Few corporations are equipped to respond to such blitzes—accurate or not—that are distributed through channels such as YouTube. When two disgruntled Domino's Pizza employees uploaded a stomach-turning video shot in the restaurant kitchen showing how they defiled the sandwiches, Domino's corporate office failed to respond for 2 days. The employees claimed it was just a prank, but before it was taken down, the video had been viewed almost 1 million times.[18] Domino's eventually tackled the crisis head on and earned high marks for limiting the damage, but their response during the first 24 hours was sluggish. Every organization's **crisis management team**, responsible for identifying, assessing, and addressing threats from unforeseen circumstances, must be on high alert for signs of any online firestorms. The teams have very little time to take action.

The way modern information systems amplify any communication may put your own reputation and livelihood at risk as well. Any e-mail you send or photo you upload can be forwarded or posted online for millions to view—and for attorneys to collect as evidence. Text, photos, and videos uploaded to your social networking site can easily be distributed to a far wider audience beyond your own network. It is also absurdly easy to make your own blunders by sending e-mail to many more people than you intended. Consider Angelo Mozilo, former CEO of mortgage giant Countrywide, who received an e-mail plea from a homeowner asking for help to restructure his mortgage. Mozilo typed that the request was "unbelievable" and "disgusting," meaning to forward his comment to one of the company executives. Instead, he clicked *reply to all*, and the homeowner promptly posted his cold-blooded response on the Internet. Countrywide, already under siege for predatory lending practices, quickly restructured the loan, but the damage to Mozilo's reputation persisted.[19]

These promises and perils make the study of information systems critically important for us all, regardless of where we work or what kind of work we do. We all share the responsibility for both harnessing the power of these systems and minimizing their risks.

✳ THE ETHICAL FACTOR Ethical Issues Surrounding Information Systems

Cases like those described in this chapter raise disquieting ethical issues:

▶ Who is responsible for damage caused by accidental leaks of private information? The United Kingdom government worker who misplaced the disks? The information systems professionals who designed a flawed system? The person who found the disks and didn't return them? The citizens who failed to check credit reports?

▶ In the Domino's case, did the employees who created and then uploaded the video violate ethical principles? Is YouTube partly responsible for allowing uploads of false, damaging, or illegal videos?

▶ In a case like Mozilo's, do people who send harsh e-mails deserve what they get if the information leaks out? Is it ethical to broadcast a message you receive that was accidentally misdirected? Should e-mail systems be redesigned to allow senders to withdraw their messages during a "pending" period?

Many of these questions have no easy answers. People tend to judge the severity of ethical violations partly on the basis of the number of people affected. When the power of information systems and the Internet are involved, the potential for harm is exponentially amplified.

MyMISLab | *Online Simulation*

The World of Mammals

A Role-Playing Simulation on Choosing a New CIO for an Animal Preserve

You volunteer at The World of Mammals, the region's largest enclosed animal preserve. Far more than a zoo, the nonprofit preserve provides a reasonably natural habitat for many endangered mammal species, and puts the visitors in the "cages" rather than the animals. Miles of chain-link-covered paths crisscross the preserve so people can safely view the animals behaving normally, not pacing back and forth in cramped exhibits. Visitors can also drive around in specially protected jeeps, equipped with night vision goggles after dark. The zoo's revenue comes from ticket and concession sales, special events, and donations, but veterinary bills keep rising, and personnel costs for the 200+ employees continue to outpace what the zoo takes in.

The zoo's chief information officer (CIO) left abruptly, and zoo director Yolanda Whalen asked you—a longtime supporter—to help select a new CIO. When you're ready, log in to meet Yolanda, learn about the zoo's needs, and start interviewing the finalists…

Meoita/Shutterstock.com

crisis management team
The team in an organization that is responsible for identifying, assessing, and addressing threats from unforeseen circumstances that can lead to crisis situations.

Chapter Summary

1 Organizations rely on information systems for a host of reasons, and they play critical roles in several contexts: operations management, customer interactions, decision making, collaboration and teamwork, strategic initiatives, an d individual productivity.

2 Data, information, and knowledge are terms along a continuum that reflect how raw facts can be combined, assembled, and analyzed to add meaning and value. Characteristics of information that add to its value include timeliness, accuracy, and completeness.

3 The four components of any information system are (1) people, (2) technology, (3) processes, and (4) data. The "people" component encompasses far more than just the IT staff. It encompasses the human element and involves people from many different parts of the organization. Customers and suppliers also participate in improving processes and eliminating waste. Customers may become contributors through user-generated content and Web 2.0 applications.

4 The young discipline of information systems attracts faculty and students from many fields, private-sector analysts, government workers, and more. Research trends show the changing nature of the field. Interest in subjects such as the role of IT in markets and in collaborative group work has increased considerably.

5 Information systems contribute to success in every functional department and in all different types of organizations. Learning how they make these contributions, and how you can lead efforts to leverage their power, are important regardless of your specialization. This knowledge will also improve your own productivity.

6 Although information systems hold extraordinary promise, they also present risks and ethical concerns, especially because of amplification effects. Privacy breaches occur frequently and the damage can affect millions. Reputations are also more vulnerable because messages, whether accurate or not, can spread so quickly.

KEY TERMS AND CONCEPTS

operations management	competitive advantage	information technology (IT)	e-discovery
customer relationship management (CRM) system	data	information and communications technology (ICT)	management information systems (MIS)
data-driven decision making	information	business process	chief information officer (CIO)
business intelligence	information system	business process management (BPM)	crisis management team
social networking sites	user-generated content (UGC)		
	Web 2.0		

CHAPTER REVIEW QUESTIONS

1. What are the six primary roles that information systems play in organizations? How are information systems used in each context?

2. How is data different from information? How is information different from knowledge? What are examples of each?

3. What are the three characteristics that make information valuable? Why is each a critical attribute of information?

4. What are the four components of an information system? Describe each component. What are the five functions that these components provide?

5. How are information systems important to managers in a variety of functional business units? What are examples of ways that information systems are important to the success of a marketing department, a human resources department, and a small business owner?

6. What are the functional areas that are common to most information technology departments?

7. What is the role of the chief information officer?

8. How do information systems offer promises to organizations? What are some of the perils of information systems? What are some of the ethical questions associated with the use of information systems?

PROJECTS AND DISCUSSION QUESTIONS

1. As customers, students, patients, taxpayers, and citizens, we are surrounded by information systems that support customer interactions. Identify and describe two such systems that you have used. Briefly describe the types of customer interactions you have experienced with these systems and compare what you found to be important features of each one. Are there features or functions that you would change or add to either system?

2. Web conferencing has been available for many years. In this market space, products from Adobe, Cisco, Citrix, IBM, and Microsoft compete with lower-cost or free web-conferencing applications from Dimdim, Yugma, and others. What are some of the advantages of using a virtual meeting space? Are there disadvantages? Search the web to learn more about online meeting rooms and prepare a 5-minute presentation of your findings.

3. Information systems play a very large role in decision making, and many would argue that you can always use more information to make better decisions. But sometimes digging deeply for more information leads to troubling ethical dilemmas. Visit 23andme.com, the website of a company that offers to read your DNA from saliva for $199 and provide reports about disease risk factors, ancestral lineage, and more. If you learn of a significant health risk, should you tell siblings who chose not to investigate their own DNA? Should you tell your fiancée? List factors you should take into account when making decisions about whether to obtain information like this, and how to use it.

4. One way to be more productive and manage time is to use the calendar feature of your e-mail system. If you use Microsoft Outlook, visit Microsoft.com and search for "Outlook tutorial" or search the Internet for an Outlook "how to" web page to learn how to set up a calendar. Then create a calendar for the semester that shows class times as well as test dates and project due dates. Which reminder option did you select for class times? Which reminder option did you select for project due dates? Briefly describe several benefits of using the Outlook calendar feature.

5. Who hasn't heard of Netflix? Although Internet users bemoan its annoying pop-up ads, the world's leading DVD rent-by-mail company has grown to more than 15 million customers who now have the option to stream movies and TV episodes instantly over the Internet to their TV, computer, iPad, or iPhone. Describe Netflix in terms of (1) the types of information technology it uses and (2) its customer-facing business processes.

6. Consider the information that is maintained by a bank. In addition to customer records, the bank maintains records on accounts and loans. Figure 1-16 and Figure 1-17 are two examples of database tables for a regional bank. How might this data be aggregated and analyzed to create information and knowledge?

7. Parking is a problem at many universities across the United States. Is it a problem on your campus? Describe the business process to acquire a parking pass at your school. Can you get a parking pass online? Can you get one in person? How does your process compare to that of a smaller school that uses a paper form to apply for a parking permit? How can the smaller school use an information system to improve this business process? Can you think of a business process at your school that can be improved with an information system?

8. A typical information technology department is comprised of common functional areas, and each requires skills and competencies unique to that area. Search the web or visit an online job search site such as careerbuilder.com or monster.com to learn more about the IT functional areas described in Figure 1-13. Select two functional areas and compare job postings for each. In a brief report, contrast the differences in education, experience, and technical certification that are required for each job.

9. In June 2010, a security breach in the AT&T network exposed the e-mail addresses of 114,000 Apple iPad 3G owners, many of whom are well-known business executives. The list of subscribers whose data were released included Diane Sawyer of *ABC News*, New York City Mayor Michael Bloomberg, and former White House Chief of Staff Rahm Emanuel. Work in a small group with classmates to consider the severity of this leak of private information. In this case, is the severity of the breach measured by the number of affected individuals or by the high-profile status of some of the subscribers? What criteria are best for judging the severity of a data leak? Prepare a brief summary of your group discussion.

10. Information systems are fundamental to the success of every functional business unit within an organization, from marketing to manufacturing to finance. Work in a small group with classmates to share your career choice and discuss how information systems support processes within your field. Can you name types of software applications that are used in your chosen career?

FIGURE 1-16

Customers table.

CustomerID	Name	Address	City	State	Zip
100001	Don Baker	1215 E. New York	Aurora	IL	60504
100002	Yuxiang Jiang	1230 Douglas Road	Oswego	IL	60543
100003	Emily Brown	632 Fox Valley Road	Aurora	IL	60504
100004	Mario Sanchez	24 E. Ogden	Naperville	IL	60563

FIGURE 1-17

Accounts table.

CustomerID	AccountNumber	AccountType	DateOpened	Balance
100001	4875940	Checking	10/19/1971	2500.00
100001	1660375	Savings	08/10/1973	1200.00
100002	1783032	Savings	05/15/1987	500.00
100002	4793289	Checking	05/15/1987	3200.00
100003	6213690	Checking	02/14/1996	6700.00
100004	1890571	Savings	10/16/2007	5300.00
100004	8390126	Checking	12/02/2008	2700.00

APPLICATION EXERCISES

EXCEL APPLICATION:
Manpower Planning Spreadsheet

Precision Products specializes in custom-manufactured metal parts. The production manager has asked you to create an Excel spreadsheet to help manage operations. The company needs a way to calculate staffing requirements (number of employees) based on different levels of production. The five manufacturing operations are fabrication, welding, machining, assembly, and packaging. One unit of production requires 1.5 hours for fabrication, 2.25 hours for welding, 0.7 hours for machining, 3.2 hours for assembly, and 0.5 hours for packaging. Create the Excel spreadsheet shown in Figure 1-18 to calculate the weekly staffing required, at 40 hours per week, for production levels of 200, 300, 400, and 500 units. How does the total required for each level of production change if Precision Products operates a 45-hour production schedule?

ACCESS APPLICATION:
Information Systems in Business

Seconds Later, a clothing consignment shop, is fast becoming a favorite place to shop. The owner has asked you to create an Access database to help manage inventory. Download and import the information provided in the spreadsheet Ch01Ex02 to create a database with two tables (Consignors and Items). The owner wants you to add a calculated field to the items table that shows the net selling price after he has paid the commission to the consignors. Start with two reports: an Inventory Report and a Consignor Report. The Inventory Report summarizes the inventory by item type. This report will include the number of items and the total selling price for each item type, plus the total sales value of each inventory type. It will also include the potential commission that the consignors will earn if the owner sells all items. The Consignor Report will list the total number of items and the total selling price and commission for each consignor. What other reports could you make with this data that would be useful to the owner?

FIGURE 1-18

Managing operations at Precision Products using Excel.

	A	B	C	D	E	F	G	H	I
1					HOURS	REQUIRED			
2			Units	Fabrication	Welding	Machining	Assembly	Packaging	Total Hours
3		Weekly Production	1	1.5	2.25	0.7	3.2	0.5	
4			200						
5			300						
6			400						
7			500						
8									
9		Weekly Manpower							Total Manpower
10	hours	40	200						
11			300						
12			400						
13			500						

CASE STUDY #1

Nasdaq OMX: Trading at the Speed of Light

With annual net sales of more than $3 billion, the world's largest "floorless" exchange handles hundreds of millions of trades every day. Buys and sells happen so fast that each trade has to be time-stamped to the nanosecond. First launched in 2000, Nasdaq OMX is, above all, a technology company, and it successfully competes against the venerable New York Stock Exchange (NYSE) on its breathtaking trading speed.

When most people think of an exchange, they think of NYSE's enormous building on Wall Street, with loud-mouthed traders on the floor shouting orders, racing stock tickers, and giant LCD screens laden with charts, numbers, and ticker symbols. In fact, most exchanges are in data centers, not in neoclassical buildings. And they are also for-profit businesses that compete for companies to list their shares, and for investors and brokers to conduct their trades.

Speed matters, and Nasdaq OMX technology can handle 1 million messages per second. It matters so much that some heavy traders, Goldman Sachs, for example, pay Nasdaq OMX for the privilege of locating their own server in its data center, just to avoid the tiny communication delay from Goldman offices. A trader's servers can instantly detect any delay and can then automatically check other exchanges to see if the trade can be rerouted.

As in other businesses, improved information systems and technology drive prices down. In the early 2000s, NYSE and Nasdaq OMX shared 90 percent of the market, but competition pushed that figure down to 45 percent. Traders can use other exchanges with cheaper prices or they can buy and sell stocks in "dark pools"—private groups whose members trade with one another. Anna Ewing, the Nasdaq OMX CIO, stresses the need to find other revenue sources and relies on her IT department to support new business strategies. She led the drive to sell Nasdaq's technology to other countries so they could start their own "floorless" exchanges.

A looming problem for Nasdaq OMX and other exchanges is computer trading based on algorithms, or "algo-trading." With machines talking to machines, racing with one another to close the deal at the best price, humans use their judgment to decide on and enter the mathematical rules that can trigger frenzied rounds of trading to yield fast profits.

Some argue that these high-frequency trades make the markets more efficient and equitable, so the big players on the trading floor don't have an advantage. While Nasdaq OMX and other exchanges compete for the growing number of algo-traders, analysts worry that the sheer technological speed introduces serious risks. When markets dropped a gut-wrenching 9 percent on one afternoon in 2010, some suspected a clumsy algo-trader who accidentally triggered the event (Figure 1-19). Though the cause of that roller-coaster "flash crash" was never clear, the huge 1-day slide back in 1987 was attributed to such programmed trades.

The Securities and Exchange Commission is studying how these rapidly advancing technologies are affecting the markets, but unlike the Nasdaq OMX trades, their work is not at the speed of light.

FIGURE 1-19

Flash crash on May 6, 2010.

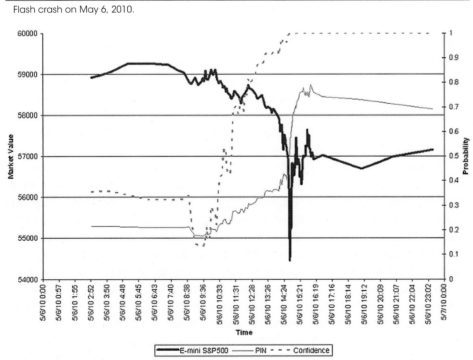

Source: http://en.wikipedia.org/wiki/File:Chart_dow_dip2.top.gif.

Discussion Questions

1. How has Nasdaq's business benefited from the use of information systems?
2. What risks do information systems pose for Nasdaq OMX's business?
3. This chapter discusses the value of information. What types of information are handled through Nasdaq systems, what are the key characteristics of this information, and how do Nasdaq customers use this information to create value?
4. What does the example of Goldman Sachs paying to locate its server in the Nasdaq data center say about the relationship between information systems and physical operations?

SOURCES: Grant, J. (2010). "Algo-trading" changes speed of the game on Wall Street. *Financial Times.* May 8, p. 2. Document ID: 2028321931. Muehlberg, R. L. (2008). How algo trading is changing the landscape. *Futures: News, Analysis & Strategies for Futures, Options & Derivatives Traders.* 37(10), 50–52. Nash, K. S. (2010). Pressure cooker. *CIO Magazine.* April 1, 29–35.

CASE STUDY #2

Breaking News: Twitter's Growing Role in Emergencies and Disaster Communications

When a city councilman in Atlanta, Georgia, spotted a woman on the street suffering a seizure, he quickly pulled out his cell phone. It showed low on battery, so instead of dialing 911 and getting stuck on hold, Councilman Hall tapped out a short tweet:

> "Need a paramedic on corner of John Wesley Dobbs and Jackson st. Woman on the ground unconscious. Pls ReTweet"

Several of the councilman's followers immediately saw his text message and dialed 911. Paramedics arrived quickly to take the woman to the hospital.

Twitter, the microblogging service best known for trivial updates on everyday events that might amuse or bore one's followers, has a growing role in emergency response. The service empowers people with the ability to gather and disseminate information about emergencies and disasters, and this information can be far timelier than anything government authorities or organizations such as the Red Cross can provide.

During the Red River Valley flood in 2009, for example, millions of tweets tracked the location and timing of flooding events, rising in volume with the water. The short messages offered on-the-ground observations of conditions, along with the worry, fear, and finally joy that residents felt when the floodwaters receded. They also passed along—or "retweeted"—official news from regular sources, such as TV or state government.

In the aftermath of the 2010 Haiti earthquake, a graduate student at the University of Colorado launched a project to improve Twitter's usefulness, called "Tweak the Tweet." Kate Starbird's goal was to develop syntax for tweets originating from the disaster sites, so they could be better organized and read by computer programs (Figure 1-20). The freewheeling unstructured tweets about victims who needed help were repurposed into more structured messages with "hash tags"—keywords preceded by a pound sign #. Computer programs can read these to categorize who is involved, what is needed, where the problem is, and what else might be happening. With this syntax, the tweets can be fed into disaster response systems that can aggregate information from many sources, mapping areas of need, the location of victims, sources of supplies, and much more.

The Red Cross and other disaster response organizations recognize that people are relying more heavily on social media such as Twitter for support during emergencies. In fact, social media are so prevalent that, in one survey, more than a quarter of the respondents said they would send a direct Twitter message to emergency responders, not realizing that aid organizations are not well prepared to monitor Twitter and other services. They also have few means to assess the value of information received in this way. It may be timely, but is it accurate? It might be a child's exaggerated report or a hoax from some scammer.

FIGURE 1-20

Reformatting tweets to improve disaster response.

Original Tweet:

Sherline Birotte aka Memen. Last seen at 19 Ruelle Riviere College University of Porter a3 story schol building

Restructured Tweet:

#haiti #ruok Sherline Birotte aka Memen. Last seen #loc 19 Ruelle Riviere College University of Porter #info a 3 story schol building

---

Despite the drawbacks, Twitter's value for emergency response and disaster communications may be phenomenal. Craig Fugate, an administrator at the Federal Emergency Management Center, said, "Social media can empower the public to be part of the response, not as victims to be taken care of."

Discussion Questions

1. What are the potential benefits of Twitter and other social media for emergency and disaster communications?

2. What are the potential risks of using Twitter and other social media for emergency and disaster communications?

3. What types of education would be necessary at the user level to make Twitter and other social media more effective for emergency and disaster communications?

4. What would need to happen on the part of aid organizations and traditional media for Twitter and other social media to be effective in emergency and disaster communications?

SOURCES: American Red Cross. (August 12, 2010). Social media grows up—Red Cross emergency social data summit. http://www.redcross.org/portal/site/en/menuitem.1a019a978f421296e81ec89e43181aa0/?vgnextoid=fa532b019666a210VgnVCM10000089f0870aRCRD, accessed April 30, 2011. Atlanta councilman chooses Twitter over 911 to report emergency. (May 19, 2009). EMSResponder.com. www.emsresponder.com/web/online/Top-EMS-News/Atlanta-Councilman-Chooses-Twitter-Over-911-to-Report-Emergency/1$9546, accessed April 30, 2011. Palen, L., Starbird, K., et al. (2010). Twitter-based information distribution during the 2009 Red River Valley flood threat. *Bulletin of the American Society for Information Science & Technology.* 36(5), 13–17. Schenker, J. L. (2009). Ushahidi empowers global citizen journalists. *BusinessWeek.com.* 12–12.

E-PROJECT 1 Analyzing the May 6 "Flash Crash" with Excel Charts

On May 6, 2010, the stock market showed mind-boggling turbulence for a few minutes, and investigators hypothesize that it was due to a flood of computer-generated trades. This e-project shows how to create charts using Excel, using downloaded stock data from that period so you can see what happened.

1. Download the Ch01_AAPL Excel file, which contains the high, low, and closing prices for Apple Computers between May 3 and May 14. (AAPL is the ticker symbol for Apple.) Open the file to see how the data are arranged in columns, with the first row showing the column headers.

   a. What was the closing price for Apple on May 6?

   b. What was the volume of trading for this stock on May 6?

2. Create a line graph from the AA PL data, in which the dates are on the x-axis (horizontal), and the stock prices are on the vertical (y) axis. Include the opening price, high, low, and closing price on the graph. Add a title to the top of your chart.

3. Download Expedia stock prices (ticker symbol EXPE) for the same time period (May 3–May 14, 2010) from http://finance.yahoo.com. (Click on Historical Prices, under QUOTES.)

   a. Create a line graph to compare the Low and Closing prices for Apple stock and Expedia stock. You do not need to include Open and High prices on this graph.

   b. How do you compare the activity on those two stocks?

E-PROJECT 2 Gathering, Visualizing, and Evaluating Reports from Twitter and Other Sources During a Disaster

The Ushahidi platform is open-source software that organizations use to aggregate, map, and visualize information about disasters or other emergencies. Originally developed to map reports of violence in Kenya after an election, software developers around the world continue to improve Ushahidi, which means "testimony" in Swahili. It can be adapted to the needs of different communities experiencing a variety of emergencies, from social unrest and violence to "snowmaggeddon," the huge snowstorm that paralyzed the eastern United States in 2010. Combined with another open-source product called "Swift River," the platform can help filter and manage real-time data coming in through Twitter, text messages, e-mail, the web, or other sources.

During the oil spill and recovery in the Gulf of Mexico, Tulane University students worked with the Louisiana Bucket Brigade and a private company to launch a site with Ushahidi to aggregate, map, and verify reports sent in by people using Twitter, text message, smartphone apps, e-mail, and web forms (Figure 1-21). Download the Excel file called "Ch01_OilSpill," which contains sample reports, and answer the following questions:

1. First, select columns B through F and reformat them with word wrap, so you can easily see the actual comments people sent in.

2. Suppose you have a friend who lives in Bay Champagne. First sort the table by LOCATION, and scroll down to Bay Champagne. How many reports do you find using this strategy? Why would this approach be limited in terms of its ability to find all the events that may have affected your friend?

3. For crisis management, timeliness is important, but so is accuracy. How many reports in this sample were not verified (NO in the Verified column)? You can use Excel's countif function to determine the number of NOs and YESes. What is the percentage of total reports that have not been verified?

4. Sort the file by CATEGORY then by LOCATION. Take a look at the reports that are categorized as Health Effects in Grand Isle. Why do you think many of these reports are not verified? Visit www.ushahidi.com/platform and examine the map showing the current and projects that are using it. Click on one near your home and explore how the organization is using the tools.

FIGURE 1-21

Mapping reports from Twitter, text messages, and other sources during the Gulf Oil Spill; www.oilspill.labucketbrigade.org, accessed May 1, 2011.

Source: www.oilspill.labucketbrigade.org. ©Louisiana Bucket Brigade.

CHAPTER NOTES

1. Stross, R. E. (2008). *Planet Google: One company's audacious plan to organize everything we know.* New York: The Free Press. pp. vii, 275.

2. Lawless, J. (2009). Villagers send Google snapper packing. *The Independent* (UK). www.independent.co.uk/news/uk/home-news/villagers-send-google-snapper-packing-1662012.html, accessed May 1, 2011.

3. Prater, E., Swafford, P. M., & Yellepeddi, S. (2009). Emerging economies: Operational issues in China and India. *Journal of Marketing Channels.* 16(2), 169–187.

4. Kilcourse, B. (2009). POS stays "front end" center. *Chain Store Age.* 85(1), 43.

5. Wailgum, T. (January 12, 2009). To hell with business intelligence: 40 percent of execs trust gut. *CIO.com.*

6. Boyd, D. M., & Ellison, N. B. (2007). Social network sites: Definition, history, and scholarship. *Journal of Computer-Mediated Communication.* 13(1), Article 11.

7. Roberts, J. (June 8, 2008). Social networking for business is next big thing. www.commercialappeal.com/news/2008/jun/08/social-networking/, accessed April 30, 2011.

8. Kornblum, J., & Marklein, M. B. (March 8, 2006). What you say online could haunt you. *USA Today.*

9. Gilroy, A. (2008). PND push: Free lifetime traffic updates. *TWICE: This Week in Consumer Electronics.* www.twice.com/article/253736-PND_Push_Free_Lifetime_Traffic_Updates.php accessed April 30, 2011.

10. Hamm, S. (2009). Big Blue goes into analysis. *BusinessWeek* (4128), 16–19.

11. Cook, S. (2008). The contribution revolution. *Harvard Business Review.* 86(10), 60–69.

12. Anonymous. (January 23, 3008). Gartner EXP worldwide survey of 1,500 CIOs shows 85 percent of CIOs expect "significant change" over next three years. *Gartner Newsroom.*

13. Mearian, L. (2009). Wall Street crisis forcing closer look at e-records. *Computerworld.* 43(3), 14–17.

14. Sidorova, A., et al. (2008). Uncovering the intellectual core of the information systems discipline. *MIS Quarterly.* 32(3), 467–482.

15. Fazio Maruca, R. (2000). Are CIOs obsolete? *Harvard Business Review.* 78(2), 55.

16. Survey finds workers average only three productive days per week. (March 15, 2005). www.microsoft.com/presspass/press/2005/mar05/03-15threeproductiveday-spr.mspx, accessed April 30, 2011.

17. Rosenoer, J., & Scherlis, W. (2009). Risk gone wild. *Harvard Business Review.* 87(5), 26.

18. York, E. B., & Wheaton, K. (2009). What Domino's did right—and wrong—in squelching hubbub over YouTube video. *Advertising Age.* 80(14), 1–24.

19. Olick, D. (May 21, 2008). Countrywide CEO Mozilo's "disgusting" email reply: OOPS! *CNBC.com.*

Information Systems and *Strategy*

Chapter Preview

COMPANIES COMPETE FOR YOUR DOLLARS, YOUR LOYALTY, AND YOUR ATTENTION, and the strategies they use often depend on innovative information systems. This chapter explores strategy, starting with the forces that shape industry competition and why some industries are more profitable than others. You will see how entire industries are occasionally transformed by events that sweep away obsolete business models and unleash a flood of new opportunities for agile players. Whether times are calm or turbulent, the reasons companies choose one strategy over another—and how they use information systems to implement them—help explain why some companies succeed and others fail.

Nonprofit organizations and governments have different missions, but they, too, develop strategies that leverage information systems to provide better services for their stakeholders. They find ways to reduce their costs, persuade donors to contribute, and engage volunteers in the mission.

Liu Jin/AFP/Getty Images/Newscom

Learning Objectives

1. Describe Porter's five competitive forces that shape industry competition.

2. Explain how disruptive innovations, government policies, complementary products and services, and other factors affect how the competitive forces operate.

3. Identify the components of the value chain and explain its extended version.

4. Describe how information systems apply to competitive strategies for business.

5. Explain how information systems apply to strategy for nonprofit organizations and governments.

6. Explain why the role of information systems in organizations shifts depending on whether the systems are deployed to run, grow, or transform the business.

Introduction

The search engine company called *Baidu* dominates the Chinese market and attracts Chinese speakers from all around the world. Its mission—to provide the best way for people to find information—is humble compared to Google's grand goal of organizing the world's information. Yet in China, Baidu far outstrips the search engine giant. Its strategy focuses directly on Chinese visitors, offering them ways to enter Chinese keywords and find relevant websites, also in Chinese.

The written Chinese language, with its tens of thousands of complex characters, poses immense challenges for human beings typing on keyboards with a standard QWERTY layout. And a syllable typed in English letters, such as *ma*, could represent different characters with quite different meanings (Figure 2-1). Baidu develops shortcuts, intelligent interfaces, and better ways to make life a bit easier for Chinese speakers struggling with a keyboard whose grandparent was the typewriter, designed in

FIGURE 2-1

The syllable "ma" typed on a QWERTY keyboard can refer to many different Chinese characters with different meanings. The spoken language distinguishes among them through tones, or slight changes in vocal pitch, as the syllable is pronounced.

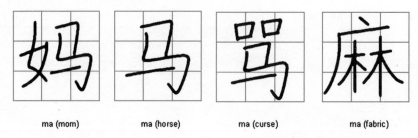

ma (mom)　　　ma (horse)　　　ma (curse)　　　ma (fabric)

the United States by English speakers. Baidu earns revenue from online marketers, much as Google does, by showing paid links relevant to the user's search terms.

It sounds simple, doesn't it? Baidu, with a clean Google-like interface, should have no trouble staying on top. But consumer-trading site Taobao has its eye on Baidu's market. Taobao offers services similar to eBay, but gained dominance over the American company in China by dropping commission fees entirely. Now Taobao's leaders want a piece of the online marketing revenue that search engines offer—and that Baidu is raking in. Joseph Tsai, chief financial officer of Taobao's parent company, said, "One of Baidu's biggest competitors is going to be Taobao."[1] Meanwhile, strategists at Google and Microsoft are making their own plans to capture a share of the Chinese Internet user market, almost 300 million strong—the largest of any country in the world. With their cash-heavy war chests and technical know-how, solving the Chinese input problem will not take long.

The strategies companies devise to win customers, earn market share, make profits, and grow their business are deeply entwined with information systems. In today's high-tech, globalized business environment, those strategies often rely heavily on innovative information technology (IT) and its application to any area, from marketing and human resources to manufacturing and supply chains. As you will see, some of the IT-related strategies have the potential to completely transform an industry, catapulting the company and its entrepreneurial founders into stardom, and pushing rivals into bankruptcy.

This chapter examines the nature of industry competition and how companies exploit openings to gain advantages, particularly with information systems. Industries differ, and in some it is more difficult to make a profit—or even survive—than others. Why this is so, and how IT can be such a powerful force for strategists, will become clear, drawing especially on Michael Porter's classic analysis of the forces that affect industry competition and shape strategy.[2, 3]

We will also see how nonprofit organizations develop strategies involving information systems to dramatically improve their ability to achieve their missions. Although the goals themselves are different, strategic thinking and strategic deployment of information systems are just as important.

1 Describe Porter's five competitive forces that shape industry competition.

Porter's Five Competitive Forces

Glancing at the industries with their average profitabilities in Figure 2-2, you might breathe a sigh of relief if you are not in the airline industry. Some industries enjoyed high return on investments during this time, with many successful companies. In others, the firms struggled just to stay afloat. For airlines, more companies went

FIGURE 2-2

Profitability of selected U.S. industries, from 2006 estimates.[3]

Industry	Profitability (average return on investment)
Soft drinks	37.6%
Prepackaged software	37.6%
Semiconductors	21.3%
Medical instruments	21.0%
Grocery stores	16.0%
Wine and brandy	13.9%
Book publishing	13.4%
Oil and gas machinery	12.6%
Hotels	10.4%
Catalog mail-order houses	5.9%
Airlines	5.9%
Average for all industries	14.9%

bankrupt than stayed in business. These conditions are not due to outstanding managerial talent in the high-profit industries and boneheaded CEOs elsewhere, though the strategies these people implement certainly play a role. Instead, based on Porter's model, the reasons lie with five interrelated forces that influence industry competition (Figure 2-3):

1. Threat of new entrants
2. Power of buyers
3. Power of suppliers
4. Threat of substitutes
5. Rivalry among existing competitors

To see how these forces play out, consider graduate students Prakash and Dana, who want to launch a new tutoring business for high school students. Needing extra money, they plan to develop an appealing and effective way for students to prepare for the SATs. Prakash and Dana know that students are notorious procrastinators, but they also have many small slots of time—usually wasted on daydreaming, game playing, or texting—throughout the day.

FIGURE 2-3

The five forces that shape competition in industries.

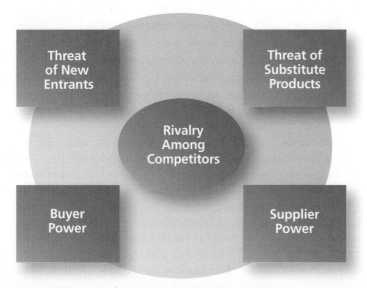

To make preparation less painful and also less costly compared to hiring personal tutors for long, tiring sessions, these cofounders want to draw on some of the compelling features of cell-phone games. Rewards, fast-paced action, competition, and special ring tones to indicate a student's advancing level as he or she gains mastery should help motivate students to practice SAT problems whenever they have a spare moment. As students improve, they can make up their own questions to add to the pool. Prakash and Dana like the name *Leveling Up Your SAT* for their company, reflecting the game world's jargon for advancing your skills or your character's capabilities. Think about how the strategic concepts in this chapter apply to their innovative idea, and then read the strategic analysis at the end of the chapter.

THREAT OF NEW ENTRANTS

The **threat of new entrants** in an industry is very high when start-ups like Leveling Up Your SAT can open shop with little capital, few employees, and next to no experience. Industry incumbents must keep their prices low to ward off newcomers, so profitability suffers.

Thinking too narrowly about who those new entrants might be can be dangerous. The big players in the SAT preparation business—Kaplan and The Princeton Review— know well that small start-ups can enter relatively easily. But new entrants might also come from established companies in other industries, whose leaders decide to diversify and encroach on another. Apple did just that when it penetrated the music distribution business with its online iTunes store. Flush with capital, companies like Apple can invest a considerable sum in a new venture outside their own industry. Apple also had the advantage of a large base of music-loving customers because of its successful iPod player.

For part, the incumbent industry players try to keep newcomers out in many different ways, often drawing on innovative use of information systems. They already have certain advantages, such as higher volumes, which can mean lower costs per unit of production. A large customer base can be significant because of **network effects**, which refer to the increased value of a product or service that results simply because there are more people using it. The value of Facebook, for example, is low if you can only connect a few people. But the more people who use that social network, the more valuable it becomes to everyone. Another example involves the wireless cellular carriers that try to foster network effects by offering free calling to any cell phone on the same network. They hope you will persuade your friends and family to select the same carrier. Their tactic also makes it cost-effective for businesses to stick with a single carrier for all its employees.

Did You Know?

Groupon, one of the world's fastest growing companies in 2011, offers daily deals by e-mail. Google offered $6 billion to buy the company, and the founders may have made a huge mistake by rejecting the offer. The threat of new entrants is huge, and hundreds of clones have already popped up. Time will tell, but loyal customers report suffering "Groupon anxiety" as they stay up late at night to see the next deal.[4]

Incumbents devise strategies to raise **switching costs**, which are the costs customers incur when they change suppliers. Carriers do this by offering a "free" cell phone with a 2-year contract, but the phone is not really free. Its cost is embedded in the monthly fees over the life of the contract, and termination fees recapture any remaining costs if the consumer stops service early.

Loyalty programs also raise switching costs and discourage new entrants. Frequent flyers earn valuable rewards for racking up all their flying miles with a single airline, including automatic upgrades and free companion tickets. Travelers go out of their way to stick with their favorite airline and continue to grow their point balance. Although these programs are effective in some industries, they have become so commonplace that any start-up can create one easily using an online service such as PointLoyalty.com. This Russia-based company handles points and bonuses for many small companies.

For information systems that organizations buy for their own use, switching costs can be extremely high. Besides the licensing costs, organizations invest considerable effort to change their business processes, migrate their data, and train their employees when they install a new system. Companies that use software such as SAP or Oracle to manage and support their business functions will be very reluctant to switch, even if their licensing costs go up and competitors offer cheaper pricing. This is one reason the prepackaged software industry enjoys very high profitability.

POWER OF BUYERS

The **power of buyers** rises when they have leverage over suppliers and can demand deep discounts and special services. If a supplier has a small number of buyers, the supplier is at a disadvantage because losing even one could be devastating. Companies whose main customer is government, for instance, must deal with a very powerful buyer. Buyer power also rises when many suppliers offer similar, undifferentiated products and the buyer can deal with any of them to get about the same product, with negligible switching costs. For airline tickets on the most popular and competitive routes, for example, buyers have considerable power. Unless passengers are tied to one airline with a loyalty program, they can search for the best price, a factor that holds down the airline industry's profitability.

The balance of power between buyers and suppliers for many industries shifted dramatically when markets went online and customers could switch from one seller to another with a single click. To make price comparisons for undifferentiated products even easier, dozens of websites gather up-to-the-minute prices from sellers so that visitors can easily compare them in a single list (Figure 2-4). On PriceGrabber.com, visitors can enter the product they want and pull up a list of all the merchants who sell it, along with their prices. To empower buyers further, the site asks visitors to rate the transaction when they purchase something from a seller on the list. These reviews tip off prospective buyers in case the seller fails to deliver or sends defective products.

POWER OF SUPPLIERS

The **power of suppliers** is high when they are just about the only game in town and thus can charge more for their products and services. Microsoft is an example. Given the dominance of its Windows operating system, PC assemblers around the world risk losing customers if they don't install it. Although Dell, IBM, HP, and Lenovo are large, there are hundreds of smaller companies that assemble components and must

---

FIGURE 2-4

PriceGrabber.com and many other websites offer comparison shopping to help consumers find the best price.

- ▶ PriceGrabber.com
- ▶ Yahoo! Shopping (shopping.yahoo.com)
- ▶ Shopping.com and partner DealTime.com
- ▶ NexTag.com
- ▶ Shopzilla.com and partner BizRate.com

---

threat of new entrants
The threat new entrants into an industry pose to existing businesses; the threat is high when start-up costs are very low and newcomers can enter easily. This is one of Porter's five competitive forces.

network effects
The increased value of a product or service that results simply because there are more people using it.

switching costs
Costs that customers incur when they change suppliers.

power of buyers
The advantage buyers have when they have leverage over suppliers and can demand deep discounts and special services. This is one of Porter's five competitive forces.

power of suppliers
The advantage sellers have when there is a lack of competition and they can charge more for their products and services. This is one of Porter's five competitive forces.

license Windows for their PCs. Not only can Microsoft demand higher prices, but it can also insist on additional perks, such as adding desktop icons for trial versions of its own software products.

PRODUCTIVITY TIP

Take a close look at the software trial versions that came preinstalled on your computer to see which products the PC manufacturer is promoting with this valuable positioning. As long as you have a recovery disk in case of problems, you can uninstall the ones you don't want to reduce clutter and improve your computer's performance.

Walmart's thousands of suppliers have far less power than Microsoft. There are few products made by a single supplier for which Walmart couldn't find an alternative close enough to please consumers. Also, Walmart's suppliers have invested in information systems that link their inventories to the company's legendary supply chain system.

High switching costs also add to supplier power. The loyalty programs described earlier do this, and there are even more dramatic strategies to lock in buyers that involve technology formats. Initially, for example, songs purchased at iTunes would only play on the iPod because of their proprietary format, and the iPod would only play songs in that format. When RealNetworks released software to convert its own music to the iPod format, Apple blasted the company as "illegal hackers." People who bought iPods had little choice but to buy music from Apple's store. The costs to switch to a different music player were also very high for consumers who had a large collection in the iTunes format. Consumer protests eventually convinced Apple to loosen its grip. The iTunes website states, "Now…the music you buy will play on iPod, Apple TV, all Mac and Windows computers, and many other digital music players."[5]

THREAT OF SUBSTITUTES

While the airline carriers compete head to head in a fierce fight to attract passengers, information systems offer a substitute for travelers, especially the ones who plan to attend a business meeting rather than lie on a beach. A news headline in *The Scotsman* read, "Video killed the passenger numbers," and a Gartner group analyst warns that video meeting solutions will cost the airlines more than 2 million seats a year. The **threat of substitutes** is high when alternative products are available, especially if they offer attractive savings.

As high-definition videoconferencing becomes available in conference rooms, natural communication can take place much more easily across vast distances (Figure 2-5). The technological advances eliminate the distracting choppiness and poorly synched voice transmissions that turned off businesspeople in the past. With rising fuel costs and tight travel budgets, videoconferencing becomes a viable substitute

FIGURE 2-5

Videoconferencing heightens the threat of substitutes to the business travel industry.

Shutterstock

for business travel, and analysts predict sales will explode. Cisco's Jacqueline Pigliucci Roy reports that the company's conferencing technology is the fastest growing product they have ever had. The systems can help slash travel costs and make international colleagues feel as though they are in the same room—without the jet lag.[6]

Substitutes, which provide the same product or service through a different means, can be quite difficult to predict and even harder to combat. What airline executives would dream that California-based Cisco, a leader in computer networking products, would grab their market? The substitute product puts even more pressure on an industry in which profitability is already low.

Information technology plays a key role in many examples of substitutional threats, from online learning modules that replace face-to-face training classes to Internet video, which threatens cable television companies. Webinars are also reducing the need for business travel. The threats may come from any direction, making it critical for strategists to pay attention to developments on a much wider scale. Although drug makers with patented products know that generic substitutes will rapidly take market share once the patent expires, other industries are taken by surprise when potent substitutes arise. The newspaper industry, for instance, failed to grasp how quickly subscribers would switch to the free news available online to save both money and trees. Cutting prices for print subscriptions or classified advertising only worsened their financial situations, and few newspapers enjoy healthy balance sheets.

RIVALRY AMONG EXISTING COMPETITORS

The profitability of an industry and its competitive structure are affected by the intensity of **rivalry among existing competitors**, particularly with respect to *how* they are competing and *what* they compete on. If firms compete mainly on price, rivalry is high and the industry as a whole becomes less profitable, because price cutting triggers rounds of retaliation and damaging price wars. Online, price cuts can occur with breathtaking speed, with no need to attach new price tags to physical merchandise. Price wars can also affect the behavior of buyers, who pay more attention to price long after the war ends, essentially reminding them to shop around for bargains and reducing profitability industry-wide.[7] The one who strikes first in a price war may benefit somewhat, but overall, all competitors are wounded while consumers enjoy terrific deals.

Slow growth can also lead to intense rivalry among existing competitors. If sales are flat, any competitive strategy from one company will steal market share from the others, so incumbents will counter every competitive move. If the companies can't or don't want to close up shop and leave the industry, rivalry remains high and competitors stay in the ring. Stubborn CEOs with big egos can lead to intense rivalry as well.

Factors That Affect How the Five Forces Operate

2 Explain how disruptive innovations, government policies, complementary products and services, and other factors affect how the competitive forces operate.

The five forces together determine industry structure and potential for profit. In addition to the strategies companies themselves implement, several external factors affect how those forces operate. Certain innovations, for example, can flood through an industry like a tidal wave, changing everything in their path and forcing every company to change its strategy.

DISRUPTIVE TECHNOLOGY AND INNOVATIONS

A **disruptive innovation** is a new product or service, often springing from technological advances, that has the potential to reshape an industry. For example, Kodak, Casio, Olympus, and other companies began offering digital cameras that needed no film in

---

threat of substitutes
The threat posed to a company when buyers can choose alternatives that provide the same item or service, often at attractive savings. This is one of Porter's five competitive forces.

rivalry among existing competitors
The intensity of competition within an industry. Intense rivalry can reduce profitability in the industry due to price cutting or other competitive pressures. This is one of Porter's five competitive forces.

disruptive innovation
A new product or service, often springing from technological advances, that has the potential to reshape an industry.

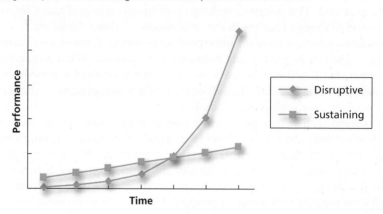

FIGURE 2-6

Comparing disruptive and sustaining innovations on performance over time.

the 1990s, transforming the industry within a few short years. Sales of film rolls and the cameras that used them plunged, along with the business of stores that processed the film. Although the early digital cameras had lower resolutions, technological advances quickly made them a very respectable substitute product that almost wiped out film cameras, along with all the services and products surrounding them.

Unlike **sustaining technologies**, which offer important improvements to streamline existing processes and give companies marginal advantages, disruptive innovation is different (Figure 2-6). Often developed by start-ups or industry outsiders, it brings a radical and unexpected breakthrough that first replaces lower end products, but then rapidly overtakes even the high end of the market. Companies that cling to the older models may eventually be out of business. Figure 2-7 shows more examples.

The Internet itself has been the kingpin of disruptive innovations in the last century, and all the innovations it supports are transforming one industry after another. It fundamentally changes aspects of the five forces by, for example, reducing entry barriers for newcomers, empowering buyers with far more information about prices and competitors, and virtually eliminating switching costs for many products. It also facilitates a vast, global marketplace in which competitors can spring from any corner of the globe, setting up shops online to compete with your neighborhood store.

Economist Joseph Schumpeter used the term **creative destruction** to describe what happens in an industry when disruptive innovations threaten the established players.

FIGURE 2-7

Examples of disruptive innovations.

Disruptive Innovation	Displaced Products and Services
Steamships	Sailing ships
Machine gun	Rifle
Truck	Horse
Digital camera	Instant cameras, such as Polaroid, and eventually most film cameras. High-end single-lens reflex cameras are still often preferred by professionals.
Desktop publishing software	Dedicated professional publishing systems
E-mail	Postal mail
Computer printer	Offset printing press
Music CD	Vinyl record, cassette tape, 8-track tape
Digital downloads of music and video	Music and video CD/DVD
Word-processing software	Typewriter
Online e-commerce	Physical retail stores
Cell phone	Landline phone

Newcomers find ways to capitalize on the new technologies, while many incumbents resist the change and seek ways to protect their old business models.

Digital music, downloaded one song at a time, is one of those disruptive innovations made possible by the Internet that led to sweeping creative destruction in the music business. Napster's file-sharing technology first made it widespread. Because sharing copyrighted songs is illegal, the record labels fought it fiercely with lawsuits, eventually forcing Napster to shut down. The labels were rightfully concerned about piracy, but they also had an urgent desire to protect the lucrative business model based entirely on CDs. As long as consumers were compelled to pay $15 to $20 for a complete album on CD, even if they only wanted one song, profits were protected. The industry did offer some single-song CDs and tapes at $3 or $4 each, but these cumbersome formats never caught on. Allowing online sales of single songs would wreak havoc on the whole industry, from the labels and artists to the retail stores and jewel case manufacturers, and the Record Industry Association of America (RIAA) resisted the trend.

From outside the music industry stepped Apple, which was about to launch what eventually became the highly successful iTunes online music store. Each song would cost 99 cents and could be instantly downloaded to your computer or iPod (Figure 2-8). During his first meeting with music company executives wearing coats and ties, the late Apple CEO Steve Jobs, in his trademark jeans and black turtleneck, interrupted their presentation after just four PowerPoint slides. From his standpoint, they just didn't get it. "You guys are all nuts," he said.

Sony's CEO, Howard Stringer, whose company lost millions to Apple by fighting this disruptive innovation, laments bitterly:

> "I'm a guy who doesn't see anything good having come from the Internet....
> (It) created this notion that anyone can have whatever they want at any given
> time. It's as if the stores on Madison Avenue were open 24 hours a day. They
> feel entitled. They say, 'Give it to me now,' and if you don't give it to them for
> free, they'll steal it." –Sony CEO Howard Stringer[8]

Clayton Christensen, author of *The Innovator's Dilemma* and *The Innovator's Solution*, argues that industry leaders need to be ever alert to these disruptive innovations, and they should build small teams that look for breakthrough opportunities themselves. The teams can't be part of the larger organizational bureaucracy, however, because that would stifle their creativity and draw them back toward improving the status quo. They need independence, a high tolerance for failure, and enthusiasm for even very small niche markets.[9, 10]

GOVERNMENT POLICIES AND ACTIONS

Government policies and funding priorities can have dramatic effects on how industries operate and how they evolve. Patents reduce the threat of new entrants, for example, while low cost loans to small business can increase that threat. In the wake of the 2009 financial crisis, governments poured money into the world economy to stimulate lending and save jobs. With good intentions, some funding was used to prop up failing companies to avoid job losses. Some revived and regained strength. But others became "zombies"—companies with no hope of recovery that stay in business anyway, dragging down prices and hurting their healthier industry competitors.[11]

Organizations frequently lobby for government action to influence how the five forces operate and to improve industry profitability. Among the large technology companies, for example, spending on lobbying has more than doubled since the late 1990s. Lobbyists concentrate on regulatory policy, taxes, government subsidies, and

sustaining technologies
Technologies that offer improvements to streamline existing processes and give companies marginal advantages.

creative destruction
What happens in an industry when disruptive innovations threaten the established players.

other issues that affect the industry. For example, companies such as Amazon, eBay, Google, and Microsoft band together to fight attempts by the telecommunications companies to sell access to an "Internet fast lane" that would provide better quality and faster transmissions for favored content providers. The telecom companies want to offer tiered service with special pricing plans to improve their own industry. The second case study at the end of the chapter explores this heated debate.

Judges and courts offer another important means by which government affects industry structure. For instance, anti-trust laws prevent dominant players from exploiting their power and becoming monopolies. The European Commission fined Intel $1.45 billion for abusing its dominant position in the computer chip industry in Europe by giving rebates to PC makers for using its chips. The court determined that this practice unlawfully disadvantaged AMD, a rival chip maker.

Many lobbying groups fight for government regulation to forestall the new entrants enabled by the Internet. Optometrists once enjoyed a lucrative business in contact lens sales, as patients used their new prescription to buy their lenses at the optometrist's store. When 1800contacts.com and other retailers began offering lenses at discounted prices, they lobbied to make it easier for customers to compare prices and buy elsewhere. However, the American Optometry Association also lobbied, and the 2004 "Fairness To Contact Lens Consumers Act" contained regulations to appease both groups. For instance, doctors must provide patients with an original, signed prescription, but online sellers may not accept faxed prescriptions from the consumer without the doctor's confirmation.

COMPLEMENTARY SERVICES AND PRODUCTS IN THE ECOSYSTEM

Many industries are interrelated and events in one can influence the structure and profitability in another. Valuable products that emerge in one industry can make products in another even more desirable. Desktop publishing software, for example, makes the computer much more useful to small businesses that save money by developing menus, signs, and brochures in-house. Manufacturers of printers and specialty paper also benefit from the software.

© Juice Images/Alamy

FIGURE 2-8

"Innovation distinguishes between a leader and a follower." –Apple CEO Steve Jobs

Companies are embedded in a complex **ecosystem**—an economic community that includes the related industries making complementary products and services, the competitors themselves, the suppliers, and also the consumers. Events in one arena—particularly a disruptive innovation—ripple through the whole community, affecting all the players and the five forces for the industries involved.

In the United States, the ecosystem for gambling consists of casinos, Indian reservations, government regulators, lobbyists, consumer groups, racetracks, financial institutions, hotels, live entertainment, and others. Moving funds from a U.S. financial institution to an online gambling site is illegal, so the online gambling sites operating in countries such as Antigua are at arms length in this ecosystem; many do not accept U.S. players to their games. But efforts are underway in the U.S. Congress to change that. American gamblers spend more than $100 billion a year on the online betting sites, but no tax revenue is collected. U.S. casinos would like to see the law changed as well so they can launch online sites of their own. Change in the law would be a ripple that spreads throughout the gambling ecosystem, damaging some members, rewarding others, and attracting new entrants with complementary services. Hotels may suffer, but the casinos will have another source of revenue. Cell-phone developers will quickly see a new, user-friendly application—live poker with real bets paid by credit card.

Some of the most powerful strategic moves come from visionaries who propose fundamental changes for all the industries in the ecosystem and persuade the others to come along. Bill Gates did just that early in his career, when he articulated a vision for moving computing away from mainframes and onto the desktop. To succeed, they would need a standard operating system so that software developers, peripheral manufacturers, and everyone else could build upon it and quickly enrich the ecosystem with a compelling set of complementary products and services. The Microsoft operating system began its ascent, eventually dominating the industry with almost 90 percent market share. Other companies that created applications to run on that operating system succeeded as well.

Another example of a strategy that leads an ecosystem into new, mutually beneficial directions involves Salesforce.com. The company's CEO promotes cloud computing (discussed in detail in the next chapter), in which an organization's information systems are not installed locally on premises. Instead, employees use the Internet to connect to their systems, hosted by a vendor in a data center shared by many other businesses (Figure 2-9). (The "cloud" is a metaphor for the Internet; a cloud-like shape is often used to depict its complex infrastructure.)

Companies can purchase subscriptions for their employees to use the Salesforce software to manage their customer relationships, and CEO Mark Benioff sees cloud computing as the future—not just for his CRM application, but for many others as well. In fact, cloud computing may be the disruptive innovation that displaces the desktop PC with its locally installed software.

One way that Salesforce.com's approach will benefit many players in the ecosystem is through the Service Cloud, which helps companies improve customer service for their own products. Service Cloud captures conversations among networks of friends on Facebook, Twitter, and other social networking sites. Friends will ask questions like, "How did you get your smartphone to access your gmail account?" in user communities devoted to those topics, and Service Cloud tracks the answers. If Salesforce agents see that the answers are worthwhile and actually resolve the problem, they can add the conversation to customer service websites for the companies involved. The approach recognizes that a considerable amount of technical support goes on behind the scenes among friends who trust one another and are willing to take time to help out. The Service Cloud leverages those friendships by making the best answers more widely available.[12]

PRODUCTIVITY TIP

You can try out one version of cloud computing with Google Docs. Your documents are stored in one of Google's immense data centers, rather than on your own PC, and you can use a web browser to access them from any computer. Keep backups, however, and avoid uploading sensitive or confidential documents. The free service offers no guarantees.

FIGURE 2-9

Cloud computing supported by the Internet. Photos/Illustrations: broukoid/Shutterstock, Alex Kalmbach/Shutterstock

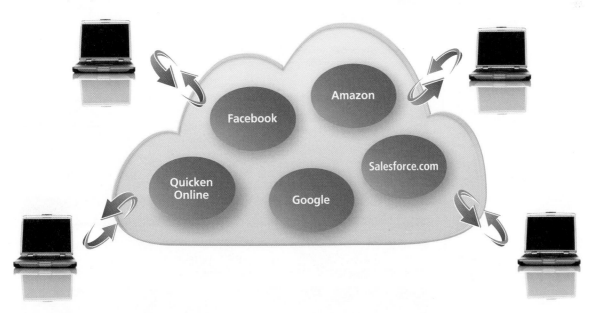

ecosystem
An economic community that includes the related industries making complementary products and services, the competitors themselves, the suppliers, and also the consumers.

ENVIRONMENTAL EVENTS AND "WILDCARDS"

Hurricanes, snowstorms, pandemics, earthquakes, strikes, and civil unrest can all have major effects on entire industries, sometimes without much warning. The H1N1 flu outbreak, for example, triggered major downturns in the travel and tourism industries. Egyptian authorities called for the slaughter of all pigs, which were thought to carry the virus, and international trade bans on pork products were implemented by many countries, even though humans can't catch flu from eating cooked pork.

Rising energy costs, conservation initiatives, and concerns over carbon emissions may also trigger waves of change. For example, supply chains that stress just-in-time deliveries may struggle to pay for the extra gas that kind of service requires. E-commerce companies that rely on many small shipments trucked to people's homes may have to raise their shipping fees, losing some competitive advantage. Information systems can help companies reduce their energy costs by optimizing routes.[13]

For an organization to develop a viable competitive strategy, its leaders take into account the nature of the industry and how the five competitive forces play out. They also consider the factors affecting those forces and how they are changing. But what are their strategic options, and where do information systems fit in? Michael Porter also developed a model that helps strategists think about how the organization actually creates value and where improvements can be made to advance the firm's competitive position.

3 | Identify the components of the value chain and explain its extended version.

The Value Chain and Strategic Thinking

Porter's **value chain model** describes the activities a company performs to create value, as it brings in raw resources from suppliers, transforms them in some way, and then markets the product or service to buyers (Figure 2-10). In the model, the company performs **primary activities** directly related to the process by which products and services are created, marketed, sold, and delivered. **Support activities** encompass all the other processes and offices the company needs, including administration and management, human resources, procurement, and technology support.

FIGURE 2-10

Components of the value chain.

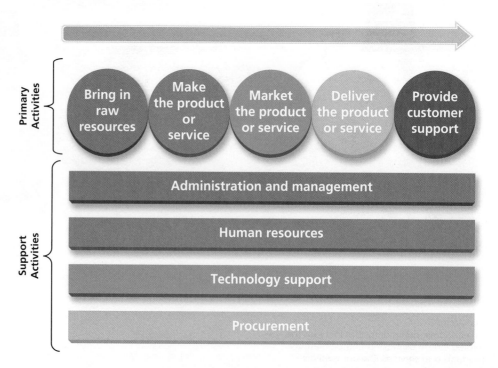

Primary Activities

Bring in raw resources | Make the product or service | Market the product or service | Deliver the product or service | Provide customer support

Support Activities

Administration and management

Human resources

Technology support

Procurement

The model may seem to suggest the activities typical in manufacturing companies but, in fact, it applies to a wide variety of settings. The "raw resources," for example, might be copper ore mined from Russia's Ural Mountains and trucked to a processing plant. They could also be digital journal articles downloaded from online libraries and summarized for a briefing paper needed by a government agency. "Making the product or service" can span many different tasks, from chemical processing of the copper to the consultants' research and analytical synthesis.

EXTENDING THE VALUE CHAIN: FROM SUPPLIERS TO THE FIRM TO CUSTOMERS

Expanding the model beyond the company's own primary and support activities leads to a better understanding of how all the processes fit together (Figure 2-11). The chain does not actually begin when a truckload of copper is dumped on a processor's doorstep, or when the analyst clicks "download" to retrieve a paper from *Harvard Business Review* online. The chain also does not end when the buyer pays for the product or service. Events in these external parts of the chain can also offer strategic opportunities.[14]

A company with shoddy suppliers might benefit from a switch or from strategic alliances with a few of them to help make them more efficient. Toyota, for example, encourages its tiny auto part suppliers to set up shop near its factories so Toyota can provide extensive training and support. Or a company that spots weakness in the suppliers' industry might decide to supply its own needs and even compete against its former suppliers.

Downstream, the value chain offers even more intriguing possibilities for strategic advantages. From the buyer's viewpoint, your company is a supplier and understanding the customers' own value chain is critical. What are the customers' needs and why are they buying the product? If the customer is another company, what is its strategy for creating value from what you provide?

Nike, the world's number-one athletic footwear maker, focuses mainly on product development, marketing, and its Nike branded stores. It leaves other activities—including actually making the shoes—to others. Its control of the stores, however, ensures that the company's ear is always to the ground to hear customer feedback early. The company is a vigorous competitor, and CEO Phil Knight is often quoted as saying, "Business is war without bullets."

Online, the extended value chain often incorporates contributions from buyers who help add value to the company's products or services. For example, Amazon's own customers enrich the retailer's site by contributing their frank and often blunt product reviews and rating the usefulness of other reviews. YouTube's entire inventory consists of this kind of user-generated content. CNN's *iReport* program solicits videos

FIGURE 2-11

The extended value chain involving suppliers, the company, and its customers.

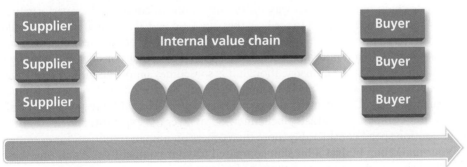

Extended value chain

value chain model
A model developed by Michael Porter that describes the activities a company performs to create value, as it brings in raw resources from suppliers, transforms them in some way, and then markets the product or service to buyers.

primary activities
Activities directly related to the value chain process by which products and services are created, marketed, sold, and delivered.

support activities
Activities performed as part of the value chain model that are not primary; support activities include administration and management, human resources, procurement, and technology support.

THE ETHICAL FACTOR Ethical Responsibility in an Extended Value Chain

As the extended value chain lengthens, responsibility for harmful consequences becomes more diffuse. Considering the length and complexity of the value chain that leads to a smartphone in a customer's hands, who is ethically responsible when it overheats and injures someone? Suppose a manager allocates smartphones to the salespeople and one person is badly burned while driving. How much responsibility would you assign to each of the links in this chain listed in Figure 2-12?

If you learned that the factory's working conditions were dreadful and the smartphone company made a deal with them anyway because their costs were so low, would your judgments change? Suppose the retailer got a tip that a recall was coming but kept selling the phones to get rid of the inventory. Increasingly, people are rejecting the "plausible deniability" excuse that companies have used in the past to avoid corporate responsibility for mishaps in their extended supply chains. Nevertheless, the drive to reduce costs, particularly for firms that compete for low cost leadership, can lead to ethically questionable decisions. The blurred boundaries along the extended value chain can make it even more difficult to allocate responsibility, and easier to point fingers.

FIGURE 2-12

How much responsibility would you assign to each of these links in the extended value chain?

	Not Responsible	Somewhat Responsible	Very Responsible
The retailer who sold it to the consumer			
The smartphone company that designs and markets it under the company name			
The factory that assembles it			
The factory worker who assembled the particular phone			
The small business that supplied battery parts to the factory			
The global shipping company that transported the phones			
The procurement manager who researched the options and selected the phones for the sales staff			
The manager who supplied the smartphones			
The user who didn't read the instruction manual			

from individuals who might just have happened to have their cell-phone camcorder turned on during breaking news. In Australia, the news site Scoopflash is based entirely on user-generated news. Web 2.0 offers countless opportunities to incorporate contributions from many different sources into the extended value chain.

BENCHMARKING COMPONENTS OF THE VALUE CHAIN

The value chain model offers a way for organizations to compare their performance against industry benchmarks to see how they stack up and also spot areas that should be targeted for improvement. A **benchmark** is a reference point used as a baseline measurement. Often it indicates a measurement that would be considered optimal, or best practices within the industry, though it is sometimes simply an industry average.

For the value chain, one benchmark might be the percent of total budget allocated to each of the primary and support activities. How does the organization's allocation compare to industry benchmarks, or average expenditures? Does your organization spend considerably more than others on human resources, for example? Is your marketing budget a bit slim compared to your competitors? Analyzing these benchmarks can point to areas that need attention—not necessarily more funding, but some thought about why the organization is spending more (or less).

In some cases, the variation may be a strategic decision intended to bolster the company's competitive advantage. For human resources, for example, some companies may try to keep salaries low, while others invest more heavily in human resources to encourage retention and develop the talent they have.

FIGURE 2-13

Average IT spending by industry.

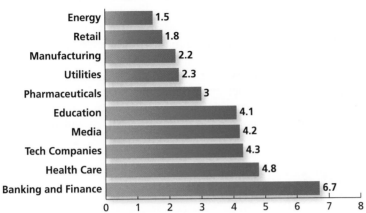

Average IT Spending as a Percentage of Revenue

Energy	1.5
Retail	1.8
Manufacturing	2.2
Utilities	2.3
Pharmaceuticals	3
Education	4.1
Media	4.2
Tech Companies	4.3
Health Care	4.8
Banking and Finance	6.7

IT BENCHMARKS

Figure 2-13 shows the average percent of total revenue allocated to IT spending for technology support activities for sample industries in 65 countries.[15] Banking and finance top the list with almost 7 percent of revenue allocated to this component of the value chain. Building online financial services is an enormously expensive proposition.

Another benchmark useful for information systems is the amount spent per employee, and Figure 2-14 shows these averages by industry. Overall, organizations spend more than $13,000 for each employee, an amount that goes well beyond the obvious computer on the desk. It includes all hardware, software, salaries for IT personnel, software licensing, data center costs, telecommunications costs, outsourced IT projects, new software and hardware, and others.

IT spending varies not just by industry, but also by region of the world. Companies in Asia spend almost 70 percent more per employee compared to those in Latin America and the Caribbean, and much of the additional expense goes to capital investment in infrastructure.

FIGURE 2-14

Average IT spending per employee in a sample of industries.

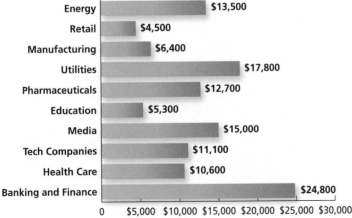

Average IT Spending per Employee

Energy	$13,500
Retail	$4,500
Manufacturing	$6,400
Utilities	$17,800
Pharmaceuticals	$12,700
Education	$5,300
Media	$15,000
Tech Companies	$11,100
Health Care	$10,600
Banking and Finance	$24,800

benchmark
A reference point used as a baseline measurement.

How should managers interpret these figures? Benchmarks like these change every year, as industries put more or less funding into IT or change their ideas about what to spend money on. In some industries, such as education, retail, and technology, the emphasis on IT is growing and organizations are spending more each year. Universities, for instance, increase spending to provide more online and mobile services to students, including e-learning. For banking and finance, though, where IT spending was already quite high compared to other industries, growth in IT spending is slowing down.

Managers can use benchmarks like these to assess components in the extended value chain and examine how much every dollar they spend is helping to create value. Each component offers opportunities for either cost savings or improved products and services that offer more value to buyers, both of which can improve the company's competitiveness and bottom line.

Did You Know?

Energy costs affect almost every link in the value chain, and organizations are testing out cheaper sources—including humans. California Fitness Gym connected all of its exercise bikes, ellipticals, rowing machines, and treadmills to generators, so customers supply up to 40 percent of the building's electricity.

Describe how information systems apply to competitive strategies for business.

Competitive Strategies in Business

Becoming a leader in an industry takes uncanny skill and strategic thinking. Although there are many variables and infinite combinations, Porter identified three basic strategies companies can adopt that are most likely to lead to success.

The **low cost leadership strategy**, which means offering a similar product at a lower price compared to competitors, is one that Walmart, Kia Motors, Southwest Airlines, E-Machine, and many others pursue. To be successful, the company has to cut every gram of fat in the value chain, using information systems to automate and streamline processes and eliminate costly human labor. Walmart's enormous success as a low cost leader in retailing comes especially from its IT-supported supply chain, the envy of its competitors.

A relentless search for ways to reduce operating expenses and achieve efficiencies pervades this strategy. Large companies can leverage their economies of scale and their powerful position relative to suppliers, but in some industries new entrants can adopt this strategy successfully as well.

ASUSTeK, a computer company in Taiwan, entered the laptop business with its "Eee PC," a stripped-down model with a tiny price tag—under $250. Founder Jonney Shih believed people wanted something lighter and cheaper, as long as it booted up quickly and had decent battery life. The major computer companies initially wrote off the netbook, as it came to be called, as a toy, but consumers thought differently. Sales skyrocketed, and not surprisingly, rival computer makers Dell, HP, Samsung, and Acer all took notice. Acer leapfrogged ahead with even lower prices, highlighting a significant downside of the low cost leader strategy. It is very difficult to sustain and can lead to the price wars described earlier. As Shih points out, "We can't forget that people are running after us" (Figure 2-15).[16]

Many companies adopt the **product differentiation strategy**—adding special features or unique add-ons for which customers are willing to pay more. The strategy tends to reduce threats from substitute products and also erects barriers to new entrants. Apple computer is a clear example that cleverly takes this path over and

FIGURE 2-15

Price competition in netbooks is fierce.

goony/Shutterstock

over again, with its Macintosh computers, iPod, iPhone, and iTunes music store. Its iPADs are now challenging lower cost netbooks, as well, despite the iPad's higher price. Pharmaceutical companies naturally adopt this strategy in their search for specialized drugs that can be patented.

Differentiating the product or service for a particular market niche is called a **focused strategy**. Research in Motion (RIM), for example, positions its BlackBerry smartphone for the business and government segment, with its conservative looks and business-oriented features. Unlike other smartphones, many RIM models lack wireless Internet capabilities, which is actually a plus for government employees and many businesspeople because of security issues.[17] Instead, they offer costlier Internet access through more secure transmissions.

Although Michael Porter thought companies should pick one of the strategies and stick with it, not everyone agrees, particularly in the digital age in which those five forces that shape competition in an industry have been shaken up considerably. Companies find successful paths with hybrid models, such as shooting for the best value for the lowest price. This contrasts with the low cost approach because it also encourages customers to compare the value of a product and its features against the competition. That can help counter deadly price wars.

Companies also achieve a different kind of success by building a large and rapt audience, gaining market share in a market that did not exist in the past. YouTube took that route by attracting millions of people who wanted to share their homemade videos with friends. The company charged nothing for its services, but venture capitalists who know the value of such a large and faithful following provided the capital. These "angel" investors hope a major company with deep pockets will acquire the new company for far more. As it turned out, Google bought YouTube for more than 40 times the sum investors contributed.

low cost leadership strategy	**product differentiation strategy**	**focused strategy**
A company strategy that involves offering a similar product at a lower price compared to competitors.	A company strategy that involves adding special features to a product or unique add-ons for which customers are willing to pay more.	A company strategy that involves differentiating a product or service for a particular market niche.

THE ROLE OF INFORMATION SYSTEMS IN STRATEGY

All of these strategies leverage information systems to succeed, and often the information and communications technology (ICT) component is at the very heart of the company's competitive advantage. Low cost leaders, for example, must automate as much as possible, from their suppliers to their customer support services. Indeed, all companies, regardless of their strategic path, benefit from the cost savings made possible through information systems.

Obvious savings accrue from implementing information systems to support all the back-office functions—payroll, benefits, accounting, procurement, inventory tracking, and asset management, for example. Indeed, major gains come from rethinking how these processes are done in the first place, by eliminating steps or avoiding duplication of effort. Converting to self-service in human resources, for instance, is a prime example. Rather than asking employees to complete paper forms that are reviewed by staff in the human resources office and then entered into systems that manage payroll and benefits, information systems let employees handle those tasks themselves. They can enter benefit selections, fill in tax forms, complete their time sheets, update contact information, register for professional development classes, and track their vacation and sick days, all online. Mercifully, phone calls to the human resources office drop considerably, and employees need not struggle with paper forms.

Information systems support strategy and reduce cost in many different ways depending on the industry. Consider how information systems streamline processes for railroads, to which shippers are gravitating because of rising fuel costs. Freight trains, after all, can move a ton of freight 400 miles on a single gallon of fuel. En route, the only busy employee is the conductor, but things change when the train stops at a terminal hub. Trucks line up to pick up or deposit their containers, and information systems coordinate their movements by scanning each one and directing it to its proper location. Thanks to these systems, truckers are in and out in 3 minutes instead of 20, and the number of accidents is dramatically reduced.

Launching a strikingly differentiated product or service often relies on innovations in IT as well, and not just for high-tech companies. Grocery stores are experimenting with various smart shopping carts with wireless access that scan shoppers' loyalty cards and then guide them through the aisles. The devices can announce special sales, scan purchases, and total the bill so customers breeze through checkout. The information is transmitted to the store's inventory system, just as the scanned data from a regular register are, so restocking is triggered as needed. Unlike the register data, though, the smart carts can report length of time in store and aisles visited, and can also deliver real-time ads that match the customer's interests. If you put hotdogs in the cart, it can offer discounts on buns and relish. Models developed by Springboard networks for a South Carolina grocery store also help customers choose recipes and then automatically add the ingredients to the shopping list.

INFORMATION SYSTEMS: RUN, GROW, AND TRANSFORM THE BUSINESS

What is that $13,000 on IT spending per employee actually used for, and how does it contribute to the company's strategy (Figure 2-16)? The computers, laptops, cell phones, and other devices support productivity throughout the organization, in every component of the value chain, whether the employee is in sales, finance, marketing, management, or human resources. The software applications touch every component of the value chain as well, streamlining processes in administration and management, creating customer friendly portals to improve loyalty, or compiling reports about the effectiveness of marketing campaigns.

FIGURE 2-16

How do organizations spend their IT dollars?[18]

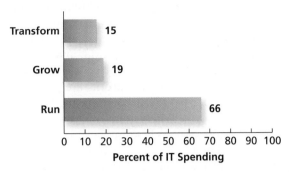

Percent of IT Spending

On average, organizations spend about two-thirds of that $13,000 to just keep things running. These costs include IT staff salaries, the data center, the help desk, software licenses, and maintenance of the company's core application software and infrastructure. They are not discretionary, in the sense that the organization can't operate without these capabilities. However, there are many ways to reduce these costs. Some companies are outsourcing their help desks, for example, or moving to cloud computing to reduce data center expenses. Indeed, managers should seek out opportunities to reduce expenses in this kind of IT spending, just as they would for any other component of the value chain.

Strategic uses of IT that consume the rest of the budget focus on growing the business (19%) or transforming the business model (15%). These can be applied regardless of whether the company strives for cost leadership, differentiation, a focused strategy, or some mix. IT is a **strategic enabler**, a role that can potentially make a far greater contribution to success compared to its role in keeping the business running. Information systems can, for example, facilitate a whole new business model, as they did for eBay in the form of specialized software to support online auctions.

Another example of a potentially game changing use of IT is the electronic medical record (EMR). The EMR is an essential ingredient to coordinate medical information so that patients, doctors, and other health care professional have easy access to it. The goal is to drastically reduce health care costs by digitizing patient history and treatment records, and making them available to health care providers as needed. Despite promising starts, however, this strategic use of information systems to transform health care lags behind almost every other industry. More than 80 percent of small medical practices keep paper records in file drawers, and prescriptions are scribbled on pads. Little information is collected or maintained about treatment results, leaving plenty of room for error and duplication of effort. To overcome the obstacles, security concerns and data exchange issues must be addressed to safeguard privacy and avoid creating a hodgepodge of incompatible systems that won't talk to each other.

Information Strategies and Nonprofit Organizations

5 Explain how information systems apply to strategy for nonprofit organizations and governments.

Dane R. Grams, the online strategy director at the nonprofit Human Rights Campaign (HRC), recognizes the need for immediacy when a legislative proposal is up for a vote and phone calls from voters can make a difference. "We wanted to call on our most active supporters to act on a moment's notice.... Most people have a single cell phone and it's always with them." HRC arranged to send messages to their members at the right moment, asking them to call their representatives about a pending bill and

strategic enabler
The role information systems play as tools to grow or transform the business, or facilitate a whole new business model.

giving them key points to use in the conversation. Once the message ended, the member was connected to the right office, vastly simplifying the mobilization process.[19]

Although nonprofit organizations have no shareholders, they do have objectives that need strategic planning and that benefit from strategic use of information systems. Running, growing, and transforming the organization are all very relevant to nonprofits, just as they are to the for-profit world, and information systems play a key role.

The operational requirements to run nonprofits are quite similar to businesses, with information systems used for payroll, accounting and finance, human resources, asset management, and related tasks. Many nonprofits also need information systems to track sales and customer transactions because they may sell products and services, either as part of their mission or as ancillary activities.

Some of the most innovative strategic uses of information systems come from the nonprofit world, among charities, schools, political groups, grassroots projects, religious organizations, government agencies, and others. Reaching out to their constituencies is fundamental to most nonprofit organizations, and ICT brings tremendous capabilities to that task. Two areas that have benefited considerably from such innovations are fund-raising and volunteer management.

FUND-RAISING

A major funding source for many nonprofits is donations, and specialized information systems help manage this critical activity. Though direct mail and telemarketing once dominated, much fund-raising is now done online. In 4 years, for example, annual online donations for Chicago's YMCA leaped from a paltry $450 to $24,000, a jump of more than 5,000 percent. Even a small nonprofit can reach out to a worldwide audience through the Internet, making a case for its mission and motivating people to help.

 Nonprofits leverage information systems to learn more about potential donors, their preferences, and their motivations, much as companies such as Amazon.com do to build relationships with customers. The Leukemia and Lymphoma Society, for example, won a contest sponsored by Google and earned free help from web design consultants. Not certain how to promote its "Team in Training" program, it conducted an experiment to compare three different web pages, with Google's help. One featured photos of team participants climbing mountains and competing in sporting events, a second version showed a video about the program, and the third contained written testimonials. During the experiment, Google randomly directed visitors to one of the three versions, and the charity analyzed how many visitors signed up to receive more information. The results showed that the sporty photos worked best, with almost 20 percent of the visitors asking for more information.[20]

Memberships and dues constitute another important source of funding for thousands of nonprofit professional associations, unions, alumni groups, and many others. Education is one of the most valuable services nonprofits offer to their members, whether it is to build awareness of legislative proposals or help members pass certification exams. A strategic use of ICT in this area is the launch of e-learning initiatives. The Public Library Association, for instance, offers online courses in web design and podcasting, and provides lessons on how to organize children's poetry readings. E-learning, discussed in more detail in Chapter 9, can be critically important to the constituents of any nonprofit, but particularly those whose members are worldwide.

VOLUNTEERING

 Attracting volunteers and sustaining their attachment to the mission are essential tasks for many nonprofits. The efforts are similar to those companies use to build customer relationships and develop employee loyalty. In fact, recognizing the similarity, Salesforce.com created a foundation to help nonprofits use their CRM software, originally designed for businesses to manage customer relationships for the salespeople.

Among the early adopters was Wildlife Victoria, an Australian nonprofit that rescues and rehabilitates injured and orphaned native wildlife. Wildlife Victoria implemented Salesforce.com to help manage and extend its network of volunteer wildlife rescuers, coordinate rescue events, and keep track of potential donors. Aiding wildlife at risk can be a complex operation, and the system helps coordinate the many components—from wildlife shelters and transporters to emergency services and rehabilitation.

Finding volunteers and helping them identify a project that needs their skills are ongoing challenges. However, both tasks have been streamlined by the volunteer's version of an online matchmaking service. VolunteerMatch.org offers search tools to help people find projects underway near their homes that match their interests (Figure 2-17). More than 62,000 nonprofits post their needs on the site, hoping to attract volunteers to teach swimming, mentor children, care for animals, guide museum visitors, and, of course, help build information systems needed by nonprofits. The site adds a Google map with pushpins showing the locations of the opportunities in your area. The founders originally wanted to promote community involvement through volunteering, with a mission "to bring good people and good causes together." Now, volunteers can also search for virtual opportunities, regardless of their own physical location.

VolunteerMatch's Greg Baldwin ignores the conventional wisdom that people don't volunteer because they don't care enough and focuses instead on creating an information system to make the whole process easier. His view of IT as a strategic enabler is clear: "To manage [technology] effectively you need to understand people first and what they need the technology to do."[21]

INFORMATION STRATEGIES AND GOVERNMENT

Like nonprofits, government agencies have similar needs for information systems to "run" the business, handling the operational requirements that all organizations share. They must manage their payrolls, budgets, procurements, assets, and inventories.

FIGURE 2-17

VolunteerMatch.org helps volunteers find opportunities in their areas.

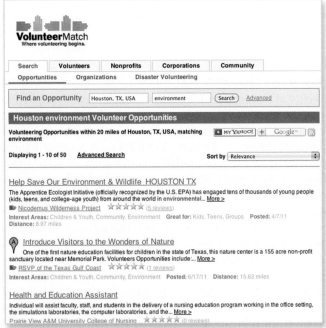

Source: VolunteerMatch.org. Used with permission.

Agencies also have some very specialized requirements that depend on their responsibilities and the varied services they provide. For example:

▶ The military needs real-time systems to manage logistics so that personnel and supplies can be rapidly deployed to trouble spots.

▶ India's Ministry of Information and Broadcasting needs systems to track export and import of films, news services, and other kinds of information broadcasts.

▶ State and local police need access to extensive information systems on criminal offenses.

▶ Canada's Department of Natural Resources offers online forms to anonymously report poachers who damage forests or hunt illegally.

▶ The U.S. Internal Revenue Service must have information systems to process more than 200 million tax returns annually.

Government missions, however, differ from those of businesses or other kinds of nonprofit organizations. They can include education, security, defense, infrastructure, justice, law making, regulation, international affairs, health and welfare, and more. They also often include a charge to break new ground in research, particularly when the project involves a substantial investment but a long-term benefit to the whole country. Citizens also expect their governments to spend taxpayer dollars wisely and provide services in a cost-effective manner.

INCREASING ACCESS AND ENHANCING SERVICES TO THE PUBLIC   **E-government** involves efforts to make unclassified information available to citizens via the Internet and offer many interactive online services to save people time-consuming visits to government offices. It has been slow getting off the ground in some areas, but U.S. agencies are required to post what they have directly to the Internet. Their websites are beginning to overflow with resources for the public. Search engines help visitors track down what they need, and USA.gov serves as a gateway.

The U.S. Census Bureau, for example, offers many summaries and tables online, and also provides tools to help researchers download data. Visitors can retrieve detailed records by county or zip code on school enrollments, educational attainments, marital status, income, native language, ethnicity, and more.

Interactive online services, from motor vehicle registration payment systems to absentee ballot requests, also enhance access and convenience for the public. The Federal Communications Commission offers an interactive service for people to conveniently submit complaints when they receive junk faxes or unsolicited telemarketing calls.

PRODUCTIVITY TIP
To block unwanted telemarketing calls, visit the National Do Not Call Registry at www.donotcall.gov to register your phone number. E-government services continue to improve, so check your state and local government websites for other time-saving services.

FUNDING RESEARCH FOR TECHNOLOGICAL INNOVATION   Government funding is critical to certain kinds of research projects that private investors might avoid because of risk, or perhaps because the payoff is very far in the future. The project that eventually led to the Internet itself is a key example. A U.S. government agency—Defense Advanced Research Projects Agency (DARPA)—created a computer research program in the 1960s, and it also funded a community of scientists working from other institutions in the United States and the United Kingdom. ARPANET was the first working network built with this funding, and it eventually grew into the vast Internet, now accessible from every corner of the globe.

Green sources of energy and the smart electricity grid receive significant funding from governments. Modernizing the grids will require advanced information systems to change the way they operate, which now is mostly one way—from power suppliers to their business and residential customers. However, as green sources of energy grow—from windmills or solar panels, for example—many customers can produce their own power. They can not only reduce their own electricity bills, but they may even earn a profit as the utility company pays them for adding more to the grid than they consumed during the month (Figure 2-18).

FIGURE 2-18

Smart meters under development can monitor power transmissions in both directions so consumers can contribute power from their own sources to the grid.

LeahKat/Shutterstock

New information systems will be a strategic enabler for the grid, with advanced capabilities to monitor power transmission in both directions. The systems will essentially enable the electric meter to run "backwards" when the customer is adding electricity to the grid, and they will make energy consumption patterns far more transparent than they are now. Consumers will be able to see exactly how much energy they use at different times of day and adjust their habits to reduce consumption during the priciest peak demand periods. The systems will also enable the grid to handle distribution challenges that come with energy sources such as wind or sun, which are intermittent and variable compared to other kinds of power generators. Although private companies are making some headway, targeted government support can speed this kind of development.

Does IT Matter?

 Explain why the role of information systems in organizations shifts, depending on whether the systems are deployed to run, grow, or transform the business.

Nicholas Carr, former editor of *Harvard Business Review*, poses a thought-provoking question: "Does IT matter?"[22, 23] His point is that IT resources have become so commonplace that their strategic importance has diminished, and they have become an infrastructure commodity—a widely available staple, much like electricity or rail transport. Initially, those two disruptive innovations gave early visionaries considerable advantage over competitors. For example, companies that understood how trains could ship large finished products across great distances invested capital in large-scale factories with efficient mass production. With economies of scale and the rail system for transport, these factories soon put the many small, local manufacturers out of business. Over time, though, competitors adopt the innovation as well, so it no longer confers any advantage. Carr argues that IT is reaching that point, and a larger danger now is overspending.

Blindly assuming that IT investments will always increase workforce productivity is also questionable. In fact, economists have struggled to explain the so-called "productivity paradox" for decades. Since the 1970s, the overall amount of IT spending in the United States has not been closely tied to increases in labor productivity. The paradox remains somewhat mysterious, and the way productivity is measured may be partly responsible. In addition, wise IT investments can lead to soaring productivity, but poorly chosen or mismanaged IT projects have the opposite effect.[24]

e-government
The application of ICT to government activities, especially by posting information online and offering interactive services to citizens.

SPENDING ON RUNNING, GROWING, AND TRANSFORMING

The benchmarks discussed earlier show that organizations are looking closely at *how* they spend their IT dollars, not just at total amounts. The funds used to "run" the business are mainly for the kinds of IT resources that now fall into the commodity category. Strategies to reduce those costs are critical, and because price competition for commodities is fierce, opportunities for savings abound. This book examines many ways organizations can avoid wasteful spending in these areas and improve productivity to get the best value for the lowest cost.

In contrast, the funds and human effort applied to growing and transforming an organization are much more closely tied to strategy, innovation, and competitive advantage. It is here where the "people" component of information systems—that human element—is most critical and central to success. Although many technologies are indeed commodities, the ability to extract their value requires human imagination; opportunities to do that are limitless. Innovative business practices, new products and services, and dramatically changed processes do not spring by themselves from technologies, but from talented people who know how to leverage them.

Whatever your role in the organization, the distinction between the different roles IT plays is very important to grasp since it affects how you allocate resources and judge the value of new initiatives. At Xerox, for example, CEO Ursula Burns cuts costs and downsizes during a business recession, just as other CEOs do. However, Xerox sustains its investment in technological innovation, particularly in areas such as color science, digital imaging, and nanotechnology.

LEVELING UP YOUR SAT: A STRATEGIC ANALYSIS

How should we evaluate the industry Prakash and Dana are trying to enter and how does IT fit into their strategy? Their industry is already dominated by very powerful and established incumbents such as The Princeton Review, Kaplan, and Cambridge. Their products include costly face-to-face classes, private tutoring, SAT prep books, and other materials. With the growth of e-learning, however, many less expensive alternatives are opening up, making the industry far more competitive. Some incumbents began offering low cost online programs, even competing with the nonprofit College Board that both administers the test and sells online practice programs to students. Newer entrants such as ePrep.com offer inexpensive video lectures to explain math problems, and number2.com offers its SAT practice questions for free. Students have many choices, and rivalry is intense.

Fortunately, *Leveling Up Your SAT* is a substitute product, quite distinct from face-to-face prep classes. Its unique mixture of fast-paced gaming features with study aids should distinguish it from the incumbents. Nevertheless, some of them already recognize that cell-phone applications may become a threat to their traditional business models, and they are developing their own products. Kaplan, for example, offers "SAT Flashcubes" for the iPhone and iPod—flash cards to practice SAT vocabulary words. Although competition may become fierce, the incumbents' cell-phone applications are relatively staid compared to the zany gaming approach of *Leveling Up Your SAT*, so they can be easily differentiated. That should help Prakash and Dana avoid the trap of competing only on price. They know they will have to move quickly and find innovative ways to market their clever approach. Viral marketing through Facebook and YouTube might work, given the customer demographic.

How can we describe the value chain Prakash and Dana are creating? It is not a simple one in which the founders buy resources from suppliers, add value to them, and then sell the product to student customers. Because user-generated content will play an important role, their value chain is more complex. They will start by writing their own practice SAT questions, drawing ideas from old SATs. The items will reach students by text message, with the software tracking correct answers and advancing levels. But students will become suppliers as they contribute good practice questions and explanations, rated for quality by other students and the cofounders. The best contributors will become high-level wizards, with special rewards and ring tones.

For Prakash and Dana, IT is a strategic enabler to launch *Leveling Up Your SAT.* They will need specialized software that works flawlessly on cell-phone platforms to deliver the SAT questions, dispense rewards, and level up the "players" as they achieve mastery and offer their own questions. The software does not exist, but their time is a major part of the capital they intend to contribute.

Leveling Up Your SAT will make an important strategic investment in the cell-phone application, and the founders will want to get it right. They should spend as little money as possible on the commodities, using free software and their own computing equipment when they can. However, the time and money spent understanding student needs, working out business processes, and creating a compelling and effective application to meet them is the key ingredient to their business model. For them, IT definitely matters.

MyMISLab │ *Online Simulation*

Leveling Up!

A Role Playing Simulation on Business Strategy for a New Smartphone App

Prakash and Dana asked you to help them brainstorm the strategic direction for their new company, Leveling Up Your SAT. As this chapter described, their idea is to create a smartphone application that will help high school students practice SAT questions and master the techniques they need to do well on such high stakes tests. The app will draw on the compelling features of games, though, with rewards, fast-paced action, competition, and special ring tones to indicate advancing levels of mastery, similar to what happens in some of the most popular action and—playing games.

Sound like fun? It's a business, though, so you'll need to think about how a company like this with a novel idea can survive, surrounded by very powerful competitors that dominate the industry.

They'll be contacting you with more information, so log in when you're ready.

Smartphone graphic from Leveling Up! simulation.

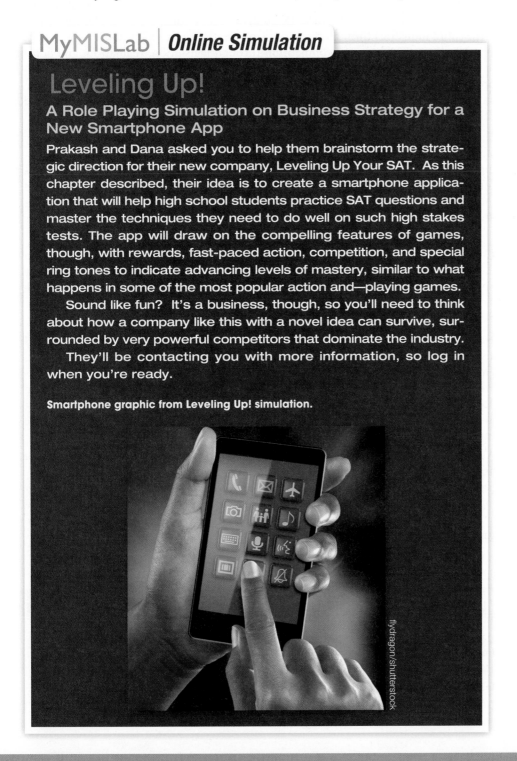

flydragon/shutterstock

Chapter Summary

1 The nature of competition in the industry forms the context for every company's strategy, and Michael Porter's model describes the five forces that shape an industry's competitive structure. They help determine how profitable companies operating in the industry will be, and they include (1) the threat of new entrants, (2) the power of buyers, (3) the power of suppliers, (4) the threat of substitute products, and (5) rivalry among competitors.

2 In addition to the strategies of the companies themselves, many external factors affect how the five forces operate. Disruptive innovations, for example, can transform entire industries through the process of creative destruction. Government policies can also affect industry competition through legislation, regulation, and court decisions. Industries that operate in a larger ecosystem are affected by the development of complementary products and services that accelerate trends. In addition, environmental events such as pandemics or earthquakes can reshape industries and call for changes in strategy.

3 Organizations can use the value chain model to understand their options as they strive to compete in an industry. Primary activities (bringing in raw resources, making the product, marketing, delivery, and customer support) and support activities form the major components of the value chain. The extended value chain, which includes suppliers and customers, offers more strategic opportunities. Benchmarks are used to compare a company's performance to industry standards on components of the value chain.

4 Competitive strategies include low cost leadership, product differentiation, and a focused strategy for a particular market niche. Information systems support all these approaches by reducing costs, streamlining processes, and adding unique value with new products or features. Their role includes running the organization and, as a strategic enabler, growing and transforming the organization.

5 Nonprofits take advantage of information systems to manage basic operations, and also as a strategic enabler in areas such as fund-raising and volunteer management. Governments use information systems extensively for e-government initiatives, especially to increase access and enhance services for the public. Governments are also deeply involved in funding initiatives that offer potential value for the country, but that may be too risky for private investors. Examples include the research that led to the Internet and funding for alternative energy.

6 As technologies become commodities, and become widely used by almost all organizations, their strategic value diminishes. The information systems used to "run" organizations, in particular, are readily available and managers should focus on reducing their cost. However, innovative information systems in which creative people leverage technology to grow and transform the organization are critical for effective strategy.

KEY TERMS AND CONCEPTS

threat of new entrants	rivalry among existing competitors	value chain model	product differentiation strategy
network effects	disruptive innovation	primary activities	focused strategy
switching costs	sustaining technologies	support activities	strategic enabler
power of buyers	creative destruction	benchmark	e-government
power of suppliers	ecosystem	low cost leadership strategy	
threat of substitutes			

CHAPTER REVIEW QUESTIONS

1. What are the five competitive forces that shape industry competition? How are these forces interrelated?

2. How do disruptive innovations, government policies, complementary products and services, and environmental events affect how the competitive forces operate?

3. What are the components of the value chain? Which components comprise the primary activities? Which components comprise the support activities? What is the extended value chain?

4. How do managers use benchmarks to analyze the value chain and IT spending?

5. How do information systems apply to competitive strategies for business?

6. How are information systems used to run, grow, and transform a business?

7. How do information systems apply to competitive strategies for nonprofit organizations?

8. How do governments use information systems to improve services and fund research?

PROJECTS AND DISCUSSION QUESTIONS

1. Although many people think electronic book readers are too expensive, there is a massive global demand for the devices, and the trend is likely to continue for some time. Search the web to learn more about how digital technology has disrupted the book publishing industry, and prepare a 5-minute presentation of your findings.

2. Is a value meal related to a value chain? The value that attracts more than 47 million customers to McDonald's every day comes from capabilities that are based in its value chain. Briefly describe McDonald's value chain and discuss how information systems facilitate each component in the chain. Can you think of a way that information technology could improve your next trip to McDonald's?

3. Information technology enables nonprofit organizations to reach out to constituents 24 hours a day, 7 days a week. Visit www.redcross.org and note the various ways this charity is using its website to communicate with volunteers, donors, and people who need assistance. Compare the Red Cross site to your university's alumni association website. Prepare a brief summary of your findings that includes a list of specific services provided on each site. How does each website support the organization's strategic goals?

4. Government agencies and corporations have similar information needs. Identify and briefly discuss specific examples of information systems typically used by a law enforcement agency such as a state or local police department. Which of these systems are used to "run" the business? Which are used to fulfill the agency's mission?

5. What are the three basic strategies that companies adopt to compete? Describe how information systems support each strategy. What is a "hybrid" strategy? Describe a company, product, or service that adopts each of these four competitive strategies.

6. What are network effects? Search the web or visit websites such as groupon.com and buywithme.com and discuss how network effects can impact the threat of new entrants. Is there a Groupon offering or a BuyWithMe deal in your hometown? How would you describe the long-term value proposition of this online shopping phenomenon? In your opinion, are there any disadvantages for an organization that offers a daily deal?

7. In 2009, the U.S. federal government collected approximately $2.9 trillion in taxes, including individual income taxes, Social Security/Social Insurance taxes, and corporate taxes. Visit www.irs.gov and describe how this website enhances services to the public. What types of services are available to individuals? To businesses? To charities and nonprofit organizations? What kind of "tax information for students" does this site provide? Prepare a 5-minute presentation of your findings.

8. Why are IT resources described as a commodity? How do IT resources "matter" in terms of the different roles they play in an organization? Which component of an information system is most critical to success in growing and transforming the business? Why?

9. According to the Computer History Museum (www.computerhistory.org), the Kenbak Corporation sold the first personal computer in 1971. Since then, several billion PCs have been sold under various brand names. Currently, HP, Dell, Acer, Lenovo, and Toshiba are the leading brands in the highly competitive PC market. Work in a small group with classmates to analyze and describe the personal computer industry using the Five Competitive Forces model.

10. Work in a small group with classmates to discuss how information technology plays a role in the competitive environment of your college or university. How do you describe the competition to attract and retain students? How do you describe the threat of substitutes in higher education? How does the threat of substitutes affect supplier power in education?

APPLICATION EXERCISES

EXCEL APPLICATION:
IT Benchmarks

Jay's Bikes is a family-owned and -operated business that stocks a wide range of bikes designed to fit the needs of professional riders, your child's first bike, and everything in between. The business has 12 full-time employees. Jay has asked you to create a spreadsheet from the data in Figure 2-19 to calculate average IT spending so that it can be compared to the retail industry average. What is the average IT spending in the retail industry? What is the average IT spending per employee in the retail industry? How do Jay's IT expenditures compare to the industry averages? How much would Jay need to increase spending in order to match the retail industry average?

ACCESS APPLICATION:
Telethon Call Reports

The volunteer coordinator of the Downtown Emergency Shelter has asked you to use the information provided in Figure 2-20 to create an Access database. (You can download the Excel file called Ch02Ex02 and import the data into your database.) The coordinator will use the database to manage donor records and help the Shelter prepare for an upcoming Phonathon fund-raising event. During the Phonathon, volunteers will call previous donors to ask for donations to this year's fund. Your instructions are to create two tables (donors and volunteers) and prepare a Phonathon Call Report for each volunteer. The shelter manager wants you to add three fields to the donor table: this year's contribution, a calculated field that shows the average

contribution per employee, and a calculated field that shows a target contribution that is 5 percent higher than last year's contribution. The report should list the volunteer's name and number, as well as the following donor information: donor number, donor name, company name, phone number, contribution amount from the prior year, number of employees, average contribution per employee, and target contribution for this year. Although address information will not be included on the report, that information will be used to send receipts to the donors at the conclusion of this year's fund-raising event.

FIGURE 2-19

Jay's Bikes revenue and IT expenditures.

	A	B	C
1	Revenue	Apparel & shoes	$ 1,250,000
2		Bike accessories	$ 550,000
3		New bikes	$ 2,650,000
4		Used bikes	$ 18,500
5		Bike repairs	$ 33,000
6			
7	IT expenditures	Hardware	$ 15,000
8		Software updates	$ 18,000
9		Software licenses	$ 4,500
10		Software support	$ 4,500
11		Employee training	$ 5,000
12		Website development	$ 5,000
13		Internet access	$ 1,200

FIGURE 2-20

Phonathon data.

	A	B	C	D	E	F	G	H	I	J	K	L
1	Donor No.	Co. Name	Street Address	City	State	Zip Code	Phone No.	2010 Contribution	Employees	Volunteer Number	Last Name	First Name
2	A226	Al's Music Shop	210 W. High Point	Aurora	IL	60506	630-555-5554	$ 945.50	8	J234	Johnson	Bob
3	A657	Downtown Bikes	34 N. Main Street	East Aurora	IL	60508	630-186-7689	$ 1,248.00	12	M173	Miller	Sara
4	C456	Carol's Beauty Shop	265 Peabody	Batavia	IL	60604	312-044-2956	$ 2,365.00	17	H042	Henry	Robert
5	D256	Do It Rental	456 Alexander	Naperville	IL	60602	630-876-3476	$ 3,465.00	19	J234	Johnson	Bob
6	E456	Edies Ice Cream Shop	2093 State Street	Batavia	IL	60604	312-345-7890	$ 5,237.76	24	M173	Miller	Sara
7	A234	All Right Auto Repair	32 N. Central Loop	Aurora	IL	60506	630-345-3333	$ 3,109.00	21	J234	Johnson	Bob
8	F234	The Barbacue Pit	423 Eastview Rd.	St. Charles	IL	60510	312-555-5445	$ 2,926.74	18	M173	Miller	Sara
9	Q349	Hollywood Pet Care	34 Glendale St.	Aurora	IL	60506	630.234.3484	$ 563.00	9	H042	Henry	Robert
10	D345	The Butcher Shop	764 Walnut Street	Batavia	IL	60604	312-456-0080	$ 928.00	5	J234	Johnson	Bob
11	L345	Mia's Nail Salon	435 Hwy. 131	Aurora	IL	60506	630-345-0080	$ 2,644.25	12	H042	Henry	Robert
12	W098	The Book Nook	415 North Second	Yorkville	IL	60607	630-345-5656	$ 5,234.00	26	J234	Johnson	Bob
13	U602	Day & Night Gym	1356 Stadium	Yorkville	IL	60607	630-434.5555	$ 2,535.90	32	M173	Miller	Sara
14	T706	The Little Card Shop	365 S. Main Street	St. Charles	IL	60510	312-455-8876	$ 1,834.00	8	M173	Miller	Sara
15	S493	Perfect Cleaners	156 Third Avenue	Batavia	IL	60604	312-451-0080	$ 2,651.00	11	H042	Henry	Robert
16	E105	Green City Grocers	394 Flood Street	East Aurora	IL	60508	630-123-4598	$ 6,234.45	32	H042	Henry	Robert
17	M697	Alternative Health Spa	3435 Race St	Batavia	IL	60604	312-341-9979	$ 878.65	3	H042	Henry	Robert
18	W456	Nelson's Gallery	345 Nettleton St.	Aurora	IL	60504	630-345-8235	$ 2,766.00	3	M173	Miller	Sara
19	HJ376	Haney Enterprises	190 Johnson Ave.	Naperville	IL	60602	630-345-3767	$ 9,345.00	36	J234	Johnson	Bob
20	A754	Say It With Flowers	3600 Southwest	St. Charles	IL	60510	312-972-3456	$ 2,500.00	14	M173	Miller	Sara

CASE STUDY #1

GameStop Fends Off Rivals with Brick, Mortar, and a Move Online

With more than 6,500 stores throughout the United States, Australia, Canada, and Europe, GameStop's management team wants to maintain its lead as the premier destination for gamers. The Texas-based retail chain's major source of revenue is the sale of games, both new and used, in its stores. The used market, which accounts for 27 percent of revenue, is important because it brings customers into the store to trade in their old games for store credits. GameStop resells the used games for more than twice what it pays for them.

The business model has, so far, survived the Internet's creative destruction that swept away other brick-and-mortar outlets selling digital products, including Egghead Software and Tower Records. GameStop's revenues topped $9 billion in 2009, but the company is surrounded by threats.

One major rival is Best Buy, which began offering customers a chance to trade in their old games for gift cards that could be used at any Best Buy store. Unlike GameStop's store credit, the Best Buy cards can be used to purchase TVs, computers, music, and any other products that Best Buy offers. GameStop executives think Best Buy won't steal many of their loyal customers, partly because GameStop stores are closer to the gamers' homes and thus easier to reach compared to Best Buy outlets. They also think gamers appreciate GameStop's narrow focus, with sales associates who know games well and love to talk about them with customers.

Another threat comes from the game developers, who fume about used-game sales because they earn no royalties. To counter used sales, many developers include a coupon with a new game so that purchasers can download special content or a game upgrade. GameStop has to charge people who buy used games a fee to get that coupon, and the total price approaches the cost of the new game. Developers will continue to find ways to combat used-game sales.

Online retailers pose another threat, especially combined with infomediary services that show up-to-the-minute price comparisons from different outlets. The free social games such as Mobster and FarmVille are also luring some gamers away from the costly titles featured at GameStop, such as Final Fantasy, Medal of Honor, and Mafia II.

Widespread access to high-speed Internet has a downside for GameStop. Companies such as Electronic Arts and Blizzard can deliver major upgrades and sequels to their high-end games digitally, instead of packaging them into boxes for GameStop to sell. Customers can buy them online, directly from the publisher, rather than making the trip to the store.

GameStop is countering these threats by moving to online games and adding digital delivery. They acquired the online game service Kongregate.com, for example, " to advance GameStop's digital strategy by providing a gaming platform for casual, mobile, and browser games," said CEO Paul Raines. He adds that the company will "continue to pursue bold directions and opportunities that establish us as one of the leading online gaming destinations." Clearly, the company appreciates the dangerous strategic waters of other brick-and-mortar media companies, such as Hollywood Video and Blockbuster who are battling rivals such as Netflix. Time will tell if GameStop's strategies will pay off.

Discussion Questions

1. Perform a five forces analysis of the online gaming industry. What are implications of the five forces analysis for GameStop?

2. What role have information systems played in the five forces you identified?

3. How has GameStop used information systems to compete more effectively?

4. What other strategic actions will GameStop need to take to protect its business?

SOURCES: Anonymous. (July 30, 2010). GameStop inks pact to buy Kongregate. *Entertainment Close-Up.* http://www. highbeam.com/doc/1G1-233507376.html, accessed May 1, 2011. Edwards, C. (July 26, 2010). GameStop suits up to battle new rivals. *Bloomberg BusinessWeek.* 4189, 23–24. Godinez, V. (2010). GameStop buys Kongregate to gain an online edge. *Dallas Morning News.* July 28. http://www.allbusiness.com/entertainment-arts/entertainment-arts-overview/14858190-1.html, accessed May 1, 2011.

CASE STUDY #2

The Open Internet Coalition and the Battle for Net Neutrality

Debates over how government should regulate the Internet's evolution heat up whenever anyone mentions "net neutrality." This principle holds that carriers selling Internet connectivity—Verizon, AT&T, and Comcast, for instance—should not discriminate for or against different content providers or applications. All traffic should be routed neutrally, and the carriers should not make special deals to favor some content by giving it priority bandwidth. The Open Internet Coalition strongly supports net neutrality and includes dozens of companies that provide content over the Internet. Amazon, eBay, Google, Lending Tree, Facebook, Skype, Paypal, YouTube, and Netflix are all members. The coalition also includes nonprofits that advocate for openness, such as the American Civil Liberties Union, American Library Association, and Educause.

This somewhat technical topic attracts ferocious lobbying efforts targeting government agencies and politicians. The outcome will affect strategy for any organization with an Internet presence, and the members of the Open Internet Coalition have much at stake. Their members do not want the risk that carriers could disadvantage their content in favor of a competitor or make it cumbersome for customers to access their sites.

On the other side are the carriers—AT&T, Verizon, Comcast, and others. They argue that incentives are needed to encourage their investment in the network infrastructure, and that their networks have to be managed to provide the best service at reasonable costs. Video downloads, in particular, hog bandwidth to the detriment of other users who just want to read the news or send e-mail. In fact, this issue gained considerable steam when Comcast began throttling download speeds for subscribers using BitTorrent, software widely used to download movies. Comcast's move, while helpful to most customers, was a violation of net neutrality.

Even though adherence to the net neutrality principle was voluntary, the Federal Communications Commission (FCC) reprimanded Comcast for what it considered an outrageous violation. Comcast sued, and the courts decided the FCC didn't actually have jurisdiction to reprimand anyone because the Commission has no authority over broadband communications. This finding led to a flurry of talks among the players and FCC heads.

When the talks broke down, two powerhouses from opposite sides of the debate—Google and Verizon—joined together to propose a new legislative framework. Their proposal gave limited authority to the FCC and reinforced the principle of net neutrality for wired services—but not wireless. Critics from all sides slammed the proposal because it exempted wireless services. On its Public Policy Blog, Google fired back that wireless services are already highly competitive, and the constraints of airwave transmission make it more critical for the carriers to manage their networks. (AT&T's wireless network, for instance, suffered badly when iPhone users began downloading videos all day long.) The Google/Verizon proposal also came under attack because it included vague terms such as "lawful" and " reasonable," without explaining how they would be defined.

As of this writing, the FCC claims authority and issued new rulings to protect net neutrality. Consumer groups and companies such as Netflix claim some carriers are in violation, but the carriers are filing their own lawsuits, so the issue remains cloudy.

Discussion Questions

1. What are the strategic interests of carriers? What are the strategic interests of websites?

2. How do the interests of carriers differ from the interests of websites? What are the implications for websites from a value chain perspective?

3. What differences between wired and wireless services are relevant to determine whether there could be a difference in the application of net neutrality?

4. What are relevant considerations on the role government could play to resolve differences between carriers and websites?

SOURCES: Nocera, J. (2010). Net neutrality: The struggle for what we already have. *The New York Times*. September 4, pp. B1, B6. Pil Choi, J., & Byung-Cheol, K. (2010). Net neutrality and investment incentives. *RAND Journal of Economics.* 41(3), 446–471. Stein, J. (September 6, 2010). Net wit. *Time*. 176(10), 68 Warner, C. (August 27, 2010). Get off the fence on net neutrality. *ECN: Electronic Component News.* 54(10), 9.

E-PROJECT 1   Identifying Company Strategy with Online Financial Chart Tools

One useful way to catch up on a company's strategy is to check out trends in its stock price, and the net offers many free tools. Type the stock ticker symbol for GameStop (GME) into the Google search bar to pull up current news about the company, including a graph of its share prices, from Google finance.

1. The letters on the graph tie to the news stories, and some of them have major effects on the company's stock. Change the graph to show 1 year of data by clicking 1y at the top left of the graph. Do you see any sudden changes in share price paired with a news story? Does the news shed light on how investors view its strategy or the execution of it?

2. One way to get an idea of how well the company is doing is to compare the trend in its share prices to the Dow Jones Industrial Average. Check the box next to Dow Jones at the top of the graph and compare the trends. How does GameStop's performance compare?

E-PROJECT 2   Analyzing Movie Download Times with Excel

In this e-project, you will obtain and analyze information about download times to assess Internet connectivity.

1. Download the file called CH02_MediaDownloads. This file shows the approximate file sizes for different kinds of media, along with estimated download times.

2. Add a column called Speed Advantage and enter the formula that shows how many times faster the download will be if one uses fast broadband (+d2/+c2). Copy the formula to the remaining rows, and then add a row at the bottom called "AVERAGE". On average, how much faster is it to download media files using fast broadband compared to regular broadband?

3. Add two more columns called Download Time per MB (Fast Broadband) and Download Time per MB (Regular Broadband). Compute these values by dividing the appropriate download time by the file size in MB, and add the average at the bottom.

a. What is the average download time per MB for fast broadband?

b. For regular broadband?

4. Download the video file called CH02_TestVideo and time how long it takes.

a. What is the file's size in MB? If the file size is represented in gigabytes (GB), multiply that number by 1,000 to convert to megabytes (MB).

b. Using the average download times you computed, what should be the download time using fast broadband? What would it be for regular broadband?

c. How does your download time compare to these estimates? Do you have fast broadband, regular broadband, or something else?

CHAPTER NOTES

1. (May 5, 2009). Alibaba says Taobao will rival Baidu in China web ads. www.cn-c114.net/579/a409358.html, accessed May 1, 2011.

2. Porter, M. E. (1998). *Competitive strategy: Techniques for analyzing industries and competitors.* San Francisco: The Free Press.

3. Porter, M. E. (2008). The five competitive forces that shape strategy. *Harvard Business Review.* 86(1), 78–93.

4. (March 2011). Business: Groupon anxiety; online coupon firms. *The Economist.* 398, 70. Retrieved March 21, 2011, from ABI/INFORM Global (Document ID: 2297561851).

5. (2009). What's new in iTunes 8. www.apple.com/itunes/whatsnew, accessed June 8, 2009.

6. Chernikoff, H. (June 2, 2008). Video conference use soars as airlines squirm. *Reuters.*

7. van Heerde, H. J., Gijsbrechts, E., & Pauwels, K. (2008). Winners and losers in a major price war. *Journal of Marketing Research.* 45(5), 499–518.

8. Rosenberg, D. (May 16, 2009). Sony Pictures CEO hates the internet. *Software, Interrupted.* http://news.cnet.com/8301-13846_3-10242526-62.html, accessed May 1, 2011.

9. Christensen, C., & Raynor, M. (2003). *The innovator's solution.* Cambridge, MA: Harvard Business School Press.

10. Christensen, C. (1997). *The innovator's dilemma: When new technologies cause great firms to fail.* Cambridge, MA: Harvard Business School Press.

11. Coy, P. (January 15, 2009). A new menace to the economy: "Zombie" debtors. *BusinessWeek.* pp. 24–26. www.businessweek.com.proxy3.library.jhu.edu/magazine/content/09_04/b4117024316675.htm?chan=magazine+channel_top+stories, accessed May 1, 2011.

12. Lager, M. (2009). The 2009 CRM Service Awards: Rising Stars–Salesforce.com: Clouding up the scene. *CRM Magazine.* p. 39. www.destinationcrm.com/Articles/Editorial/Magazine-Features/The-2009-CRM-Service-Awards-Rising-Stars—Salesforce.com-Clouding-Up-the-Scene-53333.aspx, accessed May 1, 2011.

13. Porter, M. E., & Reinhardt, F. L. (2007). A strategic approach to climate. *Harvard Business Review.* 85(10), 22–26.

14. Crain, D. W., & Abraham, S. (2008). Using value-chain analysis to discover customers' strategic needs. *Strategy & Leadership.* 36(4), 29–39.

15. Smith, M., & Potter, K. (2009). IT spending and staffing report, 2009. *Gartner Research.*

16. Tsai, T.-I., & Johnson, I. (2009). As giants step in, Asustek defends a tiny PC. *Wall Street Journal* (Eastern Edition). May 1, p. B-1.

17. Sheinberg, B. (2009, March). RIM touches off a storm. *CRN: CRNtech 25,10.* Retrieved May 25, 2009, from ABI/INFORM Global database (Document ID: 1663121481).

18. Wallace, N. (March 21, 2008). Charities urged to use cellphone messages to get in touch with supporters. *The Chronicle of Philanthropy.* http://philanthropy.com/article/Charities-Urged-to-Use/62799/, accessed May 1, 2011.

19. Wallace, N. (February 26, 2009). Google helps charity test its web design. *The Chronicle of Philanthropy.* http://philanthropy.com/article/Google-Helps-Charity-Test-Its/57281/, accessed May 1, 2011.

20. (2008). Interview with Greg Baldwin, President of VolunteerMatch. *BrownHEN/BrownHEN.org,* accessed March 15, 2009.

21. Carr, N. G. (2003). IT doesn't matter. *Harvard Business Review.* 81(5), 41–49.

22. Carr, N. G. (2004). *Does IT matter? Information technology and the corrosion of competitive advantage.* Boston, MA: Harvard Business School Press Books. p. 1.

23. Brynjolfsson, E. (1993). The productivity paradox of information technology: Review and assessment. Communications of the ACM, 36(12), 66–77.

Information and Communications Technologies:
The Enterprise Architecture

Chapter Preview

THE TECHNOLOGY COMPONENT OF INFORMATION SYSTEMS ENCOMPASSES HARDWARE, software, and telecommunications. This chapter provides an overview of information and communications technologies (ICT), showing how the parts fit together, and why they sometimes don't fit together well at all. You will see how the ICT architecture continues to evolve to support business objectives, like a house whose owner remodels the bathroom, adds a deck and garage, and replaces all the faulty wiring. You will also see how and why organizations make choices that lead down certain paths as they remodel, and why a master architectural plan is essential to guiding decisions about these very valuable assets.

The chapter will acquaint you with many of the most common terms and concepts needed to discuss information systems with colleagues, consultants, and vendors. It will also help prepare you to evaluate emerging technologies, identifying which ones are hype and which can offer real value to you and your organization.

© Peter Arnold, Inc./Alamy

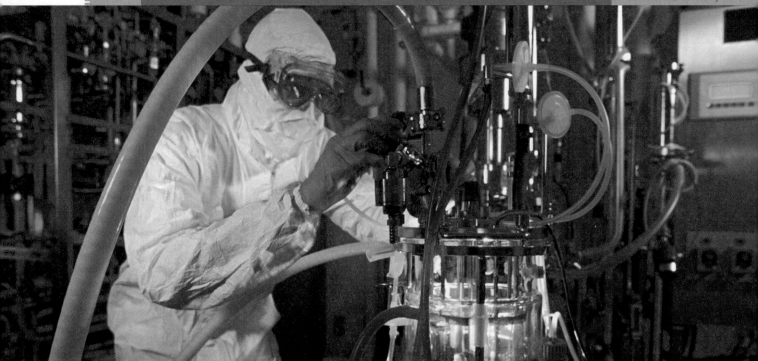

3

Learning Objectives

1. Describe the four hardware components of a computer, giving examples of each component.

2. Identify and provide examples of the two major types of software, and describe how software is created.

3. Describe the major types of networks and the transmission media they use, and give examples of network protocols.

4. Explain the importance of the enterprise architecture, describing trends in ICT architecture over time.

Introduction

Genentech, founder of the biotechnology industry, taps into the human genetic code to create new medicines for life-threatening conditions. Its sales representatives call on physicians to explain new products and answer questions about the company's drugs. Many don't carry laptops any longer and just use their iPhones to instantly access the office when they need information on the fly. Once logged in, reps can locate company staff members whose expertise they need, query the customer relationship management system, use e-mail, or check company data for a drug's latest uses.[1] Learning from Apple's success with smartphone applications, Genentech builds corporate apps that staff can download and use from anywhere. Todd Pierce, VP for information technology, says, "We're cutting down on the drag of technology so people can focus more of their intellectual energy and creativity on the important stuff."

Suppose Genentech hires a talented new sales rep who really loves the smartphone approach. She's already attached to her BlackBerry, though, and says to her boss, "It's OK if I just use this, right? That will save our department some money, too." If you were the manager, how would you answer?

The decision to deploy smartphones is one piece of a much larger puzzle: the **enterprise architecture (EA)**. The organization creates the EA to describe its current situation and where it should head to achieve its mission, focusing especially on business strategy and the technology infrastructure required to achieve it. A roadmap describing how to get from the present to that future state guides decision making about technology directions. The EA helps managers navigate the vast array of choices they integrate new information systems to support strategic objectives and retire older ones. Yet the roadmap is bound to contain many speed bumps and detours. What seems like a simple request to keep the BlackBerry could be quite significant. It could lead to costly duplication of programming efforts if the manager, eager to save a few hundred dollars for the department's budget, agrees that it's OK.

The knowledge you gain from this chapter will help you understand what the ICT options are, how they fit together, why they are changing, and how they apply to your organization. People in all parts of the organization have a role to play in designing the enterprise architecture, and leaving this task to the IT department is foolhardy. Input from all stakeholders is needed to develop the best solution and help the organization avoid very expensive mistakes.

Describe the four hardware components of a computer, giving examples of each component.

1 The Hardware

The physical basis of ICT encompasses an immense range of equipment, from mainframes and servers in giant data centers, to robots, microprocessors, smartphones, printers, scanners, digital cameras, smart cards, hard drives, and much more. These devices generally share two important features. First, they are digital, so they all process information using the same binary language of zeroes and ones. Second, they can all be considered computers or computer components.

The **computer** is any electronic device that can accept, manipulate, store, and output data, and whose instructions can be programmed. That definition covers equipment you might not ordinarily think of as a computer, such as the smartphone, a game console, or a robotic rat with cameras for eyes and highly sensitive wire whiskers.

Times have changed since 1947 when the world marveled at ENIAC, the first electronic computer. Weighing 27 tons, the behemoth was 26 meters (80 feet) long and contained more than 17,000 vacuum tubes. With every breakthrough and each succeeding generation, the overarching goal is to make technology work for human beings—reducing the "drag" by making it smaller, faster, easier to use, more intuitive, less expensive, less power hungry, and considerably more intelligent.

INPUT AND OUTPUT

Although the details vary considerably, computers have four components, as you see in Figure 3-1. Figure 3-2 includes various input devices which accept signals and convert them to a digital format that matches the signal's meaning. Some also display the output, such as digital cameras and touchscreens.

HUMAN INPUT Most input devices rely on human input, so are designed with human capabilities in mind. Hands can type on keyboards, and each key press is converted into a different string combination of zeros and ones. The **ASCII code** and its variants

FIGURE 3-1

Hardware components.

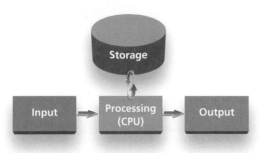

determine how characters are encoded into digital strings, so that a backspace might send 00001000 and a SHIFT + s sends 01010011, for capital S.

Productivity guru David Allen commented on twitter.com, "Communicating without knowing how to type is like talking with marbles in your mouth." As an interface for human beings, the keyboard is an underappreciated milestone in computer history. Skilled typists can type more than 100 words per minute—faster than most people speak. Managers once disdained keyboards because they seemed linked to low-level clerk-typist jobs, but typing soon became an essential productivity skill for everyone. Unfortunately, the keyboard layout evolved from the typewriter—originally designed to slow down data entry to prevent collisions of the hammers striking the paper. Because so many people already knew the QWERTY layout, though, attempts to introduce a better design failed. As sometimes happens, a superior technology solution lost out, in this case because human behavior can be so difficult to change.

The ASCII keyboard also helps explain why some countries adopted computing much earlier than others. Although a standard keyboard handily encodes languages that use the Roman alphabet with its 26 letters, 10 numerals, and a few punctuation marks, it is very cumbersome for other languages. Chinese and Japanese, for example,

FIGURE 3-2

Input and output devices.

Nikita Rogul/Shutterstock

---

enterprise architecture (EA)
A roadmap created by an organization to describe its current situation and where it should head to achieve its mission, focusing on business strategy and the technology infrastructure required to achieve it.

computer
Any electronic device that can accept, manipulate, store, and output data, and whose instructions can be programmed.

ASCII code
A code that defines how keyboard characters are encoded into digital strings of ones and zeros.

FIGURE 3-3

Keyboard shortcuts that improve productivity.

Windows	Macintosh	Function
CTRL+C	Command (⌘)+C	Copy selected text
CTRL+V	Command (⌘)+V	Paste
CTRL+S	Command (⌘)+S	Save current document
CTRL+Z	Command (⌘)+Z	Undo
CTRL+F	Command (⌘)+F	Open a Find window

use thousands of characters. Characters in the Korean language, called Hangul, are grouped as syllables and positioned in different locations. Arabic, Urdu, and Hebrew are written from right to left. These obstacles are overcome with more intelligent software, but they certainly made fax more useful in those countries compared to e-mail, and delayed widespread computer use.

The mouse, joystick, and graphics tablet are other human input devices, and these can transmit motion and location information. Touch-sensitive screens, for example, respond to finger motions and convert them to digital signals. A screen is organized into x and y axes, and locations can be transmitted as coordinates. Multitouch screens that several people can manipulate at the same time are gaining popularity as a way to collaborate. Gloves equipped with sensors can also transmit complex hand movements, such as those used in American sign language.

PRODUCTIVITY TIP

Although the mouse is very useful, it can slow you down as you move your hands from the keyboard. Try the keyboard shortcuts in Figure 3-3 to eliminate some unneeded motion.

Microphones capture human speech and transmit it in digital format. Although the sounds can be represented digitally just as sounds, speech recognition software can also dissect the words, matching them to known vocabularies or alphabets. This software is distributed with recent Windows and Macintosh PCs, and many organizations have added speech recognition to their phone answering systems so callers can speak their account numbers or menu choices.

Why hasn't speech input overtaken fingers and hands? Although spoken commands are valuable when the hands are needed for something else (like driving), most applications still rely heavily on keyboards and touchscreens. One reason is that speech recognition is less accurate, but many people also *prefer* typing to speaking, and reading to listening. Texting, e-mail, and instant messaging have outpaced voice mail, and in some organizations, voice mail is all but dead. One CEO claims he gets no more than a couple per month, and those are typically marketing calls or automated messages reminding him of overdue library books. Human preferences like these play an important role when designing the enterprise architecture.

Other parts of the body can generate input signals, as well. Nintendo's balance board captures weight shifts by the feet, and cameras can be configured to detect eye blinks, body movements, and even facial expressions. The polygraph, or "lie detector," incorporates input devices to pick up and transmit respiratory patterns, sweat responses, blood pressure, and other biological stress signals.

SCANNERS AND SENSORS **Optical scanners** capture text or images and convert them to digital format in thousands of settings. They can scan virtually anything into an image, but combined with software or special symbols, they can decipher much more detail. For example, the bar codes that appear on price tags or postal mail represent specific numbers and other symbols, and scanners transmit those details—not just the image.

Combined with **optical character recognition (OCR)** software, the actual letters and numbers on a page can be interpreted, creating a digital document that can be edited rather than a flat picture. Early adopters of this technology were the banks, which use it for processing checks. The unique font is standard throughout the industry, and magnetic ink allows scanners to read the characters even if someone writes over them.

Digital cameras are another important input device widely used for surveillance, security, and just entertainment. They monitor traffic patterns, city streets, building entrances, hallways, homes, ATM machines, bird nests, baby cribs, and much more. The British government installed more than 4 million video cameras, one for every 14 people, and private cameras installed by companies and individuals far outnumber that. Especially because tiny cameras can be easily concealed, their proliferation raises many privacy issues.

Did You Know?

Kinect from Microsoft has changed the gaming industry by being the first entertainment system that does not require an individual to use hardware to control the software. The camera tracks body movement, and the software recognizes individual faces. Interpreting facial expressions may be just over the horizon, so the system might suggest different activities according to mood.

Radio frequency identification (RFID) tags, used in supply chains to track shipments, are small chips equipped with a microprocessor, a tiny antenna to receive and transmit data, and sometimes a battery (Figure 3-4). RFID tags can store information on the object's history and whereabouts, and can be embedded in anything, including pets, livestock, and human beings. The Department of Energy relies on RFID tags to track shipments of hazardous nuclear material, something they certainly want to keep a close eye on. Although their potential is enormous, privacy advocates voice concerns over these devices as well, particularly since people may be unaware that they carry such tags. Dutch technologist Marc Boon invented the RFID "sniffer" that alerts people to the presence of nearby tags.

FIGURE 3-4

RFID tag.

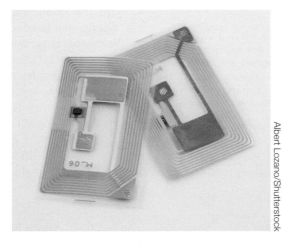

Albert Lozano/Shutterstock

---

optical scanners
Electronic devices that capture text or images and convert them to digital format.

optical character recognition (OCR)
The capability of specialized software to interpret the actual letters and numbers on a page to create a digital document that can be edited, rather than a flat picture.

radio frequency identification (RFID)
A technology placed on tags with small chips equipped with a microprocessor, a tiny antenna to receive and transmit data, and sometimes a battery, that stores information on the tagged object's history.

FIGURE 3-5

Buoy sensors collect live data that is made available on the Internet.

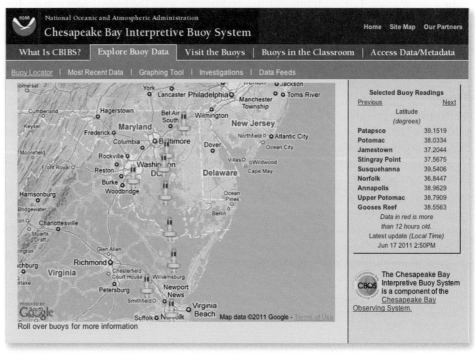

Source: www.buoybay.org/site/public accessed September 15, 2010.

Sensors are spreading so fast that analysts predict their signals will comprise 20 percent of Internet traffic. Environmental sensors, for instance, monitor temperature, humidity, and pollution. The Chesapeake Bay's smart buoys capture data on water quality, wind speed, and temperature, and their data is transmitted in real time to the Internet (Figure 3-5).

OUTPUT DEVICES   The familiar flat panel display is the most common computer output device for desktop computers. Falling prices make a large screen, or even two of them, quite affordable. For human beings, screen real estate is a valuable commodity, making it possible to view several applications at the same time.

PRODUCTIVITY TIP

Adding a second monitor can improve your productivity and also reduce the need to print output on paper. Eileen Durkin, co-owner of a New Jersey insurance agency, claims that dual monitors improved her staff's productivity by at least 10 percent. She installed them when the company moved to electronic documents, so staff could view a document and access the information system simultaneously.[2] For engineers and others who need a lot of screen real estate, productivity gains may be much higher.[3, 4] Students struggling with a small laptop screen should consider this option.

On the other end of the spectrum are the small screens used for cell phones and handheld devices, and the somewhat larger ones used in iPads and e-books. Other common output devices include computer printers and speakers, as well as an enormous variety of controllers that operate machinery, from lawn sprinklers and lights to an aircraft's landing gear. Powered USB ports open up opportunities for creative inventors, who came up with several oddball output devices: heated slippers, coffee warmers, and air darts fired off with the mouse.

PROCESSING

The computer's brain is the **central processing unit (CPU)**, which handles information processing, calculations, and control tasks. Early versions used vacuum tubes that frequently blew out, but with the invention of the **transistor**—a small electrical circuit made from a semiconductor material such as silicon—computers switched to using electrical signals to represent zeros and ones. The transistors are packed onto integrated circuits, and mass produced at low cost (Figure 3-6).

FIGURE 3-6

Integrated circuits.

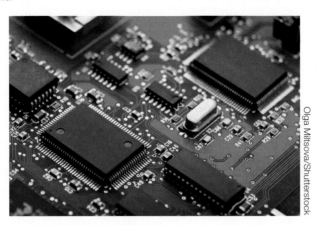

Olga Miltsova/Shutterstock

Decades ago, Intel cofounder Gordon Moore predicted that the number of transistors fitting on a chip would about double every two years, a forecast that has proven uncannily accurate. Now known as **Moore's Law**, his prediction about density also captures advances in processing speed, storage capabilities, cost, and other computer features. Today's low-cost laptop outperforms mainframes from the 1960s—and takes up far less space.

The computing architectures in Figure 3-7 illustrate how the technology has evolved, as each generation took advantage of declining costs, increasing power, and advances that support mobility. As we discuss later in this chapter, decisions about

FIGURE 3-7

Computing architectures.

Computing Architectures	Description
Mainframe	Developed for large businesses in the 1960s and often called "big iron," mainframes are still used for massive bulk processing tasks and financial transactions requiring high reliability. They are also deployed as servers for large networks. The mainframe market is dominated by IBM.
Supercomputer	Introduced in the 1960s, these high-end computers feature the fastest processors for calculation-intensive tasks in areas such as physics, weather modeling, and molecular analyses.
Minicomputer	Designed to be smaller in size and less expensive than mainframes, minicomputers and the terminals connected to them worked well for small and midsized businesses through the 1990s when many were replaced by PC servers. Now they are called "midrange computers," used as servers.
Microcomputer	Called PCs for short, these devices proliferated in organizations in the 1990s, replacing the dumb terminals and offering far more capability on the desktop. Powerful PCs are widely used as servers as well.
Laptop	Valued for their integrated display screens and portability, these battery-powered PCs became popular in the late 1980s, facilitating mobility. They could run much of the same software as their desktop cousins, though more slowly.
Netbook	Engineered to be even smaller and less expensive than laptops, netbooks gained attention in the late 2000s as a cost-effective means to wirelessly connect to the Internet. Their low cost also facilitates widespread distribution, especially in developing countries.
Smartphones	Offered initially in the 1990s, these devices combine cell-phone capabilities with data communications for web browsing, e-mail, and text messaging.
Tablet	A mobile device with a large touchscreen and virtual keyboard, a tablet is smaller and thinner than a laptop but larger than a smartphone. They gained popularity with the introduction of Apple's iPad in 2010.

central processing unit (CPU)
The brain of a computer, which handles information processing, calculations, and control tasks.

transistor
A small electrical circuit made from a semiconductor material such as silicon.

Moore's Law
A principle named for computer executive Gordon Moore, which states that advances in computer technology, such as processing speed or storage capabilities, doubles about every two years.

these computing architectures should fit into the larger picture, and choices among them depend on the enterprise architecture. For example, a company that still relies on an old software system running on an expensive mainframe would need to keep that running temporarily, but plan its replacement in the roadmap.

STORAGE

How is all this digital information stored? Fortunately, Moore's Law applies to storage technology, so it is cheaper to satisfy the voracious appetite for more space. Storage capacities are measured using the **byte**, which in most architectures holds eight zeros and ones—the equivalent of one key press for text. Figure 3-8 shows ascending storage capacities.[5]

A computer's primary storage, typically on integrated circuits located close to the CPU, includes **random access memory (RAM)**. RAM serves as a temporary storage area as the CPU executes instructions. It is a critical factor in the computer's performance, and you often find extra room so that additional RAM can be inserted. RAM is volatile storage that is erased when power is turned off or lost, but computers also have other chips that permanently store information.

The massive quantities of digital information—soon to exceed zettabytes—are written to secondary storage devices, including computer hard drives. Although easily accessible and searched, hard drives can be a million times slower than primary storage. Their rotating disks and moving heads cannot compare to solid-state integrated circuits, but capacity is higher and costs far less. Solid-state storage with no moving parts is also gaining popularity as prices drop and capacity increases. This category includes flash memory used in USB keys, memory cards for cameras, and hard drive substitutes for rugged laptops. Optical disks (CD-ROMs and DVDs) also offer low cost secondary storage as well as backups for offline storage needed for archiving, disaster recovery, and portability. Magnetic tapes provide cost-effective long-term storage capability.

The business drivers that affect storage decisions include access, speed, cost, and safety. Organizations must have their most important data easily accessible at top speed to respond to customer queries and process transactions. For safety, all the organization's data must also be backed up, and storage solutions depend partly on how much downtime the organization can risk. Reloading from magnetic tapes stored in secure warehouses will take much longer compared to reinstalling from nearby hard drives.

Considerations about storage, backup, and recovery time are included in the enterprise architecture, reflecting the strategic needs of the organization. For instance, a fast-moving e-commerce website would lose revenue if it takes an hour or more to recover from backup media. An organization whose website is more for marketing and handles no transactions might tolerate longer downtime.

FIGURE 3-8

Storage capacity measurements.

Name	Abbreviation	Capacity	Description
Kilobyte	KB	1,024 bytes	A short e-mail message
Megabyte	MB	1024^2 bytes	A digital song runs about 3MB
Gigabyte	GB	1024^3 bytes	About 1 hour of TV recording (not HD)
Terabyte	TB	1024^4 bytes	About 150 hours of HD video recording
Petabyte	PB	1024^5 bytes	eBay's database: 6.5 PB (2009)
Exabyte	EB	1024^6 bytes	Estimated size of the Internet: 500 EB (2009)
Zettabyte	ZB	1024^7 bytes	All electronic data in existence (2011)

THE ETHICAL FACTOR Ethical Implications of Airport Body Scanners

When the infamous "underwear bomber" smuggled plastic explosives onto a Christmas day flight bound for Detroit, calls for more effective screening mounted. Airports around the world stepped up installation of full body scanners that use high-frequency radio waves to create black-and-white three-dimensional images of passengers. The scanner sees through clothing, making people appear virtually nude and revealing contraband that slips through metal detectors.

Scanners improve security, but critics point to ethical questions surrounding their use, particularly invasion of privacy. For instance, Britain delayed implementing them over concerns that they violated child protection laws, which forbid the creation of indecent images of children. Maria Kayanan, associate legal director of the American Civil Liberties Union of Florida, points out that these scanners do pose ethical concerns, particularly for children.[6]

Airports in the United States and the United Kingdom are rapidly adopting the technology, but major hubs in other countries are reluctant for cultural reasons. In the United Arab Emirates, Dubai Airport rejected their use because they violate the Islamic culture's ethical principles.

Other ethical concerns include possible health hazards from the radiation for susceptible passengers and the potential use of the images for other purposes. The Transportation Safety Administration insists that images are immediately discarded, but a watchdog privacy group points to one instance in which images were stored.[7]

To address privacy concerns, airports place screeners in closed rooms so they never see the passenger in person. Passengers can also decline the scan and choose a pat-down. Despite these measures, though, ethical questions over the technology persist. How should a society balance the need for airline security against ethical concerns over privacy?

The Software

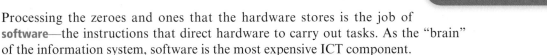

Identify and provide examples of the two major types of software, and describe how software is created.

Processing the zeroes and ones that the hardware stores is the job of **software**—the instructions that direct hardware to carry out tasks. As the "brain" of the information system, software is the most expensive ICT component.

TYPES OF SOFTWARE

Software has two major functions in an information system (Figure 3-9). **Application software** supports all kinds of individual activities, from word processing and presentation development, to video editing, e-mail, web browsing, and game playing. Databases, discussed in the next chapter, are another major example of application software. Microsoft Access is a database useful for personal or departmental applications; enterprise class databases such as Oracle can handle billions of records.

For organizations, application software supports transaction processing, human resources management, customer relationship management, collaboration, corporate training, financial modeling, manufacturing processes, supply chain management, customer support, and all the other processes along the value chain. Many programs are industry specific, such as the intelligent software that helps physicians diagnose illnesses, the iTunes software Apples uses for its online store, or the routing software used by trucking companies. Businesses spend considerable time and money developing or modifying application software to streamline their operations and deliver excellent services.

Drawing an analogy to the human brain, application software is like the neocortex, the top two-thirds that supports consciousness, language, decision making, analysis, and imagination, for instance. Deeper brain structures, such as the cerebellum or medulla, support breathing, heart rate, sleep cycles, and other activities below the level of

---

byte
Measurement unit for computer storage capacity; a byte holds eight zeros and ones and represents a single character.

random access memory (RAM)
A computer's primary temporary storage area accessed by the CPU to execute instructions.

software
The computer component that contains the instructions that directs computer hardware to carry out tasks.

application software
The type of software used to support a wide range of individual and business activities, such as transaction processing, payroll, word processing, and video editing.

FIGURE 3-9

Types of software.

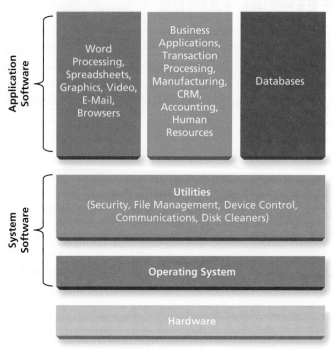

consciousness that keep us functioning smoothly. **System software**, the second category of software, plays a similar role in the computer. It controls basic operations such as file management, disk storage, hardware interfaces, and integration with the application software. It ensures that the technology tools involved in the information system all work together smoothly, though most of the time you need pay no attention to its activities. Software in this category includes operating system software and utilities.

The **operating system (OS)** performs a variety of basic tasks, without which the computer would not function at all. It handles input and output to devices such as keyboards and monitors, maintains file structures, and allocates memory for its own activities and the needs of application software. It may support multiple processors, multiple concurrent users, and multiple applications running simultaneously. The OS also provides a software platform for application developers, which means that application software is typically developed to run on one OS and optimized for that platform. Figure 3-10 shows market shares for common desktop operating systems.

FIGURE 3-10

Desktop microcomputer operating systems' market share as of 2011.

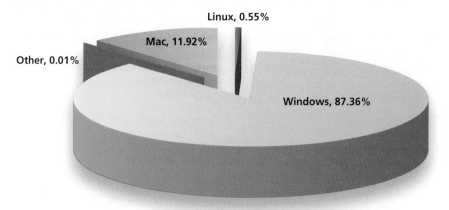

FIGURE 3-11
Smartphone operating systems.

Operating System	Comment
Android	Google's fast growing open source operating system for mobile devices, based on Linux
iPhone OS	Apple's mobile operating system
Research In Motion (RIM) BlackBerry	Very popular OS for business use
Symbian OS	Large but declining market share worldwide; used by Nokia, Motorola, LG, and others
Windows Mobile	Microsoft product that emphasizes Windows applications
Palm OS	Used for Palm devices and some others; based on Linux

To increase adoption of their applications, however, developers often create versions for two or more operating systems. Much software for microcomputers, for example, is offered in Windows and Mac versions.

Operating systems for mobile smartphone s (Figure 3-11) are battling for market share and some may become extinct. Unlike desktop computer operating systems where Windows dominates, numerous smartphone operating systems flood an unstable market. Developers have to decide which platform their new application will run on, and the choice is like playing smartphone roulette. Should they write their nifty new financial calculator for the iPhone, Android, or one of the others? Writing multiple versions is costly, but developing for a dying OS is even worse.[8] Santiago Becerra, chairman of a company that develops such applications, predicts, "The industry will have room for three or four at the most."

Utility software encompasses a large variety of programs that perform specific tasks to help manage, tune, and protect the computer hardware and software. Utilities scan for viruses, perform cleanup routines, log events, compress and back up files, encrypt information, and perform many other tasks. Some of these utilities can significantly improve your own productivity by speeding up your computer and automating tasks (Figure 3-12).

HOW IS SOFTWARE CREATED?

Software is created by teams of programmers working with business analysts, end users, and other stakeholders who envision what the software is intended to do. Creating something like Salesforce.com, or a virtual world such as Second Life, takes intensive collaboration among people with very different areas of expertise. Although

FIGURE 3-12
Examples of utility software.

Utility Software	Description
Antivirus software	Protects against viruses and other malicious code
Disk defragmenter	Optimizes disk performance by moving parts of the same file to contiguous sectors on the hard drive
Compression software	Reduces file sizes to conserve disk space
Shredder	Makes deleted files completely unrecoverable
Recovery	Assists with the recovery of deleted files
File management	Assists with tasks such as renaming groups of files, changing file attributes, and others

system software
The type of software that controls basic computer operations such as file management, disk storage, hardware interfaces, and integration with the application software.

operating system (OS)
The category of system software that performs a variety of critical basic tasks, such as handling device input and output, maintaining file structures, and allocating memory.

utility software
The category of system software that includes programs to perform specific tasks that help manage, tune, and protect the computer hardware and software.

Chapter 11 explores the systems development process in detail, this section introduces the technical side of the process, especially to show how software fits into the larger picture of an organization's overall architecture.

PROGRAMMING LANGUAGES AND DEVELOPMENT ENVIRONMENTS Software is written in one of many **programming languages**, which are artificial languages that provide the instructions for the computer about how to accept information, process it, and provide output. Figure 3-13 lists some common ones, along with some that are nearly defunct. These older languages still survive in **legacy systems**—applications that are still in use because they work reasonably well and are costly to replace.

The **source code** includes all the statements that the programmers write to communicate with the computer and provide instructions. You can see the source code for a web page by right-clicking the page in your browser and selecting "view source." A simple web page might only be a few lines long, but a complex information system might contain millions of lines of code.

Advances in programming languages make it easier for developers to write reliable and easily maintained code. For instance, **object-oriented programming** focuses on "objects" rather than lists of instructions and routines to manipulate data. Programmers define the nature of the data each object contains and also the kinds of operations or behaviors it can do. The modular, reusable objects often simulate real-world objects along with the various states and behaviors they display. For example, the states of a "dog object" might include the dog's name, its color, its breed, or its hunger level. Behaviors could include run, jump, bark, and eat. A "counter object" could be reused in many different settings. The counter's state could specify that it uses only whole numbers, and its behaviors could include resetting to zero, incrementing its value by one, or displaying its current value. An important benefit of object-oriented programming is modularity, so that an object can be independently maintained, reused, or replaced if it breaks down or causes problems. Also, programmers have no need to understand the object's inner workings—only the rules that determine how other objects can interact with it.

Other improvements emerge when software development environments add helpful features that make programmers more productive, much like spell checkers help writers. Microsoft's .NET framework (pronounced "dot net"), for example, offers numerous shortcuts and a large library of canned code that solves common problems, such as displaying a calendar so the user can pick a date.

The Java development environment is popular with developers who want to create software that can easily be adapted to run on any platform, not just Windows. Initially created by Sun Microsystems, Java's mantra is "write once—run anywhere." The language is often used to provide instructions for set-top cable boxes, mobile phones, car navigation systems, lottery terminals, medical devices, and web cams.

FIGURE 3-13

Examples of programming languages, using Gartner Research terminology for age.[9]

Programming Language	Description	Age
COBOL	One of the oldest languages, but more than 200 billion lines of code are still in use for legacy business applications	Elderly
FORTRAN	Used in special projects involving intensive calculations	Elderly
C++	Widely used object-oriented language with considerable support from vendors	Mature
Java	Object-oriented language widely used in web development projects, and designed to run on many different platforms	Adult
Python	Dynamic object-oriented language that runs on a variety of platforms, including smartphones, and growing in popularity	Adult
.NET	Microsoft's proprietary language used in its development environment	Adult

Choosing a programming language for a project depends partly on the tools available and the kinds of tasks to perform. It also depends on the skills of the staff, the availability of vendor support and training, and the overall "age" of the language (Figure 3-13).[9] Older languages like COBOL are poor choices for new projects because more powerful languages are available, and also because continued support will be a problem. The baby boomers who learned COBOL years ago are retiring.[10]

SOFTWARE DEVELOPMENT AND DEPLOYMENT STRATEGIES   Much software is developed commercially by IT companies and offered for sale or licensed to buyers who pay fees for its use. Familiar products such as Microsoft Office, Adobe Premiere, or Quicken are all considered **commercial off-the-shelf (COTS)** software, which means they are ready to buy, install, and use. Although some products, like Excel, are designed for the mass market, others are more specialized for particular business processes. SAS, for example, offers software for statistical analysis, and Cardiff produces software that scans handwriting on paper forms. Much COTS software is also produced for particular industries with features they need. Practice-web, for example develops specialty software for dentists. It includes features such as appointment scheduling, insurance tracking, and the capability to capture dental images as part of the patient's history.

Many of these COTS products allow buyers to configure the software so it better matches their personal preferences or organizational setting. However, the source code is not usually included, so the buyer can't dig into the code to make fundamental changes independently. Indeed, the source code is often a closely guarded trade secret.

A fast-growing variety of commercially produced software is called **software as a service (SaaS)**, which is an information system that is owned, hosted, and managed remotely by a vendor.[11] Organizations pay subscription fees to access it via the web, based on their own volumes. The approach is part of an emerging trend in enterprise architecture that relieves the need for an organization to maintain its own data center, discussed later in this chapter.

On the other end of the spectrum is custom software development, in which an organization works with developers to build software tailored specifically to its needs. For example, the nonprofit HIVConnect needed a specialized social networking site to support people around the world suffering from HIV, and also to encourage and accept online donations. They worked with the software development firm Web Global Net to define the exact requirements and build the site for them. Most custom software is owned by the client who pays for its development or builds it in-house, so changes to the source code can be made as needed.

OPEN SOURCE SOFTWARE   Another approach to software development and distribution is called *open source*. To be considered **open source software**, the licensing terms must comply with several criteria, one of which is free redistribution. The code underlying the program must be freely distributed along with the program, or at least must be easily obtainable, so that other people can improve it, build upon it, or use it in

---

programming language
An artificial language used to write software that provides the instructions for the computer about how to accept information, process it, and provide output.

legacy systems
Older information systems that remain in use because they still function and are costly to replace.

source code
All the statements that programmers write in a particular programming language to create a functioning software program.

object-oriented programming
A type of software programming that focuses on "objects" rather than lists of instructions and routines to manipulate data.

commercial off-the-shelf (COTS)
Commercially available computer software that is ready to buy, install, and use.

software as a service (SaaS)
A type of commercially available software which is owned, hosted, and managed by a vendor, and accessed by customers remotely, usually via the Internet.

open source software
A type of software whose licensing terms comply with criteria such as free distribution, so other people can access the source code to improve it, build upon it, or use it in new programs.

new programs. In practice, this means that licensing costs for open source software are zero, though organizations incur other costs for modifications, implementation, training, and maintenance. It also means that developers who work on the software don't expect any revenue from licensing fees.

Many open source products enjoy considerable success, earning respectable market shares against commercial heavyweights with competitive products and large marketing budgets. Examples include the Linux operating system, the Apache web server, the Firefox web browser, and the Moodle learning management system. Analysts forecast continued growth in the use of open source products.[12]

The question of why people would build open source software nagged the industry for years, but talented developers contribute their time for more than gold. Enormous developer communities, often thousands strong, materialize around products such as Apache, and social recognition for valuable contributions is an important motivator. The communities may be organized as nonprofits, with a leadership team that determines policies about priorities for enhancement. The nonprofit Apache Software Foundation, for example, supports the collaborative efforts of its members who elect the leaders.

Describe the major types of networks and the transmission media they use, and give examples of network protocols.

3

Networks and Telecommunications

Waiting for her class to begin, part-time student and marketing manager Becca Wells wants to catch up with e-mail on her laptop. She clicks on her wireless icon and then refreshes the list of nearby connections (Figure 3-14). The university's StudentNet signal is usually strong, but today it does not show up at all. Instead, she clicks hopefully on a network called "garage" that she never noticed before and waits a few seconds before trying her e-mail. Downloading attachments is a bit slow, but not too bad. She hopes the connection holds up for the video chat with her coworker to discuss a client's marketing campaign, scheduled for 2 p.m.

Becca's e-mail is on a server more than 3,000 kilometers away. The shapes those zeros and ones take and the paths they travel are of little concern to her—as long as the information moves fast and arrives safely. Though networks and telecommunications often stay hidden in the background, this component of ICT is transforming the workplace in every organization—especially through the Internet and wireless computing. Every industry is affected by these transformations, and the companies providing telecom services are experiencing major upheavals.

In the context of telecommunications, a **network** is a group of interconnected devices (such as computers, phones, printers, or displays). To understand how networks operate, we begin with the media and protocols they use to move the zeros and ones.

TRANSMISSION MEDIA AND PROTOCOLS

Networks can take advantage of either wired or wireless transmission media, and often include a mix of both—as Becca's situation shows. Just as hardware devices use different means to store zeros and ones, transmission media convert digital data to different kinds

FIGURE 3-14

Example of wireless networking connection display. The colored bars indicate the strength of the signal, and the lock symbol indicates that the secured network requires password authentication.

Wireless Networks Found

garage **g**　　　NorthEnd **n**

of signals depending on the nature of the medium. Each has strengths and weaknesses, as well as speed and capacity limitations. Transmission speed is measured in **bits per second (bps)**, and **bandwidth** refers to the maximum amount of information in bits per second that a particular channel can transmit. A bit is a single zero or one, and a string of eight bits makes a byte. For text information, a byte represents a single letter, number, or other character.

WIRED MEDIA   The three major wired media are twisted pair wire, coaxial cable, and optical fiber (Figure 3-15). **Twisted pair wires** are the insulated copper wires also used for ordinary telephones. They are the most common wired medium, partly because the phone companies already installed them for voice communications long before they were used to transmit digital data. Transmission speeds have been improved and these wires remain popular for apartment and office buildings as well. They are somewhat fragile and susceptible to interference, but their thin, flexible shape lets them wind easily through ceilings, walls, and cubicles.

Coaxial cables have a single inner conductor wire (typically copper), surrounded by insulation, which is then surrounded by a mesh-like conductor. These are thicker and sturdier than twisted pair wire, and were deployed by cable companies to carry television signals. As a result, they too were installed in many homes and buildings.

Optical fiber cables transmit bits by means of light pulses along a glass or plastic fiber, rather than electrical signals over a conductor. This medium is ideal for very long distances since the signals do not attenuate as much as electrical signals do. The thin fibers can also carry many more channels simultaneously using different wavelengths of light, so bandwidth is very high. Fiber-optic cables the size of a garden hose span all the planet's oceans and form the major arteries for worldwide telecommunications. Although some have occasionally suffered shark bites or other damage, they are proving extremely durable.

WIRELESS MEDIA   Electromagnetic waves, the radiation associated with electric and magnetic fields, can transmit digital information wirelessly (Figure 3-16). These

asharkyu/Shutterstock

FIGURE 3-15

Optical fiber cables

FIGURE 3-16

The electromagnetic spectrum.

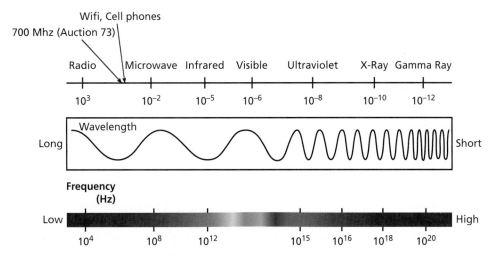

Source: Adapted from http://www.kollewin.com/blog/electromagnetic-spectrum/

network
A group of interconnected devices, such as computers, phones, printers, or displays, that can share resources and communicate using standard protocols.

bits per second (bps)
The measurement of transmission speed, defined as the number of bits transmitted each second; each bit is a single zero or one, and a string of 8 bits makes up a byte.

bandwidth
The maximum amount of information in bits per second that a particular channel can transmit.

twisted pair wires
The most common form of wired media, these wires consist of thin, flexible copper wires used in ordinary phones.

coaxial cables
Wired medium, initially used for cable TV, consisting of a single inner conductor wire (typically copper) surrounded by insulation, which is then surrounded by a mesh-like conductor.

optical fiber
Cables that transmit bits by means of light pulses along a glass or plastic fiber instead of electrical signals over a conductor; ideally suited for long distances.

FIGURE 3-17

Cell-phone infrastructure.

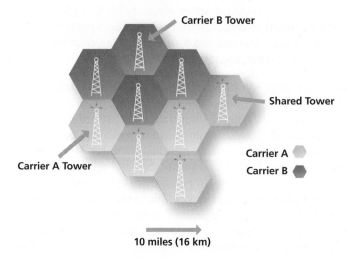

waves include the tiny, atom-sized gamma rays with very rapid frequencies, to very long waves with wavelengths stretching to thousands of miles. Electromagnetic waves are also simply called *light*, but what human eyes perceive as light is actually just a small part of this spectrum. **Wavelength** refers to the distance between one peak of the wave to the next, and frequency, measured in **hertz (Hz)**, is the number of cycles per second.

The waves we use for wireless telecommunications are longer than visible light—in the ranges of radio waves and microwaves. **Microwave transmission** sends signals in the gigahertz range to relays in the line of sight. The signals can hop about 70 kilometers when earthbound, but they can also be transmitted to satellites, vastly increasing their flexibility. Networks of microwave relays have been constructed to transmit wireless data, especially in cities where the dishes can be installed on tall buildings.

The cell phone infrastructure (Figure 3-17) relies on radio waves in the 800 to 1900 megahertz range. Different cell-phone networks use different bands along this range, with separate technologies to encode the transmissions and take best advantage of the frequencies available. Cell-phone towers are constructed about 10 miles apart, and carriers often negotiate agreements to share the towers and install their own equipment at the tower's base, though not all carriers have equipment at every tower. That explains why carriers publish separate coverage maps for their own networks. Transmission speeds keep increasing with improved technology, and carriers are beginning to roll out 4G (4th generation) systems that support wireless Internet access as fast or faster than home cable connections.

Wifi, short for wireless fidelity, refers to a computer network in which connections rely on radio waves at frequencies of 2.4 GHz or 5 GHz for transmission. The 2.4 GHz frequency range is also widely used by cordless phones, which is why they can interfere with one another. The radio signals emanate from the antennae of a **wireless router**, which has a wired connection to the network. They broadcast out to devices within a few hundred feet, getting fainter as the distance increases. If your laptop has a wireless adapter to receive the signal, your software alerts you when one is in range. The router can be configured to prevent unauthorized access by means of passwords or other security measures. For Becca, though, the "garage" wireless network was unsecured so she was able to connect without any password. Perhaps whoever installed "garage" in some nearby dwelling simply forgot to set security, or maybe they were offering the free wifi connection as a public service.

Did You Know?

CoffeeCompany in Holland chooses names for its free wifi networks to cleverly market its menu items and also make people feel a little guilty if they just freeload. When customers in the cafe open their laptops to connect, they see wifi networks with names like "HaveYouTriedCoffeeCake?" or "BuyAnotherCupYouCheapskate."

Bluetooth, a technology that also uses radio waves in the same range as wifi, is commonly used for wireless connections over very short distances. Devices equipped with Bluetooth adapters, such as a printer and computer, or a cell phone and earpiece, can detect one another and communicate.

THE WIRELESS SPECTRUM AS OCEANFRONT PROPERTY   The frequencies used for these technologies may seem dreadfully dull, but think of them as oceanfront real estate, where supply is short and location is everything—at least in terms of what can be done with the bandwidth. Governments usually regulate the spectrum's use and its allocation because it is a limited public good. Much of the spectrum usable for wireless transmission is already reserved for TV, cell phones, radio, law enforcement, emergency services, defense, and various government agencies. Some of it is left unlicensed and available for any devices to use, such as the bandwidth used for wifi. Since no carrier has control, no fees are charged to use that bandwidth, though some router owners, such as hotels, might want some payment for using their Internet connection.

Governments also auction these licenses, and the high bidder wins the right to build services using the bandwidth and sell them to customers. The infrequent auctions are often high-stakes events. Some bandwidths have more potential than others for technical reasons, and every company involved in wireless networks and applications, from Google and Yahoo! to AT&T and T-Mobile, pays very close attention. Innovation in wireless is exploding, and no one wants to be left out of the next new thing. In a recent auction of some valuable bandwidth in the 700 MHz range that became available because of the switch to digital TV, Verizon won a particularly valuable block with its $9.4 billion bid. As downloading videos to smartphones and other wireless devices spreads, this invisible oceanfront property will only grow in value.

THE LAST MILE   Another tense issue involving transmission media is that last mile— the final leg of cabling that connects the communications provider to the customer. For rural areas, that leg can be quite long and expensive to traverse with wired solutions. The phone carriers, as regulated companies, had an early edge because their twisted pairs were already in place, an infrastructure subsidized by regulated fees. These could be repurposed for two-way digital communications, using **digital subscriber lines (DSL)**. This technology significantly improves transmission speed over twisted pair wires.

However, cable TV companies had also deployed their thicker coaxial cables to homes and businesses, especially in more densely populated areas. They had more trouble transforming their infrastructure to accommodate two-way digital communications because their systems were originally designed for one-way transmission of TV signals. Their advantage, though, was greater bandwidth and higher transmission speeds.

wavelength
The distance between one peak of an electromagnetic wave to the next.

hertz (Hz)
The number of cycles per second of a wave.

microwave transmission
The technology involving signals in the gigahertz range that are transmitted to relays in the line of sight.

wifi
Short for wireless fidelity; refers to a computer network in which connections rely on radio waves at frequencies of 2.4 GHz or 5 GHz for transmission.

wireless router
A device connected to a computer network that emits signals from its antenna and enables wireless connectivity to the network.

Bluetooth
A technology that uses radio waves for connectivity, commonly used for wireless connections over very short distances.

digital subscriber lines (DSL)
Technology that supports high speed two-way digital communication over twisted pair phone lines.

The competition between cable companies such as Comcast or Time Warner Cable and the carriers that started as phone companies, such as Verizon and AT&T, remains very fierce as they all try to improve their services, increase speed, and provide the best value. Verizon, for example, is deploying optical fiber for that last mile in some locations, and cable companies add voice service to their networks. As people drop landline service in favor of cell phones and Internet-based services such as Skype or Yahoo! Messenger, the carriers are losing landline customers, along with the monthly fees they paid. Making the carriers' business model even less stable is the growing availability of high-speed wireless networks. In some locations, customers need no wires at all to enjoy phone and fast Internet service. As we saw in the last chapter, though, agile companies can revamp their strategies and reinvent themselves to meet the challenge of disruptive innovations. Verizon will certainly try to use its precious oceanfront spectrum in innovative ways.

TYPES OF NETWORKS

Connecting computers or other devices to transmit and receive digital information over any of the media involves creating a network, and many different configurations are used. The industry categorizes network types based on their scale and scope, and how much geographic area they encompass. The **local area network (LAN)** typically connects computers, printers, scanners, and other devices in a single building or home. To describe networks that span smaller or larger geographic areas, the terms in Figure 3-18 are common.

CIRCUIT-SWITCHED AND PACKET-SWITCHED NETWORKS The approach used to transmit data between computers is another characteristic that distinguishes networks. In a **circuit-switched network**, nodes communicate by first establishing a channel, as though there were a single pipe leading between them. Once established, the two devices can communicate very quickly and reliably. The phone system used this approach, as do various specialty applications that require high speed and secure data transmission. Although many improvements make circuit switching more efficient, it does tend to waste capacity. Waiting on hold, for example, occupies the channel even though no information is transmitted.

Most networks now use **packet switching**, in which strings of digital data are broken into segments called *packets* before they are transmitted. The packets contain information about their destination and position in the whole message, and they are reassembled at the receiving end. They may travel different routes, weaving around offline servers or taking longer paths if they confront traffic congestion. Packet switching is quite flexible and it makes networks far more survivable against natural or manmade disasters.

Packet switching can be configured to handle connections that once required circuit switching, including voice phone calls. **Voice over IP (VoIP)** refers to the technologies that make voice communications across networks using packets

FIGURE 3-18

Types of networks.

Type of Network	Geographic Area
Personal area network (PAN)	20–30 feet, for devices within reach
Local area network (LAN)	Home, office, school, building
Campus (or Corporate) area network (CAN)	Interconnected LANs encompassing several buildings for a university or a corporate campus
Metropolitan area network (MAN)	Interconnected LANs or CANs for a city
Wide area network (WAN)	Interconnected LANs, CANs, MANs covering a wide geographic area
Global area network (GAN)	Supports mobile communications across the globe, using a mix of satellite or other strategies

feasible, including over the Internet. This disruptive innovation started out as many of them do, attracting people with small budgets and lots of patience for dropped calls or bad audio due to the bursty way packets travel. However, making free phone calls to anyone in the world who has a computer and Internet connection is a compelling draw. Skype is now the market leader for VoIP, accounting for 12 percent of all international calls.[13] The technology continues to improve—adding video, conferencing capabilities, voice mail, low cost calls to landlines and mobile phones, and better security and voice quality. Businesses can integrate their voice and data communications, making it unnecessary to install separate systems. As you will see later, this feature opens up new possibilities for cost savings and innovative business applications.

CLIENT-SERVER AND PEER-TO-PEER NETWORKS   Beyond geographic span and connection styles, we can describe networks in terms of how centralized they are, and how the devices on the network share the workload and provide services to others. A **client-server network** has one or more high-performance hosts running programs and storing data that clients—such as desktop computers, laptops, or smartphones—can access. The workload is shared, and the client runs software that performs some of the work of interpreting, displaying, and analyzing the data (Figure 3-19). A web browser such as Mozilla's Firefox, for example, is client software that runs on a microcomputer. When you open your browser and connect to a host, your client sends the request to the web server, which then sends back the instructions for displaying the page you requested.

The server in a client-server network can be around the corner, deep in your organization's data center, or perhaps across the planet. With any particular request, more than one server may be involved in the response, each specialized for its particular purpose. For instance, the web server may receive your request

---

FIGURE 3-19

Client-server network. Photos/illustrations: ArchMan/Shutterstock, Pokomeda/Shutterstock, Sashkin/Shutterstock.

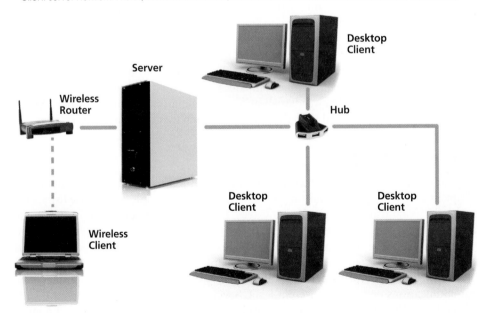

---

local area network (LAN)
A network that connects devices such as computers, printers, and scanners in a single building or home.

circuit-switched network
A type of network in which the nodes communicate by first establishing a dedicated channel between them.

packet switching
A technology used by networks in which data is broken into segments called packets, for transmission. The packets contain information about their destination and position in the whole message, and they are reassembled at the receiving end.

Voice over IP (VoIP)
The technologies that make voice communications across networks using packet switching feasible, including over the Internet.

client-server network
A type of network in which the workload for running applications is shared between the server and the client devices, such as desktop computers, laptops, or smartphones.

to display your bank balance, but the data itself is retrieved from a database on a different server. This kind of architecture is called **n-tier**, with a client and one or more servers involved.

The client in a client-server network can do more or less work, depending on how the software is designed, but the trend is to reduce its workload. In fact, much business software now only requires a web browser. This eliminates the need to install and configure special software on all the different types of clients throughout an organization.

The highly decentralized approach is called the **peer-to-peer network**, in which there is no central server and computers can share files, printers, and an Internet connection with one another. The networks for homes or small offices are often set up this way, and most operating systems support it. The nodes on a decentralized network are peers in the sense that each one can offer services to the others and none is the centralized server.

On a larger scale, peer-to-peer networks support file sharing and other services on the Internet. BitTorrent is one example, used to move large files rapidly from one computer to another by breaking them into smaller pieces called *torrents*. The software allows its more than 160 million users to locate a song, movie, game, or other digital product stored on peer computers, download the pieces, and then make the pieces available for others to download. Implications for copyright violation are acute, and lawsuits very common. For example, the four men who launched Pirate Bay, a Swedish website that facilitates the use of BitTorrent, were sentenced to a year in jail and a $3.6 million fine by a Swedish court in 2009. However, the defendants argue that no copyrighted material is stored on their own servers. Because the network is peer-to-peer, the material is stored only on the users' computers. That decentralization makes them hard to shut down and the appeals will likely take years.[14]

BitTorrent solved a human obstacle associated with peer-to-peer networking—freeloading. On other peer-to-peer networks, people eagerly found files to download, but were reluctant to share them with others. Legal issues aside, letting your computer act as a server can degrade its performance, slow down transmissions, and introduce security threats. However, BitTorrent software requires sharing before a user can enjoy good download speed, so the technology incorporates incentives. Those who never share are eventually cut off.

Skype also uses peer-to-peer networking for VoIP, borrowing a bit of their users' computer power and Internet connections as calls are routed around the globe, hopping from node to node. Unlike the phone companies, which built the vast, wired infrastructure and manage servers that handle call switching, billing, and technical support, Skype enlists the aid of its users and their equipment—though they may not realize it.

NETWORK PROTOCOLS

Transmitting data over any medium requires protocols that both the sender and recipient use. When you power on your cell phone, for example, the device listens for a control signal transmitted via radio waves. If no signal is received, your phone will report "No service." The signal also includes a code that indicates the carrier, and if your phone is using the same carrier, the codes will match, indicating your phone is on its home network and not roaming on some other carrier's network.

Networking protocols perform their work in layers, each of which defines how communications occur at a different level. Several models have been proposed, such as the Open Systems Interconnection (OSI) model with the seven layers, shown in Figure 3-20. The lowest level determines how a device will physically connect using a transmission medium and plug layout. Higher layers define how other connection issues are resolved, such as how the bits will be organized and transmitted, how errors will be corrected, and how the connection will be established and then broken off when finished. The highest level defines how software applications interface with the user. That "http://" preceding the website is a protocol at this highest level, and it tells your browser how to interpret the data so you can view it properly.

FIGURE 3-20

Layers defined by the OSI model.

OSI Model
7. Application layer
6. Presentation layer
5. Session layer
4. Transport layer
3. Network layer
2. Data link layer
1. Physical layer

ETHERNET   **Ethernet** is the protocol widely used for local area networks, dominating the market since the 1980s. Technology improvements have increased transmission speed, now in the gigabit per second range. The familiar cabling that leads from the back of your office desktop to a jack in the wall is very likely an ethernet cable, connecting to your organization's local area network, then to the data center. It resembles a phone jack, which often appears on the same wall plate, but is a little wider.

TCP/IP AND THE INTERNET'S HOURGLASS ARCHITECTURE   The suite of protocols used for Internet communications that connect ethernet and other networks together includes the Transmission Control Protocol and Internet Protocol, or **TCP/IP** for short. These two deal especially with the middle networking layers that define how data are packaged and transported, leaving plenty of room for innovation at the lower and upper layers.

The core design principle of the Internet is its hourglass structure, so the network protocols themselves are really very simple (Figure 3-21). As long as bits are transmitted

FIGURE 3-21

The Internet's hourglass architecture.

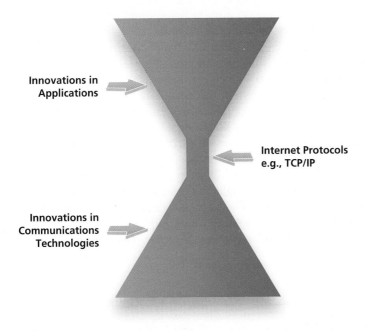

Innovations in Applications

Internet Protocols e.g., TCP/IP

Innovations in Communications Technologies

n-tier
Type of network architecture in which several servers, specialized for particular tasks, may be accessed by a client computer to perform some activity, such as retrieving a bank balance.

peer-to-peer network
A type of network in which there is no central server and computers can share files, printers, and an Internet connection with one another.

ethernet
A communication protocol widely used for local area networks.

TCP/IP
Abbreviation for Transmission Control Protocol and Internet Protocol; used for Internet communications.

using the Internet's suite of standardized protocols, new applications for the top end and new communications technologies for the bottom can all be incorporated. For example, long after the Internet was launched using standard phone lines, dozens of new wiring and wireless schemes emerged to increase speed, serve remote areas, or leverage some existing wiring such as coaxial cable. (Some say the Internet is so flexible that two cans and a string will do the trick.)

At the top of the hourglass, the Internet's open architecture leads to astonishing creativity and new applications. In fact, the World Wide Web is one of those innovations that came along to sit atop the Internet in the application layer. Streaming video, e-commerce, and VoIP are other examples, and no doubt more are on the way.

Although the Internet's original design was extremely clever, some features later caused regret. One problematic element is simply the number of addresses available. The current protocol assigns an IP address to each node or device as a string of four numbers, such as **157.150.190.10,** which is currently the United Nations' website (www.un.org). The scheme supports about 4 billion different addresses, which seemed like more than enough at the time. However, with explosive growth and innovations that demand addresses for so many new devices, the pool will soon be exhausted. The next generation addressing scheme, called **Internet Protocol Version 6 (IPv6)**, offers several improvements, including much more breathing room for addresses— quadrillions for each man, woman, and child on the planet, in fact.

WIRELESS PROTOCOLS Wireless protocols determine how the electromagnetic spectrum is used to transmit data. A family of standards called *802.11* is widely used for wifi connections, with different versions indicated by a letter appended after the 11. Figure 3-22 compares the standards on several features. The newer 802.11n standard supports wider coverage and also much higher transmission speeds, though not as high as the theoretical 600 Mb/s. Nevertheless, the extra speed certainly lured many customers to the 802.11n standard even when it was still in draft mode. The fact that it can be set to transmit at 5 GHz is another plus, to avoid the interference from cordless phones and other home appliances that use 2.4 GHz.

For larger geographic areas, mobile broadband technologies use licensed spectrum in different ways. **WiMax**, for example, relies on microwave transmissions to blanket large metropolitan areas from microwave towers, usually on buildings. Cellular networks offer rival services since they can also carry IP traffic. If your cell phone gets a signal from a cell tower, your smartphone or computer (with an adapter) will also be able to access the net. Emerging technologies are leading to the 4th generation of cellular networks, with greater transmission speed and coverage. People who want to boost signal strength in their home or office, perhaps so they can eliminate their landlines, can even extend cellular coverage by installing their own base station that connects to their carrier's network through their home Internet connection.

The future for wireless is very bright and customer demand high, but the industry will be tumultuous for some time. Competing technologies, standards, and protocols lead to fierce battles as allied companies with complementary products and services line up to support one protocol or another. Network effects make the outcome critically important to all of us.

FIGURE 3-22

Comparing 802.11 standards.

Standard	Indoor Range	Frequency	Maximum Data Rate
802.11a	~35 meters	3.7 or 5 GHz	54 Mb/s
802.11b	~38 meters	2.4 GHz	11 Mb/s
802.11g	~38 meters	2.4 GHz	54 Mb/s
802.11n	~70 meters	2.4 or 5 GHz	600 Mb/s

The Enterprise Architecture

Explain the importance of the enterprise architecture, describing trends in ICT architecture over time.

Reputed to be haunted, The Winchester House in California has about 160 rooms, some set inside another. Countless staircases lead nowhere, and a chimney stops short of the ceiling. Closets open to blank walls and doors open to steep drops to the garden far below. The weird house is a tourist attraction, but it wasn't built to be amusing. Its oddities occurred because Sarah Winchester had no master architectural plan for the house and just improvised its construction, day after day, year after year. As heiress to the Winchester rifle fortune, she could afford those gaffes. But businesses cannot.

Nevertheless, the architecture of an enterprise often evolves just as haphazardly, as managers change their strategies and drop ongoing projects, people duplicate work they don't realize has already been done somewhere else in the company, and new information systems overlap existing functionality. Recall from the beginning of the chapter that to avoid missteps, organizations are increasingly thinking in terms of the **enterprise architecture (EA)**. In the United States, all federal agencies are required to develop an EA plan, and you can find examples of them on the web.

The enterprise architecture is the big picture for the organization, the blueprint that describes the current environment and the target environment the organization hopes to reach to achieve its mission. It also includes a roadmap for transitioning from the baseline to the target, to help managers make better decisions that focus on long-term benefits and not just short-term gains. The architecture is not just about ICT assets, though that is a key component. It encompasses the people, technology, processes, and data that make up information systems, and it should be driven by business requirements and the organization's mission.

Figure 3-23 illustrates the enterprise architecture as layers, in which the business mission at the top drives decisions about data and applications architectures. These should then shape the ICT architecture, to include hardware, software, and communications.

FIGURE 3-23

Components of an enterprise architecture.

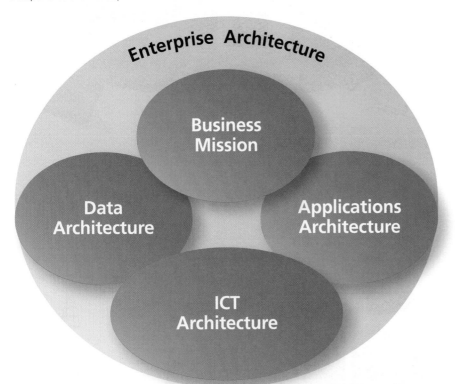

Internet Protocol Version 6 (IPv6)
The next generation protocol for the Internet, that will support far more IP addresses compared to the current scheme.

WiMax
Technology that relies on microwave transmissions to blanket large metropolitan areas from microwave towers, usually on buildings.

TRENDS IN ICT ARCHITECTURES

The ICT component of the enterprise architecture changes over time as new technologies emerge and businesses build more effective and efficient processes to achieve their missions. Figure 3-24 plots some of the major architectural approaches, and many organizations have mixed versions.

FIGURE 3-24

The evolution of ICT architectures. Photos/illustrations: Pokomeda/Shutterstock, broukoid/Shutterstock, Ilona Baha/Shutterstock, Nasonov/Shutterstock, Mad Dog/Shutterstock.

FROM MAINFRAMES TO MICROCOMPUTERS Beginning in the 1960s, mainframes were the foundation of the ICT architecture. Dumb terminals, with their glowing green and black screens, accessed the data center's mainframe, and private leased lines were used to transmit information between corporate sites. When microcomputers entered businesses in the 1980s, they swiftly replaced typewriters, despite how clunky the early word processing software was. The electronic spreadsheet was so compelling that businesses began tossing their dumb terminals out. The PC could emulate a dumb terminal to access the mainframe's applications, but it could also run its own software locally.

CLIENT-SERVER ARCHITECTURES Local area networks, more powerful PCs, and the development of PC operating systems that could support many users concurrently opened the path for the client-server architecture described earlier. Software applications that tap the resources of both server and client emerged, with more user-friendly, colorful, and graphical interfaces replacing the staid black screens so familiar to mainframe users.

Businesses enjoyed major savings by retiring expensive mainframes with their costly software and peripherals. They replaced aging systems with new software that ran on PC-based servers and local area networks. Because PC hardware could be obtained from many manufacturers (Dell and H-P, for example), prices stayed competitive. Organizations settled on ethernet as the local area networking standard and adopted strategies for using the Internet for communications rather than leasing private lines from the telecommunications carriers. They also gravitated toward a handful of server operating systems, namely Windows Server, Unix, and Linux. These trends initially introduced many cost savings.

VIRTUALIZATION The organization's data center, once home to a mainframe computer and all its components, quickly became jammed with rack after rack of PC servers. Because many servers in n-tier client-server architectures specialize in one kind of task or one software application, much capacity remains unused. The CPUs might sit idle much of the time, though still drawing electricity and generating heat. To address this, companies implement **virtualization** using software that allows multiple operating systems to run concurrently on a single physical PC server. To the users, each one appears as a separate, self-contained server that may handle only one software application, but they are actually virtual servers.

Virtualization can cut costs dramatically, not just by lowering electricity bills and hardware expenses, but also through reduced maintenance. IT staff must tend every server in the data center, and each one needs backup, communications, software installations, upgrades, virus protection, patches, and more. Kevin Brown of Service Corporation International reported $1.5 million in savings in the first 6 months after implementing virtualization.[15]

Virtualization is also an important element in the drive toward environmentally friendly information systems. With improved use of capacity, energy consumption drops.

INTEGRATION OF VOICE AND DATA COMMUNICATIONS Since the mainframe era, the infrastructure for voice communications was separated from data. Buildings have been constructed with two sets of cabling to each office or cubicle—one for data communications and the other for voice (Figure 3-24A and 3-24B). The twisted copper pair wiring for voice typically leads to **private branch exchange (PBX)** equipment in the data center or off site, which manages all the office phone lines, voice mail, internal billing, call transfers and forwarding, conferencing, and other voice services. This equipment might be provided and managed by the phone company or, for larger companies, purchased outright and operated by IT staff. Figure 3-24A shows a PBX right next to the mainframe, and then later, as a smaller, rack-based model (Figure 3-24B).

virtualization
Cost-cutting approach to servers in which multiple operating systems run concurrently on a single physical PC server.

private branch exchange (PBX)
Technology that manages all the office phone lines, voice mail, internal billing, call transfers, forwarding, conferencing, and other voice services.

With VoIP, however, organizations can design the enterprise architecture quite differently. Voice communications can be integrated with data, traveling over the same networks and managed by software applications on the same servers. Although the trend is still early, managers have many more options about how to handle voice traffic, and the PBX will eventually fade out. Voice communications will be closely integrated with the other software that a company uses.[16] Embedding communications capabilities into business software is especially attractive, because those systems already store contact information for customers, suppliers, and employees.

CLOUD COMPUTING The emerging ICT architecture called **cloud computing** moves IT resources out of the corporation's own data centers or desktops and into the so-called "cloud"—a term borrowed from drawings that depict the Internet (Figure 3-24C). The concept is confusing because it encompasses many different styles and technologies, and some are not actually new.[17] One approach, for example, involves leasing IT resources, such as hardware capacity or software applications, from vendors rather than building corporate data centers and installing software locally. Customers can access the services they lease through the Internet. Vendors such as Amazon, Google, eBay, and Salesforce.com are creating cloud computing capabilities in which business customers can lease the IT resources they need on "multitenant" servers, sharing each server's capacity with the vendor's other customers.

Amazon's Elastic Compute Cloud, for example, sells flexible server capacity on which a company can install whatever software it chooses. Companies can expand or contract quickly, leasing just what they need from Amazon's immense data centers. Virtualization is a particularly important enabler for this version of cloud computing—customers probably won't even know the neighbors who share the same physical server.

Beyond hardware capacity, vendors are scrambling to offer software as a service (SaaS) in the context of cloud computing, described in the previous chapter. They build a software application in a way that allows many tenants to use it for their own organizations, and access it from computers or smartphones through wired or wireless Internet connections. Salesforce.com offers its customer relationship management software this way.

A drawback of cloud computing is that an extremely reliable Internet connection is a must. Organizations that can't count on that for their operations, perhaps because of their location or harsh weather conditions, would find themselves without access to their mission critical systems when the net connection failed.

For individuals, an attractive feature of cloud computing is how it frees information that is often stranded on a hard drive at work, a common fate for files created with PC software. If the file is saved in the cloud, it can be accessed from home, office, hotel, or on the road, using any device with a net connection. It can also be shared with coworkers. Google Docs is one service that offers cloud-based word processing, spreadsheet, and presentation software.

To some extent, the drive to rebrand some familiar services as "cloud computing" is more about marketing hype than a brand new architecture. However, improvements in virtualization, security, and mobile access are very real, and they may offer compelling opportunities to reduce costs and empower the workforce. Eliminating even one corporate data center, for example, can offer substantial savings in capital expenditures and IT personnel costs. For employees and customers, the switch can mean far more freedom of mobility. Blue Cross of Northeastern Pennsylvania, for example, is switching to cloud computing for its 300,000 members, so they can access medical histories and claims information on their smartphones. Chief Medical Officer Dr. Leo Hartz said, "In this area, we're a bit behind, so this is a huge step for us.... It's new, but I expect to see some big changes."

As the shift to the cloud gathers momentum, the richness and variety of services will continue to grow. Gartner predicts the market will explode to more than $150 billion by 2013, provided vendors can satisfy customer concerns that their data and applications are safe, secure, and utterly reliable. Those concerns are not trivial, considering how valuable these resources are.

GUIDING THE ARCHITECTURE

Creating the roadmap to guide the enterprise from its current architecture to its target is a formidable task, especially for organizations that have a mix of platforms already in place. Peek behind the counter at your dentist's office, for example, and you may see a PC emulating a dumb terminal, with an old-fashioned text-based display showing your last three appointments. On another desk, you see someone logging into a graphical software application to check on insurance for your dental visit. In the chair, you might watch your dentist pull up vivid X-ray images and medical records on a flat screen. And in a few days, you may be able to check on the insurance claim yourself with your smartphone. Many organizations carry a mix of architectures, implemented over time, and with limited integration among them.

The task of creating and guiding the architecture is often led by an enterprise architect (Figure 3-25). This new (and well-paid) position requires a person with deep knowledge of the organization's mission and strategy, and a clear understanding of how different ICT architectures can support the company's goals. Some architects rely on frameworks developed to guide the process, such as the Federal Enterprise Architecture Framework used by many U.S. agencies. The architect's role is to lead the effort, promote the value of EA concepts, and coordinate decision making so the organization stays on track.

The enterprise architecture for Genentech, the company described at the beginning of this chapter, would help managers make smarter decisions that benefit the whole company, although they sometimes might not benefit each manager's department. When the sales rep wanted to use her own BlackBerry and save the department the cost of an iPhone, a red flag should have gone up. The architect would weigh the costs of developing applications for more than one smartphone platform against the benefits of allowing employees to use their own devices. One BlackBerry may be a trivial detour from the roadmap, but hundreds of such detours add up, delay progress, and lead to chaos. In Chapter 12, we discuss strategic planning, and the enterprise architecture plays a major role.

The architectural shifts now underway have a major impact on industries, organizations, their employees, and their customers. Cloud computing offers many valuable business capabilities and the potential for cost savings. But drafting a blueprint that erases the underground data center is far easier than actually dismantling it and reconfiguring in the cloud. Managers worry about the safety of their data and the reliability of the services. They wonder whether their old legacy applications will still run, or whether they can get the help they need as the IT department shrinks. IT staff struggle with reduced budgets and staffing, and also a loss of control over the company's mission-critical systems. The enterprise architect must take into account these human elements, designing a road map that will guide the organization into a successful future.

With this overview of information and communications technologies, and the different kinds of enterprise architectures we can create with them, we can now move deeper into information systems and the data architecture. The database is a central feature, and the next chapter shows how it works.

FIGURE 3-25

Job opening: Enterprise architect.

Job Opening: Enterprise Architect

As enterprise architect, you will lead the effort to analyze our company's business strategy, define the ICT architecture to support it, and create the roadmap for getting there. You must be familiar with business objectives and how technology solutions align with them. Superb communications and negotiation skills are essential. You will interact with business leaders in every department to understand needs, and develop a governance structure to guide decision making about technology investments. Salary in the low to mid $100s. Bachelor's degree in business with strong background in information systems required. MBA preferred.

---

cloud computing
ICT architecture in which users access software applications and information systems remotely over the Internet, rather than locally on an individual PC or from servers in the organization's data center.

MyMISLab | *Online Simulation*

Devil's Canyon

A Role-Playing Simulation on Enterprise Architecture for a Mountain Resort

A team of entrepreneurs is building a deluxe mountain resort from the ground up and they need your help to plan the enterprise architecture. Devil's Canyon is a breathtaking location, and the resort will offer everything from skiing and snowboarding in the winter, to rock climbing, white water rafting, hiking, swimming, and fishing in the warmer seasons. These young and enthusiastic entrepreneurs aren't really sure what they'll need, but they want Devil's Canyon to be the premier, 21st century resort, well equipped with technology to please their demanding target market.

Your job is to get a sense of their vision and how much they can afford, and then help them design the enterprise architecture using the interactive design tools. You'll meet the team at the kickoff session, so log in when you're ready to start...

Ilja Mašík/Shutterstock

Learning Objectives

1 The four hardware components of every computer include input, output, the central processing unit (CPU), and storage. Input devices convert signals such as a key press on a keyboard or finger motion on a touchscreen into digital information and transmit it to the CPU. Output devices include display screens and printers, and many devices serve both purposes. Computing architectures vary in terms of size, processing speed and capacities, portability, and other factors. They include mainframes, minicomputers, supercomputers, microcomputers, laptops, netbooks, smartphones, and tablets. Storage devices include random access memory, hard drives, solid state drives, optical disks, and magnetic tape.

2 Two types of software include applications software, which support all business processes and specific tasks, and system software, which includes the operating system and utilities. Software is written in various programming languages and software development environments. Managers make choices by taking into consideration staff skills; the availability of training, support, and tools; and other factors. Software created by IT companies such as Microsoft or Oracle and licensed to customers is called commercial off-the-shelf (COTS). Increasingly, web-based applications are licensed as software as a service (SaaS). Unique applications or business processes sometimes call for custom software development. Open source software, with licensing terms that call for free redistribution, is developed by volunteer communities and carries no licensing costs.

3 Networks connect computers and other devices, and their transmission media can be wired or wireless. Wired media include twisted pair, coaxial cable, and optical fiber. Wireless transmission relies on the electromagnetic spectrum, using segments that are either licensed or unlicensed. Networks can be classified by their geographic areas (such as LAN or WAN), by whether they use packet or circuit switching, and by their degree of centralization (client-server and peer-to-peer). To connect, devices rely on protocols, such as ethernet and TCP/IP. These protocols determine how different layers address connection issues, from the physical layer to the application layer. The Internet's protocols support ongoing innovation because they address mainly the middle layers.

4 The enterprise architecture is the organization's master blueprint that describes its current environment, its future state, and the roadmap for achieving it. It is driven by business needs and helps define and guide the ICT architecture needed to support it. ICT architectures have evolved over time with changes in business needs and technological innovations. Emerging trends include virtualization, the integration of voice and data, and cloud computing. Developing and guiding the enterprise architecture requires a keen understanding of the business mission and how ICT architectures can support it.

KEY TERMS AND CONCEPTS

enterprise architecture (EA)	transistor	utility software	network
computer	Moore's Law	programming language	bits per second (bps)
ASCII code	byte	legacy systems	bandwidth
optical scanners	random access memory (RAM)	source code	twisted pair wires
optical character recognition (OCR)	software	object-oriented programming	coaxial cables
radio frequency identification (RFID)	application software	commercial off-the-shelf (COTS)	optical fiber
central processing unit (CPU)	system software	software as a service (SaaS)	wavelength
	operating system (OS)	open source software	hertz (Hz)
			microwave transmission

wifi	circuit-switched network	peer-to-peer network	WiMax
wireless router	packet switching	ethernet	virtualization
Bluetooth	voice over IP (VoIP)	TCP/IP	private branch exchange (PBX)
digital subscriber lines (DSL)	client-server network	Internet Protocol Version 6 (IPv6)	
local area network (LAN)	n-tier		cloud computing

CHAPTER REVIEW QUESTIONS

1. What is the function of each of the four components of a computer? Give an example of each component.

2. What is the meaning and significance of Moore's Law?

3. What are the two major types of software and how do they differ? Give an example of each.

4. What are the different strategies for creating and deploying software?

5. What are the major types of wired and wireless transmission media? What are the strengths, weaknesses, and potential of each?

6. What are two types of networks and how are they used?

7. What is a network protocol? What are the roles of Ethernet, TCP/IP, and wireless protocols?

8. What is an enterprise architecture and what is its role in an organization?

9. How have ICT architectures changed over time as new technologies have emerged?

10. What is cloud computing? How does it support business objectives?

PROJECTS AND DISCUSSION QUESTIONS

1. Why did people stand in ridiculously long lines for hours in hopes of buying a $300 iPhone 4? Despite widespread reports of reception issues, Apple struggled to meet the demand for its latest smartphone. Describe the latest iPhone in terms of hardware components (input, processing, storage, output) and its operating system and application software.

2. When the "StudentNet" wireless Internet signal did not appear on the list of nearby connections (Figure 3-14), Becca Wells used the "garage" network to check her e-mail. What issues should Becca have considered before connecting to that unknown network? For example, is it ethical to connect through someone's service without permission, even if they didn't password protect the access point? What security issues should she be concerned about? Search the web to learn more about "wardriving" and prepare a brief summary of your findings.

3. Twenty years ago, analysts predicted the death of mainframe computers. Today, however, many public and private enterprises throughout the world rely on the mainframe as the backbone of large-scale computing. For example, the U.S. Census Bureau uses mainframe computers to process data about the nation's people and economy. On the other hand, many of today's data centers run on racks of PC servers or large-scale PC server farms. How are mainframe computers different from PCs? How are they similar? Search the web or visit websites such as openmainframe.org and ibm. com to learn more about how mainframes support an IT infrastructure. List and discuss the major uses of mainframe systems.

4. Although vendors describe the cloud as a cost-effective solution to increase IT capabilities, some critics describe it as marketing hype. The implementation of cloud computing to replace in-house computing generally requires:

   a. Leasing IT resources

   b. Depending on a third party to store data

   c. Depending on a third party to provide services

   List the positive and negative results of these factors as they affect organizations that adopt cloud computing. Outline several reasons why a company might decide to use cloud computing. Are there other issues related to cloud computing? In your opinion, what is the strongest argument against cloud computing?

5. Consider the many types of computer input devices available today. Identify two general categories of input devices and provide several examples of each. List and describe several input devices that also serve as output devices. List several input/output devices that you own. Which are your favorites? Why? Which are your least favorites? Why?

6. Why are there different programming languages? What is the fundamental difference between Java and .NET? Search the web to learn the origin of the name "COBOL." How is COBOL used today? How strong is the case that "COBOL is dead"? Why or why not?

7. Jackson Real Estate is relocating to new office space and owner Bella Jackson must decide between a wired or wireless network for 35 on-the-go agents. What are the pros and cons of each type of network for this business environment? Consider the cost, security, and mobility issues of this decision and make a recommendation.

8. Work in a small group with classmates to compare three office productivity applications: Microsoft Office, a commercial off-the-shelf software product; Google Docs, software as a service; and Open Office, a free, open source office suite (available at openoffice.org). What are the benefits, costs, and risks of each application? Discuss why a small business or nonprofit organization may prefer one application instead of another.

9. Work in a small group with classmates to explain the effects of Moore's Law on information and communication technology. What is the impact of Moore's Law on your life? Prepare a 5-minute presentation on your findings.

10. Work in a small group with classmates to consider the differences between commercial off-the-shelf software and custom software. What are the advantages and disadvantages of each type of software? Why would a company decide to develop its own software rather than use COTS? Investigate the student information system used by your college or university to learn whether the software was custom developed or purchased.

APPLICATION EXERCISES

EXCEL APPLICATION:
Analyzing Growth in Computer Storage Capacities

Since the computer hard drive was invented in 1956, a constantly increasing data storage capacity has been available at an ever-decreasing cost. Use the historical data of hard drive capacities and prices shown in Figure 3-26 to create an Excel spreadsheet that includes formulas to calculate a common measure of disk size (GB) and the cost per GB for each year. You can also download the Excel file that contains this data, named Ch03Ex01. Recall 1 gigabyte = 1,024 megabytes; 1 terabyte=1,024 gigabytes. Create two line charts to present trends in the cost of data storage, using the data for years 1980–1999 for one chart and the data for years 2000–2010 for the second chart. Write a brief summary of the trends you found. What factors have contributed to these trends? What are the implications of these trends?

ACCESS APPLICATION:
Managing ICT Assets with a Database

Steve Adams Design is an architectural design firm specializing in corporate design projects such as commercial building architecture, interior design, master planning, and sustainable design and consulting. As part of its ICT asset management program, the IT director has asked you to build an Access database to manage the devices used by employees. The database will contain information about each device, such as manufacturer, model, date acquired, condition, purchase price, and current value.

FIGURE 3-26

Hard drive capacities and costs by year.

Year	Size	Price
1980	26 MB	$5,000
1983	20 MB	$3,495
1984	20 MB	$2,399
1987	40 MB	$1799
1989	20 MB	$899
1995	1.7 GB	$1,499
1996	3.2 GB	$469
1997	7.0 GB	$670
1998	8.4 GB	$382
1999	19.2 GB	$512
2000	27.3 GB	$375
2001	40 GB	$238
2002	100 GB	$230
2003	120 GB	$168
2004	250 GB	$250
2006	390 GB	$106
2008	1 TB	$200
2010	1.5 TB	$220

Create an empty database named "Adams." Download the Excel file Ch03Ex02 and import the two worksheets to tables in your database. Create a totals query to summarize the current value of equipment for each category. Create a report displaying the names and locations of employees who use laptop computers. Create a report displaying the names and locations of employees who use CAD systems.

CASE STUDY #1

Einstein@home: Harnessing the Power of Voluntary Distributed Computing

With more than 1 billion PCs around the world that are often idle, the planet is not short of computer processing power. To tap this immense distributed computer architecture, projects such as Einstein@Home invite volunteers to download some software that will run in the background, analyzing astronomical data from observatories and other sources. The project splits the work into small chunks and sends it out to the volunteered PCs. Einstein@home director Bruce Allen points out that, collectively, this architecture surpasses the power of the supercomputers, creating a cheap way to look for rare and unusual oddities hidden in the vast mounds of data collected from the skies.

Einstein@home hunts for the gravitational waves that Einstein predicted, but so many volunteers offer their PC's services that the project also feeds them data from an observatory in Puerto Rico to look for pulsars. Helen and Chris Colvin of Ames, Iowa, loan out time from their aging PC for the project, and it won the "golden packet" with the first newsworthy discovery made through voluntary distributed computing. It found a dense, rapidly rotating pulsar about 17,000 light years away that pulses much like a lighthouse beacon. This was no ordinary pulsar, however. It was once part of a pair of stars that finally broke free when its partner exploded as a supernova. A few days later, the data were analyzed again by the computer volunteered by Daniel Gebhardt in Germany, and the discovery was confirmed.

The idea to tap the distributed power of volunteer PCs started with a team at the University of California, Berkeley. They devised an open source program to deliver data packets to computers around the world, which then perform analyses with spare processing power. The Berkeley Open Infrastructure for Network Computing (BOINC) was first used to manage the analysis of radio telescope data in a hunt for extraterrestrial intelligence. The SETI@home project attracts hundreds of thousands of volunteers in an effort to detect narrow bandwidth radio signals that would not occur naturally. Because supercomputers are costly and the detective work might take decades, or might never find anything, SETI turned to distributed computing, and built an enterprise architecture that spans the globe.

The distributed computing model's success, along with the willingness of so many people to volunteer some computer time to scientific research, has facilitated many other projects. Rosetta@home, launched by the University of Washington, harnesses the donated computer power to analyze the three-dimensional shapes of proteins in an effort to find cures for HIV, malaria, cancer, and other diseases. The University of Houston's Virtual Prairie project simulates complex ecosystems, analyzing data from plant growth and water quality. Oxford University scientists send weather and climate data to the volunteers, in a project called Climateprediction.net.

Since BOINC is open source, many organizations have launched projects, including private companies with massive data to analyze. If you choose to participate, check out the goals of the project and its findings, and also look at the project's security practices. Visit http://boinc.berkeley.edu for more tips on getting involved and lists of current projects.

Discussion Questions

1. How do the hardware and software architecture of a supercomputer differ from the architecture of distributed computing?

2. What are the advantages of distributed computing over supercomputers for the types of applications discussed in this case?

3. What are the risks of distributed computing compared with supercomputers for these types of applications?

4. Based on examples described in the case, can you think of other applications that may be amenable to distributed computing?

SOURCES: Berkeley Open Infrastructure for Network Computing. http://boinc.berkeley.edu, accessed May 8, 2011. Ehrenberg, R. (2010). Finding a pulsar in their spare time. *Science News.* 178(6), 10. Einstein@home. http://einstein.phys.uwm.edu, accessed May 8, 2011. Knispel, B., et al. (2010). Pulsar discovery by global volunteer computing. *Science.* 329(5997), 1305. Matson, J. (August 12, 2010). Volunteers' idle computer time turns up celestial oddball. *Scientific American.* www.scientificamerican.com/article.cfm?id=einstein-at-home, accessed May 8, 2011. Reed, S. (2010). Astronomical find by three average Joes. *Science Now.* http://news.sciencemag.org/sciencenow/2010/08/astronomical-find-by-three-avera.html?ref=hp, accessed May 8, 2011.

CASE STUDY #2

Rolling Out Its "4G" Network, Sprint Struggles with the Human Element

Sprint, AT&T, Verizon, and T-Mobile play leapfrog as they upgrade their networks with new technologies that offer faster speeds, more bandwidth, and better coverage for mobile smartphones. The carriers are adopting different solutions to achieve what they brand as 4G, or 4th generation cellular service. Sprint invested heavily in WiMax, and the company pins its hopes for a turnaround on its early-to-market advantage. The technology relies on Clearwire's WiMax network with download speeds that promise to beat 3G networks, and also outdo the services from rivals Verizon and AT&T, companies that use different technologies.

A major hurdle, though, is in the rollout. Clearwire has control of the wireless spectrum it needs, but Sprint must install the towers and equipment that will send and receive the wireless signals. Before installing 4G antennas, the company has to identify the sites that will provide best coverage for the area. For cities with tall buildings, large bodies of water, many hills and valleys, and high foliage, those choices are engineering brainteasers. In New York City, for instance, the urban "canyons" create dead spots that cause coverage problems. Sprint and Clearwire may need thousands of sites to provide adequate service.

Once sites are identified, Sprint must navigate a labyrinth of government agencies, local building codes, citizens' groups, and landowners to obtain approvals. In San Francisco, multiple bureaucracies may be involved, depending on the tower's location. The company may need approval from the California Coastal Commission for sites near the ocean, or from the California Department of Transportation. Municipalities may also compete with one another for towers, since they are a source of revenue, or they might insist they be constructed on city-owned property.

Some community and homeowner associations may also protest tower construction. Although Californians want 4G, they may value neighborhood aesthetics even more. The "NIMBY" mentality (Not In My Back Yard) further delays rollouts. Sprint and other carriers deal with this human element by hiding their equipment in church steeples or masking their appearance in other ways. Some are built to resemble trees (Figure 3-27) or their construction matches the historical architecture of the neighborhood.

Despite all these nontechnical hurdles, Sprint is making good progress. Although the network may not be "real" 4G, defined by the nonprofit International Telecommunications Union (ITU) as an all IP packet-switched network with speeds in the 1 GB/s range, smartphone users eagerly anticipate the service in their cities. A New York blogger tipped off readers that a weak WiMax signal was detected on a smartphone near Coney Island for the first time, and then again in midtown Manhattan. Step by step, Sprint is jumping through all the hoops to serve its customers and compete with rivals.

Discussion Questions

1. What is the relationship between physical infrastructure and services as described in this case study?

2. What is the relationship between regulatory considerations and wireless services?

3. In the placement of infrastructure, how do the interests of an individual as a customer conflict with the interests of the same individual as a homeowner?

4. What other considerations must Sprint consider as it puts its infrastructure in place?

SOURCES: German, K. (August 20, 2010). Where's my 4G? *CNET.com.* www.cnet.com/8301-17918_1-20014302-85.html, accessed August 23, 2010. Sheth, N., Das, A., & Cheng, R. (2010). Sprint scrambles as 4G race tightens. *Wall Street Journal.* 256(24), p. B3. Sullivan, M. (2010). 4G's speed short of hype. *PC World.* pp. 10–11.

FIGURE 3-27

A cell tower disguised as a pine tree.

Christina Richards/Shutterstock

E-PROJECT 1   Building a Voluntary Distributed Computer Architecture for the Planet

The voluntary distributed computing architecture model relies on the participation of millions of people who offer their computer time in exchange for an interesting screen saver and, of course, the good feeling that comes with contributing to a worthy goal. To engage enough people, the projects must find ways to build enthusiasm and commitment, a task that may be especially difficult for long-term projects that potentially continue for decades with no notable findings. The lists of BOINC projects can be found at http://boinc.berkeley.edu.

1. Visit several BOINC project sites and examine the ways in which the project leaders are engaging volunteers and sustaining commitment. What strategies are they using and how well do they appear to be working?

2. Trust is a significant element for voluntary distributed computing, especially because users are warned about the dangers of downloading executable programs to their computers from unknown sources. Pick two BOINC projects, compare their privacy policies, and look for other ways in which they attempt to convince potential participants that their computer will not be harmed and their privacy will not be violated. How do the two projects compare?

E-PROJECT 2   Using Excel to Analyze Cost Effectiveness for 4G Rollouts

For this e-project, you will analyze data on U.S. municipalities to estimate approximately how many cell-phone towers the city will need and how many people would be able to access each tower. This kind of information helps the carriers decide which markets are most cost effective.

Download the Excel file called Ch03_Cities and answer the following questions.

1. Sort the cities by land area in square miles, largest to smallest. Which city has the largest land area? Which has the smallest?

2. Insert a column after Land Area in Square Miles and label it "Cell Towers Needed." For the first city in that column, enter the formula to divide the Land Area in Square Miles by 10, assuming that one tower will serve about 10 square miles. Copy the formula down to the remaining cities. About how many cell towers will Baltimore require?

3. Insert another column to the right of Cell Towers Needed, labeled "Estimated Cost." Enter the formula for the first city as "Cell Towers Needed" * 150000. Format the cell to currency with no decimals, and copy it down the whole column. About how much will it cost to build out the cell tower infrastructure in Chicago?

4. Insert one more column to the right of Population, labeled "Cost Per Customer." Insert the formula Estimated Cost/ Population for the first city, and then copy the formula down the column. What is the estimated cost per customer for Houston?

5. Sort the table on Cost Per Customer, from smallest to largest.

   a. Which city would have the lowest cost per customer, and what is the cost?
   b. Which city has the highest cost per customer?
   c. If you live in the U.S. and your city is listed, which one is it, and what is the estimated cost per customer? If your city is not listed, please select the closest city that is listed.
   d. What is the main factor that accounts for the dramatic differences in cost per customer?

> **PRODUCTIVITY TIP**
>
> If you live in the U.S., visit www.antennasearch.com and enter your own address. The program will map the locations of all the nearby cell towers. Click on the towers nearest your home to obtain some information about them, such as the building they are on or their owner. Knowing their locations will help you avoid unpleasant call interruptions for important conversations.

CHAPTER NOTES

1. Hamm, S. (June 15, 2009). Cloud computing's big bang for business. *BusinessWeek.* pp. 42–48.

2. Thibodeau, P. (2007). Multiple-monitor proponents point to productivity benefits. *Computerworld.* 41(13), 12.

3. Ganssie, J. G. (2006). Multiplying monitors. *Embedded Systems Design.* 19(7), 61–63.

4. JPR Special Report. (nd). *The multiple display market and consumer attitudes.* Tiburon, CA: Jon Peddie Research. http://jonpeddie.com/publications/multiple-display-market/, accessed May 8, 2011.

5. *Decimal and Binary Prefixes.* (nd). http://wolfprojects. altervista.org/articles/binary-and-decimal-prefixes/, accessed May 8, 2011.

6. Anton, L. L. (July 18, 2010). Airport body scanners reveal all, but what about when it's your kid? *St. Petersburg Times.*

7. Center, E. P. I. (2010). Whole body imaging technology and body scanners. http://epic.org/privacy/airtravel/backscatter, accessed May 8, 2011.

8. Hamm, S. (2009). Smartphone roulette. *BusinessWeek.* 4136, 28.

9. Duggan, J. (December 14, 2008). Assessing the age of software languages and tools. Gartner Research, DOI: ID Number: G00151340.

10. Vecchio, D., & Duggan, J. (August 8, 2008). IT modernization: The changing COBOL market could affect your decision. Gartner Research, DOI: ID Number: G00159385.

11. Desisto, R. P., & Pring, B. (May 30, 2008). Essential SaaS overview and guide to SaaS research. Gartner Research, DOI: ID Number: G00158249.

12. Natis, Y. V., Weiss, G. J., Driver, M., Wurster, L. F., Prentice, B., & Igou, B. (November 23, 2010). Predicts 2011: Open-source software, the power behind the throne. Gartner Research, DOI: ID Number: G00209180.

13. Grant, I. (April 14, 2009). Skype targets businesses. *Computer Weekly*, p. 6.

14. Raphael, J. R. (2009). File sharing's future after the Pirate Bay verdict. *PC World.* 27(7), 13.

15. Dubie, D. (February 5, 2009). How I slashed costs with virtualization management software. *CIO.com.*

16. Johnson, G. (March 5, 2008). Understanding the emerging communications supply chain. Gartner Research, DOI: ID Number: G00153548.

17. Austin, T., Smith, D. M., & Cappuccio, D. J. (April 24, 2009). Cloud computing constituencies and inconsistent perspectives. Gartner Research, DOI: ID Number G00166134.

Managing Information Resources
with Databases

Chapter Preview

EVERY ORGANIZATION IS AWASH WITH INFORMATION RESOURCES OF ALL KINDS, and it takes considerable effort to bring together the people, technology, and processes needed to manage those resources effectively. This chapter explores the structure and quality of information, and how people organize, store, manipulate, and retrieve it. Earlier approaches created information "silos," and their drawbacks led to the integrated enterprise database—an information repository that everyone in the organization shares. Creating a database takes skill in technology and also a keen understanding of what the company needs. As organizations change, they implement multiple databases and need integration strategies to avoid lapsing back into the poorly integrated "silos" of days gone by.

© Iain Masterton / Alamy

4

Learning Objectives

1. Explain the nature of information resources in terms of structure and quality, and show how metadata can be used to describe these resources.

2. Compare file processing systems to the database, explaining the database's advantages.

3. Describe how a relational database is planned, accessed, and managed, and how the normalization process works.

4. Explain why multiple databases emerge, and how master data management helps address the challenge of integration.

5. Describe why a data warehouse is valuable for integration and strategic planning, and explain the three steps involved in creating one.

6. Explain how the human element and ownership issues affect information management.

Introduction

YouTube, one of the most visited websites in the world, had humble beginnings. In 2005, the founders built a website whose popularity exploded. Within a year of its launch, visitors accessed well over 100 million videos per day. Steve Chen and Chad Hurley never expected their company to grow so large, but they had an idea that what people would really want to see on video was themselves. They had little money to start and chose mainly free software, including the open source database management system MySQL, for their backend. Their goal was not just to create a database of videos— it was to build a worldwide community of people who would share, comment on, and celebrate videos contributed by anyone wanting to show off creative talent. The information resources they gathered for their business strategy were certainly unusual, but the database was their backbone, as it is for almost every organization.

Kathy Burns-Millyard/Shutterstock

FIGURE 4-1

The modern workspace: An information storehouse.

Information resources, such as those that YouTube manages, are central to any organization's success. And like that company's visitor count, these resources are growing at an astounding rate. Data stored in digital format are multiplying everywhere on a vast array of physical media, ranging from the organization's own computers to hosts that might be located almost anywhere on the planet. Data also reside on DVDs, CD-ROMs, and tapes, and inside people's digital cameras, cell phones, iPods, personal digital assistants, memory cards, and even flash drives on a keychain. On your own workspace, for instance, objects that *don't* store or display information of some kind are scarce—perhaps the coffee cup or stapler (Figure 4-1).

People understand that some information is powerful and valuable, but far more is useless junk that should be tossed. We need a strategy to manage information resources so that what is important is secure, organized, and easily accessible to managers, employees, customers, suppliers, and other stakeholders. This enormous challenge is the subject of this chapter.

Explain the nature of information resources in terms of structure and quality, and show how metadata can be used to describe these resources.

The Nature of Information Resources

STRUCTURED, UNSTRUCTURED, AND SEMI-STRUCTURED INFORMATION

Every organization relies on **structured information**, the kind that is usually considered to be facts and data (Figure 4-2). It is reasonably orderly, in that it can be broken down into component parts and organized into hierarchies. Your credit card company, for example, maintains your customer record in a structured format. It contains elements such as last name, first name, street address, phone number, and e-mail address. It would also maintain transaction records, each with a transaction date, description, debit or credit amount, and reference numbers.

Straightforward relationships among the data are also relatively easy to identify. A customer's order would be related to the customer record, and the items purchased as part of the order would be related to the order itself. This kind of information is the heart of an organization's operational information systems, with electronically stored customer records, orders, invoices, transactions, employee

FIGURE 4-2

Types of information resources.

Type of Information Resource	Example
Structured information	A sales transaction with clearly defined fields for date, customer number, item number, and amount
Unstructured information	Manila folder containing assorted items about a lawsuit, such as photos, handwritten notes, newspaper articles, or affidavits
Semi-structured information	A web page with a title, subtitle, content, and a few images

records, shipping tables, and similar kinds of information. It is the kind that databases are designed to store and retrieve.

In contrast, **unstructured information** has no inherent structure or order, and the parts can't be easily linked together, except perhaps by stuffing them in a manila folder or box. It is more difficult to break down, categorize, organize, and query. Consider a company involved in a touchy lawsuit. The information related to that could include letters, e-mails, business cards, post-it notes attached to legal documents, meeting minutes, phone calls, voice mail messages, video recordings, progress reports, project timelines, resumes, and photos in file cabinets.

Drawing information out of unstructured collections also presents challenges. A catering business might have a back room stacked with boxes containing unstructured information on hundreds of contracts. If the owner wants to know which contracts went over budget, and then see whether most of those were handled by people who had less experience in project management, every box would have to be opened. Because unstructured collections have no means to enforce rules about what types of information must be included, the owner may find little to go on.

A vast gray area exists between the extremes of structured and unstructured information, in which **semi-structured information** falls. This type includes information that shows at least some structure, such as web pages and documents, which bear creation dates, titles, and authors. Spreadsheets maintained by different people containing similar kinds of information, such as contact lists, are also semi-structured. Their creators might use familiar column names to identify attributes such as name or phone number, but there would be many inconsistencies. For instance, one might put work phone and mobile phone numbers in separate columns, and another might just put all types of phone numbers in a single column. These collections don't have the strong structure, enforced by advance planning, to clearly define entities and their relationships, and they lack controls about completeness and formatting. Nevertheless, such data are easier to query and aggregate compared to the unstructured variety.

METADATA

Metadata is data about data, and it clarifies the nature of the information. For structured information, metadata describes the definitions of each of the fields, tables, and their relationships. For semi-structured and unstructured information, metadata are used to describe properties of a document or other resource, and are especially useful because they layer some structure on information that is less easily categorized and classified. YouTube's MySQL database, for example, contains metadata about each of its videos that can be searched and sorted. A library's card catalog provides metadata

structured information
Facts and data that are reasonably orderly, or that can be broken down into component parts and organized into hierarchies.

unstructured information
Information that has no inherent structure or order, and the parts can't be easily linked together.

semi-structured information
Information category that falls between structured and unstructured information. It includes facts and data that shows at least some structure, such as web pages and documents, which bear creation dates, titles, and authors.

metadata
Data about data that clarifies the nature of the information.

FIGURE 4-3

Metadata for a beach scene photo.

Photo Metadata	Description
Photo title	Ocean beach scene
Date taken	12/15/2011
License type	Royalty free
Photographer	Felipe DiMarco
Key words	ocean, waves, outdoors, sunshine, beach, vacation, swimming, swimmers, fishing, surf

Rigucci/Shutterstock

about the books, such as where they are physically shelved. Word-processed documents are easier to organize if they include title, author, and subject in their properties.

Flickr, a popular photo-sharing website with more than 4 billion queries per day, relies on metadata to search its enormous photo collection. A father's beach scene photos, with filenames such as "image011.jpg," become more accessible, meaningful, and sharable for friends and family when metadata are added to their properties, such as location, subject, date taken, and photographer (Figure 4-3).

PRODUCTIVITY TIP

Adding metadata to the properties of your documents, photos, and videos makes them easier to search and locate later. Right-clicking on the filename usually brings up a menu that includes Properties, with a Details tab. You can also remove information from a file's properties so others will not see it.

THE QUALITY OF INFORMATION

Not all information has high quality, as anyone who surfs the net knows. Following are the most important characteristics that affect quality in different settings:

▶ *Accuracy*. Mistakes in birth dates, spelling, or prices reduce the quality of the information.

▶ *Precision*. Rounding to the nearest mile might not reduce quality much when you are estimating distance to the shopping mall. But for property surveys, "about 2 miles" would be unacceptable.

▶ *Completeness*. Omitting the zip code on the customer's address record might not be a problem because the zip can be determined by the address. But leaving off the house number would delay the order.

▶ *Consistency*. Reports that show what appears to be the same information may conflict because the people generating the reports are using slightly different definitions. When results are inconsistent, the quality of both reports is in question.

▶ *Timeliness.* Outdated information has less value than up-to-date information and thus is lower quality unless you are specifically looking for historical trends. The actual definition for what is up-to-date varies. In stock trading, for example, timeliness would be measured in fractions of a second.

▶ *Bias.* Information that is biased lacks objectivity, a feature that reduces its value and quality. A sales manager might want to put the most positive spin on a tally of recent orders, so might choose to include ones that had been canceled.

▶ *Duplication.* Information can be redundant, resulting in misleading and exaggerated summaries. In customer records, people can easily appear more than once, if their address changes or they use a different credit card, for example.

The data collected by the ever-present online pop-up surveys illustrate many of the problems surrounding information quality. The sample of people who actually respond is biased, and people may quit before completing or turn in more than one survey. Virtual Surveys Ltd., a company that specializes in web-based research, discovered that one person completed an online survey 750 times because a raffle ticket was offered as an incentive.[1] To avoid relying on poor quality data like that, managers must define what constitutes quality for the information they need.

Managing Information: From Filing Cabinets to the Database

> **2** Compare file processing systems to the database, explaining the database's advantages.

Human ingenuity was applied to the challenges of information management long before the digital age. Before Edwin Siebels invented the lateral filing cabinet in 1898, businesses often organized documents by putting them in envelopes, in rows of small pigeonholes that lined entire walls from top to bottom. Storing documents in vertical folders neatly arranged in cabinet drawers was quite an improvement for record keeping, and much appreciated by file clerks (Figure 4-4). The real revolution, however, occurred in the 1960s when digital technologies used to manage structured information entered the picture. These relied on an organizing strategy built around the concept of the record.

FIGURE 4-4

Early information management approaches.

Edwin Verin/Shutterstock

deepspacedave/Shutterstock

RECORDS, FIELDS, AND TABLES

The **record** is a means to represent an entity, which might be a person, a product, a purchase order, an event, a building, a vendor, a book, a video, or some other "thing" that has meaning to people. The record is made up of attributes of that thing, and each of the attributes is called a **field**. For a record intended to represent an event, common fields are event name, start date, end date, and sponsor. Fields typically contain numeric data or text, or a combination of the two. Each field should have a **data definition** that specifies its characteristics, such as the type of data it will hold or the maximum number of characters it can contain.

Consider, for example, an employee record. The fields might include the person's first name, last name, birth date, employee number, gender, e-mail address, and office phone. A group of records, with one record for each employee of the company, would be logically organized into a **table**, so that each unique employee is a row and the fields are the table's columns.

THE RISE AND FALL OF FILE PROCESSING SYSTEMS

Initially, electronic records were created and stored as computer files, and programmers wrote computer programs to add, delete, or edit the records. Each department maintained its own records with its own computer files, each containing information that was required for operations. For example, the payroll office maintained personnel records and had its own computer programs to maintain and manage its set of files. At the end of the month when it was time to generate payroll checks, the payroll system's computer programs would read each record in the file and print out checks and payroll stubs for each person, using the information contained in the files for that department. That kind of activity is called **batch processing**. The program is sequentially conducting operations on each record in a large batch.

Accounts payable and receivable, personnel, payroll, and inventory were the first beneficiaries of the digital age. Compared to the manual method of generating a payroll, in which deductions and taxes were computed by hand and each check was individually typed, the monthly batch processing of computer-generated checks was revolutionary. However, it didn't take long for problems to surface as other offices began to develop their own file processing systems. Understanding what went wrong is crucial to grasp why the database offers so many benefits.

DATA REDUNDANCY AND INCONSISTENCY Because each set of computer programs operated on its own records, much information was redundant and inconsistent (Figure 4-5). The payroll office record might list your name as ANNAMARIE, but the personnel office that handles benefits shows you as ANN-MARIE. Further, the extra workload involved in resolving redundant records was not trivial, and often never got done.

FIGURE 4-5

Data redundancy problems. Separate file processing systems often contain redundant and inconsistent data.

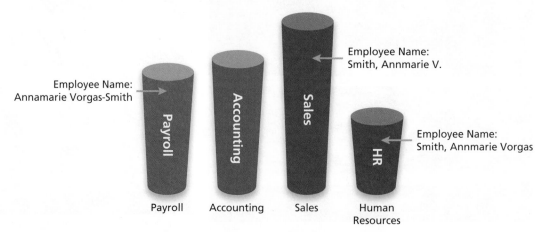

Employee Name:
Annamarie Vorgas-Smith

Employee Name:
Smith, Annmarie V.

Employee Name:
Smith, Annmarie Vorgas

Payroll   Accounting   Sales   Human Resources

FIGURE 4-6

Information in separate file processing systems is difficult to integrate. For example, a report listing hourly rates by gender would need extra programming effort in this business.

Employee Name:
T. Douglas Guarino

Salary: 25.50/hr

Payroll

Employee Name:
Guarino, Theodore (Doug)

Gender: M

Human Resources

LACK OF DATA INTEGRATION   Integrating data from the separate systems was a struggle (Figure 4-6). For example, the payroll system might maintain information about name, address, and pay history, but gender and ethnicity are in personnel records. If a manager wanted to compare pay rates by ethnicity, new programs were written to match up the records. This clumsy integration affects customers, as well, who fume when they can't resolve inconsistencies in their accounts (Figure 4-7).

FIGURE 4-7

Separate file processing systems lead to a fragmented customer interface, frustrating customers who have to contact several offices to straighten out inconsistencies. Photo: William Casey/Shutterstock.

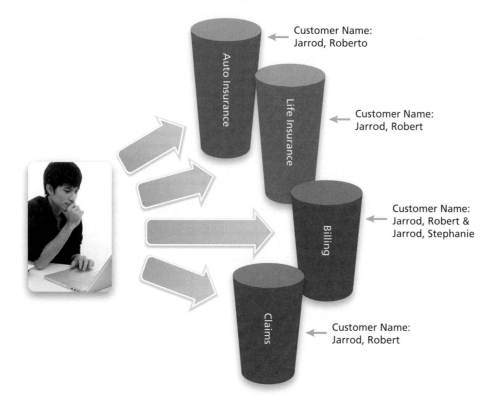

Customer Name:
Jarrod, Roberto

Auto Insurance

Life Insurance

Customer Name:
Jarrod, Robert

Billing

Customer Name:
Jarrod, Robert &
Jarrod, Stephanie

Claims

Customer Name:
Jarrod, Robert

record
A means to represent an entity, which might be a person, a product, a purchase order, an event, a building, a vendor, a book, a video, or some other "thing" that has meaning to people. The record is made up of attributes of that thing.

field
An attribute of an entity. A field can contain numeric data or text, or a combination of the two.

data definition
Specifies the characteristics of a field, such as the type of data it will hold or the maximum number of characters it can contain.

table
A group of records for the same entity, such as employees. Each row is one record, and the fields of each record are arranged in the table's columns.

batch processing
The process of sequentially executing operations on each record in a large batch.

database
An integrated collection of information that is logically related and stored in such a way as to minimize duplication and facilitate rapid retrieval.

FIGURE 4-8

When data definitions are inconsistent, the meaning of different fields will vary across departments and summaries will be misleading. Note how the three departments use categories in different ways.

Department	Object Code	Amount	Category	Description
Sales	4211	1888.25	Computers	Desktop Computers
Sales	4300	249.95	Computer supplies	Image editing software
Sales	4100	29.99	Office supplies	Flash drive
Personnel	4211	59.00	Computers	Stastical software
Personnel	4300	14.95	Computer supplies	Flash drive
Personnel	4211	2500.21	Computers	Laptop Computers
Warehouse	4211	59500.00	Computers	Web server
Warehouse	4211	2500.00	Computers	Printer/copier/scanner/fax

INCONSISTENT DATA DEFINITIONS   When programmers write code to handle files, differences in format inevitably creep in. Phone numbers in one system may include the dashes and be formatted as a text field, but are treated as numbers in another. A more subtle problem involves the way people actually choose to use the system. Data definitions may seem similar across systems, but they are used differently and summaries become misleading. For example, employees in the personnel department at a retail chain categorize software purchases as "computers." Their coworkers in sales prefer to lump software with pencils, staplers, and clocks as "supplies," because less paperwork is needed to justify the purchase. The CEO lamented that there was no way anyone could possibly know how much this chain was spending on technology because of the human element in information systems (Figure 4-8).

DATA DEPENDENCE   These early systems became maintenance nightmares because the programs and their files were so interconnected and dependent on one another. The programs all defined the fields and their formats, and business rules were all hard-coded or embedded in the programs. Even a minor change to accommodate a new business strategy was no trivial undertaking. IT staff were constantly busy, but kept falling behind anyway.

The disadvantages to the file processing approach led to a better way of organizing structured data, one that relies on the database.

DATABASES AND DATABASE MANAGEMENT SOFTWARE

The foundation of today's information management relies on the database and the software that manages it. The **database** is an integrated collection of information that is logically related and stored in such a way as to minimize duplication and facilitate rapid retrieval. Its major advantages over file processing systems include:

▶ Reduced redundancy and inconsistency
▶ Improved information integrity and accuracy
▶ Improved ability to adapt to changes
▶ Improved performance and scalability
▶ Increased security

Database management software (DBMS) is used to create and manage the database and this software provides tools for ensuring security, replication, retrieval, and other administrative and housekeeping tasks. The DBMS serves as a kind of gateway to the database itself, and as a manager for handling creation, performance tuning, transaction processing, general maintenance, access rights, deletion, and backups.

FIGURE 4-9
Relationship types.

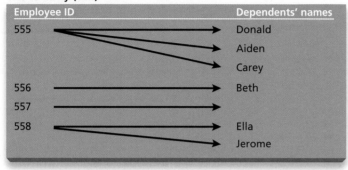

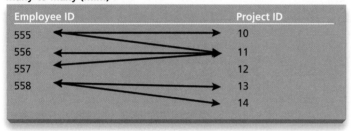

DATABASE ARCHITECTURE To be most useful, a database must handle three types of relationships with a minimum of redundancy (Figure 4-9):

- ▶ One to one (1:1)
- ▶ One to many (1:M)
- ▶ Many to many (M:M)

The *one-to-one relationship (1:1)* is relatively easy to accommodate, and even file processing systems could handle it. For instance, each person has one and only one birth date. The *one-to-many relationship (1:M)* between records is somewhat more challenging. A person might have one or more dependents, for example, or one or more employees reporting to him or her. The *many-to-many relationship (M:M)* is also more complicated to support. This might involve a situation in which a person might be working on any number of projects, each of which can have any number of employees assigned to it.

Earlier database architectures offered different strategies to organize and link records (Figure 4-10). For example, one intuitive way to organize information is to follow the organizational chart, and the **hierarchical database** did just that (Figure 4-11). This approach worked well for 1:M relationships, but stumbled when M:M links complicated the chart, such as when a person worked for two bosses. The **network database** (Figure 4-12) had more flexibility to link entities that didn't fall along a neat hierarchy, and was better able to support these M:M relationships. But another inventive approach—the relational model—soon won out.

database management software (DBMS)	hierarchical database	network database
Software used to create and manage a database and that also provides tools for ensuring security, replication, retrieval, and other administrative and housekeeping tasks.	An early database approach that linked records based on hierarchical relationships, such as those in the organizational chart.	An early database approach that allowed flexible links to support M:M relationships.

FIGURE 4-10

Types of database architectures.

Early Database Architectures	
Hierarchical	Resembles an organizational chart or an upside down tree, with the root record the company itself with attributes such as name and address. Departments are the root's child records, and staff members are children of the departments (Figure 4-11).
Network	Resembles a lattice or web rather than the upside down tree. Records can be linked in multiple ways, supporting many-to-many relationships (Figure 4-12).
Modern Database Architectures	
Relational	Maintains records in rows within tables, and links between the tables are created by linking a field in one table to a field in another table with matching data (Figure 4-13). The relational database is the most widely used.
Object-oriented	Represents information in the form of objects, and uses object-oriented programming languages to access them; used especially for organizing complex data types such as graphics and multimedia.
XML	Organizes data using XML tags; used especially for managing web content and web-based resources.

FIGURE 4-11

Hierarchical database.

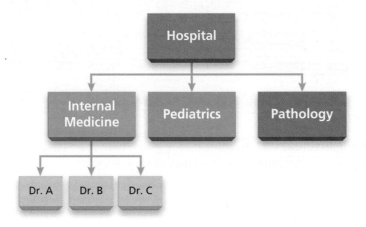

FIGURE 4-12

Network database.

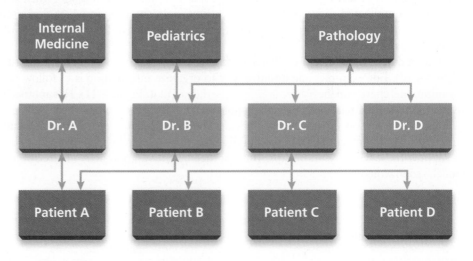

FIGURE 4-13
Relational database.

Students

StudentID	LastName	FirstName	BirthDate
54001	Chong	Kevin	12/01/1987
65222	Danelli	Douglas	01/05/1986
54555	Burton	Stephanie	11/12/1978
25553	Washington	Nikia	10/02/1981
96887	Perez	Louis	07/25/1982

StudentRegistrations

StudentID	ClassCode	Grade
54001	20083BMGT300A	A
54001	20083HIST450B	C
54001	20083ECON200F	B
54555	20083ECON200F	A
96887	20083HIST410B	I

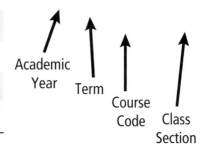

ClassCode
2008 3 BMGT300 A

Academic Year · Term · Course Code · Class Section

THE RELATIONAL DATABASE E. F. Codd, a British mathematician working at IBM, invented the **relational database**, which organizes information into tables of records that are related to one another by linking a field in one table to a field in another table with matching data (Figure 4-13). The approach separates the data from the paths to retrieve them, thus making the database less dependent on the hardware and its particular operating system. His invention eventually came to dominate the field, though it was not well received in the beginning, especially by his bosses at IBM. That company had much invested in selling and supporting its older hierarchical database and the mainframe computers it ran on, and IBM executives were quite critical of Codd's approach. Nevertheless, the relational database survived and flourished, and is now a standard in most organizations.[2]

To see how the relational database works, consider the tables about students in Figure 4-13. The first table shows the student ID, last name, first name, and birth date. The second table shows student registrations with fields that display student ID, class code, and grade. Note that student ID is also included in this table, making it possible to link the records in the two tables together.

If you have Microsoft Access on your personal computer, you have an offspring of Codd's ingenious approach. Other common relational DBMSs include Microsoft SQL

relational database
The widely used database model that organizes information into tables of records that are related to one another by linking a field in one table to a field in another table with matching data.

Server, Oracle, and MySQL. These relational databases continue to improve, each adding support for large files containing images, video, or audio. Relational systems now also support XML data types, as well as spatial information and mapping coordinates. Count on the relational database to be the mainstay for organizations in the years ahead.

Describe how a relational database is planned, accessed, and managed, and how the normalization process works.

3

Developing and Managing a Relational Database

The database is the central information repository, a mission-critical asset of any enterprise. To see how a database is designed and created, we will help Devon Degosta and her colleagues build the database to support DD-Designs, a small business that offers web design services.

PLANNING THE DATA MODEL

The first step is to sit down with Devon and her team to develop the **data model**, identifying what kind of information they want to track and how it is related. The process starts by defining all the entities that will be included, their attributes, and their relationships. A challenging process even for a small business, this model-building step is critical because the database will be the backbone of the company. Also, time spent planning reaps enormous benefits in time saved making changes later.

ENTITIES AND ATTRIBUTES   What entities should be represented for this small business? Employees, clients, projects, websites, invoices, events, and transactions are all candidates, and many more may come to mind as we work with Devon and her team to understand the business and its strategies. Each of the entities represented in the model will have attributes, or fields, that describe the entity. "Employees," for example, is a relatively straightforward entity with attributes such as employee ID number, last name, first name, birth date, e-mail address, and phone number. The "Client" entity might include attributes such as company name, client ID number, contact person, company phone number, and company address.

> **PRODUCTIVITY TIP**
> When you give names to tables and fields, use a consistent naming convention to make it easier for you to remember the names and for others to understand their meaning. Naming conventions vary, and your organization may already have policies on this. One common convention is "CamelCase," which combines capital and lowercase letters to clarify compound words, such as LastName or SalesRegion. The camel's humps are the capital letters in the string. Another convention separates words with an underscore.

A single entity, such as the employee Thomas Jackon and that employee's attributes (or fields), will become a record, and a collection of records will become a table in the relational model. Terms such as "rows" and "columns" are also used to describe the components of a table, but records and fields are widely understood.

PRIMARY KEYS AND UNIQUENESS   Each record in a table must have one **primary key**, which is a field, or a group of fields, that makes the record unique in that table. Devon suggests using each person's last name as the primary key since that is unique. But as the organization grows, there might be two people with the same name. Devon nods, thinking she might invite her brother to join the company. Some organizations have used Social Security numbers (SSN) to uniquely identify employees, but that has serious drawbacks as well. Non-U.S. citizens might not have one, and that number is confidential and should not be released. Database developers also avoid meaningful information for primary keys, such as an SSN or name. If the key is mistyped or changes, fixing it throughout the database is a complicated affair. Many systems instead simply use **autonumbering** to assign primary keys, in which the DBMS assigns incremental numbers to records as they are created. This approach ensures that each record has a unique primary key and that no one accidentally gives the same ID number to two different people (Figure 4-14). Because the autonumber has no other meaning, there would be no reason to ever change it.

FIGURE 4-14

Primary and foreign keys in the Employees and Departments tables.

Employees

EmployeeID	LastName	FirstName	BirthDate	DepartmentID
1011	Jackson	Thomas	12/01/1981	200
1012	Zuniga	Raul	01/05/1983	300
1013	Delany	Nora	11/12/1968	300
1014	Degosta	Dana	10/02/1975	400
1015	Park	John	07/25/1985	200

Primary Key (pointing to EmployeeID)
Foreign Key (pointing to DepartmentID)

Departments

DepartmentID	DepartmentName	DepartmentPhone
200	Marketing	251-3621
300	Human Resources	251-1102
400	Finance	209-6656
500	Sales	512-5555
600	Facilities	207-8787

Primary Key (pointing to DepartmentID)

NORMALIZING THE DATA MODEL   The next step is to work with Devon to further refine the entities and their relationships. The process is called **normalization**, and it helps minimize duplication of information in the tables—a condition that can cause many kinds of problems that diminish the database's integrity. It also helps avoid a number of anomalies that can happen when users try to insert, edit, or delete data.

In the Employees table, for example, one goal of normalization is to make each attribute **functionally dependent** on the employee ID number, which uniquely identifies each employee. Functional dependence means thats for each value of employee ID, there is exactly one value for each of the attributes included in the record, and that the employee ID determines that value. For DD-Designs, Devon agrees that there would be just one employee e-mail address, one birth date, one last name, one first name, and one department. In another business, such as theater, that might not work. Actors work under several stage names.

Devon also wants to add the departmental phone number, and we first consider adding it as a field to the Employees table. On second thought, however, the departmental phone number is not functionally dependent on employee ID, but on department ID. If we put it in the Employees table, it might not be too cumbersome with only five employees. With hundreds, however, we would create considerable redundancy. Instead, we will normalize by adding a field to Employees called DepartmentID, and then create a new table called Departments, with department ID as the primary key. Departmental phone number becomes an attribute of department ID, along with other functionally dependent attributes of that key, such as department name, department office number, and department office building (Figure 4-15).

data model
A model used for planning the organization's database that identifies what kind of information is needed, what entities will be created, and how they are related to one another.

primary key
A field, or a group of fields, that makes each record unique in a table.

autonumbering
Process that assigns incremental numbers to records as they are created to ensure that each record has a unique primary key.

normalization
A process that refines entities and their relationships to help minimize duplication of information in tables.

functionally dependent
For each value of the table's primary key, there should be just one value for each of the attributes in the record, and that the primary key determines that value; the attribute should be functionally dependent on the value of the primary key.

FIGURE 4-15

Normalizing the Employees table by removing Department Phone (A) and placing this field in the newly created Departments table (B).

Employees

EmployeeID	LastName	FirstName	BirthDate	DepartmentPhone
1011	Jackson	Thomas	12/01/1981	251-3621
1012	Zuniga	Raul	01/05/1983	251-1102
1013	Delany	Nora	11/12/1968	251-1102
1014	Degosta	Devon	10/02/1975	209-6656
1015	Park	John	07/25/1985	251-3621

A

Employees

EmployeeID	LastName	FirstName	BirthDate	DepartmentID
1011	Jackson	Thomas	12/01/1981	200
1012	Zuniga	Raul	01/05/1983	300
1013	Delany	Nora	11/12/1968	300
1014	Degosta	Devon	10/02/1975	400
1015	Park	John	07/25/1985	200

B

Departments

DepartmentID	DepartmentName	DepartmentPhone
200	Marketing	251-3621
300	Human Resources	251-1102
400	Finance	209-6656
500	Sales	512-5555
600	Facilities	207-8787

RELATIONSHIPS AND FOREIGN KEYS The relational model's elegance really shines when the entities are connected to one another in meaningful ways, relying on **foreign keys**. Notice that the field "DepartmentID" is an attribute in the Employees table, and a primary key in the Departments table (Figure 4-16). When a primary key appears as an attribute in a different table, as department ID does, it is called a *foreign key*. It can be used to link the records in the two tables together. In DD-Designs so far, we have two tables, Employees and Departments, linked through the primary key in Departments and the foreign key in Employees. This relationship allows us to enter information about employees and information about departments, and then link the two together with a minimum of redundancy. It would be easy, for example, to find the list of employees who worked in a particular building, perhaps to make announcements about a broken water pipe.

HANDLING COMPLEX RELATIONSHIPS Normalization uncovers one-to-many and many-to-many relationships, and the relational model can handle them with a minimum of redundancy. Devon considers project management to be extremely crucial for the company's success, and she wants to track many details about the specific web design project each employee is currently involved in. We might choose

FIGURE 4-16

DepartmentID is the primary key for Departments, but appears as a foreign key in the Employees table so the two tables can be linked together.

Employees

EmployeeID	LastName	FirstName	BirthDate	DepartmentID
1011	Jackson	Thomas	12/01/1981	200
1012	Zuniga	Raul	01/05/1983	300
1013	Delany	Nora	11/12/1968	300
1014	Degosta	Devon	10/02/1975	400
1015	Park	John	07/25/1985	200

DepartmentID is a foreign key in Employees, and the primary key in Departments

Departments

DepartmentID	DepartmentName	DepartmentPhone
200	Marketing	251-3621
300	Human Resources	251-1102
400	Finance	209-6656
500	Sales	512-5555
600	Facilities	207-8787

to create a Projects table to manage those attributes, and then add Project ID as a foreign key in the Employees table, similar to what we did for Departments. But we first ask whether Devon's team members might oversee more than one project at a time, which would make it a 1:M relationship. She nods enthusiastically, thinking that it is already happening. She plans to bring on a graphic artist who will probably spend time on all the projects. That comment also makes it clear that it is not just a 1:M relationship of one employee to many projects. It is M:M. Each employee can be assigned to more than one project, and each project can have more than one employee assigned. And of course, the sales staff may have no projects, and some projects may not have any assigned employees (yet).

A messy approach would be to create two or more records for the employee, each of which lists a different project. However, this would create redundancy because the other attributes are all functionally dependent upon employee ID number and would simply be repeated. When an entity is repeated in the table, updates and deletions are tricky. For example, should Raul's address change, the new address would need to be edited in all the duplicated records for his projects to remain consistent.

Another unfortunate solution, which is sadly rather common in sloppily designed databases, is to include several fields for projects in the record, such as Project1, Project2, Project3, and so on. This introduces other problems, such as difficulties in data retrieval. If we are trying to find all the people assigned to the Moon Landing Project, where would we look? It might appear as Project1 for some, but in the Project2 or Project3 field for someone else. We would need rather complex queries to go through each of the fields, and we'd waste a lot of storage space with many empty fields.

foreign keys
Primary keys that appear as an attribute in a different table are a foreign key in that table. They can be used to link the records in two tables together.

FIGURE 4-17

Managing M:M relationships.

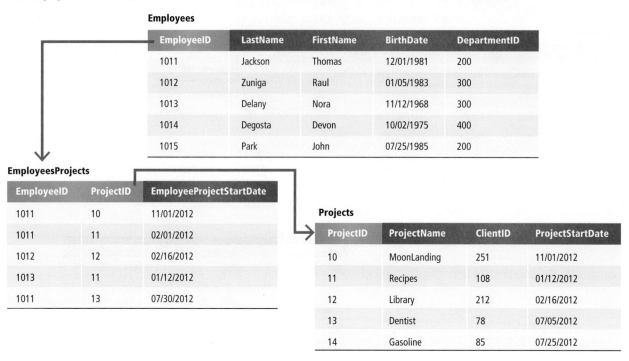

Employees

EmployeeID	LastName	FirstName	BirthDate	DepartmentID
1011	Jackson	Thomas	12/01/1981	200
1012	Zuniga	Raul	01/05/1983	300
1013	Delany	Nora	11/12/1968	300
1014	Degosta	Devon	10/02/1975	400
1015	Park	John	07/25/1985	200

EmployeesProjects

EmployeeID	ProjectID	EmployeeProjectStartDate
1011	10	11/01/2012
1011	11	02/01/2012
1012	12	02/16/2012
1013	11	01/12/2012
1011	13	07/30/2012

Projects

ProjectID	ProjectName	ClientID	ProjectStartDate
10	MoonLanding	251	11/01/2012
11	Recipes	108	01/12/2012
12	Library	212	02/16/2012
13	Dentist	78	07/05/2012
14	Gasoline	85	07/25/2012

A more efficient approach is to normalize the relationship between Employees and Projects (Figure 4-17). Projects will use ProjectID as its primary key and will include attributes that Devon wants to track—project name, start date, budget, and client. Then, to support the M:M relationship between employees and projects, we create a third table, EmployeesProjects, to contain the two attributes that link together employees with their projects: Employee ID and Project ID. This new table is very flexible. Thomas Jackson (EmployeeID 1011) is working on three projects, but Devon works on none. Also, a single project such as Recipes (ProjectID 11) can involve more than one employee. Gasoline (ProjectID 14) has no employees assigned. Adding the EmployeesProjectStartDate to EmployeesProject lets Devon track when each employee actually joined the project. DD-Designs will be prepared for rapid growth.

✱ THE ETHICAL FACTOR

Ethical Issues in Database Design: The Case of Ethnic Identification

When a database includes ethnicity, should the designers create a one-to-one relationship with each person? Or should it be one-to-many? For decades, most databases constructed this as a 1:1 relationship with the individual, much like birth date or gender. In the Medicare system, for example, this variable can take one of six different values:

- ▶ White
- ▶ Black
- ▶ Asian
- ▶ North American Native
- ▶ Hispanic
- ▶ Other

Only one category can represent each individual in the Medicare files, but ethnicity is clearly not so easily categorized for many people with mixed heritage. Studies of Medicare coding, for example, show that people of Hispanic, Asian, and American Indian ancestry are often miscoded. When Medicare data are used to study ethnic differences in health outcomes, the results can be misleading and biased. The confusion can also affect conclusions about ethnic discrimination in the workplace, scholarship awards, or any other programs that consider ethnic subgroups.

Converting ethnicity to a 1:M relationship may be feasible in some settings, but how might that affect decisions about program eligibility or conclusions about health care needs? Understanding the human consequences of database design choices takes considerable skill.[3]

ACCESSING THE DATABASE AND RETRIEVING INFORMATION

Most people access the database through an application interface with user-friendly web-based forms they can use to securely enter, edit, delete, and retrieve data. The web-based forms make it easy to let customers and suppliers access the database along with staff, with appropriate security controls. The customer account records and product catalog on eBay, for instance, are drawn from the relational database, and buyers and sellers have access to certain tables and fields to update their accounts, add purchases, or upload their own product photos.

The application software can be created in many different development environments and programming languages, and DBMS software vendors include their own tools for creating applications. In MS Access, for example, form-generating and report-writing tools help you enter and retrieve the data. Oracle and others provide application development tools as well.

As the front end or gateway, the application software performs a number of duties in addition to allowing users to enter, edit, or retrieve information. It may have modules for access control, determining which users can access which parts of the database, and what rights they have with respect to viewing or manipulating data. This interface may also help ensure the integrity of the database by enforcing rules about completeness, validity, or format. For example, it might require users to enter a valid zip code for the address and state.

Although the application software can be developed in any number of programming languages, the main way that they interact with a relational database is through a query language, and SQL is the most popular.

SQL: STRUCTURED QUERY LANGUAGE   Pronounced either as letters, or as "sequel," **Structured Query Language (SQL)** is a standard query language, widely used to manipulate information in relational databases. A simple query to retrieve the record for all the people whose last name is "Park" would look like this:

```
SELECT LastName, FirstName, EmployeeID
FROM Employees
WHERE LastName = "Park"
```

More complex queries can insert and edit data, or delete records. To link tables together, SQL relies on their primary and foreign keys. For example, to retrieve Devon's phone number, which is a field in the Departments table, you would join the Employees and Departments tables on DepartmentID—the primary key in Departments and foreign key in Employees.

The SQL is embedded in the application itself, written by programmers. When you click "SUBMIT" on a web-based survey, for instance, the application will trigger an SQL command that inserts your record into the database.

Did You Know?

Each year, thousands of IRS refund checks are returned undeliverable, often because the taxpayer moved and left no forwarding address. In 2009, the IRS began making these records available to the National Taxpayers Union, which launched a database that people can query very easily. If you think you missed a refund check, visit www.ntu.org and go to Tax Basics. Enter your last name, state, and tax year, and a quick SQL query brings up a list of matches. You might be one of them.

Structured Query Language (SQL)
A standard query language, widely used to manipulate information in relational databases.

OTHER ACCESS AND RETRIEVAL TOOLS Although the web is a common platform for application software, other platforms are widely used as well. For example, **interactive voice response (IVR)** takes advantage of signals transmitted via the phone to access the database, retrieve account information, and enter data. Callers can make selections from menus, enter numbers, confirm transactions, and sometimes pound on the "0" key in a desperate attempt to reach a live person. Though they can be frustrating for customers, these systems are often the only way to handle massive call volumes.

Canal Satélite Digital, Spain's leading satellite TV operator, launched an IVR system to handle the flood of cable customers who wanted to watch a pay-per-view soccer match but procrastinated until the last minute to order it. Boris Levy, who helped build the IVR interface to the cable company's Oracle database, points out that Europeans are historically less amenable to IVR than Americans. But "if you need to handle 25,000 or 50,000 calls in an hour or two, there's no way you can put in an army of people to attend all that."[4] *American Idol* call-in voting, of course, dwarfs those numbers. Mobile phones are also growing in importance as a platform for database access, not just through IVR, but by means of their web capabilities—tiny screens notwithstanding. The ability to access a database anywhere, anytime, is a compelling advantage for everything from handling customer orders to voting for your *Idol* favorite.

Another database access strategy takes advantage of mobile digital assistants that can use wireless cellular networks to connect. Annemiek Ballesty, managing director at Fossil Group Australia, wanted her account executives to have this kind of access to their backend database containing real-time information on customer accounts and clothing inventory. With styles constantly changing, and account executives traveling all over Australia, they need up-to-the-minute data for time-sensitive orders. To ensure accuracy, they also use a bar-code scanner attached to the digital assistant to identify the product and enter the order into the database.[5]

NATURAL LANGUAGE INTERFACES To many, the holy grail of query languages is the capability to understand and correctly reply to natural language queries, either spoken or typed. Although vendors have attempted to make end-user queries easier to do, the ability to correctly interpret a person's question is still limited, though many promising applications are underway for specific settings. For example, Gartner Group ranks as one of the "cool" new technologies a product called VoiceBox that offers voice commands sequenced like a natural conversation, as a means to access a database. In a car, drivers may ask, "Who is singing that song?" or say, "Play a similar blues song." Automakers are especially interested in this kind of technology given its importance for "hands-free" settings, such as driving. For instance, many navigation systems let drivers speak their destination rather than laboriously type it in.[6]

The natural language query systems work well when the questions use a limited vocabulary. For example, a natural language query that asks, "Which employees make more than $100,000 per year?" could be translated into SQL with reasonable accuracy. However, problems arise when the vocabulary is vague, the attribute names can be confused, or the question itself is not clear. Even the question about the high-earning employees is not unambiguous. For example, did the user intend to include benefits and stock options? Should "employees" include part-time people? Natural language query systems are improving very rapidly, however, as the next "Did You Know?" anecdote shows.

Did You Know?

After its Deep Blue chess-playing computer beat the world champion Garry Kasparov, IBM went on to develop a system that can answer natural language questions by interpreting human speech and accessing an immense database of human knowledge. Named "Watson" after IBM's founder, the supercomputer trounced the top two human players in the TV game show *Jeopardy*. Player Ken Jennings wrote next to his final Jeopardy answer, "I for one welcome our new computer overlords."[7]

FIGURE 4-18

Job opening: Database administrator (DBA).

Applicants Wanted: Database Administrator

The DBA is responsible for the efficient operation of the company's databases: monitoring and optimizing performance, troubleshooting bottlenecks, setting up new databases, enhancing security, planning capacity requirements, designing backup and disaster recovery plans, and working with department heads and the IT team to resolve problems and build innovative applications. Starting salary: $65K and up.

MANAGING AND MAINTAINING THE DATABASE

According to the Bureau of Labor Statistics, the job of database administrator (DBA) is one of the fastest growing careers in the United States, and projections from other countries point to the same promising future for people who can tend this critically important asset (Figure 4-18). The analysts who work closely with the DBA to link business needs and IT solutions also have very attractive job prospects. Figure 4-19 shows some examples.

The DBA must be very familiar with the DBMS software the organization uses. This software will offer many different administrative tools to help keep the databases running smoothly.

PERFORMANCE TUNING AND SCALABILITY The database needs tuning for optimal performance, and the tuning process takes into account the way the end users access the data. For example, fields that they use to search for records should be indexed for maximum performance. Although a customer has an ID number, chances are they can't recall it, so the database should index other fields that will help the representative find the record quickly, such as home phone number or e-mail address. Although the DBA might be tempted to index everything, that would slow the system down when records are added, so a balance is needed. DBAs are constantly making trade-offs to add speed to certain activities while slowing down others, always attentive to the needs of the employees, customers, and other stakeholders. Optimizing performance for speedy retrieval of information, for example, may require slowing down other tasks, such as data entry or editing. Although managers who query the database frequently would want to optimize for retrieval speed, those who are entering data would have a different preference.

Scalability refers to a system's ability to handle rapidly increasing demand, and this is another performance issue. Cuong Do at YouTube faced this when the trickle of visitors became a tsunami. Bigger servers would have helped, but he and his team did something that would scale even further. They split the database into "shards," or slices that could be stored separately and accessed on different computers to improve performance. Shards

FIGURE 4-19

Careers in database administration and related areas.

Occupation	Projected Increase to 2018	Median Salary (2008)	Suggested Education & Training Requirements
Database administrators	Much faster than average	$66, 310	BS in MIS, computer science, or information sciences; training in DBMS software
Management analyst, Information systems focus	Much faster than average	$73,570	BS with IS concentration, or MBA (MIS); industry experience
Computer systems analysts	Much faster than average	$75,500	BS in technical field or business with MIS concentration; MBA (MIS focus).

Source: Bureau of Labor Statistics, U.S. Department of Labor. *Occupational outlook handbook.* (2010–2011 ed.). www.bls.gov/oco/, accessed May 9, 2011.

interactive voice response (IVR)
A technology that facilitates access to the database from signals transmitted by telephone, to retrieve information and enter data.

scalability
A system's ability to handle rapidly increasing demand.

also break with tradition by storing denormalized data, in which information that users typically retrieve as a whole is stored in the same place, rather than separate, normalized tables. When growth is that fast, the DBA must solve one bottleneck after another.

INTEGRITY, SECURITY, AND RECOVERY   The DBA manages the rules that help ensure the integrity of the data. For example, a business rule may require that some fields may never be empty, or the input must adhere to a particular format. The software can enforce many different rules, such as the **referential integrity** constraint, which ensures that every foreign key entry actually exists as a primary key entry in its main table. For example, when Devon adds a new employee to the employee table and attempts to enter a department ID that doesn't exist in the Departments table yet, the DBMS integrity constraint would prevent the insertion. She must create the record for the new department before assigning people to it. The constraint would also stop Devon from deleting a department if employees are assigned to it, even if they left the company.

A DBMS will also provide tools to handle access control and security, such as password protection, user authentication, and access control. Although application software often shares the responsibilities for ensuring integrity and security, or even handles most of those jobs, the database management software may perform some of them.

When the database locks up or fails, the DBMS offers tools to get it back up and running quickly or to reload all the data from backup media. Some systems use mirroring, so that users are directed to a copy of the database when the main one fails. Werner Vogels, the chief technology officer at Amazon, said, "Stuff fails all around you, that's reality, why don't we embrace it? For example, go more with a fast reboot and fast recovery approach. You need to have a self-healing environment."[8] That's good advice.

DOCUMENTATION   Even a small start-up like DD-Designs will need a database with dozens of tables and many complex relationships. The data model can be documented using a **database schema**, which graphically shows the tables, attributes, keys, and logical relationships (Figure 4-20). The **data dictionary** should contain the details of each field, including descriptions written in language users can easily understand in the context of the business. These details are sometimes omitted when developers rush to implement a project, but the effort pays off later. End users will start to develop their own queries and will become frustrated when the exact meaning of fields is not clear. What does a field named "CustomerTerminationFlag" mean? The DBA may recall the thinking that went into it, but end users will be puzzled.

FIGURE 4-20

Sample database schema.

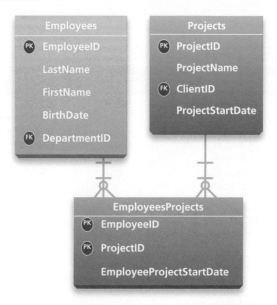

Multiple Databases and the Challenge of Integration

4 Explain why multiple databases emerge, and how master data management helps address the challenge of integration.

The database was intended to end the frustrations of those early departmental information silos, and it succeeded. However, as organizations grow, some of the same disadvantages creep back into the mix because the number of databases used to handle operations multiplies, especially when companies merge.

Robert Rosholt, the CFO at Nationwide Insurance Company, complains, "When you're dealing with 14 general ledger platforms and over 50 applications, it was enormous work to get the financials out." Nationwide's CIO, Michael Keller, wasn't optimistic. Keller said, "One of the first questions I was asked when I joined was, how much money do we spend, total, on IT? The answer was we didn't know. It took weeks to put that answer together."[9]

Does that sound familiar? With multiple databases, software applications, and inconsistent data definitions for similar entities, integration is a major challenge. Mergers and acquisitions contribute to the complexity, leading to many different databases operating under the same corporate umbrella. Sometimes partially redundant databases spring up in an organization simply because a fast-moving business needs support for an innovative idea immediately. The managers may choose to buy a separate system for it rather than take the time to build the support into the enterprise database and integrate it fully.

SHADOW SYSTEMS

Although the integrated enterprise database is a critical resource, changes to support new features can be painfully slow. People want to get their jobs done as efficiently as possible, and sometimes the quick solution is to create a **shadow system**. These are smaller databases developed by individuals or departments that focus on their creator's specific information requirements. They are not managed by central IT staff, who may not even know they exist. Shadow systems proliferate because people see advantages to managing their own information resources, especially the ability to control their data and make changes rapidly. They can retrieve information whenever they need it, in just the formats they want, and respond quickly to their customers. With Excel, Access, and other desktop software, the tools to create a shadow system are widespread. A hazard, though, is that the department may be left hanging when the creator leaves, because documentation and support are lacking.

All these business, technical, and human issues can add up to a serious headache for managers who need enterprise-wide summaries for strategic planning and executive decision making. They are confronted with many "versions of the truth," since the information is coming from multiple sources with inconsistent data definitions and data quality. Reports that attempt to add apples and oranges can't be trusted. One data source might include student interns as employees, while another may omit them, so executives are unable to obtain a consistent personnel summary. Or one department's report on sales growth may differ from another department's version because they are using slightly different definitions of sales. These problems call for an enterprise-wide integration strategy to resolve the differences and reduce the arguments about which version of the truth is "correct," especially about important pieces of information needed for strategic planning.

referential integrity
A rule enforced by the database management system that ensures that every foreign key entry actually exists as a primary key entry in its main table.

database schema
A graphic that documents the data model and shows the tables, attributes, keys, and logical relationships for a database.

data dictionary
Documentation that contains the details of each field in every table, including user-friendly descriptions of the field's meaning.

shadow system
Smaller databases developed by individuals outside of the IT department that focus on their creator's specific information requirements.

INTEGRATION STRATEGIES AND MASTER DATA MANAGEMENT

Organizations approach integration challenges in several ways. Some build interfaces, or bridges between different databases, to link common fields. Using this approach, a field that is updated in one database, such as an e-mail address, is then copied over to the same fields in other databases that maintain that information. In the "downstream" databases, the e-mail address would be in read-only format, so that end users could not update it there.

An approach that addresses the underlying inconsistencies in the way people use data is **master data management**. This effort attempts to achieve consistent and uniform definitions for entities and their attributes across all business units. For example, the units must agree on how everyone will define "an employee" or "a sale." For a nonprofit, clear definitions of "donation" and "volunteer" are needed.

The most successful efforts at master data management focus mainly on a key area, such as customers, or on a limited number of entities that are most important. Teams from different business units participate in master data management to negotiate and resolve differences. **Data stewards** may then be assigned to ensure that people adhere to the definitions for the master data in their organizational units. They become a combination watchdog and bridge builder, to keep the reconciliation process on track.

Master data management has less to do with technology than with people, processes, and governance. It requires constant coordination among organizational units that are building, buying, or modifying databases. The stewards need savvy leadership and persuasion skills to reconcile different formats and meanings in the multiple databases, especially because the benefits may seem somewhat remote to those less concerned about summary reports that conflict. The human element often enters into the negotiations, especially when the definitions affect promotions or raises.

Nationwide launched a master data management initiative to resolve its fragmented environment. Team members, including CFO Rosholt, who sponsored the project, met weekly over pizza, talking out the changes that were needed and developing new policies. Rosholt's presence was critical to reinforce the importance of the project, and also settle disputes. As one team member put it, "We needed that hammer to remove some of the bottlenecks." The results were slow in coming, but eventually were dramatic. In 2006, it took the company 30 days to close the books, with much hair pulling to reconcile reports. Within a year, Nationwide cut that time in half and is shooting for even more improvement in the years ahead.

Another integration strategy, one that is even more effective when master data management efforts are helping to reconcile data inconsistencies and improve data quality from multiple sources, is the data warehouse.

 Describe why a data warehouse is valuable for integration and strategic planning, and explain the three steps involved in creating one.

Data Warehouses

The **data warehouse** is a central data repository containing information drawn from multiple sources that can be used for analysis, intelligence gathering, and strategic planning. Figure 4-21 shows examples of the many sources that might contribute to the warehouse.

Rachael LaPorte Taylor, the senior technology architect at FedStat.gov, is a leader in the U.S. Census Bureau's effort to make its vast storehouse of data accessible to the public. With a MySQL backend, the FedStat website handles thousands of self-service queries from people around the world who have specific questions about economic and population trends, health care costs, aviation safety, foreign trade, and much more. This enormously valuable data warehouse combines data from many different sources within and outside the U.S. Census Bureau.[10]

The ability to draw high-quality information from an organization's databases to spot trends, identify patterns, generate reports for compliance purposes, do research, and plan strategy is critical to the stakeholders of any organization. Although the

FIGURE 4-21

The data warehouse. Illustrations: Colorlife/Shutterstock, Bryan Solomon/Shutterstock.

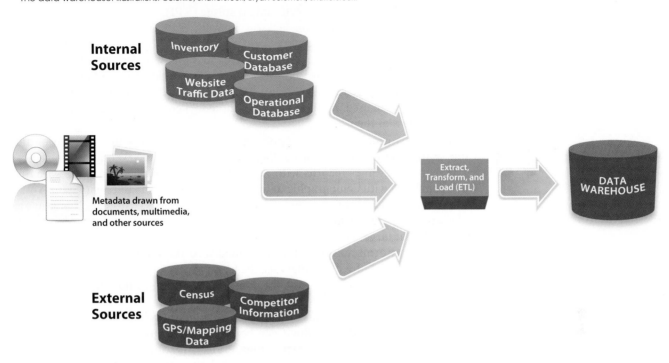

operational databases that support the day-to-day business contain much of the information that managers need, they are typically not in a format that is easily applied to broader analyses and what-if–type questioning. And as we saw earlier, organizations often have more than one database. Reports that span the enterprise must integrate data from many sources.

Another reason the operational database is not a good candidate for high-level management reporting is that the DBA has to optimize its performance for operations. Fast customer response and data entry come first, not complex queries for strategic planning. Those queries can be CPU hogs that slow everyone else down, so it makes sense to run them on a separate data warehouse, not the operational database.

BUILDING THE DATA WAREHOUSE

How do we create a data warehouse? A common strategy for drawing information from multiple sources is abbreviated **ETL**, short for **extract, transform, and load**. The first step is to extract data from its home database, and then transform and cleanse it so that it adheres to common data definitions. As we discussed, this is not a minor challenge, and computer programs rarely can handle it alone. Data drawn from multiple sources across organizations, or even within the same organization, will be defined or formatted differently. If the organization has already made progress with master data management, this transformation process is smoother. Indeed, attempts

master data management
An approach that addresses the underlying inconsistencies in the way employees use data by attempting to achieve consistent and uniform definitions for entities and their attributes across all business units.

data steward
A combination of watchdog and bridge builder, a person who ensures that people adhere to the definitions for the master data in their organizational units.

data warehouse
A central data repository containing information drawn from multiple sources that can be used for analysis, intelligence gathering, and strategic planning.

extract, transform, and load (ETL)
A common strategy for drawing information from multiple sources by extracting data from its home database, transforming and cleansing it to adhere to common data definitions, and then loading it into the data warehouse.

to build a data warehouse often expose a lot of "dirty data"—inconsistent name spellings, for instance. That leads to more interest in master data management, which is what happened at Rensselaer Polytechnic Institute (RPI).

RPI's president, Shirley Ann Jackson, knew the institute needed better data for strategic planning, and her executive team was frustrated by untrustworthy reports. The institute's data warehouse initiative uncovered many underlying problems that needed cross-functional teams to resolve before data could be loaded into the warehouse. Once they agreed on definitions, data stewards were appointed to watch over how the fields were used. As the project lead noted, "People are not going to do it out of the goodness of their hearts."[11]

The transformation process applies to external resources that will enrich the value of the data warehouse for intelligence gathering and marketing. For instance, a company's customer records with zip codes could be made even more valuable when combined with demographic data from the U.S. Census Bureau (Figure 4-22). The company might want to send a special promotion to customers living in zip codes with high average incomes, and adding this external resource makes it possible to identify that target group.

After transformation, the data is loaded into the data warehouse, typically another database. At frequent intervals, the load process repeats to keep it up to date. The DBA optimizes the warehouse for complex reporting, without having to worry about slowing down customers and staff.

Many data warehouses take advantage of standard relational database architectures, and most DBMS products can be optimized for use as a warehouse. Some include tools to help with the extractions, transformations, and loading, as well. Organizations also use alternative data warehouse architectures, such as those described in Figure 4-23.

STRATEGIC PLANNING, BUSINESS INTELLIGENCE, AND DATA MINING

The data warehouse makes data easily accessible for strategic planning. Along with the tools and approaches described in Chapter 7, the data warehouse opens up a wealth of opportunities for managers seeking insights about their markets, customers, industry,

FIGURE 4-22

Demographic data downloaded from the U.S. Census Bureau can make a data warehouse more valuable.

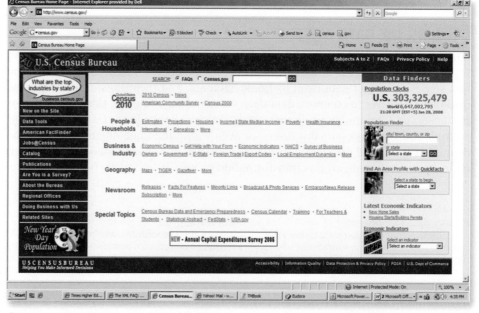

Source: www.census.gov, accessed March 5, 2011.

FIGURE 4-23

Data warehouse architectures.

Data Warehouse Architectures	
Relational database	Companies often use the same relational DBMS for their data warehouse as they use for their operational database, but loaded onto a separate server and tuned for fast retrieval and reporting.
Data cubes	This architecture creates multidimensional cubes that accommodate complex, grouped data arranged in hierarchies. Retrieval is very fast because data are already grouped in logical dimensions, such as sales by product, city, region, and country.
Virtual federated warehouse	This approach relies on a cooperating collection of existing databases; software extracts and transforms the data in real time rather than taking snapshots at periodic intervals.
Data warehouse appliance	The appliance is a prepackaged data warehouse solution offered by vendors that includes the hardware and software, maintenance, and support.

and more. It often becomes the main source of business intelligence that managers tap to understand their customers and markets, and make strategic plans.

For example, **data mining** is a type of intelligence gathering that uses statistical techniques to explore records in a data warehouse, hunting for hidden patterns and relationships that are undetectable in routine reports. Business analysts work with the statisticians to suggest areas to explore, so the software doesn't resort to "data dredging," that is, trekking blindly into terabytes of data to sniff out meaningless relationships that occur just by accident. Guided by security experts, for instance, data mining can spot elusive patterns in credit card transaction records that point to fraud so the company can block further purchases.

The Challenges of Information Management: The Human Element

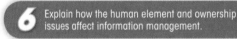

6 Explain how the human element and ownership issues affect information management.

Information resources reach their top value only if they are high quality and can easily be integrated, searched, and analyzed in productive ways. The move from file processing to databases was an important step for organizations to achieve these goals, reducing redundancy and improving integration.

As with all technology-related activities, however, managing information resources is not just about managing technology. It is also about people and processes, and understanding how people view, guard, and share information resources is a critical ingredient for any successful strategy.

OWNERSHIP ISSUES

In the workplace, information resources are found almost everywhere, from file cabinets and desk drawers, to the electronic files on portable media and computer hard drives. Although a company may set the policy that all information resources are company-owned, in practice, people often view these resources more protectively, even when compliance and security don't demand tight access controls. Norms about how records are used and shared emerge over time, and though many are unwritten, they can certainly affect employees' behavior.

Salespeople may feel protective about their own customers' records, or whole departments might want to control who has access to records that they are mainly responsible for maintaining. They may prefer that employees outside the department have the right to only view one of "their" records, but not change it. Now that customers themselves can enter and update their own records, how much control should they have over them? If a customer insists his name should be entered in all lowercase,

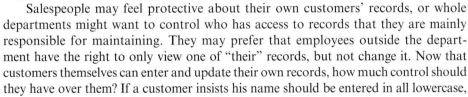

data mining
A type of intelligence gathering that uses statistical techniques to explore records in a data warehouse, hunting for hidden patterns and relationships that are undetectable in routine reports.

for example, should the DBA change the database's rules for those fields? Should last name be made an optional field for an entire database because some customers claim they don't have one? What entries should the database accept as valid for gender or ethnicity? Ownership issues have to be negotiated among many stakeholders.

Another challenge is simply the time required to make changes to an integrated enterprise database because those changes affect many more people who want to have input. This process takes time, not just for IT staff to analyze the impact, but for all the stakeholders to discuss it, as well. Changes to the old file processing systems were time-consuming for the IT staff because of the way the code was written. Changes to the integrated database take less time from IT, but more from the end users.

DATABASES WITHOUT BOUNDARIES

Another example of how the human element interacts with database management involves databases without boundaries, in which people outside the enterprise enter and manage most of the records. These contributors feel strong ownership over their records. Craigslist is one example.

Craig Newmark, founder of Craigslist.com, initially sought to help people in San Francisco find apartments and jobs. Starting on a shoestring, Newmark watched his site grow into the largest online database of classified ads in the world, causing the revenues that newspapers once earned from their paper-based classified sections to plummet. Craigslist is very customer-centric, and although the enterprise "owns" the database, the records are almost completely created by its customers. The site relies on the community of users—not just to generate all the ads, but also to reply privately to inquiries outside the Craigslist site.

Newmark also depends on the end users to generate new ideas for the site. In fact, compared to other websites with the same level of traffic, Craigslist employs extremely few people. It is the community of users that makes the site so successful. Newmark's concerns are less about the technology to support this wildly successful idea than about the health of the community and the relentless threats from spammers and fraudsters who can destroy trust in the site.[12]

Emergency disaster relief illustrates another way a database without boundaries comes into being. Online databases can help victims find missing family members, organize volunteers, or link people who can provide shelter to those who need it. In the aftermath of Hurricane Katrina, for example, volunteers began launching blogs and online databases, but missteps were common. Without any central coordination, the information about victims and sources of aid were scattered all over the web in many different formats, with no integration. David Geilhufe of the Social Source Foundation quickly worked with other volunteers to create a standardized data format—the People Finder Interchange Format—and enlisted more volunteers to enter all the unstructured data about evacuees into it so it could be integrated and reliably searched in a database. The army of volunteers grew to more than 3,000, and within a few weeks after the disaster, the database counted more than 600,000 records of missing and found people.[13]

A valuable lesson from the efforts to build databases without boundaries is simply the need to plan for scalability. In fact, the People Finder project had to be halted until a stronger database backend could be implemented. Ethan Zuckerman, a technical lead on the People Finder Project, was not at all prepared for the volunteer turnout. He commented, "… when net people try to solve a problem, they bring their posse with them. …" Another important lesson is the need for standard data formats and coordination among all the players.[14] Although small groups can be very agile in a disaster, coordination is needed to make sure the efforts don't add to the confusion with fragmented data in unstructured and incompatible formats.

BALANCING STAKEHOLDERS' INFORMATION NEEDS

How should managers balance the information needs of so many stakeholders? Top-level management needs clear, consistent, and accurate reports that summarize information from across the enterprise; conflicting "versions of the truth" are a major frustration. Operating units must have accurate reports on transactions that match their operations, and they need information systems that are easily changed to support fast-moving business requirements. Customers want simpler user interfaces that work quickly and reliably, and don't want to be told that "we just merged and our computer systems don't work together yet. " Government agencies want enterprises to provide compliance reports using government's definitions, because they have their own summaries to do.

Meeting all these needs is a balancing act that requires leadership, compromise, negotiation, and well-designed databases. As a shared information resource, the database fulfills its role exceptionally well to provide a solid backbone for the whole organization and all its stakeholders.

MyMISLab | *Online Simulation*

Volunteer Now!

A Role-Playing Simulation on Designing the Database for a Volunteer Matching Service

Star and Khaled started their volunteer matching service a year ago, making lists of local organizations that needed assistance and then posting calls for help on bulletin boards around campus and in local stores. Animal shelters, art museums, soup kitchens, a wildlife rescue station, a children's hospital, and many other worthy organizations benefit from the enthusiastic people who sign up, and students often earn community service points for participating.

The Volunteer Now! loose-leaf notebook is overflowing and mistakes keep happening. Last week a volunteer called from his cell phone to complain that the address he was given for the soup kitchen was a deserted warehouse, and Star had to pick him up rather than let him wander around on foot. They need a reliable information system with a backend database to organize the records.

As a frequent volunteer who has some knowledge of databases, you've been asked to offer your input. Log in to meet this well-meaning and energetic team, so you can help them get organized...

mangostock/Shutterstock

Chapter Summary

Learning Objectives

 An organization's information is a critical resource, and strategies to manage it are essential. Information resources can be described as structured, unstructured, or semi-structured, depending on their characteristics. Structured information is most easily captured by database management systems, since it can be broken down into component parts and organized in logical ways. Metadata, or data about data, describes the nature of information and provides details about its structure and properties. The quality of information is affected by several characteristics, such as accuracy, completeness, and timeliness.

 Early attempts to manage digital information resources used file processing systems, in which each department maintained its own records. Although they were very valuable, file processing systems had several disadvantages, including data duplication, lack of integration among departmental systems, inconsistent data definitions across departments, and data dependence. The database approach addresses these disadvantages and creates a shared resource with minimal redundancy. Several different database architectures have been developed, and the relational database is now the most widely used. Information is organized into tables in which each row represents a record. Relationships between tables are created by linking a field in one table to a field in another table with matching data.

 The development of a relational database begins with the planning phase, to identify the entities, their attributes, and their relationships. The process involves normalization, in which tables are created in such a way as to eliminate redundancy as much as possible and ensure that tables can be related to one another in a way that reflects their actual relationships. Primary keys ensure that each record in a table is unique, and foreign keys help establish relationships among tables. Most databases are accessed through application software, which serves as a user-friendly gateway to the underlying tables. The database management system (DBMS) provides tools for monitoring and maintaining the database in areas such as documentation, performance tuning, disaster recovery, and security. Information is retrieved from the database using query languages, such as SQL.

 As organizations grow and expand, they launch many databases, including shadow systems. Integration strategies, such as master data management, are needed to provide enterprise-wide summaries for strategic planning. A data steward helps maintain data consistency across the organization.

 The data warehouse draws information from multiple sources to create one information storehouse that can be used for reporting and analysis. Sources can be both internal and external. Extract, transform, and load are the three steps used to create the warehouse, which is refreshed with updated information daily or more often.

6 Enterprise information management is not just about technology. It involves a variety of challenges that touch on the human element. Data ownership issues arise, for example, because data have to be shared by all the stakeholders in the organization. Ownership issues also play a major role for databases without boundaries, such as Craigslist, in which most records are entered by people outside the enterprise. Leadership, cooperation, negotiation, and a well-designed database are all needed to balance all the stakeholders' requirements.

KEY TERMS AND CONCEPTS

structured information	field	database management software (DBMS)	data model
unstructured information	data definition	hierarchical database	primary key
semi-structured information	table	network database	autonumbering
metadata	batch processing	relational database	normalization
record	database		functionally dependent

foreign keys	scalability	shadow system	extract, transform, and
Structured Query Language (SQL)	referential integrity	master data management	load (ETL)
	database schema	data steward	data mining
interative voice response (IVR)	data dictionary	data warehouse	

CHAPTER REVIEW QUESTIONS

1. What are three categories that describe the nature of information resources? Give an example of each. How do you characterize the relationships within each category of information?

2. What is metadata? What does metadata describe for structured information? For unstructured information? Give an example of each type of metadata.

3. What are the characteristics of information that affect quality? What are examples of each?

4. What were the early design approaches to managing information resources?

5. What are the major disadvantages of file processing systems? What are four specific problems associated with file processing systems?

6. Following the file processing model of data management, what three architectures emerged for integrated databases? What are the advantages of each? Are there disadvantages?

7. Which database models have been developed to handle unstructured information? What are examples of unstructured information that may be handled by these specialized database models?

8. What are the steps in planning a relational data model? Are there benefits to the planning stage?

9. What are primary keys and foreign keys? How are they used to create links between tables in a relational database?

10. What is the typical strategy to access a database? How do users access an Access database? Are there other strategies to access database systems?

11. What is the role of the database administrator in managing the database? What is the career outlook for this job?

12. What is SQL? How is it used to query a database?

13. What is a shadow system? Why are shadow systems sometimes used in organizations? How are they managed? What are the advantages of shadow systems? What are the disadvantages?

14. What is master data management? What is a data steward? What is the role of master data management in an organization's integration strategy?

15. What is a data warehouse? What are the three steps in building a data warehouse?

16. What are three examples of data warehouse architectures? Which approach is suitable to meet today's growing demand for real-time information?

17. What is data mining? What is the difference between data mining and data dredging? What is the goal of data mining?

18. What are examples of databases without boundaries?

19. How do ownership issues affect information management? How do information management needs differ among stakeholder groups?

PROJECTS AND DISCUSSION QUESTIONS

1. Why is metadata becoming increasingly important in this age of digital information? What types of metadata would you expect to see attached to these information resources?

   a. Book
   b. Digital photograph
   c. MP3 file
   d. Zappos.com web page for men's athletic shoes

2. The concept of relationships is fundamental to relational database design. Briefly describe three relationships that explain how records in a database might be logically related to one another. What are examples of each type of relationship? At your university, what is the relationship between students and courses? What is the relationship between advisors and students?

3. Target marketing uses databases and data warehouses to identify potential customers that a business wants to reach based on factors that describe a specific group of people. For example, target markets may be identified by geographic area, by age group, by gender, or by all three factors at one time. One of the leading providers of business and consumer information is infoUSA.com. Visit their website at www.infousa.com to learn how they compile data from multiple sources. How does their process compare to extract, transform, and load (ETL)? Prepare a brief summary of your findings that describes the infoUSA five-step process of building a quality database.

4. Visit YouTube.com and search for "R. Edward Freeman Stakeholder Theory" to learn more about stakeholder groups. Are you a stakeholder at any of the following organizations? List several stakeholders at each of these organizations and describe the kind of information each stakeholder needs.

   a. A university
   b. A regional bank
   c. Toyota Motor Corporation

5. The idea of data warehousing dates back to the 1980s. Today, data warehousing is a global market worth billions of dollars. What is the relationship between operational databases and data warehouses? Why are data warehouses created, and how do organizations use them? What types of decisions do data warehouses support? Have you ever searched a data warehouse? Visit FedStats. gov and search "MapStats" to see what facts are available for your home state. Prepare a list of five interesting facts about your home state to share with your classmates.

6. Lisa Noriega has a problem with unstructured data. As her catering business grows, Lisa wants to analyze contracts to learn if over-budget projects result from using inexperienced project managers. Lisa wants to set up a database and she wants you to identify the records she will need. Work in a small group with classmates to identify the three entities that have meaning for her catering business. What are the attributes of these entities? What are probable data definitions of the attributes? What is the relationship between records and tables?

What is the relationship between fields and attributes? Prepare a 5-minute presentation of your findings.

7. The Drexel Theatre is a small, family owned cinema that screens independent and classic films. The lobby is decorated with vintage movie memorabilia including an original poster of Arnold Schwarzenegger, the Terminator, and his famous quote, "I'll be back." The theatre has a collection of 5,000 movies on DVD. It hires part-time workers for ticket and concession sales, and janitorial and projection services. It shows one of its movies every evening at 7:00 p.m. The owner of the Drexel plans to implement a relational database to handle operations. He has asked you to develop the data model for managing the film inventory. He wants to track movies, genres (categories), actors, and languages. He wants a description of each entity's attributes, and he wants an explanation of how to use primary keys and foreign keys to link the entities together. Work in a small group with classmates to plan the data model. Prepare a 5-minute presentation that includes an explanation of primary keys and foreign keys.

APPLICATION EXERCISES

EXCEL APPLICATION:
Managing Catering Supplies

Lisa Noriega developed the spreadsheet shown in Figure 4-24 so that she can better manage her inventory of disposable catering supplies. Download the spreadsheet named Ch04Ex01 so you can help her with the inventory analysis.

Lisa listed her inventory items in "Case" quantities, but she now wants to analyze items according to "Pack" quantities and create a price list to show to her customers. For example, a case of Heavy Duty Deluxe Disposable Plastic Knives has

12 packs of 24 knives each. She wants to calculate a "Sales Price per Pack" based on her cost plus a 25 percent markup.

Lisa asks that you complete the following operations and answer the following questions.

▸ Create columns that list Case Pack, Packs on Hand, and Cost per Case Pack for each item. Use a formula to calculate the Cost per Case Pack.

▸ Create a column that lists Sales Price per Pack. Use a formula to calculate a 25 percent markup. Set up an

FIGURE 4-24

Catering supplies spreadsheet.

Item No.	Description	Color	Unit	Unit Cost	On Hand
630K-C	Deluxe Heavy Duty Disposable Plastic Knives	Clear	Case (12 pk/24 each)	13.61	3
630F-C	Deluxe Heavy Duty Disposable Plastic Forks	Clear	Case (12 pk/24 each)	13.61	3
630S-C	Deluxe Heavy Duty Disposable Plastic Spoons	Clear	Case (12 pk/24 each)	13.61	3
630K-B	Deluxe Heavy Duty Disposable Plastic Knives	Black	Case (12 pk/24 each)	13.61	2
630F-B	Deluxe Heavy Duty Disposable Plastic Forks	Black	Case (12 pk/24 each)	13.61	2
630S-B	Deluxe Heavy Duty Disposable Plastic Spoons	Black	Case (12 pk/24 each)	13.61	2
5454W	54" × 54" Plastic Table Cover	White	Case (24)	19.15	1
5454B	54" × 54" Plastic Table Cover	Beige	Case (24)	19.15	2
5454BL	54" × 54" Plastic Table Cover	Black	Case (24)	19.15	1
549W	54" × 108" Plastic Table Cover	White	Case (24)	30.24	4
549B	54" × 108" Plastic Table Cover	Beige	Case (24)	30.24	2
549BL	54" × 108" Plastic Table Cover	Black	Case (24)	30.24	1
72W	72" Round Plastic Table Cover	White	Case (24)	52.08	3
72B	72" Round Plastic Table Cover	Beige	Case (24)	52.08	3
72BL	72" Round Plastic Table Cover	Black	Case (24)	52.08	1
537	13" × 17" Linen-Like Napkins	White	Case (6 pk/50 each)	45.90	6
28500	10" × 10" Linen-Like Napkins	White	Case (8 pk/50 each)	42.00	3
1010W	10" × 10" 2-ply Beverage Napkins	White	Case (12 pk/50 each)	18.14	6
1010B	10" × 10" 2-ply Beverage Napkins	Black	Case (12 pk/50 each)	18.14	1
1010R	10" × 10" 2-ply Beverage Napkins	Red	Case (12 pk/50 each)	18.14	1
1313W	13" × 13" 2-ply Luncheon Napkins	White	Case (12 pk/50 each)	25.20	3
1313B	13" × 13" 2-ply Luncheon Napkins	Black	Case (12 pk/50 each)	25.20	2
1010WED	10" × 10" Wedding Bells Print Napkins	White	Case (12 pk/50 each)	26.46	3
1313WED	13" × 13" Wedding Bells Print Napkins	White	Case (12 pk/50 each)	37.80	4
CC12	12 oz. Classic Crystal Tall Plastic Glasses	Clear	Case (12 pk/20 each)	78.33	1
CC16	16 oz. Classic Crystal Tall Plastic Glasses	Clear	Case (12 pk/20 each)	107.73	1
CCR9	9 oz. Classic Crystal Plastic Rocks Glasses	Clear	Case (12 pk/20 each)	53.90	3

assumption cell to input the percentage markup rather than include the markup value in the formula.

▶ Format the spreadsheet to make it easy to read and visually appealing.

1. What is Lisa's total investment in disposable catering supplies?
2. What is the total sales value of her inventory?
3. How much profit will she make if she sells all of her inventory at a 25 percent markup?
4. How much profit will she make if she uses a 35 percent markup instead?

ACCESS APPLICATION:
DD-Designs

Devon Degosta set up an Access database to manage her web design business. She has asked you to create a report that summarizes and identifies projects that are assigned to more than one employee. Recreate the Access database with the table names, attributes, and relationships as illustrated in Figure 4-25. Download and use the information in the spreadsheet Ch04Ex02 to populate the tables. Create a report that lists each project by name and the names of the employees assigned to it. Devon wants the report to include the client name and the project budget. What other reports would Devon find useful?

FIGURE 4-25

DD_Designs database schema.

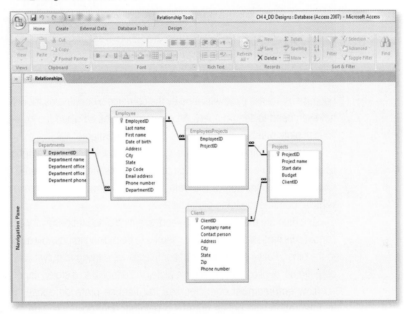

CASE STUDY #1

U.K. Police Track Suspicious Vehicles in Real Time with Cameras and the License Plate Database

Almost every city street in London is under constant video surveillance, partly as a reaction to terrorist attacks. These closed-circuit cameras initially created tapes that could be viewed later, but the technology now is far more capable. The cameras are equipped with automatic number plate recognition (ANPR) capabilities, which use optical character recognition to decipher the license plate numbers and letters (Figure 4-26).

The camera's data is sent to the national ANPR Data Centre in north London, which also houses the Police National Computer. Cameras, some obvious and others covertly hidden, are widespread throughout the city, and many are mounted on police vehicles. Each camera can perform 100 million license plate reads per day, and they are sensitive enough to work well at night and in rainy weather. Each vehicle's plate number is combined with the camera's GPS location and a timestamp, so the Oracle database at the Data Center contains detailed information about the whereabouts of almost every vehicle.

Since the database is linked to the Police National Computer, police on the beat can query it to see whether a nearby vehicle is flagged for some reason. Cross-checking the license plate information against the crime database can turn up vehicles involved in crimes or registered to wanted criminals. In one case, a police constable was killed during a robbery, and police were able to track the getaway car

Ann Cantelow/Shutterstock

FIGURE 4-26

Capturing license plate numbers for law enforcement.

because its license plate was read by the cameras. For cameras mounted on vehicles, the officer does not even need to send a query. An audio alert goes off when the camera's image matches a flagged license plate number, prompting the police to investigate.

Beyond criminal activity, the police database contains extensive information linked to the license plate data. For instance, a car might show that it is registered to someone who owes parking fines, or who is uninsured. The data might also show that the license plate is attached to the wrong vehicle, pointing to stolen plates.

The data are maintained for 5 years, creating a rich repository for data mining. One study found that certain cars triggered no flags, but seemed to be making impossibly quick journeys from one end of town to the other. Police discovered that car thieves were trying to outwit ANPR by "car cloning," in which the perpetrators duplicate a real license plate and attach it to a stolen car of the same make and model.

Law enforcement agencies see the license plate database, the cameras that feed it, and its integration with police data as a revolutionary advance, one that dramatically improves their effectiveness. Police departments in the United States and other countries are rapidly adopting the system, buying camera-equipped cars and developing smartphone access to the database.

Privacy advocates, however, are concerned about the mounting power of integrated databases and surveillance technologies to scrutinize human behavior. One judge remarked, "A person who knows all of another's travels can deduce whether he is a weekly churchgoer, a heavy drinker, a regular at the gym, an unfaithful husband, an outpatient receiving medical treatment, or an associate of a particular individual or political groups." The United Kingdom is tightening regulations to provide better protections for citizens in an attempt to balance privacy concerns against the enormous value these databases offer to law enforcement.

Discussion Questions

1. Describe the manner in which data elements are linked across databases.

2. What technical and physical challenges has this system overcome to date? What are some remaining technical and physical challenges?

3. What human capital capabilities for law enforcement are necessary to make the database more effective?

4. What are the relevant considerations to balance the police's ability to investigate versus the citizens' need for privacy?

SOURCES: Anonymous. (August 5, 2010). Maryland to create statewide database for license plate readers. *Government Technology.* http://www.govtech.com/public-safety/Maryland-to-Create-Statewide-Database-for.html accessed May 9, 2011. National Vehicle Tracking Database. http://wiki.openrightsgroup.org/wiki/National_Vehicle_Tracking_Database, accessed May 9, 2011. Savage, C. (2010). Judges divided over rising GPS surveillance. *New York Times.* August 14, p. 12.

CASE STUDY #2

Colgate-Palmolive Draws on Its Global Database to Evaluate Promotions and Drive Investment Decisions

With more than $15 billion in annual sales, Colgate-Palmolive's global operations span dozens of countries. The consumer products giant makes and markets iconic brands such as Colgate toothpaste, Irish Spring soap, Palmolive dish detergent, and Softsoap shower gel and sells them around the world. Besides taking a "bite out of grime" with its soaps and personal hygiene products, the company also makes Science Diet pet foods.

Founded by William Colgate in 1806, the Manhattan-based company specialized in soap, candles, and starch. The "Palmolive" brand, featuring fragrant soaps made from palm and olive oils rather than foul-smelling animal fats, was added in mid-century through a merger. The company began expanding abroad by purchasing local soap and toothpaste companies in the 1930s, first in Europe, and then later in emerging economies in Asia and Latin America. In Latin America, for example, Colgate-Palmolive captured 79 percent of the market for oral care products after it acquired companies in Brazil and Argentina. More than 80 percent of its net sales now come from other countries, many in Latin America.

Managing this sprawling global empire requires a dedication to consistency, not just in the products themselves, but in the data they use to track every aspect of the company's operations and performance. Colgate's integrated backend database and enterprise software, supplied by SAP, supports a consistent approach to master data management. CIO Tom Greene says, "With SAP, the product masters and the customer groupings are all driven by the same master data." With everyone using the same integrated system, Greene avoids the problem of redundant and inconsistent data entered into separate systems. Disputes about which is the correct "version of the truth" disappear.

Greene relies on this consistent backend database for the Colgate Business Planning (CBP) initiative, which guides Colgate's investment decisions around the world. Marketing managers for consumer products confront a bewildering array of choices to promote products, from advertising campaigns and TV spots to discount coupons, rebates, and in-store displays. Most companies judge the success of such investments by measuring "uplift"—the difference between actual sales with the promotion and a projection of what sales might have been without the promotion. But CBP, combined with the integrated master database, allows Colgate management to dig far deeper, measuring actual profit, loss, and return on investment.

The detailed metrics can be broken down for individual products, regions, and retailers, providing a very clear window into how much any investment contributed to the company's profit. Corporate headquarters taps these finely tuned results to plan new investments. It is not a cookie cutter approach, however. Guided by their knowledge of local markets, subsidiary managers can tweak the plans to better fit local conditions. Since the results are all tallied consistently, drawing on the database, managers know what works and what doesn't.

Margins are critical in consumer products, so this deeper insight pays off. Thanks to CBP, Colgate reinvested $100 million in promotions found to be more profitable, and its long-term goal is $300 million—a sum that could be reinvested in promotions, or added to the company's bottom line. As Greene puts it, "You have to understand the technology, but the most important thing ... is to understand the business so you can marry the two together."

Discussion Questions

1. What type of data does Colgate-Palmolive use, and what types of decisions does Colgate-Palmolive make based on the data?
2. Why is it important for Colgate-Palmolive for the data to be integrated across systems?
3. What business benefits does Colgate-Palmolive achieve through use of this data?
4. What types of business knowledge would be necessary for a Colgate-Palmolive manager to analyze the data?

SOURCES: Colgate-Palmolive Company. (September 21, 2010). Hoover's Company Records. Retrieved September 21, 2010, from LexisNexis. Colgate world of care. www.colgate.com, accessed September 21, 2010. Henschen, D. (September 13, 2010). Data drives Colgate investment decisions. *Information Week*. 1278, 38–39.

E-PROJECT 1 Identifying Suspects with a License Plate Database: Constructing Queries with Access

An Access database from a hypothetical small island nation contains simulated license plate information and violation records, and it will illustrate how police are identifying cars involved in crimes or traffic offenses. Download the Access file called Ch04_Police to answer the following questions.

1. What are the three tables in the database? For simplicity, the LicensePlates table in this e-project uses LicensePlateNumber for its primary key. Why might that work for a small island nation, but not for the United States?

2. Why is PlateImagesID the primary key for the PlateImages table, rather than LicensePlateNumber?

3. A police officer spots a car illegally parked on a dark street, with license plate LCN5339. Query the database and list any crimes or other violations that are linked to this license plate.

4. A citizen reports a robbery to the police, but she can only remember the first three letters of the car's license plate (JKR). She thinks it was a black or dark blue Toyota. Which car is the best candidate, and who is the owner?

5. Letters such as G and C are often confused by eyewitnesses. Some witnesses to a hit-and-run accident reported that the license plate started with LGR, but they said they weren't sure. Construct a query to retrieve records that might match either LGR or LCR, and list the candidates.

6. The homicide division learned that a vehicle with a license plate number DYV4437 was observed near a murder scene, and they would like to speak to the owner, who might be able to shed light on the case. If the cameras have picked up the license plate at some time, it should be in the PlateImages table. Construct a query to retrieve the latitude and longitude of the car's most recent location.

E-PROJECT 2 Building a Database for Customer Records

In this e-project, you will construct a database of customer purchases for a small concession stand near "Four Corners," the point in the United States at which Utah, Colorado, Arizona, and New Mexico state lines meet. Much of the data will be imported from Excel files.

1. Open Access and create a new database called FruitStand.

2. Create a table called Products with the following fields:

ProductID (The first field defaults to the name ID, as the table's primary key. Change the name to ProductID. Leave it as autonumber and as the primary key.)
ProductName (Text data type, field size 25 characters)
Price (Currency data type)

3. Enter the records in the following table. Note that you do not enter the ProductID; it is an autonumbering field that generates the next value. Save your work.

ProductID	ProductName	Price
1	apple	$.45
2	pear	$.70
3	watermelon	$2.75
4	grapefruit	$1.50
5	avocado	$1.25

4. Download the Excel file Ch04_FruitStand, and import the two worksheets, labeled Customers and Purchases. Identify the CustomerID as the primary key for Customers, and

PurchaseNumber fields as the primary key for Purchases, rather than letting Access create its own primary keys.

a. What fields are contained in the Customers table? Generate a list of all your customers, sorted by CustomerID.

b. What fields are contained in the Purchases table? What are the foreign key(s) in the Purchases table, and which table(s) do they reference?

5. Use Access Create Query (Query Design), join Customers to Purchases (on CustomerID), and Purchases to Products (on ProductID), and answer the following questions:

a. Create a query that returns all the purchases from customers from Nevada (NV). Which fruit do people from that state seem to prefer?

b. How many pears have been sold? (Click on Totals in the Design Ribbon to bring up options to report grouped totals. Your query should Group By ProductName. Include the Quantity field, and in the Total row, select Sum for Quantity.)

c. How many watermelons have been sold?

d. List all the states your customers come from, and the number of customers from each one. (Use COUNT under the CustomerID field from Customers.) From which state do most of your customers come?

6. List the countries your customers come from, sorting the data by CountryName. What problem do you encounter? What would you do to the database to improve your ability to analyze the data by country?

CHAPTER NOTES

1. Ilieva, J., Baron, S., & Healey, N. M. (2002). Online surveys in marketing research: Pros and cons. *International Journal of Market Research.* 44(3), 361–376.

2. National Research Council. (1999). *Funding a revolution: Government support for computing research.* Washington, DC: National Academy Press. www.nap.edu/readingroom/books/far/notice.html, accessed May 7, 2008.

3. Waldo, D. R. (2005). Accuracy and bias of race/ethnicity codes in the Medicare enrollment database. *Health Care Financing Review.* 26(2), 61–72. www.cms.gov/HealthCareFinancingReview/downloads/04-05winterpg61.pdf, accessed February 19, 2011.

4. Muraskin, E. (nd). It's a fax server! No! It's an IVR platform. www.copia.com/voicefacts/canal_casestudy.html, accessed May 9, 2008.

5. Mobile access to inventory data reduces back orders by 80 percent. (August 2007). *Windows Mobile Customer Solution Case Study.* www.microsoft.com/casestudies/casestudy.aspx?casestudyid=4000000611, accessed April 2, 2008.

6. Raskino, M., Fiering, L., Dulaney, K., Jones, N., & Koslowski, T. (2007). Cool vendors in user-interface technology innovation. Gartner Research, DOI ID Number: G00146423.

7. Feldman, S. (2011). Watson beats Jeopardy's best: What next? *PCWorld.* www.pcworld.com/article/220056/watson_beats_jeopardys_best_whats_next.html, accessed February 19, 2011.

8. *Software Engineering Radio.* Interview with Werner Vogels. Audio available at http://se-radio.net/podcast/2006-12/episode-40-interview-werner-vogels (38:00).

9. Wailgum, T. (2008). How master data management unified financial reporting at Nationwide Insurance. *CIO Magazine.* www.cio.com/article/print/167452, accessed May 9, 2011.

10. U.S. Census Bureau counts on MySQL. www.mysql.com/why-mysql/case-studies/mysql-cs-us-census-casestudy.pdf, accessed May 7, 2008.

11. Daniel, D. (2007). The secret to successful business intelligence: A top-notch data warehouse. *CIO Magazine.* www.cio.com/article/151601/The_Secret_to_Successful_Business_Intelligence_A_Top_Notch_Data_Warehouse/3, accessed May 9, 2011.

12. Craigslist's Craig Newmark: 100% of what we do is based on community. Knowledge@Wharton, University of Pennsylvania, Wharton School of Business. http://knowledge.wharton.upenn.edu/article.cfm?articleid=1775 accessed May 9, 2011.

13. Geilhufe, D. (2006). Personal history of the Katrina PeopleFinder Project PART I. http://socialsource.blogspot.com/2005/10/personal-history-of-katrina.html, accessed May 10, 2008.

14. Jones, C., & Mitnick, S. (May 1, 2006). Open source disaster recovery: Case studies of networked collaboration. *First Monday.* 11(5). www.uic.edu/htbin/cgiwrap/bin/ojs/index.php/fm/article/view/1325/1245, accessed May 4, 2008.

Information Systems for the *Enterprise*

Chapter Preview

MANAGING ANY ORGANIZATION, LARGE OR SMALL, MEANS KEEPING RECORDS. Those records track transactions, income, expenses, employees, customers, taxes, assets, and much more, providing a solid backbone for the company's activities. The records also form the data repository needed to generate the endless reports that stakeholders require, both inside and outside the organization. Fortunately, information systems to support most common business processes are widely available, even for start-ups. This chapter examines those systems, showing the business processes they support, the functionality they offer, and the value they can provide.

© Kevin Foy/Alamy

5

Learning Objectives

1 Explain the role that financial and asset management information systems play in an organization, and the importance of financial reporting.

2 Define human capital management, identify its major components, and describe several metrics used to quantify aspects of human capital.

3 Define supply chain management, and describe the metrics, technologies, and information systems that support supply chain processes.

4 Define customer relationship management and its role in an organization, and describe the metrics and information systems that support it.

5 Explain the importance of ERP systems and describe how they are created, integrated, and implemented.

Introduction

Blogger Christopher Sciacca was pondering the "Made in …" stickers on all the IKEA bags and boxes as he struggled to assemble furnishings for his new Vienna flat. The shelves said "Made in Russia," the computer desk came from Poland, the chair hailed from Thailand, the screws were imported from China, and the carpet arrived from India.[1] He wondered how IKEA orchestrates all these complex global inventories and avoids the dreaded "Out of Stock" sign. Enterprise-class information systems must be the key.

Why did IKEA choose a Russian supplier for the desk, and transport the screws all the way from China to the Vienna store? IKEA's supply chain managers use their information systems to constantly juggle these choices, sorting out predicted demand, supplier commitments, transportation costs, labor expenses, strikes, and more.

FIGURE 5-1

Major information system categories for operational management.

Business Process	Sample Functionality for Information System
Finance and Asset Management	Accounts payable, accounts receivable, general ledger, inventory, procurement
Human Capital Management	Human resources management, payroll, benefits, time sheets, talent development, training programs
Supply Chain Management	Supply chain planning software, warehouse management, transportation management
Customer Relationship Management	Contact management, marketing campaign management, e-mail marketing, sales force management, customer service

Companies like IKEA need robust and flexible information systems to run their businesses, striving for the perfect balance between efficient operations and effective results. Every organization that handles money and hires people must rely on systems to manage accounting, finances, assets, procurement, and human resources. Most companies, especially global retailers, must also deal with intricate supply chains. Organizations that serve customers of any kind—clients, students, patients, citizens, association members, patrons, or donors—need information systems to manage operations and build enduring relationships.

This chapter explores the four major categories of information systems that underlie fundamental business processes common to most organizations, shown with sample functions for each in Figure 5-1. The four are finance and asset management, human capital management, supply chain management, and customer relationship management. Companies that handle these processes well gain an edge over competitors by reducing costs, adding value, and satisfying employees and customers. Organizations that stumble over these basic functions, dragged down by cumbersome, incompatible, and inconsistent systems, may not stay in business at all, let alone reach the top of their industries. They may struggle just to pay employees, balance the books, comply with government regulations, handle returns and refunds, or track their suppliers.

Although these back-office systems are absolutely necessary, managers can easily underestimate how difficult they can be to implement and maintain. Their functions weave a path through every organizational unit from the finance office to the sales desk, touching, transforming, and sometimes eliminating business processes. First we will look at individual systems that support major business processes, and then at attempts to integrate the processes into full-featured suites of applications.

||||||||||||||||||||||||||||||||||||||||||||||||||||||||||||||||||||||||||||||||||||||||||||||||||||||||||||||||||||||||

Explain the role that financial and asset management information systems play in an organization, and the importance of financial reporting.

Finance Management

Any organization that handles money—and few do not—needs a robust **financial management system**. In the wake of disastrous bank failures and government bailouts for those deemed "too big to fail," financial information systems—and the way people use them—are under more scrutiny than ever. These systems lie at the heart of the organization, and companies are held fully accountable for the accuracy of their records. Fuzzy math and accounting tricks that make companies look more profitable than they really are can destroy trust, even if they are legal. Though the endless tabular outputs may seem dry to some, their accuracy, reliability, and trustworthiness concern every stakeholder.

COMPONENTS OF FINANCIAL INFORMATION SYSTEMS

Accounts payable, accounts receivable, procurement, cash management, budget planning, asset management, and the general ledger are examples of the modules typically included in a full-featured financial management system (Figure 5-2). Beyond those, the system may support many other finance-related activities and processes, such as collections, debt management, travel and expense management, installment payments, and contracts management.

Nonprofits and government need additional modules for their financial systems. These could track and manage taxes and customs revenue, or perhaps grants and gifts from foundations or individuals.

INTEGRATING THE COMPONENTS Integration among the modules is especially important to avoid inconsistencies. For example, the details from accounts receivable and accounts payable transactions should automatically update the general ledger, to streamline reconciliation and consistent reporting. Bridges and interfaces to other systems, especially human resources and payroll, also vastly improve accuracy. Time periods and data definitions should match so that, for instance, a monthly report with year-to-date expenditures shows the same payroll totals in both systems.

FINANCIAL WORKFLOWS The integration of these components supports the development of streamlined and paperless workflows in an organization. In many organizations, procurement and accounts payable were the first targets for this kind of process improvement. Staff can now use online shopping carts to generate procurements from established vendors, routing their requests to supervisors and then to the vendors themselves if supply chain relationships are in place. The software builds in online, interactive forms so staff can make corrections along the way, with customized workflow tables that determine the routes.

Let's buy some Bluetooth headsets for sales reps in a hypothetical travel company—Gulf Travel—to see how this works:

FIGURE 5-2

Sample components for a finance management system.

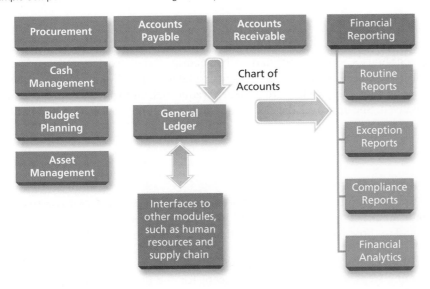

financial management system
Enterprise information system that supports financial accounts and processes, including accounts payable, accounts receivable, procurement, cash management, budget planning, assets, general ledger, and related activities.

Shaun, the office manager in the sales department, browses the web for the best models and then logs in to the financial system. He requests price comparisons for the model he's chosen and finds the lowest prices from TechSmart, Inc., which has a special supplier arrangement with Shaun's company. Shaun enters the order for 10 headsets into the shopping cart, selecting TechSmart as the vendor. Totals and taxes are all computed, and Shaun splits the purchase against two budget numbers—40 percent for the Northern sales group with four sales reps, and 60 percent for the Southern sales group for their six reps.

Rania, Shaun's supervisor, logs in and sees a message in her inbox— "Shopping cart approval needed." She is authorized to approve purchases for both budgets, and when she does, the electronic order goes straight to the sales department at TechSmart, since the supplier's contact information is all filled out in Gulf Travel's system.

TechSmart staff receives the order and electronically delivers it to the warehouse for fulfillment. Gulf Travel's system is linked to TechSmart's inventory information, so Shaun already knew that TechSmart had the headsets in stock. TechSmart's warehouse ships the box to Gulf Travel.

Sven, the goods receipt clerk at Gulf Travel, signs for the 10 headsets and logs in to the system to indicate they have been received. He drops the headsets off to Shaun, who hands them out to the sales reps.

TechSmart's system automatically generates the invoice and sends it electronically to Gulf Travel accounts payable, where Takia can see immediately that the goods were properly requested, approved, shipped, and received. She approves the electronic transfer of funds to TechSmart's bank account.

The system automatically updates the general ledger and asset records to indicate the company now owns 10 Bluetooth headsets. Other staff may add detail to those records, such as serial numbers or warranty data.

 Humans are part of the loop, making decisions, approving actions, and confirming steps in the process. But except for the package's wrapping, paper is not. All the players have real-time access to the same underlying information, so inconsistencies are unlikely. Compare this scenario with one in which orders, approvals, invoices, and payments are all handled manually, moving paper from one person's in-tray to the next, with massive filing cabinets, handwritten signatures, inked stamps, and endless voicemail tag to clarify stock levels, prices, and shipping dates.

FINANCIAL REPORTING AND COMPLIANCE

Reports are the lifeblood of people in finance and accounting, and information systems routinely generate detailed and summary reports on all the organization's transactions and assets.

EXCEPTION REPORTING Financial systems generate exception reports that automatically tag unusual events—ones that human beings must review. Such reports are often used to spot fraudulent transactions, including any committed by employees. In an accounting industry survey, almost 40 percent of the respondents said they knew about employees who submitted inaccurate travel and expense vouchers for reimbursement. Average losses per incident may not be huge, but the same employees repeat the fraud over and over, causing slow fiscal hemorrhages. Sales reps may exaggerate mileage for trips, or travelers may submit receipts twice.[2] Exception reports can help identify events that fall outside accepted ranges.

COMPLIANCE REPORTING Financial systems also carry the major burden of compliance reporting, and in doing so they must conform to local, national, and international regulations. The Sarbanes-Oxley Act, for example, passed in 2002, dramatically enhanced U.S. reporting standards for public companies. Following the 2008–2009 financial crises, countries around the world are mandating stricter financial reporting as well. Indeed, the ratcheting up of compliance reporting is a major driver for companies seeking to implement integrated, commercially supported financial software.

In the United States, the Security and Exchange Commission (SEC) mandates many aspects of compliance reporting, and the paper reports are no longer enough. Electronic reporting is required, relying on **eXtensible Business Reporting Language (XBRL)**. XBRL is part of the XML family of standardized languages and is specialized for accounting and business reports. The goal is to develop a common language for financial reporting, one that tags every individual item of data to make it understandable, transparent, and also computer-readable for further analysis. "Net Profit," for instance, is defined clearly and given a tag, so when it appears on an electronic compliance report, both humans and computer programs know its meaning. This is a huge advance over paper reports, and even electronically delivered text reports. Although managers can download some output into Excel spreadsheets for further analysis, the lack of tags to define the data limits its usefulness.

XBRL can help eliminate manual processes, but its enhanced transparency and standardization are even more valuable for other stakeholders. Governments, regulators, auditors, investors, and creditors can compare "net profit" from one company to the next, with more assurance that all the figures have been calculated in the same way.

The International Accounting Standards Board (IASB) exists to develop and promote a single worldwide set of understandable and enforceable financial reporting standards. Information systems incorporate these as much as possible, though differences among countries still remain. Local political and economic factors can affect a country's decisions about the proper way to report financial figures. In China, for example, different accounting standards have been used to judge the value of companies that come about as a result of mergers between state controlled and privately held enterprises.[3]

Nevertheless, the growing body of widely accepted accounting standards throughout the world, combined with the use of robust financial information systems and languages such as XBRL for business reporting, are promising steps. Worldwide trade and investment rely on trust, and the importance of reliable and consistent financial reports can hardly be overstated.

eXtensible Business Reporting Language (XBRL)
Part of the XML family of standardized languages specialized for accounting and business reports; tags identify data elements to make them transparent and also computer-readable.

Define human capital management, identify its major components, and describe several metrics used to quantify aspects of human capital.

2

Human Capital Management

Human capital management (HCM) encompasses all the activities and information systems that support effective management of an organization's human capital. The HCM information system includes a growing suite of applications with the employee record as the central element. Together, these applications support recruitment, hiring, payroll, benefits, taxes, career development, training programs, employment histories, employee self-service, and more (Figure 5-3).

COMPONENTS OF HUMAN CAPITAL MANAGEMENT SYSTEMS

HUMAN RESOURCES MANAGEMENT   The **human resources management system (HRM)** is typically the heart of the HCM system, tracking each employee's demographic information, salary, tax data, benefits, titles, employment history, dependents, and dates of hire and termination. Some systems also keep track of performance evaluations, professional development, and training. HRM systems are quite mature, and almost all organizations integrate this information system with the financial system, especially to track payroll expenditures, taxes, and benefits.

WORKFORCE MANAGEMENT   The broader term *human capital management* reflects the fact that traditional human resources management systems have grown into larger software systems that support other employee-related functions. The **workforce management module**, for example, draws on the data in the core human resource records and adds features to keep track of time and attendance, sick leave, vacation leave, and project assignments. This module is especially useful for labor scheduling and workforce planning and for making sure, for instance, that the proper number of clerks is assigned to specific shifts. The goal is to match staffing with requirements, optimizing the schedules so that employees are assigned when they are most needed but are not standing around with nothing to do during slack periods. This system can also draw on information stored in sales records that shows when peak demand occurs.

TALENT MANAGEMENT   **Talent management** applications focus on the employee life cycle, beginning with the recruitment phase and extending into performance evaluations, career development, compensation planning, e-learning, and succession planning after retirement or departure. Visualization and charting tools are adding richness to the way managers view the organization's talent (Figure 5-4). For instance, a constantly updated organizational chart, drawing from the core human resources records, can help with succession planning by showing managers where depth might be lacking, or which units are particularly vulnerable due to a high number of relatively inexperienced hires. Managers can see the talent throughout their organizations in a more intuitive way, pulling data from many different corners of the organization's information systems.[4]

FIGURE 5-3

Components of human capital management systems.

HCM Module	Description
Core human resources management application	Demographic information, human resources management, payroll, benefits, professional development, education
Workforce management applications	Time and attendance, sick and vacation leave, task and activity tracking, labor scheduling capabilities
Talent management applications	E-recruitment and position applications, employee performance management and tracking, career development, compensation management, e-learning and professional development tracking; visualization and organizational charts
Service delivery applications	Employee and managerial self-service, typically web-based, for entering data and retrieving reports
Social software	Wikis, blogs, social networks

FIGURE 5-4

Talent management applications include visualization and charting tools to display key metrics for human resource professionals.

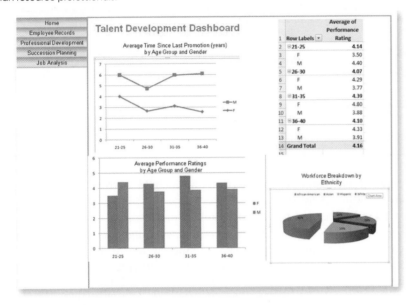

SOCIAL NETWORKING AND HCM   HCM systems are increasingly incorporating social networking software, and organizations are finding innovative ways to leverage it to nurture talent. Dow, for instance, wanted to tap the extensive knowledge and skills of its retirees, employees on maternity leave, and others who were loyal to the company but not currently working. It launched a social "alumni" network for this population—well over 40,000 people—and invited them to reconnect with colleagues, search for job opportunities, share news, and mentor less-experienced workers. Part of the company's motivation was the looming skills shortage, given that experienced baby boomers will retire in the coming years.[5]

The project continued to grow, and Dow even invited employees who had been laid off during a business downturn. Some managers feared these members might just vent on the alumni network, but most did not. In fact, some laid-off workers—called "boomerangs"—are being hired back when business recovers, based on their positive attitude and networking capabilities.[6]

HCM METRICS

Buried in the HCM information system is a wealth of data that can reveal how well the organization is managing and nurturing its human capital.

▶ Do we have the talent we need to succeed in the future?
▶ Can we weather the departure of that star over in marketing?
▶ Are training expenses growing so much because turnover is too high?
▶ How productive are our full-time employees compared to the part-time people?

human capital management (HCM)
Encompasses all the activities and information systems related to effectively managing an organization's human capital. The HCM information system includes applications and modules with the employee as the central element.

human resources management system (HRM)
Typically the heart of the HCM system, the HRM system tracks each employee's demographic information, salary, tax data, benefits, titles, employment history, dependents, and dates of hire and termination.

workforce management module
As part of the HCM system, the workforce management module helps track time and attendance, sick leave, vacation leave, and project assignments.

talent management
As part of the HCM system, the talent management module focuses on the employee life cycle, including recruitment, performance evaluations, career development, compensation planning, e-learning, and succession planning after retirement or departure.

FIGURE 5-5

Metrics drawn from the human capital management system can reveal important information about how well the organization is managing human capital.

Human Capital Metric	Description
Turnover	The percentage of workers who left and were replaced during a time period
Turnover costs	The total of termination costs, hiring costs, training costs, and other costs related to replacing a worker
Cost per hire	Average advertising costs + agency fees + recruiter's salary and benefits + relocation expenses for new employees
Human capital return on investment	The return on investment produced by the organization's expenditures on salaries, benefits, bonuses, and other costs for human talent
Employee satisfaction	Measures of job satisfaction, usually assessed through employee surveys or exit interviews

Figure 5-5 shows some examples of common HCM metrics, ones that most organizations will want to investigate.

Any metrics intended to quantify human performance or productivity can be controversial. A study of New Zealand companies found considerable disagreement about what exactly to measure and what the metrics meant. For example, it may be easy to use sales volume as a metric to assess performance for a customer account executive, but it is harder to find metrics for positions with less tangible output, such as scientists or graphic designers. These metrics get quite personal and employees often refused to accept them, citing problems in accuracy or relevance.[7]

Despite the obstacles, metrics that capture the elusive aspects of human performance are vitally important to an organization. When managers and staff work together to devise metrics that people agree are fair, relevant, and aligned with business goals, everyone knows what to do to improve. They also have a much clearer understanding of the organization's human capital and how best to deploy it.

Define supply chain management, and describe the metrics, technologies, and information systems that support supply chain processes. ③

Managing the Supply Chain

IKEA's teams watch inventory levels, weather reports, political news, and customer trends around the world in their quest for excellence in **supply chain management (SCM)**. This term refers to strategies that optimize the flow of products and services from their source to the customer. Depending on your type of business, the chain can be long indeed, stretching from your supplier's suppliers all the way to your customer's customer. The ultimate goal is to align supply with demand so that the right product is delivered to the right place, at just the right time, and at the right price.

✴ THE ETHICAL FACTOR Ethics and Talent Management

Scenario: The CEO of a large media entertainment company with more than 10,000 employees decides to buy out a small business that created a spectacularly successful online role-playing game. The smaller company has about 50 software engineers, and the CEO wants to retain about 20 top performers. The rest will be laid off. The CEO can't obtain performance ratings for the 50 engineers at the online game company, so instead asks the human resources director to analyze the performance metrics of software engineers at the media company. The CEO's goal is to identify common characteristics of star software engineers to help guide the decision about who should be retained. With the new talent management system, the director can quickly analyze average ratings by job position, years of experience, age, gender,

ethnicity, educational background, university attended, marital status, and many more variables.

Suppose the graphs show that within the media company, average performance ratings are slightly higher for male software engineers under 35 years old compared to women of all ages, and men over age 35.

Relying on this information to decide who should get job offers to stay on would not only be unethical, but it could also lead to poor decisions. For instance, the results could stem from past and present discrimination at the media company against people who don't fit a stereotype about software engineers. Human resource professionals need sharp critical thinking skills and thoughtful decision making to use these powerful systems ethically and wisely.

SUPPLY CHAIN FUNDAMENTALS

Optimizing the flow of products and services includes myriad activities as they move along the value chain, particularly to ensure that the flow meets customer demand. Consider Nintendo's Wii videogame console, which was a huge success the day it was released. While customers laughed about the name, they lined up to buy one—often in vain, since stores were notoriously out of stock. Walmart, Target, and Gamestop repeated the same litany to frustrated buyers: "We don't know when the Wii will be in, but it's first come, first served." Conspiracy theorists accused Nintendo of deliberately withholding the consoles to boost demand while stockpiling them in secret warehouses. But SCM failures were the more likely culprit.

Drawing on the steps in the value chain described in Chapter 2, the **Supply Chain Operations Reference (SCOR)** model illustrates five processes that underlie successful management of a next-generation supply chain. These are (1) plan, (2) source, (3) make, (4) deliver, and (5) return (Figure 5-6). Developed by the nonprofit Supply Chain Council, the model standardizes terminology to improve communications among suppliers and customers, and also draws attention to the interrelationships and trade-offs among all the chain's elements, not just the more obvious inventory levels or transportation costs.

SCM starts with planning, with the goal of building a nimble supply chain that aligns with actual business goals. If the corporate strategy calls for low-cost leadership, for example, the company will favor cost efficiencies for transportation and inventory storage. IKEA holds costs down by shipping flat boxes containing furniture parts rather than bulky, fully assembled bookcases or tables. The boxes fit nicely into far fewer containers traveling by ship or rail. (IKEA also grants customers the honor of assembling the products themselves, another huge cost saver for the firm.)

In step 2, managers make decisions about sources, and which suppliers to use. Again, the business strategy should guide many choices, such as whether to commit to long-term contracts or encourage frequent and fierce competition among potential suppliers. For safety, managers may also want to make arrangements with more than one supplier for the same resource in case one fails. Today's global supply chains must

---

FIGURE 5-6

Supply Chain Operations Reference (SCOR) model.

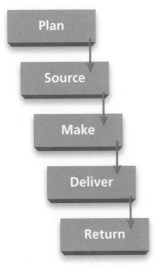

---

supply chain management (SCM)
Strategies that optimize the flow of products and services from their source to the customer.

Supply Chain Operations Reference (SCOR)
A model that illustrates five processes that underlie the supply chain: (1) plan, (2) source, (3) make, (4) deliver, and (5) return. The model standardizes terminology to improve communications among suppliers and customers, and also draws attention to the interrelationships and trade-offs among all the chain's elements.

be chaos-tolerant; hurricanes, earthquakes, political turmoil, or pandemics can cause major interruptions. Sometimes companies choose to go upstream and become their own suppliers, as Pepsi did in China when it wanted to hook consumers on salty Lay's potato chips—a sure way to push soda sales. Unable to find local potato growers, Pepsi branched out with its own potato farms in Inner Mongolia to ensure a reliable supply.

Managers also factor quality and purity of suppliers' products into their sourcing decisions. Faulty sourcing decisions for food and medicines could be disastrous. For example, vegetable protein contaminants harmful to animals were introduced into the pet food supply chain in 2007, resulting in major product recalls, hundreds of deaths, and widespread fear about pet food safety.[8] The ingredients came from tiny suppliers in China, but because the SCM systems lacked details about them, the investigations were especially difficult.

Corporate responsibility is another factor, and it affects IKEA's decisions about where to buy wood. In its "Position on Forestry," the company explains how it audits suppliers to ensure wood is harvested from renewable sources.[9]

The "make" step transforms the resources into something with more value. Supply chain managers track inventory at each stage, fine-tuning the flow so that some parts don't run short while others are overstocked. Managers' keen interest in inventory levels continues through the delivery step, as products are transported to distribution centers and retailers. Finally, SCM includes returns. A very low cost leader might post the "All sales final!" sign, hoping to reduce the cost of that final process to near zero. An online shoe retailer would design a very user-friendly return process, so customers will feel more comfortable about purchasing shoes they haven't tried on.

MEASURING PERFORMANCE IN SUPPLY CHAINS

While company strategy guides decision making throughout the five supply chain steps, accurate and well-chosen metrics tell how well those decisions are working out. How do IKEA's managers know their inventory levels are optimal, and that their supply chains are humming along as well as they should?

SUPPLY CHAIN VISIBILITY **Visibility** describes how easily managers can track timely and accurate supply chain metrics. Some metrics, such as total sales by product, are easy to get, but a maddening lack of transparency plagues many others. The data might be housed in a supplier's or customer's database with no real-time access, and only slow-moving paper reports transmit critical information. Data might also be intentionally hidden in an upstream supplier's operation, as the pet food contaminants may have been. Valuable metrics may also be invisible simply because no one is collecting them. Many are fleeting time durations that are costly and cumbersome to collect.

Netflix, the DVD rental company, strives for better visibility on metrics for a critical leg in its supply chain: the U.S. Postal Service. Subscribers choose videos online and Netflix sends them by mail. When a customer returns a DVD, Netflix processes the return and promptly mails out the next one in the customer's queue. However, the delivery step is highly dependent on USPS timeliness. Customers who wait days to get their new film are annoyed, but Netflix managers may not even know it. Figure 5-7 shows

---

FIGURE 5-7

Netflix surveys customers with e-mails like this one to improve visibility in the supply chain.

Thank you for your recent return of *Slumdog Millionaire*. Please tell us when you mailed back this movie by clicking on the appropriate link below.

I mailed the movie Thursday, Apr 12, 2012
I mailed the movie Wednesday, Apr 11, 2012
I mailed the movie Tuesday, Apr 10, 2012
I mailed the movie Monday, Apr 09, 2012
I mailed the movie before Monday, Apr 09, 2012

a sample automated e-mail from Netflix, sent in the hope that customers themselves will make that critical metric more visible. As you will see, a major goal of SCM information systems is to use technology-supported collaboration to improve visibility for both suppliers and customers.

Did You Know?

Netflix introduced a new supply chain that cuts out the U.S. Postal Service when it launched "Instant Play," offering subscribers the option to download movies via the Internet and watch them immediately. By some estimates, Netflix accounts for 20 percent of Internet traffic on most evenings in the United States.[10]

SUPPLY CHAIN METRICS How do managers decide which metrics to track, and how do they use them to fine-tune their supply chains? Theoretically, thousands of metrics could be candidates, a fact that contributes to the challenge of building SCM information systems. The SCOR model emphasizes about a dozen that touch on all the major characteristics of overall supply chain performance, such as reliability, responsiveness, and cost. No company can excel at all of them, though; SCM is about optimization, which means trade-offs.

The metric that matters most is **demand forecast accuracy (DFA)**—the difference between forecasted and actual demand. Supply chain managers work with the sales and marketing teams to forecast demand for products, drawing on historical sales patterns, marketing campaign plans, advertising budgets, seasonal promotions, focus groups, demographic shifts, gut instincts, and crystal balls if they have them. Underestimating demand leads to lost sales and frustrated customers. Overestimates lead to higher inventory costs, and ultimately discount blowouts to get rid of excess merchandise.

Sophisticated computer models incorporate dozens of variables to predict demand, drawing on data from sources inside and outside the company. Sales of AT&T cell-phone plans, for example, depended heavily on iPhone sales, and they skyrocketed whenever Apple released a new model. In 2009, for instance, 1.4 million new subscribers wanted AT&T plans for their iPhones, and AT&T's network and customer support services were stretched to their limit under the onslaught.[11]

One reason DFA is so critical is the **bullwhip effect**, which describes the distortion in the supply chain caused by changes in customer demand as the orders ripple upstream (Figure 5-8). Small fluctuations in retail sales trigger large swings in inventory levels, as the retailer sends orders to the distributor to replenish the stock, and the distributor follows up with orders to the manufacturer. As orders are filled and products shipped, inventory builds up in some places, but shortages occur in others. At times, warehouse shelves are stocked full, but the retailer's display is empty.

Reducing operating cost is another major priority, so costs must be visible (Figure 5-9).[12] Total costs are difficult to grasp, though, since they span transportation, inventory storage, warehouse management, distribution centers, customer service for refunds and exchanges, and direct operational costs. Knowing where along the supply chain costs are high is the first step to finding ways to reduce them. If inventory storage costs are high, a bullwhip effect may be operating and managers will look into better demand forecasting to synchronize the chain's links.

visibility	demand forecast accuracy (DFA)	bullwhip effect
Describes how easily managers can track timely and accurate supply chain metrics.	The difference between forecasted and actual demand.	Describes the distortions in a supply chain caused by changes in customer demand, resulting in large swings in inventory levels as the orders ripple upstream from the retailer to the distributor and manufacturer.

FIGURE 5-8
The bullwhip effect in a supply chain.

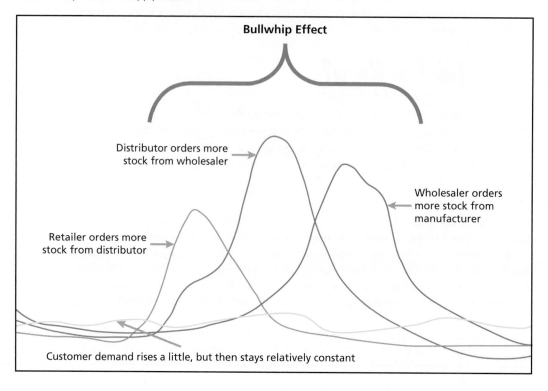

Groundbreaking interventions can sometimes dramatically reduce supply chain costs, especially by omitting whole segments. For example, Walmart adopted "cross-docking," an approach that almost eliminates the costs of storing goods in regional warehouses. Goods are unloaded directly from railcars or trucks and immediately packed into smaller trucks standing by, ready to head to retailers. No warehousing is needed, and software synchronizes the timing and logistics.

Dell started with a different approach to SCM. Other computer manufacturers built several models, shipping them first to distributors and then out to retailers such as Best Buy, Staples, or Costco. Dell bypassed those middlemen altogether. At dell.com, the customer selects the computer online, customizes it, clicks the "Buy" button, and then tracks the order until it arrives at the front door, shipped directly from the manufacturer. The monitor, shipped in a separate box, may come from a different manufacturer, but Dell synchronizes the delivery so all the hardware arrives at the same time (Figure 5-10). The trade-off, which sacrifices instant gratification of taking the new PC home the same day in favor of lower cost and customization, was a gamble. But it worked, at least for awhile. Dell dominated the PC market with its low cost strategy until rivals mastered their own supply chains. and companies like Apple lured customers back into stores to try out their classy, innovative products.[13]

FIGURE 5-9

Major priorities identified by supply chain managers for 2012.[14]

Supply Chain Priority	Percent of Respondents Rating Priority Among Top Three
Improve efficiency and/or productivity	56%
Reduce operating costs	42%
Improve customer service	46%
Target supply chain contributions to drive business growth	53%

Based on Payne, T., Klappich, C. D., & Eschinger, C. (April 23, 2010). Key issues for SCM IT leaders 2010. Garner Research. ID Number: G00175430.

FIGURE 5-10

Dell's supply chain synchronizes delivery of the monitor with the PC, so they both arrive at the same time.

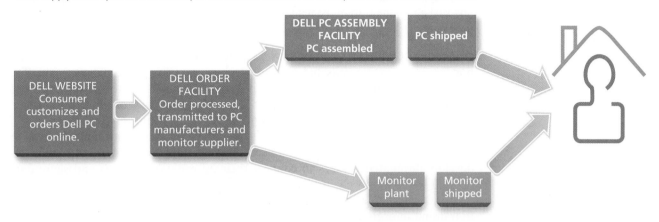

The longer the chain becomes, the more susceptible it is to disruption. A survey of manufacturers in North America, Europe, Asia, and Latin America found that 58 percent reported major disruptions in their global supply chains, with significant financial losses.[15] The most common causes are listed in Figure 5-11. Fuel prices, along with any future restrictions on carbon emissions, will have major impact on global supply chain costs. Managers may need to reconsider the small, expedited deliveries that help keep inventory costs low and supply in sync with demand because their energy cost is high. The e-retailers that rely on small, speedy deliveries to residences will also need to find ways to conserve gas and avoid unnecessary trips.

INFORMATION SYSTEMS AND TECHNOLOGY FOR SUPPLY CHAIN MANAGEMENT

Supply chain management software evolved as a patchwork quilt of specialized tools and applications, often developed to address one aspect of the supply chain puzzle in a single industry. A software collection for a manufacturing company, for example, might include:

▶ Supply chain planning software, to predict demand, synchronize with supply, and optimize the whole network

▶ Warehouse management software (WMS), to manage and optimize inventories, space allocation, shipments, cross-docking, and other warehouse activities

▶ Transportation management software (TMS), to optimize shipping, logistics, and fleet routing and scheduling

▶ Manufacturing execution system, to manage activities and flow through the manufacturing process

▶ Global trade management software, to ensure compliance for cross-border transactions for importers and exporters

Making all these specialized software applications work together is very challenging, but managers need a clear, end-to-end picture of supply chain performance, not fragmented

FIGURE 5-11

Major causes of supply chain disruptions.[15]

Supply Chain Disruption	Percent Reported
Supplier capacity did not meet demand	56%
Raw materials price increase or shortage	49%
Unexpected changes in customer demand	45%
Shipment delayed, damaged, or misdirected	39%
Fuel price increase or shortage	35%

Based on Blanchard, D. (February 1, 2009). Portrait of best-in-class risk management. *IndustryWeek*.

views of each component. Increasingly, vendors are building software that combines several SCM applications and share data. Also, the major vendors that offer comprehensive financial and human resource management suites are integrating SCM functionality into their suites.

COLLABORATION IN THE SUPPLY CHAIN   The secret to excellence in SCM is collaboration, internally among units and externally with partners, suppliers, and customers. The bullwhip effect, for example, can be tamped down if suppliers have real-time access to up-to-date retail sales data, instead of an occasional faxed purchase order from the retailer.

How can organizations share information about real-time inventories and sales? CEOs are understandably reluctant to just hand over a login name and password to suppliers or customers so they can access the company's databases. Instead, firms develop automated bridges to connect their information systems and share data relevant to the supply chain.

Since the 1970s, companies have been using **electronic data interchange (EDI)** to transmit information about orders, inventories, invoices, and other data electronically between partners in a supply chain. This approach to bridge building, which predates the Internet, often relies on private networks and proprietary software and is time-consuming to set up. While it dramatically improves supply chain performance by alerting suppliers and customers about real-time demand, it also tends to lock the partners into their relationship. Having spent so much time and energy building that data bridge, they are less likely to switch partners.[16]

A more recent and flexible way to share information is through electronic markets, relying on the Internet's inexpensive communications and open standards for defining data. Here, buyers can browse products, prices, and stocks for many sellers, electronically placing orders and completing transactions. Electronic markets rely on a shared language, usually XML, to define data and processes. Buyers benefit considerably because suppliers compete for orders. The U.S. Federal Supply Service, for example, is where government agencies can place orders for more than 4 million products using one of three methods: paper forms, EDI, or the Internet-based e-market called GSA *Advantage!* The e-market channel is the clear winner in terms of an perfect orders and timeliness.[17]

Collaborative systems can develop over time as the partners come to trust one another. They also emerge through sheer power, when one dominant partner demands to share information with smaller players. Walmart, Dell, and other very large buyers can insist that suppliers collaborate electronically to improve the overall supply chain. In fact, some large players not only require participation, but they also charge fees for the privilege. Although trust and coercion may seem like strange bedfellows, a study of Chinese companies found they worked together. The best and most integrated supply chains resulted when one company coerced the other, but they still built trust through shared forecasting and planning.[18]

SENSING TECHNOLOGIES   Supply chains benefit from sensing technologies that improve visibility during transit and in storage. Commercial shippers deploy handheld wireless scanners to read the bar codes on packages and upload the tracking number, date, time, and place to servers. On delivery, the scanners capture the signature and upload that as well, to close the loop (Figure 5-12).

The RFID chip attached to the package transmits its own data as it passes by readers throughout the supply chain, at seaports, railway stations, and warehouses. When error-free efficiency is mandatory, the extra expense for RFID tags is justified. Blood banks, for example, can ill afford mistakes. Blood products move through a complex supply chain that starts with the donor and usually ends with a transfusion to a hospital patient. But the process is fraught with errors arising from manual, handwritten forms.[19] In the United States, more than 40,000 units of blood are discarded each year due to record-keeping errors. German and Italian hospitals are piloting RFID tracking to reduce such errors and ensure patients receive the right blood type.

FIGURE 5-12

Wireless scanner captures bar-code information and uploads to supply chain management system.

© Anatoly Vartanov/istockphoto.com

For high-risk supply chains, organizations use a combination of sensors and tracking software. Dow Chemical, for example, must closely monitor the location and status of hazardous materials moving by train. They use satellite communications and sensors in the tank cars, watching for any temperature changes or security breaches. The satellite images also update the nearest emergency facilities in case of an accident.[20]

Global positioning systems (GPS) are a critical feature of navigation and transportation systems. These devices receive signals from 32 orbiting satellites that transmit time and location data, and the GPS receiver computes its own 3-dimensional location based on distances from the three or four closest satellites (Figure 5-13). Location is accurate within a few meters. GPS devices help drivers navigate to their destinations and keep managers apprised of their fleets. Live GPS tracking software shows the speed and location of every vehicle overlaid against live traffic maps (Figure 5-14).

FIGURE 5-13

GPS devices receive signals from nearby orbiting satellites and triangulate location based on the distance each signal travels. Photos/Illustrations: cobalt88/Shutterstock, Mechanick/Shutterstock.

electronic data interchange (EDI)
An electronic bridge between partner companies in a supply chain that is used to transmit real-time information about orders, inventories, invoices, and other data.

global positioning systems (GPS)
Electronic devices which receive signals from orbiting satellites that transmit time and location data; GPS devices help drivers navigate and keep managers in touch with their transportation fleets.

FIGURE 5-14

GPS software tracks the locations of vehicles in a fleet in real time.

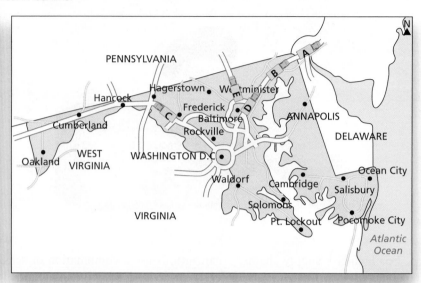

Vehicle	Driver	Start Time	Speed
A	5786	4:05 AM Owings Mills	55 MPH
B	5633	7:15 AM Owings Mills	62 MPH
C	6777	9:00 AM Frederick	41 MPH
D	6554	9:21 AM Owings Mills	68 MPH
E	4001	9:45 AM Baltimore	32 MPH

The supply chain includes the customer, and even the customer's customer. But an organization's relationships with its customers are so critical that special information systems have been developed to help manage them, as we see in the next section.

Define customer relationship management and its role in an organization, and describe the metrics and information systems that support it.

4 Customer Relationship Management

A former World of Warcraft game master who handled in-game customer support lamented the sheer volume of absurd trouble tickets that players submitted:

> "Stupid tickets, yep. As with pretty much every customer service related job, stupid people are to be expected—especially with the main [Warcraft] age bracket. Everything from, 'Rojer called my character fat' to big flaming guild fights, it's all there."[21]

Blizzard, the company behind the massive, multiplayer online role-playing game, recognizes that customer support—even for "stupid" customers—must be first rate. Blizzard's game masters are well trained and equipped with sophisticated technology to help their 10 million+ subscribers. Their software allows them to see the player's quest, check game histories, access vast knowledge bases, chat with players' avatars, return lost weapons, and ban violators. For the videogame industry, in-game customer support is one piece of a much larger picture: customer relationship management.

Customer relationship management (CRM) encompasses the strategies, processes, and information systems an organization uses to build and maintain relationships with its current and prospective customers. Those who have direct interactions with the customer, such as sales reps or customer support staff, are on the front lines, but processes in marketing, sales, accounting, product development, and manufacturing can all benefit from a customer-centric focus.

CRM GOALS AND METRICS

To devise a strategy for building customer relationships, managers need clarity about their actual goals. Some common objectives are:

► Improving customer retention
► Improving profitability
► Growing revenue
► Listening to the customers

IMPROVING CUSTOMER RETENTION Attracting new customers is often more difficult and expensive than retaining existing ones, and the new customer may be less profitable than the old. Strategies for improving retention stress customer satisfaction, loyalty rewards, and perks for returning customers. Farmers Insurance Group, for example, uses analytical software from SAS to analyze customers' lifetime loyalty rates and profitability. Its analysis led to a 14 percent increase in the company's rate of return.[22]

Loyalty and retention can be encouraged in many ways. The U.K.-based holiday travel site called "On The Beach" uses CRM to track customer behavior when they visit the site, noting the travel deals they linger over. Using the data, the company carefully tailors every e-mail to help customers find a perfect beach holiday that matches their tastes. Average retention rate for most travel sites is 18 to 20 percent, but On The Beach boasts retention approaching 27 percent.[23]

Analysts project that companies can reduce the loss of profitable customers by at least 10 percent if they develop a good retention management strategy, which is a very fast return on investment. One metric that organizations gather is simply the number of repeat customers. However, beneath that figure lie other metrics showing *why* customers are returning (or staying away). Close monitoring of the customer satisfaction index is critical, which is why we are bombarded with requests to complete a survey when we visit a website or make a purchase.

IMPROVING PROFITABILITY Finding ways to reduce the costs of serving each customer—without also diminishing customer satisfaction—is another important CRM goal. For instance, innovations that encourage customers to stop phoning the company and use other channels instead are worth the investment. A customer who calls FedEx to ask what happened to her package costs the company $2.40 in human resource time, but the same query submitted to the company's website costs FedEx just pennies to answer.[24] Online self-service applications, such as FedEx's package tracker, improve profitability and also please customers who enjoy unparalleled visibility into their package's journey.

Empowering customers with easy access to inventory levels can improve profitability and boost customer satisfaction even more. Software that shows customers current stock levels at their local stores can save the company a phone call, and save the customer a disappointing trip to the store. As we discussed earlier in this chapter, Apple experienced delays in delivery of its iPhone when it underestimated demand for the new model. The company helpfully posted an "iPhone Availability Tool" to let buyers select their colors and options, and then check whether a nearby store had the model in stock. That window into real-time inventory helped forestall a line of frustrated customers at the mall.[25]

PRODUCTIVITY TIP
Many libraries offer online catalogs with "availability" tools to let students and faculty know whether the book they want is on the shelf or already checked out. Some allow you to reserve or recall the book, and will send you an automated e-mail when it becomes available.

GROWING REVENUE CRM strategies to grow revenue often include finding new customers and markets, as well as earning more revenue from existing customers through tactics such as cross-selling and upselling. The marketing and sales departments champion these efforts, finding new leads, identifying marketing segments, managing campaigns, and building the customer base. They also grow revenue by learning everything they can about each customer and using the data to introduce new products and make additional sales.

Capturing new leads, particularly people who show some interest in your service, is crucial to building your customer base. One innovative strategy to capture motivated buyers at just the right time is the "click to chat" button on a website, which opens up a live chat window staffed by a company agent. Although it is widely used by customers who are having trouble completing a transaction, a more proactive use is to intervene

customer relationship management (CRM)
Encompasses the strategies, processes, and information systems an organization uses to build and maintain relationships with its current and prospective customers.

FIGURE 5-15

Click-to-chat functionality to provide just-in-time customer service.

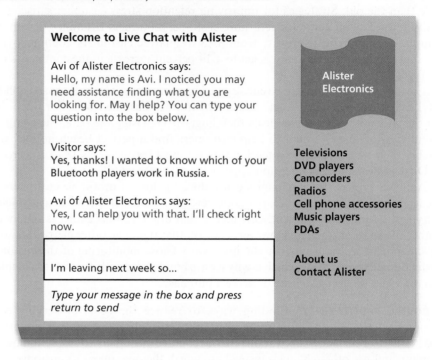

Welcome to Live Chat with Alister

Avi of Alister Electronics says:
Hello, my name is Avi. I noticed you may need assistance finding what you are looking for. May I help? You can type your question into the box below.

Visitor says:
Yes, thanks! I wanted to know which of your Bluetooth players work in Russia.

Avi of Alister Electronics says:
Yes, I can help you with that. I'll check right now.

I'm leaving next week so...

Type your message in the box and press return to send

Alister Electronics

Televisions
DVD players
Camcorders
Radios
Cell phone accessories
Music players
PDAs

About us
Contact Alister

when the visitor is just browsing. A pop-up (Figure 5-15) can appear, offering the customer a chance to chat with a live agent who asks, "Can I help you?" Some research indicates that proactive live chat can increase sales as much as 20 percent.

Some visitors find the sudden and uninvited pop-up alarming, so companies need to think through the psychological aspects carefully. Configuring the software and training the agents properly are critical. For example, the software might be set so that the live chat invitation appears only after the visitor has been browsing for a period of time or seems to be stuck. Knowing when to interrupt is the key to success, and a live chat window should never just appear out of thin air without asking the visitor's permission first.[26]

Live chat in the customer support context offers considerable savings as well. The Internet service provider EarthLink claims savings of $3 to $5 per customer contact, partly because agents can multitask with several customers in different chat windows, rather than just one on the phone.

Total revenue is an obvious metric for evaluating CRM strategy, but that can be broken down further. For instance, managers can collect revenue by product, by sales team, by customer category, or by geographic area. Organizations need finely tuned sales data to learn how their cross-selling or upselling approaches are working. A company whose auto insurance division keeps separate records from its life insurance division will be at a serious disadvantage when its agents are trying to build a well-rounded relationship with the customer.

 LISTENING TO CUSTOMERS When customers answer one of your surveys, CRM software can easily capture and analyze what they say. Some systems can also do **sentiment analysis**, with software that scans the text comment boxes, blogs, or other user-generated content and employs algorithms to classify the opinions as pro, con, or neutral (Figure 5-16). Companies want to know whether customers' online chatter is rising wherever it appears, and especially if it is negative. For example, an online ticketing company called StubHub used sentiment analysis software from Scout Labs to spot a surge in complaints from baseball fans. The stadium mistakenly announced to some ticket holders that a Yankees–Red Sox game was rained out, so the ticket holders requested refunds. The game was only delayed, however, and StubHub initially denied

FIGURE 5-16

Sentiment analysis dashboards can show daily trends in positive or negative blog posts, recent Twitter activity, and other relevant information drawn from social media.

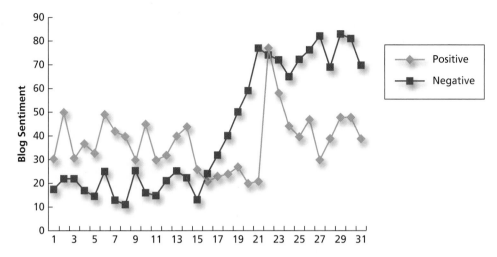

fans' requests. The company quickly reversed that policy when sentiment analysis caught the growing tide of negative posts about StubHub on sports blogs.[27]

CRM STRATEGIES AND TECHNOLOGIES

Since CRM touches so many different metrics and areas of the company, the information systems it uses can be quite fragmented, much like those that manage supply chains. These systems cluster into several categories, shown in Figure 5-17, based especially on the business unit that drives the need for them, the kinds of related services they offer, and the metrics they track.

MARKETING   Marketers treasure CRM applications, drawing on them to manage marketing campaigns, loyalty programs, and customized e-mail programs. Companies use Web 2.0 technologies for marketing as well—publishing blogs, launching social networking sites, and hosting events in virtual worlds.

FIGURE 5-17

Customer relationship management systems support activities in several areas of the company, and integrated suites bring these applications together.

sentiment analysis
A capability of specialized software to scan text input surveys, blogs, or other user-generated content and classify the opinions as pro, con, or neutral towards the company or product.

E-mail marketing is a major focus for CRM applications. JangoMail, for example, offers e-mail marketing software that connects to the company's database to personalize each message. This kind of information system also helps marketing managers tailor each message so that customers who show some particular interest based on their purchases can receive tailored cross-selling messages. A customer who recently purchased a tennis racket might receive an offer for discounted tennis balls. But another customer's golf ball purchase would trigger an e-mail with deals on golf clubs.

E-marketing information systems provide extensive tracking capabilities as well, with detailed reports about customer behavior, showing how many opened the message, forwarded it, or clicked on a link.

Technically, the software accomplishes this tracking by embedding in the HTML e-mail a **web beacon** or **web bug**, which is a tiny, invisible image, typically a single pixel with a unique identifier. The image is actually located on the e-marketing server, and when the customer opens the message, a request is sent from the recipient's computer to retrieve the invisible image and download it. The request includes the date, time, and IP address of the computer making the request, and the unique identifier links the request to the customer's e-mail address as well. Beacons are widely used on websites to track visitors.

PRODUCTIVITY TIP

Although web beacons in e-mail provide very useful metrics for marketers, they raise privacy issues, especially since most people will not realize their e-mail contains the invisible web bug and that their behavior is being tracked. Marketers prefer the term "web beacon" since it sounds less threatening than "web bug," but spammers use the approach routinely to verify that e-mail addresses are valid. To avoid sending tracking information when you open your e-mail, you can set your e-mail client to "text only" so it does not download any graphics, or you can go offline before you open the mail. Unfortunately, neither option is very convenient.

One promising technology that has had a thorny start among marketers hoping to build relationships with hip customers is the virtual world, such as Second Life or Active Worlds. Early attempts to harness these intriguing habitats for CRM failed, partly because of their risqué image, but also because the "inhabitants" objected to any commercialization of their social site. Some protested by holding virtual gunfights inside stores showcasing digital versions of new running shoes. An especially vehement resident detonated a simulated atomic bomb outside the American Apparel outlet in Second Life. Companies pulled out, leaving vacant storefronts.[28]

Some companies are now returning, but they are tightly controlling the marketing venue. Virtualis, Second Life's convention center with large auditoriums, stages, exhibit halls, and breakout rooms, is attracting organizations hoping to reduce travel expenses for "invitation only" events (Figure 5-18). The center offers business-oriented event planning services, and expenses for a 2-day virtual conference for 75 people are a tiny fraction of what a hotel-based event would cost.[29]

FIGURE 5-18

Conference room in a virtual convention center.

Source: Used with permission of VenueGen. VenueGen immersive virtual environments for training and collaboration.

SALES FORCE AUTOMATION   Sales force automation systems boost performance of an organization's sales reps by helping them track and manage their accounts, contacts, leads, and to-do lists. Some systems also help salespeople develop proposals and quotes for their clients and assist managers in evaluating the success of their sales teams. For mobile sales reps, access to CRM applications via the web and by smartphone is essential.

CNN, for example, deployed Salesforce.com to help its sales teams deal with more than 2,000 clients who advertise on the television network. The system is configured with human motivation in mind, especially to encourage sales reps to reach new goals. For example, it provides real-time web-accessible metrics showing number of new accounts for each rep, and it automatically sends e-mails to the whole organization to recognize and congratulate the top performers.

CUSTOMER SERVICE AND SUPPORT   CRM can help organizations make major improvements in customer service and support and reduce costs as well. The click-to-chat feature described earlier is widely used to interact with customers having login problems or other issues. Online knowledge bases and support sites let customers help themselves at any time of day or night, downloading instruction manuals and software drivers. Many companies also try to nurture user communities so that customers can answer each other's questions about the products. IBM, for example, hosts dozens of such communities for developers who use their software tools. The participants discuss issues online and also meet face-to-face in major cities.

Twitter is a handy tool for some kinds of customer support, because followers pick up messages frequently. Washington, DC's Metro subway, for instance, keeps customers informed about service disruptions with tweets to their mobile phones, in addition to the automated e-mails that go out to subscribers. Though tweeting can be very useful and cost-effective, occasional blips occur. Twitter truncates any message down to 140 characters, but Metro workers sometimes forget to shorten the message they just sent out via e-mail:

> "No Line: There is no Blue line train service between Rosslyn & King Street. Shuttle bus service is established. Customers are encouraged to "

Amused followers started tweeting possible endings, such as "go to the closest bar …" or "… ford the Potomac River at their own risk." Cathy Asato, a company spokesperson, said Metro was working with IT to shorten the messages. "It's an evolving tool and we want to make it be the most useful thing it can be."[30]

Call center software can queue calls, let callers know the approximate waiting time, offer menu options for call routing, and retrieve customer data based on the caller's information so agents can quickly find answers. The software can track performance metrics for the agents as well, such as time spent per call or number of escalated calls. Some even assess the caller's stress level through voice analysis, so managers can intervene early. The capabilities of call center systems are expanding to full-featured contact center systems in which agents can interact with customers by phone, through online chat, through e-mail, and inside social networks and community forums mentioned earlier.

Did You Know?

Twitter and the Library of Congress announced in 2010 that every tweet sent since the website's founding will be stored digitally to record how we communicate with 140 character snippets. Will you rethink your tweets? "I could really go for some pancakes" probably isn't a tidbit that merits a place in the annals of American history, but we're sure to find it there.

web beacon (or web bug)
A tiny, invisible image, typically a single pixel with a unique identifier, used on websites to track visitors.

MOBILE CRM APPLICATIONS Mobile access to CRM for employees is essential, but what about customers? Incorporating cell phones into marketing campaigns is certainly feasible, but fraught with hazards. Most people object to unsolicited cell-phone calls and text messages. Sending an invitation to visit a pizza parlor, known from the cell-phone's location to be close by, might provoke irritation unless it also comes with a hefty discount coupon. Offering customers the choice to opt-in helps avoid negative reactions.

PRODUCTIVITY TIP

Many colleges and universities invite students, alumni, and parents to opt-in to particular types of targeted messages, such as sports scores, college news, events, or reminders. Universities typically use opt-in even for emergency notifications transmitted via text messages to cell phones, something you should consider if available.

The cell phone offers endless CRM possibilities, and customers welcome certain approaches. In Germany, for instance, where drivers are legally required to buy snow tires, BMW dealers send customers photos of their car models with options to "try on" different snow tires to see how they look. From within the same cell-phone message, customers can set up an appointment with the dealer, and about one-third of those who receive this customized message come in to buy their tires from BMW.

 Offering something the customer really values is essential. To promote its Huggies diapers, Kimberly-Clark created a program to help with toilet training. Parents can text "bigkid" from their cell phones and then request a free toilet training kit. The website has resources and tips for parents, who can also sign up for the second part of the program to schedule cell-phone calls at designated times—for the toddler. On the other end, a Disney character congratulates the child on his or her progress. To encourage sales, the company tempts parents with more Disney voices and phone messages if they submit proof of a Huggies purchase.[31]

The dazzling array of information systems for finance, human capital, supply chains, and CRM offers tremendous value, but some major challenges as well. Lack of integration is the most severe one, a drawback that enterprise resource planning attempts to solve.

<table>
<tr><td>Explain the importance of ERP systems and describe how they are created, integrated, and implemented.</td><td>5</td></tr>
</table>

Enterprise Resource Planning (ERP): Bringing It All Together

As you saw in Chapter 4, early information systems started out in the last century supporting individual departments: accounting, payroll, human resources, inventory, manufacturing, or sales. Accountants could quickly tally the day's receipts and reconcile their bank deposits. The payroll officer could update salaries in the afternoon and output the payroll checks that evening.

 Nevertheless, the departmental information systems operated as separate "silos," and information sharing was difficult. Business processes that crossed departmental boundaries were fragmented and disjointed, and employees grumbled about delays as paperwork passed from inbox to inbox. Confronted with contradictory reports, managers wondered which ones were correct. Inconsistencies might be due to variations in data formats, definitions, or data-entry procedures. The integrated database for the organization's backend surmounts these silos and provides much more consistency. However, when departments are implementing separate systems from different vendors, each one has its own backend database.

Responding to the need for better integration, major software vendors stepped in to build integrated application suites with functionality for two or more of the core business processes. Early suites arose from systems that supported "manufacturing resource planning," which was software designed for manufacturing companies that helped manage inventories and materials. When the software vendors added capabilities for sales transactions, accounting, human resources, and other common business functions, the software's name was elevated to **enterprise resource planning (ERP)**, to underscore its growing breadth. ERPs have grown well beyond their manufacturing roots and now support back-office business processes for retailers, universities, hospitals, government agencies, and many other organizations.

ERP COMPONENTS

ERP suites, at a minimum, provide a solid, integrated backend that supports the company's core functional requirements. Modules typically include financials and asset management, human resources management, and, if applicable, manufacturing. Increasingly, ERPs add CRM, SCM, and many other applications to create a "suite of suites." Figure 5-19 shows examples of the kinds of functionality that an ERP might include.

Major ERP vendors include SAP, Oracle, Microsoft, Epicor, Infor Global, and others. SAP's Business Suite, for example, offers a vast array of applications going well beyond the basics. Its expanding list encompasses electronic document management, RFID and bar-code tracking, event management, product design, business intelligence, data mining, and more. The company also partners with companies such as Nakisa, which has a rich application for visualizing and managing talent throughout the organization. The partnership makes it easier for clients to integrate Nakisa's product into their SAP environment.

FIGURE 5-19

Enterprise resource planning (ERP) systems typically include financials and human resources and often also support many other business processes.

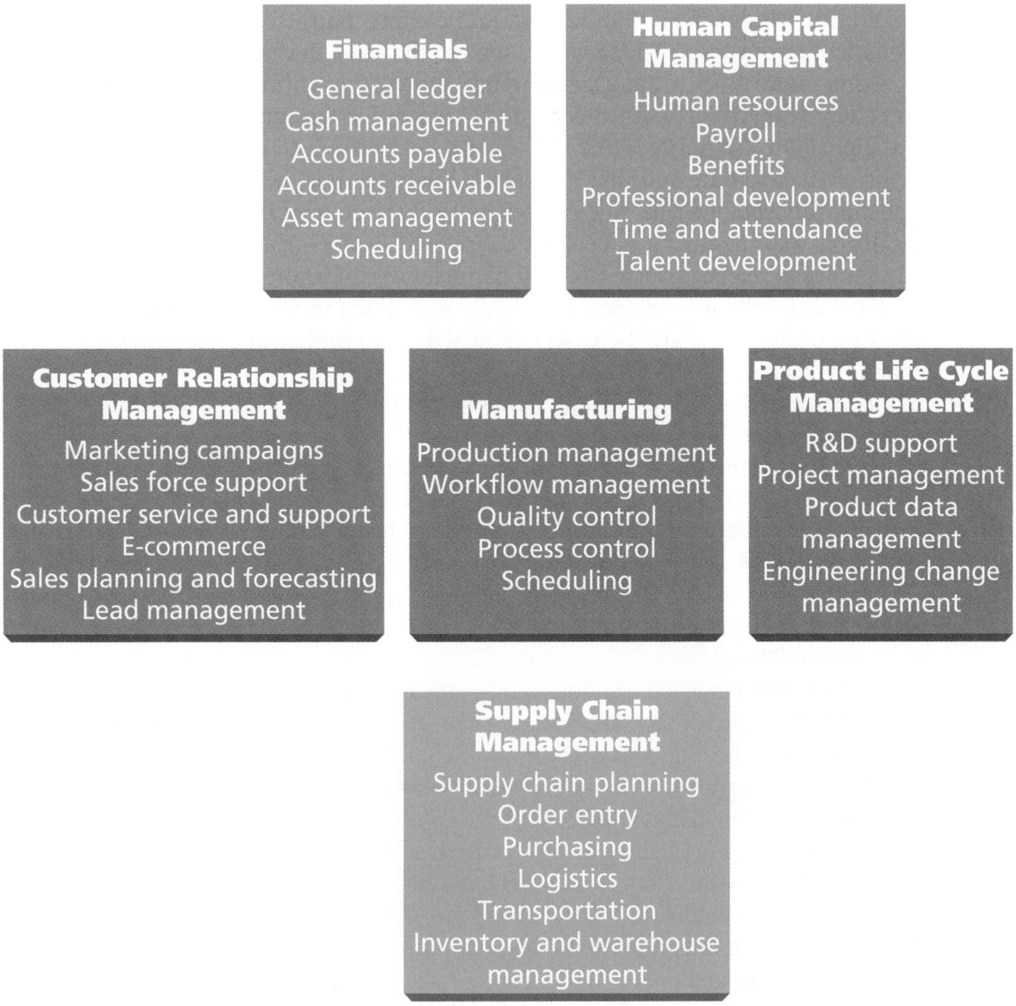

Financials
General ledger
Cash management
Accounts payable
Accounts receivable
Asset management
Scheduling

Human Capital Management
Human resources
Payroll
Benefits
Professional development
Time and attendance
Talent development

Customer Relationship Management
Marketing campaigns
Sales force support
Customer service and support
E-commerce
Sales planning and forecasting
Lead management

Manufacturing
Production management
Workflow management
Quality control
Process control
Scheduling

Product Life Cycle Management
R&D support
Project management
Product data management
Engineering change management

Supply Chain Management
Supply chain planning
Order entry
Purchasing
Logistics
Transportation
Inventory and warehouse management

enterprise resource planning (ERP)
Integrated application suite to support the whole enterprise that includes modules to manage financials, human resources, supply chain, customer relationships, and other business processes.

FIGURE 5-20

Components of an ERP with modules specialized for higher education.

Module	Description
Financials	Tailored for nonprofit, educational institutions, using fund accounting
Human Resources	Human resources and payroll, benefits, time and attendance; system is customized to manage faculty employment conditions, such as tenure and joint appointments
Student Academic Records	Manages classes, courses, student admissions, student registrations, grades, class rosters, faculty assignments
Enrollment Management	CRM tailored to higher education, managing recruitment and retention
Financial Aid	Manages financial aid applications, awards, budgets, and interfaces with aid sources, such as government agencies
Institutional Advancement	Tracks donations, pledges, and gifts, and manages contacts and donor relationships
E-Learning	Provides support for online classes with multimedia presentations, discussion forums, blogs, wikis, assessments, grade books, and other features

ERPs specialized for particular industries are rapidly evolving as well. An ERP for real estate management can manage a portfolio of rental properties, for instance. ERP suites for higher education include modules for managing admissions, grades and academic records, registrations, student advising and degree tracking, financial aid, grants, scholarships, fund-raising, and campus portals. These are bundled with the human resources and financial systems so they can all share data.

Sophomore Ellen Chang's experience shows how an integrated ERP works at her college (Figure 5-20). Ellen is eager to register for the spring semester and logs in to the portal to get started. She first checks her account to confirm that her tuition payment is up to date and that her partial scholarship is there. Next, she checks the academic advising module. She can see how all the courses she's taken so far fit into her degree plan to earn a bachelor's degree in business. Ellen notes that she needs another social science course to fulfill her general education requirements, and since her focus is marketing, she decides to take something in sociology. She searches the schedule of classes, finds SOC 411: Social Demography, and sees that Professor Arnaud is teaching the Monday–Wednesday section that meets at 10 A.M. Clicking on the section, Ellen brings up a map that shows the room location, and a click on the course shows the required textbooks.

When Ellen tries to register, though, she receives a message saying she lacks the prerequisites. Instead, she looks into SOC 100: Introduction to Sociology, and figures she can take the demography course next year. The display shows which sections still have seats, and she registers for one that meets in the afternoon. Professor Darshan teaches that one, and Ellen clicks on the name to bring up a brief bio, office hours, photo, and contact information. She clicks to register and within seconds receives a confirmation e-mail.

Professor Darshan's portal for faculty offers many other self-service tools, such as the ability to update contact information, manage health benefit choices, record expense statements, and view class lists. The class list for SOC 100 now includes Ellen's name and student ID number, with links to Ellen's contact information. When the class is filled, Professor Darshan will send an e-mail to everyone, welcoming them to the class.

On the backend, Ellen's and Professor Darshan's clicks are generating requests to retrieve information from several ERP modules—registrations, academic advising, human resources, financials, and financial aid. The campus portal controls access for each user, and the integrated database ensures that information is consistent, up to date, and unduplicated.

INTEGRATION STRATEGIES

How are the ERP modules integrated so the end users have seamless access to whatever organizational data they need? Figure 5-21 shows the major approaches, each of which has pros and cons.[32]

FIGURE 5-21

Strategies for integrating ERP modules.

Integration Approach	Description	Pros	Cons
The engineered suite	Built from the ground up with consistent user interfaces, integrated backend database, and a single architectural foundation.	Data integrity is high, with consistent, up-to-date, and nonduplicated elements.	Modules are highly interdependent so organizations have to implement and/or upgrade all systems together. Switching costs are high.
Suite with synchronized modules	Vendor provides middleware to connect and synchronize systems that may be running on different platforms.	A common, vendor-provided architecture overlays the systems to improve consistency across the modules.	Modules are integrated at the edges, and the bridges can be fragile.
Vendor-branded or best of breed suites	Separate systems, deployed because they each match user requirements closely, but integration is weak and architectural foundations can be very different.	Modules can have very rich functionality and can be implemented individually, reducing risk.	Processes, interfaces, and data may not be consistent across systems. Connections and synchronization, which can be error-prone and costly, may be done in-house or by vendor.

Some products are built from the ground up, so they are engineered with a single architectural foundation. All the components have similar user interfaces and the backend database shares common data elements. An employee's e-mail address, for instance, is stored in one place and can be accessed by any module that needs it.

Some vendors enhance their ERPs through mergers or acquisitions, so integration must be added later. SAP and Oracle, the two largest ERP vendor, have both bought numerous smaller companies with attractive software. The two giants fought bitterly over Retek, whose specialized software for large retailers fills a gap in the ERP suite. Oracle won, and then the company's programmers raced to build the software bridges between Retek's retailing software and the Oracle financial suite.

Organizations may also implement a more limited ERP from one vendor, but select "best of breed" software for managing customer relationships, supply chain, or some other aspect of their operations. Many universities, for instance, implement an ERP for finances and human resources, but build or buy a separate student information system to match their particular requirements. In these cases, the integration effort is often done by in-house IT staff.

The bridges that attempt to connect different components that might be running on different servers and operating systems are created with software called **middleware**. This software allows one application to access data in another system's database, and it synchronizes data across multiple systems. A customer's e-mail address might be stored in both the finance and CRM modules, and middleware can synchronize the data and propagate an update from the originating system to all the others.

These different approaches have pros and cons. The engineered suite offers solid integration on the backend and consistent user interfaces throughout. Its single architectural foundation can translate to lower IT support costs because staff can focus on just one platform. However, the individual modules may lack all the rich features users want. Also, switching costs are far higher for ERPs in which all the modules are so interdependent.

Another drawback is that tightly integrated ERP systems can be more difficult to modify to meet changing business needs, compared to more loosely linked best of breed systems. What seems like a simple change in the structure of a field will ripple throughout the organization with unintended consequences. In one survey, business leaders complained that the ERP's rigidities were costing them millions in lost opportunities by delaying product launches, mergers, and acquisitions.[33]

Organizations that use either the synchronized or best-of-breed approach must pay close attention to master data management, since the same information will

middleware
Software used as a bridge to integrate separate information systems and synchronize data across multiple systems.

appear in more than one system. Avoiding the fate in which the different systems report inconsistent versions of the "truth" is a constant challenge.

IMPLEMENTATION ISSUES

Implementing an ERP strikes fear into the hearts of CEOs, CFOs, and CIOs alike. Research shows that more than 70 percent of such implementations go over budget and take longer than expected.[34] An alarming number fail altogether. Some studies report failure rates as high as 51 percent.[35] Finger-pointing about what or who is responsible for such dismal success rates and runaway costs is rampant. Even when an organization successfully launches an ERP, the expected benefits and reduced operating costs may be disappointing.

The engineered suite, in particular, can be breathtakingly complex and difficult to implement because the tightly integrated modules are hazardous to launch in phases, one at a time. Instead, organizations use the "big bang" approach, going live with all the core modules at the same time. Simultaneously changing all four tires on a moving car is an apt analogy.

 To a large extent, the software requires people throughout the organization to change the way they handle processes, so extensive training before going live is the essential key to success. In principle, the ERP's way of dealing with any particular process embodies best practices, but the organization's old way of doing things might be quite different. It is not just a matter of learning a new software interface to buy some sandwiches for the company's retreat, or hire a temporary receptionist. The new processes can involve massive changes in terminology, workflow, approvals, and accounting entries.

Success also depends on choosing the ERP that best matches the company's needs. For instance, failures are not uncommon when an ERP developed in one country is marketed to businesses in other locations. Language problems are just one obstacle. The best practices might also be different, and the complexity far more than needed. Some Chinese companies, for instance, gave up on implementing foreign-developed ERPs such as SAP. Yu Min, board chairman of a Chinese furniture company, said, "[SAP] is like a Ferrari sports car which runs great on the highway. But it cannot run fast on China's bumpy road. Besides, you cannot find a Ferrari auto shop when it has problems."[36]

ERPS AND SOFTWARE-AS-A-SERVICE (SAAS) The drive to lower implementation costs is pushing vendors toward offering ERPs as software-as-a-service (SaaS) products, in which companies pay subscription fees to access the vendor's software remotely, via the web. Small and medium businesses with limited IT budgets are especially interested in this model because they can usually get up and running more quickly, and they don't need their own data center. Salesforce.com, with its online CRM applications, was an early SaaS vendor, and NetSuite offers access to its online ERP. Larger enterprises are looking closely at the model as well, and market leaders SAP and Oracle are developing SaaS versions of their own products.

Although SaaS has many advantages, security and privacy are significant concerns. CEOs are reluctant to house their most valuable assets on servers in the cloud, especially when other companies, even competitors, might be tenants sharing the same servers. Although data on a company's own servers are certainly vulnerable to leaks and attacks, management at least feels some sense of control.

SaaS ERP solutions also may take longer to implement than managers expect. They are not really "instant on" products, and they require just as much training and reengineering of workflows as the on-premise versions. Though IT staff don't install and maintain servers and software, people must configure the software, prepare data for migration, manage the implementation, and train everyone on the new procedures. Interfaces with other systems in place may also be needed to synchronize data.

ERP PROS AND CONS Despite the implementation hurdles, the ERP, at least to integrate finance and human resources, is becoming a near necessity for most organizations. Once in place, it can dramatically enhance operational efficiencies and reduce costs. A key ingredient, of course, is that the organization's employees actually change the way they work to take best advantage of the integrated backend. Indeed, while companies such as Dow Corning, IBM, and Texas Instruments reaped huge savings from their implementations, others are disappointed by lackluster results.[37]

With all its pros and cons, the ERP is, as one business leader put it, something you can't live with and can't live without. Used properly, it can standardize and streamline business processes across the whole enterprise, eliminating the waste and redundancy that creep in when everyone's work is so focused on a single department. An ERP helps people appreciate the full process, spanning departments, not just the part that touches their unit.[38]

Compared to a tangled thicket of poorly integrated systems with rickety electronic bridges running between them, the ERP is an elegant racehorse. It certainly needs a new name, though, given that few remember its roots or what the acronym stands for.

MyMISLab | *Online Simulation*

Custom Cakes

A Role-Playing Simulation on Enterprise Information Systems and the Supply Chain

The CEO of Custom Cakes is not happy. "Not again! Seems like every day we are either out of stock— which makes our customers mad—or we're loaded with excess inventory that didn't sell. So today it's the line of frustrated customers. I hope you can fix this supply chain and get a handle on that bullwhip effect!"

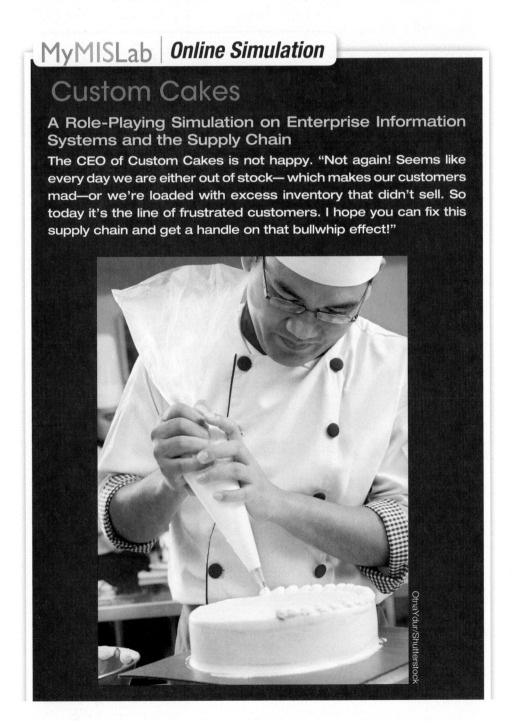

OtnaYdur/Shutterstock

Custom Cakes is a store in the mall that sells delicious layer cakes with white icing. Inside each box is a special kit with a packet of decorations and several tiny tubes of colored icing that customers use to write their own message on top. Procrastinating customers who forget to order party cakes in advance really appreciate those kits, and also buy templates so their cake writing looks more professional.

The company is growing fast, and most of its information systems are supporting business processes well. But its growth is hampered by lost revenue because of supply chain problems. The former assistant manager did his best, but now its your turn. As the new assistant manager, your job is to get familiar with the company and its information systems, and then take on the supply chain problem. Log in when you are ready to get to work...

Chapter Summary

1. The four major categories of information systems that support business processes common to most organizations include finance and asset management, human capital management (HCM), supply chain management (SCM), and customer relationship management (CRM). Finance and asset management systems incorporate modules to support accounts payable, accounts receivable, procurement, cash management, budget planning, asset management, general ledger, and financial reporting. Compliance reporting has become especially important for financial systems, with stringent regulations that require electronic reporting using XBRL, a business report language in the XML family intended to make reports more transparent, consistent, and computer-readable.

2. Human capital management systems include core human resources functionality, along with other modules that support a broader range of employee-related applications. Workforce management software offers labor-scheduling tools, and also tracks time and attendance, leave, and project assignments. Talent management helps map the employee life cycle, from recruitment through career development, and to retirement. Social software is also sometimes included, especially to encourage mentoring. Metrics from these systems, including performance and productivity measures, can help reveal how well an organization is managing and nurturing its human capital.

3. Supply chain management supports processes that optimize the flow of products and services from their source, through the company and to the customer. The Supply Chain Operations Reference model describes five steps for supply chain management: (1) plan, (2) source, (3) make, (4) deliver, and (5) return. Improving visibility in a supply chain helps managers see metrics that help assess overall effectiveness, in a retailer's real-time sales, for example. The bullwhip effect occurs in a supply chain when visibility is low. Collaboration to improve visibility among suppliers and customers uses electronic data interchange (EDI) or XML. Sensing technologies such as RFID and GPS also help improve visibility.

4. Customer relationship management revolves around customer records, especially to improve retention, increase profitability, grow revenue, and listen to customer sentiments. CRM's diverse software applications are especially useful in marketing, sales force automation, and customer service and support. Included in this category are software tools to support e-mail marketing, loyalty programs, marketing campaigns, online customer service, contact management, sentiment analysis, mobile phone advertising, and more.

5. Enterprise resource planning (ERP) systems integrate two or more of the applications that support major business processes common to most organizations, especially finance and human resources. ERPs from major vendors incorporate functionality for CRM, SCM, manufacturing processes, analytics, and other business requirements as well. Some ERPs have tightly integrated modules, while others synchronize data across modules that are more loosely integrated, using middleware. Implementing an ERP is a major challenge, partly because so many applications are replaced and so many processes affected at the same time. SaaS versions are being offered, which can be easier for some organizations. Despite the hurdles, most organizations find the integrated ERP solution very valuable, especially for finance and human resources.

Learning Objectives

KEY TERMS AND CONCEPTS

financial management system	workforce management module	demand forecast accuracy (DFA)	sentiment analysis
eXtensible Business Reporting Language (XBRL)	talent management	bullwhip effect	web beacon (web bug)
human capital management (HCM)	supply chain management (SCM)	electronic data interchange (EDI)	enterprise resource planning (ERP)
human resources management system (HRM)	Supply Chain Operations Reference (SCOR)	global positioning systems (GPS)	middleware
	visibility	customer relationship management (CRM)	

CHAPTER REVIEW QUESTIONS

1. What are the four major categories of information systems that support business processes common to most organizations? Which basic business functions does each provide?

2. What role does a financial and asset management information system serve in an organization? Why is financial reporting important? What are exception reporting and compliance reporting? Why is each important?

3. What is human capital management? What are the major components of a human capital management information system? What are examples of metrics used to quantify human capital? How are these metrics used?

4. What is supply chain management? What is the most important metric in supply chain management? What does it measure? What are examples of supply chain management software? How is each used to support supply chain processes?

5. What is customer relationship management (CRM)? What are the objectives of CRM? How do organizations measure their customer relationship? How do information systems support each objective of CRM? What are three basic categories of CRM technologies? How do information systems support activities in each area?

6. Why are ERP systems important to organizations? What are the typical components of an ERP system? What is meant by the term "a suite of suites"? What are three approaches to ERP integration? What are some of the issues associated with an ERP implementation? What is the success rate for ERP implementation? What is the primary benefit of a successful ERP implementation?

PROJECTS AND DISCUSSION QUESTIONS

1. Sensing technologies are everywhere in the supply chain. Describe some of these sensing technologies and discuss the benefits they provide. Search the Internet to learn more about one of these technologies and how it is used in the supply chain. Prepare a 5-minute presentation of your findings.

2. Do you tweet? Twitter claims its users are sending 50 million tweets a day. That's a lot of Twitter chatter! What is sentiment analysis? How do organizations use sentiment analysis to manage customer relationships? Visit www.tweetfeel.com and enter the name of your city to learn what Twitter users are saying about your hometown. Then visit www.tweetfeel.com/biz to learn how organizations can use this online tool to improve customer relations. Describe how TweetFeel works. What are search sets? Does TweetFeel work in real time? How do you think Twitter chatter will change when users learn it is being monitored?

3. Does your college or university let you sign up to receive emergency alerts on your cell phone? What are the advantages of this system? How does this differ from using mobile devices for marketing purposes? What are the challenges of implementing mobile CRM targeted to customers? Describe several approaches to mobile CRM that are welcomed by customers. What are the advantages to employees of providing them mobile access to CRM?

4. Many colleges and universities use Banner, a higher education software ERP system. Describe the ERP system at your college or university. Compare the modules described in Figure 5-20 to the system components that you access during the semester. Which modules do you use? How do you use those modules? Which modules are used by university faculty and staff?

5. Many CRM systems are integrating social networking technologies to improve customer relationships. Search several social networking sites such as Facebook, Twitter, and YouTube to identify how a specific company such as Dell, Coca-Cola, or McDonald's is using social media to interact with customers. Prepare a 5-minute presentation of your findings.

6. Work in a small group with classmates to identify the types of information that you would need for an HCM module to help you identify individuals in an organization that have the potential for promotion. How would you use this information to manage high potential employees?

APPLICATION EXERCISES

EXCEL APPLICATION:
Performance Bicycle Parts

Ted Stevens owns an Internet-based bicycle accessories website that sells bicycle tires, tubes, chains, sprockets, and seats, as well as helmets and water bottles. The bicycle parts aftermarket is very competitive, and Ted realizes that having both a low price and sufficient inventory to offer same-day shipping are critical to his success. He has a global supply chain and relies on many different supplier sources for the quality products his customers demand.

FIGURE 5-22

Suppliers for Performance Bicycle Parts.

Supplier	Shipping Days	Per Unit Base Cost	Per Unit Shipping Cost	Import Duty %	Per Unit Import Duty Cost	Per Unit Warehouse Cost	Average Inventory (Units)	Average Inventory Value	Total Inventory Carrying Cost	Average Per Unit Carrying Cost	Per Unit Total Cost	Gross Profit	Percent Gross Profit
United States	4	$ 3.90	$ 0.25	0									
South Korea	120	$ 1.70	$ 0.80	4%									
India	160	$ 1.60	$ 1.10	3%									
Russia	140	$ 1.35	$ 0.95	6%									
Vietnam	100	$ 1.55	$ 0.75	4%									
China	110	$ 1.65	$ 0.85	5%									

Ted sells more replacement tubes than any other product. For this item, customers expect high quality at a competitive price. Ted spent several months evaluating the quality and performance of six potential suppliers for the most popular replacement tube, the 29 × 1.85−2.20" presta tube. These suppliers manufacture replacement tubes of comparable quality and performance. With the right price, quality, and availability, Ted expects to sell an average of 12,000 tubes per month, or 400 tubes per day for $6.50 each. However, he is concerned about the amount of cash or working capital required to support the level of inventory he needs to provide same-day shipping.

Use the information provided in Figure 5-22 to create a spreadsheet to analyze the replacement tube cost structure for six potential suppliers. Per unit import duty cost equals the import duty rate multiplied by the sum of per unit base cost and the per unit shipping cost. The per unit warehouse cost is the sum of the per unit base cost and the per unit shipping cost and the per unit import duty cost. The per unit total cost is the sum of the per unit warehouse cost and the average per unit carrying cost.

Required inventory levels are based on projected daily sales times the number of shipping days required for delivery from the supplier to Ted's warehouse. A longer delivery time requires Ted to maintain a higher level of inventory. Thus he wants to include inventory carrying costs in the analysis. Ted maintains average inventory (units) based on 150 percent of projected daily sales multiplied by the number of shipping days from the supplier. The average inventory value equals the per unit delivered cost multiplied by the average inventory (units).

Inventory carrying costs include the cost of putting away stock and moving material within the warehouse, rent and utilities for warehouse space, insurance and taxes on inventory, and inventory shrinkage. Ted calculates his total inventory carrying costs at 24 percent of the average inventory value. The average per unit carrying cost equals the total inventory carrying cost divided by the total number of units sold per year (144,000).

Which supplier source requires the highest investment of working capital or cash for average inventory? Which supplier source provides Ted with the highest percentage of gross profit on the presta replacement tube?

ACCESS APPLICATION:
VSI Consultants

VSI Consultants Group, Inc., is a professional IT consulting firm that provides business and nonprofit organizations with the highly skilled IT professionals they need to complete IT projects and resolve staffing problems. VSI matches employees with client projects based on employee education, skills, and experience. Emily Loftus, the HR manager, has asked you to use the information provided in the spreadsheet shown in Figures 5-23, 5-24, and 5-25 to create an Access database to manage employees and projects. You can download the Excel file Ch05Ex02, and import the worksheets to tables in your database. Emily wants you to create two queries. The first query identifies the best candidates for three client projects: U.S. Brokerage, Helen's Clothiers, and Solar Systems. The second query matches employees with projects. Specifically, she wants to match projects for two employees: Y326 and T871. What other queries may be useful to Emily?

FIGURE 5-23

Employee data.

	Employee ID	Last Name	First Name	Undergraduate Degree	Advanced Degree	Yrs. Exp.	Skills
				Employee Data			
3	V321	Victor	Albert	BS Computer Sciences	MS Computer Sciences	3	1,3
4	J045	Johns	Carl	BS Mathematics		2	2,5
5	B195	Barton	Alice	BS Management	MBA	1	1,5
6	C013	Cox	Amanda	BS Accounting		3	2,5
7	Y326	Yee	Han	BS Accounting	MS Accounting	6	5
8	W821	Watson	Helen	BS Computer Sciences		8	2
9	J342	Johnson	Sally	BS Education		7	3,4
10	T078	Thornton	Robert	BS History		4	3
11	R430	Randal	Joyce	BS Economics	MBA	2	5,6
12	N541	Nottingham	Henry	BS Mathematics		3	1,2
13	C427	Cary	Jane	BS Computer Sciences	MS Computer Sciences	5	1,5
14	U039	Underwood	Frank	BS Accounting		2	4,5
15	M432	Morgan	Thomas	BS Mathematics		7	4
16	P549	Palmer	James	BS Electical Engineering		5	2,4
17	B130	Boston	Matt	BS Computer Sciences	MS Computer Sciences	3	4,5
18	S0343	Soloman	Robert	BS Computer Sciences		6	2
19	F430	Francis	Tom	BS Logistics		2	4,5
20	T871	Trenton	Mary	BS Mathematics	MS Mathematics	3	2,4
21	A321	Alverez	Hernando	BS Computer Sciences		4	1,2,4

FIGURE 5-24

Skills data.

	A
1	**Skills**
2	1 = Data base management
3	2 = Business Intelligence
4	3 = Web-design
5	4 = ERP Systems
6	5 = Project management

FIGURE 5-25

Open projects data.

	Client	Project Type	Min. Exper.	Basic Skills	Add'l Skills	Preferred Degree
1			**Open Projects**			
3	JM Logistics Inc.	1	4	1	4	BS CS or Math
4	Jefferson Automotive	4	5	4,5	1	MBA
5	World-wide Sourcing	2,4	5	2	4	BS Accounting or MBA
6	Solar Systems	2	2	2		BS Math, BS CS, BS Acctg.
7	Robert's Heating Supply	3	2	3		none
8	Casual Dining, Inc.	2	3	2	1	BS CS
9	U.S. Brokerage	1,2	5	1,2	5	BS CS, BS Math. Or MBA
10	Computer Chips, Inc.	4	3	4,5	1	none
11	Southeast Region Youth Ministries	1,2	4	2	1	BS CS or Math
12	Huston Power Co.	1	5	1		none
13	Helen's Clothiers	4	3	4	1	BS CS, BS Acctg., BS Math.
14	McMasters Printing	3	2	3		none
15	United Grocers	4	5	1,4	5	MBA
16	Shelby County Women's Shelter	1	2	1	5	none
17	National Distributors	1,3	5	1,3	2	BS Accounting

CASE STUDY #1

Helping the Homeless: A Customer-Centric Approach with CRM Software

Banita Jacks and her daughters fell through one crack after another in the maze of government-funded human services in the District of Columbia. Jacks sought help at least 23 times from 11 different agencies, but their separate information systems made it difficult for any of them to obtain a complete understanding of the family's desperate plight. Federal marshals finally visited their row house, where the mother had been living with her dead daughters' bodies for more than 7 months. At her trial, Jacks claimed the children were possessed by demons, and she is now serving a 120-year prison sentence.

The poorly integrated systems left giant information gaps that hampered agencies trying to help. For example, Child and Family Services received an anonymous hotline tip that the mother must be neglecting the girls, but since the agency didn't have any home address, no caseworker followed up. Other agencies had an address, but their systems didn't track the complaint. Teachers at the girls' school attempted unsuccessfully to contact the family when they were absent, but they knew nothing about the neglect charge. Information wasn't shared, and service workers who handled the family's requests rarely followed up.

Although the outrage over these agency blunders led to investigations and a round of firings, the real problem was in the information systems. Agency directors want to transform the way these systems work by implementing an integrated information system to share data. The agencies need the same kind of customer-centric systems that private industries have when they install customer relationship management (CRM) software. In a financial institution, for example, employees in different departments might see individual events that could be warning signs pointing to a dissatisfied customer. The broker might know that the customer sold stocks and moved the funds to a cash account, or the retirement counselor might receive a call from the same customer, inquiring how to roll over an IRA. With an integrated system, these individual events will paint a picture so that company reps can follow up.

Nevertheless, CRM efforts in human services agencies face challenges that go well beyond those that a company encounters when implementing a CRM and a coordinated approach to customer service. First, lawmakers must approve the project and provide funding. A project of this magnitude could run $10 million or more, and city officials are reluctant to spend such a huge sum on IT when budgets for shelters are being cut, despite overcrowding.

Another concern involves privacy. The Child and Family Services worker, for example, would need access to data on a family's food stamps, disabilities, homelessness, and schooling. Privacy advocates object to legislation that allows widespread access to so much personal information about children at risk and homeless families because it impinges on confidentiality. Special legislation is required to permit such access, and many people oppose it.

Finally, former DC Human Services Director Clarence Carter points to a mindset that resists change. Many people just want to keep doing what they do, because that's how they've always done it. "We are hired and held accountable for the administration of programs, not for the well-being of individuals. That has got to change," said Carter.

Discussion Questions

1. How did the previous lack of integration impact the District of Columbia Department of Human Services' ability to serve its clients?

2. How do challenges of the public sector compare with challenges of the private sector?

3. How do privacy challenges of the social service context compare with challenges of other public services such as traffic enforcement?

4. If you were the D.C. Human Services Director, what rationale would you use to gain approval for the multimillion-dollar investment?

SOURCES: Cherkis, J. (October 8, 2009). Banita Jacks is behind bars. Now comes the $6 million legislation honoring her children. *Washington City Paper.* www.washingtoncitypaper.com/blogs/citydesk/2009/10/08/banita-jacks-is-behind-bars-now-comes-the-6-million-legislation-honoring-her-children, accessed May 15, 2011. Nash, K. S. (2010). Government IT: Fixing service delivery to put customers first. *CIO Magazine,* May 14.

CASE STUDY #2

Winning the War for Talent: The Mandarin Oriental's Talent Management System

"Colleagues" is the term that the Mandarin Oriental Hotel Group uses to refer to employees, and a major goal for this luxury chain is to recruit, train, and retain the most productive people in the hospitality industry. Starting in 1963 with a single luxury hotel in Hong Kong called the Mandarin, the company expanded slowly, acquiring a stake in the landmark Oriental Hotel in Bangkok. That hotel first opened in 1865 and enjoyed a grand tradition, having survived several wars and hosted countless authors, celebrities, and government leaders.

Over the years, the Mandarin Oriental Hotel Group grew to over 40 properties in more than 25 countries, and each became as distinctive as the first two. The company does not want a mono-culture, so each property takes on its own personality to match the local market. But the company's leaders also strongly believe in establishing clear standards and performance indicators for every position and job function. The Hotel Group's HR department in Hong Kong oversees the process so that, for instance, the chef at the Mandarin Oriental in Singapore will be subject to the same standards as the chefs in Boston, Bangkok, and Bermuda. Locally, each hotel's human resources team can tweak policies and procedures, especially because employment law and cultural factors differ. But the underlying standards are global.

To manage this empire and ensure that every hotel contributes to its reputation for unsurpassed customer satisfaction, the company needed a global approach to talent development. With more than 10,000 colleagues speaking many different languages in Asia, Europe, the Americas, and North Africa, the company implemented a specialized talent management system called Profile from the software company SuccessFactors.

Profile provides the building blocks to assess each colleague's performance, and the system also adds a means to determine career development paths and training needs. Both staff and managers can input information about performance, and they can add notes about development plans so that colleagues know what they should do to move ahead. The system also supports succession planning, because every individual's capabilities and career progression are easily accessed. Group Director of HR Paul Clark says, "The system is doing the job of tracking careers with the [Mandarin Oriental] group. It helps us to determine who is ready for the next career step and then actively promote internally." A major advantage is that colleagues are well aware that they have attractive career opportunities, and they know what training they need to pursue them. A side benefit of systems such as this is that the emphasis on career development and interactivity increases the motivation of executives to do performance appraisals with more care.

Companies may never actually win the war for talent, but they must engage in it continually to attract and retain the most productive people. Talent management systems can help them do that.

Discussion Questions

1. How does the talent management system help Mandarin Oriental balance the needs between global coordination and local responsiveness?
2. Why would it be important for Mandarin Oriental to have an integrated HR database?
3. What are the benefits for Mandarin Oriental executives? What are the benefits for Mandarin Oriental employees?
4. What further uses could be possible for the data in this system?

SOURCES: Anonymous. (2009). SuccessFactors supports Mandarin Oriental Hotel Group global growth strategy. S. C. Study. www.successfactors.com/docs/Mandarin_CaseStudy_final_art_CRAIG_approved_JM_0121.pdf, accessed May 15, 2011. Anonymous. (March 2010). Mandarin Orientalwhere. *HRM Asia*. www.: Talent everyhrmasia.com/case-studies/mandarin-oriental-talent-everywhere/40527, accessed May 15, 2011. Needleman, S. E. (2008). Demand rises for talent management software. *Wall Street Journal*. January 15.

E-PROJECT 1   CRM for Human Services Agencies

This e-project explores how human services agencies strive to improve customer relationship management capabilities.

Make a table like the one in Figure 5-26, and then visit the websites of those Departments of Human Services. Attempt to answer the questions for each site, but if you can't find the answer to a question within 3 minutes, enter "Not found."

http://www.oregon.gov/DHS/
http://www.dhr.georgia.gov/portal/site/DHS/
http://www.dhs.dc.gov/

1. How do you compare these departments in terms of how customer-centric their websites are for visitors with different goals?
2. What measures are these human services agencies taking to make it easier for people to obtain services that are designed for them?
3. In what ways could CRM help agencies improve services and reduce costs?

FIGURE 5-26

How customer-centric are human services agencies' websites?

	Oregon	Georgia	District of Columbia
How do I apply for food stamps?			
Where can I find the nearest homeless shelter?			
What services are available for deaf people?			
What should I do to apply if I only speak Korean?			

E-PROJECT 2   Evaluating Employment and Recruitment Websites

In this e-project, you will compare the major publicly accessible career management websites and test their capabilities.

Founded in 1995, Careerbuilder.com holds resumes for more than 30 million job seekers and posts ads from over 300,000 employers about 1 million+ job openings. A chief rival is Monster.com, which pioneered digital recruitment in 1994. Its parent company, Monsterworldwide.com, also offers similar services in other countries with local listings. Both companies earn revenue from fees charged to employers for posting jobs and searching through resumes for qualified candidates, and also from online advertising.

1. Visit each site and check out the "About Us" sections to better understand how the two companies differ. Compare and contrast their vision statements.
2. Imagine you are a hotel manager looking for a job in a major U.S. city of your choice. Compare the positions you find with Monster to those you find with Careerbuilder.
3. Now enter each site as though you are a human resources manager for a luxury hotel, and would like to post a job for hotel manager. Compare the various services and packages that each site offers employers. Which one would you choose to post your ad, and what factors led to your decision?

CHAPTER NOTES

1. Sciacca, C. (2008). IKEA and the suppy chain super hero. http://supplychainsrock.blogspot.com/search?q=ikea, accessed August 16, 2009.

2. Schaeffer, M. S. (2009). Putting expense fraud under the microscope. *Financial Executive.* 25(10), 42–44.

3. Baker, C. R., Biondi, Y., & Zhang, Q. (2010). Disharmony in international accounting standards setting: The Chinese approach to accounting for business combinations. *Critical Perspectives on Accounting.* 21(2), 107–117.

4. Otter, T. (2008). HCM visualization. Gartner Research, DOI: ID Number: G00159248.

5. Otter, T., & Drakos, N. (March 27, 2008). Case study: Dow's formula for social software. Gartner Research, DOI: ID Number: G00156018.

6. Baker, S. (April 23, 2009). You're fired—but stay in touch. *BusinessWeek.* p. 54.

7. Beth, T., et al. (2009). Metrics: HRM's Holy Grail? A New Zealand case study. *Human Resource Management Journal.* 19(4), 375–392.

8. Roth, A. V., et al. (2008). Unraveling the food supply chain: Strategic insights from China and the 2007 recalls. *Journal of Supply Chain Management.* 44(1), 22–39.

9. IKEA. (February 2009). *The IKEA position on forestry.* http://www.ikea.com/ms/en_CN/about_ikea/pdf/IKEAPosForestry_2009.pdf, accessed May 15, 2011.

10. Burrows, P. (December 2, 2010). Will Netflix kill the Internet? *BusinessWeek.* http://www.businessweek.com/magazine/content/10_50/b4207043617708.htm accessed, May 15, 2011.

11. AT&T beats forecast on strong iPhone. *CNNMoney.com.* http://money.cnn.com/2009/07/23/news/companies/ATT_earns.reut/index.htm?postversion=2009072310, accessed May 15, 2011.

12. Klappich, C. D., et al. (December 17, 2008). Supply chain management vendor guide, 2008. Gartner Research, DOI: ID Number: G00163287.

13. Edwards, C. (October 16, 2009). Dell's Do Over. *BusinessWeek.* DOI: 4152, 36–40.

14. Payne, T., Klappich, C. D., & Eschinger, C. (April 23, 2010). Key issues for SCM IT leaders 2010. Gartner Research, DOI: ID Number: G00175430.

15. Blanchard, D. (February 1, 2009). Portrait of best-in-class risk management. *IndustryWeek.*

16. Wallace, P. (2004). *The Internet in the workplace: How new technologies transform work.* Cambridge, UK: Cambridge University Press.

17. Yao, Y., Dresner, M., & Palmer, J. (2009). Private network EDI vs. Internet electronic markets: A direct comparison of fulfillment performance. *Management Science.* 55(5), 843–852.

18. Yeung, J. H. Y., et al. (2009). The effects of trust and coercive power on supplier integration. *International Journal of Production Economics.* 120(1), 66–78.

19. Rodeina, D., et al. (2009). Tracking blood products in blood centres using radio frequency identification: A comprehensive assessment. *Vox Sanguinis.* 97(1), 50–60.

20. Aitoro, J. R. (2009). Unplugged. *Government Executive.* 41(9), 37–38.

21. Gaston. (2007). Interview with a WoW. *GM.* www.notaddicted.com/forums/showthread.php?t=930, accessed September 6, 2009.

22. (2008). Farmers Insurance analyzes customer lifetime value with SAS®. www.sas.com/success/farmers.html, accessed May 15, 2011.

23. (2010). The frontline. *Marketing Week* (01419285). 33(41), 29.

24. (2003). On the shop floor. *The Economist.* 368(8341), 62.

25. Coursey, D. (July 22, 2009). Apple can't meet iPhone demand amid record profits. *PCWorld.*

26. Magill, K.E.N. (2009). Time for a chat? *Multichannel Merchant.* 5(5), 49–51.

27. Wright, A. (August 24, 2009). Mining the Web for feelings, not facts. *New York Times.* p. B.1.

28. Semuels, A. (May 10, 2008). Corporate America's Second Life, *Los Angeles Times.*

29. Morrison, S. (August 19, 2009). A second chance for second life—Northrop, IBM use virtual world as setting for training, employee meetings. *Wall Street Journal,* pp. B.5-B.5. Retrieved from http://search.proquest.com/docview/399087268?accountid=11752

30. Hohmann, J. (August 21, 2009). Metro tweets far from short and sweet (or decipherable). *The Washington Post.*

31. Chang, R. (August 2009). Getting personal with mobile marketing can boost sales, loyalty. *Advertising Age.* 80(27), 14.

32. Genovese, Y., et al. (July 28, 2008). ERP, SCM, and CRM: Suites define the packaged application market. Gartner Research, DOI: ID Number: G00158827.

33. Wailgum, T. (December 15, 2009). ERP's paralysis problem and the repercussions for businesses everywhere. *CIO.com.*

34. Plaza, M., Ngwenyama, O. K., & Rohlf, K. (2010). A comparative analysis of learning curves: Implications for new technology implementation management. *European Journal of Operational Research.* 200(2), 518–528.

35. Chen, C. C., Law, C. D. H., & Yang, S. C. (2009). Managing ERP implementation failure: A project management perspective. *IEEE Transactions on Engineering Management.* 56, 157–170.

36. Yajiong, X., et al. (2005). ERP implementation failures in China: Case studies with implications for ERP vendors. *International Journal of Production Economics.* 97(3), 279–295.

37. Karimi, J., Somers, T. M., & Bhattacherjee, A. (2007). The impact of ERP implementation on business process outcomes: A factor-based study. *Journal of Management Information Systems.* 24(1), 101–134.

38. Woods, J. (February 5, 2010). ERP key initiative overview. Gartner Research, DOI: ID Number: G00173623.

The Web and *E-Commerce*

Chapter Preview

THE INTERNET AND THE WORLD WIDE WEB CONTINUE TO GENERATE WAVES OF CREATIVE DESTRUCTION AS SOME ORGANIZATIONS FLOURISH AND OTHERS STRUGGLE TO SURVIVE. Every enterprise needs a well-thought-out web strategy, one that features its website as its front door. Whether the enterprise actually sells products, solicits donations, or tries to build mindshare and loyalty, its web presence is a focal point for stakeholders—customers, vendors, investors, donors, employees, students, and even competitors. In this chapter, you will learn how organizations develop a web strategy, and how they build and market the site. The web's capabilities and importance continue to grow with Web 2.0 applications that engage users in participation and interaction, and that draw on immense quantities of data from people and sensors.

© Lourens Smak/Alamy

Learning Objectives

1 Identify and provide examples of four goals an organization might choose as it develops its web strategy, and explain how websites are named.

2 Provide examples of different website information architectures, explain the importance of usability and accessibility, and describe how websites are created with various software tools.

3 Explain how e-commerce works, and why security and trust are critical ingredients.

4 Explain how organizations market their websites using search engine optimization and web advertising, and describe some of the challenges of online marketing.

5 Explain how Web 2.0 attributes such as crowdsourcing, expanded data sources, and machine learning capabilities are changing the nature of the web.

Introduction

Beset by readership losses, layoffs, and plummeting advertising revenue, print newspapers are in deep trouble. Some have already gone bankrupt or drastically cut back their activities. It's not that people aren't interested in news. Rather, most won't buy the print version when they can access news from all over the world online for free. Even more appealing, they can now join the conversation, adding comments, debating opinion pieces, and contributing their own breaking stories.

The Internet bulldozed the business model for print newspapers in less than a decade, taking down much of the ecosystem that surrounds it. Advertisers pay less and less for space to reach a dwindling readership, and printing presses stand idle. Reporters, columnists, and editors wonder how they will earn a living when everyone can read their work for free and pass it along to all their friends. Comedian Dave Barry's columns, published by the *Miami Herald* and widely syndicated, are also freely disseminated online. Barry jokes that he once wrote a column about the Oregon State Highway Department's struggle to remove a dead whale, and a youthful fan posted a copy on the Internet without citing him as the author. Years later, people still find it and forward it to him, suggesting he write a column about it. A manager at the *New York Times* lamented, "When a 14-year-old kid can blow up your business in his spare time, not because he hates you but because he loves you, then you have a problem."[1]

The Internet's waves of creative destruction are far from over. To thrive, every organization needs a sound web strategy, one that uses the net to engage customers, motivate employees, compete against rivals, and earn revenue. The website is the centerpiece of an organization's online presence, but the strategy should take into account all the other ways in which people interact or absorb information, from smartphones and e-readers to social media, blogs, and tweets. Even some newspapers have found ways to navigate these choppy waters. *The Wall Street Journal's* successful business strategy combines print with fee-based online subscriptions.

Identify and provide examples of four goals an organization might choose as it develops its web strategy, and explain how websites are named.

1 Developing a Web Strategy

Barely two decades old, the web offers an inexpensive virtual home to any organization, accessible 24/7. An effective website requires a clear vision of the site's goals. Who do you want to attract as visitors, and what do you want them to do while there? What do you want to learn about them, to find ways to improve the site's effectiveness and lure them back?

CHOOSING A GOAL

The primary web goals of most organizations fall into four broad categories:[2]

- ▶ Inform or entertain the audience
- ▶ Influence the audience
- ▶ Sell products or services
- ▶ Facilitate offline relationships

INFORM OR ENTERTAIN THE AUDIENCE Organizations that aim to inform an audience, or entertain people in some way, offer content that drives traffic to the site. To earn revenue, many sell advertising, or offer premium access to specialized content for fee-paying members. Online magazines, newspapers, and video sites usually adopt this goal. The video site hulu.com provides access to thousands of videos, all easily searchable by popularity, category, or genre. Addictinggames.com offers casual amusement, such as shooting games and celebrity spoofs. The games are free, but the site's ads target the likely demographic of the players.

Huffington Post, acquired by AOL in 2011, had been making a profit as an online-only, ad-supported source of news, commentary, blogs, and entertainment, partly by keeping costs way down. Cofounded by socialite and media personality Ariana Huffington in 2005, "HuffPost" hires few paid journalists, relying instead on unpaid citizen journalists and celebrities for much of its content. Actors Alec Baldwin, Ron Howard, Jamie Lee Curtis, and other stars blog there, along with several well-known authors and politicians.

An **infomediary** focuses on informing visitors and empowering them with aggregated information about products from different suppliers. *Consumer Reports*, for instance, tests consumer products in its labs and disseminates information on the results so consumers can compare brands. Many infomediaries are also **e-marketplaces** that facilitate transactions by bringing together buyers and sellers, often from all over the world. Bizrate.com, with its "Search, compare, conquer" slogan, compares sellers on thousands of items, showing buyers who has the best price. Research from PriceWaterhouseCoopers found that a family in the United Kingdom can save £560 (about $888) a year by using such tools.[3]

E-marketplaces are often classified based on the buyers and sellers they serve (Figure 6-1). Bizrate and Expedia, for instance, focus mainly on **business to consumer (B2C)** transactions, in which many suppliers post their wares and consumers can compare them on pricing and features. E-marketplaces also support **business to business (B2B)** relationships. On AliBaba.com, a retailer who needs to restock the inventory for a product can compare wholesale prices, minimum order quantities, payment terms, and delivery times from suppliers in dozens of countries.

Consumer to consumer (C2C) e-marketplaces include eBay and Craigslist. Individual sellers can post their wares, and shoppers use the search tools to find what they want. **Consumer to business (C2B)** relationships, in which consumers sell products or services online to business, are also facilitated by e-marketplaces. A blogger, for instance, might add a link on the blog to a product sold by an e-commerce company. If a blog visitor clicks on the link and buys the product, the company will pay the blogger a small fee.[4] Individual buyers have growing power to negotiate and demand their own terms, thanks to the net.

Government websites also support online interactions, so terms such as G2C, G2G, and C2G have appeared. For example, G2C encompasses services such as online payment for car registration renewals, and C2G might include electronic filing of tax forms.

INFLUENCE THE AUDIENCE   Companies that are not actually selling directly to the public online hope to influence their audience in subtle ways. They might want to increase brand awareness, or persuade visitors to consider new technologies and upgrades. For instance, automobile manufacturers offer numerous tools to construct a virtual car, choose accessories, read reviews, and learn about new options. Procter & Gamble's website (www.pg.com) focuses more on investor relations, business partners, and strategic initiatives in areas such as sustainability.

Nonprofit organizations, political blogs, campaigns, and public service initiatives might also emphasize influence as the primary goal of their web presence, disseminating information and encouraging visitors to get involved with local activities and events.

FIGURE 6-1

Types of e-marketplaces.

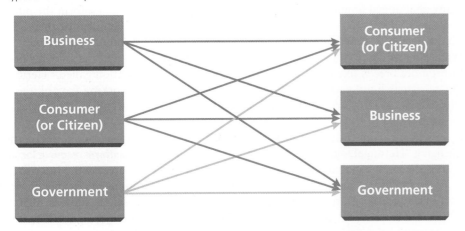

---

infomediary
Focuses on informing visitors and empowering them with aggregated information about products from different suppliers.

e-marketplace
A website that facilitates transactions by bringing together buyers and sellers from all over the world.

business to consumer (B2C)
E-commerce relationship in which businesses offer products for online sale to consumers.

business to business (B2B)
E-commerce relationship in which businesses can buy and sell products or services online to one another.

consumer to consumer (C2C)
E-commerce relationship in which individual consumers can buy and sell to one another over the Internet.

consumer to business (C2B)
E-commerce relationship in which individual consumers can sell products or services to businesses.

SELL PRODUCTS AND SERVICES Selling is the primary goal of organizations whose websites live and die by e-commerce transactions. Overstock.com, iTunes, and Amazon include many features to help visitors find what they are looking for, read product information or reviews, compile wish lists, and buy online. The checkout process on these sites is critical to customer satisfaction. It must include several payment options, easy shipping solutions, package tracking, and simple returns.

Many nonprofit websites feature e-commerce as well, although the emphasis is on donations to worthwhile causes rather than product sales. They must make a convincing case, and then make it very easy for visitors to donate. For instance, a "Donate Now" button is prominently featured on SPCA International's website, an organization dedicated to the safety and well-being of animals.

FACILITATE OFFLINE RELATIONSHIPS For companies such as Royal Bank of Scotland, Takashimaya Department Store in Japan, Abercrombie and Fitch, and Hyatt Hotels, the website's goal is to facilitate and extend offline relationships. The site should build customer awareness of the brand and encourage stronger and broader offline connections. Retail stores might offer online buying with in-store pickup, and restaurants provide directions and discount coupons. India's Taj Mahal Hotel website features special deals, event planning, virtual tours, reward programs, and food preference surveys, along with online reservations.

Websites for colleges and universities typically create engaging tours for prospective students and portals for current students, faculty, alumni, and staff. Along with many online self-service applications, the sites include college news, sports scores, access to digital libraries, and online learning support.

The goal an organization emphasizes for its website will help drive choices about its design, navigation, features, and effectiveness metrics. For example, Suzanne Brace, executive director of Hopewell Cancer Support in Ohio, stressed that the main focus of the group's website should be to get newcomers to attend a welcome meeting. That simple goal drove her team's decision making and helped them avoid costly distractions when choosing features.[5]

NAMING THE WEBSITE

To understand how an organization conceptualizes and implements its web strategy from the start, we'll follow a group of dog lovers who met while on a study abroad program in Thailand. Sharing their interests, they learned about dog breeds that originated in their different home countries, and they also became aware of the fate many abandoned animals suffer. The team brainstormed a way to inform the public about local dog breeds and help fund rescue services in each country for them. The Thai Ridgeback, Japanese Akita, Chinese Pekingese, English Pointer, and American Water Spaniel all play a special role in each country's history, and the students hope to promote breeds like these by creating a nonprofit organization called "Heritage Dogs." Their lighthearted approach will feature social networking capabilities in which dogs get their own profiles and personalities, and owners can post messages on the pet's behalf.

Selecting a name for the website is a critical first step, and the team hopes to grab the name "HeritageDogs.org," if it hasn't been taken yet. The **uniform resource locator (URL)** is the unique global address for a web page or other resource on the Internet.

Every device connected to the net, whether it is your home videogame console or a major corporation's mainframe, has a unique, numerical IP address, such as 10.181.25.56. These IP addresses are not human-friendly, though, so the Internet's designers added the **Domain Name System (DNS)**—the hierarchical naming system that maps a more memorable URL, such as HeritageDogs.org or cnn.com, to the actual IP address. Mapping responsibilities are distributed to many different servers across the Internet, each of which maintains the mappings within its own domain. A great advantage of DNS is that the URL stays the same even if the organization moves the website to a new server with a different IP address. The new mapping will propagate to all the other name servers on the Internet.

COMPONENTS OF A URL   The URL itself is a string of characters, and each component has a specific meaning (Figure 6-2). The letters followed by the colon and forward slashes indicate the transmission protocol used to connect to the resource. The most common is **hypertext transfer protocol (http://)**, which specifies that the resource is a web page containing code the browser can interpret and display. In fact, the http:// is so common that most browsers add it automatically if you enter a string of letters, such as www.mysite.com, without the protocol. Another is **file transfer protocol (ftp://)**, which indicates that the resource is a file to be transferred.

The actual name of the site follows the protocol, as in www.southwest.com, alumni.umd.edu, www.timesonline.co.uk, or whitehouse.gov. The last string of letters is the **top-level domain**, and this can indicate the type of organization or country code. The students chose .org because this top-level domain usually signifies a nonprofit organization, which is what they plan for Heritage Dogs.

The Internet started in the United States as a rather obscure technology used mainly by academics and government researchers, and as a result, the naming conventions are somewhat U.S.-centric. For instance, the top-level domains ".gov" and ".mil" refer only to U.S. government agencies and military. The net's astounding growth led to the adoption of hundreds of additional top-level domains, including all the two-letter country codes from the Ascension Islands (.ac) to Zimbabwe (.zw). Many more have been added to reflect diverse organizations, such as ".museum" or ".travel." Alternatives to the overcrowded ".com" domain include ".biz" and ".info," and new rules passed in 2011 open the door to even more options.

MANAGING DOMAIN NAMES AND VIRTUAL REAL ESTATE   As the maxim goes, the three most important features of real property are location, location, and location. Online property is not that different. Though many more top-level domains are available now, there is still fierce competition to grab the "best" names, those that visitors will most easily remember.

FIGURE 6-2

Components of the web address, or uniform resource locator (URL).

Component	Examples	Description
Protocol Identifier	http://microsoft.com (web page) ftp://myfiles.org (file transfer) https://olympiabank.com (secure web page, supporting encrypted transmission)	Identifies the protocol that will be used to connect to the address following the forward slashes.
Registered domain name	http://mysite.com http://www.etrade.com http://www.umd.edu http://www.edu.cn	Maps to the unique IP address of the destination location.
Top-level domain	http://youtube.com http://www.whitehouse.gov http://www.army.mil http://redcross.org http://www.dw-world.de http://canada.gc.ca	The top-level domain typically indicates the type of organization or the country of origin, such as those below. New rules passed in 2011 clear the way for using brand names, cities, or general keywords as well. .com—commercial .edu—education .org—nonprofits .gov—US federal government .ca—Canada .de—Germany .cn—China .tn—Tunisia
Filename (optional)	http://mysite.com/FAQ.htm	Specifies a particular web page within a site, in this case, one with the file name of FAQ.htm.
Port (optional)	http://mysite.com/FAQ.htm:8080	Directs the connection to a specific port on the server. If absent, the default http port (80) is used.

uniform resource locator (URL)
The unique global address for a web page or other resource on the Internet.

Domain Name System (DNS)
The hierarchical naming system that maps a more memorable URL to the actual IP address.

hypertext transfer protocol (http://)
A URL component which specifies that the resource is a web page containing code the browser can interpret and display.

file transfer protocol (ftp://)
A URL component which indicates that the resource is a file to be transferred.

top-level domain
The last string of letters in a URL that indicates the type of organization or country code.

The students want heritagedogs.org because it nicely reflects their mission and is easy to remember. They can go to one of the domain name registrars, such as www.networksolutions.com, register.com, or www.godaddy.com, to see whether that URL is available. If it is, they can pay a small fee to register it.

The **Internet Corporation for Assigned Names and Numbers (ICANN)** is the nonprofit organization charged with overseeing the net's naming system. ICANN works out contracts with the organizations that manage URL assignments within each of the top-level domains, accredits the registrars who sell domain names, resolves disputes, and establishes policies. For instance, the net's naming system originally accepted only domain names written with the Roman alphabet. Recently, however, ICANN opened the door for domain names in other scripts. Egypt was one of the first to apply to use Arabic script for domain names under its ".eg" top-level domain.[6] In 2011, ICANN also ruled to accept applications from organizations that want to use brand names, city names, or general keywords as top-level domains. URLs may soon end in descriptive strings such as ".nyc," ".paris," or ".Hitachi."

Domain name disputes can be contentious, and complaints escalate every year. Legal battles are common, and companies take quick action if a name is registered with even a whiff of trademark infringement. An Indian travel portal called MakeMyTrip registered oktatabyebye.com, but Tata Sons, the giant Mumbai-based holding company, objected. A Delhi court ruled against MakeMyTrip, even though "ta ta" is a widely used colloquial expression for "goodbye."[7]

A related offense is "cybersquatting," in which someone registers a domain name that is a company's trademark, hoping to resell it to the company at an exorbitant profit. Although laws have been enacted to prohibit such activity, variations on the practice can still confuse web surfers.[8] "Typosquatting," for instance, is registering a replica site with a misspelling in the trademark name that users might easily mistake for the real thing and enter personal information and passwords for the squatter's fraudulent use. The squatter might also display negative information about the actual company, hoping the CEO will pay a ransom to get the name back. Damage to the brand can be extensive, and many companies want to get control over those rogue sites. Verizon, for example, reclaimed thousands of false domain names related to its business and placed links on them to the company's real site. Sarah Deutsche, vice president and associate general counsel at Verizon, thinks the effort well worthwhile: "We're on track to bring in 9 million new visitors, just from the names we've been able to get back."[9]

> **PRODUCTIVITY TIP**
> Your future plans may or may not require you to have your own website, but you might consider reserving a good domain name now for a few dollars a year. Independent consultants and other self-employed individuals might benefit from having their own website, using a common pattern such as www.FirstnameLastname.com. You might also choose other top-level domains, such as .net, .org, .biz, or your country code.

Provide examples of different website information architectures, explain the importance of usability and accessibility, and describe how websites are created with various software tools.

2 Building the Website

Once confined to experienced programmers, the task of building the website has been simplified considerably. Nevertheless, creating a professional and well-designed site containing features that support the site's major goals requires skill and careful attention to visitors' interests and motivations.

WEBSITE DESIGN

The best-designed website is the one that achieves its goals, and many different approaches work. TripAdvisor.com's strategy has made it one of the most trusted sources of travel advice on the web, with more than 25 million monthly visitors and 30 million reviews and opinions. Visitors can quickly tap into the collective knowledge of reviewers to read their unvarnished opinions on restaurants, hotels, cruises, and more. Advertisers in the hospitality and travel industries pay top dollar to post ads relevant to the visitor's query.[10] Someone reading reviews for hotels with golf courses in Scottsdale, Arizona, will see ads for just those hotels, and perhaps special deals on golf clothing. The site can also identify the visitor's location (from his or her IP address) and serve ads about air travel at the same time. The candid reviews contributed by other travelers help build trust in the site, though they can certainly make advertisers squirm. Commenting on a London restaurant, one reviewer said, "Overrated rubbish. Maybe it was just my bad experience but I don't want to go back to see if things have changed. ..."

WEBSITE INFORMATION ARCHITECTURE AND NAVIGATION   Just as an architect designs buildings that are easy to use and aesthetically pleasing, web designers strive to reach similar goals with their site's information architecture. Designers must find ways to organize the information, provide navigational tools, and ensure visitors don't struggle to find what they are looking for and complete a transaction.

Figure 6-3 shows some examples of website architectures. Although visitors can enter a website at almost any location, designers consider the home page as the

FIGURE 6-3

Information architectures for websites.

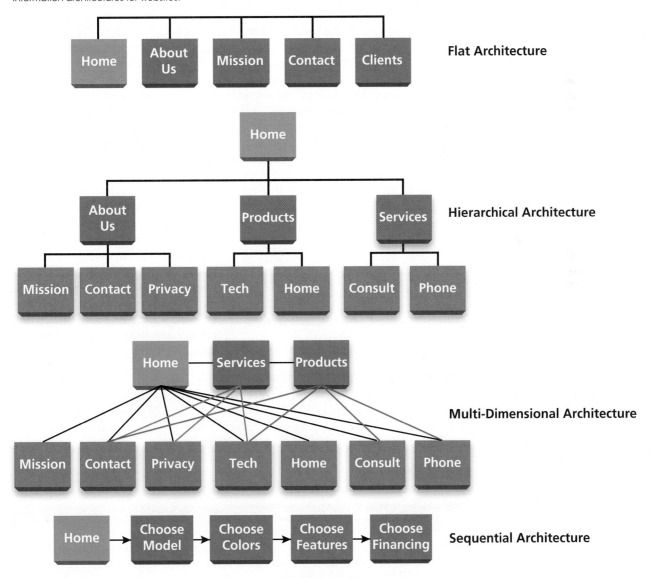

Internet Corporation for Assigned Names and Numbers (ICANN)
The nonprofit organization charged with overseeing the Internet's naming system, establishing policies, and resolving disputes.

conceptual gateway and entrance point, and they build out the information architecture from there. For a very small site, a flat architecture serves well, with a home page linking to four or five additional pages. For larger sites, a common design is the **hierarchical website architecture**, in which the top-level home page contains links to second-level pages, which then link to further relevant pages. For example, Heritage Dogs will use a hierarchy based on countries, so visitors to the home page can drill down to the images and rescue operations for dogs in each nation. Many organizations start out with a hierarchical design, following their own organizational charts or product lines.

The strict hierarchy has appeal, but frustration mounts if visitors drill down the wrong path, looking for information that doesn't easily fit or that spans categories. A prospective student visiting a college website who wants to learn more about the art major will be stumped when the second-level categories list College of Arts and Sciences, School of Performing Arts, and College of Architecture and Allied Arts. Or someone hunting for a horse race's start time in an online newspaper would not know whether to click on Sports, Entertainment, Events, or Activities.

The **multi-dimensional website architecture** recognizes that information can be categorized in many ways, and that visitors need multiple paths through the site. Panasonic's website, for instance, offers links to different visitor categories in the top navigation bar, including consumers, business, and industrial. Along the right navigation bar, it offers links to product lines, such as printers, audio and video electronics, and others. The Maryland Motor Vehicle Administration has links to generic information across the top, including Contact Details, Hours and Locations, Fees, and Forms. Links along the left guide visitors to different types of services such as online registration renewals or information for disabled drivers. Amazon.com helps users browse by department, keyword, and sales promotions. Once in the "Books" department, visitors can browse by even more dimensions relevant to the category, such as best-sellers, bargain books, textbooks, or new releases.

A **sequential architecture** is useful in some settings, particularly when designers want the visitor to proceed step by step through a transaction, survey, or learning module. The example in Figure 6-3 shows how a website might help a shopper design his or her own dream car. Each page would have only one link, often labeled "Next Step."

Search functionality that confines the search to the website rather than the whole web dramatically improves the visitor's ability to find relevant material, particularly on very large websites. One drawback is that a search may retrieve obsolete pages the organization neglected to delete.

PRODUCTIVITY TIP

Search is a powerful tool, but it works best when you use less common words or strings that are as specific as possible. Search for *graphic design* and you retrieve more than 72 million web pages. *Graphic design jobs New York City* retrieves far fewer, and they are more relevant to your search. Putting quotation marks around a string will return web pages with an exact match.

USABILITY AND USER INTERFACE DESIGN **Usability** refers to the ease with which a person can accomplish a goal using some tool, such as a website, a mobile phone, or a kiosk. Does the user struggle to find directions to the company's address? Do many visitors abandon their shopping carts? Figure 6-4 lists several elements of usability that apply to websites.

FIGURE 6-4

Elements of website usability.

Element	Sample Metrics
Ease of learning	To what extent can a user accomplish simple tasks on the first visit?
Efficiency	After learning the site's basic design, how quickly and efficiently can a user perform tasks?
Memorability	When a user returns to the site after a period of time, how much effort does it take to regain the same level of proficiency?
Error rates	How many mistakes do users make when they attempt to accomplish a task, and how easy is it to recover from those mistakes?
Satisfaction level	How do users rate their experiences on the site? Do they describe it as pleasant and satisfying, or frustrating?

FIGURE 6-5

Designers use color to manage the visitor's attention on a web page.

Usability relies partly on clear information architecture, and also on the user interface design. For example, designers use color to manage the user's attention, drawing on principles of visual perception. Bright red—especially against a darker background—attracts the eye. That color is very often used for the DONATE NOW! button on nonprofit websites. Note how the red button on the left side of Figure 6-5 seems to leap out, even though it is the same size as the dark blue button on the right. Figure 6-6 lists basic tips for designing an effective user interface.

A good way to assess a site's usability is to ask visitors to perform a sequence of tasks and observe the problems they encounter. At the University of Nevada, Las Vegas, for instance, researchers assigned students tasks related to library research, such as these:

1. Find a journal article on the death penalty.
2. Check whether the library is open on July 4.
3. Locate the most current issue of *Popular Mechanics.*

Even when the designer puts much thought into the website's information architecture and user interface, results from usability tests are frequently disquieting. Visitors easily found the library's hours, but they had trouble finding content because they could not easily distinguish between "Journals" and "Articles and Databases," or between "E-Reserves" and "Other Reserves." They tended to ignore the navigation tabs at the top, and they also found little use for "Subject Guides."[11] Usability tests are critical to help designers improve the site for the people who actually use it, not the ones who design it.

FIGURE 6-6

Tips for effective user interface design.

▶ Keep it structured. Use a clear and consistent design that is easy for users to recognize throughout the site.

▶ Keep it simple. Make the common tasks very simple to do, so users can accomplish them on the first try without frustration.

▶ Keep users informed. Let users know in clear language when something on the website changes, or the user has completed an action.

▶ Be forgiving of errors. Let users easily undo their actions or return to previous states.

▶ Avoid distractions. Especially when the user is engaged in a sequential task, avoid adding unnecessary links or options.

hierarchical website architecture
Website structure in which the top-level home page contains links to second-level pages, which then link to further relevant pages.

multi-dimensional website architecture
Website structure with multiple links to pages at all levels, allowing visitors multiple paths through the site.

sequential architecture
Website structure that guides visitors step by step through a transaction, survey, or learning module.

usability
Refers to the ease with which a person can accomplish a goal using some tool, such as a website, a mobile phone, or a kiosk.

Did You Know?

Sixdegrees.org simplifies donations by offering four easy ways to do it. Click here to donate or volunteer; click here to buy a gift card for a friend to donate to a charity of his or her choice; click here to use a gift card; and click here to create a charity badge. It's a creative approach, with effortless usability.

WEB ACCESSIBILITY FOR PEOPLE WITH DISABILITIES **Web accessibility** refers to how easily people with disabilities can access and use web resources. Impaired vision, hearing loss, limited motor skills, and other kinds of disabilities can hinder or even block people from using the web. In the United States, the disabled comprise almost 20 percent of the population, a figure expected to grow as the population ages. Studies of *Fortune* 100 websites show that while most large companies have made some improvements, hurdles remain for many users.[12]

The Web Accessibility Initiative (WAI) develops guidelines for web accessibility that are widely regarded as international standards. It also offers tutorials and tips to help organizations improve their sites and understand how design techniques can radically alter a site's accessibility. Its site (www.w3.org/WAI) offers links to a variety of software tools that designers can use to check a site's accessibility against the guidelines and that provide useful reports. Fujitsu, for instance, offers free software to assess how legible text and background color combinations will be for people with cataracts or color blindness (Figure 6-7).

Assistive technologies to help people with disabilities range from the low-tech magnifying glass for the visually impaired to motorized wheelchairs. For using the web, mouse foot pedals, screen readers, Braille displays, head-mounted pointers, joysticks, and speech-to-text translators for the deaf can all improve access. Figure 6-8 shows a wireless device that tracks small head motions and converts them to mouse movements, designed for people with limited use of their hands.

Designers should address accessibility issues in the site's information architecture, with design elements that meet the needs of a wider range of users and work well with assistive technologies such as screen readers. Figure 6-9 lists some dos and don'ts for web designers.

PRODUCTIVITY TIP
Browsers incorporate a variety of accessibility features you can configure. For example, the Windows shortcut to increase text size for Internet Explorer and Firefox is to hold the Control key down and press the plus sign. On a Macintosh, the shortcut for Safari is Command+.

✹ THE ETHICAL FACTOR Corporate Social Responsibility and Website Accessibility: Why Is Progress So Slow?

Why are organizations so slow to make their websites accessible to people with disabilities? In a survey of corporate web masters and other specialists, a majority cited lack of knowledge and inadequate training.[13] But more than half also agreed that there is a conflict between usability and accessibility, suggesting that many developers assume an accessible website will have to bypass many of the rich features and graphical elements that make them pleasing and attention-getting. Forty-nine percent agreed that "it is impossible to cater to all users' needs."

Although the challenge of creating accessible websites is not trivial, organizations can make tremendous progress by building in accessibility from the start. A common obstacle for visually impaired people, for instance, is a button that can only be accessed with the mouse. One university's new virtual student union had that flaw on its "Let's get started!" button, so blind students couldn't ever get started.[14] But it is just as easy to program the button to also respond to a key press, if the designers keep that feature in mind.

Though many organizations see efforts to improve accessibility for people with disabilities as additional costs, others are learning that accessibility adds strategic benefits in the form of heightened corporate social responsibility and Internet visibility. Making the site more accessible from the beginning also broadens the potential base of customers and thus makes good business sense.

FIGURE 6-7

Software tools can help designers audit website accessibility. Fujitsu's free color selector software alerts developers when their color combinations for background and text may be unreadable for people with cataracts or one of several types of color blindness.

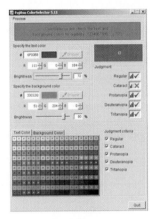 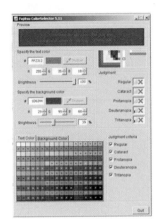

Source: www.fujitsu.com

FIGURE 6-8

Wireless sensor mounted on the laptop picks up tiny head movements from the small blue tracking dot on the boy's forehead, and converts the motion to mouse movements. The HeadMouse® Extreme from Origin Instruments is designed for people with limited use of the hands.

Source: Provided by Origin Instruments Corp.

FIGURE 6-9

Design tips for improving website accessibility.

Do:
Add alternative text tags for every image, so visually impaired people know what the image is.
Use self-explanatory links. Use "More on cosmetic dentristy" rather than "click here for more."
Make bold headings, short paragraphs, and orderly paragraph arrangements, so screen readers follow the flow correctly.
Create text-only alternative versions for devices such as PDA or mobile phone.

Don't:
Use fixed text sizes, which may make it impossible for visually impaired people to use the site.
Create very tiny clickable areas, which hinder those with limited mobility or motor function.
Implement forms that require a mouse click, which prevents keyboard-only users from typing in their information.
Use overly complicated designs with no simple alternative for browsing on a PDA or mobile phone.

web accessibility
Refers to how easily people with disabilities can access and use web resources.

assistive technologies
Devices and software that help people with disabilities, such as screen readers for the visually impaired.

FIGURE 6-10

Major web browsers.

Web Browser	Market Share	Description
Microsoft Internet Explorer	65%	Microsoft bundled its browser with the Windows operating system in 1995 and established dominance in the "browser wars."
Mozilla Firefox	25%	Developed in the open-source model, Firefox has a loyal following with its many useful add-ons, such as one that blocks all advertising.
Apple Safari	4%	Dominant browser for Macintosh computers.
Opera	2%	Not widely used on PCs, but installed on many mobile phones due to its "lightweight" footprint.
Google Chrome	4%	Google's web browser, developed using the open-source model.
Netscape Navigator	~0%	Introduced in 1994 by Marc Andreessen, the leader of the Mosaic team. Netscape quickly captured 90% of the market but eventually lost the battle with Microsoft.
Mosaic	~0%	Introduced in 1993, the now defunct Mosaic was one of the first graphical web browsers. It helped fuel the explosion in web use.

SOFTWARE DEVELOPMENT STRATEGIES FOR THE WEB

Creating the website can be as simple as typing into a word processor and uploading some files, or as complicated as writing thousands of lines of code from scratch. The goal is to create pages that a visitor can access with a **web browser**—the software application that retrieves, interprets, and displays web resources. Figure 6-10 lists some examples of web browsers, all of which are free to end users.

PRODUCTIVITY TIP

Common browsers support an enormous variety of add-ons you can install to boost your productivity and customize your web browsing. Ad blockers, Flash blockers, spyware protection, Facebook toolbars, to-do lists, reminders, web page previews, and news feeds are just a few examples. Be selective, though, since some add-ons, or just too many of them, can impede your browser's performance.

HTML The original language used to create web pages is called **hypertext markup language (HTML)**, which specifies the web page's format and helps put it into reader-friendly output. The language uses tags in angle brackets that browsers can interpret (Figure 6-11), such as <p>, to indicate the start of a new paragraph. Usually, the page will still appear even if you have many mistakes in the tags, though it may not be formatted quite the way you intended in all the browsers. Competitive battles for market share often lead browser developers to add special features and proprietary tags that work only with their own browser, creating headaches for software developers who must test their code in one browser after another.

Variations and improvements on HTML are released periodically, particularly to extend the language's capabilities and integrate it more closely with XML, the

FIGURE 6-11

Example of how hypertext markup language (HTML) formats text and a link on a web page.

language used for defining data on the web described in Chapter 4. Change can be frustratingly slow, however, because people around the world use so many browsers and browser versions, and websites containing older features are widespread.

CREATING INTERACTIVE, MEDIA-RICH WEBSITES Static web pages with just text and graphics are just the beginning, and many other approaches are used to bring media-rich, interactive experiences to the web. For example, **Javascript** is a very popular language used to add interactivity to web pages written in HTML. Pop-up alert boxes, lively images that appear when your mouse rolls over the page, and validation for your input on forms are all examples of what Javascript can do.

AJAX is a mix of technologies that builds on Javascript and enlivens the web even more, adding instant intelligence drawn from live data to create interactive displays. Go to www.google.com and try typing the word "computer" into the search box, but type slowly. You will see a rapidly changing list of words as you enter each letter, showing suggestions even before you finish typing. Many interactive maps and charts that show updated data as you move the mouse over different regions also use AJAX, drawing the data from a database (Figure 6-12).

The Flash development platform from Adobe Systems offers web designers another way to add rich media, animations, and interactivity. The animated ads that appear on websites are often developed in Flash, and an ecosystem of related tools help people make Flash files to put on their websites with no programming needed. For example, some products convert bloated PowerPoint files into smaller Flash files. Nevertheless, Flash animations can be distracting and take time to load, so designers use them sparingly.

Several major web development environments have emerged to add interactivity and database interfaces. For example, if you see .php somewhere in the URL, it means the underlying software is written in the programming language called PHP. Facebook uses this language, as you can see in the address bar if you log in. If you see .aspx buried in the URL, as you would if you logged into the online dating site

FIGURE 6-12

Interactive chart comparing net job creation by state since the 1980s, using AJAX.

Source: www.ces.cencus.gov/index.php/bds/state_line_charts

web browser
The software application that retrieves, interprets, and displays web resources.

hypertext markup language (HTML)
The original language used to create web pages; HTML specifies the web page's format using tags in angle brackets that browsers can interpret and put into reader-friendly output.

Javascript
A language used to add interactivity to web pages.

AJAX
A mix of technologies that builds on Javascript and draws on live data to create interactive online displays.

called Match.com, you know the web software was created with Microsoft's .NET framework. Java is also widely used to develop software for the web.

 The **World Wide Web Consortium (W3C)**, of which the Web Accessibility Initiative is one part, is an international body that establishes and publishes standards for programming languages used to create software for the web. Headed by Tim Berners-Lee, the inventor of the World Wide Web, the W3C strives to make sure the web continues to support communication and commerce for all people, regardless of their hardware, software, native languages, or geographic location. So far, its work has helped developers avoid the fate in which the web fragments into islands that can't interact with one another, but there is more to do. Berners-Lee says, "The Web as I envisaged it, we have not seen it yet. The future is still so much bigger than the past."

WEB CONTENT MANAGEMENT SYSTEMS As websites grow in size and incorporate audio, video, text, graphics, and other kinds of unstructured content, organizations need better ways to manage not just the content, but the many tasks and people required to maintain the site. **Content management systems** encompass a large group of software products that help manage digital content in collaborative environments. The web content management system supports website development and maintenance for larger teams.

These systems enable multiple people, often with limited web development and HTML skills, to contribute to the website from any place in the world. The site's overall look and feel, including the navigation bars that should appear on each page, are created as templates with consistent fonts, colors, and layout. The templates include **cascading style sheets (CSS)** that control the fonts and colors to appear when an editor identifies some text as a page heading, a paragraph title, or some other style.

Website editors can create new pages using a software environment similar to word processing, and their content is converted to HTML so it will appear nicely formatted on the website, inside the appropriate template. The content management system and its CSS can enforce a consistent look and feel throughout the site, preventing contributors from straying too far from the designer's templates.

Content management systems have many other features to support collaborative website development. For example, they prevent two people from trying to edit the same page at the same time, and they save older versions of each page as the website evolves. The systems also include workflow functionality so that new content can require a supervisor's approval before publication to the actual website.

Explain how e-commerce works, and why security and trust are critical ingredients. **3**

E-Commerce

E-commerce refers to the buying and selling of goods and services over the Internet or other networks, encompassing financial transactions between businesses, consumers, governments, or nonprofits. Analysts project worldwide e-commerce sales will reach almost $1 trillion by 2013, with average yearly increases of almost 20 percent.[15] Canny marketing promotions, well designed websites, increased consumer confidence in online payments, and even paralyzing snowstorms help steer shoppers to the Internet.[16]

THE ONLINE TRANSACTION AND E-COMMERCE SOFTWARE Websites whose main goal is selling, or that offer visitors opportunities to buy products or donate money, need e-commerce capabilities. Many software vendors offer information systems to support online stores and secure web-based financial transactions. These systems help web developers create a catalog of products using a backend database, conduct online marketing and sales promotions, manage the financial transactions, and handle reporting (Figure 6-13).

E-commerce systems typically include **shopping cart software** that tracks purchases as customers navigate the site and click "add to cart" as they go. When the customer is ready to check out, the software tallies the purchase, calculates taxes based on the customer's location, computes shipping costs, and also posts a discount if the customer enters a valid promotional code. The shopping cart analogy and the software underlying it work well for nonprofits like Heritage Dogs, though it may seem odd to add your donation to a "cart."

FIGURE 6-13

E-commerce software helps retailers manage their online store. This screen from Modular Merchant shows how a new product is added to the store's catalog.

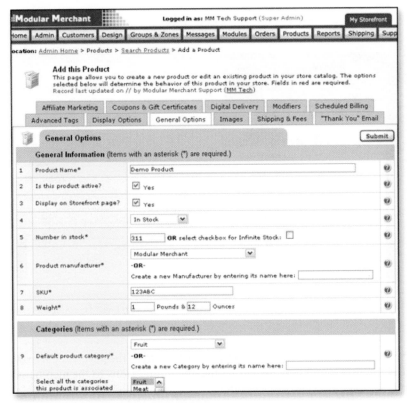

Source: www.modularmerchant.com/screenshots_detail.php?count=21, accessed May 16, 2011.

Retailers find that the online checkout process dramatically affects how customers perceive the site. If the checkout is cumbersome or unexpected charges appear, the shopper often abandons the transaction altogether. In one survey, 8 of 10 retailers targeted the checkout process as the area that needs most improvement on their websites, and many planned to offer free shipping to avoid surprising the customer with extra costs.[17]

E-COMMERCE SECURITY   The success of e-commerce depends heavily on its security and the perceptions people have about its trustworthiness. Fraud steals billions of dollars from unwary buyers and sellers. In one of the largest breaches on record, Albert Gonzales (who used the screen name "soupnazi") devised ingenious strategies to penetrate retail networks and capture data on more than 130 million credit and debit cards, sending the information to servers in California, Latvia, the Ukraine, and other locations.[18]

An e-commerce transaction must be secure from end to end, despite including several steps on different servers that can be geographically quite distant. The web address originating the transaction should show the https:// protocol, indicating the transmission to that server is encrypted and secure.

PRODUCTIVITY TIP

The secure connection confirmed by the https:// protocol relies on a certificate issued by a recognized authority such as the VeriSign Trust Network. Most browsers offer buttons so you can quickly display additional information about the certificate and the secure connection, including the level of encryption. They will also warn you if they detect security problems, such as an expired certificate (Figure 6-14).

World Wide Web Consortium (W3C)
An international body that establishes and publishes standards for programming languages used to create software for the web.

content management system
Software used to manage digital content in collaborative environments. The web content management system supports teams that develop and maintain websites.

cascading style sheets (CSS)
The part of a website template that controls the fonts, colors, and styles which appear when an editor identifies some text as a page heading, a paragraph title, or some other style.

e-commerce
The buying and selling of goods and services over the Internet or other networks, encompassing financial transactions between businesses, consumers, governments, or nonprofits.

shopping cart software
Computer software that tracks purchases as customers navigate an e-commerce site and click "add to cart" as they go. The software tallies the purchase, calculates taxes based on the customer's location, computes shipping costs, and also posts a discount if the customer enters a valid promotional code.

FIGURE 6-14

Details about the website's security, Note also the https:// protocol in the URL, indicating transmission is encrypted.

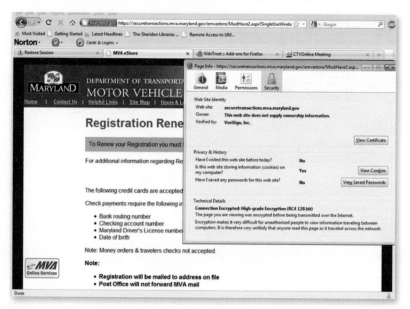

Source: securetransactions.mva.maryland.gov/emvastore/MustHave2.aspx?SingleUse WindowGuid=e00d5b0e-bb7f-4d1d-9234-d9b3dbdd7308&DeepLink=true

The credit or debit card information is transmitted to the **payment gateway**, which facilitates online shopping by mediating the interconnections to the merchant's bank, the bank or other entity that issued the card, and then back to the original website. If the transaction is approved, a confirmation is returned to the seller's site. All these connections must also be encrypted and secured. "Soupnazi" exploited holes in an early step in the process, when data from the online forms the buyers filled out with their personal financial information was compromised. Chapter 10 explores security in more detail.

E-COMMERCE TRUST   Trust is an essential element of e-commerce—buyers need assurance that an organization selling products online is reputable and secure. Well-known brands such as Macy's, Borders, and Walmart can rely on their own reputations, built from years of operating physical stores. Some large online retailers that lack actual retail locations, such as Amazon.com and Overstock.com, struggled to build trust over time but now enjoy solid reputations and loyal customers.

Building trust is a daunting task for less well-known organizations and requires close attention to consumers' motivations and buying behavior. For instance, the level of trust plays a larger role for women than for men in deciding whether to make a purchase online.[19] Men, however, rely more on online word-of-mouth reviews than women. Cultural factors also come into play. Although Australians develop some trust in an online store based on its association with a portal, such as Yahoo!, Chinese in Hong Kong are far less impressed. They are more likely to trust an unknown website based on favorable endorsements from peers.[20,21]

Businesses can apply for a "seal of approval" from independent organizations that audit websites to verify their compliance with minimum trust requirements in different countries. TRUSTe gives its approval to U.S. websites that follow strict privacy standards, such as explaining to visitors how personal data is collected. In the Philippines, a service called Sure Seal endorses sites that comply with local laws and Internet trading ethics, and e-commerce sites targeting Philippine shoppers are eager to obtain that seal.[22]

Marketing the Website

4 Explain how organizations market their websites using search engine optimization and web advertising, and describe some of the challenges of online marketing.

How do organizations attract people to their site, as buyers if the site's main goal is to sell, or as visitors for sites with different goals? Marketing majors certainly need a deep understanding of how the web works to develop creative and effective approaches. They also need to know how different kinds of people use the web, and why they return again and again to some sites but ignore others.

SEARCH ENGINE OPTIMIZATION

Seeing your website at the top of the first page on the results list from a search engine is a joyful experience for web marketers. Research shows that 62 percent of search engine users don't look beyond the first page of results, and the sites at or near the top get the most hits.[23] **Search engine optimization (SEO)** uses strategies to increase the quantity and quality of traffic from search engines, often by improving the site's position in result lists.

Search engines such as Google and Bing continually send out "spiders"—software programs that crawl the web, visiting sites to analyze the key words, headers, content, and links to other sites. The spiders update their own databases, and the search engine uses the new information to compute relevance when people submit a search term to the search engine. Web marketers must understand not only what data search engines collect and how they use it to judge relevance, but also how people use the web to find what they want.

SEARCH TERMS AND KEY WORDS   For users, search terms are key. Developers must guess what people who would be interested in their site might type as a search term, and then make sure their site gets a high relevance rating for that term. Choosing the most effective key words for the descriptors on your pages is critical. The students creating Heritage Dogs should ask what search terms a user who is interested in native dog breeds might enter, and they can use software tools to help them make good choices. For instance, Quintura offers an easy way to sort out possible key word combinations and see what results will appear. Figure 6-15 shows a **tag cloud** generated from the search term "country dog breeds." The tag cloud is a visual depiction of key words related to the search, with font size and position indicating relevance.

Very general key words such as "travel" or "pets" are not as helpful as more specific terms. A Montana car dealership found that most people learned of its site through a search engine using the search terms "Montana Toyota," so the staff reviewed their website to make those words more prominent in the page headings and content.[24]

FIGURE 6-15

Software tools can help web developers brainstorm appropriate key words for their site. These key words were generated by software from www.quintura.com.

Source: © Quintura, www.quintura.com.

payment gateway
An e-commerce application that facilitates online shopping by mediating the interconnections to the merchant's bank, the bank or other entity that issued the card, and then back to the original website to approve or decline the purchase.

search engine optimization (SEO)
An Internet marketing strategy used to increase the quantity and quality of traffic from search engines, often by improving the site's position in result lists.

tag cloud
A visual depiction of key words related to the search, with font size and position indicating relevance.

PAGERANK AND RELEVANCE Search engines rely partly on popularity to determine relevance, and the rules they use to rate popularity take into account the number and quality of external links to the site from other websites. Google's PageRank system, for example, named for cofounder Larry Page, interprets a link from Site A to Site B as a vote, thereby improving B's rank. The ranking system also considers the page that casts the vote, weighing votes more heavily if they come from pages that are themselves highly ranked.

PRODUCTIVITY TIP
You can see the actual PageRank of any site you visit if you install the free Google toolbar for Internet Explorer or Firefox.

Web marketers launch link-building campaigns to improve their search results, contacting sites that might add a link and making deals to do reciprocal linking. Online tools such as www.linkdiagnosis.com provide developers with detailed information about which sites are linking to them and the PageRanks of those sites.

SEARCH ENGINE SCAMS The drive to improve search results gets so heated that some unscrupulous developers launch devious strategies to outwit the engine's ranking system. For example, one technique to build valuable external links is to look for guest books on authoritative sites whose votes would be particularly valuable, such as those in the .gov or .edu domains, and then include a link to the scammer's site in an area that lets any visitor add comments. Scammers also build giant link farms out of servers whose only purpose is to increase the number of external links. Such techniques draw the ire of the search engine developers and often result in penalties or outright bans.

An even more insidious approach is to get a competitor's site banned, or at least move its site lower in the results. The scammer might inject some code onto a competitor's site that repeats the same key word over and over in a header, which spiders can easily spot and penalize as an unacceptable trick to make the page seem extremely relevant. Scammers might also invite raunchy adult-oriented or gambling sites to add links to the competitor, which can result in penalties and lower ranking.

WEB ADVERTISING

Pop-up ads, floating images, banners, music, and flashy animations appear on many websites, and overall spending for online ad campaigns worldwide is higher than for television. For example, a fitness company that wants its banner ad to appear on top of a sports website pays a fee for a certain number of impressions, perhaps 50 cents per 1,000. Prices vary depending on factors such the site's popularity or how likely the company thinks people who see the ad will click on it and perhaps buy a product. The **click-through rate (CTR)** is an important metric for such ads, computed as the number of visitors who click on the ad divided by the number of impressions. Typical click-through rates for banner ads are not high, typically less than 1 percent.[25]

USING COOKIES TO TARGET ADVERTISING A **cookie** is a small text file that the website's server leaves on your computer when you visit and then retrieves when you visit again, usually to personalize the site for you. The file typically contains a unique ID and information such as date and time, or the page you visited. The cookie can also store information you yourself provide, such as the zip code for a city you intend to visit on a weather site. When you return, the site can immediately display that city's weather.

E-commerce sites rely on cookies to keep track of the products a customer places in a shopping cart. As you collect items, the web server retrieves your unique ID and stores it with the item number in its own database. If you leave the site and return later, the software can retrieve your ID and refill your shopping cart. The site can also deliver targeted ads and recommendations, without asking you to log in, by retrieving your cookie and checking to see what that ID has viewed in the past.

Ad networks such as Brightroll and Casale Media have sprung up that facilitate even better targeting. They deliver banners and other ads to their clients' websites and also deposit their own cookies whenever someone visits one of the client sites. These are called **third-party cookies**, because they are not tied just to the site you are visiting. They let the ad network track you as you visit any client site and then serve targeted ads at other sites.

Suppose on your favorite news site you click on an ad for Caribbean cruises designed to appeal to single women in their twenties. The ad network associates that information with the unique ID for you. If you move to a travel site that is also a network client, your cookie will be retrieved and you will see more ads about cruises for young singles. With more information about what sites an individual visits, marketers can better understand that person's motivations and deliver more effective advertising. Click-through rates improve and online ad prices climb.

SEARCH ENGINE MARKETING   Google pioneered a simple marketing approach that relies on your search terms rather than on cookies. On the theory that the terms you enter reveal your current motivations, Google developed the Adwords program, which serves small ads related to your search in a list of sponsored links. Type in "shiba inu" for example, and you will see sponsored links offering puppies for sale. Whether the ad actually appears to someone who submits a key word the organization has chosen for its ad depends partly on how much the company is willing to spend each day. Unlike buyers of most banner-type ads, these advertisers pay only when someone actually clicks on the ad, not each time it appears.

The ads are text only and quite short, so they are far less intrusive than flashy banner ads or pop-up windows. They are also extremely well targeted and effective. Income from this source accounts for the vast majority of Google's annual revenue of more than $20 billion, and other search engines such as Bing and Yahoo! have followed suit with their own search engine marketing programs.

For Tiny Prints, an online store selling custom holiday cards, search engine marketing works extremely well. The company selected "holiday cards" and "photo cards" as its key words for a week in November, and sales soared. Hoping sales would stay high with a smaller ad budget, the company cut back for just one day. Its competitors did not cut back, however, and Tiny Prints' sales suffered. CEO Ed Han said, "We knew we had made a bad decision."[26]

Figure 6-16 shows the global market shares for the major search engines. In specific countries, however, different search engines may dominate, especially if

> **PRODUCTIVITY TIP**
> You can adjust the settings in your browser to control how it handles cookies as you browse—to prohibit third-party cookies or prompt you for permission to download them, for example. Try overriding automatic cookie handling to see how your favorite sites are using cookies.

FIGURE 6-16

Search engine market shares, December 2010.

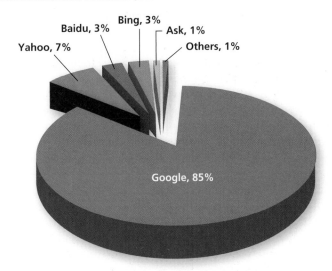

Source: Data from www.netmarketshare.com, accessed December 2010.

---

click-through rate (CTR)
A metric used to assess the impact of an online ad; computed as the number of visitors who click on the ad divided by the number of impressions.

cookie
A small text file left on a website visitor's hard drive that is used to personalize the site for the visitor, or track web activities.

third-party cookies
Small text files which a website leaves on a visitor's computer that are not deposited by the site being visited; used by ad networks to track customer behavior across all their client websites.

people can enter their search terms in the native language. Baidu does this for Chinese and holds over 60 percent market share in China.[27] Because search engine marketing can be so effective and lucrative, the companies compete fiercely to attract users. They also encourage websites to place text boxes for their search engines on their own sites, configured to search just the local site.

ONLINE MARKETING CHALLENGES   Trying to drive up the operating expenses of a rival airplane charter service, employees at Blue Star Jets clicked repeatedly on the competitor's sponsored link—without, of course, intending to charter anything.[28] Organizations worry about scams like that, and they also wonder whether their ad networks are exaggerating the number of impressions, or worse, putting their ads on inappropriate sites. An adult-oriented site is no place for children's ads, and candy manufacturers don't want their ads appearing next to articles on obesity.

Although online marketing offers tremendous promise, it also poses new challenges. Fraud is certainly one, but unfortunate or embarrassing product placements are another. Microsoft, for instance, was not thrilled when an ad featuring the company's butterfly icon appeared adjacent to a *New York Times* story about troublesome corporate promotions. The reporter criticized Microsoft for releasing a swarm of 12-inch-wide adhesive butterflies into the city, creating a costly nuisance and cleanup.[29]

Third-party cookies are controversial from a privacy standpoint, as well. Yahoo! Canada, for instance, has agreements with more than 30 different ad networks, creating a web of interconnections that can follow people's tracks as they browse different sites. As we discuss in Chapter 10, your online tracks reveal quite a bit about you that can also be tied back to publicly available offline data—your address, phone number, age, marital status, net worth, and political donations. Although web surfing may seem anonymous, digital tracks are much deeper than most people realize.

Explain how Web 2.0 attributes such as crowdsourcing, expanded data sources, and machine learning capabilities are changing the nature of the web.

5 Web 2.0 and Beyond

In its early days, people compared the web to a vast and rapidly growing library with unlimited shelf space, in which valuable documents could be published alongside trivial junk. As businesses entered and e-commerce matured, the web emerged as a global shopping mall in which tiny start-ups could share space with giant retailers. Marketers and advertisers developed the business approaches, and giant web portals such as Yahoo! and America Online dominated visitors' online experiences.

Innovation exploded and the web also became home to innumerable services that offered people opportunities to participate in new ways—gaming, photo sharing, blogging, menu planning, restaurant reviewing, community building, and much more. Web 2.0, as we discussed in Chapter 1, refers to the next generation, in which the emphasis is on interaction, conversation, participation, collaboration, and endless sources and streams of data. While new technologies continually emerge that support these activities, Web 2.0 is less about the technologies than about the ways in which people and organizations are using the web.[30]

One significant trend for Web 2.0 is that the web serves as a platform not just for delivering software as a service or for presenting useful applications online, but for harnessing the collective intelligence of its users as well. Websites that find ways to leverage this wisdom tap into a vast reservoir of talent and knowledge that can continually improve the site's services.

CROWDSOURCING AND COLLECTIVE INTELLIGENCE

The term **crowdsourcing** describes how tasks can be delegated to large diffuse groups or communities, who often volunteer their contributions. Unlike outsourcing, in which an organization contracts with a vendor to do work, crowdsourcing depends on engaging people in tasks they find interesting or rewarding, or collecting data about what people are doing anyway as they go about their daily work. Google, for instance, relies on everyone who clicks on links or embeds links in their websites to continually improve its ranking system. All those clicks and external links are votes that adjust relevance rankings for every website.

Amazon harnesses collective intelligence by inviting your product reviews, summarizing the ratings, and then encouraging people to rate the value of each review as well. The publisher HarperCollins used crowdsourcing to replace some editors, and Miranda Dickinson's novel *Fairy Tale in New York* was discovered this way. Over 135,000 people around the world were invited to read more than 10,000 submitted manuscripts and enter their ratings and comments.[31]

Amazon's Mechanical Turk site goes one more step, bringing organizations that need human wisdom together with all the people who have a few moments to spare and want to earn a bit of money. Visitors sign up to receive payments and then browse through the thousands of available tasks that are best done by humans rather than computers. VideoJug, an online site with free "how to" videos, offers 15 cents to people who will re-title, tag, and write a description for a video. A university lab studying computer vision hopes to attract some humans to track a basketball with their mouse, collecting data for a research project. Amazon named the site after the eighteenth-century mechanical chess-playing machine that handily defeated most human opponents, including Napoleon Bonaparte and Benjamin Franklin. The Turk was actually a hoax, with a human chess master hiding inside.

Wikipedia is another well-known site that amasses collective intelligence and volunteer labor, in this case to create a vast online encyclopedia with more than 3 million entries, far more than Britannica or other competitors. Debates over its accuracy continue to rage, with one early study finding that Wikipedia entries compared favorably to Britannica articles, with about the same number of major errors but more minor ones.[32]

Wikipedia demonstrates some of the downsides of crowdsourcing. Bias and self-interest can motivate authors, particularly for trendy, controversial topics or hot political issues. For instance, staff of U.S. Congress members have been caught editing articles about their bosses and deleting references to campaign pledges they never fulfilled.[33]

PRODUCTIVITY TIP

Citing Wikipedia entries in academic papers as part of the bibliography is controversial. Many universities and faculty object, due to concerns about bias, reliability, accuracy, and the lack of identified authors. Also, encyclopedias target a general readership, so material from any of them may be considered too low level for college papers. If you do use such citations, include your evaluation of its quality as a source for that topic, just as you would for other web-based sources with unknown authorship. You can also use Wikipedia for general background on a topic and useful links to more detailed primary sources.

EXPANDING DATA AND SENSORY INPUT

Another important trend for Web 2.0 and beyond is the exponential growth of data and innovations in the way organizations collect, use, and value it. The flood of human participation is one contributor to the growing volume, through crowdsourcing and social media, for example. New sensors are adding far more, through RFID technology, smartphones, cameras, camcorders, GPS devices, and other sensory input. The original IP address system is overwhelmed because so many new devices need unique addresses, but the new numbering scheme described in Chapter 3 will make room for quadrillions more.

Companies can achieve distinct competitive advantages when they manage to get control over valuable data collected by all these people and sensors, organize it into a database, and find ways to use it to deliver and improve their products. Ebay succeeds largely because of its critical mass and control over data—contributed by users—about items for sale and sellers' reputations. Facebook earns enough to cover its costs and brings in millions more in venture capital, thanks to the millions of users worldwide whose contributions make the site the most popular social network on the net.

Navteq, a company that creates digital maps for navigation devices, strives to build the best geographic database in the world. It relies first on easily available maps from local governments or satellite photography and then deploys geographic

crowdsourcing
Delegating tasks to large diffuse groups or communities, who often volunteer their contributions.

FIGURE 6-17

For China's urban residents, GPS geography analysts add map details relevant to pedestrians or bicyclists who want the quickest routes through crowded streets.

Bartlomiej Magierowski/Shutterstock

analysts to collect more detailed data. In developed countries where car travel is most common, the analyst collects images with a camera perched on the car's roof. In densely populated cities, navigation details relevant to pedestrians, bus riders, or bicyclists may be more useful (Figure 6-17). Analysts armed with GPS-equipped mobile phones document the quickest walking routes from the train station to the shopping mall. Some of these mapmaking tasks are crowdsourced as well, relying on volunteers to submit corrections or add features. Tim Akinbo is one such volunteer who contributes his own time to add details about banks, churches, movie theaters, and other features to maps of Lagos, where he lives.[34]

Did You Know?

Metropolitan areas are offering smartphone bus and train schedule widgets that predict the placement of your desired means of transportation every 30 seconds. You can even watch the bus and train icon move down the map on your phone. With this technology, you'll know just when your ride will arrive.

THE LEARNING WEB

The massive and ever-growing mounds of data are valuable not just in their own right, as revenue sources for companies or as features to attract more users. They also provide resources for machine learning, making the web and its applications ever smarter. One example shows how Google taught software to translate texts from Arabic to English and back and then pushed it to learn on its own.

Drawing on an enormous volume of already-translated texts and documents on the web, Google developed a text translator that acquires its skills directly from the data. The software is not programmed with any rules about Arabic semantics or syntax. Instead, it statistically compares phrases from text in one language to its parallel in text that has already been translated by humans into English. Feeding it more paired, translated texts from United Nations documents and other sources makes the translator ever more powerful. The more data it has to learn from, the smarter it gets.

Google claimed it didn't even use native speakers to double-check any translations, a fact that astonished the CEO of Systran, a rival company that develops translation software relying on language rules and syntax. In one competition, Systran's software translated an Arabic headline into:

Alpine white new presence tape registered for coffee confirms Laden.

Google's translation read,

The White House Confirmed the Existence of a New Bin Laden Tape.

Peter Norvig, who worked on the project at Google, remarked, "We don't have better algorithms. We just have more data."[35]

The translator also continually learns. For example, it produces more natural English phrasing by looking for patterns in large quantities of professionally written documents. To find the smoothest way to render a phrase in English, the program might search a million possible word combinations from news stories or other text, picking the one used most often by highly regarded sources.

The web grew from a document-publishing environment to one that supports secure financial transactions and interactivity. Now it is transforming again, even surprising its own creators. As Tim O'Reilly, the person credited with coining the term *Web 2.0*, says, "The Web is growing up and we are all its collective parents."[36]

MyMISLab | *Online Simulation*

Cruisin' Fusion

A Role-Playing Simulation on Website Development for a Chain of Concession Stands

You inherited a mobile concession truck from your uncle, who sold tacos and bottled drinks at lunchtime. Uncle Al liked talking to people and his stand had become a local legend. He served only top of the line mahi mahi, chicken, and cheese tacos in freshly baked shells. He also grew his own herbs to make "fusion" sauces that blended flavors from Mexico, Thailand, Korea, and India. His curried chicken taco was a favorite and long lines formed every day.

Charlotte Lake/Shutterstock

You're not sure what to do with the concession truck, but a couple of your friends think Al was onto something with his unusual taco food truck. They want to partner with you to expand, targeting sports events, outdoor concerts, political rallies, holiday marches, and other events where customers might pay a little more for a very distinctive and healthier meal. With the right marketing, this could be a promising business venture. Log in when you're ready to start planning the website....

Chapter Summary

1 The Internet is a disruptive technology that causes waves of creative destruction, and an organization's web strategy is increasingly critical to its success. Four major goals that organizations choose to stress for their websites include (1) inform or entertain the audience; (2) influence the audience; (3) sell to the audience; and (4) facilitate or extend offline relationships. The website's name in the form of its URL uniquely identifies the site on the Internet, mapping to its numerical IP address. The URL's components include the top-level domain, such as .com, .gov, .org, .cn, or .de, which reflects the organization's mission or country code. Name disputes are common and are resolved by ICANN.

2 Building a website requires paying attention to the site's information architecture, which might adopt a hierarchical, multi-dimensional, flat, or sequential structure. Usability should be assessed early, and the user interface should follow design principles that will make it easier for visitors to accomplish their goals on the site. The website should also support accessibility for people with disabilities. Software development for websites starts with HTML, the programming language used to format web pages. Media-rich and interactive websites are created with other programming tools, such as Javascript, AJAX, Flash, and programming languages that interface with backend databases. Web content management systems enable teams to work together on a website, offering simple ways to format content and providing support for version control and other features.

3 E-commerce is the buying and selling of goods and services on the Internet. E-commerce software, including shopping carts, can support secure and encrypted transmissions, manage product catalogs, and track transactions. Trust is a critical element in e-commerce, and independent organizations audit websites, granting a seal of approval to those that meet minimums standards.

4 Marketing strategies on the web start with search engine optimization (SEO), which seeks to improve a website's position on result lists returned by search engines. Organizations choose appropriate key words and encourage links from external sites to achieve higher rankings in the search results. Web advertisers also use pop-up ads, banners, floating ads, and other techniques. Ad networks use third-party cookies to track user behavior across multiple websites, gathering data used to improve targeting. Search engine marketing, in which relevant text ads are served alongside results for the user's query, are most effective. Online marketing raises ethical issues, especially because tools such as third-party cookies can threaten privacy.

5 Web 2.0 represents the next generation of web capabilities, which rely particularly on crowdsourcing and collective intelligence, expanded data sources and sensory input, and machine learning. As the web matures, the massive amount of data contributed by individuals and sensors is greatly enhancing its power and potential, opening new opportunities for innovation.

KEY TERMS AND CONCEPTS

infomediary
e-marketplace
business to consumer (B2C)
business to business (B2B)
consumer to consumer (C2C)
consumer to business (C2B)
uniform resource locator (URL)
Domain Name System (DNS)
hypertext transfer protocol (http://)

file transfer protocol (ftp://)
top-level domain
Internet Corporation for Assigned Names and Numbers (ICANN)
hierarchical website architecture
multi-dimensional website architecture
sequential architecture

usability
web accessibility
assistive technologies
web browser
hypertext markup language (HTML)
Javascript
AJAX
World Wide Web Consortium (W3C)
content management system

cascading style sheets (CSS)
e-commerce
shopping cart software
payment gateway
search engine optimization (SEO)
tag cloud
click-through rate (CTR)
cookie
third-party cookies
crowdsourcing

CHAPTER REVIEW QUESTIONS

1. What are four primary goals an organization might choose to develop its web strategy? What is an example of each?

2. How is a URL related to a registered website name? Why does a URL include a protocol identifier? What are the components of a website address? What are typical suffixes that identify top-level domains?

3. What is website architecture? What are examples of website architecture?

4. What is the difference between usability and accessibility? How do website developers test for usability? How can website design improve accessibility? How do text and background color combinations relate to website accessibility? What are the benefits of designing accessible websites?

5. List some software development strategies used for websites. What is an advantage to using basic HTML? What is an advantage to using Java? Why is AJAX used to develop websites? What role does a content management

system play in website development? Why do content management systems use templates?

6. What is e-commerce? What activities does it include? How do online transaction sites use databases and shopping cart software? Why is security critical for e-commerce success? Which protocol supports secure Internet transactions? Why is trust critical for e-commerce success? Aside from having a well-known brand name, how do online sellers signal their trustworthiness to potential customers?

7. What is search engine optimization (SEO)? What are two examples? How do organizations improve their position on search result lists?

8. How does web advertising work to target ads for individuals? How can users avoid targeted ads?

9. What is Web 2.0? What is crowdsourcing? What is an example of crowdsourcing? How do Web 2.0 capabilities change the way in which people and organizations use the web?

PROJECTS AND DISCUSSION QUESTIONS

1. VeriSign is a recognized authority on website security, and the VeriSign seal tells online customers they can trust the website to encrypt sensitive data that is transmitted over the Internet. Visit versign.com to learn more about the VeriSign Trust Seal. In addition to verifying encryption, what else does this seal tell consumers about the websites on which it appears? What is SSL security? How does it work? Prepare a brief report of your findings.

2. Pop-ups, such as windows that open to provide a return shipping label, and web browser add-ons, like the Google toolbar, can make browsing more fun or more effective, but sometimes they can slow down your computer or cause the browser to shut down unexpectedly. Most add-ons require user consent before they are downloaded, but some might be downloaded without your knowledge and some may be tracking your browsing habits. How do you know which add-ons are running on your computer? Click on Tools to learn about your browser's settings. How do you allow some pop-ups and disallow others? Review your add-ons. Which ones are allowed on your browser? What specific functionality does each provide? Did you disable any add-ons? Which ones and why?

3. Visit a site that uses AJAX to create interactive maps, such as www.MeasureofAmerica.org. What features does this technology add to make the site more interactive? How might you use this technology to present an interactive map showing the changing incidence of reported cases of flu by geographic area, as the flu season progresses?

4. Visit an e-commerce site such as Amazon.com, a nonprofit site such as the Cancer Research Institute (www.cancerresearch.org), and a government website, such as California Department of Motor Vehicles (www.dmv.ca.gov). For each site, assume you want to accomplish an e-commerce task: purchase a travel guide to Peru; donate $10 to cancer research; and pay a traffic fine online. Compare your overall experiences on each site, and how easy it is to accomplish the tasks. How do these sites track purchases or donations as users navigate the site? Do all the sites use secure transmissions for e-commerce (https://)? What improvements would you recommend for these sites?

5. Visit joomla.com to learn more about this open-source content management system. What types of content does it manage? Who uses Joomla, and what are its advantages? Visit two sites that use Joomla and compare them. How are they similar? How are they different? Prepare a 5-minute presentation of your findings.

6. Work in a small group with classmates to evaluate website accessibility issues. Select a website to evaluate, and then choose three pages from the website for your sample. Your sample should be varied, but should ideally include pages that contain tables, images, multimedia (e.g., a video or sound file), and a form. Conduct the following tests, using at least two different browsers.

   a. Turn off images (usually under Tools). Do all the images have alternative text that properly describes the image? Screen readers for visually impaired people will need accurate verbal descriptions to grasp the content of the image.

b. Turn off sound. Is there a text transcription for the narration that hearing impaired people will need?

c. Use the controls on the browser to increase the size of the fonts. Can the fonts be adjusted using the browser? Visually impaired people often need larger fonts to read, but some websites use fixed font sizes.

d. Using just the keyboard, not the mouse, try navigating through the links and the fields on a form. Can you reach all the links, and do they describe what they link to? Can you navigate through the form with the keyboard, without using the mouse? This is a good test to see if screen readers will work properly.

e. Print out the three pages using only black, white, and gray. Is there sufficient contrast without color to accommodate color-blind visitors?

f. Compare the results for the different browsers you tested, and prepare a 5-minute presentation of your group's results.

7. What do people look for on the front page of a university website? Randall Munroe, the comic artist at xkcd. com, created the cartoon in Figure 6-18 about university websites. Work in a small group with classmates to review your university's website. What is the goal or goals of the site? What type of architecture does it have? Describe its usability. Do you struggle to find specific information or is navigation easy? How many clicks does it take to locate holiday hours of operation for your library? Prepare a list of suggestions for the university web master that describe specific ways to improve your university's website.

FIGURE 6-18

Designing the university website.

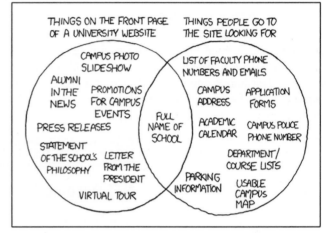

Source: Cartoon by Randall Munroe.

APPLICATION EXERCISES

WEBSITE APPLICATION:
Heritage Dogs

Use Microsoft Word to create a simple website for Heritage Dogs. Launch Word and type "Heritage Dogs" into the document. Click File > Save As > Other Formats and select Web Page. Save the file as "index.html." (Depending on your version of Word, the default for the file extension may be "htm," which is also recognized as a web page.) Click New to create another page and type "Thai Ridgeback" into the document. Save it as "Thai Ridgeback.html." Create additional web pages for each breed that Heritage Dogs plans to promote. Return to the index page and type "Thai Ridgeback" into the document. Highlight "Thai Ridgeback" and click Insert > Hyperlink and locate "Thai Ridgeback.html." Select the file and click OK. You have just created a hyperlink. After you create additional hyperlinks for each breed, save and close the files. To view the website in a browser, right-click on the Start button in the lower-left corner of your screen and select "Open Windows Explorer." Browse to locate and open the index file you created. Check the hyperlinks. Do they work? What type of website architecture did you create? Explain how this simple website can be expanded to provide additional content for visitors to HeritageDogs.org.

EXCEL APPLICATION:
Heritage Dogs Website Metrics

The board of directors at Heritage Dogs is meeting to consider how its website is serving the needs of volunteers, donors, and potential adoptive pet owners. The website coordinator has asked you to create an Excel spreadsheet to help her analyze quarterly data for several key indicators including percentage of repeat visitors, page views per visit, and bounce rate. The bounce rate is the percentage of visitors who view only one page. Together, these are a measure of website "stickiness"—the ability to keep visitors interested and coming back for more. Additionally, she wants two line charts that display website usage statistics.

Create the spreadsheet shown in Figure 6-19 and add calculations for Total Visitors, Percentage Repeat Visitors,

FIGURE 6-19

Heritage Dogs Website Metrics.

	A	B	C	D	E	F	G	H	I
1				Heritage Dogs					
2				Website Metrics					
3									
4		Q1	Q2	Q3	Q4	Q5	Q6	Q7	Q8
5	Visits	128	143	275	290	365	468	605	681
6	First Time Visitors	82	98	162	172	218	304	436	439
7	Repeat Visitors	12	24	48	28	58	56	98	110
8	Page Views	210	200	480	520	569	780	1004	1265
9	Single Page Views	65	55	125	154	160	250	305	425

Page Views per Visit, and Bounce Rate. To calculate Bounce Rate, divide Page Views by Single Page Views.

Create one line chart that shows Visits, Total Visitors, and Page Views. Create a second line chart that shows the Bounce Rate and the Percentage Repeat Customers. For both charts select a layout that includes a chart title, axis title, and a legend.

How would you describe the pattern of website usage in terms of visits, total visitors and page views? How would you describe the website in terms of "stickiness"?

ACCESS APPLICATION:
Springfield Animal Shelter

The Springfield Animal Shelter manages a volunteer foster program in which volunteers care for sick and immature animals in their homes and take in injured or abused animals when the shelter facility is full. Animals may be in foster care for a few weeks or a few months, depending on the need. When the animal is healthy and ready to be adopted, the shelter will post its picture and story on the website. Foster parents are given first choice to adopt the animal but are not required to do so. Volunteers enroll in the program on the shelter website, and the information they provide is stored in an Access database. Download the Springfield Animal Shelter database Ch06Ex03 and create three detail reports for the shelter manager. A detail report displays all information for each volunteer.

The first report will list all active volunteers who specified they wish to care for a cat. The second report will list all active volunteers who wish to care for a dog. The third report will list all inactive volunteers regardless of animal preference. Review the information being collected about volunteers and suggest other types of information that may be useful to the shelter manager.

CASE STUDY #1

NTT Docomo Pioneers the Cell-Phone Wallet in Japan

In a country where cash is king and almost everyone owns a cell phone, Japan's NTT Docomo led a major drive into mobile e-commerce, or m-commerce. The mobile phone carrier pioneered the use of "near-field communications" (NFC) chips inside its cell phones, enabling them to exchange data wirelessly over a few centimeters. More than 54 million people subscribe to Docomo's wireless voice network, and they can all pay for their cappuccinos at participating stores by tapping their cell phone against a special terminal or just waving it nearby.

When a customer taps the cell phone to pay, the expense is automatically logged into a digital expense report and charged to the customer's account. Called *osaifu keitai* in Japanese, the cell-phone wallet frees people from carrying cash. Consumers use their cell-phone wallets to buy subway, train, and airline tickets, and the phone's chip also serves as an electronic key to control access doors to buildings or homes. Cell-phone wallet holders can check their balances, loyalty point totals, and purchasing history from the handset and receive promotional discounts.

Visa and Mastercard have offered NFC payment capabilities on key fobs and cards in the United States and other countries, and some wireless carriers are promoting chips that stick to the back of existing cell phones or their cases. But NTT Docomo's approach has far more potential because of the phone's processing power and communications features. The software can combine and integrate data, including location, from many sources.

The technology to pay bills and buy products by mobile phone is well established, but the use of the cell phone to handle in-store transactions and track purchases and reward points is still in its infancy in most countries. Analysts predict that most cell-phone manufacturers will soon embed the chips in their handsets, transforming in-store payments and marketing. Although NTT Docomo had to take over a bank to build its *osaifu keitai* service, other carriers will probably partner with credit card companies, with their extensive fraud-protection capabilities. A new ecosystem is evolving in which financial institutions, wireless carriers, brick and mortar retail stores, technology companies, savvy online marketers, and innovative start-ups will be vying for a piece of the cell-phone wallet market and all its services. As NFC chips become commonplace on cell phones around the world, those lines at checkout counters may get shorter and shorter, and real wallets stuffed with credit cards, loyalty cards, photos, and cash may become extinct.

Discussion Questions

1. What are the potential benefits of this technology for consumers? What are the potential benefits for retailers?

2. What are the risks for consumers and retailers? What are some ways that these risks could be overcome?

3. How could this technology impact the telecommunications and consumer banking industries?
4. Do you believe this technology would work in the United States? Why or why not?

SOURCES: Anonymous. (2004). Coming soon: The cell phone wallet. *Community Developments Online*. www.occ.treas.gov/cdd/cellphonewallet.html, accessed August 30, 2010. *Internet Retailer*. www.internetretailer.com, accessed August 28, 2010. Macsai, D. (September 2010). Pocket change. *Fast Company*. 148, 40–41. NTT Docomo, Inc. Hoover's Company Records. (August 31, 2010). LexisNexis Academic. Retrieved September 6, 2010.

CASE STUDY #2

Pandora Radio: The Net Threatens the Music Business (Again)

Music CD sales collapsed when Napster began its online music site, where visitors could find the song they wanted and download it for free. Though Napster ran afoul of copyright law and was shut down, the demand for single-song downloads was so intense that Apple's iTunes store became an instant hit. Reluctantly, record labels such as Sony and Warner made royalty deals with iTunes, Amazon, Rhapsody, and even Walmart, but the music industry's business model is under assault once again. Song download sales are shrinking, and analysts predict that streaming Internet radio services such as Pandora will take a chunk out of the market.

Billed as the station that "plays only music you like," Pandora.com offers music lovers access to their own customized "radio stations." Pandora's website visitors can submit a favorite song, artist, or composer, and Pandora's software builds a playlist of similar songs.

The software that powers the playlist emerged from the Music Genome Project, launched by Pandora founder Tim Westergren. He and a team of musicians and musicologists analyze 10,000 songs a month for hundreds of attributes—harmony, rhythm, lyrics, instrumentation, vocals, genre, and others. The result of their efforts is an immense and continuously growing database that powers a recommendation engine to suggest music with similar attributes—the same musical "DNA." A visitor who asks to hear Glenn Miller's music of the 1940s will be offered old favorites such as "Heart and Soul" or "Smoke Gets in Your Eyes." An Usher fan's playlist will fill with songs by artists such as Chris Brown and T-Pain. The musicologists don't count popularity as an attribute, so unknown bands appear regularly, giving them a welcome opportunity for exposure. Though artists earn a royalty from Pandora each time their song plays, the service is far less profitable for them than song downloads. A song must be streamed at least 200 times to earn the same royalty as one download.

With more than 50 million users, Pandora relies on targeted advertising and premium subscriptions for revenue. Westergren says, "If you're a car or beverage company, you can come to Pandora and say I'd like to put this advertisement in front of men in their 30s listening to rock music in Kansas." People can buy subscriptions for a few dollars a month to omit the ads.

Although most users initially enjoyed Pandora's services while sitting at their computer at home or work, they can now add the streaming, customized radio service to their smartphones. The shift makes their "radio" mobile, and this is what threatens to disrupt the music industry's business model again. "It's impossible to overstate [the smartphone]," says Pandora's founder. "The iPhone has ... almost doubled our growth rate overnight." This time around, the online stores that sell MP3 downloads will also have some adapting to do.[37-39]

Discussion Questions

1. What are the various components of Pandora's business?
2. What are some shortcomings of downloading music?
3. How does Pandora address some shortcomings of downloading music?
4. How could music labels and online stores use the web to respond to Pandora?

SOURCES: Grossman, L. (2010). If you liked this. *Time*. 175(22), 44–48. Grover, R., & Satariano, A. (July 1, 2010). The fall of music downloads. *Bloomberg Businessweek*. http://www.businessweek.com/magazine/content/10_28/b4186037467816.htm, accessed May 21, 2011. Rose, C. (July 5, 2010). Charlie Rose talks to Tim Westergren. *Bloomberg Businessweek*. p. 39.

E-PROJECT 1 Examining the Top M-Commerce Sites

The success of m-commerce depends partly on the quality of the user's experience when accessing the site from an Internet-enabled mobile phone. Some key metrics for several popular m-commerce sites are shown in Figure 6-20, including load time and success rate. The score is computed by equally weighting the load time and success rate.

1. Visit each of the sites in Figure 6-20 using an Internet-enabled mobile phone, and time how long each one takes to load, using a stopwatch. You can use an online stopwatch at www.online-stopwatch.com if you don't have one of your own.

2. Create a spreadsheet with four column headers: Retailer, Load Time 2010, Current Load Time, Percent Change.

3. Enter the four retailers and add your data for the third column.

4. Enter the formula to compute the Percentage Change in the QVC row (fourth column) and copy the formula to the other cells in the column.

5. Which retailer's m-commerce site has shown the most change since 2010?

FIGURE 6-20

Key metrics for m-commerce sites.

Retailer	Load Time (Sec)	Success Rate	Score Out of 1,000
QVC	1.95	98.60	953
Walmart.com	3.20	98.98	926
Best Buy	6.81	97.38	565
Target	5.13	98.58	782

Source: Data drawn from www.internetretailer.com for week beginning August 30, 2010, accessed October 3, 2010.

6. What factors contribute to a site's load times? Why would your data be different from a classmate's when accessing these sites?

7. Conduct an experiment to compare m-commerce at Walmart and Target. Start the stopwatch, load Walmart's site, and search for a Fodor's travel guide to Mexico. Add the product to your cart, check out up to the point at which you would enter a credit card number, and then write down the time from the stopwatch. Do the same experiment at Target's site. How did your time estimates compare for the two m-commerce experiences? Overall, which site do you think offers the best user experience?

E-PROJECT 2 Exploring Pandora's Web Analytics

In this e-project, you will explore the Pandora website to learn more about its web model. Then, you will examine the site's analytics using Alexa, a web information company that offers free information about traffic to websites.

1. Visit www.pandora.com and click on Register. (You don't need to register unless you would like to.) Why does the site ask for your birth year? Why does it collect your zip code? Why does it ask for gender?

2. Visit www.alexa.com and search for Pandora.com to retrieve the website's analytics. Click on Get Details.

3. What is Pandora's Alexa Traffic Rank, and what does that term mean? (It's above the graph.) Compare the Alexa Traffic Rank, which is worldwide, to the Traffic Rank in the United States. What accounts for the large difference?

4. Traffic Stats Tab. Check out the weekly and monthly trends under Traffic Rank, Reach, and Pageviews. On what days of the week does Pandora have relatively few visitors? What does that suggest about how people use the service?

5. Audience Tab. How would you generally describe Pandora's main market?

6. Clickstream Tab. These charts show which other websites Pandora visitors come from before entering Pandora.com (upstream), and also which ones they enter when they leave Pandora (downstream). What are the most common upstream and downstream sites?

CHAPTER NOTES

1. Shirky, C. (2009). *Newspapers and thinking the unthinkable. Risk Management.* (56), 3, 24–26, 28–29.

2. Maoz, M. (November 6, 2009). *The top ten ways to make a website customer-centric.* Gartner Research, DOI: ID Number:G00172127.

3. Williams, K. (2009). *Families could save pounds 560 a year by using internet to shop around; But website owner says figure is higher. The Western Mail.* p. 16.

4. *Breen, Howard.* (2008). *Marketing Magazine.* Rogers Publishing Limited. p. 22.

5. Gammel, C.D. (2009). *What's driving your web strategy? Associations Now.* 5(13), p. 19.

6. ICANN. (November 16, 2009). *Global Internet leaders welcome internationalization of Internet address names.* http://www.icann.org/en/news/releases/release-16nov09-en.pdf accessed May 21, 2011.

7. Shamni, P. (2009, October). Fight over Oktatabyebye. com: What's in a name? *Business Today.* DOI: ID Number: 1878135471.

8. Wilbers, E. (2009). What's next as the UDRP turns 10. *Managing Intellectual Property.* (193), 104–107.

9. Mitchell, R.L. (2009). Domain Wars. *Computerworld.* 43(27), 18–23.

10. Nah, F. F.-H. (2004). A study on tolerable waiting time: how long are Web users willing to wait? *Behaviour & Information Technology.* 23(3), 153–163.

11. Ipri, T., Yunkin, M., & Brown, J. M. (2009). Usability as a method for assessing discovery. *Information Technology & Libraries.* 28(4), 181–183.

12. Loiacono, E. T., Romano, J.N.C., & McCoy, S. (2009). The state of corporate website accessibility. *Communications of the ACM.* 52(9), 128–132.

13. Lazar, J., Dudley-Sponaugle, A., & Greenidge, K.-D. (2004). Improving web accessibility: A study of webmaster perceptions. *Computers in Human Behavior.* 20(2), 269.

14. Parry, M., & Brainard, J. (2010). Colleges lock out blind students online. *Chronicle of Higher Education.* 57(17), A1–A8.

15. Davis, D. (2011). Global e-commerce sales head for the $1 trillion mark. *Internet Retailer.* January 4.

16. comScore. (January 6, 2010). comScore reports $29.1 billion in U.S. retail e-commerce spending for full November-December holiday season, up 4 percent vs. year ago. *comScore.* http://www.comscore.com/Press_Events/Press_Releases/2010/1/comScore_Reports_29.1_Billion_in_U.S._Retail_E-Commerce_Spending_for_Full_November-December_Holiday_Season_Up_4_Percent_vs._Year_Ago, accessed May 21, 2011.

17. Anonymous. (October 2009). Online retailers focus on checkout to increase sales. *Apparel.* (51), 16. DOI: ID Number: 1898713071.

18. Anonymous. (November 2009). Alleged international hacker indicted for largest data breach ever. *Computer and Internet Lawyer.* 26(11), 31–32.

19. Awad, N.F., & Ragowsky, A. (2008). Establishing trust in electronic commerce through online word of mouth: An examination across genders. *Journal of Management Information Systems.* 24(4), 101–121.

20. Lim, K.H., et al. (2006). Do I trust you online, and if so, will I buy? An empirical study of two trust-building strategies. *Journal of Management Information Systems.* 23(2), 233–266.

21. Sia, C.L., et al. (2009). Web strategies to promote Internet shopping: Is cultural-customization needed? *MIS Quarterly.* 33(3), 491–512.

22. Anonymous. (January 5, 2010). Verification service seen to spur online transactions. *BusinessWorld.* DOI: ID Number: 1933444041.

23. iProspect. (2006). *iProspect search engine user behavior study.*

24. Lancaster, J. (2009). The secret of SEO success. *Ward's Dealer Business.* 43(12), 32–33.

25. Morrissey, B. (2009). A banner move. *Adweek.* p. 7.

26. Helft, M. (2009). Ads tied to Internet search results hold big stakes for small businesses; Companies scramble to win prominent spots on Google and Yahoo. *The International Herald Tribune.* p. 4.

27. (2009). Baidu to boost search engine market share with new services. *Chinadaily.com.cn.* http://www.chinadaily.com.cn/business/2009-11/26/content_9053270.htm accessed May 21, 2011.

28. Delaney, K. J. (2005). In "click fraud," web outfits have a costly problem. *Wall Street Journal.* 245(67), A1–A6.

29. (2003). Backspace. *PC Magazine.* 22(8), http://www.pcmag.com/article2/0,2817,1034132,00.asp, accessed May 21, 2011.

30. O'Reilly, T., & Battelle, J. (2009). Web squared: Web 2.0 five years on. *Web 2.0 Summit.* http://www.web2summit.com/web2009/public/schedule/detail/10194, accessed May 21, 2011.

31. Bradshaw, T. (January 4, 2010). Original ideas prove customer knows best. *Financial Times.* p. 4.

32. Giles, J. (2005). Internet encyclopaedias go head to head. *Nature.* (438), 900–901.

33. Goldsborough, R. (2009). Internet encyclopedias in flux. *Tech Directions.* 69(2), 12–13.

34. (September 2009). The digital geographers. *The Economist.* 392(8647), 12. DOI: ID Number: 1853056401, Retrieved from ABI/INFORM database, August 13, 2010.

35. Stross, R.E. (2009). *Planet Google.* New York: The Free Press.

36. O'Reilly, T., & Battelle, J. (2009). Web squared: Web 2.0 five years on. Web 2.0 Summit. http://www.web2summit.com/web2009/public/schedule/detail/10194, accessed May 21, 2011.

37. Grossman, L. (2010). If you liked this. *Time.* 175(22), 44–48.

38. Grover, R., & Satariano, A. (July 1, 2010). The fall of music downloads. *Bloomberg Businessweek.*

39. Rose, C. (July 5, 2010). Charlie Rose talks to Tim Westergren. *Bloomberg Businessweek.* p. 39.

Business Intelligence and *Decision Support*

Chapter Preview

MAKING SMART DECISIONS TAKES MORE THAN GOOD JUDGMENT.
It takes a clear understanding of the information relevant to solving the
problem, and knowledge about where that information can be obtained.
It also takes insightful analysis, often relying on sophisticated software
tools that can do much of the work. This chapter explains what business
intelligence is, why you need it, where you can find it, and what decision
support tools are available to help you analyze it all. You will also learn how
to organize and display the information that is most important to you, to
avoid the trap of information overload.

© Ocean/Corbis

Learning Objectives

1 Define business intelligence and describe the three levels of decision making that it supports.

2 Describe the major sources of business intelligence and provide examples of their usefulness.

3 Explain several approaches to data mining and decision support that help managers analyze patterns, trends, and relationships, and make better data-driven decisions.

4 Explain how web analytics are used as a source of business intelligence, and why they are so valuable for understanding customers.

5 Describe how dashboards, portals, and mashups support decision making, and explain the role that the human element plays in using these tools.

Introduction

Every New Year's Eve, Virginia's Richmond Police Department had been flooded with citizen complaints about random gunfire. But once the department began using data mining software to decide how and where to deploy its officers, the complaints dropped by 47 percent and the number of weapons recovered increased by 246 percent. By analyzing historical crime trends and adding recent data to the analysis, the department saved $15,000 in human resource costs alone during that one 8-hour shift.[1]

Data continues to pile up, drawing from databases, the web, videocameras, smartphones, RFID sensors, digitized books, and more. The information systems we use to tap this mother lode intelligently are the subject of this chapter, and particularly the ways we can identify trends and patterns to make better decisions. Determining how to schedule officers on New Year's Eve is just one decision that can be improved with business intelligence and decision support tools. Here are more:

▶ How much should we spend for online ads this season? Which ads work best?

▶ Should we create more fish dishes for our menu? How much can we charge?

▶ When should we start our phonathon to raise money for disaster relief? Should we invite celebrities to promote it?

▶ How should we address the bad publicity about our product recalls? Should we ignore it?

Business intelligence (BI), introduced in Chapter 1, is an umbrella term that includes the vast quantities of information an organization might use for data-driven decision making, from within its own data repositories and also from external sources. The term also encompasses the software applications, technologies, and practices that managers apply to the data to gain insights that help them make better decisions.

Define business intelligence and describe the three levels of decision making that it supports.

Levels of Decision Making

Consider the roles that these three people play in a busy city hospital:

▶ Monica works the evening shift in the call center, scheduling appointments, referring patients, registering callers for hospital seminars, and routing calls.

▶ Colin just joined the hospital as assistant director of marketing. He will track online campaigns intended to call attention to the hospital's top-ranked specialties, such aws sports medicine and cardiology. His business major in college, with its focus on information systems and marketing, was critical to his selection for this post.

▶ Bora is the hospital administrator, responsible for the hospital's overall financial and operational health. She plans budgets, sets rates, recruits and hires the medical and administrative staff, and, working with the different teams, develops hospital policies. She earned her MBA, and also holds an MS in health care administration.

Each of these people makes dozens of decisions every day, at different levels of the organization and across business units. They draw on written policies, formal training, unwritten norms, business intelligence, and their own insights and gut instincts to make the best decisions they can. Collectively, their decisions determine the success or failure of the whole organization. Figure 7-1 illustrates typical decision-making levels.

OPERATIONAL LEVEL

Employees working primarily at the operational level make countless decisions as they deal directly with customers and handle all the routine transactions. Many decisions follow predetermined policies and procedures that spell out how to handle different situations. Monica took training for her call center position, in which rules for dealing with each type of call were specified. She learned how to deal with angry callers, impatient callers, and callers who appear to be in severe physical or mental distress. Within this structure, however, Monica also makes decisions independently, such as how long to spend with each caller, how to encourage a caller to attend a hospital event, and how sympathetic to sound in each situation.

FIGURE 7-1

Different levels of decision making in an organization rely on different mixes of structured and unstructured information.

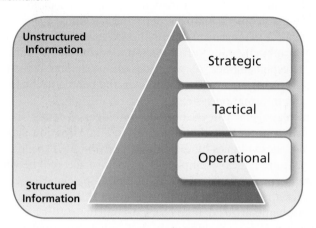

Business intelligence for use at the operational level is attracting considerable attention as organizations find ways to bring meaningful, performance-related information to all employees. Timely data showing the outcome and effectiveness of their decisions can dramatically affect performance.[2]

At 1-800-CONTACTS, the world's largest contact lens store, operational business intelligence fine-tunes the decision making of every call center agent. Each one has access to a customized screen with color-coded gauges showing daily metrics, such as his or her average calls per hour and average sale size. Bar charts show these metrics, comparing them to the agent's monthly averages. The screens also contain displays updated from a data warehouse every 15 minutes so agents get quick feedback. Bonuses are tied to a formula based on these measures, so motivation to move the needles on their dials is high. After the system was implemented, revenues increased $50,000 per month, with consistently high call quality.[3] Figure 7-2 shows an example of the kinds of screens used in call center settings.

FIGURE 7-2

Call center agents can see timely data on their own and their coworkers' activities, especially to support operational decision making and improved performance.

Metric	Minutes and Seconds
Current call length	**13:42**
Your average call length today	12:41
Today's average call length, for all agents	10:25
This week's average call length, all agents	13:32

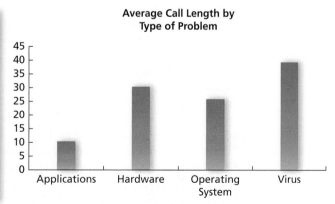

Average Call Length by Type of Problem

Time on current call

Average for all calls

Escalation rate

Resolved rate

TACTICAL LEVEL

People at tactical levels draw on business intelligence to make mid-level decisions, the kind that may guide individual business units. Decisions about marketing plans, product development, membership drives, departmental budgets, and other initiatives are generally tactical. A management information system (MIS) supports this kind of decision making, combining data, software, and reporting tools that managers need to carry out their responsibilities. As we discussed in Chapter 1, the term MIS also describes the academic discipline that focuses on the people, technology, processes, and data making up information systems.

Much useful management-level business intelligence comes from the routine weekly or monthly reports that the organization's information systems generate. Weekly reports on sales volumes by region and year-to-date expenditures compared to the previous year are typical examples. For Colin to succeed, he will need weekly reports on the number of patients admitted, organized by clinical area. If his department is conducting a marketing campaign featuring the sports medicine clinic, for instance, he can use summarized data to check his outcomes.

Operational-level decision making requires detailed structured information about actual transactions by customer, so staff can follow up and track each transaction. At the tactical level, decision makers need more aggregated information, sorted and tallied in different ways, to monitor success and plan next steps.

STRATEGIC LEVEL

The organization's leadership guides longer-term strategy. Decisions made at this level can have widespread effects throughout the organization and beyond, to suppliers, customers, and even the whole industry. Each decision could commit huge amounts of capital and people to major initiatives. For instance, hospital administrator Bora may need to decide whether to open a new pediatrics wing or use those resources to enlarge sports medicine.

A high-tech CEO might ask, should we make an offer to buy out a rival? A pharmaceutical company's CFO may wonder how much the company should invest in R&D over the next 5 years. A college president will need extensive data from financial analysts, faculty, and students—both current and prospective—to weigh whether to eliminate one of the academic departments with very few majors rather than lay off people or raise tuition.

The business intelligence that executives need to make better decisions is often less structured than at the operational or even management level. Top-level execs certainly need summary and historical data from the company's own transactional systems and data warehouses. But they also need competitive business intelligence about their rivals, broader information about the industry landscape, and a forecast of overall economic and business conditions.

The term **executive information system** refers to the software tools that support strategic-level decision making for senior managers. However, distinctions between management and executive information systems are difficult to make, since their functionality is often similar. Time horizons or levels of aggregation might differ, but the systems offer displays and retrieval capabilities that people can customize to their own decision-making needs. For example, a senior executive might want to see graphs showing 10-year trends, while a finance department manager is more concerned with the current year.

In any case, most people in an organization need decision support at more than one level, depending on the situation. A CEO will want to see the detailed transaction records of a high-value client, and the call center staff can suggest process improvements if they have access to reports showing longer-term patterns. Colin, who usually operates at the tactical level, will be very interested in analyzing the sports blogs to see what people say about the hospital. He'll need tools to tap such external information sources as much as any CEO.

Sources of Business Intelligence

2 Describe the major sources of business intelligence and provide examples of their usefulness.

A hurdle for business intelligence projects is not too little information. It's too much. Throughout the organization and well beyond its borders, valuable information sources that can improve decision making at all levels abound.

TRANSACTIONAL DATABASES, DATA WAREHOUSES, AND INTERNAL DATA SOURCES

The heart of BI is the transactional system used for daily operations. Within the organization's own databases is a treasure trove of data about its customers, employees, suppliers, and every financial transaction. Databases maintained by suppliers or customers are also critical BI sources.

As we discussed in Chapter 4, transactional systems must be tuned for best operational performance. Agents must be able to retrieve a customer's screen in microseconds, and updates to a record must not bog the system down. But BI reports can be very resource-hungry; a single query to summarize sales totals by region and product could bring the operational system to its knees. When a call agent has to say, "I'm sorry, but the system is really slow now," a good guess is that some unwitting manager is running summary reports.

To avoid slowing down operational systems, most organizations build data warehouses by extracting part or all of the data from those databases and moving it to another server. This process offers an opportunity to combine the data housed in separate systems into one, cleanse and transform it, and then load it to a database optimized for complex queries.

Moving and transforming an enormous volume of data can take time, so many organizations do extractions just once a day, or even once a week. But with a growing need for real-time intelligence, businesses are finding ways to freshen their data warehouses much more frequently. Satellite TV provider DIRECTV, for instance, needed to monitor call center activity without bogging down the work of its 1,500 agents, who support customers in several cities. The firm implemented GoldenGate's data management software to capture the transaction logs and post them to the warehouse in near real-time. Within seconds of any transaction, the new data is streamed to the gigantic data warehouse, where it becomes available for reporting.

The advantage became obvious immediately. Jack Gustafson, DIRECTV's data warehouse director, said, "Analysts are just raving about how great we're doing compared to our competitors in this area. A lot of it comes down to using this real-time copy to do analysis on customers, and to [make a fresh] offer to them the same day." DIRECTV reduced the churn common among premium TV providers, as customers switch from one to the other chasing the best promotions.[4] Oracle purchased GoldenGate to enhance its own data warehousing capabilities.

Valuable intelligence may also be housed in departmental systems, e-mail, electronic documents, filing cabinets, individually maintained spreadsheets, and PC hard drives. These are more difficult to dig into, but as you will see, some progress is being made to unleash these sources.

EXTERNAL DATA SOURCES

As individuals put more and more information online, and organizations deploy software as a service, considerably more data that is useful for BI exists in the "cloud"—on servers that could be quite distant from the company's headquarters. Managers need strategies to access these sources and feed the

executive information system
The software tools that support strategic-level decision making for senior managers.

FIGURE 7-3

Data useful for business intelligence can be downloaded from the U.S. Census Bureau's website.

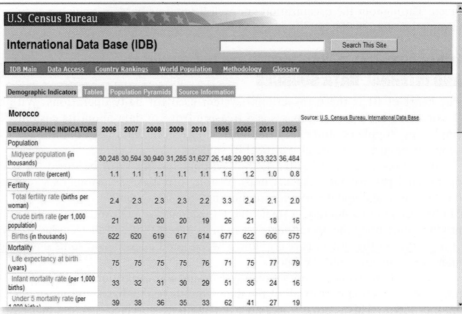

Source: www.census.gov/ipc/www/idb/country.php

data into BI systems for analysis. A company that uses a CRM product such as Salesforce.com, for instance, will have important data hosted on Salesforce's servers. The company will need to integrate the customer data maintained on the remote server with its other systems that handle finance, human resources, and other business functions.

External databases that are either purchased or publicly accessible are also excellent sources of business intelligence. The U.S. Census Bureau, for instance, maintains many searchable databases with information about demographics, educational levels, income, ethnicity, housing, employment, and more. Figure 7-3 shows an example of output from a query to its extensive international database.

Besides retrieving downloadable files from online sources, companies can also use **intelligent agents** to extract useful business intelligence from publicly accessible websites. These software programs, often called "bots," are sent out to conduct a mission and collect data from web pages on behalf of a user. For example, a tour operator in China might want competitive business intelligence about airline ticket pricing between the United States and Hong Kong, updated daily. Using robot-building software, the operator can design an agent to interact with each airline's website, recording all the steps a human performs to get a listing of first- and coach-class ticket prices (Figure 7-4). The agent can be sent on its mission every day, bringing competitive pricing information home to the company's own data warehouse.

Intelligent agents are useful for many tasks and are growing smarter and more capable each year. Search engines use them to classify and index web pages, and infomediaries deploy them to retrieve current product prices from different vendors.

Information resources include semi-structured and unstructured information in addition to the structured information found in databases

PRODUCTIVITY TIP

You can create an agent to carry out online searches for articles relevant to your term paper, business plan, research project, hobbies, job hunts, or anything else. Yahoo, Google, and many online library databases offer this service, usually called "alerts." Once you refine your search criteria to retrieve the results you want, you save the search as an alert, schedule it to run daily, and e-mail you whatever it finds.

FIGURE 7-4

To build a bot, the designer carries out the steps a human being would perform to capture data on public websites, and the software creates the agent that will carry out the tasks on its own.

Search for flights

From: LAX

To: HKG

Departure Date: [ ] Return Date: [ ]

Economy ○ Business ○ First ○

Get Prices

or retrieved by agents. The mind-boggling volume of websites, blogs, wikis, social networks, photo sharing sites, video repositories, discussion forums, and text messages may contain insights that managers can use, and business intelligence can draw from all these sources. Fortunately, technological advances are applying more structure to make these sources easier to access and analyze. For example, transactional systems add scanned images to their customer records, such as the check you wrote by hand. Most banks scan checks so you can see the images when you log in to your online bank account. Paper documents can be scanned and read with optical character recognition software that converts the image to searchable text. Crowdsourcing is also adding structure, as millions of individuals voluntarily tag online photos and videos with names, keywords, places, and dates.

PRODUCTIVITY TIP

Planning a strategy to gather and organize your own business intelligence will dramatically improve your productivity. The bookmarks you add to your browser as you surf the web, for example, represent sources of semi-structured information that may be useful for an upcoming research paper or job search, if you take time to organize them. If you use different browsers and computers, you may want to keep track of them with a cloud-based service, such as Digg or StumbleUpon.

✴ THE ETHICAL FACTOR The Ethics of Tagging Faces in Photos

Tagging online photos of faces with people's names is wildly popular and very helpful as a means to add structure to information. Those old group photos come alive when you don't have to struggle to recall long-forgotten names. However, these tags are raising serious privacy concerns and ethical dilemmas.

Although you may have no reluctance to tag yourself in your own photos, will your friends and family want you to tag them? They may think the photo is unflattering. Or they may be concerned that their employers will stumble upon tagged images you thought were amusing, but that employers think show poor judgment. Parents may also object to tagged images of their children appearing online.

Though photo sharing sites offer assurances and many choices about privacy, the potential for harm is not trivial, especially because you can't control what others are doing. Uploaded photos might include metadata that you may not even know is attached, such as GPS coordinates that

can "geotag" your photo to indicate location, and the date and time the photo was taken.

The services offer facial recognition software to ease the tedium of individually tagging each photo. After you tag some faces, the software can find those people in other photos and tag them on its own. Though very handy, this tool greatly amplifies the chance that people will be tagged without their knowledge or consent, and the information used in unpredictable ways by marketers, employers, relatives, or even law enforcement. Former Google CEO Eric Schmidt slammed facial recognition technology as "even too creepy for Google," and claimed the company would not build a database that could recognize individual faces online, even though it is feasible. But at the same time, Google bought PittPatt, a startup company that specializes in such software. With cell phone cameras widespread and photo uploads so simple and quick, the "anonymous face in the crowd" may become rare indeed.

intelligent agents
Software programs or "bots" that are sent out to conduct a mission and collect data from web pages on behalf of a user.

Explain several approaches to data mining and decision support that help managers analyze patterns, trends, and relationships, and make better data-driven decisions.

3

Data Mining and Decision Support Systems

Once a firm has identified the sources of business intelligence, the next step is to start mining them to better understand trends and patterns. The software tools to do this are becoming extremely powerful and user-friendly. Many are stand-alone BI platforms that the organization can add to its environment to support decision making and link to its data warehouses. Other tools are offered as part of enterprise information systems, and ERP vendors are adding BI capabilities to their product suites. Microsoft adds BI functionality to its SQL Server database, integrating it with its other products, especially Excel. In fact, Excel is so common in business that many of the BI products use Excel as the front end for data retrieval and analysis. Opensource BI tools are also available for free.

ANALYZING PATTERNS, TRENDS, AND RELATIONSHIPS

Looking deeply into the data and analyzing it from different perspectives is a fundamental role of decision support systems. The choice of tool depends on the kind of data and the needs of the user.

ONLINE ANALYTICAL PROCESSING (OLAP) Exploring the data warehouse, with its hundreds of tables, thousands of fields, and dozens of relationships among the tables, is not for the fainthearted. Although programmers and some power users can write SQL code to frame complex queries, most business users need views into their data that are more intuitive. They want to be able to sort and summarize it in many different ways to find patterns and relationships that don't easily show in routine reports from the transactional system.

Online analytical processing (OLAP) systems allow users to interactively retrieve meaningful information from data, examining it from many different perspectives and drilling down into specific groupings. The software allows users to "slice and dice" massive amounts of data stored in data warehouses to reveal significant patterns and trends. Managers might check sales transactions by customer gender and age group and find relationships that can guide marketing campaigns.

OLAP systems help spot suspicious activity as well. Medicare anti-fraud strike forces, for example, use such systems to detect unusual billing that might point to illegal scams. One analysis uncovered a disturbing relationship in three south Florida counties. With just 8 percent of the nation's HIV/AIDS patients residing there, the counties accounted for more than 72 percent of the entire country's Medicare charges for the disease. Another analysis found that charges for home health care services in Miami jumped a startling tenfold in just 2 years, though the city showed no comparable increase in the number of elderly residents. That insight led investigators to bills totaling $155,000 for nurses to help an elderly Miami man inject insulin twice a day. They discovered the man was not diabetic and the nurses did not exist.[5]

PRODUCTIVITY TIP
Excel is a powerful OLAP tool itself, thanks to its pivot tables and charting capabilities. You can create pivot tables from an Excel worksheet, an Access database, or your own organization's data warehouse.

OLAP systems achieve their speed and their slice-and-dice capabilities by building **multidimensional cubes**. These are data structures that contain detailed data, and also aggregated values for the dimensions, metrics, and hierarchies the users need. A company might want a cube that managers could use to analyze total sales by store location, by product, or by time period (Figure 7-5). These categories could be represented as dimensions of the cube, and time period could also be structured in the cube as a hierarchy. Managers might want to see sales by product, by month, by quarter, or by year. Although the term "cube" suggests that three is the limit for dimensions, these structures can actually incorporate dozens.

STATISTICS AND MODELING TECHNIQUES Data mining and decision support systems rely on statistical analysis and models, not just to display averages or changes over

FIGURE 7-5

Multidimensional cube created from tables in a data warehouse and used for OLAP.

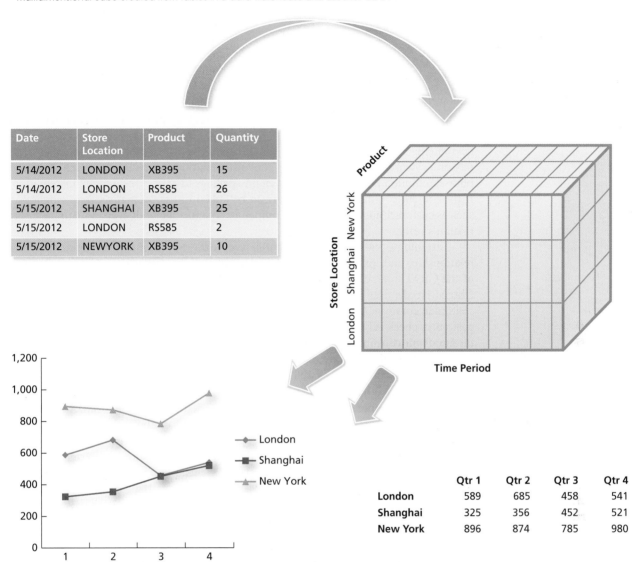

Date	Store Location	Product	Quantity
5/14/2012	LONDON	XB395	15
5/14/2012	LONDON	RS585	26
5/15/2012	SHANGHAI	XB395	25
5/15/2012	LONDON	RS585	2
5/15/2012	NEWYORK	XB395	10

	Qtr 1	Qtr 2	Qtr 3	Qtr 4
London	589	685	458	541
Shanghai	325	356	452	521
New York	896	874	785	980

time, but also to identify real patterns—ones that probably did not occur just by chance. Colin's survey of patient families suggests that women rate the pediatrics ward somewhat more favorably than men. But before launching a campaign based on this finding, Colin would use statistics software to analyze the data more closely, not just view it on a graph. If the difference is significant, Colin would be confident about a decision to target men in the next campaign.

Statistical relationships can be especially useful to spot. For example, a technique called **market basket analysis** looks for such relationships to reveal customer behavior patterns as they purchase multiple items. Are customers who buy soda more likely to also buy candy? Do men who buy shoes also tend to buy matching socks? Are people who buy larger TVs more likely to also purchase high-priced speaker systems?

Results like these can show meaningful patterns that help retailers decide where to place products in a store. Online, retailers make very obvious use of market basket analysis.

online analytical processing (OLAP)
Software that allows users to "slice and dice" or drill down into massive amounts of data stored in data warehouses to reveal significant patterns and trends.

multidimensional cubes
Data structures used for online analytical processing that permit very rapid analysis from different perspectives and groupings.

market basket analysis
A statistical technique that reveals customer behavior patterns as they purchase multiple items.

For instance, Amazon's product screens conspicuously show sections titled, "Frequently Bought Together" and "Customers Who Bought This Item Also Bought."

PRODUCTIVITY TIP
Microsoft has added considerable statistical power to Excel, both in its functions and formulas and with an add-in called "Data Analysis." Tools include descriptive statistics with mean, mode, median, standard deviation, correlation, and several modeling and hypothesis-testing tools. Some knowledge of statistics is helpful to use these tools.

TEXT MINING Dipping into the vast storehouse of unstructured text-based data contained in e-mails, blogs, tweets, online product reviews, and comments yields critical business intelligence. **Text mining**, a variation of data mining, is a discovery process in which unstructured text information is the source of business intelligence, rather than structured data (Figure 7-6). Text mining software tools rely on keywords, semantic structures, linguistic relationships, parts of speech, common phrases, emotion-laden words, and even misspellings to extract meaningful information. If the content contains some text that can be linked to the company's data warehouse, such as customer name, location, or competitor's name, that adds even more to the information's value.

Text mining that monitors web chatter is especially important for managing customer relationships and spotting crises early. Sentiment analysis, discussed in Chapter 5 as part of the CRM suite, can help detect positive and negative remarks about the company. Choice Hotels uses text mining software to make sense of the comments section of customer surveys. Although it is easy to analyze the quantitative scales on which customers check off responses ranging from "Very satisfied" to "Very dissatisfied," it is far more time consuming to analyze the comments from hundreds of thousands of survey responses. With the software, managers can retrieve graphical displays of problem types expressed in the comments, as well as positive and negative comments sorted by location, time of year, and other variables.

Sarah Hofstetner, a strategist at a digital marketing company, thinks companies are rightfully concerned about what customers might say about them in public blogs or reviews. Even if a complaint is unfair, such comments can spread widely and cause serious damage to the brand. A dissatisfied traveler, for instance, can anonymously submit a complaint to The Bedbug Registry, a website that publishes bedbug reports by state so tourists can avoid those hotels. "Fear has been the core of the motivation for daily active listening," she points out. "The challenge is information overload. You can set up alerts to the point of crashing your inbox…. It depends on the frequency of conversations about your brand and your threshold for pain."[6]

Did You Know?

Yahoo! offers a free service you can use to monitor web chatter and do some active listening of your own (alerts.yahoo.com). For example, you can enter your name, college or university, hobby, or club as keywords, and the service will send you an e-mail or text message whenever it finds a match.

FIGURE 7-6

Text mining software can extract useful business intelligence from blogs.

From a blog:

"The sales rep at Reliance was really rude. He kept insisting that I add more services when all I wanted was a lower price. Made me mad so I canceled completely. "

New London Mom

SIMULATING, OPTIMIZING, AND FORECASTING

Beyond gathering, analyzing, and displaying the data, decision support systems encompass a range of approaches that help managers simulate events and make forecasts for the future.

WHAT-IF ANALYSIS A simulation category called a **what-if analysis** builds a model that establishes relationships between many variables and then changes some of the variables to see how the others are affected. Excel is popular for building relatively simple models, such as the one in Figure 7-7. Bora is considering launching the hospital seminar series and uses this what-if analysis to play with the variables that contribute to revenue and expenses. She can estimate and change any of the variables in yellow, and the worksheet computes revenue, expenses, and net profit or loss. For example, she calculates parking fee revenue as:

(# attendees per seminar/average # attendees per car)
*# seminars per year * parking fee

If Bora wants to advertise free parking as part of the program, she can immediately see the result by entering zero as the parking fee. Or she can experiment with different marketing costs per session, to see how much she can spend before landing in the red.

GOAL SEEKING **Goal seeking** is similar to what-if analysis, but in reverse. Instead of estimating several variables and calculating the result, the user sets a target value for a particular metric, such as profit/loss, and tells the program which variable to change to try to reach the goal. For instance, Bora might wonder what the average attendance at each seminar needs to be for the project to break even. She can use the goal-seeking tool in Excel on her what-if spreadsheet, as shown in Figure 7-8. She enters net profit/loss as the cell to set, zero as the goal, and the estimated attendees per session as the changing cell. When she clicks OK, she learns that she'll need an average audience of about 31 people to break even.

FIGURE 7-7

What-if spreadsheet to estimate revenue and expenses for a hospital seminar series. The user can change the estimates for any variables in yellow, and the spreadsheet recomputes.

Hospital Seminars What-If Analysis Estimated Annual Revenue and Expenses		Variables	
Revenue		$500	Speaker's fee per session
Registration Fees	$16,800	$150	Tech support cost per session
Parking Fee	$960	12	Number of seminars per year
Subtotal	$17,760	$35	Registration fee per attendee
		40	Estimated attendees per session
Expenses		$250	Room rental per seminar
Speaker's Fees	$6,000	$5.00	Parking fee per car per session
Tech Support	$1,800	2.5	Average number of attendees per car
Marketing	$3,000	$250	Marketing costs per seminar
Room Rental	$3,000		
Subtotal	$13,800		
Net Profit/Loss	$3,960		

text mining
A technique used to analyze unstructured text that examines keywords, semantic structures, linguistic relationships, emotion-laden words and other characteristics to extract meaningful business intelligence.

what-if analysis
A simulation model, often constructed using Excel, which calculates the relationships between many variables; users can change some variables to see how others are affected.

goal seeking
A decision support tool, often based on an Excel model, in which the user sets a target value for a particular variable, such as profit/loss, and tells the program which variable to change to try to reach the goal.

FIGURE 7-8

Goal seeking using Excel.

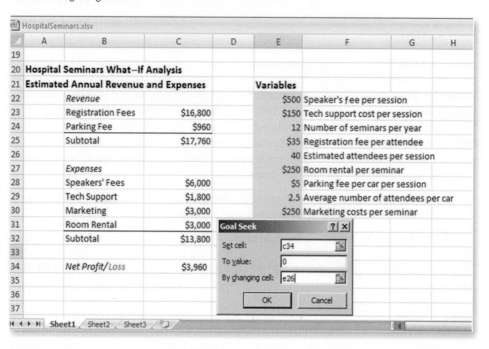

OPTIMIZING An extension of goal seeking is **optimization**, in which the user can change many variables to reach some maximum or minimum target, as long as the changes stay within the constraints the user identifies. For example, Bora might use Excel's optimization tool, called "Solver," to find the best schedule for her evening nurses, the one that minimizes human resource costs (Figure 7-9). All schedules include two consecutive days off, and Bora uses the software to determine how many nurses to assign to each schedule, with the constraint that enough nurses are available each day.

FIGURE 7-9

An Excel add-in called "Solver" can help Bora optimize the schedule for the evening nurses. She sets Solver to minimize total payroll (target cell) by changing the number of nurses assigned to each schedule with different days off. The constraint is that the total available nurses each day must equal or exceed the total required.

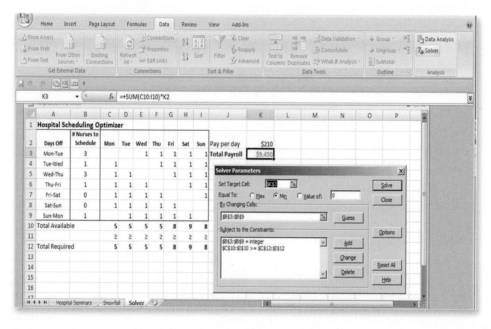

Optimization is used in decision support in many settings in which the best solution must meet many constraints that are difficult to juggle. Airlines, for instance, try to optimize profit per flight, taking into account constraints such as fuel costs, ticket discounts, gate availability, airport congestion, and connections. The list grows ever longer and complex as the decision support tools try to balance many competing variables. For example, a Department of Transportation regulation about publicizing each airline's on-time record adds a new constraint. To keep their on-time rating high, most airlines decided to pad their published flight durations so even delayed flights count as "on time." One puzzled traveler remarked, "If you leave late, you know you will arrive late. But now you leave late and arrive early."[7]

FORECASTING   Forecasting tomorrow's demand, next month's sales, or next year's stock price relies especially on statistical decision support tools. **Forecasting** tools usually analyze historical and seasonal trends and then take into account existing and predicted business conditions to estimate some variable of interest, such as customer demand or projected revenue. For example, Figure 7-10 is a simple model that shows the historical relationship between weekly snowfall and sales revenue from ski lift tickets. Although not perfect, the correlation between them is reasonably high (+.64): the more snow, the higher the revenue. Using the graph, the weather report for 15–16 centimeters next week forecasts revenue of about $60,000. More sophisticated models incorporate many other variables that affect the forecast, drawing widely on business intelligence sources.

DECISION SUPPORT AND ARTIFICIAL INTELLIGENCE

Artificial intelligence (AI) describes the capability of some machines that can mimic human intelligence, displaying characteristics such as learning, reasoning, judging, and drawing conclusions from incomplete information. For business, AI makes valuable contributions in areas such as financial monitoring and customer relationship management. Amazon's software, for example, continually learns about each customer to make more relevant recommendations for new purchases. An ongoing project called ALADDIN is working out ways for large collections of intelligent agents to draw on incomplete information from sensors, share what they learn, and collaborate on decision making. This kind of AI is especially valuable for fast-moving

FIGURE 7-10

Fore casting ski lift ticket revenue from historical weekly snowfalls.

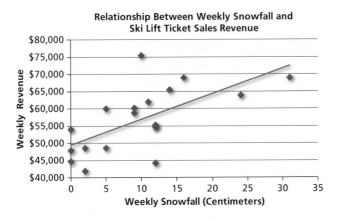

optimization
An extension of goal seeking in which the user can change many variables to reach some maximum or minimum target, as long as the changes stay within the constraints the user identifies.

forecasting
A statistical decision support tool used to analyze historical trends and other business intelligence to estimate some variable of interest, such as customer demand.

artificial intelligence (AI)
The capability of some machines to mimic aspects of human intelligence, such as learning, reasoning, judging, and drawing conclusions from incomplete information.

emergency situations when the volume of incoming data could overwhelm human decision makers. After an earthquake, for instance, these agents might analyze information from fire alarms, cameras, 911 calls, and other sources to quickly decide how best to allocate ambulances across a city.

The AI underpinnings for Watson, IBM's supercomputer that beat human champions in the game show Jeopardy! in 2011, show extraordinary promise. The stunt demonstrated that AI has a very bright future for interpreting human language and drawing on an immense knowledge base to find answers. The next step is to apply Watson's capabilities to the real world beyond Jeopardy! and plans are underway to create a physician's assistant service.

AI is also a lively field within computer science. At MIT, for example, the Sociable Machines Project created Kismet, an expressive "infant" robot that perceives social cues from its human caregivers and responds with social signals of its own, indicating fear, surprise, pleasure, interest, or boredom. Kismet uses facial expressions, body posture, gaze, and other cues in its social interactions. Together, the human and robot learn from one another, just as a human baby and parent learn from and adapt to each other's moods. Although AI has not quite delivered on the early optimistic hope of producing true thinking machines that can masquerade as human beings, these recent advances are very promising.

One downside of the growing power of AI is that scammers use the same techniques to gain access to sites, gather information, or overwhelm a service. Companies that offer free e-mail services, for example, do not want bots registering for thousands of accounts. In fact, web developers increasingly add obstacles they hope will block these rogue intelligent agents.

One such obstacle that thwarts most software bots is the **CAPTCHA**, a test the visitor must pass before continuing to register or enter the site. One variety presents an image of some letters and numbers, and the user must correctly read and enter them before proceeding (Figure 7-11). The image is fuzzy and the fonts are irregular, making it difficult for optical character recognition software to read. Audio CAPTCHAs are also in use. Visitors listen to an audio file and type the phrase they hear.

Did You Know?

Each time you decipher a CAPTCHA, you're helping libraries struggling to digitize old books, but whose optical character readers are stumped by those odd fonts and blurry characters. Every day, some 10 million CAPTCHAs are solved by human beings, giving a big boost to the effort to make these valuable texts searchable. The human solutions also save the cost of workers who would otherwise be needed to resolve fuzzy text.[8] CAPTCHA is an acronym for "Completely Automated Public Turing test to tell Computers and Humans Apart," coined by researchers at Carnegie Mellon University.

FIGURE 7-11

A CAPTCHA designed to ensure visitors are actually human beings and not bots.

Enter the words above [   ]
Get another CAPTCHA
Get an audio CAPTCHA

Some of the most useful applications of AI for businesses and other organizations are found in robotics, expert systems, and neural nets, described next.

ROBOTICS The robots that creep around Mars, vacuum airports, assemble autos, assist the disabled, and perform countless other services have become ever smarter and more useful. The challenges of mobility, sensation and perception, balance, obstacle detection, navigation, memory, and battery life are being overcome. Rather than focusing on creating an artificial human, researchers now apply robotics to specific arenas. Industrial robots have been in use for decades to assemble cars or clean up floors, but service robots with more intelligence and mobility are appearing in business, government, and other sectors.

Service robots that can take on military or rescue operations are particularly in demand as they become more mobile and capable of replacing humans on dangerous assignments. The Precision Urban Hopper, for example, is a shoebox-sized rover that looks like a toy truck, but it has one mighty leg that propels it over obstacles as high as 25 feet, which stopped earlier robots in their tracks. Guided by GPS, the Hopper carries a video camera and microphone for urban surveillance operations.[9]

EXPERT SYSTEMS An **expert system** mimics the reasoning of a human expert, drawing from a base of knowledge about a particular subject area to come to a decision or recommendation. To build an expert system, developers work with experienced and specialized professionals as they provide answers to questions and explain their reasoning processes. The output is fine-tuned continually as the experts contribute more knowledge to the base, refine the rules, and add additional questions. The process is challenging, often because experts don't quite know exactly how they reach their conclusions. Formally identifying the actual steps is harder than you might think, but the results can be quite dramatic and enormously useful for decision support.

Medical diagnostics reap huge benefits from expert systems. Now, with cell phones so widespread, people can access diagnostic systems from anywhere. In Kenyan villages, for example, health workers carrying a small test kit visit rural households looking for signs of malaria. They send the results via text message to the expert system, which in just a few seconds returns an automated response about the proper course of treatment based on its analysis. The system sends additional messages about follow-up treatments and clinic appointments.[10]

NEURAL NETS Neural networks attempt to mimic the way the human brain works, with its vast network of interconnected neurons. Each of the 10 billion+ neurons connects with thousands of its neighbors, receiving chemical signals from them. Each neuron constantly summarizes the input it receives and the results determine its outgoing transmissions. When repeated input causes signals to travel the same pathway again and again, the connections grow stronger and the pathway becomes more permanent and easier to activate. When you use flash cards to memorize vocabulary words in Japanese, for instance, you are reinforcing the paths connecting the neural underpinnings for the English word with its Japanese equivalent. After many repetitions, when you see *dog* you easily recall the Japanese word *inu*.

Neural networks are far simpler than the human brain, of course, but they borrow the brain's approach, using digital signals in place of neural ones. The neural net learns from training data selected by humans that contain cases defining the paths from input to output. The net's success depends largely on the number and quality of the cases it can learn from. For example, a neural net being trained to predict housing values could absorb millions of cases in which the input includes location, sales price,

CAPTCHA
A test created by software developers that the visitor must pass before continuing to register or enter the site; designed to thwart software bots.

expert system
Software that mimics the reasoning and decision making of a human expert, drawing from a base of knowledge about a particular subject area developed with the expert's assistance.

FIGURE 7-12

The neural-net called "20Q" plays the game 20 Questions with visitors, very often guessing correctly. The training data includes the millions of games users play at the site. (www.20Q.net, from 20Q.net Inc.)

Source: ©1988-2011. 20Q, I can read your mind…, and the neural-net on the internet, are registered trademarks of 20Q.net Inc. All related titles, logos and characters are trademarks of 20Q.net Inc. All rights reserved.

square footage, number of bathrooms, and more. For the training data, the output is the actual sales price. Once the net is up and running, the output will be predicted house value.

Neural-nets are widely used where massive data sets are available, such as in the finance industry where detecting fraud is an important application. Analyzing each card transaction in real time, neural-nets compare the specific purchase to the cardholder's regular spending habits and also to fraudulent spending patterns. The neural net will certainly pick it up if a retiree who hasn't traveled beyond Costa Rica starts racking up charges for hip blue jeans in Bucharest.

> **PRODUCTIVITY TIP**
> Before you travel outside your home country, it's wise to let your credit card company know where you are headed. A neural-net may automatically block your card if unexpected foreign charges appear and the card company is unable to reach you.

An amusing neural-net that encourages Web visitors to contribute cases is 20Q (www.20Q.net), based on the game called Twenty Questions. The player thinks of an animal, vegetable, or mineral, and the game asks yes or no questions until it makes a correct guess or gives up (Figure 7-12). Relying on the millions of cases visitors have added, the neural net's accuracy is, as one reviewer put it, "scary." From a single English version, 20Q now has neural-nets in more than 20 languages covering the classic game, as well as domains for Star Trek, Harry Potter, TV, movies, and more.

Explain how web analytics are used as a source of business intelligence, and why they are so valuable for understanding customers. **4**

Web Analytics

The sheer volume of business intelligence available from an organization's own website can be overwhelming. The **clickstream data** includes every single click by every visitor, along with associated data revealing customer behavior patterns, such as time spent on the page, the URL the visitor just left, and the visitor's IP address. With potentially millions of clicks per day, clickstream data adds up quickly. Let's first take a look at what metrics can be gathered from this rich source of business intelligence.

WEB METRICS

Like the proverbial kid in a candy store, analysts have access to an astonishing number of metrics about clickstream activity to draw upon. Each measure reveals something a little different that can help describe how people are interacting with the site, and how well the site is meeting the goals set for it.

FIGURE 7-13

Website metrics.

Web Visitor-Related Metrics	Description
Visitors	Number of visitors to the website. (Returning visitors will be counted again if they return within the time period.)
Unique visitors	Number of unique visitors. (Returning visitors are not counted again.)
Average time on site	Average amount of time visitors spent on the site.
New visitors	Number of new visitors to the site.
Depth of visit	The number of page views per visit, which shows how extensively visitors interact with and navigate around your site.
Languages	The number (or percentage) of visitors based on the language they configured to use on their computer.
Traffic sources	The sources from which visitors arrive at your site, such as a keyword search in a search engine, an ad, or from a link on related sites. Direct traffic is a visit from someone who used a bookmark or typed the URL in the browser.
Service providers	The number of visits coming from people using different Internet service providers.

Web Content-Related Metrics	Description
Page views	The number of visits per page on the site, showing analysts the most popular content.
Bounce rate	Percentage of visits in which the user left the site from the same page he or she entered it. This can mean that the page the user landed on was not very relevant.
Top landing pages	The number of entrances to your site for each page.
Top exit pages	The number of exits from the site for each page.

ORGANIZATIONAL WEBSITE METRICS Figure 7-13 lists several measures of traffic on their own websites that are important to all organizations. All the measures refer to a particular time period the analyst selects, such as the previous week, month, or year.

These web metrics come from server logs, and each entry contains detailed information about the date and time, the page, the source, and any clicks on the page itself. The logs also contain information about each user, including his or her IP address and browser. If the site uses cookies, it can collect more information about each user.

SOCIAL MEDIA METRICS For interactive websites with registered members who contribute their own materials and build friendship networks, even more metrics may be available to analysts. Number of active users, posts per user, photo tags, profile information, purchases, data on friends, group memberships, and product ratings are examples of what these sites can collect. Privacy settings may prevent the release of some of this information, but increasingly, users allow its release in return for some benefit, such as access to games or discounts. We discuss these kinds of privacy issues in more detail in a later chapter.

Lively real-time social media such as Twitter produce their own set of metrics that analysts may want to capture. Figure 7-14 shows some examples.

FIGURE 7-14

Sample metrics for Twitter activity.

Twitter Metric	Description
Updates	The number of updates the user published within the most recent time period.
Followers	The number of followers reported by Twitter at last count.
Following	The number of individuals the user is following at last count.
ReTweeted	The number of times a user has been retweeted by other people.
Referenced	The number of times a particular user has been referenced or cited by other people in their tweets.

clickstream data
Business intelligence data that includes every click by every visitor on a website, along with associated data such as time spent on the page and the visitor's IP address.

FIGURE 7-15

E-commerce metrics.

E-Commerce Metric	Description
Conversion rate	The ratio of visitors who complete some activity (such as buying a product) divided by the total number of visitors.
Clickthrough rate (CTR)	The ratio of clicks on an ad divided by the number of times the ad was delivered.
Cost per clickthrough (CPC)	The amount an advertiser pays each time a visitor clicks on the ad to navigate to the advertiser's site.
Cost per impression (CPM is cost per thousand impressions)	For banner and display ads, the cost the advertiser pays each time the ad loads onto a user's screen from any site on which it appears.
Position on page	The position in which a sponsored link appears on a page in keyword advertising on search engines.

E-COMMERCE METRICS If the site includes advertising or e-commerce capabilities, many of the metrics about visitors and content will certainly be relevant, such as the characteristics of the visitors, how they found you, how long they stayed at the site, and what pages they lingered on. Some other useful measures are shown in Figure 7-15.

ANALYZING TRAFFIC AND ACHIEVING SUCCESS

Making sense of these numbers takes considerable skill, and the web analyst who has it is in great demand. Although spending for analytical software tools is projected to more than double from 2009 to 2014, spending on salaries for talented analysts will far outpace that. Figure 7-16 shows part of a job posting for this type of position for an online retailer in New York.

ANALYTICS SOFTWARE To reap value from all this information, especially given its volume, organizations must rely on analytical tools. Products specifically designed to analyze clickstream data are growing ever more powerful, with easy-to-use interfaces, graphing capabilities, and advanced statistical techniques. Analysts can quickly see important details about their web traffic, their visitors, and the links that bring customers to their site.

Some products are embedded in content management systems, some are stand-alone products, and others are offered as software as a service. Google's free web analytics, for instance, is a software-as-a-service product. It requires only a short string of code on each page to direct the clickstream data to Google's servers, where the analytical engine does its work. Figure 7-17 shows one example of the kinds of graphs and tables available with web analytics.

REACHING GOALS Web analytics software spews out thousands of aggregated graphs, tables, and charts. To use it wisely to make decisions, companies should have a clear notion of the major goals for the site so they know what to look for. These goals will guide them toward the appropriate metrics, so they can see whether their decisions bring about improvements.

Rail Europe, the company that promotes and sells European train travel tickets in the North American market, wanted U.S. visitors to spend more time planning their trips on its site and eventually buy train tickets. North Americans, however,

FIGURE 7-16

Job posting for a web analyst.

Director, Business Intelligence and Web Analytics

- Analyzes web traffic and customer behavior using clickstream and business intelligence tools
- Creates clear and comprehensive reports showing data and trends
- Provides recommendations on maximizing revenue and improving customer experience
- Leads efforts to integrate clickstream data into marketing campaigns
- BA required, MBA a plus

FIGURE 7-17

Sample output from web analytics software, describing the number of website visitors by day and the most keywords used to reach the site.

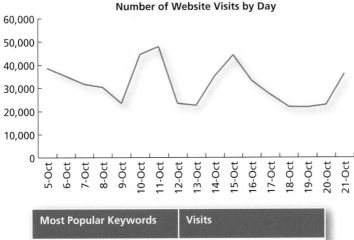

Number of Website Visits by Day

Most Popular Keywords	Visits
Peru	987
Latin America	745
South America	158

are used to driving, so they rarely went to a railway site for travel advice. When Rail Europe began analyzing the site's clickstream data, the results were discouraging. "We saw some trends that would basically put us out of business," said the company's VP for e-business.

Rail Europe learned, for example, that most U.S. visitors stumbled onto the site from a general keyword search, using vague phrases such as "Paris travel." Guided by such analytics, the company added much more travel-related advice, interactive maps, and content to the site, hoping to attract U.S. travelers earlier in their trip planning.

The site's metrics showed major improvements. Bounce rate decreased from 33 to 23 percent, and conversion rates grew 28 percent during the critical April to May period. **Stickiness**, a term that refers to how long visitors linger at the site, jumped from 6 to 8 minutes in less than a year. U.S. visitors were especially intrigued by the interactive maps showing railway lines, so Rail Europe continued to expand these sections.[11]

ANALYZING THE EFFECTIVENESS OF ADS The e-commerce metrics that summarize data on advertising campaigns are essential for marketers. Cost per clickthrough, conversion rates, and other measures reveal how well ads are doing and whether advertising dollars are being spent wisely. Over time, historical patterns can also predict how much the company needs to spend on online campaigns to achieve sales goals.

Online advertising is a moving target, though, and analysts should track overall changes in user behavior patterns. For example, the number of people who click display ads dropped 50 percent in a 2-year period. Just 8 percent of Internet users do most of that ad clicking. However, although display ads may not attract many clicks, research shows they do raise brand awareness, much like TV or print ads. One study found that web users exposed to ads notice the brand name and are 65 percent more likely to visit the company's site within a week.[12] Findings like these help web advertisers make smart decisions about how to spend their online marketing budget.

stickiness
The measurement of how long visitors linger at a website.

FIGURE 7-18

Online ads can include variables to customize the text according to the phrase the user entered as the search term.

Search term: phones for children	Search term: kids' phones
Phones for Children The Fun & Easy Way to Find **Phones** for **Children** at Low Prices *www.goodgifts.biz*	**Kids' Phone** 100s of Kids Phone Top **Brands** at **Low** Prices! *www.goodgifts.biz*

Keyword advertising, in which relevant text ads appear as sponsored links along with the results of a keyword search in a search engine, is seeing much higher growth than display advertising. The lion's share of Google's and Yahoo!'s revenue comes from these tiny text ads, and marketers achieve generally good results. Their effectiveness, though, depends on variables such as the position in which the sponsored ad appears. The top spot is most effective, with diminishing returns for ads appearing under that.[13]

Clear relevance to the user's search term is also an important variable that contributes to success. A user who enters "phones for kids" is interested in phones for kids, or possibly cell phones for children, but not kid's bedroom furnishings. To help advertisers improve their results, search engines allow the text ads to include variables that will be replaced by the user's actual search terms. An online gift store, for instance, will program the ad to display "Phones for Kids" as the title, or "Phones for Children" if that was the user's search term (Figure 7-18).

 Describe how dashboards, portals, and mashups support decision making, and explain the role that the human element plays in using these tools.

5 Putting It All Together: Dashboards, Portals, and Mashups

Staying on top of this endless stream of data from so many business intelligence sources can be an immense challenge. Transactional records, competitive business intelligence, clickstream data, news, blogs, tweets, government regulations, and legal cases combine in a barrage of information overload. Access to this universe of information relevant to your job and organization may be a wonderful thing, but you also need strategies for sorting it out and staying apprised of the most useful parts that will help you make good decisions.

DASHBOARDS

Like a plane or car dashboard with its dials, gauges, and other displays of real-time data, the IT **dashboard** is a graphical user interface that organizes and summarizes information vital to the user's role and the decisions that user makes (Figure 7-19).

Colin, for instance, wants to track hospital seminar registrations and attendance, and also results from the online evaluations each attendee is asked to complete. A dashboard combines those metrics with updated graphs showing clickthroughs for his keyword ads and the number of unique visitors to the web pages he designed as landing pages for the ads.

The dashboard should summarize **key performance indicators (KPIs)**, which are the quantifiable metrics most important to the individual's role and the organization's success. For instance, a chief of police might want to see frequently updated charts showing criminal activity by week or number of crimes solved by type. A regional sales manager launching a major discount promotion might want hourly updates on sales volume by product.

Dashboard capabilities come with most business intelligence software, but users will quickly ignore them if the dashboard isn't relevant, timely, and useful. Figure 7-20 lists some tips on best practices for dashboard design.[14]

FIGURE 7-19

A graphical dashboard example, showing summarized and updated information relevant to a project manager.

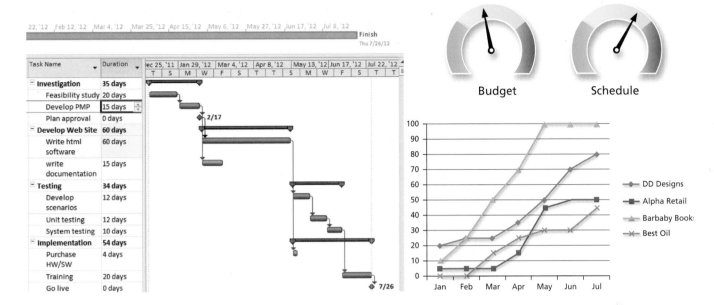

PORTALS

Portals are gateways that provide access to a variety of relevant information from many different sources on one screen. They are content aggregators, making it easier for users to view and drill down into company dashboards, weather announcements, news, traffic reports, stock reports, to-do lists, e-mail, and discussion groups. Each bit of content or functionality that a user can customize and add to the display is called a "portlet."

The enterprise portal (Figure 7-21) is a gateway to the organization's resources, usually built and maintained by the IT department using portal software. Working with the business units, IT develops default pages with commonly requested content and builds interfaces to the organization's resources. Communications or human resources offices often play leading roles in the launch, viewing the portal screen as a precious opportunity to disseminate corporate information and reminders quickly. The "Daily Announcements" portlet is often front and center.

FIGURE 7-20

Dashboard design tips.

Dashboard Feature	Design Tip
Key performance indicators (KPIs)	Choosing KPIs that are most important to the organization and the person using the dashboard is the most important success factor.
Data quality	Dashboards make data look good, but the charts and graphs are only as useful as the quality of the underlying data. Users should ask for warnings when data is stale or not altogether reliable.
Timeliness	Update the dashboard as often as needed for the user's situation—daily, hourly, or minute by minute, if necessary.
Density	Use seven or fewer graphs, charts, maps, or tables on one dashboard, to avoid information overload.
Chart formats	Keep tables small and charts simple, using familiar types. Avoid 3D and unnecessary animations. Be cautious about pie charts, which can be more difficult to interpret.
Maps and visual displays	When relevant, populate actual maps, seating plans, campus layouts, or other visual displays that combine real images with data.

dashboard
A graphical user interface that organizes and summarizes information vital to the user's role and the decisions that user makes.

key performance indicators (KPI)
The quantifiable metrics most important to the individual's role and the organization's success.

portal
A gateway that provides access to a variety of relevant information from many different sources on one screen; for an enterprise, the portal provides a secure gateway to resources needed by employees, customers, and suppliers.

FIGURE 7-21

An enterprise portal.

Source: © 2011 SAP AG. All rights reserved.

Portal users, who include customers and suppliers as well as employees, access the portal with a company-supplied login ID and password. That login determines which applications users are able to access and what level of access they are granted. From within the portal, users can personalize the display, choosing, for example, e-mail accounts, transactional databases, dashboards, 401(k) retirement accounts, benefits summaries, W-2 tax forms, and other applications. Portlet choices often include some external content as well, such as news, traffic reports, and weather.

> **PRODUCTIVITY TIP**
>
> If your university or college offers a portal, you can experiment to see what portlets are available, what functionality you can access, and how much you can customize it. You may be able to do much more than register for courses and check grades.

Enterprise portals were inspired by the consumer portals offered by several major web companies that help people aggregate content to their liking. MyYahoo!, MyMSN, and iGoogle are examples in which users can custom design their own portals with blocks containing snippets of e-mail, news, instant messenger chat, calendars, horoscope, movie show times, stock prices, to-do lists, favorite bookmarks, and more. Depending on the portal, the portlets might be called "gadgets," "widgets," "modules," or just "stuff." Many social network sites develop interfaces for these portals, so a block for Twitter, Facebook, or another site can appear on the consumer's portal page as well.

MASHUPS

Increasing demands for more flexible and customizable gateways stretch the limits of portal technology. They also tax IT departments responsible for development and maintenance. Users want to easily aggregate an exploding array of content from countless business intelligence sources, merging maps with customer data, combining dashboards, news sources, and Excel spreadsheet data, adding live camera feeds, and blending all kinds of information that supports their work roles.

A newer approach to aggregating content from multiple internal and external sources on customizable web pages is the **mashup**. This approach relies on Web 2.0 technologies and programming standards such as XML to blend content and updated feeds from various inside and outside sources in flexible ways.

Mashups can easily incorporate a **web feed**, for example, which is standardized and regularly updated output from a publisher, such as CNN or Weather.com. Rather than going to the website itself, users can embed the web feed in their own mashup so they can always see a little content block with the major headlines. Online publishers, news agencies, weather stations, investment companies, magazines, and many other organizations create and maintain such feeds. The feed includes the text for each update, plus XML metadata for some structured data, such as date and author.

How would end users envision a useful mashup? Sometimes too much flexibility stumps people, so they must understand what information is available, how it might be displayed, and how often it can be updated. Armed with that knowledge, they can focus on the information they need most to do their jobs.

Hospital administrator Bora, for example, might benefit from a mashup that shows KPIs summarized from the hospital's transactional systems, something she can access from a dashboard. She could link seminar attendee data to maps, showing where people who attend the seminars reside. Then during major storms, she might envision maps drawn from city data sources that could affect emergency room requirements—from traffic accidents or fires, for example. Real-time web feeds showing emergency notifications might improve readiness.

Simple consumer-oriented mashups with maps, feeds, data, and other elements can be created using free online tools such as Yahoo! Pipes (pipes.yahoo.com). Once they have created the mashup, users can share it or make it public, and other users can clone, reuse, or tweak the modules (Figure 7-23).

For enterprise mashups, IT departments must ensure security, data quality, and reliability, especially since free services may not provide any assurance of continued existence.[15] Organizations use software, such as the IBM Mashup Center, which make it easier for developers to build secure and robust modules that draw on enterprise resources as well as external content. The workload is reduced,

FIGURE 7-22

This symbol indicates that the website offers a web feed.

PRODUCTIVITY TIP

When you visit a website that displays the orange symbol (Figure 7-22), you can subscribe to that publisher's web feed for your own consumer portal or website. Adding too many, though, could cause your portal to load more slowly.

FIGURE 7-23

Mashup modules can be created using software tools such as Yahoo! Pipes. In this example, the module will display updated business news from CNN with the word "China" in the description.

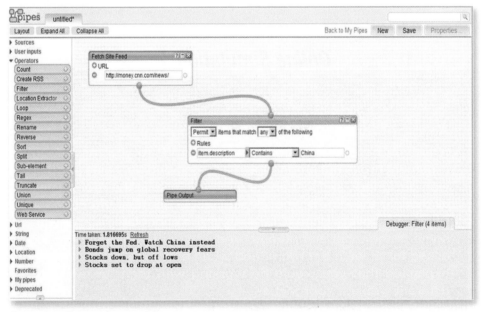

Source: http://pipes.yahoo.com/pipes

mashup
An approach to aggregating content from multiple internal and external sources on customizable web pages that relies on Web 2.0 technologies.

web feed
Standardized and regularly updated output from a publisher, such as CNN or Weather.com, that can be embedded in a customized mashup.

though, partly because mashup software already includes pre-built interfaces for common ERPs and other enterprise systems. Also, interfaces are already built for many commonly used external resources, such as Google maps, YouTube, Facebook, Twitter, and Amazon. Users can mix and match them for their own customized mashups, retrieving timely data as needed.

DECISION MAKING: THE HUMAN ELEMENT

With targeted, timely, and well-summarized business intelligence at our fingertips, we have much of what we need to make smart decisions. With the information systems described in this chapter, we can use computers to analyze information, drawing on our own organization's structured and unstructured resources. We can also tap the growing mounds of data online, combining public and private information in meaningful ways to sort out options and reveal new trends.

Decision support tools aren't crystal balls, and human beings are not always rational creatures weighing evidence the way a computer weighs input. Yet humans are the critical element in decision making, choosing what intelligence to rely upon, what tools to use, and how to interpret the results, and we will still sometimes make poor decisions, even disastrous ones. Research shows, for example, that people in positions of power are more likely to seek out information that confirms what they already believe and steer clear of information that could refute it.[16] An executive who leans toward opening a new plant in a country with lower labor costs may just click "delete" on the mashup's foreign news feed reporting political turmoil there and add graphs showing that country's rosy economic conditions and weather reports.

For our community hospital, similar biases might emerge. Eager to demonstrate that the hospital seminar series is adding value so Bora will fund more of them, Colin might distribute the widget showing the glowing attendee survey results but downplay the graphs that show low attendance.

As we discuss further in the upcoming chapters on collaboration, knowledge management, and e-learning, people are a central component of all information systems. That means we must consider human motives, foibles, and capabilities when designing and implementing effective information systems.

MyMISLab | *Online Simulation*

Chocolate Lovers Unite

A Role-Playing Simulation on Web Analytics

"Can you believe this?" whispered the VP to you, as a loud argument broke out among the marketing people, sales people, web designers, and just about everyone else in the room. They all thought they knew what design would be most effective for Chocolate Lovers Unite (CLU)—an online chocolate retailer with some of the most sumptuous products on the market. The VP asked for quiet in the room, and when everyone settled down, explained that you would be working with them to evaluate different website approaches.

Adisa/Shutterstock

As a web analyst, you were asked to help CLU resolve these arguments using data-driven decision making and business intelligence. Which marketing pitch will work best? Your job is to find out with real data, not guesswork. Time is short with the gift-giving holiday season fast approaching, so you better get started. Check your e-mail and voice messages after you log in ...

Chapter Summary

1 Business intelligence encompasses a vast array of information sources that can contribute to better decision making, along with the software applications, technologies, and practices used to analyze it. Levels of decision making that draw on different types of information sources include operational, tactical, and strategic.

2 A primary source of business intelligence is the transactional database, or data warehouse, used by the organization itself for operations, or by its suppliers and customers. Data available online can also be sources, including websites, blogs, e-mail, downloadable tables, wikis, and business reports. Both internal and external sources can include structured, semi-structured, or unstructured data.

3 Data mining and decision support tools used to analyze patterns, trends, and relationships include online analytical processing (OLAP), statistics and modeling techniques, and text mining software. These software systems can analyze immense quantities of data to identify patterns, spot relationships, test hypotheses, and assess sentiments in online comments. Several software approaches are useful for simulating business events, forecasting the future, or determining optimal solutions to business problems given a set of constraints. The what-if analysis, for example, involves building a model based on relationships among variables that the user can change. Other tools in this category include goal seeking, optimization, and statistical forecasting. Artificial intelligence research contributes many important decision support tools, especially in the fields of robotics, expert systems, and neural nets. These all mimic some aspects of human intelligence, such as learning or expert decision making.

4 The organization's website is a key source of business intelligence with its own metrics. Total visits, number of unique visitors, traffic sources, page views, bounce rates, and other measures reveal how well the site is meeting its goals. For e-commerce and advertising, web analysts rely on display ads and search engine ads, with their own metrics and payment schemes. Web analytic software tracks and summarizes all the clickstream data.

5 Dashboards provide graphic displays that summarize key performance indicators (KPIs), and their content can be customized to meet the needs of individual users. These help reduce information overload and focus attention on the most important metrics. Portals are gateways that aggregate content on the screen and provide access to the individual's resources from a personalized website. Enterprise portals control access to the organization's resources, and the login determines access rights. Mashups also aggregate content and are similar to portals in concept. However, they use Web 2.0 technologies and standards that provide more flexibility to incorporate external resources of all kinds. The human element plays a critical role in decision making, and only people can decide which intelligence to draw on, which tools to use, and how to interpret the results.

KEY TERMS AND CONCEPTS

executive information system	market basket analysis	artificial intelligence (AI)	key performance indicators (KPIs)
intelligent agents	text mining	CAPTCHA	portal
online analytical processing (OLAP)	what-if analysis	expert system	mashup
	goal seeking	clickstream data	web feed
multidimensional cubes	optimization	stickiness	
	forecasting	dashboard	

CHAPTER REVIEW QUESTIONS

1. How do you define business intelligence?
2. What are the three levels of decision making that business intelligence supports?
3. What are the most important sources of business intelligence inside the organization? What makes them useful?
4. What are some examples of external sources of business intelligence?
5. How can managers use data mining techniques to analyze patterns, trends, and relationships? How does this lead to better data-driven decision making?
6. What is text mining?
7. What are examples of statistical techniques that managers can use to simulate business situations, optimize variables, and forecast sales or other figures?
8. What are examples of applications that draw on artificial intelligence for decision support?
9. How are web analytics used to assess the effectiveness of websites?
10. How do dashboards, portals, and mashups support decision making?
11. How does the human element affect decision making?

PROJECTS AND DISCUSSION QUESTIONS

1. Why do organizations use external data as a source of business intelligence? What are examples of sources of external data? How might retail giant Walmart use external data to make tactical-level decisions? How might its decision makers use external data to make strategic-level decisions?

2. How can an intelligent agent assist with a term paper? Visit your university library's home page to locate the "Search Databases" feature. If your library offers the "ABI/INFORM Complete" database, choose that and enter several keywords (for example, "social media in organizations") into the Basic Search dialog box. (If your library does not offer ABI/INFORM, try doing this exercise on a different database.) Review the results, then select "Refine Search" to select additional databases and/or specify additional search criteria. When you have the results you want, select the "Set Up Alert" option to schedule an alert. Prepare a brief report that describes the alert options that are available for your search. How frequently can you receive updates? How long can you receive updates? Are there options other than frequency and duration? Would you recommend using this intelligent agent to other students working on term papers?

3. First Class Salons maintains a company website to promote its chain of 12 health salons. The website includes links to information about its locations, special offers, and FAQs about its services, as well as "About Us" and "Contact Us" links. How can First Class Salons use information from its website to gain business intelligence? Consider the various visitor-related and content-related web metrics and suggest at least six specific metrics that First Class Salons would want to analyze. Prepare a brief report of your suggestions.

4. The Springfield Family Community Center has an outdoor pool that operates May through October. The director is interested to learn whether the center can afford the $57,000 cost of installing a pool-covering dome so patrons can swim year-round. It will also cost about $200 a month for power to keep the dome inflated for 6 months each year. How can the director use forecasting to evaluate the likelihood of selling sufficient tickets to pay for this improvement? Prepare a brief report to the director that explains forecasting. Be sure to include suggestions on both internal and external data that would be useful for this analysis.

5. Digital dashboards began to appear in the 1990s as organizations looked for ways to consolidate and display data to make it accessible and useful for busy executives. Visit www.digitaldashboard.org or www.dashboardsbyexample.com or search the Internet to learn more about digital dashboards. What is the relationship between digital dashboards and key performance indicators? Work in a small group with classmates to consider how a digital dashboard can be used by a Radio Shack or other electronics store manager. What specific daily performance indicators would he or she want to see on a digital dashboard? What design tips would you offer to the dashboard developer? As a group, create a hand-drawn sketch of a dashboard design for the Radio Shack manager.

APPLICATION EXERCISES

EXCEL APPLICATION:
Analyzing Revenue and Expenses for City Hospital Seminars

Figure 7-24 shows the Excel spreadsheet that Bora uses to evaluate the variables relating to the hospital seminar series. She has asked you to use Excel to create a similar spreadsheet to conduct additional what-if and goal seek analyses. You will need to use the following formulas:

Revenue

Registration Fees = Attendees per seminar × Registration fee × Seminars per year

Parking Fees = (Attendees per seminar / Average number attendees per car) × Seminars per year × Parking fee

Expenses

Speakers' Fees = Speaker's fee per session × Seminars per year

Tech Support = Tech support cost per session × Seminars per year

Marketing = Marketing cost per seminar × Seminars per year

Room Rental = Room rental per seminar × Seminars per year

What-If Questions

After answering each question, be sure to return the variables to their original values shown in Figure 7-24 before testing the impact of changing another one.

1. What is the impact on net profit if the average attendance per seminar increases to 45?

2. What is the impact on net profit if the average attendance drops to 35?

3. What is the impact on net profit if the parking fee is reduced to $3?

4. What is the impact on net profit if the speaker's fee increases to $550 per seminar?

5. What is the impact on net profit of increasing the marketing expense per seminar to $350, which increases average attendance per seminar to 50?

6. What is the impact on net profit of an increase in room rental per seminar to $300?

7. If Bora can negotiate a room rental fee of $160 per seminar, how much will net profit increase?

8. If technical support is included in the room rental per seminar, what is net profit?

FIGURE 7-24

The hospital seminar series data.

	A	B
1	**Hospital Seminars Revenues and Expenses**	
2		
3	**Revenue**	
4	Registration Fees	$16,800
5	Parking Fees	$ 960
6	Subtotal	$17,760
7		
8	**Expenses**	
9	Speakers' Fees	$ 6,000
10	Tech support	$ 1,800
11	Marketing	$ 3,000
12	Room rental	$ 3,000
13	Subtotal	$13,800
14		
15	**Net Profit/Loss**	$ 3,960
16		
17	**Variables**	
18	Speaker's Fee (per session)	$ 500
19	Tech Support cost per session	$ 150
20	Seminars per year	12
21	Registration fee	$ 35
22	Attendees per seminar	40
23	Room rental per seminar	$ 250
24	Parking fee	$ 5
25	Average number attendees per car	3
26	Marketing cost per seminar	$ 250

Goal Seek Questions

1. Given the expenses and variables presented in the figure, how many attendees per seminar are required to generate a net profit of $5,500?

2. What parking fee results in a net profit of $4,150?

3. What registration fee per attendee results in a net profit of $5,750?

ACCESS APPLICATION:
Marketing City Hospital Seminars

Colin is the assistant director of marketing at a hospital that conducts seminars on topics such as sports injuries, arthritis, hip and knee pain, knee replacement, and joint replacement. He is working on a marketing campaign for a new seminar on minimally invasive knee surgery that the hospital is planning to offer. Colin has asked you to help identify potential patients who may be interested in this seminar.

Download the City Hospital database, Ch07Ex02. Write a query that sorts registrants by the type of seminar they have attended. Include the session date as well as attendee information. Modify the query to identify registrants who attended a Knee Replacement seminar. Use the report wizard to create a report that lists the session dates and the names and phone numbers of those who have attended Knee Replacement seminars. This report serves as a "patient contact sheet" that hospital staff will use to call previous attendees to invite them to attend the new seminar. How many patients are listed on the report? Review the attendees table. Is there additional patient information the hospital could collect that may be useful for future marketing campaigns?

CASE STUDY #1

Combating Insurance Fraud with Data Mining and Analytics

About 3 percent of the $2 trillion spent on health care in the United States is wasted on fraud every year. Insurers recover only a fraction of that $68 billion, but the information systems they use to spot suspicious claims are improving dramatically. Data mining and analytics are their most important weapons. They arm the insurer's special investigative units with information about potentially fraudulent billing patterns buried in millions of legitimate claims, spotting unusual trends that no human being working alone could ever see.

Health Care Service Corp. (HCSC), for example, implemented a fraud detection system that drew on software from IBM and SAS, and it paid off almost immediately. An allergist in Illinois was submitting fraudulent bills, but the individual amounts were never high enough to trigger any suspicion. Something was amiss, however, and the system helped Mone Petsod find it. As senior investigator for the insurance company, Petsod drew on comparative analytics that showed what other allergists were charging for the same procedures. "It was so different," she said of the Illinois practitioner's billing history, and that finding helped uncover the $800,000 scam.

Fraud detection systems rely partly on rules developed by human beings, and partly on patterns and trends that the analytic engines detect. A key step is to spot fraud before any claim is paid, because it is much easier to deny payment than to recover funds that have already been paid out. The time window is short, however, given pressure on payers to reimburse quickly. For example, Medicare acknowledges paying almost $50 billion per year in questionable claims, a figure that is much higher than the private sector's fraudulent claims rate. Government agents go after scammers once they see a pattern of abuse, but if the money was already paid, it is difficult to recover. Fraud detection systems, on the other hand, can operate quickly enough to catch suspicious claims before they are paid.

Although data mining and analytics are potent weapons, it takes time for insurance company investigators to understand them and use them wisely. At HCSC, for example, the analysts must work closely with investigators to apply human judgment as they create new rules and follow data leads. Ongoing training is essential, especially because the fraudsters continue to launch novel and increasingly complex schemes, changing their tactics to stay a step or two ahead. Knowing when, where, and how to drill down into the data to see meaningful patterns is a skill that agents must learn. But the investigators who master these skills will be able to combine their own experience and judgment with an immensely powerful information system to help reduce health care costs for everyone.

Discussion Questions

1. What are some ways that data mining could be used to detect fraud in health insurance claims?

2. How could private insurance companies and public government agencies collaborate to combat insurance fraud?

3. What types of business skills would be necessary to define the rules for and analyze the results from data mining?

4. What business processes are necessary to complement the IS component of data mining?

SOURCES: Babcock, C., & McGee, M. K. (June 28, 2004). Filter out the frauds. *InformationWeek*. (995), 45+. Bridgewater, P. (June 30, 2010). Beware of Medicare and health insurance scams. *Michigan Chronicle*. B3. DOI: ID Number: 2087933781. Retrieved from Ethnic NewsWatch(ENW) May 21, 2011. Matthews, M. (2010). Scamming Uncle Sam. *Forbes*. 185(8), 20.

CASE STUDY #2

Real-Time Dashboards Track the Action at New York Jets Games

While fans are watching the play on the field, New York Jets managers, owners, and operations staff are glued to the "Command Center," a master dashboard that tracks everything from hotdog sales at concessions to traffic jams in the stadium's parking lots. Built by web development company Roundarch, the Command Center will help the stadium's management track merchandising and customer behavior.

The four-panel touchscreen display shows real-time data aggregated from ticket sales, concession stand sales, heat maps, parking lots, and other sources. One screen, the dashboard software can access historical data and add comparisons to the same metrics taken at the last game and the overall season averages.

The operator can zoom in on these metrics to drill down to individual concession stands and their sales figures by product. A manager can learn which t-shirts are selling fastest or where souvenirs are in great demand. If one corner of the stadium is in the sun and its concessions are running low on hats and sunscreen, managers can spot the trend quickly and replenish inventories.

With incoming real-time data, the Command Center can also compare metrics from game to game based on time periods. How does spending after the 2-minute warning compare to the last game? For games that are not close, what percent of ticket holders leave the stadium at half-time?

Fans are offered their own dashboards to track football action, using a handheld device called "FanVision." Besides real-time stats and comparisons, the device can show different camera angles and replays. It works only in the stadium or nearby parking lots, however, supporting a strategy to encourage fans to attend live games rather than watch them at home on giant high-definition TVs. The New York Jets and other professional teams are also rolling out smartphone applications to keep fans up to date on their team's events and stats.

At New Meadowlands, fans will also appreciate seeing some Command Center data along with the football statistics. The stadium is working to make relevant information—such as current waiting times at concession stands—available on its immense outdoor screens. Customers can see where the choke points are and avoid the longest lines at concessions and exit gates. For the New York Jets, all these dashboard applications not only keep fans happy; they also increase revenue for the team, its owners, the stadium, the concessionaires, and all the other businesses that rely on the excitement of live football.

Discussion Questions

1. What types of decisions can managers make based on data from the dashboards?

2. What decisions can fans make based on data from the dashboards?

3. What data is common between the manager dashboard and the fan dashboard? What data is different between the two dashboards?

4. What are complementary processes necessary for both dashboards?

SOURCES: Carr, A. (September 3, 2010). NY Jets' Command Center offers real-time analytics for sales, stats freaks. *Fast Company*. www.fastcompany.com/1686697/ny-jets-high-tech-command-center-offers-real-time-analytics-of-fans-and-sale, accessed May 22, 2011. Dempsey, C. (August 26, 2010). FanVision a must for football junkies. *The Denver Post*. www.denverpost.com/sports/ci_15896209, accessed May 22, 2011. Manassy, E. (August 30, 2010). Jets fans can purchase in-game video unit "FanVision" for $200. *Jets Twit* blog. http://jetstwit.com/2010/08/30/jets-fans-can-purchase-in-game-video-unit-fanvision-for-200-00, accessed May 22, 2011.

E-PROJECT 1   Detecting Suspicious Activity in Insurance Claims

Detecting unusual patterns in drug prescriptions is the focus of this e-project. To begin, download the Excel file called ChO7_MedicalCharges.

The worksheet contains columns showing a sample of hypothetical prescription drug claims over a period of years.

1. Create a pivot table and chart to show the total amounts paid by year for this pharmacy, by dragging Year to the Axis Fields box and Amount to the Values box. Be sure you are looking at the sum of Amounts in your chart. Which year had the highest sales for prescription drugs?

2. Change the pivot table to show total sales by month by removing Year from the Axis Fields and dragging Month to that box. During which month of the year does this pharmacy tend to sell the most prescription drugs?

3. Remove Month and put Prescriber ID in the Axis Field box. Which prescriber generates the most income for this pharmacy?

4. Remove PrescriberID and put PatientID in the Axis field box. Which patient generates the most income for the pharmacy?

5. Let's take a closer look at this patient by filtering the records. Click on PatientID in the PivotTable Field List and uncheck all boxes except for this patient. Drag Year under PatientID in the Axis Fields box so you can see how this person's spending patterns have changed. Which year shows the most spending?

6. Let's see who is prescribing for this patient. Remove Year from the Axis Fields box and drag PrescriberID to the box. Which Prescriber has the highest spending total?

7. Now, let's see what is being prescribed. Drag DrugName to the Axis Field box under Prescriber ID. What might you conclude from this chart?

E-PROJECT 2   Analyzing Football Statistics with Excel

In this e-project, you will explore some online sources of football statistics and gain practice in analyzing them using Excel. Download the Excel file called ChO7_FootballStatistics. This file contains 2009 statistics for NFL quarterbacks from the National Football League's website (www.nfl.com).

1. Sort the table by Rank.

   a. Who is ranked #1 according to this metric?
   b. Who is ranked at the very bottom?

2. Sort the file by the column labeled "Avg" from largest to smallest, to see how the quarterbacks compare based on the average yards per pass attempt.

   a. Who would be in the # 1 spot?
   b. Who is at the bottom?

3. Insert a new column called "Att/I" and compute the ratio of pass attempts to interceptions (Att/Int). Sort on this column, from largest to smallest.

   a. Who has the highest ratio of pass attempts to interceptions?
   b. Who has the lowest ratio of pass attempts to interceptions?

4. List the quarterbacks you identified along with their teams in the previous questions, and then check www.nfl.com or other online sources to determine which ones are still playing quarterback.

CHAPTER NOTES

1. McCue, C. (nd). Data mining and crime analysis in the Richmond Police Department. www.spss.ch/eupload/File/PDF/Data%20Mining%20and%20Crime%20Analysis%20in%20the%20Richmond%20Police%20Departement.pdf, accessed May 22, 2011.

2. Davis, J. R., Imhoff, C., & White, C. (2009). Operational business intelligence: The state of the art. B. R. Report, BeyeNETWORK. www.beyeresearch.com/executive/11012, accessed June 18, 2011.

3. Watson, H. J., & Hill, J. (July 2009). What gets watched gets done: How metrics can motivate. *Business Intelligence Journal*, 14(3), 4–7. Retrieved May 22, 2011, from ABI/INFORM Global (Document ID Number: 1849906461).

4. Briggs, L. (January 2009). DIRECTV connects with data integration solution. *Business Intelligence Journal*. 14(1), 14–16. Retrieved May 22, 2011, from ABI/INFORM Global (DOI: ID Number: 1673554871).

5. Sutton, J. (July 1, 2009). Government moves to staunch massive Medicare fraud. *Reuters*. www.reuters.comarticle/2009/07/01/us-usa-medicare-fraud-idUS-TRE5604FL20090701, accessed May 22, 2011.

6. Wasserman, T. (September 2009). Text mining firms' golden opportunity. *Adweek*. 50(34), 8.

7. McCartney, S. (February 4, 2010). The Middle Seat: Why a six-hour flight now takes seven. *Wall Street Journal (Eastern Edition)*. p. D1.

8. Morse, G. (2009). The power of unwitting workers. *Harvard Business Review*. 87(10), 26–27.

9. Cohen, A. (2010). U.S. military develops hopping robots. *The Futurist*. 44(2), 13–14.

10. Sachs, J. D. (2010). Expert systems fight poverty. *Scientific American*. 302(4), 32.

11. McKay, L. (October, 2009). Analytics are just the ticket. *Customer Relationship Management*, 13(10), 45.

12. Patel, K. (October 5, 2009). Number of web users still clicking display ads declines by half. *Advertising Age*. 80(33), 24.

13. Misra, S., Pinker, E., & Rimm-Kaufman, A. (2006). An empirical study of search engine advertising effectiveness. The RKG Rimm-Kaufman Group. www.rimmkaufman.com/content/4A2_Pinkeretal WISE2006.pdf, accessed May 33, 2011.

14. Richardson, J. (November 19, 2009). Tips for implementers: The basics of good dashboard design. Gartner Research, DOI: ID Number: G00171685.

15. Fichter, D., & Wisniewski, J. (2009). They grow up so fast: Mashups in the enterprise. *Online*. 33(3), 54–57.

16. Flynn, F. J., & Wiltermuth, S. S. (2009). How executives can make bad decisions. *MIT Sloan Management Review*.

Collaborating with *Technology*

Chapter Preview

MANY HUMAN RELATIONSHIPS NOW HAVE SOME VIRTUAL COMPONENT, even for people who see one another every day. Collaborative technologies support these interactions, and they go well beyond e-mail, text messages, and telephone. They transform the way people in organizations work together, whether they are in the next office or across the globe. They open new possibilities for productive work and social activity, but to use them successfully we should recognize that online environments affect human behavior and group dynamics in subtle and often unexpected ways. This chapter explores the major collaborative technologies, the facets of human interaction they support, and the factors that make them different from face-to-face interactions.

nmedia/Shutterstock

Learning Objectives

1 Describe the major collaborative technologies, and explain the features that each one offers for communications and productivity.

2 Identify and describe Web 2.0 technologies that facilitate collaboration.

3 Explain how unified communications contribute to collaboration.

4 Describe features of online environments that can affect human behavior and group dynamics, and identify strategies to make virtual teams more productive and successful.

Introduction

It's 7:30 A.M. in Dallas, Texas, and Tamara opens a mapping application on her cell phone to find out where all her team members are. The team is developing an ad campaign for a chain of nightclubs, and they hold a weekly meeting online. The tiny map shows that Allen is already in the building, but Freda looks like she is stuck on the beltway. Jun's icon shows him at the Hong Kong headquarters. A "ding" alerts Tamara to an incoming text message. It's Jun, saying he and his colleague Liu can start anytime.

Tamara boots up the computer and logs in to their virtual meeting space, waving when she sees Jun in the webcam. Allen's presence indicator shows he's at his desk, so she sends a quick instant message to say they're starting without Freda. The team members in Hong Kong, staying late for this meeting because their workday is already over, have launched the document under discussion, showing each person's edits in a different color. When Allen walks into the conference room carrying two cups of coffee, he glances at the screen and laughs. "That's a sea of red! You all didn't like what we wrote yesterday." Jun smiles and says, "Don't worry. Most of that red is our British spell checker correcting your American spellings."

Information and communications technologies, like smartphones and virtual meeting spaces, transform the way people collaborate and open up countless opportunities for interactions unhindered by time and location constraints. These virtual environments attempt to reproduce some aspects of face-to-face interactions, and they can add new features that were barely possible earlier. They enable global virtual teams like Tamara's, for example, but they can also introduce unexpected stumbling blocks that hinder group dynamics and inter-personal relationships. The "people" component for collaborative technologies is critically important, perhaps more so than for any other information system category.

Describe the major collaborative technologies, and explain the features that each one offers for communications and productivity.

The Evolution of Collaborative Technologies

Samuel Morse inaugurated his telegraph in a grand public demonstration in 1844. Keenly aware of the history-making potential of this technology, Morse chose a dramatic phrase as his first message: "What hath God wrought!"

Ray Tomlinson, widely credited with sending the first e-mail message, can't even remember what it was, but he suspects it was something like "QWERTYUIOP." Despite the lack of fanfare, Tomlinson's invention triggered a tidal wave of online collaboration, and billions of messages are now sent daily. Figure 8-1 shows the major generations in the evolution of tools that support online collaboration. Many of them rely heavily on the database and database management systems, discussed in Chapter 4. In fact, without a shared database, tools like calendaring, contact management, and social networks could not exist.

E-MAIL

Technically, e-mail transmission is relatively simple (Figure 8-2), although the steps vary depending on the type of email server that is hosting your mail. You usually start by identifying the servers that will handle your outgoing and incoming mail. For outgoing, you enter the name of the **SMTP server**, which stands for "simple mail transfer protocol." For example, Tamara's e-mail may be hosted by her university, so she enters smtp.myuniversity.edu. When she types a message to jun.chang@

FIGURE 8-1

Evolution of collaborative technologies.

1990   2000   2010   2020

1st Generation
- E-mail
- Contact management and address books
- Time management and calendaring
- Discussion forums

2nd Generation
- Instant messaging
- Texting
- GDSS
- Web conferencing
- Interactive video
- Shared workspaces

3rd Generation Web 2.0
- Blogs
- Wikis
- Social networks and profiles
- Microblogging
- Virtual worlds

4th Generation
- Unified communications
- Universal dashboards

FIGURE 8-2

Sending e-mail. Photos/Illustrations: Lana Rinck/Shutterstock, Shutterstock, Bryan Solomon/Shutterstock.

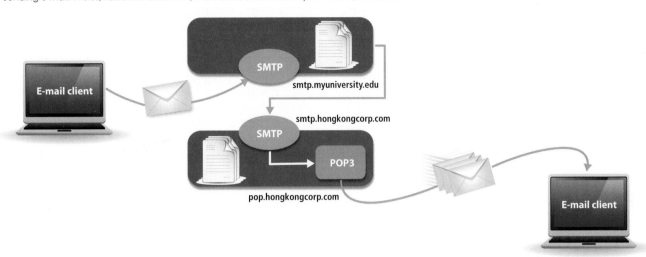

hongkongcorp.com and clicks "send," her message is first transmitted to a special port on the university's SMTP server, and the server software takes over.

Tamara's SMTP server adds date and time information, and then reads the server name to the right of the @ sign in the recipient's address. The server checks a domain name server to retrieve the IP address for hongkongcorp.com and then transmits. If Jun's server is down for some reason, Tamara's message is kept in a queue and her SMTP server will try to send it again later. Jun's SMTP server transfers it as incoming mail to his inbox.

Mailbox accounts also specify the name of the server that handles incoming mail. Many begin with "pop," such as pop.hongkongcorp.com, reflecting a common mail protocol called post office protocol. To retrieve his mail, Jun connects to the pop server and then downloads all the incoming messages to his local computer. Depending on how he set up his account, the server might then delete everything he just downloaded.

A newer protocol for incoming mail is **IMAP (Internet mail access protocol)**, in which mail is actually maintained on the server and organized into folders there. IMAP is especially useful when you use more than one device to access your mail. Instead of being stranded on one computer, all your sent and received mail, drafts, folders, attachments, and indicators are readily accessed from any device. Another advantage is that the symbols indicating you read or replied to a message are maintained on the server, too, so you can see them from your laptop, desktop, smartphone, or public computer. Proprietary e-mail systems that target business users, such as Microsoft's Exchange Server, offer many other features as well, such as advanced integration with calendaring, appointment scheduling, and contact management.

Although most e-mail clients offer web interfaces so users can retrieve and send from any computer, the web versions may have more limited features. Web-based e-mail services, however, such as Google's Gmail or Microsoft's Hotmail, are built from the ground up to work within the browser rather than with client software installed on your computer. One drawback is that some organizations block access to those sites, over concerns about productivity. Some governments have blocked access as well, such as those in Iran and Myanmar.

THE ADDRESS BOOK, BUSINESS CARDS, AND CONTACT MANAGEMENT   E-mail's explosive success led to enhancements and new features, making the e-mail system the indispensable tool on which many workers rely every day. The simple address book

PRODUCTIVITY TIP
When you delete e-mail, remember that copies are stored elsewhere, such as on the server's backup media. Legal authorities can retrieve it, and so can employers if it is company e-mail.

SMTP server
Mail server using the simple mail transfer protocol; handles outgoing e-mail.

IMAP (Internet mail access protocol)
A protocol for handling incoming e-mail.

expanded to a rich contact management system that supports distribution lists and groups and offers new fields for storing contact's job titles, company names, birth dates, URLs, mobile phone numbers, instant message IDs, names of assistants, children's names, and more. Keeping all this information about clients and coworkers together, synched to a smartphone, boosts productivity considerably.

The ability to seamlessly share and update contact information electronically is fundamental to contact management. But the paper business card with all its nonstandard formats, typefaces, and shapes is not going away soon. Sales calls, business meetings, and introductions typically start with an exchange of business cards, and protocol for each exchange may be rigidly prescribed by custom and tradition. Japanese businesspeople, for example, use both hands to offer their cards as a show of respect, and they always make certain the card is oriented so that the recipient can immediately read it.

People can use scanners and optical character recognition software to decipher which field on a business card is which, and then upload the structured data into the address book along with the card's image. Another strategy is to exchange electronic files with your contacts that software can easily read. The vCard, for instance, is a file format used to exchange business card information electronically. The format defines metadata properties such as N (name), TEL (telephone), and ORG (organizational unit) so that e-mail clients can read and load them properly into the address book. A vCard can be attached to e-mail or imported into a contact management system. A more recent and versatile approach uses **microformats**, which rely on the XML family of standards to represent metadata in HTML code. The microformat called hCard, for instance, embeds tags such as <street-address> and <email>.

PRODUCTIVITY TIP

Start building your contacts database in a structured format early. In some email systems, you can add a contact by right clicking or scrolling over the person's email address. Most e-mail clients also include tools to create your own vCard, which will help friends and colleagues add you as a contact. Many websites help you build your own vCard or hCard, such as http://microformats.org/hcard/creator.

Standardized file formats with business card information can also be exchanged over wireless networks or by means of Bluetooth or infrared connections. In some companies, these electronic exchanges are quite common. However, the business card protocol lives on in most organizations around the world, so it's best to keep some handy.

CALENDARING AND TIME MANAGEMENT Adding calendars and appointment scheduling capabilities to e-mail clients is a major breakthrough for time management. Although the paper appointment book served well, it could not trigger a "ding" as an alert for an upcoming event. Nor could it send an e-mail, synch with a smartphone, or flag recurring events that stretch out over months or years.

PRODUCTIVITY TIP

Enter monthly reports, bills, birthdays, and any other recurring events into your calendar software so you'll always get reminders of them in advance.

Like contacts, calendar events can be transmitted and exchanged using standardized file formats. The iCalendar format is widely used to transmit calendar data. The .ics extension indicates that the plain text file contains iCalendar code, so the programs can recognize it (Figure 8-3). The hCalendar format, which can contain iCalendar data, is another microformat relying on the XML family, and cousin to the hCard. The hCalendar code tags the event title, date, time zone, location, and other

FIGURE 8-3

Example of plain text iCalendar event.

```
BEGIN:VCALENDAR
VERSION:2.0PRODID://HongKongCorp//NONSGML//EN
BEGIN:VEVENT
DTSTART:20130709T170000Z
DTEND:20130709T190000Z
SUMMARY:Tiger Team Meeting
END:VEVENT
END:VCALENDAR
```

information so the code can be placed on web pages or in e-mail. Clicking on the "Add to my calendar" link enters the event into the user's calendar.

The calendar's collaborative features eliminate much frustration for event managers. Consider, for example, the struggle to schedule a team meeting, even with the help of e-mail. Asking people for the times and dates they have available can be fruitless and time-consuming, with many false starts and delayed responses. But if everyone is sharing their calendars, it becomes a simple matter to find a time when all team members are free and then trigger an e-mail to invite them to the meeting. If conference rooms or study areas are also managed under the electronic calendar, the meeting coordinator can retrieve their schedules, too, and reserve an empty one for the meeting. Personal preferences, cultural factors, and corporate norms all affect the use of calendaring software and how much it is able to add to overall productivity. Some corporations require its use to streamline meeting arrangements and also to show everyone's whereabouts.

DISCUSSION FORUMS

The asynchronous discussion forum evolved from the earlier bulletin board as an online site in which people could post text messages, reply to others at any time, and discuss a topic of interest. Employee discussion forums are often used to share company information and coordinate activities or to serve as an online suggestion box. Forums may be moderated, with someone nurturing the discussion, deleting unacceptable posts, and blocking users who violate the rules. The forum rules may allow people to post under a pseudonym, so members feel more anonymous and less identifiable during discussions. That changes how they behave, as we discuss later in this chapter.

Posters and "lurkers" are both part of the forum community. Some people contribute the majority of posts while others just read them. On one university's discussion forum devoted to its sports programs, students, alums, faculty, and fans discuss games and share information about their teams. The heavy posters like the social recognition they get from other sports fans for their contributions.[1]

Employee discussion forums can be unpredictable. Most are used productively, but occasional posts can tip in a negative direction. At a large European petroleum company, the forum was initially used to post helpful tips about new technology, but some employees used it to criticize the leadership (Figure 8-4). Discussion forums can be quite valuable when managed properly, with an understanding of how the human element unfolds in online collaboration discussed later in this chapter.

INSTANT MESSAGING AND TEXTING

Instant messaging (IM), also called "chat," consists of real-time text-based interactions over a network. For quick answers in the workplace, it can be very useful. IM can save you a walk down the hall to a colleague's office, or a costly phone call to someone in another country.

IM grew dramatically with the net and the launch of free IM software clients, such as AOL Instant Messenger, Google Talk, Yahoo! Messenger, Skype, and other products targeted to internal business communications or B2B interactions. Some universities provide the service for their students, faculty, and staff so they can chat with one another.

FIGURE 8-4

Sample post from an employee discussion forum.

> What happened at Epsilon was almost a Manual of How Not to do Change in Companies … People were ill-treated in the face of a restructuring and a merger with another company. They were then left without knowing anything about what to expect […] and ending up learning that there was a "confidential" (!) plan for the restructuring through reading the newspapers."[2]

microformats
A set of formats that rely on the XML family of standards to represent metadata in HTML code, and that support electronic exchange of business cards, calendar appointments, and other kinds of data.

instant messaging (IM)
Also called "chat." IM consists of real-time text-based interactions over a network.

IM AND INTEROPERABILITY   Unlike e-mail, which was designed to be fully open so that anyone can send messages to anyone else regardless of which e-mail software they used, the IM world tends toward proprietary islands. Each product uses different protocols that the others may not understand without special conversion software. Although some major players develop agreements to allow interaction, the nature of the underlying technology continues to hamper interoperability. In addition, IM providers' competitive strategies are not necessarily leaning toward a more open architecture, since these firms are not eager to reduce consumers' switching costs.

PRESENCE AWARENESS   IM software introduced a critically important collaborative feature called **presence awareness**, which allows users to display their current status to their contacts, colleagues, or buddy list. The software shows whether the person is logged in and the user can elaborate, adding "working on the team project," "out to lunch," or "pretending to work...." Arguably, this feature is the killer app of IM, since it shows whether the person is available to answer a question, pick up the phone, or stop by for a brief meeting.

Presence awareness is one of the subtle advantages that co-located teams have over virtual teams. For example, companies grasp the value of a **war room**, the large area in which team members on the same project work closely together, surrounded by whiteboards, large digital displays, and other tools to facilitate impromptu meetings and smooth collaboration. Working on fast-moving, intense projects, team members in the war room are constantly aware of one another's presence so they can get an immediate response, rather than sending out e-mails, leaving voice messages, and delaying work. Although not quite as reliable, presence awareness indicators add an important human element to online collaboration, and they are a key reason people adopt the tool within organizations.[3]

IM is a common collaborative tool even for people in the same building, who may keep the IM client active all day long to receive brief text messages from coworkers in the next cubicle or around the world. An IM is much faster than a phone call or conference call for short questions or pithy remarks, and it requires none of the social courtesies or dedicated attention that phone calls demand (Figure 8-5). People can also multitask during IM exchanges.

PRODUCTIVITY TIP
Use proper spelling and grammar in your IMs at work, at least until you're sure you have a clear understanding of the corporate culture. Also, avoid "textisms," such as "cul8tr" (see you later).

TEXT MESSAGING OR "TEXTING"   Jun's text message to Tamara's cell phone, to say he and Liu were ready to start, demonstrates how people seamlessly blend this technology into any collaborative setting. During the meeting, Liu sees Allen in the webcam glancing down several times and guesses he is checking some incoming text messages as inconspicuously as possible so as not to disrupt the flow.

Interconnections between cellular networks and the Internet now blur the distinction between IM and texting, but the origins of texting were in mobile communications. Texting transforms a cell phone from a single-purpose mobile device into a one that can send brief text messages to other mobile devices, transmit photos and videos, and broadcast messages to large groups, as with Twitter. The sender may assume that most people will notice the buzz or vibration on their mobile device that signals an incoming text and, if the situation permits, will take a moment to view it immediately.

Text messaging first gained momentum in Europe and Asia, where it goes by names such as SMS or Short Mail. It now outpaces voice phone calls, with heavy users sending and receiving hundreds of text messages daily. Although texting can be a substitute for a phone call, its characteristics make it a different kind of collaborative tool with its own advantages and limitations. Because people usually carry

FIGURE 8-5

Comparison of time elapsed for a query handled by phone call or IM.

Phone Call	IM
Look up number.	
Dial number.	*Allen clicks on Tamara's icon and types into the chat box:*
Voice mail responds. Allen decides to try again in a few minutes rather than leave a message, not knowing how often Tamara checks her voice mail.	Allen: Tam, can you send me your copy of the August report?
Wait 10 minutes.	*Tamara is on the phone, but can easily multitask.*
Dial number.	Tamara: Sure.
Ring … ring …	*Wait 10 seconds.*
Tamara: Hello	Tamara: AugustReport.xlsx
Allen: Hi, this is Allen, is this Tamara?	Allen: Got it, thanks.
Tamara: Hi Allen, yes this is Tamara. How are you doing?	*Allen clicks on the file and opens the report.*
Allen: Good, and you?	
Tamara: Not too bad, though I'm glad it's Friday!	
Allen: I just had a quick question.	
Tamara: Shoot.	
Allen: I can't find my copy of the August report. Do you have one?	
Tamara: Yes, I'll e-mail it to you.	
Allen: Thanks!	
Tamara: No problem. I'll do that now.	
Allen: That's great. OK, I'll see you later at the meeting.	
Tamara: Talk to you soon.	
Allen: Bye.	
Tamara composes a brief e-mail message to Allen, attaches the report, and clicks send.	
Allen waits for the message to arrive, saves the attachment on his hard drive, and opens the report.	
Time elapsed: ~15 minutes	Time elapsed: ~15 seconds

their cell phones, texting can assist in emergency situations and disaster recovery. During the SARS (Severe Acute Respiratory Syndrome) in China, text messages were the primary means by which citizens kept one another informed of outbreaks in different districts, since official communications on television or radio were sparse and unreliable.[4]

Text messages also multiply the power of informal networks by allowing users to broadcast information not yet available through traditional means. The first report of the plane that crash-landed on the Hudson River in New York City in 2009 came from a witness who sent a text message to his Twitter followers: "There's a plane in the Hudson. I'm on the ferry to pick up the people. Crazy."[5] The message spread virally as the followers re-sent it to all their networks.

The features of texting also make it extremely valuable for real-time micro-coordination, letting people know where and when activities are to be held, and Jun's text message was one example.[6] Texting is also used widely to coordinate fast-moving crowds. Protesters used it in Egypt to organize their activities in early 2011.

presence awareness
IM software feature that allows users to display their current status to their contacts, colleagues, or buddy list.

war room
A large area in which team members on the same project work closely together, surrounded by whiteboards, large digital displays, and other tools to facilitate impromptu meetings and smooth collaboration.

GROUP DECISION SUPPORT SYSTEMS (GDSS)

A collaborative technology that helps groups brainstorm and make decisions is called a **group decision support system (GDSS)**. These systems are used for face-to-face group meetings in which each individual is equipped with a computer connected to a shared server, and the group facilitator structures the tasks during the session. The software allows each member to type his or her contributions anonymously as the group moves through the stages of identifying the problem to be solved, brainstorming possible solutions, rating the alternatives, and coming to some consensus about the best course of action. As the contributions, comments, and votes unfold, they appear on the screen with no names attached.[7]

In a typical session to decide which candidate to hire for a position, group members might begin by entering the criteria they think should be used to evaluate each candidate, followed by a weighting for each criterion. Members might discuss their differences and then redo the task to achieve consensus, or they might rely on majority voting. Next, they rate each candidate on the criteria and finally attempt to come to a consensus.

GDSS was designed to promote novel ideas and high-quality, rational decisions, especially by altering some of the group dynamics that can cause groups to function poorly. High-status members, for instance, have a disproportionate influence even when they are wrong. Group pressure can also squash expression of independent viewpoints that differ from the majority. The anonymity of GDSS helps reduce these effects.

WEB CONFERENCING

Another synchronous collaboration technology is **web conferencing**, which supports online meetings, sometimes called "webinars," via the Internet. Participants join the meeting from their own computers or smartphones and use headsets with microphones or phone conferencing to speak to one another. Browser-based conferencing software, such as WebEx or Go To Meeting, have enriched their offerings to include features such as the following:

- Real-time video support, using web cameras
- Support for PowerPoint or other slide presentations
- Interactive whiteboards, with drawing tools and color coding for each participant
- Text-based chat
- Polling software
- Web-based clients for both desktop computers and mobile phones
- Desktop application sharing, in which the meeting participants or audience can see whatever application the host is running on the desktop
- Archiving recordings so participants who missed the event can play it back
- Registration systems for fee-based enrollments

Web-conferencing applications take advantage of mashups to support shared web browsing, chat windows, video, news feeds, and other modules the meeting participants might need. At Reuters, for example, stock traders in the United States send market data to Asia-based traders as U.S. markets close. The traders can put a webcam image in one corner, a rolling feed of stock prices in another, and an application that calls up news about a particular stock when one of the traders, either in the United States or in Asia, clicks on that ticker symbol.[8]

Web-conferencing tools can make a dramatic dent in travel budgets, and the services see particularly fast growth during economic downturns. They are widely used for corporate training, global project teams, product announcements, virtual sales calls, and other events.

INTERACTIVE VIDEO

Interactive video chats for collaboration are freely available via webcams and software such as Skype. This capability fundamentally changes an online collaboration by allowing participants to see facial expressions and other nonverbal aspects of communication.

The free and lower-end systems often have transmission delays that make it impossible to synchronize the speaker's voice with lip movements, so they may not work well for delicate negotiations. Higher-end interactive video systems can dramatically improve the interaction, with crystal-clear images and audio. Many systems rely on leased communications lines to ensure high definition; broadcast-quality images and sound are transmitted to produce the "you are there" feeling of a face-to-face meeting.

The most powerful systems create a sense of **telepresence**, in which the remote participants are almost life-sized and images are vividly clear. Eye contact is more natural, and voices are well synched to lip movements. An executive can turn on the desktop camera and interact with someone across the planet almost as though the person were sitting on the other side of the desk. For meeting rooms, larger screens can add remote participants almost as though they are sitting at the same table (Figure 8-6).

Baxter Healthcare Corporation, for example, deployed high-end interactive video to support its R&D teams, with members located in many different countries. Given cultural barriers, Baxter execs found that traditional conference calls and other collaborative technologies were not working well. They needed in-person meetings, but travel costs were prohibitive. They launched a system with telepresence to see and hear the nonverbal nuances, to create much richer interactions that helped bridge the cultural divides. The system can also show life-size images of new-product components for the company's medical equipment.[9]

FIGURE 8-6

High-end interactive video systems create a sense of telepresence.

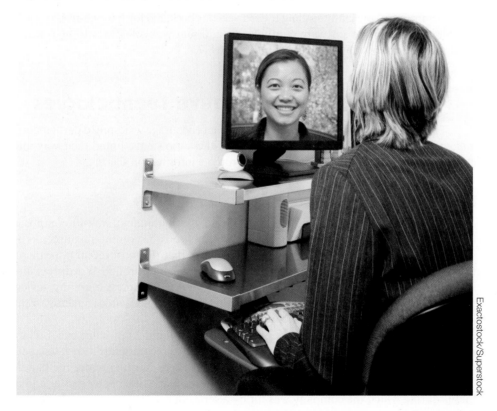

Exactostock/Superstock

---

group decision support system (GDSS)
Collaborative technology that helps groups brainstorm and make decisions in face-to-face meetings, led by facilitators. Participants can contribute anonymously via their computers.

web conferencing
Technology that supports online meetings or "webinars" via the Internet. Participants join the meeting from their own computers or smartphones.

telepresence
The impression created when remote participants in an interactive video meeting are almost life-sized and vividly clear; useful for sensitive negotiations.

FIGURE 8-7

Functionality offered by shared workspaces to support teamwork.

Shared Workspace Capabilities for Teams

▶ Discussion forums
▶ Team calendars
▶ Team announcements
▶ Shared task lists with task status, due dates, priorities, and assignments
▶ E-mail alerts to inform team members of updates to the shared workspace
▶ Member lists with contact information
▶ Search functionality
▶ Content management capabilities with checkout and version control
▶ Collaborative document editing
▶ Workflow management

With increasing bandwidth available for cellular networks, the transmission of clear video signals to smartphones with powerful processors is much more feasible. Multisite conference calls with interactive video are possible on these tiny devices.

SHARED WORKSPACES

Organizing all the information resources and communications for a team of people takes another kind of collaborative technology. The **shared workspace** is an area on a server in which team members can post documents, maintain membership lists, feature news and announcements, and collaborate on edits and updates.

The core of a shared workspace is the document library, where members can store important information assets and keep track of all the edits. Some software for shared workspaces, such as Microsoft's Sharepoint, includes features for version control to ensure that older copies are maintained and no changes are lost. This centralized document library goes a long way toward eliminating the confusion and duplication that arise when team members are constantly sending revised versions back and forth over e-mail.

Shared workspace software continues to add many new features to help teams collaborate. Some examples are listed in Figure 8-7.

Identify and describe Web 2.0 technologies that facilitate collaboration.

2

Web 2.0 Collaborative Technologies

Web 2.0 introduces powerful tools that encourage widespread participation and end-user contribution to the web. Many of these tools have found their way into corporations to facilitate collaboration and promote information sharing.

BLOGS

A **blog**, short for "web log," is one example. The blogger maintains a website composed mainly of ongoing commentary, images, and links to other online resources. The posts are displayed in reverse chronological order so that the most recent appears on top. Blogging software, such as the free versions available through Wordpress and Blogger, simplifies the task of creating your own website to express opinions, review products, discuss hobbies, or just rant. Readers can add their own comments to the blogger's posts, joining in the asynchronous discussion.

For organizations, blogs are a popular means of building knowledge bases, as we discuss in Chapter 9. They are also used for marketing and communications, to create a more intimate connection with customers and suppliers. Writing under the handle "Morizo," the president of Toyota Motor Corporation updated his blog after a long hiatus during which the company was hit by a series of recalls. Akio Toyoda posted, "Good evening everyone, this is Morizo. I'm deeply sorry to have caused inconvenience and concern to so many of our customers, to so many of you."[10] He was blogging as Morizo before he became president, and he continued the tradition as an unofficial and personal way to engage with Toyota's stakeholders.

The blogosphere, as pundits call it, also benefits from blogger networks and cross-linking. An intriguing post on one blog may be picked up by many others, creating a viral spread of the item and a rapid increase in page views. When a popular blog links to a post on a relatively unknown site, traffic to that site suddenly skyrockets.

Some blogs are labors of love for friends, family, or other hobbyists, with bloggers earning a little revenue when visitors click on ads or contribute to a "tip jar." Other blogs belong to conventional media organizations and employ teams of contributors to update frequently. AOL, for instance, continues to expand its blog empire devoted to finance, politics, music, and other topics, all staffed by freelancers and journalists. These blogs are more like online, interactive magazines, earning revenue from display ads. They are quite different from earlier homegrown blogs started by individuals struggling to reach an audience.[11]

A key reason people return again and again to favorite blogs is to check for updates, so frenetic posting is the hallmark of the most popular and influential blogs. This volume of posting can lead to quite a lot of junk. One blog reader commented,

> "Give an infinite number of monkeys typewriters and they'll produce the works of Shakespeare. Unfortunately, I feel like I'm reading all the books where they didn't."[12]

Others see it quite differently, noting that user-friendly blogging software gives voice to millions of people outside the mainstream media, strengthening the democratic vision the web's designers had in mind and preventing it from becoming a one-way broadcast vehicle controlled by major corporations or governments. Whether you see the blogosphere as a blessing or calamity depends on your point of view, but there is no question that this relatively simple collaborative technology has an immense impact.

WIKIS

Another significant Web 2.0 technology that facilitates end-user contributions and collaborative editing is the **wiki**, a website that allows users to add and edit interlinked web pages. Wiki software usually offers simple text editing tools so users need not know HTML. It keeps track of versions and lets users view the history of changes to each page, along with discussions about the page's content. Users navigate within a wiki by doing a keyword search or by clicking on the many embedded links to related wiki pages.

Wikis have also emerged as extremely valuable tools within organizations, especially to centralize documents and create knowledge storehouses that employees can edit as needed. The wiki makes it easy for people in any unit or any level of the organization to make contributions from their own personal experience or to update existing articles with current information. Such wikis can become a substantial base of knowledge for an organization, useful for training new employees and organizing all the how-to guides.

The online encyclopedia called "Wikipedia" is the best-known publicly accessible wiki. With more than 15 million articles contributed and edited by volunteers around the world, the nonprofit Wikipedia is the most popular general-purpose reference work on the net. Critics point to problems with accuracy and bias, exacerbated by the site's open structure that allows anyone promoting an agenda to edit articles. Corporations and government agencies are known to quietly edit entries about themselves to put out the best spin wherever possible. The site locks out external editing for some articles, especially when they deal with controversial current events.

---

shared workspace
An area on a server in which team members can post documents, maintain membership lists, feature news and announcements, and collaborate on edits and updates.

blog
Short for "web log," and used to facilitate collaboration and knowledge sharing. Posts are displayed in reverse chronological order so that the most recent appears on top.

wiki
Web software frequently used to build knowledge bases that allows users to add and edit interlinked web pages.

FIGURE 8-8

WikiTrust color-codes segments of text in Wikipedia articles that have been recently edited, suggesting they may not be as reliable as uncolored text.

> Angry Birds is a puzzle video game developed by Finland-based Rovio Mobile. Inspired primarily by a sketch of stylized wingless birds, the game was first released for Apples's iOS in December 2009. Since that time, over 12 million copies of the game have been purchased from Apple's App Store, which has prompted the company to design v ersions for other touchscreen-based smartphones, such as those using the Android operating system, among others.

Source: http://en.wikipedia.org/wiki/Angry_Birds?trust, accessed March 24, 2011.

Did You Know?

More than 85 percent of Wikipedia's contributors are men, and the lopsided gender ratio appears to lead to some bias in coverage. For instance, articles on baseball cards and videogames are longer and more detailed compared to articles that might have more appeal for women. The site is actively encouraging more women to participate.[13]

Wikipedia illustrates how technology can be tweaked to address human issues of trust and bias. Its leadership developed a means to show how reliable entries are and also to prevent vandalism by gangs of new users who repeatedly edit pages they want written a certain way. One strategy is to add color coding to the text, to indicate each phrase's level of trustworthiness—computed from the article's and editors' histories. Text that has been untouched for quite some time earns a higher trust score and appears in black, under the assumption that others agree with it. An editor's reputation is computed based on how often his or her contributions are preserved or edited out. Bright orange indicates frequent changes, suggesting that editors are battling over a controversial passage (Figure 8-8).

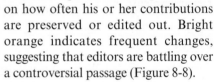

PRODUCTIVITY TIP

You can download an add-on for Firefox that adds a link to Wikipedia pages called "WikiTrust." Clicking on the link displays the color coding, with orange highlights to indicate which sentences were recently changed.

SOCIAL NETWORKING

More than three of four millennials, members of the generation born from about 1980 to 1995, have created profiles on one or more of the social networking sites, such as Facebook, LinkedIn, Classmates.com, MySpace, Ning, Orkut, or Buzz. People outside that age group, particularly the over-50 crowd, are these sites' fastest-growing demographics. Social networks have become the de facto platform for collaboration and online asynchronous interaction. If Facebook were a country, it would be the third-most populous after China and India, with 500 million + members in 2011.

The core element of these sites is the individual or organizational profile. Tamara maintains one on Facebook, and she enhanced her profile with a photo and information about her hobbies and educational background. The site also usually includes a "wall" on which the user can post updates, adding commentary, links, or images about current happenings.

The value of these sites, though, is that the profiles are nodes in a vast, interdependent network of links to other nodes created by other people or organizations (Figure 8-9). The users build this network themselves, as they link to friends or colleagues. Some connections may be suggested by the software itself, so Tamara has no difficulty finding and linking to alumni from the same graduating class or to former coworkers at her previous position, even if she never actually met them. She might add others from her address book, from e-mail messages, from instant messaging contacts, or by searching for potential friends or colleagues by name, e-mail address, or other characteristic. Wondering whether an old friend she met in New York had a Facebook profile, Tamara searched the site by name and then sent that person a request to become friends on the site, adding yet another link to her ever-growing social network.

FIGURE 8-9

Interconnected nodes in a social networking site. Emiko's connection to Isabel leads to four more connections, but her link to Stella does not expand Emiko's network yet.

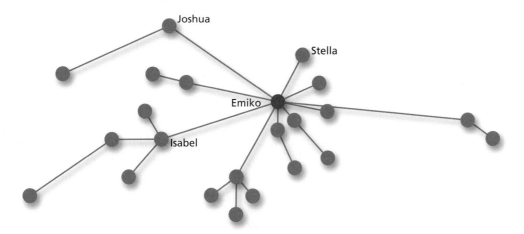

Tamara adds an update to her wall almost daily to describe what she's doing, and her friends can comment on it or add their own posts. Depending on her privacy settings, visitors to Tamara's wall might be able to view everything or very little.

For users, the value of social networking sites can be quite high, offering a platform to nurture or renew connections that might otherwise fade away. Network effects, described in Chapter 2, increase the value of these services, simply because more people use them. Social network developers ensure that finding friends is easy, since their goal is to increase membership and internal links.

For companies, these sites offer a means to support knowledge sharing in the company and to reach people who may be interested in their products or services. Network interconnections help messages leap from one network of friends to the next. Ads can be tailored to reach precise target groups based on their members' profiles. Tamara and her teammates, for instance, plan to launch an ad targeted to people on their 21st birthday, inviting them to a nearby club for a celebration. Since social network sites collect birth dates, this precise targeting is feasible. To leverage the friendship networks, their ad offers free admission to the recipient and 50 percent off to five friends who come along.

Beyond advertising, organizations create their own profiles as a means to connect with their customers, recruit new employees, announce new products, and generally promote their brands. Even traditional brick and mortar corporations take advantage of social media to build relationships with their online communities. Procter & Gamble, which makes household products such as diapers and laundry detergent, effectively used its social networking presence to coordinate messages about its 2010 Winter Olympics sponsorship. Links to the company's emotional and poignant YouTube video ad about young athletes, "To their moms, they'll always be kids," appeared on all P&G's social media sites, dramatically increasing the commercial's exposure.[14]

MICROBLOGGING

Lady Gaga, with millions of followers on Facebook and Twitter, skyrocketed to the pinnacle of pop culture in record time.[15] Her microblogging on Twitter, in particular, with impromptu, intimate, and often hourly tweets, created a constant connection with youthful fans in a way that broke through the static and surpassed the one-way websites most other celebrities create (Figure 8-10).

Microblogging is a form of blogging in which the posts are quite short, containing a brief sentence fragment and perhaps a link to another web resource or video.

microblogging
A form of blogging in which the posts are quite short, and especially suitable for mobile devices. As in a blog, the entries appear in reverse chronological order.

FIGURE 8-10

Sample tweets from Lady Gaga.

> **Lady Gaga**   REPLY
> Its so silly, I do these interviews, + they say Gaga
> "arent u sick of the life," I think to myself, if they only
> knew how much I love my fans
> **Lady Gaga**   REPLY
> since im living nowhere right now and live on the
> road with my props+wigs.(which is everything I
> own) i suppose my fans, in a way, livewithme

As in a blog, the entries appear in reverse chronological order. The topics range widely, from simple updates about what the poster is currently doing to informative links to resources about current events, hobbies, companies, services, and more. The social media aspect exists because users are able to "follow" other users, whose posts constantly appear on followers' computer screens or mobile devices. Followers can reply to posts or repeat them for the benefit of their own followers.

Twitter has the largest number of users and its vocabulary terms "tweet" and "re-tweet" are widely used to describe the basic elements of this collaborative technology. As simple as it sounds, the real-time updates enrich online group dynamics with a level of connectedness that many consider a significant leap for social media, especially since they extend the advantages of text messaging to interconnected social networks. Microblogging offers features that few thought would be valuable when the services were first launched. The news that a distant friend had pancakes for breakfast turned out to be more interesting than expected, at least for some. Even what seems to be pointless babble can serve a role in human interaction.

Companies find innovative ways to reach out to customers using Twitter, especially as social referrals dent the impact of sponsored search term advertisements, which are relevant to your search but not endorsed by someone you know. SponsoredTweets.com, for example, is a marketplace that brings together people with large followings and advertisers who would like them to tweet something nice about their products. Pro basketball player Jon Brockman earns revenue this way and says, "Having the opportunity to share great deals with my fans is a lot of fun." He earns money only if a follower actually clicks on the advertiser's link, making this marketing tool very attractive for business.[16]

The users themselves have added their own conventions to make microblogging more useful. For example, users invented the **hashtag**, in which posts on a similar topic all include a keyword prefixed by a #. At one educational conference in Manhattan called "Hacking Education," attendees agreed to tweet their comments during the conference and include the hashtag "#hackedu" in each post. Searching for the tag on Twitter revealed their ongoing reactions and thoughts, documented online for the attendees as well as others interested in the topic. The tag continued in use after the conference, as attendees and others extended the discussion.[17]

VIRTUAL WORLDS

The **virtual world** is a graphical, often 3-D environment in which users can immerse themselves, interacting with virtual objects and with one another using avatars. Sitting at a computer screen with a keyboard, mouse, joysticks, console controls, steering wheels, or foot pedals, users can explore digitally constructed worlds or pilot vehicles through realistic terrain. They can also change the camera perspective to see their own avatar, a virtual representation of themselves that could be fantastical or quite lifelike.

These simulated environments create **virtual reality**, a term that describes what people experience when some of their sensory input is not from the real world, but from a computer-generated one. Advanced virtual reality systems enhance the illusion of physical immersion in a virtual world even further by adding other technologies. Stereoscopic goggles, for instance, can present aspects of the virtual world that match the user's actual body posture, movements, or head turns. Specially wired gloves can reproduce the sensations of actually touching and manipulating virtual objects.

Virtual-world inhabitants can often tailor their avatar's appearance and control its movements, facial expressions, and body postures. They type into text chat boxes to communicate or use microphones to speak with other characters in the world, who may be automated bots or avatars controlled by other users.

These engaging online spaces are widely used for multiuser games such as World of Warcraft, in which the fantasy environments feature imaginative creatures and brilliant terrain. They also serve as simulations for training. The U.S. Air Force, for instance, launched its own virtual world on Second Life, one of the biggest commercial virtual-world providers. Visitors to "MyBase" can take a virtual tour of an Air Force base, fly a P-51 Mustang, and learn more about job possibilities. MyBase is a starting point for the Air Force, with many other virtual training programs on the drawing board. One major advantage is that virtual worlds are extremely useful for simulating dangerous situations such as combat or urban warfare. They also offer safe ways to train people who work in environments such as offshore drilling platforms and chemical manufacturing plants (Figure 8-11).

Although many organizations have set up a presence in Second Life or other virtual worlds, their initial efforts focused more on customer relationship management, as we discussed in Chapter 5. These have not had tremendous success. The software can be buggy and complicated, making it frustrating to make a quick visit to an organization's site to gain more information. These worlds have also been mainly used as social venues, so some inhabitants are fiercely opposed to any commercial squatting on the space.

Most virtual-world products and the servers that host them are privately owned by software vendors, so when they go out of business, the digital properties vanish, wasting the effort that went into building them. Unlike the pages for a website created in HTML, the virtual-world environment can't easily be moved to a different host.

FIGURE 8-11

Virtual worlds can be used to train workers who fight fires or tackle other problems in dangerous environments.

Source: Used with permission of Abient Performance.

hashtag	**virtual world**	**virtual reality**
Microblogging tool invented by web users in which posts on a similar topic all include a keyword prefixed by a #.	A graphical, often 3-D environment in which users can immerse themselves, interacting with virtual objects and one another using avatars.	Describes what people experience when some of their sensory input is not from the real world, but from a computer-generated one. Technologies such as stereoscopic goggles and specially wired gloves enhance the illusion of physical immersion.

FIGURE 8-12
Business meeting in a virtual world.

Source: Used with permission of VenueGen. VenueGen immersive virtual environments for training and collaboration.

However, open-source projects are underway to create virtual-world software platforms that may be less susceptible to the fates of individual software companies.

Despite rocky starts, virtual worlds hold much promise for collaboration. Business users who want to hold meetings are attracted to them as a way to simulate a live conference with speakers, breakout rooms, and small-group sessions. Venuegen, for instance, offers a business-oriented virtual world for such events, in which attendees can upload their own photos to make their avatars more realistic. They can enter meeting rooms to share content, show slides, and engage in conversations in which the sound appears to come from the speaker's direction, and eye contact shifts to the appropriate avatar (Figure 8-12).

Beyond business meetings, virtual worlds can recreate any environment for humans to explore, from a tiny blood cell to the vast emptiness of space. For engineers, the ability to collaborate on the design of component parts, regardless of how small or large, offers exciting possibilities. The opportunities for educators to simulate live classrooms are equally intriguing.

Did You Know?

A virtual reality program called the "Comprehensive Deepwater Oil and Gas Blowout Model" is used during oil spills, such as the 2010 spill in the Gulf of Mexico. Not only can scientists predict the direction the oil will spread, but they can also add virtual chemicals to the VR model to see how each one affects the oil's dissipation.[18]

Explain how unified communications contribute to collaboration. **3**

Unified Communications

A major recent advance in collaboration is less about the technologies themselves and more about how they are integrated with one another, and how people use them. **Unified communications (UC)** integrates multiple applications and communications channels into a single interface, accessible from many different devices. Although the technologies are not new, a unified approach can bring together real-time communication services such as instant messaging and video conferencing, with asynchronous e-mail, voice mail, and fax. Making all these accessible regardless of the device simplifies collaboration considerably.

CONTEXT INDICATORS

One important feature of unified communications is the context indicator, which lets senders know whether the individual is available to communicate at the moment, and which mode he or she prefers. On a long car trip, for instance, a driver might signal his or her availability for hands-free cell-phone conversations, but not IM or videoconferencing. The driver could direct e-mail to the cell phone's text-to-speech application, to have it read aloud. Microsoft offers unified communications with its Exchange platform, building on the feature-rich Outlook interface to simplify and streamline the variety of collaborative technologies that exist in most organizations.

UNIVERSAL DASHBOARDS

Universal dashboards are emerging that help people manage their unified communications, providing quick access to context indicator, e-mail, secure instant messaging, voice and video calling, conference calling, corporate RSS feeds, and more. The Mitel Unified Communicator Advanced, for instance, is a software client that integrates those features, and allows employees to choose the best method of communicating with coworkers based on their context indicator. When a colleague is talking on the phone, the person's status will automatically switch to "in a call" so coworkers know that phoning the person at that moment would be a waste of time. The software can also integrate with the company's ERP and customer relationship management system to launch detailed contact information on the screen, based on the incoming caller ID. That could help eliminate long pauses when a caller says "Hi, this is Bill," and you can't quite place the voice. Accessible from desktops or smartphones, the dashboard creates a constant link between the individual and his or her contacts and information resources, one that can be configured based on personal preferences and current status.

Collaborative technologies are constantly improving, not just because bandwidth is increasing, but because developers adapt the technologies to human needs and add features that accommodate human behavior, as we see in the next section.

The Human Element and Collaborative Technologies

4 Describe features of online environments that can affect human behavior and group dynamics, and identify strategies to make virtual teams more productive and successful.

Human beings have had thousands of years to refine their strategies for productive interactions in face-to-face settings, but only a couple of decades to figure out how best to collaborate virtually. Much communication is through typed text, and without the nonverbal cues that add richness and meaning to any communication, the unexpected can happen. Missteps lead to miscommunication, hurt feelings, flame wars, dysfunctional teams, lost jobs, and even lawsuits. A key reason for these problems is that online communication is not the same as face-to-face conversation. We also underestimate how much the online environment can affect behavior, just as any environment—from the beach to the office—affects how we behave.

PSYCHOLOGICAL CHARACTERISTICS OF ONLINE ENVIRONMENTS

Online environments vary a great deal, but some common themes that affect behavior appear in many of them (Figure 8-13).

UNFAMILIAR TOOLS   We use unfamiliar tools to interact online, often stumbling over them in the effort to make our interactions productive. The QWERTY keyboard is one example. Typing is not the same as speaking, though people often try to use the

unified communications (UC)
Technology that integrates multiple communications channels and applications into a single interface, accessible from many different devices.

FIGURE 8-13

Characteristics of online environments that distinguish them from face-to-face settings.

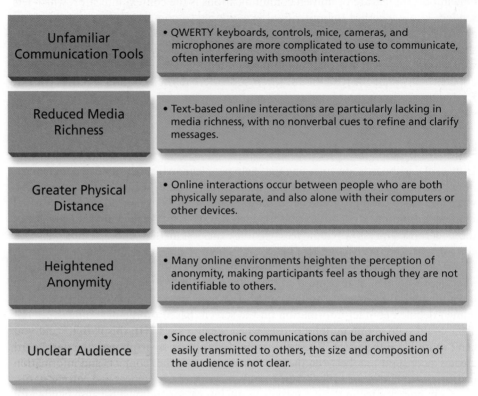

Unfamiliar Communication Tools	• QWERTY keyboards, controls, mice, cameras, and microphones are more complicated to use to communicate, often interfering with smooth interactions.
Reduced Media Richness	• Text-based online interactions are particularly lacking in media richness, with no nonverbal cues to refine and clarify messages.
Greater Physical Distance	• Online interactions occur between people who are both physically separate, and also alone with their computers or other devices.
Heightened Anonymity	• Many online environments heighten the perception of anonymity, making participants feel as though they are not identifiable to others.
Unclear Audience	• Since electronic communications can be archived and easily transmitted to others, the size and composition of the audience is not clear.

keyboard to simulate spoken conversations rather than more formal written correspondence. As collaborative technologies add new capabilities, people struggle with complex controls and settings that can cause frustration.

MEDIA RICHNESS **Media richness** measures how well a communication medium can reproduce all the nuances and subtleties of the message it transmits. Media richness is usually starkly lower online than face-to-face. Many communications are text only, leaving out facial expression, eye contact, voice pitch and tempo, gestures, body posture, and hand gestures. Although words carry meaning, most of what people communicate is actually nonverbal. Jun's text message to Tamara, "you won't be late??" could be interpreted as a simple question about start time or a criticism about tardiness. The second question mark might be a keyboard slip or a way to emphasize the criticism.

Figure 8-14 compares various technologies with respect to their support for media richness and interactivity.

PHYSICAL DISTANCE Another important variable is the combination of physical distance and lack of physical presence. Online interactions typically take place between people who are geographically separate, not just from one another, but from other people as well. There is no human face looking straight at you as you type, no smile, arched brow, or puzzled expression to signal with immediate nonverbal cues how the other person is reacting. There is only the screen and the keyboard. Distance also contributes to a sense of physical safety, so people may take more risks with their words.

ANONYMITY A feature common to online games, public discussion forums, and some other venues is anonymity. When people have a sense that others will not be able to identify who they are, their behavior can change considerably. In some settings, this is helpful. GDSS, for instance, relies on a modicum of anonymity in a small workgroup to encourage people to participate and contribute freely. Many very successful

FIGURE 8-14

Interactivity and media richness in different collaborative technologies.

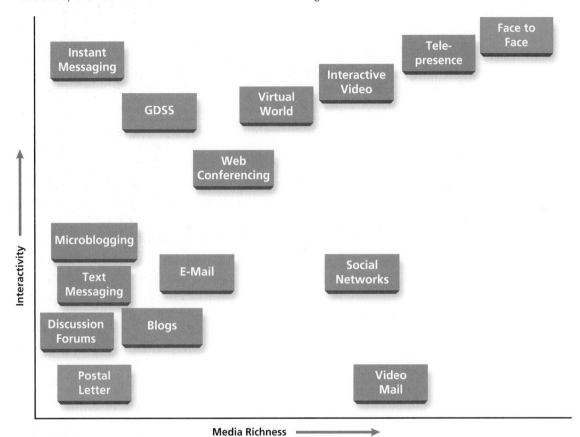

online support groups for people with HIV/AIDS or other disorders ensure privacy by making all contributions anonymous. But in other settings, anonymity can lead to problems because people feel less accountable for their actions.

AUDIENCE Finally, online interactions are always somewhat blurry in terms of who is in the audience. When you receive an e-mail with a large distribution list, you might easily click "reply to all" by mistake when you intended to just reply to the sender. This common blunder might be just a minor embarrassment or it could wreck a career. People also often treat online interactions as casual chats, forgetting that e-mail is archived on company servers and backup media where it can be resurrected years later.

Electronic communications can also be forwarded to others or publicly released. For instance, an impatient CEO fired off an abrupt e-mail to his 400+ managers, saying, "We are getting less than 40 hours of work from a large number of our KC-based employees. The parking lot is sparsely used at 8 A.M. Likewise at 5 P.M.... NEVER in my career have I allowed a team which worked for me to think they had a 40-hour job." After ranting for another page, the CEO threatened firings if the lot was not full by 7:30 A.M. and half-full on Saturdays. "You have two weeks. Tick Tock." Within hours, someone posted the e-mail on a Yahoo! financial forum, and alarmed investors reacted by selling their shares. The stock plummeted almost 30 percent.

PRODUCTIVITY TIP

The characteristics of the online environment should help you decide what kind of communication tool to use for different interactions. For example, when the discussion is sensitive, or when it must be completely confidential, text-based communication is a poor choice.

media richness
A measure of how well a communication medium can reproduce all the nuances and subtleties of the messages it transmits.

✳ THE ETHICAL FACTOR
Flash Mobs and Free Speech: Should Police Block Mobile Messenging Services?

Flash mobs, whether they erupt for a benign celebration or a violent riot, are difficult to stop and are spreading to more and more cities. Concerns about the violent variety are mounting, particularly when the rioters smash store windows, loot shops, and attack bystanders. Government officials are struggling to find ways to counter these spontaneous eruptions.

In certain cases, the participants use mobile group messenging services such as Twitter to organize. The nature of text-based communications promotes a certain amount of disinhibition, and people feel less accountable for their actions—particularly when they are part of a large group.

Some authorities advocate cutting off mobile services in danger zones. Addressing the problem of violent flash mobs in London, British Prime Minister David Cameron proposed imposing limits on communications channels that the rioters were thought to be using to organize—in this case, Blackberry Messenger services. In San Francisco, the Bay Area Rapid Transit system shut off cellular signals at some stations, hoping to block riders from using group messenging to organize a protest about police shootings. Cleveland's

City Council voted unanimously to criminalize the use of social media tools to organize unruly flash mobs.

The ethical implications of such measures, and even their constitutionality with respect to free speech, are under severe scrutiny. Cutting off mobile service to certain areas is a drastic move that would also hinder normal communications and emergency cell phone calls to 911 as well. Shutting down the Blackberry service in parts of London, for instance, would prevent innocent people from warning their families to stay away. Cleveland mayor Frank Jackson vetoed his Council's proposal, saying, "To make a criminal activity of just having a conversation, whether some acts of criminal activity are associated with it or not, it goes beyond reason." When the Council voted again, most took a second look and agreed with the mayor.

Police departments are learning how to monitor group messenging and other social media for signs of criminal activity, and these strategies may be more effective than trying to block the services when the flash mob appears. Philadelphia's Police Commissioner stressed that, "Social networking is not the issue. It's how people are misusing it to gather and then commit a crime." [19,20]

How do these characteristics of electronic communication influence human behavior, social interactions, and virtual teamwork? These technologies are enormously valuable in allowing communication to occur anytime, anywhere, but they also introduce new twists that may cause uncomfortable bumps in the relationship-building process.

MANAGING ONLINE IMPRESSIONS

Although Tamara first met Jun and Liu at a conference in Dallas, Allen's first impression of Jun came from his e-mail message at the start of the project (Figure 8-15). Without quite realizing why, Allen saw Jun as an older Chinese businesswoman who preferred formality and liked to get right down to business. He hoped the two teams would work smoothly together, though he and Tamara were more laid back. When Allen later looked up Jun on the social networking site Orkut, he was stunned by the profile photo showing a hip young man wearing t-shirt, jeans, and sunglasses.

> **PRODUCTIVITY TIP**
> According to surveys, about half of employers visit a candidate's social networking site as a screening tool before making a hiring decision. Thirty-five percent said they found material on the site that caused them not to hire the candidate.[21] To manage your online persona, take into account the impression it makes on different audiences and carefully review your privacy settings.

FIGURE 8-15

Managing impressions with introductory e-mails.

1 February 2012

Dear Mr. Barron,

It is with great honour that we join you in this important project to develop a marketing campaign for clients. Please be kindly aware that Hong Kong time zone is 13 hours later than you so we hope to agree on acceptable meeting times to create the programme.

Yours faithfully,
Jun Chang

People form impressions quickly using social categories, particularly age, gender, ethnicity, and physical attractiveness. When those cues are not obvious, they use whatever they can to form some kind of impression, and so miscalculations are common online. In the e-mail, Jun's formal, businesslike approach with its British tilt conveyed the impression of someone quite different.

Social media with photos and videos add physical appearance back into the mix, and studies show the level of attractiveness dominates the impression they create. In fact, people are more interested in meeting those whose profile shows no photo at all than those with unattractive images.

Social networking adds an unusual feature to online impression management that has no parallel in face-to-face settings. Visiting Jun's Orkut site reveals his friendship network, which includes dozens of college-age buddies, one with pink hair and another with tattoos. The wall posts showed a few outrageous comments from friends, with many LOLs (laughing out loud). People will form an impression of Jun based not just on his own profile, but also on whatever is visible about his friendship network. The contrast between Jun's professional e-mail and his Orkut impression was quite puzzling to Allen.

GROUP DYNAMICS IN VIRTUAL TEAMS

Organizations are eager to leverage collaborative technologies to create virtual teams, drawing on people's expertise regardless of their physical locations and reducing travel expenses in the bargain. But how do these groups fare compared to the face-to-face variety? How does the online environment affect group dynamics, and the success of the group's efforts?

DEVELOPING GROUP NORMS   Within organizations, people usually learn norms from one another as they watch what others do and experience subtle praise or rebuke, often nonverbal. At a face-to-face meeting, for instance, a stony silence from group members when a latecomer arrives will forcefully communicate a "let's always start on time" norm. Online, though, group members can't perceive the nonverbal cues, so group norms can be more difficult to establish. For example, virtual team members often complain that one or two members are free riding and failing to do their share of the work. Norms about how workload should be shared are more difficult to transmit and enforce online.

> **PRODUCTIVITY TIP**
> Student project teams usually conduct a great deal of their work online, through e-mail, text messages, and shared workspaces, for instance. A team charter that includes elements such as those listed in Figure 8-16 will help establish norms that build productive and trusting relationships, and avoid misunderstandings.

Successful virtual team leaders compensate for weak norms by making the expectations much more explicit. They may prepare a written team agreement or team charter with very precise language, because it helps clarify exactly what is expected from team members without having to rely on nonverbal communication to convey norms.[22]

FIGURE 8-16

Tips for developing a team charter.

Elements of a Team Charter	Sample Questions to Answer
Leadership	What role does the leader play? How is the leader chosen? What happens when the leader is unavailable?
Meeting Protocols	How often will the group meet using synchronous technologies, and how will meeting times be decided? Will meetings start on time?
Communication	How will the group interact, and what collaborative technologies will it use? How often should each member check e-mail or team workspaces? How quickly are members expected to respond to e-mail? Is it OK for team members to IM each other during meetings? What information is considered confidential, for team members only?
Conflict Resolution	How will the team members resolve disagreements among members? How will members communicate dissatisfaction with the performance of other team members?
Decision Making	How will the team members come to decisions?
Task Definition, Work Allocations, and Deadlines	How will the team define the task, and what constitutes a successful outcome? How will the team allocate work and determine deadlines?
Team Member Evaluation	How will team leaders and members evaluate the performance of each team member? What significance will evaluations have in terms of grade or other outcome?

DISINHIBITION   Online environments often lead to disinhibition, in which people express themselves more bluntly, abruptly, or aggressively than they would in face-to-face settings. Their messages lack the verbal softeners and nonverbal nuances that make consensus easier to reach. Allen might type, "I disagree with Jun," rather than the less assertive, "I am not quite sure I can agree completely with what Jun said." But Allen can't see Jun wince or roll his eyes, so he doesn't know his remark's impact. A smiley face icon may soften the message a little, but that same icon might also be interpreted as sarcasm. And accidentally pressing the CAPS LOCK key so that the communication is sent in all capital letters equates to shouting.

The other aspect of disinhibition is heightened self-disclosure, and this, too, appears more often in online interactions. On blogs, for example, endless streams of highly personal updates are common, partly because the writer can't see his or her followers yawning.

Disinhibition is more extreme in relatively anonymous text-based environments, which is why outrageous flame wars break out in open online forums. Virtual teams are less affected, but distance and lack of media richness contribute to this phenomenon, so misunderstandings can occur even in long-standing teams.

STATUS EQUALIZATION   The online world tends to flatten out hierarchies and equalize status, partly because many of the cues used to establish status are less apparent. A text message, for example, doesn't draw attention to the sender's top-floor corner office or CFO title. Collaborative technologies also empower people to communicate with others and participate on virtual teams regardless of hierarchical boundaries.

Status doesn't go away, of course, but virtual team leaders know they do not have the same power as they might in a face-to-face setting. For example, it is easier for a team leader to bring a face-to-face meeting to closure and end the discussion of a controversial topic than it is to terminate an ongoing e-mail exchange.

Status is partly conveyed through physical appearance, and even variables such as height matter. Social science research shows that, other things being equal, taller people tend to have a slight advantage over shorter ones in group discussions because height conveys a sense of power and status. For online interactions in which height is visible, status can be manipulated in subtle ways by altering how tall and powerful the person appears to be. When people use interactive video to discuss an issue and come to agreement, for example, camera position can influence whose views carry more influence. Placing the webcam a little too high can make you look shorter, but placing the camera a little lower enhances height, improves your status, and adds to your power to persuade.[23] In cinematography, the extremely low-angle camera shot can convey considerable power and also threat. It is often used for villains.

PRODUCTIVITY TIP
When you use a webcam or smartphone camcorder for interactive video sessions, consider the position of the lens. A little below eye level will enhance height without creating an eerie, threatening look. You should also look directly into the lens to simulate eye contact.

The use of avatars adds another fascinating element to perceptions of status in online group dynamics. When people negotiate as avatars, researchers can change their heights far more than a shift in camera angles. When people are given a taller avatar to control, they tend to negotiate aggressively and win against people assigned to shorter ones, regardless of their actual heights. Interestingly, the effect spills over to subsequent face-to-face interactions, so that the person manipulating the tall avatar continues to negotiate more forcefully after resuming his or her own physical stature, at least for a short period.[24]

TRUST   Trust develops over time, and it is not easy for virtual teams to create it. Working in the same building, Allen and Tamara see each other often—at lunch, in the elevator, at nearby shopping centers. They have considerable "face time," even when they are not working on the same project. Allen knows he can count on Tamara to get the job done, and he also knows she'd lend a hand in other ways. When his car wouldn't start, for instance, she volunteered to jump start it with battery cables.

For virtual teams, especially newly created ones containing members who have never met, trust is fragile and challenging to create. The team can develop a less robust form of swift trust, based on the members' strong task orientation, their willingness to share information and volunteer for assignments, and their frequent communications. But it can break down when people have little knowledge of their teammates' context. A monsoon in Hong Kong might prevent Jun from getting online, but Allen and Tamara would not know that. They might assume he was slacking off or partying if they didn't know much about his work habits.

Technology glitches are not uncommon, and they also can weaken trust. In one case, a team at an organization's California headquarters planned an interactive videoconference with a remote team in Oregon and began by playing a videotape for both teams to see. The technology wasn't working properly, however, and the screen in Oregon was blank. The Oregon team assumed they were being intentionally excluded. Miffed, they got up and left. When the tape ended, the California participants saw only the empty couch in Oregon on their screen, which made it look as if the Oregon teammates didn't think the meeting was important.[25]

Research shows that an initial face-to-face meeting can enhance trust in virtual teams, often dramatically. Meeting the people you are about to work with, even through interactive video, makes a difference. Instead of having only typed words in an e-mail, your teammates can match a name with a face and a smile.

MAKING VIRTUAL TEAMS WORK

Knowing how group dynamics unfold online, and how collaborative technologies can best support teamwork, will help improve the chances for success. Whether the team is composed of students working on a class project, or employees from far-flung corners of a multinational company, these principles can greatly facilitate a team's productivity. They can also make virtual teamwork more satisfying, and more resistant to the pitfalls of online collaboration.

FIGURE 8-17

Tips for making virtual teams work.

Tips for Virtual Team Members	▶ Appoint a leader (if one has not already been appointed) and clarify the leader's role.
	▶ Develop a written team charter to ensure team members agree on goals, expectations for work styles, conflict resolution, and team member evaluation strategies.
	▶ Agree on a decision-making strategy.
	▶ Practice with the technologies before they are needed for intense tasks with upcoming deadlines.
	▶ Proactively volunteer for assignments, focusing especially on how your own skill sets can best contribute to the team's success.
	▶ Use a high-tech, high-touch approach. Hold an in-person meeting or interactive video session at the start of the project to build trust.
	▶ Communicate and share information frequently, even more than required by the team agreement.
	▶ Review your communications for any effects of disinhibition that may inadvertently offend.
	▶ Let team members know about any change in your context, such as a family emergency, blizzard, or illness.
Tips for Virtual Team Leaders	▶ Get to know each team member, both to build trust and to understand how each person can best contribute.
	▶ Arrange a synchronous session and invite members to introduce themselves to kick off the project, using interactive video, in-person meetings, conference call, or chat.
	▶ Use the kick-off meeting to raise awareness of any differences in culture or working styles.
	▶ Use a relatively structured leadership style, with clearly documented assignments, deadlines, and expectations.
	▶ Enhance group cohesiveness and team identity through team-building exercises, team charter, and other means.
	▶ Choose collaborative technologies wisely and arrange training to ensure team members know how to use them. Use synchronous collaborative tools, preferably with video, to discuss sensitive topics.
	▶ Encourage participation by all members, contacting any who have contributed little to learn why.
	▶ Send out frequent reminders about upcoming events and deadlines.
	▶ Use encouragement and praise publicly, but convey constructive criticism privately.

MyMISLab | *Online Simulation*

Department of Social Services

A Role-Playing Simulation on Collaborative Technologies and Virtual Teamwork

Everyone at the Department of Social Services in Newton is really tired of wasting time in traffic and paying high gas prices, and they want to convince the management to allow them to use virtual teamwork part of the time. They have to travel enough as it is, visiting homes, hospitals, shelters, and the county jail. Why do they have to drive to the office every day when they could be meeting virtually to review case files, or submitting their paperwork electronically? That would also give them more time to be out in the community. They think the benefits far outweigh the drawbacks, and virtual teamwork would save the department money, too. But it's important to start off right.

As someone who knows something about collaborative technologies, your coworkers asked you to join a task force to discuss how to proceed. Log in when you're ready to start brainstorming...

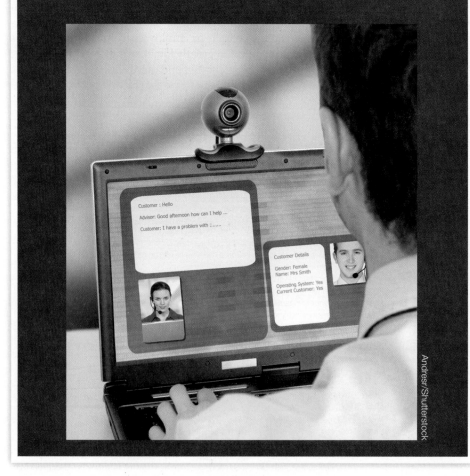

Andresr/Shutterstock

Chapter Summary

1 Collaborative technologies have evolved rapidly, beginning with e-mail and its enhanced features that support contact management with address books, and time management with calendaring. Discussion forums, instant messaging, and texting provide support for text-based collaboration, and each technology adds slightly different features to support human interaction. IM, for instance, adds presence awareness, so colleagues can see one another's current status. Texting is widely used for mobile communications and emergency alerts. Collaborative technologies designed for groups include group decision support systems (GDSS), web conferencing, and shared workspaces. GDSS is usually used for face-to-face group meetings, in an attempt to promote brainstorming by allowing members to make contributions anonymously via their computers. Web conferencing supports synchronous online meetings for people at different locations using webcams, audio, interactive whiteboards, desktop application sharing, and other features. Shared workspaces provide teams with server space to support information resource libraries and asynchronous interactions. Interactive video is included in many of these technologies. High-end systems can create a sense of telepresence.

2 Web 2.0 technologies provide extensive collaborative support, with blogs, wikis, social networking, microblogging, and virtual worlds. Organizations are using these tools to support their own collaborative efforts, but also to reach out to customers and suppliers. Social networking sites, for example, offer endless possibilities for targeted marketing based on users' profiles.

3 Unified communications bring together multiple collaborative technologies and applications, simplifying the interfaces, and making them accessible through many different devices. With context indicators, users can signal the best way to communicate with them at particular times. Universal dashboards aggregate the collaborative services into a single customizable interface.

4 Key characteristics of online environments that affect human behavior include the unfamiliar tools used to communicate, reduced media richness, greater physical distance, heightened perceptions of anonymity, and unclear audience. Managing impressions can be challenging because of these characteristics. Virtual teams may experience more difficulty developing group norms and building trust, and their members may show more disinhibition. However, online groups tend to show more status equalization. Strategies for making virtual teams work more effectively stress the need to take into account the way online environments affect human behavior.

KEY TERMS AND CONCEPTS

SMTP server	presence awareness	telepresence	hashtag
IMAP (Internet mail access protocol)	war room	shared workspace	virtual world
microformats	group decision support system (GDSS)	blog	virtual reality
instant messaging (IM)	web conferencing	wiki	unified communications (UC)
		microblogging	media richness

CHAPTER REVIEW QUESTIONS

1. What are the seven major collaborative technologies? What feature or features does each technology offer for communication and productivity?

2. What are the five Web 2.0 technologies that facilitate collaboration? What features does each technology provide?

3. What is presence awareness? How does it add value to instant messaging? What are examples of ways that presence awareness facilitates collaboration?

4. What are unified communications? How do they contribute to collaboration?

5. What are the five distinguishing features of online environments? How does each affect human behavior?

6. What are group norms? How does the online environment affect group norms? What is disinhibition? What are other ways in which the online environment influences group dynamics?

7. How can virtual team members make their teams more successful? What are some of the things virtual team leaders can do to make their teams more successful?

PROJECTS AND DISCUSSION QUESTIONS

1. E-mail: Do you love it or hate it? How much time do you spend processing your e-mail every day—deciding what it is, deleting it, filing it, answering it, or deferring it for later action? Are there occasions when you would prefer to use instant messaging? Describe the basic functionality of e-mail and instant messaging and discuss the primary uses/purposes of each. What are the advantages of e-mail? Of instant messaging? What are the disadvantages of each? Prepare a 5-minute presentation of your findings.

2. The first GDSS was developed in the early 1980s, but not by a business; the first GDSS was developed by a university. What is a GDSS? What are the advantages of using a GDSS? Are there disadvantages of using a GDSS? Can you think of specific problems with meetings that cause groups to function poorly that may be overcome by using a GDSS?

3. Draw a square and divide it into four equal sections. Label the horizontal axis "Interactivity" and the vertical axis "Media Richness." Label the first column "Low" and the second column "High." Label the first row "Low" and the second row "High." Use this 2-by-2 grid to group the different collaborative technologies into four categories: (1) low interactivity, low media richness; (2) high interactivity, low media richness; (3) low interactivity, high media richness; (4) high interactivity, high media richness. Can you think of a specific organizational communication task that is best suited to the type of technology in each category?

4. Social networking sites are fast becoming corporate resources. Consider how Facebook may be used by an organization. Can you think of different ways in which organizations such as Coca-Cola, KFC, or Bank of America can use social networking? What are network effects? Search your favorite social networking site to learn how organizations are using the site and prepare a 5-minute presentation of your findings.

5. Visit YouTube.com and search for "What is Sharepoint?" View one or more of the videos you find and prepare a summary that describes how Microsoft® SharePoint is used by organizations. What are the key features of SharePoint? What are "tags" and how are they used? What is version control? What are the advantages of using SharePoint rather than a shared network drive?

6. Sorority meetings. Basketball practice. Your part-time job. Your social life. Is it challenging to find time in your schedule for a group project meeting? Work in a small group with classmates to implement shared calendars. Visit calendar.google.com and click on "Create an Account" to get started, or sign in with your Google account. Add your classmates' calendars by entering their contact e-mail addresses. Create a calendar for one full month by adding events for future dates (i.e., classes, work schedule, social events) by using the various options for adding events, and then schedule a group study meeting at a time that is convenient for everyone in your group. Prepare a five minute presentation of your group's experience with Google Calendar that includes a list of specific features that are available. What are the advantages of shared calendars? How do they facilitate collaboration?

7. Online communication has evolved from newsgroups and listservs to the discussion boards of today where people post and reply to posted messages. Consider the many discussion boards that are available. Search the Internet for "music discussion board" or "movie discussion board" to locate sites such as musicboards.com, a site for musicians and music fans, and chasingthefrog.com, a site with movie games as well as discussion boards. Or visit www.big-boards.com to see a list of the most active discussion boards on the web today. Work in a small group with classmates to consider the use of discussion boards and how they may be used effectively by businesses, nonprofits, and governments. Discuss different ways in which discussion forums may be used internally and externally. Does your university use online discussion boards? If so, how are they used?

APPLICATION EXERCISES

EXCEL APPLICATION:
Going Green!

Everybody talks Green ... but some really do it. Marie Chong is a Green home designer and builder who is producing a webinar to share her knowledge of Green building. She learned that web conferencing requires only a PC and an Internet connection; however, audio conferencing capability is required if she wants to chat with attendees by telephone. Marie is working with a webinar hosting company that charges 10 cents per participant/per minute (ppm) for web conferencing, 15 cents ppm for audio conferencing, and $175 for online registration support. Although Marie will present some content herself, she will hire a professional speaker who is an expert on wind turbines for home use, and she will include audio conferencing so that attendees can interact with the speakers. The registration fee for a 60-minute webinar is $159. Create the Excel spreadsheet shown in Figure 8-18 to determine the number of attendees required for Marie to make a profit. How does that number change if Marie reduces the registration fee to $149? Use formulas for all calculations and Goal Seek to set profit to $1 by changing the number of attendees. If the registration fee is $159, how many attendees are required for Marie to make a profit of $10,000?

ACCESS APPLICATION:
Cloud 9

The ad campaign that Tamara and her team developed for the Cloud 9 chain of nightclubs was a smashing success! Club owners Sally and John Gilbert report membership

FIGURE 8-18

Going Green spreadsheet.

	A	B	C
1	**Going Green!**		
2			
3	Revenue		Total
4	**Number of Attendees**		
5	Registration Fee	$ 159.00	
6			
7	**Expenses**		
8	Speaker Fee		$ 1,500.00
9	Audio Conference Service Fee (ppm)*	$ 0.10	
10	Web Conference Service Fee (ppm)*	$ 0.15	
11	Online Registration Support Costs		$ 175.00
12	Webinar Length (minutes)	60	
13			
14			
15	**Profit**		
16			
17	*per participant/per minute		

has doubled and event bookings are sold out months in advance. The Gilberts have implemented an Access database to track membership and events at four nightclubs. Download the Cloud 9 database Ch08Ex02 and use the Report Wizard to create reports that identify which location has the most members and which has the most bookings. Review the structure of the Cloud 9 database. Can you suggest other reports that may be useful to Sally and John?

CASE STUDY #1

Mozilla Corporation Deploys "Telepresence Robots" for Collaboration

"It's not every day that you see a machine autonomously rolling around your office [carrying] a disembodied head of one of your colleagues," said Mike Beltzner, product director for Mozilla's Firefox browser project and owner of the displayed head. The Silicon Valley company is experimenting with ways to improve collaboration for remote workers, and the rolling machine is a "telepresence robot."

Beltzner logs in to the robot from his Toronto office, controlling its movements and cameras with his laptop. At meetings, he can swivel the camera around to see everyone present, and the other attendees can see and hear him. The robot, which looks a little like a vacuum cleaner topped by an LCD screen, has a second camera facing down so the remote operator can avoid bumping into coffee tables or toppling over objects left in the hallway. The 5-foot-tall machine is also equipped with speakers about chest high, and a microphone to pick up conversations.

When Beltzner rolled his robot into a staff meeting with more than 100 engineers, his presence was barely noticed until Mozilla's marketing manager began speaking to him. She asked whether he would be interested in leading tours for visitors to Mozilla, thinking that would make quite a hit.

In terms of the psychological aspects of collaboration, the telepresence robot is a significant improvement over the speakerphone and even over stationary videoconferencing facilities. Beltzner recalls that at first, "The general response was that it was kind of creepy." But very soon colleagues were asking him to roll by their cubicles for a chat. He insists it is far better for collaboration than prearranged video calls. When he is rolling his robot through the halls, people can approach him to start a spontaneous conversation or ask a quick question. "As you walk around you bump into Jeff or Frank, who you haven't seen in a while, and you remember that thing," Beltzner says. He can get around to all the offices and cubicles and can even move from floor to floor if someone will press the elevator buttons for him. The robot has no arms, at least not yet.

Some workers raise concerns about privacy when they imagine camera-equipped devices creeping up behind them. The robot's design, however, can help mitigate such concerns. A large screen that clearly displays the remote operator's face will probably be perceived as a telepresence, but a mobile device with just a tiny camera lens would be interpreted as surveillance. You would wonder who was viewing you, and why.

The prototype robot, called a "Texai," comes from Willow Garage and was loaned to Mozilla to see how it might work in office settings. Remotely operated systems like this one have been in use by the military for some time to disarm explosives, but their costs are coming down and their value in other settings is growing. For example, some hospitals use them to bring medical specialists into an examining room so they can speak directly to the patient, see the monitors, and interact with the patient's family members. If Beltzner's experience with the Texai is a good predictor, the units will soon become a common collaborative technology in business as well.

Discussion Questions

1. What are the benefits of telepresence robots for Mozilla?

2. What are the limitations of telepresence robots for Mozilla?

3. How does the use of telepresence robots compare with traditional video conferencing?

4. In what other settings might telepresence robots be applicable?

SOURCES: Dempsey, A. (September 8, 2010). Tele-robot connects workers separated by distance. *Thestar.com*. www.thestar.com/news/gta/article/857967--tele-robot-connects-workers-separated-by-distance, accessed May 23, 2011. Markoff, J. (September 4, 2010). The boss is robotic, and rolling up behind you. *New York Times*. www.nytimes.com/2010/09/05/science/05robots.html, accessed September 9, 2010. Willow Garages website. www.willowgarage.com, accessed May 23, 2011.

CASE STUDY #2

Leveraging the Advantages of Collaborative Technologies: The Virtual Workplace at Sun Microsystems

With gas prices soaring and traffic congestion stealing hours from every commuter's day, companies around the world are moving toward collaborative technologies and the virtual workplace. Sun Microsystems, a subsidiary of Oracle Corporation, was an early adopter of the virtual workplace with its "Open Work" program. About 17,000 employees—more than half the company's workforce—work at least part of the time from home. They collaborate with their coworkers using Sun's technologies, including Open Office and web conferencing.

The virtual workplace benefits the employee, company, and community as well (Figure 8-19). For example, employees save as much as $1,700 per year in gasoline and other car expenses, and they add many hours to their days by eliminating commutes. Expenses for clothing, restaurant lunches, parking fees, and tolls also drop. Virtual workers enjoy greater flexibility to balance work and personal lives, which appears to reduce both stress and health problems. Dealing with child and elder care responsibilities is simplified, and disabled workers also benefit.

FIGURE 8-19

Sample benefits of virtual work, assuming 40 percent of U.S. workers could work from home half of the time.

> ▶ Costs for imported oil would drop by $23 billion per year.
> ▶ Greenhouse gas emissions would drop by taking almost 10 million cars off the road.
> ▶ Costs for traffic accidents would drop by $11 billion per year.
> ▶ Highway maintenance costs would drop by about $2 billion per year.

Source: Lister, K., & Harnish, T. (2010). Workshifting benefits: The bottom line. *Telework Research Network. com.* www.workshifting.com/downloads/downloads/Workshifting%20Benefits-The%20Bottom%20Line.pdf, accessed May 23, 2011.

For Sun, the Open Work program offers considerable cost savings. The company has saved more than $68 million per year in real estate costs since it drastically reduced office space and implemented "hoteling," in which workers log in to a central reservation system to reserve an office whenever they want to work on site, choosing the office that best meets their needs. Although that office is often the closest one, it might also be one that facilitates a face-to-face meeting of workers who otherwise meet virtually. Kristi McGee, Sun's Open Work program manager, says, "We just don't need as much real estate because we don't have assigned offices that are sitting empty when people are working from home or in another location."

For the community, the virtual workplace can lead to reduced traffic congestion and energy use. Sun found that electricity usage, which averages about 130 watts per day per office worker, drops to just 64 watts for the home office. On a national scale, implementing more virtual workplaces would have major effects on oil imports, pollution, traffic injuries and deaths, and highway maintenance costs.

Sun and other organizations recognize that many jobs are not suitable for home-based virtual work—retail sales, nursing care, construction, and work requiring access to classified documents, for instance. But even for jobs that fit the virtual model well, objections and barriers exist. Some managers think they need to be in the office to supervise, and many are still not comfortable with collaborative technologies that support virtual work. Managers worry that they can't judge the output and productivity of virtual workers and wonder whether people working from home are devoting the full eight hours to their workday. One manager remarked, "I allow [virtual work] for people who perform well. People who do not perform well, I forbid to work from home since it is not visible what they do." Her attitude, though, illustrates another obstacle: liability. Many managers are reluctant to approve any virtual work because employees who are denied may file costly and time-consuming grievances.

Despite the obstacles, the benefits of virtual work to the employee, the company, and the community are substantial, as Sun's experience demonstrates.

Discussion Questions

1. How can Sun workers collaborate without being in the same physical location?

2. What types of tasks may require Sun workers to be in the same physical location?

3. One limitation of rolling out the virtual workplace to all Sun employees appears to be the need for supervision of some employees. How can Sun managers address this issue?

4. In what other types of settings could a virtual workplace be applicable? In what settings would a virtual workplace not be applicable?

SOURCES: Anonymous. (2010). Compensation: Virtual work options could result in $10,000 savings per employee per year. *Institute of Management & Administration Controller's Report.* 2010(8), 3–5. Bednarz, A. (June 20, 2008). Sun's "Open Work" program sheds light on telecommute savings. *Computerworld.* www.computerworld.com/s/article/print/9105218/Sun_s_Open_Work_program_sheds_light_on_telecommute_savings?taxonomyName=Mobile+and+Wireless&taxonomyId=15, accessed May 23, 2011. Lister, K., & Harnish, T. (2010). Workshifting benefits: The bottom line. *TeleworkResearchNetwork.com.* www.workshifting. com/downloads/downloads/Workshifting%20Benefits-The%20Bottom%20Line.pdf, accessed May 23, 2011. Peters, P., den Dulk, L., et al. (2010). May I work from home? Views of the employment relationship reflected in line managers' telework attitudes in six financial sector organizations. *Equality, Diversity and Inclusion: An International Journal.* 29(5), 517–531.

E-PROJECT 1 Estimating Breakeven Pricing for Telepresence Robots Using a Spreadsheet

In this e-project, you will use a spreadsheet and goal seeking to estimate at what price telepresence robots will become affordable, meaning they generate enough savings to pay for themselves in one year. Download the Excel file called Ch08_Robots, which includes variables that affect how much savings will be generated, including the number of employees who will use the systems, how many trips will be saved, and average travel expenses per trip. For costs, the spreadsheet shows the current cost for a robot, which is about $400,000 each. The spreadsheet also estimates that the organization will need one robot for every two employees who will be using them.

1. Use goal seeking (under Data/What If Analysis) to determine how much the company can pay for each robot and break even, so that savings minus costs = 0. You will set the cell containing the (Savings – Cost) as the Set Cell, and enter 0 in the To Value input box. The cell that can be changed is the one that represents the unit cost of a telepresence robot. How much can the company pay for each robot, using the assumptions in the spreadsheet?

2. If travel expenses increase to $6,000 per trip, what should the company be willing to pay for each robot and still break even? You can change the average travel expenses, and redo the goal seeking analysis.

3. To be conservative, the CEO insists that any project to implement robots should have a return on investment of at least $100,000. Assuming $6,000 per trip, 20 employees, and 12 trips per year per employee, how much should the company be willing to pay for each robot?

4. It is possible the robots will be so useful that the company needs to assign one for every employee, instead of sharing them. Change the number of robots required so that all 20 employees get their own robot. Then recompute the cost the company can pay per robot, still assuming $100,000 return on investment and $6,000 travel costs. Under these assumptions, how much should the company be willing to pay per robot?

E-PROJECT 2 Estimating Savings for Virtual Work Using an Excel Model

Calculating the effects of a virtual work program requires making many assumptions about gas prices, commuting distances, productivity gains or losses, and other factors. For this e-project, you will create an Excel spreadsheet that models the effects of implementing virtual work for a hypothetical organization.

Download the Excel file called Ch08_VirtualWorkSavings Model.

1. How does the model calculate the gasoline savings per virtual worker per year? Click on cell B21 and press F2 to display the variables used in the calculations.

2. Using the assumptions in the model, how much would each virtual worker save in gasoline each year?

3. If the leadership decides to implement a smaller pilot program in which those eligible work at home just one day every two weeks (0.5 day per week), what would be an employee's average savings on gas per year?

4. Add more variables to the model, to show:
   a. Average cost per square foot per year ($200)
   b. Average square foot per person in an office (80 square feet)

5. Add a conclusion, "Average cost per office per year," and enter the formula to compute this. What is the average cost per office per year?

6. Assume that the company can eliminate an office for every 200 virtual workdays per year (regardless of who is not there). Add another conclusion, "Savings in real estate costs per year," and enter the formula that will compute it.
   a. How much could this organization save in real estate per year if they stick with one virtual workday per eligible employee per week?
   b. How much could they save if they raise that to three virtual workdays?

CHAPTER NOTES

1. Marett, K., & Joshi, K. D. (2009). The decision to share information and rumors: Examining the role of motivation in an online discussion forum. *Communications of AIS*. (24), 47–68.

2. da Cunha, J. V., & Orlikowski, W. J. (2008). Performing catharsis: The use of online discussion forums in organizational change. *Information and Organization*. 18(2), 132–156.

3. To, P.-L., et al. (2008). An empirical investigation of the factors affecting the adoption of instant messaging in organizations. *Computer Standards & Interfaces*. 30(3), 148–156.

4. He, Z. (2008). SMS in China: A major carrier of the nonofficial discourse universe. *The Information Society*. 24(3), 182–190.

5. Deards, H. (January 19, 2009). Twitter first off the mark with Hudson plane crash coverage. *Editorsweblog.org*. http://www.editorsweblog.org/multimedia/2009/01/twitter_first_off_the_mark_with_hudson_p.php, accessed May 23, 2011.

6. Jones, C., & Wallace, P. (2007). Networks unleashed: Mobile communication and the evolution of networked organizations. In Kleinman, S. (Ed.). *Displacing place: Mobile communication in the twenty-first century*. New York: Peter Lang Publishing.

7. DeSanctis, G., et al. (2008). The Minnesota GDSS research project: Group support systems, group processes, and outcomes. *Journal of the Association for Information Systems*, 9(10/11), pp. 551–608.

8. Fletcher, O. (2010). New Markets: Mash it up yourself: Global teams could benefit from evolving web conferencing tools that allow individuals to jointly use browser-based apps. *CIO Insight*. 23(10). DOI: ID Number: 1973263621. Retrieved January 14, 2011, from ABI/INFORM Global.

9. (2008). *Global healthcare company improves communication for dispersed employees*. Cisco Customer Case Study. http://www.cisco.com/en/US/prod/collateral/ps7060/ps8329/ps8330/ps8333/case_study_c36-496658.pdf, accessed May 23, 2011.

10. Tabuchi, H. (March 17, 2010). Toyota's chief returns to his blog. *New York Times*.

11. Learmonth, M. (June 2009). AOL cracks web publishing-sans Time Warner. *Advertising Age*. 80(24), 6.

12. Rosenberg, S. (2009). *Say everything: How blogging began, what it's becoming, and why it matters*. New York: Crown Publishers.

13. Cohen, N. (January 30, 2011). Define gender gap? Look up Wikipedia's contributor list. *New York Times*.

14. Neff, J. (February 2010). Once skeptics, brands drink the Facebook Kool-Aid. *Advertising Age*. 81, 40.

15. Hampp, A. (February 2010). Gaga, oooh la la: Why the lady is the ultimate social climber. *Advertising Age*. 81, 42.

16. IZEA. (June 5, 2010). SponsoredTweets unlocks "AdWords for Twitter" with CPC launch. *Marketing Weekly News*. p. 197.

17. Johnson, S. (2009). How Twitter will change the way we live (in 140 characters or less). *Time International (Atlantic Edition)*. 173(24), 28–33.

18. Schwartz, A. (May 4, 2010). Scientists harness virtual reality to aid oil spill cleanup effort. http://inhabitat.com/scientists-harness-virtual-reality-to-aid-gulf-oil-spill-cleanup-effort, accessed May 23, 2011.

19. Sarker, S., et al. (2010). Media effects on group collaboration: An empirical examination in an ethical decision-making context. *Decision Sciences*. 41(4), 887–931.

20. Millian, M. (August 19, 2011). *Little evidence links mob violence to social media*. CNNTech. http://www.cnn.com/2011/TECH/social.media/08/19/flash.mob.violence/, accessed August 20, 2011.

21. (2009). Nearly half of employers use social media to research candidates. *HR Focus*. 86(12), 8–8.

22. Sookman, C. (2004). Building your virtual team. *Network World*. 21(25), 91–91.

23. Huang, W., Olson, J. S., & Olson, G. M. (2002). Camera angle affects dominated in video-mediated communication. *Proceedings of CHI 2002, Short Papers*. New York: ACM Press. Retrieved January 11, 2011, from ACM Digital Library.

24. Yee, N., Bailenson, J. N., & Ducheneaut, N. (2009). The Proteus effect: Implications of transformed digital self-representation on online and offline behavior. *Communication Research*. 36(2), 285–312.

25. Wallace, P. (2004). *The Internet in the workplace: How new technologies transform work*. Cambridge, UK: Cambridge University Press.

Knowledge Management and *E-Learning*

Chapter Preview

ALTHOUGH INFORMATION SYSTEMS DO A SUPERB JOB OF TURNING DATA INTO INFORMATION, the processes of creating, organizing, sharing, and acting on meaningful knowledge are more challenging. Much of the valuable intellectual capital and know-how possessed by an organization's workforce attempt to capture semi-structured data. A skilled web designer's hard-earned insights about a customer interface might be found in e-mails, drawings, videoconferences, blackboard scribbles, presentation slides, or hallway conversations. A salesperson's success at building a vast social network that links to new clients might be equally difficult to encapsulate and hand over to others. This chapter explores the nature of intellectual capital and the technologies and processes that help capture, organize, and make best use of it. As a critical component of an organization's approach to building intellectual capital, e-learning is included in this chapter as well.

© Carol and Mike Werner/Alamy

Learning Objectives

1 Describe the three types of intellectual capital and show how both explicit and tacit knowledge contribute to intellectual capital.

2 Describe the steps in launching a knowledge management program, providing examples of the applicable technologies.

3 Explain how the human element can pose challenges for knowledge management projects, and how managers can overcome them.

4 Describe three different approaches to e-learning.

5 Explain how to create an e-learning program and the kinds of technologies that can be applied, including the learning management system.

6 Compare and contrast corporate and educational e-learning, and e-learning and classroom-based learning.

Introduction

The World Bank fights poverty in developing countries by providing financial help and low-interest loans, and also by sharing knowledge.[1] With more than 10,000 employees speaking dozens of languages in more than 100 offices around the world, sharing knowledge is no mean feat. The bank leverages information and communications technologies (ICT) to nurture and manage its intellectual capital, however, creating dozens of online communities whose far-flung members share their expertise in international migration, civil service reform, water sanitation, private-sector development, and legal issues. For example, an aid worker in Bangladesh starting a micro-loan program for local entrepreneurs can tap into the experiences of others who have implemented similar programs and avoid their mistakes.

A company's assets—land, inventory, cash on hand—are all listed on its balance sheet and are relatively easy to valuate. Its intellectual capital, arguably its most valuable asset, is much more difficult to pin down. But what exactly is intellectual capital?

Describe the three types of intellectual capital and show how both explicit and tacit knowledge contribute to intellectual capital.

1

The Nature of Intellectual Capital

Intellectual capital (IC) includes all the intangible assets and resources of an enterprise that are not captured by conventional accounting reports, but that still contribute to its value and help it achieve competitive advantage. A company such as Apple, for instance, might show $50 million in net tangible assets on its balance sheet, but the firm's estimated market value is over $250 billion. The term "intellectual capital" highlights the notion that intangible factors, such as the knowledge and expertise of employees, are assets just like other kinds of capital that a firm can apply to the production of goods and services, and that help determine its market value. In many cases, it is the one asset that truly distinguishes a successful company from its competitors.

TYPES OF INTELLECTUAL CAPITAL

Sally H., a baby boomer born in 1950, looks forward to her retirement after 22 years with a midsized employment services firm. She and her veterinarian husband are all packed, ready to move to Panama to set up a sloth rescue shelter and fulfill their life-long passion to help endangered animals. Sally gave 30 days' notice, but her swamped coworkers do not have much time to go over all her accounts. They haven't learned her secrets for keeping clients happy or recruiting the best temporary staffer for every position. Sally entered notes about each client into the company's customer relationship management (CRM) system, but the notes are just a pale shadow of her knowledge. She is also concerned that she can't pass on the strong relationships she developed with her contacts, especially in regional business schools where she recruits so much talent.

Sally possesses all three of the main types of intellectual capital, shown in Figure 9-1. They reflect the ways human beings contribute intellectual power to an organization.

 HUMAN CAPITAL **Human capital** includes the competencies and knowledge possessed by the organization's employees. E-learning plays a key role in building this capital, as do years of experience working in the field and acquiring successful strategies from experiment or mentors. Sally's vast knowledge of interview techniques, negotiating strategies, mentoring, and coaching is all part of the human capital she adds to the company.

FIGURE 9-1

Types of intellectual capital.

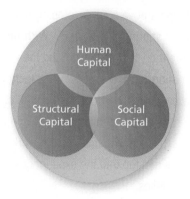

SOCIAL CAPITAL Social capital describes the number and quality of all the relationships an organization's employees maintain, not just with one another but with clients, customers, suppliers, and prospective employees. Sally has built significant social capital through her network of university contacts, working closely with the advisors who help students find employment. They have learned to trust her to place students in career-enhancing temp or intern positions that build skills and resumes and often turn into full-time jobs after graduation. Sally knew her success depended not just on her relationships with employers with hiring needs, but on her long-term ability to find talented students to fill those needs, as well. She invited the students to be "friends" on her social networking site and checked in on them from time to time. Her offers of advice and coaching based on her knowledge about each organization's unique culture helped the students make outstanding impressions from day one.

STRUCTURAL CAPITAL Structural capital includes the knowledge stored as documentation about business processes, procedures, policies, contracts, transactions, patents, research, trade secrets, and other aspects of the organization's operations, often stored electronically. Essentially the knowledge left behind when an employee goes home for the day, it is built up over years of operations, although it may not always be well organized. Sally contributed in many ways to the company's structural capital over the years by developing a handbook that explains legal aspects of temporary employment, for example, and frequently updating it as laws changed.

TYPES OF KNOWLEDGE

In Chapter 1, we discussed the continuum from data to information and finally to knowledge. Knowledge is not just data. At each step along the continuum, the bits and pieces are further refined, analyzed, and combined to create something much more valuable and meaningful: actionable knowledge. Much intellectual capital is knowledge of one kind or another, and it is helpful to clarify the two major types of knowledge since they require different management approaches.

EXPLICIT KNOWLEDGE The notes Sally entered into the CRM, and the handbook she updated, encompass explicit knowledge, or knowledge that can be documented and codified. It is often stored in information systems, on websites, in spreadsheets, or in handbooks and manuals. This kind of structural capital includes all the summarized data that information systems can provide, along with documentation on business processes, procedures, and policies. It can include both structured and unstructured information, as well as multimedia content. Sally's notes touched on a wide range of information about each client, as she updated contact data, anticipated hiring needs, and documented work policies, benefits packages, and the skill sets each client needed most. The information system already contained each client's hiring history, pay scales, and contract terms, so she didn't need to add that.

TACIT KNOWLEDGE Employees like Sally and the many World Bank aid workers possess another kind of knowledge that is more elusive, called tacit knowledge. This encompasses the insights, judgment, creative processes, and wisdom that come

---

intellectual capital (IC)
All the intangible assets and resources of an enterprise that are not captured by conventional accounting reports, but still contribute to its value and help it achieve competitive advantage.

human capital
The competencies and knowledge possessed by the organization's employees.

social capital
The number and quality of all the relationships an organization's employees maintain, not just with one another, but with clients, customers, suppliers, and prospective employees.

structural capital
The knowledge stored as documentation, often electronically, about business processes, procedures, policies, contracts, transactions, patents, research, trade secrets, and other aspects of the organization's operations.

explicit knowledge
Knowledge that can be documented and codified, often stored in information systems, on websites, in spreadsheets, or in handbooks and manuals.

tacit knowledge
Knowledge that encompasses the insights, judgment, creative processes, and wisdom that come from learning and long experience in the field, and from many trials and errors.

from learning and long experience in the field, and many trials and errors. The water sanitation specialist in Bangladesh, for instance, knows a great deal about how to set up a new project for a small village, from balancing the interests of local leaders to finding the best spot for the equipment. Sally's tacit knowledge, which is so critical to the human capital she contributed to the company, includes her insights about how to interview prospective recruits for different clients, drawing on years of experience in which some recruits did exceptionally well for one client, but bombed at another work site.

Some tacit knowledge is so ingrained that the person may not even be consciously aware he or she possesses it, or that other people don't share it. A person who is very familiar with the gentle sliding finger motions that control a heat-sensitive smartphone screen might never think to mention that to a new user, who fruitlessly taps the screen harder and harder to get a response.

The distinction between explicit and tacit knowledge can be blurry, partly because strategies to make tacit knowledge more explicit are improving dramatically. Organizations are eager to use technology to prevent so much tacit knowledge from "walking out the door" at retirement or whenever a competitor lures away a talented professional.

MANAGING INTELLECTUAL CAPITAL

The growing realization that intellectual capital is a critical asset, one that can easily vanish as employees depart, led to strategies to manage and use it more effectively. Collaborative technologies, in particular, offer exciting possibilities that help coworkers share knowledge and avoid the immense gaps that open when key employees leave. Particularly in knowledge-intensive industries like employment services, these losses can be devastating. The disappearance of Sally's social capital alone may be a major setback as her replacement starts fresh to build trusting bonds with suppliers and clients.

 Knowledge management (KM) refers to a set of strategies and practices organizations use to become more systematic about managing intellectual capital. It is also a field of study in which researchers investigate all the roles these intangible assets play, how they contribute to competitive advantage and productivity, and how human behavior interacts with efforts to capture and share knowledge. It's a spirited field, drawing people from many different disciplines—computer science, information systems, sociology, business administration, management, psychology, and more. Some focus heavily on the role technology plays in capturing and managing intellectual capital. Others stress the human and organizational elements, noting that the success of knowledge management efforts depends less on technology than on people's willingness to participate.

"Knowledge management" is also one of those buzzwords that is often overhyped and oversold, leading to frustration and abandoned projects. Nevertheless, the failures present key lessons, and the mismanagement of intellectual capital can be so damaging that KM strategies will continue to flourish, although they might appear under different names.

Did You Know?

Knowledge management is not just for organizations. The leaders of the United Arab Emirates are pursuing strategies to transform the country into a knowledge-based economy, by nurturing innovation and creativity in all citizens. The Ministry of Economy is building a knowledge repository of best practices for achieving these aims, drawing on lessons from countries such as Sweden, Singapore, Denmark, and South Korea.[2]

Knowledge Management Strategies and Technologies

2 Describe the steps in launching a knowledge management program, providing examples of the applicable technologies.

Let's take a look at the steps in a knowledge management project, pointing out how different projects can take advantage of various technologies, and what pitfalls can spell trouble along the way. Figure 9-2 shows the major steps, beginning with the project's goal.

IDENTIFY THE GOAL

The first step is to identify the precise goal of the project, which can best be determined by studying the organization's specific needs.[3] A project with a specific goal and clear aims is more likely to achieve success. The nature of the intellectual capital the organization hopes to capture also guides later steps in the process, such as the methods to capture it and technologies used.

For instance, as electronics, safety, and emissions systems become increasingly complex, Hyundai's leadership recognized a need for a central call center that could help technicians in all its dealerships diagnose and repair problems. To be effective, the call center agents needed to be fully expert, supported by an extensive knowledge basis with quick and reliable answers.[4]

Sally's manager identifies a different goal, one that targets the priceless social capital built up by employees who retire or leave the company. With social networking sites so prevalent and lending themselves so readily to mixing personal and business ties, employees create complex relational webs that can make substantial contributions to the company's success. These sites could help spread news about the company through word of mouth to an employee's social network ties, for example, and they can extend connections to new clients based on recommendations from happy customers.

FIGURE 9-2

Knowledge management steps.

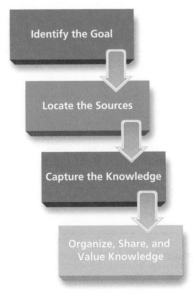

Identify the Goal

Locate the Sources

Capture the Knowledge

Organize, Share, and Value Knowledge

knowledge management (KM)
A set of strategies and practices organizations use to become more systematic about managing intellectual capital. It is also a field of study in which researchers investigate all the roles these intangible assets play, how they contribute to competitive advantage and productivity, and how human behavior interacts with efforts to capture and share knowledge.

The aging population is the driver for some KM projects. The trend is creating a workforce crisis for companies in many developed countries. Mass retirements trigger a hemorrhage of human capital knowledge, business contacts, and goodwill. Departing workers take with them decades of experience, and remaining employees struggle to reinvent wheels and deal with questions that were answered long ago. Companies in countries such as Australia and Japan, where the demographic shifts are most acute, are eagerly embracing projects that target a transfer of knowledge from retiring workers.

Other KM goals, focused more on structural capital, might include documenting and centralizing the organization's policies and procedures, building a collection of presentation templates for salespeople, or creating an online repository for patent ideas.

LOCATE THE SOURCES

Once the organization identifies its goal, it next locates the sources of relevant knowledge. For projects focused on explicit knowledge and structural capital, much may already be in electronic form, although scattered about in different formats and media types. A common problem is redundancy, worsened by the ease of copying and editing electronic files so that different versions contain inconsistent information. Figure 9-3 shows some possible information sources inside most organizations. These can become excellent starting points for a successful KM project.

The tacit knowledge that employees may not even know they possess is more challenging to locate. Much of it is in the minds of the company's experts, those people everyone else has learned to turn to when they have a stubborn question in the expert's domain. Locating these sources means finding the experts, wherever they may be working in the organization, and at whatever level.

EXPERT LOCATION SYSTEMS   **Expert location systems** offer one way to apply technology to finding people in an organization with specific types of expertise, based on their education, experience, and activities. Many expert locator tools draw on directories, in which each employee maintains an online profile that includes details about projects, publications, or other hints of expertise. A researcher struggling with a problem on solar panels, for instance, can enter some keywords into a search engine and retrieve a list of contacts in the company who might have the answers. These systems often include workflow tools so that if the first expert doesn't answer, the query is routed to the next. Some include means to control volume, so the experts aren't drowned with repetitive questions.

Expert location systems can crawl through databases, websites, e-mail, project summaries, and other electronic documents to refine their expertise ratings, and sometimes they add candidates who would not have occurred to human beings. For instance, CIO Ron Remy introduced an expertise location system to Lockheed Martin scientists by asking them to pose a question. One asked about how to insulate a spacecraft from a very hot power source. The system returned 20 names, and excellent suggestions poured in within a day. One idea came from someone who had never

FIGURE 9-3

Potential sources of explicit knowledge from structural capital.

Sources of Structural Capital	
Information system	Employee directories
Intranet	Annual reports
Employee manuals	Calendars
Employee handbooks	Presentation slides and videos
Operating manuals	Department bulletin boards
Strategic plan	Marketing materials
Policies and procedures documents	Vendor lists
Lists of frequently asked questions	Human resource forms

FIGURE 9-4

Characteristics people look for when they seek out an expert.[6]

Expert's Characteristic	Average Relative Importance to Users Seeking an Expert
Extent of knowledge	25%
Trustworthiness	19%
Communications skills	14%
Willingness to help	12%
Experience	12%
Currency of knowledge	9%
Awareness of other resources	9%

worked on spacecraft at all. But the system picked him because after the Cold War, he studied how to dismantle Russian rocket motors—a job that used similar insulating materials. Although human beings wouldn't think to tap his expertise on the spacecraft question, the expert location system made the connection.[5]

What makes an expert helpful, however, turns out to be more than knowledge about the subject. Trustworthiness, communication skills, and willingness to help are all very important according to user surveys (Figure 9-4). No matter how knowledgeable, a grouch who curtly rejects newcomers' questions will be dropped by the expert locator system.

Social media, in particular, can be helpful to flush out desirable traits. Employees who maintain blogs in a specialty area, and who respond to comments and questions, demonstrate not only their expertise, but their communication skill and willingness to help as well. Wikis are another powerful means to identify experts. As entries evolve over time, users can see who makes the most substantive contributions, along with the contributor's tact and writing abilities.

PRODUCTIVITY TIP

If you maintain a profile on a social networking site, consider how you would modify it if the site were used as an expert location system. How would you feature your expertise so software could easily find you?

SOCIAL NETWORK ANALYSIS Tracking down those key individuals who are tightly integrated into the informal networks through which information flows is a challenge, but **social network analysis (SNA)** can be very useful. This technique maps and measures the strength of relationships between individuals and groups, represented as nodes in the network. The measures provide insights into network clusters and the roles different people play as leaders or connecting bridges to other networks. They also pinpoint the loners who interact with very few others. These connections are apart from any individual's actual position on a hierarchical organizational chart. Experts who earn respect and recognition, and who are also willing to provide assistance, will show dense connections in such maps. The technique also uncovers those who play pivotal roles as bridges to other groups, both inside and outside the organization.

Figure 9-5 shows an example of how this kind of network analysis reveals underlying communication patterns. Though Rudy is not a VP, his connections suggests he is a key hub for his unit, and also a bridge to Finance that goes around the normal reporting lines.

The raw material of a social network analysis is usually data from surveys that ask people to identify the people they work most closely with, or the experts they trust most for advice on different subjects. Data drawn from social networking sites is useful as well. The food-packaging giant Mars, for instance, used SNA to trace its scientists' informal networks, asking them with whom they interacted most often and to whom they went for answers. Some kind souls were found to be much overburdened with

---

expert location system
An information system that can find people in an organization with specific types of expertise based on their education, experience, and activities.

social network analysis (SNA)
A technique that maps and measures the strength of relationships between individuals and groups, represented as nodes in the network. The measures provide insights into network clusters and the roles different people play as leaders or connecting bridges to other networks.

FIGURE 9-5

Social network mapping shows relationships within a network, which can differ from the organizational chart.

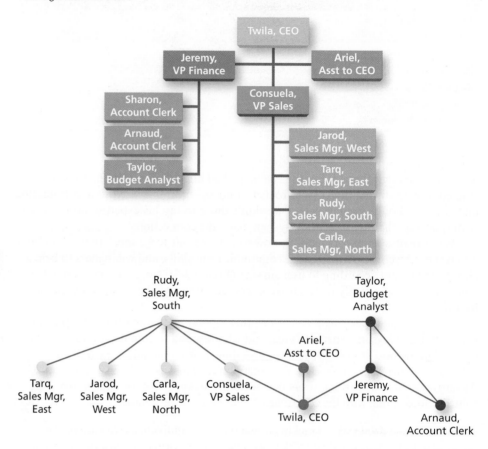

repetitive questions from advice-seekers. The SNA also suggested that Mars's scientists were becoming too insulated, perhaps too comfortable with their small social cliques. Research shows that having many network connections, even weak ones, contributes to innovation since connections expose people to a wider range of diverse viewpoints and ideas.[7] To try to expand its networks, Mars launched an unusual convention to encourage the introverted scientists to break out of their usual clusters and meet new people. Attendees wore RFID badges that lit up whenever they approached someone they hadn't yet met. Giant screens in the ballroom dynamically graphed new connections on people's growing social networks as they introduced themselves to new people.[8]

PRODUCTIVITY TIP

Build a social network that includes a wide variety of people, not just those in your own area of interest. Even weak ties may contribute to your innovative capacity.

CAPTURE THE KNOWLEDGE

Before people can take advantage of intellectual capital, it must be captured. The best strategies for doing this depend on the kind of knowledge we seek and how we can store it.

BUILDING A KNOWLEDGE BASE FOR STRUCTURAL CAPITAL Hyundai's technical knowledge base shows how an organization can gather its structural knowledge assets, organize them electronically, and make them productive for the company. The system started with legacy information from technical bulletins and repair manuals, but it grew rapidly as technicians found the best ways to resolve problems and answer dealers' questions and then added that knowledge to the system.

FIGURE 9-6

NOAA's Answer website is a massive, easily searchable knowledge base containing information about oceans and weather.

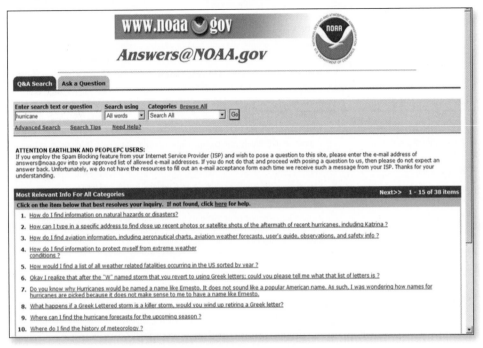

Source: answers.noaa.gov, accessed June 10, 2011.

The National Oceanographic and Atmospheric Agency (NOAA) created an immense knowledge base of its information about hurricanes and other extreme weather events for anyone who visits the site at answers.noaa.gov. The site is an easily searchable database, built from existing data and frequently asked questions, but it is continually expanded as new information becomes available. Visitors who can't find their answers can also e-mail a question to NOAA scientists from the site and receive a reply within a few days. But the expanding knowledge base is becoming so extensive that 99 percent of visitors find what they need through the search engine. Those visitors (Figure 9-6) include professionals and scientists, as well as interested citizens, underscoring the depth of content the site contains.[9]

STRATEGIES FOR CAPTURING TACIT KNOWLEDGE   Attempts to capture tacit knowledge benefit from less structured approaches that encourage people to describe their knowledge in their own words or through their own actions. The goal is to uncover knowledge the person may not even know he or she has and then find ways to organize, tag, and categorize it so others can access it.

Figure 9-7 describes strategies organizations use to capture tacit knowledge. Some in the table, such as after-action reviews, best-practice sessions, narratives, and shadowing, use little technology at this stage, except perhaps to video some of the action. The techniques are powerful, though, because they help shed light on bits of knowledge people may not have considered important and so would not have brought up in a more formal setting.

Collaborative technologies capture and share both explicit and tacit knowledge. For instance, **communities of practice**, which are groups of individuals who come together to learn from one another and share knowledge about their professions, typically rely

communities of practice
Groups of individuals who come together to learn from one another and share knowledge about their professions; they typically rely on online discussion forums, shared workspaces, wikis, blogs, and other social media.

FIGURE 9-7

Strategies for capturing tacit knowledge.

Knowledge Capture Strategy	Description
After-action review	A meeting held after a project has been completed to document what worked well and what did not.
Best-practice session	A meeting of people in the same field, or who contribute to the same business process. They share and document their tips for best practices in accomplishing the goal.
Wiki	A website in which users add and edit articles about specific topics and discuss the contents of each article with other editors.
Shadowing	A mentoring strategy in which a new employee works side-by-side for weeks or months with one who is leaving, allowing the veteran to impart knowledge in the context of the actual work.
Community of practice	A group of individuals with common interests who share knowledge because they are in the same profession or job role, often using online tools.
Blog	In the context of knowledge management, a blog can serve to keep coworkers up to date about recent developments, new initiatives, and new ideas.
Narrative	An oral history or commentary, often presented as a video interview.
Team workspaces	A collection of online tools that organize and collect a variety of activities for a team, such as team calendars, document and multimedia repositories, blogs, announcements, chat, and discussion boards.

on online discussion forums, shared workspaces, wikis, blogs, and other social media. Nancy Kinder, the knowledge manager for Science & Technology at U.K. confectionary manufacturer Cadbury, has created more than 30 such communities for colleagues to share ideas about product development and new recipes. Communities such as CHOCNET, which focuses on chocolate products, engage more than 800 people in 36 countries. The chewing gum community became especially valuable when Cadbury acquired Intergum, a Turkish manufacturer. Colleagues could immediately begin interacting with the Turkish employees to generate new ideas and integrate the newcomers quickly into the company.[10]

Wikis are gaining popularity in corporate settings as a means to capture and share knowledge as well.[11] IBM managers launched wikis for employees as an experiment, just to see how they would be used. The growth rates were extremely high as people flocked to the easy-to-use interface to build document repositories, share information about projects, and manage events. Nokia has also had good success with a homegrown wiki, one that caught on very quickly with employees around the world who used it to collaborate on mobile phone designs.

ORGANIZE, SHARE, AND VALUE THE KNOWLEDGE

The bits and pieces of knowledge that emerge from all these meeting notes, interviews, documents, and videos will be like a chaotic library with no searchable catalog until they are organized into some kind of repository. The technologies vary considerably, though many companies establish their intranet as the gateway to their knowledge management efforts. Contrasted with the open Internet, an **intranet** is an organization's private web space. It relies on TCP/IP and web browsers, but it is password-protected and accessible only to authorized individuals through the organization's portal. Intranets started as a way to organize and distribute employee forms and announcements, but they have grown considerably with knowledge management initiatives.

ORGANIZING AND SHARING STRATEGIES   Within the intranet an organization might use a variety of technologies as an organizing framework for their knowledge repositories. Many so-called knowledge management systems are actually powerful **document management systems**, which manage electronic documents, often converted from paper sources, making them searchable and easily transmitted. In the financial industry, for instance, document management systems are essential, not just because they save so much in printing and storage costs, but because they help institutions more easily

FIGURE 9-8

Examples of properties tracked by document management systems.

- ▶ Date created
- ▶ Date last modified
- ▶ Author(s)
- ▶ Title
- ▶ Document status
- ▶ File size
- ▶ Keywords
- ▶ Latest version
- ▶ Date last accessed
- ▶ Date last printed
- ▶ Security level

meet increasingly stringent compliance requirements. A small bank in Alabama saves thousands each year simply because electronic files eliminate the need to pay travel expenses for auditors to physically visit the bank and pore over filing cabinets stuffed with loan files, investment documents, and other paper records.[12]

Users can add tags and metadata to the contents of a document management system, track document versions, assign roles, and establish security rules. The systems include extensive search capabilities and also offer workflow tools so the content can be reviewed and approved before publication. Figure 9-8 shows examples of document properties that are tracked.

Using optical character recognition, which reads typed text, the systems can quickly do much of their own indexing and tagging to process forms, reading specific zones that have been identified on each form to decipher the keywords and document identifiers. The forms-processing software shows the scanned form along with the fields the software has read, so human beings can verify the results. Figure 9-9 shows an example in which the software is programmed to capture text in zones where key information appears, such as PO number, date, zip code, and vendor name.

Some systems also incorporate **intelligent character recognition (ICR)**, provided by software that can interpret handprinted text written on paper forms. The digital version of the document is displayed on a screen for a human viewer, with recognized letters displayed and question marks for letters that the software is unable to decipher. The human being can make corrections and then store the record (Figure 9-10).

Document management systems may also include extensive content management features, along with the tools to convert paper-based records into well-organized electronic libraries. Less formally organized repositories, such as those that might emerge in wikis, blogs, social networks, and other social media, can use other methods that make it easy to search and share the contents. Wikis use keywords and metadata, and Web 2.0 conventions are also in wide use. For instance, people can add tags to photos to indicate names, locations, and other characteristics, making the images much more valuable from the standpoint of corporate knowledge and history.

Image recognition technology is advancing rapidly as well. The software that scans facial features and returns possible matches from a database is widely used in law enforcement, for example. For consumers, Google draws on its unrivaled access to data to offer an image-matching service called "Google Goggles." The user uploads an image taken with a cell-phone camera, and the service searches for possible matches. A photo of a bar code is easy to decipher and will immediately return an image of the product along with web links about it. Popular monuments also hit correct matches, such as the easily recognizable Washington Monument (Figure 9-11).

---

intranet
An organization's private web space. It relies on TCP/IP and web browsers, but it is password-protected and accessible only to authorized individuals through the organization's portal.

document management systems
Systems that manage electronic documents, often converted from paper sources, making them searchable and easily transmitted.

intelligent character recognition (ICR)
Software that can interpret handprinted text written on paper forms.

FIGURE 9-9

Document management systems include forms-processing software that reads the text in specified zones on a scanned form so they can be indexed properly.

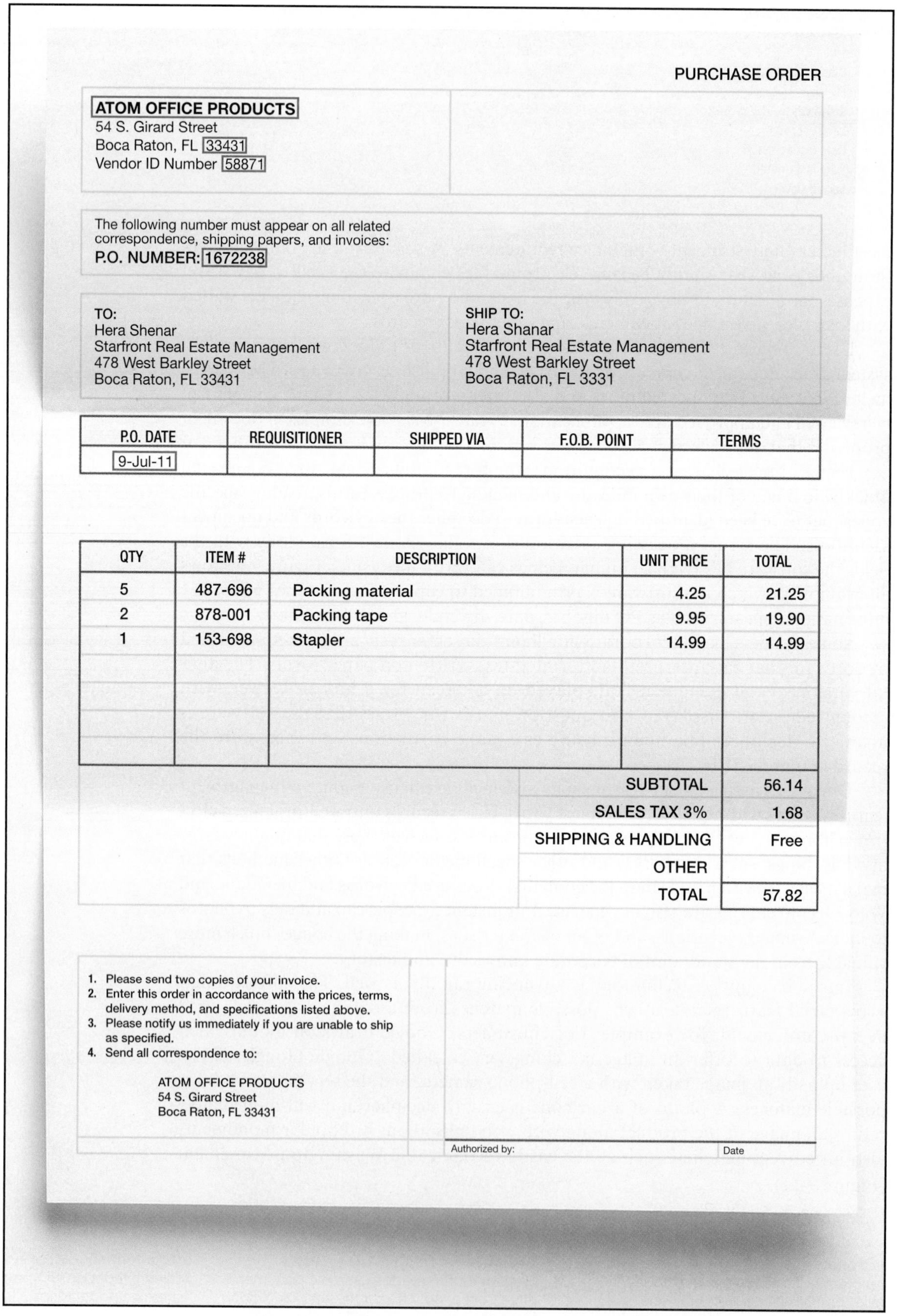

PURCHASE ORDER

ATOM OFFICE PRODUCTS
54 S. Girard Street
Boca Raton, FL 33431
Vendor ID Number 58871

The following number must appear on all related correspondence, shipping papers, and invoices:
P.O. NUMBER: 1672238

TO:
Hera Shenar
Starfront Real Estate Management
478 West Barkley Street
Boca Raton, FL 33431

SHIP TO:
Hera Shanar
Starfront Real Estate Management
478 West Barkley Street
Boca Raton, FL 3331

P.O. DATE	REQUISITIONER	SHIPPED VIA	F.O.B. POINT	TERMS
9-Jul-11				

QTY	ITEM #	DESCRIPTION	UNIT PRICE	TOTAL
5	487-696	Packing material	4.25	21.25
2	878-001	Packing tape	9.95	19.90
1	153-698	Stapler	14.99	14.99
			SUBTOTAL	56.14
			SALES TAX 3%	1.68
			SHIPPING & HANDLING	Free
			OTHER	
			TOTAL	57.82

1. Please send two copies of your invoice.
2. Enter this order in accordance with the prices, terms, delivery method, and specifications listed above.
3. Please notify us immediately if you are unable to ship as specified.
4. Send all correspondence to:

ATOM OFFICE PRODUCTS
54 S. Girard Street
Boca Raton, FL 33431

Authorized by: _____ Date _____

FIGURE 9-10

Intelligent character recognition interprets handprinted text on documents such as this application for additional passport pages.

Attention: Read WARNING on page 1 of instructions
Please select the 48 page option only if you prefer to add 48 visa pages in lieu of the standard 24 extra pages to your passport book. The larger book is appropriate for those who anticipate very frequent travel abroad during the passport validity period and is recommended for applicants who have required the addition of visa pages in the past. **NOTE:** If pages have been added to your passport book previously, we may not be able to accomodate your request.

☐ 48 Pages

☐ VP1 ☐ VP2 **DOTS Code** _____

End. # _____   **Exp.** _____

1. Name as Listed on Passport: Last

First   Middle

2. Date of Birth *(mm/dd/yyyy)*   **3. Sex**   M   F   **4. Place of Birth** *(City & State if in the U.S., or City & Country as it is presently known.)*

Source: www.state.gov/documents/organization/80/20.pdf

Did You Know?

Google uses its image recognition technology to take on e-retailers such as Amazon.com and eBay. With Google Product Search, you can snap a photo of a product and retrieve similar items that match its physical attributes. If you spot some shoes you like, take a picture and you may learn which store sells them.[13]

FIGURE 9-11

Google Goggles uses image recognition software to analyze an uploaded snapshot of the Washington Monument and then returns relevant web pages from the National Park Service about the familiar landmark.

MosamMoments/Shutterstock

FIGURE 9-12

Strategies for determining the value of captured knowledge.

Type of Content	Knowledge Management Strategy
Strategically Valuable Information	Develop strategies to experiment with and invest in this information
Operational Information	Systematically collect and organize, ensuring wide availability throughout organization
Compliance Information	Automate collection and archiving to achieve cost-effectiveness
Low-Value, Nuisance, Redundant Information	Delete

DECIDING WHAT TO KEEP: VALUATION STRATEGIES Knowledge is not always valuable or useful, and much that is captured should be edited or just tossed out. Even as storage costs plummet, the cost, in terms of time wasted, for employees to sift through piles of electronic junk as they search for what they need can be quite high. Figure 9-12 breaks down different ways of handling content, based on its potential value.

Engaging users to help determine the value of a knowledge repository's contents is one way to sift out the junk. In a knowledge base, for instance, users who call up an entry and use it to solve a problem can rate its value directly in the system. Over time, the ratings determine how the system chooses which entries to promote to the top and which to review for possible deletion.

Explain how the human element can pose challenges for knowledge management projects, and how managers can overcome them. **3**

Knowledge Management: Pitfalls and Promises

Success stories in which companies reap immense benefits from their knowledge management efforts abound, and their metrics show glowing results (Figure 9-13). Yet many projects do fail. These cases add to lessons learned, however, and they can help others avoid the same mistakes. Let's start with the role of the human element, and how to manage it.

THE HUMAN ELEMENT: WHY SHARE KNOWLEDGE?

From a senior manager's perspective, capturing valuable intellectual capital and sharing it with all the employees seems like a magnificent idea. But the employee may feel differently. A person's knowledge is a large part of what makes that individual valuable to any organization, and it helps determines salary, title, status, and promotion opportunities. Sally H. spent decades building up her expertise about how to make every temporary employment contract succeed, and she was consistently promoted for it. Would she think twice about sharing all her secrets on a blog, or

FIGURE 9-13

Metrics to assess the success of knowledge management projects.

Knowledge Management Project Metrics
Growth in resources attached to the project
Growth in the volume of content
Growth in usage by employees
Survival even after the loss of particular champions who started the project
Evidence of return on investment

contributing tips to the company's knowledge base? She would, at least until she is ready to retire. And unlike all the formal documents and contracts she generates, her tacit knowledge is difficult to impart to others. It would take a lot of her time, and she'd prefer to spend that time gaining new clients to earn another raise or bonus.

Some employees will actively hoard knowledge, perceiving that their value to the organization drops as they share expertise with others. A software developer who knows the code inside a specialized financial application may be the only person who can repair bugs and add features. This creates a very risky situation for the organization, but it can certainly translate to job security for the programmer.

Employees may also judge that time spent adding to any knowledge base means time away from their other productive activities. They calculate that it's wiser to contribute as little as possible and instead make that extra call to a client or polish their latest proposal. They may become free riders and actively use the knowledge base to achieve their own goals, but they don't add to it. Their free riding eventually causes others to drop out as well, as they observe the inequity.

Another obstacle is that people may be reluctant to share information that saves them time because employers might then require higher workloads. For instance, an accountant developed a nifty what-if spreadsheet that dramatically cut down the time to produce cost estimates for clients. Sharing this innovation might make requests for last-minute estimates skyrocket, raising the accountant's workload. Figure 9-14 shows another example of this kind of dilemma.

Finally, enthusiastic early contributors to the knowledge base may get turned off as their content is critiqued or corrected by others. Lukewarm ratings by users may discourage contributors, and no one likes to be publicly contradicted. A wave of comments that point out faults in a contributor's carefully crafted entry is embarrassing. That scenario also raises a red flag to others, who observe that generous sharing can lead to unpleasant consequences. As we discussed in the chapter on collaboration, online discussions can seem more abrupt and harsh, compounding the problem.

INCENTIVES FOR KNOWLEDGE SHARING

Most successful projects incorporate incentives to counteract people's reluctance to share knowledge.[14] Monetary rewards such as cash bonuses, reward points, and gift certificates, and nonmonetary rewards such as praise and public recognition can all influence sharing.

Incentives can have unintended consequences, however. For instance, an accounting firm tried offering mousepads to people who contributed, but the employees viewed this as a laughable reward for their valuable time and knowledge, so they refused to contribute. Bigger monetary rewards can encourage participation, but they can also lead to an organizational culture in which employees don't share at all unless they earn what they think is a fair payment. Some will start gaming the system by adding

FIGURE 9-14

A knowledge sharing dilemma. What would you do?

Evan manages installations of videoconferencing systems for his clients and after long experience has developed a detailed checklist that almost guarantees the installation will go smoothly and will come in under budget. A coworker who saw his checklist suggested he add it to the knowledge base, but Evan is reluctant.

He thinks the company will use this checklist to tighten its future cost proposals and win more contracts. Evan will lose his edge, his margin for error, and his 99% rating for completing projects on time and within budget.

Evan should put the checklist in the knowledge base:

__Strongly agree
__Agree
__Not sure
__Disagree
__Strongly disagree

© Alex Slobodkin/istockphoto.com

✷ THE ETHICAL FACTOR   Knowledge Sharing in Fast-Paced Industries: The Case of Formula One Racing

In the brutally competitive Formula One racing industry, Ferrari, Mercedes, Honda, and other top automakers vie to build the fastest car on the planet. The engineering teams closely track every tiny change to their rivals' cars, taking photos and videos, chatting with drivers who race for other companies, or picking up tips about technology improvements from suppliers who work with several automakers.

Each company relies heavily on its human capital. The companies value sharing when the results lead to a faster car, even if the "sharing" came from someone they just recruited from a competitor who slipped out carrying the rival's design documents. As one CEO put it, "Every time we take an employee from BMW, or we lose one to Honda, or a Renault man goes to so-and-so, there's always some transfer in information…. sometimes it's of tiny value, and sometimes it's worth a tenth or two of a second per lap."[15] The leaks continue despite employment contracts that strictly forbid such knowledge transfers.

Employees are under tremendous pressure to manage their own intellectual capital, hoarding or sharing depending on how they judge the advantages. They may hoard knowledge for job security, but freely offer what they know about their former employer's technology. In a fast-moving innovative industry like Formula One, patents and other legal protections are not very useful. By the time a lawsuit is resolved, the intellectual property that was improperly transferred is worth little anyway, so claims of espionage or intellectual property theft are uncommon. Questionable ethical decisions become very tempting in this environment.

trivial contributions, or splitting their content into smaller bites so they get paid more for it. If people earn different amounts based on managers' subjective judgments of knowledge value, protests about fairness erupt.

Done well, incentives can be very effective, however. Praise and recognition are essential, and moderately priced rewards can also encourage participation. Larger cash rewards might be offered for detailed contributions from particular experts. Rewarding teams rather than individuals for their contributions can be an effective way to balance competition and cooperation. Management support for a knowledge sharing culture is also important, and evaluating sharing in annual performance reviews so it can affect raises and promotions can reinforce that support.

TECHNOLOGY HURDLES AND CONTENT ISSUES

Overly complicated technology with long learning curves and high price tags stalls many KM projects. Especially given human concerns about knowledge sharing, systems with novel or awkward user interfaces can easily turn people away. An intuitive, user-friendly interface encourages people to actually use the system. If the technology is smoothly integrated into the systems people use everyday anyway, it is more likely to be used.

The quality of the content in the knowledge repository is another key element in its success. If it is stale or inaccurate, people will quickly learn to distrust the entries. Particularly for structural knowledge, a review process should ensure the contents are up-to-date and accurate.

Too little content can also cause people to abandon the project. If they repeatedly search the repository for answers that aren't there, they will look elsewhere and the knowledge base will eventually wither. A critical mass of content is needed from the outset so people see value right away. Hyundai, for instance, populated its knowledge base with stacks of technical documentation that already existed, then rapidly expanded it to incorporate real tips from actual repair jobs.

THE SEMANTIC WEB

Managing knowledge on the web involves building the **semantic web**, which is a web with meaning, in which online resources and their relationships can be read and understood by computers. The web now offers links from one page to the next, and the meaning of that link is clear to human beings who are reading the page. The semantic web will make that relationship clear for software agents as well, so they can be far more effective at more complex tasks.

The semantic web relies on the **resource description framework (RDF)** to describe resources and their properties. RDF is written in XML and was developed by the World Wide Web Consortium. It describes a resource and its properties like a sentence, so that the actual relationship between the parts of the sentence can be understood:

- ▶ Flipper *is a* dolphin.
- ▶ Homo sapiens *is a member of* mammalia.
- ▶ Shoes *cost* $25.99.

The semantic web will also make it possible for agents to integrate information from many different databases and collections with different structures, terms, and entity names. For example, a semantic web developed at the University of Texas Health Science Center in Houston, Texas, integrates information on emerging health issues from scientific journals, hospital records, emergency room cases, electronic health records, and other sources. Called SAPPHIRE, the web's automatic reporting alerts health workers of any threats. The system replaced nine nurses who were doing this tedious job manually, and its reports are delivered much more quickly.[16]

Although not widely adopted yet, futuristic scenarios about the semantic web show how it might transform how consumers and businesses interact. If you're hungry, you could send out your agent to check which restaurants are open, which have special deals, and which friends are nearby who might want to join you. It could also check where you ate last night and based on your past choices, assume you don't want the same type of food. If you like your agent's choices, it will reserve the table. Your agent will be immune to TV and online advertising so marketers will have to alter their promotion strategies.

PRACTICAL TIPS FOR LAUNCHING A KNOWLEDGE MANAGEMENT PROJECT

Although the challenges are great, the value organizations can reap by better managing intellectual capital are far greater. The competitive advantages companies strive to maintain are tied up with the knowledge their employees possess, and also with the capacity of those employees to leverage collective knowledge for innovation. Every organization is different, and knowledge management efforts will not be the same. Drawn from years of lessons learned, the practical tips in Figure 9-15 will help managers get projects off to a good start, and avoid common missteps.

FIGURE 9-15

Practical tips for launching a KM project.

- ▶ Identify a clear and specific goal, and start small.
- ▶ Get management buy-in for the project.
- ▶ Find the assets and human experts in the organization that can help start up the knowledge base, and populate it with valuable, accurate, and up-to-date information.
- ▶ Choose technology that is simple and user-friendly, and that integrates easily with existing systems.
- ▶ Introduce the project as a pilot, with a smaller subset of receptive employees.
- ▶ Develop knowledge-sharing incentive strategies appropriate for the organization.
- ▶ Actively encourage people to participate, suggest improvements, and add to the organization's collective intellectual capital.

---

semantic web
A web with meaning, in which online resources and their relationships can be read and understood by computers as well as human beings.

resource description framework (RDF)
Part of the XML family of standards, RDF is used to describe online resources and their properties for the semantic web.

Describe three different approaches to e-learning. **E-Learning**

Carlos, human resources manager at Sally's employment services firm, is eager to expand the company's training program. Thinking about Sally's skills, he asks her to develop a short course on work visas for noncitizens. Most employees already see her as the resident expert and e-mail her their questions, so Carlos's goal is to both capture this intellectual capital and turn it into a short online course to train new employees. Since Sally had been a trainer earlier in her career, she is happy to give it a try. She taught face-to-face classes, so e-learning will be something new. She also realizes it could help many more people learn the basics compared to the classroom version. And people can still learn from the course after she leaves for Panama on her mission to save the sloth.

Learning is central to an organization's capacity to build intellectual capital, and ICT can transform the process through e-learning. The constraints of time and space that come with a face-to-face classroom session vanish, but new challenges emerge. Technological glitches are not uncommon, with connections breaking down or microphones failing. But organizations can reap huge benefits if they find ways to take best advantage of the online medium for learning and not just try to replicate a class session.

COMPARING E-LEARNING APPROACHES

E-learning refers to a varied set of instructional approaches that all depend on ICT, especially the Internet, to connect trainees with learning materials, and also with their instructors and other trainees. E-learning approaches can be quite different, and the jargon used to describe them can be confusing. Let's sort out the major categories.

SELF-PACED E-LEARNING   Instruction might be designed as self-paced e-learning, in which students use online materials independently, with little or no instructor involvement. They might read texts, watch narrated presentations, play videos, and then take quizzes. Their successful completion of the course demonstrates mastery of the material and readiness to move on to more advanced topics.

These self-paced learning programs are especially useful for gaining structural knowledge, such as how to use the company's enterprise resource planning (ERP). Rather than waiting for HR to schedule a face-to-face class, new employees can log in to take a self-paced course whenever it suits them. SAP, for instance, maintains a vast inventory of online, self-paced courses in several languages that teach how to navigate the software, design reports, add records, and use each of the ERP's components. Self-paced learning is also widely used for technical training. At nuclear power plants, employees who work long shifts in remote areas can log in to take self-paced courses on nuclear physics, refrigeration, power plant fundamentals, and other subjects.

INSTRUCTOR-LED E-LEARNING   Instructor-led e-learning, as its name suggests, involves a teacher who guides students through the course, often using e-mail, phone, discussion forums, and other collaborative technologies. The course can include synchronous events in which students and instructors interact using online tools at the same time, although from different geographic locations. One of the early versions of e-learning was the interactive video network, in which classrooms equipped with video cameras and TV monitors were constructed in different locations, and proprietary network lines connected them to one another (Figure 9-16). The instructor taught as usual from one classroom location, and could see the students at the remote location in a large TV monitor. At the other location, the students could see the instructor on their own TV monitor.

With increasing Internet bandwidth, synchronous e-learning events were no longer limited to specially constructed interactive video classrooms and networks.

FIGURE 9-16

Interactive video network linking physically separated classes.

Instead, they could bring together instructors and students wherever they resided, using their own computer screens, speakers, microphones, webcams, and Internet connections. Instead of viewing the instructor speaking from a podium on a TV monitor, students might view presentation slides while the instructor narrates, or they might share an online, interactive whiteboard.

Instructor-led e-learning can also incorporate considerable asynchronous activities, in which students can log in at any time to work through online course materials, submit assignments, take assessments, or send messages. Some modules developed for self-paced learning might be embedded in an instructor-led course. Also, synchronous activities might be recorded so students can log in to review them later.

e-learning
A varied set of instructional approaches that all depend on ICT, especially the Internet, to connect trainees with learning materials, and also with their instructors and other trainees.

HYBRID PROGRAMS Hybrid e-learning blends online activities with in-class sessions to create a rich learning experience. Trainees might attend a day-long class at the corporation's national conference and then continue to advanced topics using e-learning after they go home. Or they might enroll in an instructor-led e-learning course that includes a weekend at the plant for hands-on activities and class sessions.

Face-to-face courses increasingly use online tools to communicate and store materials as well. An instructor might post the course's PowerPoint slides, for instance, so students do not need to take detailed notes during the class session.

Explain how to create an e-learning program and the kinds of technologies that can be applied, including the learning management system.

5 # Creating an E-Learning Program

Almost any technology used to develop web resources, collaborate online, or organize existing resources into a coherent course can add to e-learning programs. The array of tools is mind-boggling. Carlos relies on a well-designed strategy that focuses first and foremost on the content and how best to present it. He wants it to be clear, cohesive, lively, and easy to update as work visa policies change.

COURSE DEVELOPMENT

Unlike a face-to-face class, where the learning experience relies so heavily on the instructor's knowledge of the content and skill as a teacher, a successful e-learning course needs a team.

Sally will fill the role of **subject matter expert**, the person who knows just what should be included in the course and possesses the content expertise. She has all the government checklists and forms, and extensive knowledge about all kinds of visa scenarios and immigration issues.

Peyton from Carlos's office will join the team as **instructional designer**, the person who brings the knowledge and skills about what strategies work best for e-learning. Peyton will help Sally clarify the goals of the course, develop an effective e-learning strategy based on the needs of the trainees, and design assessments that will confirm the trainees have mastered the material (Figure 9-17). The designer helps bring the content to life, and also makes sure the content is accessible to people with disabilities.

The project's sponsor is typically the manager who defines the project's goals and pays the bills. In this case, Carlos fills that role, as head of the HR office where the corporate training budget resides. Depending on the project, skills might also be needed from writers, programmers, technicians, videographers, and graphic artists. Finally, a project manager coordinates all these activities, tracking progress from kickoff to completion. Peyton, the instructional designer, will handle that role.

The team strives to create a course that will effectively accomplish its goals and that instructors and students will find easy to use—and also to adapt and modify as needed. Figure 9-18 shows some items often used to judge whether an online course is properly designed.

FIGURE 9-17

Job description for an instructional designer.

> **Job Opening: Instructional Designer**
>
> As instructional designer, you will join the Human Capital Development Office to help create engaging e-learning courses for corporate training. You will work with subject matter experts and corporate sponsors to assess learner needs, develop learning content, create assessments, and evaluate e-learning programs. Knowledge of content authoring tools, web-based application development, and learning management systems required. Bachelor's degree in instructional design or related field required.

FIGURE 9-18

Sample items from online course assessments.

	strongly agree	agree	disagree	strongly disagree
▶ The introduction to the course provides a clear orientation for the student.	☐	☐	☐	☐
▶ Course layout is easy to navigate and understand.	☐	☐	☐	☐
▶ Course policies, such as grading standards, plagiarism, attendance, and late penalties, are clear.	☐	☐	☐	☐
▶ Guidelines for contributing to group discussions are clearly stated.	☐	☐	☐	☐
▶ Self-introductions are encouraged to help build the learning community.	☐	☐	☐	☐
▶ Instructions for obtaining technical support are readily available.	☐	☐	☐	☐
▶ The learning objectives for the course are clearly stated.	☐	☐	☐	☐
▶ Course resources are easily accessed.	☐	☐	☐	☐
▶ Course resources and activities are relevant and closely tied to learning objectives.	☐	☐	☐	☐
▶ All instructional resources are appropriate for the online environment.	☐	☐	☐	☐
▶ Technologies used support the learning objectives.	☐	☐	☐	☐
▶ Course technologies support and encourage interaction.	☐	☐	☐	☐

LEARNING OBJECTS

Sally brings her PowerPoint slides and a collection of documents to the kickoff meeting with Peyton and Carlos, and they can see she has already started to flesh out the substance. As they go through the material, Sally's outline is falling into place, with six major units and four or five topics under each one. She estimates people will need about eight hours to go through all the material.

The goal is to take each topic and create a **learning object**, a digital resource that can be embedded in Sally's course in its proper place, and that can be edited and reused for other purposes if needed. Unlike a lengthy classroom lecture, the learning object is smaller, more self-contained, and more reusable. Each learning object will have metadata to describe its contents, author, date created, and other features, making it easy to locate later and reuse. An employee who just needs to brush up on the requirements for the H2B visa program, for instance, will not have to trudge through long texts, videos, or slide presentations. The learning object in Sally's course that deals just with that topic will be readily found. If policies for that visa change, staff can update just that learning object without major surgery on the whole course.

CONTENT-AUTHORING TOOLS

A learning object might be as simple as a text document converted to a web page or a PowerPoint presentation, or as complicated as a multiplayer interactive game, custom-built with Java. A common theme in e-learning is that "content is king," so the substance should always drive the technologies, not the other way around.

NARRATED PRESENTATIONS   Presentations with an audio soundtrack are popular for e-learning, especially because many people are familiar with PowerPoint. Narrating

---

subject matter expert
The person on an e-learning development team who knows what content should be included in the course and possesses the content expertise.

instructional designer
The person on an e-learning development team who brings the knowledge and skills about what strategies work best for e-learning.

learning object
A self-contained digital resource embedded in an e-learning course that can be edited and reused for other purposes.

FIGURE 9-19

Interactive diagram as a learning object. Clicking on each segment of the visa triggers a pop-up and audio, explaining that segment means.

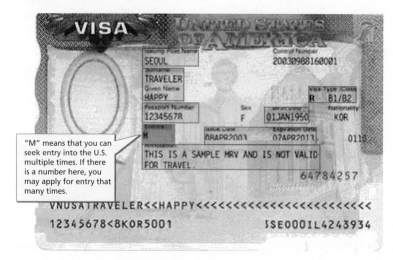

Source: http://travel.state.gov/images/HowtoRead_clip_image002.gif

the presentation is essentially what instructors would do during a face-to-face class session, so this type of learning object can be easy to develop. The presentation can include text, images, diagrams, videos, animations, and other features.

INTERACTIVE PRESENTATIONS   A number of content-authoring tools support interactivity beyond just moving slides forward or turning the audio on or off. For instance, some software helps developers create interactive diagrams that students can explore with the mouse, pop-up text boxes, or narration that explains each component (Figure 9-19). Other varieties might include flash cards that the student can click to turn over, crossword puzzles, fill-in-the-blank interactions, drag-and-drop matching exercises, and guided tours through a series of images, with a question to answer at the end of each series.

Computer programmers were once essential to develop interactive learning objects, but with advances in content authoring tools, people with no programming knowledge can create engaging resources. For instance, templates for flash cards require you to enter only the number of cards on the page and the contents of both sides.

SCREEN CAPTURES   The computer screen itself can be an important element in any e-learning program, especially if the topic is about software or programming. A trainer might want to walk students through the process of adding a record to a database, for example, or show them how to download files from a website. Screen-capture software is used to make a video of such sessions, complete with audio soundtrack for the narration and special effects that highlight events such as mouse clicks.

For one of her learning objects, Sally wants to create a 10-minute virtual tour of the resources available online from the Department of State, and screen-capture software will work well. As she is explaining how to access the site and navigate through the materials, she will capture the tour in a video file that can be added to her course.

SIMULATIONS   Online activities that simulate a scenario and invite the learner to make choices that lead to different consequences can make engaging learning objects. For example, in the role-playing simulations that accompany this text, students enter situations that call for smart decisions and quick action, as they interact with the characters through simulated smartphones, web conferencing, e-mail, and other methods. Figure 9-20 shows the start of a simulation that will be part of Sally's course.

Simulations can also be quite elaborate and costly to create. For instance, Sun Microsystems developed "Rise of the Shadow Specters," a 3-D simulation set in an alternate universe that helps new hires learn the company's structure, values, and innovative culture. Wandering colonists settle one of the worlds, and their goal is to create an information network with a knowledge base to make sure colonists don't get lost again. In the game world, Sun is the groundbreaking company that founds the network.[17]

FIGURE 9-20

For each choice the student makes in a simulation, the program proceeds down that path and provides feedback at the end.

Jeanne is a citizen of the Philippines and a highly qualified nurse. City Hospital would like her to join their staff, and is relying on you and your team to help her obtain the visa she needs.

Select an appropriate visa type to proceed.

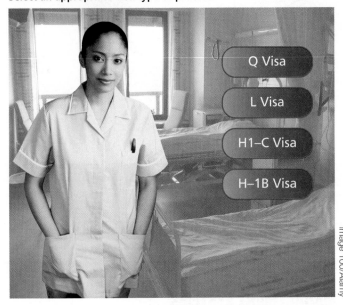

Q Visa

L Visa

H1–C Visa

H–1B Visa

image 100/Alamy

Business simulations can also help students see how their decisions on allocating budgets for marketing, new product development, employee training, or other areas can affect the organization's outcomes. After each time period, students can revise their allocations and get feedback about the consequences.

A great advantage of simulations is that they offer people a chance to practice skills without risk to themselves or to others. Medical simulations allow physicians to diagnose and prescribe for simulated patients, and military ones let officers try out battle tactics in different settings.

COLLABORATION TOOLS

E-learning, especially when it is instructor-led, takes advantage of most of the collaboration tools we described in Chapter 8. Discussion forums, shared workspaces, blogs, and wikis offer useful ways for instructors and students to interact asynchronously. Virtual worlds, web conferences, and interactive video systems support synchronous interaction.

Web-conferencing systems are widely used for virtual business meetings, but they have features that make them ideal for e-learning as well (Figure 9-21). Participants all see what the meeting host selects to show—presentation slides, a software application, a website, or an interactive whiteboard, for example. They can interact using webcams and microphones or submit comments and questions using text chat. The host might want to walk them through a budget in Excel, show some websites, or conduct a brainstorming session in which all participants can contribute their color-coded notes on the whiteboard. Other features include file sharing, polling, and the ability to create "breakout rooms" so small groups can work together privately and then come together with the other groups later to report.

The virtual classroom offers features to accommodate the human element and gives students ways to express themselves with those nonverbal nuances that help teachers gauge how the class is going. Even if they aren't using their own webcams, students can indicate status by clicking icons to signal they are currently laughing, clapping, raising their hand, or nodding their heads in agreement. They can also pass "notes" to one another during the class. When they use the text chat box, they can choose who in the class should receive the message—everyone, just the presenter, or just one other student.

FIGURE 9-21

Virtual classroom session.

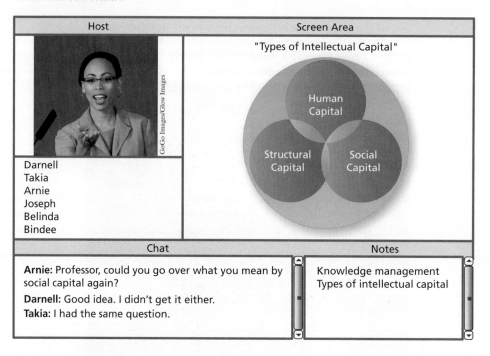

LEARNING MANAGEMENT SYSTEMS

Carlos manages the company's whole e-learning program with a corporate **learning management system (LMS)** as the platform. The LMS is an information system used to deliver the e-learning courses, track student progress, and manage educational records. Many offer other features, such as online registration, assessment tools, collaborative technologies, and payment processing. They also can provide a wealth of tools for content authoring or ways to import content from other sources so it can be added to the e-learning environment.

Once considered niche software, the LMS has grown in importance as organizations focus on knowledge management and talent development, striving to nurture their employees and build intellectual capital. It also has become a crucial feature in industries such as hazardous materials or financial services, where compliance with regulations requires many specialized training programs and certifications.

LEARNING OBJECTS, ASSESSMENTS, AND STANDARDS The LMS hosts the e-learning content and assessments and provides a range of tools to create learning objects, quizzes, and tests. For a lesson, the instructor might insert text, images, or video into a sequence of pages through which the student will progress. For an assessment at the end of the lesson, the instructor can create a series of questions, enter the answers, and choose a grading strategy. The LMS may also offer extensive options for the testing conditions, such as whether the test is timed or whether students can repeat it to improve their score.

Learning objects created with content-authoring tools in the LMS work nicely in that environment, but they may not be usable in another LMS. A student's score on a quiz, for example, might not be captured correctly. As LMS vendors strove to raise switching costs by adding proprietary features that made it difficult for clients to move their content to a rival LMS, the need for interoperability and industry standards for e-learning content became clear.

PRODUCTIVITY TIP
Choose content-authoring tools that at least support SCORM and, if possible, at least one other widely used standard. This will increase the chances that your e-learning module will work in different learning management systems.

Several standards for learning objects emerged, and the LMS vendors added tools so clients could export and import learning objects. A widely used set of standards that originated with work in the U.S. Department of Defense is called the **Sharable Content Object Reference Model (SCORM)**. These guidelines govern how e-learning objects communicate with the LMS on a technical level, so a user can import a SCORM-compliant object to any LMS that supports the standard.

SOCIAL LEARNING PLATFORMS   The long history of knowledge management efforts makes it clear that people learn at least as much from their peers and mentors on the job as they do from formal learning programs and instructors. People are so accustomed to social networking and other Web 2.0 applications that it is an easy step to build these tools into e-learning environments. Many LMS vendors are doing this by adding support for wikis, blogs, personal profiles, discussion forums, and virtual classrooms.[18] Organizations that already have social software in place for knowledge sharing can tie the activities that happen in those venues to their e-learning programs. For example, an instructor leading a course on web analytics can start a blog accessible to the whole organization to highlight key points from the course and how they apply to current events in the company. Using social software to blend the e-learning programs with what happens day-to-day is a powerful way to make learning timely, relevant, and just-in-time.

E-Learning in Education

6 Compare and contrast corporate and educational e-learning, and e-learning and classroom-based learning.

Sally is no stranger to e-learning. When she and her husband decided to move to Panama, she enrolled in an online course on nonprofit management. She registered online and then received her login name and password to the college's LMS. Her course hadn't started, but she could click on links to view the syllabus, assignments, textbooks, and also an introductory video. Professor Altman encouraged all the students to complete their profiles and upload a photo so classmates could get to know one another. Sally thought she'd be the oldest one in the class, but browsing through the completed profiles suggested otherwise. There were students from several states and a few foreign countries as well. E-learning attracts students of all ages and backgrounds, and it is especially appealing to older, nontraditional students who have jobs, families, and little time to commute to face-to-face classes on campus. Several retirees seeking second careers were among Sally's classmates.

On the first night of class, Sally logged into the virtual classroom and was immediately welcomed by the professor using a webcam: "Welcome, Sally, I'm glad you could make it tonight. Can you hear me OK? Try using your mike to make sure it works." Several other students were already there, conversing in the scrolling chat window.

As the class progressed, Sally and her classmates read the textbook, visited websites, watched videos, completed assignments, sent endless e-mails and text messages, and contributed to discussions in the forum. They added comments to the professor's blog, worked on team projects, and posted informal messages to the Student Lounge discussion area. "I'm getting married next week," said one student. The rest offered hearty congratulations.

For each assignment, the professor sent detailed feedback and talked with Sally by phone as well. They held virtual classes weekly, but the classes were all recorded so Sally could skip a few when she was busy at work and watch them later. That feature was especially helpful for the student in Korea. Given the 13-hour time difference, he woke up early enough for only a couple of sessions. Twelve weeks later, Sally felt she had had more interaction with this professor and these classmates than she ever had in those large classes she took years ago as an undergraduate. She invited everyone in the class to visit if they ever came to Panama.

---

learning management system (LMS)
An information system used to deliver e-learning courses, track student progress, and manage educational records. Such systems also support features such as online registration, assessments, collaborative technologies, payment processing, and content authoring.

Sharable Content Object Reference Model (SCORM)
A set of standards that govern how e-learning objects communicate with the LMS on a technical level, so a user can import a SCORM-compliant object to any LMS that supports the standard.

DIFFERENCES BETWEEN CORPORATE AND EDUCATION E-LEARNING

Initially, universities and corporations took different approaches to e-learning. Corporations built many self-paced e-learning modules that employees could take on their own time to improve their skills or achieve certifications. Many modules were professionally developed with excellent production values or licensed from providers who developed specialized commercial software. Instructor-led training was conducted mainly in classrooms, not online.

In contrast, colleges and universities leaned toward simulating the learning experience of a face-to-face class led by a faculty member. The faculty pioneers who experimented with e-learning created their own courses and pushed vendors to add tools and features that matched their needs.

One consequence was that LMS developers targeted *either* the corporate market *or* the educational market, and the products were different for each. The LMS for business emphasized integration with human resources, compliance training, and professional development tracking, while the educational products followed a course model, with syllabus, library access, gradebooks, test banks, and many collaborative tools—wikis, blogs, forums, profiles, and more. While business software developers built market share for corporate LMSs, the educational market became dominated by companies such as Blackboard and Angel, and also open-source products such as Moodle and Sakai. Over time, however, the different learning management systems used in corporations and education are beginning to converge, especially as corporations seek to build social software into their e-learning programs and LMS vendors respond.

COMPARING E-LEARNING AND CLASSROOM LEARNING

E-learning is one of those disruptive innovations with the potential to overturn existing industries in waves of creative destruction, not just in corporations, but in colleges and schools as well. Fiery debates about it are not uncommon. Educators and corporate trainers worried that they could suffer the same fate as travel agents, whose numbers diminished as people migrated to online services to plan trips and buy tickets.

Many argued that e-learning is a poor substitute for a live classroom in which students and teacher can interact face-to-face. The lecture method of teaching and learning is more than 700 years old, first used in medieval universities in Paris. Perhaps its resilience speaks to its effectiveness as a gold standard for learning. Indeed, a nagging question for corporations and educational institutions alike is whether e-learning "works." Do students learn and retain as much from an e-learning course as from one offered in a face-to-face classroom? Budget allocations make this question very pertinent. Is it more cost-effective to allocate scarce resources to subject matter experts, instructional designers, and e-learning infrastructure? Or should the funds be directed to instructor salaries, classroom buildings, and employee travel expenses?

Years of research that compares student outcomes for e-learning and classroom-based learning show few differences. In many studies, students taking the e-learning course actually do better.[19] However, the results are variable, and as we discussed, e-learning comes in many forms. Conventional classrooms vary dramatically as well, due especially to the talent, expertise, and energy of the teacher. Even the technologies of e-learning cover a wide range. Figure 9-22 shows which ones might be useful in different settings, from the asynchronous e-learning conducted at "different times, different places, to the "same time, same place" classroom experience.

Finally, the nature of the student counts. Success in e-learning courses depends heavily on the students' ability to adapt to this learning format and especially to apply top-notch time-management skills. Figure 9-23 offers some useful tips.

E-learning and classroom learning are complements to one another, not competitors. Organizations can blend them in creative ways by offering online resources to students enrolled in classroom-based programs, for instance. They can also tie in-person events into e-learning or develop hybrid programs that leverage the best aspects of each.

FIGURE 9-22

Comparing e-learning and classroom-based instructional technologies based on whether students and instructor are in the same or different locations, and whether their interactions occur at the same time (synchronous) or different times (asynchronous).

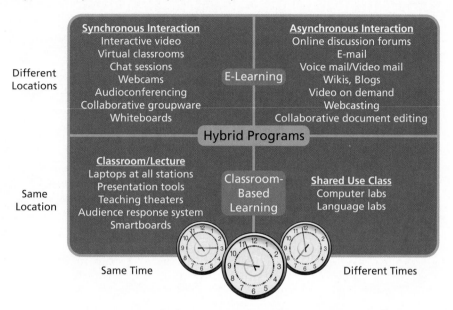

Learning is an essential building block in any effort to manage intellectual capital in a broader sense, and e-learning is a powerful tool for knowledge management. It supports formal courses, and combined with social media tools, it promotes informal, just-in-time learning among colleagues. To speed learning for a new CRM system, for instance, the company might offer face-to-face classes, e-learning courses, and also an easy-to-use wiki in which employees can ask each other questions about specific screens, post their own solutions and tips, and access the training manuals and videos. When information systems help integrate learning smoothly into day-to-day work, it does not feel like "learning" at all. Instead, it adds to the organization's culture of knowledge sharing and cooperation and constitutes real progress toward effective knowledge management.

FIGURE 9-23

Tips for succeeding in e-learning courses.

▶ Manage your time effectively. Create a calendar with to-do list and deadlines that match the course requirements and your own schedule. (Time management mishaps are a major cause of failure in e-learning.)

▶ Practice navigating the course and the learning management system before class starts. Be sure you know how to turn in assignments and take online tests. Locate any FAQs or online help files and keep them handy.

▶ Post a personal profile that humanizes your presence in the class, adding hobbies and career interests. Include any special expertise to help with expert location.

▶ Polish your skills with the collaborative technologies offered. Try practicing with one classmate first to avoid making a major blunder that all will see.

▶ Communicate often in the class discussions, wikis, blogs, virtual classroom, or whatever medium is offered. This is your only way to show that you are "present" in the class.

▶ For group projects, build trust and develop agreement by creating a team charter, volunteering, meeting deadlines, offering assistance, and documenting work assignments. (See Chapter 8 for more tips on virtual teamwork.)

▶ Help build the learning community by asking questions and offering comments, not just to the instructor, but to other students.

▶ After the course ends, invite classmates you worked well with to join your social network, continuing to build your social capital.

MyMISLab | *Online Simulation*

Criminal Investigations Division

A Role-Playing Simulation on Knowledge Management for Crime Scene Police Work

The Deputy Police Commissioner who heads the Criminal Investigations Division looks over the roster and sighs. "So, another rookie just brought in a suspect's computer as evidence, but forgot to initial the sealing tape. With so few experienced officers, we just can't afford to put one on every team to avoid mistakes like that. And we're going to lose them in a year or two, anyway, and that means an awful lot of knowledge going out the door. We've got to do something now, before that happens."

The Commissioner chimed in. "The recruits have some savvy of their own that they could share. They're right on top of the way flash mobs are using Twitter and Facebook. Our older officers don't know much about that."

Much of what those veteran detectives know about solving cases comes from many years of investigating crime scenes, interviewing witnesses, interrogating suspects, gathering and processing forensic evidence, and chasing down leads. The training the new recruits receive helps, but there is so much to remember and little time to look things up when officers are out in the field. For their part, the recruits could really be helpful to show the other officers how the flash mobs organize so quickly, and how police could get to the scene more quickly.

The Commissioner thinks you should be able to bring in new ideas about how to capture this priceless intellectual capital, and make it available to the all the officers. The leadership is open to suggestions, so log in when you're ready to learn more about the challenges they face and how you can help...

Brian A Jackson/Shutterstock.com

Chapter Summary

1 Intellectual capital includes all the intangible assets and resources of an enterprise that are not captured by conventional accounting reports, but that still contribute to its value and help it achieve competitive advantage. The three types are structural, human, and social capital. Explicit knowledge can be documented and codified, but tacit knowledge is more difficult to capture because it includes insights, judgment, creative processes, and even wisdom from experience. Organizations launch knowledge management initiatives to better manage their intellectual capital.

2 A knowledge management (KM) project begins with the identification of the goal; projects with clear and focused objectives are more likely to succeed. The second step is locating the sources of knowledge. Expert location systems assist in this area, along with social network analysis. The third step is to capture the knowledge using a variety of techniques such as after-action reviews, best-practice sessions, wikis, shadowing, and blogs. Communities of practice are also widely used to capture knowledge. Knowledge must be organized, shared, and valuated to be most useful to an organization, and the organization's intranet often becomes the focal point for these steps. Document management systems rely on optical character recognition (OCR) and intelligent character recognition (ICR) to convert paper-based information to searchable electronic format. To determine value and decide what to keep, organizations consider compliance requirements, operational effectiveness, and strategic value.

3 The human element's role in KM efforts is critical, especially because many incentives exist to hoard valuable knowledge rather than share it. The right incentives can encourage employees to share. KM projects are also prone to fail when the technologies underlying them are too complicated or the content is not useful. The semantic web offers considerable potential for large-scale knowledge management across enterprises by describing relationships among entities with the resource description framework (RDF).

4 E-learning is an important ingredient for building intellectual capital and developing talent. Approaches include self-paced e-learning, instructor-led e-learning, and hybrid programs that combine face-to-face classes with e-learning.

5 E-learning programs begin with clear objectives, and courses are created by teams that include subject matter experts, instructional designers, a sponsor, and others. Learning objects are digital resources that each cover one topic. Technology helps developers to easily create narrated slide presentations, interactive presentations, screen captures, and simulations. E-learning courses also may include collaborative technologies to support synchronous and asynchronous interactions between instructors and students. Learning management systems (LMS) support e-learning programs with features such as online registration, content-authoring tools, tools to create tests and assessments, progress tracking, gradebooks, social networking, and other Web 2.0 technologies. Standards such as SCORM help ensure compatibility with multiple learning management systems.

6 Corporate e-learning emerged with an emphasis on self-paced modules, while e-learning in higher education tended to replicate a classroom experience. The two are growing more similar as corporations add more collaboration. Although there are many varieties of both e-learning and classroom-based learning, research generally confirms that outcomes for e-learning are equal to or slightly better than face-to-face classes.

KEY TERMS AND CONCEPTS

intellectual capital (IC)	structural capital	knowledge management (KM)	social network analysis (SNA)
human capital	explicit knowledge		communities of practice
social capital	tacit knowledge	expert location systems	intranet

document management
  systems

intelligent character
  recognition (ICR)

semantic web

resource description
  framework (RDF)

e-learning

subject matter expert

instructional
  designer

learning object

learning management
  system (LMS)

Sharable Content Object
  Reference Model (SCORM)

CHAPTER REVIEW QUESTIONS

1. What is intellectual capital? What are the three main types of intellectual capital? How is each type of intellectual capital acquired?

2. What is explicit knowledge? What is tacit knowledge? How does each contribute to intellectual capital? Why do they require different management approaches?

3. What are the steps in launching a knowledge management program? What types of information technology can be used in a KM program?

4. How can human behavior pose challenges for a KM project?

5. What is the semantic web?

6. What are three approaches to e-learning? How are these approaches similar? How are they different?

7. How are e-learning programs created? What types of technology are used to create e-learning programs? What is a learning management system? What role does it serve?

8. How are corporate learning and educational learning similar? How are they different?

9. How are e-learning and classroom-based learning similar? How are they different?

PROJECTS AND DISCUSSION QUESTIONS

1. In 1998, Buckman Labs was recognized for its leadership in building knowledge communities. In 2000, Bob Buckman was named one of the 10 Most Admired Knowledge Leaders for world-class knowledge leadership. Buckman Labs has received the Most Admired Knowledge Enterprise (MAKE) Award eight times, and Buckman's book, *Building a Knowledge Driven Organization* (2004), is regarded as one of the seminal books on knowledge management. Search the Internet (search "Fast Company Buckman knowledge management") to learn how Buckman created a culture of knowledge sharing. Why did he develop a KM system? How did he motivate employees to share their knowledge? Prepare a 5-minute presentation of your findings.

2. Are you one of the 500 million active users of Facebook? Consider your Facebook page and what it may look like in the future when you have completed your degree program and become an expert in your field. Log on to Facebook, select "Profile," and then select "Edit Profile." How would you change your basic information, profile picture, featured people, and philosophy to reflect your future professional status? Would you change the information in other categories such as activities and interests or contact information? Describe how your profile could be part of an expert location system. Prepare a 5-minute presentation of your new profile to share with the class.

3. Microsoft maintains a vast searchable knowledge base containing information about its various products and services. Visit support.microsoft.com and select "Visit our Solution Center." Note the different product categories including Windows, Internet and MSN, and Office Products. Select a product such as "Windows Phone" and then search the top solutions to see various support topics that range from general issues (Getting Started) to specific issues (How to troubleshoot photo upload issues on a Windows Phone 7). Return to the product categories and select a Microsoft product you use. Search the solutions to find a topic relevant to your use of the product. What are the advantages of using this site? What are the disadvantages? Prepare a brief summary in which you recommend (or don't recommend) this knowledge base to your coworkers.

4. How can collaborative technologies facilitate knowledge management? Recall the types of collaborative technology discussed in Chapter 8. Work in a small group with classmates to create a list of suggestions for your university, outlining how it could use different types of collaborative technology to manage knowledge.

5. Work in a small group with classmates to explore the kinds of graduate programs in business that are available online. Are e-learning programs offered online, or in hybrid formats? Choose three programs and prepare a brief summary to compare and contrast the way each one uses e-learning that you can share with the class.

APPLICATION EXERCISES

EXCEL APPLICATION:
Top Talent

Top Talent Employment Services provides both temporary and permanent employees to clients in a tri-state area. Top Talent uses an online customer satisfaction survey that makes it easy for clients to provide feedback about the services and the employees provided by Top Talent. Jill Simons, sales and marketing manager at Top Talent, has asked you to analyze the survey data from the last three months to identify areas of company performance that may need improvement. Download the TopTalentSurvey Excel file Ch09Ex01 and provide descriptive statistics (mean, mode, minimum, maximum, standard deviation) for each survey item. Use formulas to calculate statistics. Create a line chart to display the survey results (the means of all survey items). Which areas have shown the greatest improvement in customer satisfaction? Which have shown a decline in customer satisfaction?

ACCESS APPLICATION:
Top Talent

Recall the e-learning course that Sally was asked to develop at the beginning of this chapter and assume it was a success. Now her firm has decided to create a simplified version of an expert location system in order to capture the experience of its professional staff. Carlos plans to launch the system using an Access database. His goal is to identify members of the staff who have specialized expertise and to provide access to that knowledge in a searchable format. Download the TopTalent Excel file Ch09Ex02 and import the worksheets to create the database shown in Figure 9-24. Create a report that lists each expert by name within each category of expertise.

FIGURE 9-24

Access database for Top Talent.

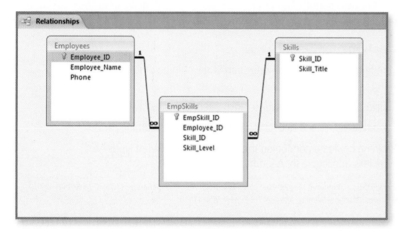

CASE STUDY #1

Developing Talent at Arkadin Through E-Learning

As organizations strive to reduce operating expenses by cutting travel budgets, companies such as Arkadin are reaping the profits. Founded in 2001, Arkadin provides audio and web-conferencing services that support virtual meetings and online collaboration. With offices in 22 countries in Asia, Europe, and North America, the company's 500+ employees serve more than 8,000 active clients.

Customized service and attentive customer support distinguish Arkadin's product offerings, which is why they have so many offices around the world. Their growing workforce speaks 12 different languages, and most of their new recruits are young people. Training new people and developing their talents are enormous challenges for this globally dispersed company, and their approach had been chaotic and ad hoc. What training occurred was inconsistent across the offices, and there was no attempt to measure success. Anticipating about 100 new people per year, the human resources office established these objectives:

▶ Integrate new employees quickly and easily.

▶ Create professional development plans to improve retention.

▶ Standardize training programs.

Arkadin's business model and experience with online collaboration pointed to e-learning. The company's own IT staff is heavily invested in developing products for customers, however, so they decided the best approach would be to find an innovative and flexible training company that offered a hosted solution, one that could also support all the languages they needed. They chose CrossKnowledge, a European company whose distance learning products are developed by business experts working with educators. They helped Arkadin build several "academies," each with online content that is highly practical and available 24/7, and also tailored to different employee groups. More than 65 percent of Arkadin's staff is in customer service or sales, so pragmatic, just-in-time learning is essential.

A major challenge in developing the academies was different skill levels. Arkadin decided to deploy self-assessment pretests that would steer employees toward material they needed to learn and away from content they already knew. Another challenge was achieving buy-in and promoting the program. Arkadin used their own web-conferencing and communications tools to boost awareness throughout the organization.

Arkadin plans to implement performance measures that will determine how effective these training programs are, but they are already finding that employees value the service. They now have anytime, anywhere access to the courses, and many who complete a program go on to become mentors for the next cohort. The praise newcomers are hearing from their colleagues through word of mouth beats any corporate promotion campaign.

Discussion Questions

1. Why does Arkadin fit the profile of an organization that would be amenable to e-learning?

2. What other initiatives would be necessary to make e-learning successful?

3. What challenges did Arkadin need to overcome to implement e-learning?

4. What types of training could be conducted through e-learning? What types of training may be less applicable for e-learning?

SOURCES: Arkadin Company Dossier. Retrieved May 29, 2011, from LexisNexis Academic Database. Mulin, C., & Reen H. (2010). Arkadin develops employee talent through e-learning. *Strategic HR Review.* 9(5), 11–16.

CASE STUDY #2

Diplopedia: Managing State Department Knowledge with a Wiki

Shooting past a milestone of 10,000 articles, the State Department's Diplopedia wiki is a huge success. First launched in 2006 with just a handful of articles, the project was promoted by Condoleeza Rice, then the Secretary of State. Improvements in collaboration and knowledge management were also strongly recommended by the 9/11 Commission.

U.S. diplomats and other State Department employees move frequently from country to country, and they needed a much better way to capture and transmit knowledge. They might take six months to a year to get up to speed when they were transferred to a new country. They could e-mail or phone other department employees who had lived there, but the wiki solution is far superior.

The wiki is a rapidly mounting collection of constantly updated articles on subjects critical to diplomats. For instance, it contains the desk officer manual that helps newcomers decipher departmental jargon or tips on getting a newly nominated ambassador confirmed by the Senate. As an internal wiki, Diplopedia is only accessible to authorized employees.

FIGURE 9-25

Strategies for KM success for Diplopedia.

Diplopedia's Guidelines

- ▶ If something is wrong, change it.
- ▶ If something is missing, add it.
- ▶ Use plain language.
- ▶ Use the Discussion tab to discuss an article.
- ▶ Use a neutral point of view.

The idea for the State Department's wiki as a knowledge repository came from Jimmy Wales, founder of Wikipedia. Diplopedia uses the same open-source software and also follows many of its guidelines, shown in Figure 9-25. Unlike Wikipedia, however, the State Department's wiki requires very strict governance, given the sensitivity of this kind of information. Wikipedians rely on people behaving like adults, so their guidance to the department about governance was basically to tell employees: "Don't be a jerk." That doesn't work for a government agency, but a founding principle of Diplopedia is to assume people's good intentions. As a check, however, Diplopedia does not permit anonymous contributions, as Wikipedia does, and no "sock puppets" are allowed. Also, Diplopedia's security is extremely tight, especially so after Wikileaks obtained and publicly released thousands of classified diplomatic documents in 2010.

Diplopedia's success surprised many observers because the department was not known for any pioneering IT initiatives. Chris Bronk, a professor at Rice University who studies the agency, remarked that "science and technology have a somewhat tarnished history at State." Even though the department is fully wired, its communication patterns have changed little since the days of the telegraph and cable, although e-mail is used instead.

Diplopedia provides a platform for diplomats to go well beyond summarizing the local news to higher-ups back in Washington. They can capture and document the richness of their experiences and expertise about their country, annotating conversations with local government officials, academics, and taxi drivers. Most important, their knowledge will not be lost when their plane takes off for the next assignment. And it won't go out of date, either, as newly assigned members of the diplomatic corps correct, expand, and enrich the wiki knowledge base.

Discussion Questions

1. In 2010, the website WikiLeaks posted more than 250,000 U.S. diplomatic cables. What are some potential implications of this posting for Diplopedia?

2. What key issues will need to be addressed for Diplopedia to be more widely used by diplomatic personnel?

3. How can the State Department benefit from Diplopedia?

4. What types of knowledge are appropriate for Diplopedia?

SOURCES: Anonymous. (May 21, 2010). Wiki platforms touted for gov't. *Investors Business Daily.* p. A02. Bronk, C. (March 2010). Diplomacy rebooted: Making digital statecraft a reality. *Foreign Service Journal.* 43–47. Bronk, C. (2010). Diplopedia imagined: Building State's diplomacy wiki. *Proceedings of the 2010 International Symposium on Collaborative Technologies and Systems.* Ruth, D. (May 20, 2010). Diplopedia a success at US Department of State. www.eurekalert.org/pub_releases/2010-05/ru-das052010.php, accessed May 29, 2011.

E-PROJECT 1   Exploring the World of Online Courses

Thousands of courses are available for free on the web, and in this e-project, you will explore some of them to learn what technologies they use and how they compare to your own courses.

1. Visit the MIT Open Courseware project (http://ocw.mit.edu) and review the many courses available. Note the icons at the top of the course listings that explain what resources are included. Find a course that you have already taken at your college or university.

   a. What resources are included in the online course?
   b. What technologies does the course rely on for its learning objects?
   c. How does this course compare to the one you took at your university?

2. Visit the Khan Academy (www.khanacademy.org) to learn more about a growing list of online course materials posted on YouTube. Salman Khan started this nonprofit organization with the aim of making education freely available to anyone who wants it, at any time. Courses are arranged as "playlists" and students are encouraged to start from the beginning unless they need a quick refresher on a specific topic. Choose a course that you have already taken, look over the list of topics, and watch the first video.

   a. What technologies does the course rely on?
   b. How does this approach to online courses compare with MIT's open courseware?
   c. How does it compare to the course you took?

E-PROJECT 2   Managing the Human Element on Wikipedia with Technology

In this e-project, you will explore Wikipedia's strategies for managing the largest online knowledge repository in the world, learning more about how technology is used to manage the human element.

First, visit Wikipedia's main page (http://en.wikipedia.org/wiki/Main_Page) for an overview of the site. Next, go to the article titled "Smartphone" (http://en.wikipedia.org/wiki/Smartphone).

1. Click on the Discussion tab at the top.

   a. What is the purpose of this section?
   b. What issues and debates are underway regarding the content of the article on smartphones?
   c. How does this technical support for discussion about the contents of an article help manage the human element?

2. Click on the Edit tab and read the policies at the top regarding disclosure of your IP address if you want to edit the contents of an article without logging in.

   a. What is Wikipedia's policy regarding the disclosure of your IP address if you are not logged into your account and choose to edit the contents of an article?
   b. Why would Wikipedia's leadership allow account holders to hide their IP addresses?

3. Follow the links to create an account and then review the benefits of being an account holder (http://en.wikipedia.org/wiki/Wikipedia:Why_create_an_account%3F). Read the section on Reputation and Privacy.

   a. How does Wikipedia encourage contributors to create an account, make worthwhile contributions, and build trust and respect?

4. Return to the Smartphone page and click on the View History tab.

   a. How many edits have been made in the past month? What percent are made by registered users whose username shows in the entry versus unregistered users whose IP addresss shows?
   b. Use the Compare Selected Revisions button feature to examine what the most recent contributor decided to edit. What was changed?

5. The History log sometimes shows a very active "edit war" for controversial topics, as editors vie to present the topic as they see it. Read Wikipedia's policies about edit wars at http://en.wikipedia.org/wiki/Edit_war.

   a. What is the three-revert rule?
   b. In 2011, the Wikipedia entry on Wikileaks was deemed "semiprotected." What is Wikipedia's policy regarding "semiprotected" pages? Visit the Wikileaks article to see its current status.
   c. Overall, how do you evaluate Wikipedia's strategies for managing the human element?

CHAPTER NOTES

1. McFarlan, F. W., & Delacey, B. (2003). Enabling business strategy with IT at the World Bank. *Harvard Business School Case Study*. Harvard Business School: Cambridge, MA.

2. Kumar, H. M. (May 16, 2011). Knowledge-based economy is UAE's strategic objective. Gulfnews.com. http://gulfnews.com/business/economy/knowledge-based-economy-is-uae-s-strategic-objective-1.808295, accessed May 29, 2011.

3. Atwood, C. G. (2009). *Knowledge management basics*. Alexandria, VA: ASTD Press.

4. Call center case study. www.knowledgesys.com/solutions/print-call-center-case.pdf, accessed April 25, 2010.

5. D'Agostino, D. (2004). Who knows about this? *CIO Insight*, 1(41), 59.

6. Nevo, D., Benbasat, I., & Wand, Y. (October 20, 2009). Who knows what? *MIT Sloan Management Review*.

7. Byosiere, P., et al. (2010). Diffusion of organisational innovation: Knowledge transfer through social networks. *International Journal of Technology Management*. 49(4), 401–420.

8. Patton, S. (June 15, 2005). Who knows whom, and who knows what? *CIO*. 18(17), 1.

9. Reid, C. K. (November 2009). KM at work: A look at how organizations maximize knowledge to deliver results. *Econtent*.

10. Twentyman, J. (November 2009). Connecting people is a recipe for innovation at Cadbury. *Knowledge Management Review*. DOI: ID Number: 2002767681.

11. Arazy, O., et al. (Summer 2009). Wiki deployment in corporate settings. *IEEE Technology and Society Magazine*. 57–64.

12. Adams, J. (2010). Small Banks Take to Document Management. *American Banker*. 175(9), 11.

13. Efrati, A. (November 4, 2010). Google vies for shoppers. *Wall Street Journal*.

14. Wolfe, C., & Loraas, T. (2008). Knowledge sharing: The effects of incentives, environment, and person. *Journal of Information Systems*. 22(2), 53–76.

15. Solitander, M., & Solitander, N. (2010). The sharing, protection and thievery of intellectual assets: The case of the Formula 1 industry. *Management Decision*. 48(1), 37–57.

16. Feigenbaum, L., et al. (2007). The semantic web in action. *Scientific American*. 297(6), 90–97.

17. Zielinski, D. (March 2010). Training games. *HR Magazine*. 55, 64–66. DOI: ID Number: 1973995931.

18. Otter, T., et al. (July 24, 2009). Hype cycle for human capital management software, 2009. Gartner Research, DOI: ID Number: G00169635.

19. Means, B., et al. (2009). Evaluation of evidence-based practices in online learning: A meta-analysis and review of online learning studies. Office of Planning and Policy Development. U.S. Department of Education: Washington, DC.

Ethics, Privacy, and *Security*

Chapter Preview

A TINY USB DRIVE CAN HOLD INFORMATION ABOUT MILLIONS OF CUSTOMERS, CITIZENS, STUDENTS, OR PATIENTS, and its value far exceeds the few dollars the device costs. Safeguarding information is an enormous challenge, one whose solution goes well beyond mere locked doors and surveillance cameras.

This chapter explores the responsibilities organizations and individuals share to treat such data with care, make ethical decisions about its use, and protect it from countless threats. We examine ethical dilemmas in the collection and use of information, explore the elusive concept of privacy, and discuss the critical importance of information security in all organizations.

©TomBham/Alamy

WIKIPEDIA
The Free Encyclopedia

Main Page   Discussion

Welcome to Wikipedia,
the free encyclopedia that anyone can edit.

3,516,706 articles in English

Main page

10

Learning Objectives

1 Define ethics, describe two ethical frameworks, and explain the relationship between ethics and the law.

2 Explain how intellectual property and plagiarism pose challenges for information ethics, and describe technologies that are used to deal with them.

3 Describe information privacy and strategies to protect it, and explain why organizations may implement surveillance.

4 Explain the steps that organizations use to manage security risks, identify threats, assess vulnerabilities, and develop administrative and technical controls.

5 Explain why human behavior is often the weakest link for ethics, privacy, and security, and provide examples of strategies that can be used to counteract the weaknesses.

Introduction

Jimmy Wales's ethical dilemmas sometimes shake Wikipedia's foundations. As the inspirational leader and cofounder of the website, Wales vehemently supports freedom of speech, including the principle that anyone can contribute any information to the world's largest open-source public reference work. But circumstances sometimes gnaw away at ethical commitments. When *New York Times* reporter David Rohde was kidnapped by the Taliban, the newspaper's editors begged Wales to suppress mention of it on Wikipedia, fearing it would reduce Rohde's chances of survival. Although the manager of any traditional news outlet could oblige, Wales can't easily prevent the site's thousands of editors from adding the event, at least not without red flags and cries of protest about censorship. Instead, he asked his team to sanitize updates that mentioned the kidnapping as fast as they popped up, playing a deadly game of "whack the mole." When that failed, he blocked Rohde's Wikipedia entry, securing it against *any* editing. Contributors were deeply divided over Wales's decision to censor, with some offering praise and others arguing that he would never have caved in for other kidnapping victims. (Rohde eventually escaped to safety.)

Another ethical dilemma finally forced Wales to step down. His estranged cofounder, Larry Sanger, complained to the FBI that some entries featured child pornography. Without discussing it with the site's administrators, Wales rushed to delete the images. "We were about to be smeared in all the media as hosting hardcore pornography and doing nothing about it. Now the storyline is that we are cleaning up…. I'm sorry I had to step on some toes to make it happen." In the ensuing uproar, Wales chose to relinquish his all-powerful access rights and downgraded his own account to a low-level administrator, so the software's security systems would prevent him from deleting anything.[1]

Ethics, privacy, and security issues underscore how the human element is so tightly interwoven with the other three components of information systems: technology, processes, and data. People decide how to build a system, manage it, secure it, and use the potentially priceless information it contains. In this chapter, we explore this serious responsibility and the difficult choices people make as they navigate increasingly uncharted and murky waters.

Define ethics, describe two ethical frameworks, and explain the relationship between ethics and the law.

1

Ethics

How do people decide on the right course of action? What makes an action right or wrong? Jimmy Wales tried to do the right thing in both cases described earlier, but it is not always easy to decide what that is. **Ethics** refers to a system of moral principles that human beings use to judge right and wrong and to develop rules of conduct.

ETHICAL FRAMEWORKS

Innumerable ethical frameworks have arisen throughout human history and culture, but two are especially widely adopted (Figure 10-1). One framework emphasizes **natural laws and rights**. It judges the morality of an action based on how well it adheres to broadly accepted rules, *regardless* of the action's actual consequences. "Thou shalt not steal," for example, is one of Christianity's Ten Commandments, and religious principles form the basis for many underlying rules. Others, such as "Keep your promises," "Protect private property," and "Defend free speech," emerge from beliefs about fundamental and natural rights that belong to human beings. The U.S. Declaration of Independence, for instance, lists life, liberty, and the pursuit of happiness as inalienable human rights.

A second framework, called **utilitarianism**, considers the *consequences* of an action, weighing its good effects against its harmful ones. "First, do no harm" is a precept of medical ethics ensuring physicians will heavily weigh the possible harmful

---

FIGURE 10-1

Major ethical frameworks.

Ethical System	Description	Examples
Natural laws and rights	Actions are judged to be ethical or unethical according to how well they adhere to broadly accepted rules derived from natural law.	Thou shalt not kill. Right to privacy. Right to a free press. Liberté, égalité, fraternité.
Utilitarianism	Actions are ethical or unethical based on their consequences and outcomes.	The greatest good for the greatest number. The needs of the many outweigh the needs of the few.

consequences of each remedy. When you try to judge what action would create the greatest good for the greatest number, you are using a utilitarian scheme.

In many situations, both ethical approaches will lead people to the same conclusion about the proper action. But ethical dilemmas can arise when the application of different systems leads to different judgments about what is the ethical thing to do. That's what happened to Jimmy Wales. When he founded Wikipedia, he made a commitment to principles that favored democratic governance and free speech. But his ethical framework was sorely challenged when the consequences of sticking to those rules might cause grave harm.

ETHICS AND THE LAW

Laws are often grounded in ethical principles, such as the prohibition against murder and theft or the protection of private property and free speech. The U.S. Bill of Rights codifies many ethical principles into the Constitution, such as freedom of religion, freedom of the press, and the right to trial by jury. Its Fourth Amendment, about protection from unreasonable search and seizure, helps shape expectations about privacy, as we discuss later in this chapter.

However, some laws have less to do with ethics and instead come into existence from the pushes and pulls of lobbying efforts and other political pressures. For example, when cable television was first introduced, the TV networks lobbied hard for laws to slow cable's growth. The dairy industry fought for laws to limit how "yellow" margarine could look to protect market share for real butter.[2] The Internet's growth triggers efforts to erect barriers for special interests, especially to protect industries that suffer when people can obtain services online. An Oklahoma law once required casket sellers to be state-licensed funeral directors, essentially cutting out Internet sales by independent casket retailers.[3]

Laws don't cover all ethical principles, so just because an action is legal does not mean it is ethical. Depending on the circumstances, lying might be legal, but at the same time, grossly unethical. A Missouri woman created a fake profile of a fictitious teen boy on the social networking site MySpace and then used the account to torment a neighbor's daughter, who eventually committed suicide. The woman could not be prosecuted for murder, but a jury did find her guilty of computer fraud. Even that misdemeanor was thrown out when the judge determined that her only misbehavior, according to law, was a violation of the MySpace terms of service.[4]

ETHICAL ISSUES AND INFORMATION AND COMMUNICATIONS TECHNOLOGIES

Before reading this section, take the short survey in Figure 10-2.

For questions like number 1, both ethical frameworks would lead to the conclusion that stealing a book is not right and warrants punishment. In a few areas, though, questions could lead to a debate that depends on the ethical framework. On number 5, for instance, a natural law approach would lead people to say punishment is warranted, similar to the punishment assigned to the theft in question 1. But a utilitarian approach might argue that helping a sick friend is a greater good compared to the harm done to the copyright owner, so a lesser or even no punishment is warranted.

Information and communications technologies (ICT) also add important new elements to ethical decision making. First, they change the scope of effects, especially for the consequences of an action. Their worldwide, viral reach amplifies the extent of both good and harm, turning what might be a minor blunder into something far greater. The job-search firm J. L. Kirk Associates discovered this when one of its clients blogged about what she thought were the firm's unethical business practices.

ethics	**natural laws and rights**	**utilitarianism**
A system of moral principles that human beings use to judge right and wrong and to develop rules of conduct.	An ethical system that judges the morality of an action based on how well it adheres to broadly accepted rules, regardless of the action's actual consequences.	An ethical system that judges whether an act is right or wrong by considering the consequences of the action, weighing its positive effects against its harmful ones.

FIGURE 10-2

Take this short survey on ethical decision making. Do you judge these actions as completely right, completely wrong, or somewhere in between?

	Completely right, no punishment 1	2	3	4	5	6	Completely wrong, severe punishment 7
1. In a book store, accounting student K.F. slips an expensive CPA Exam Prep book into a shopping bag, then leaves the store without paying for the book.	●	●	●	●	●	●	●
2. Marketing manager L.D. posts some negative reviews about a competitor on a review website, pretending to be various dissatisfied customers.	●	●	●	●	●	●	●
3. Business student F.W., who asked to take the midterm early due to travel, meets several friends for coffee after the test, to tell them all the questions on it.	●	●	●	●	●	●	●
4. Late for work, Assistant Manager J.T. cuts and pastes large segments from a website to finish a report on time, without citing the source.	●	●	●	●	●	●	●
5. A sick friend asked M.B. for a special book on alternative medicines, so M.B. downloads a pirated copy without paying, and e-mails it to the friend.	●	●	●	●	●	●	●
6. Frustrated by incompetent managers who only promote their relatives, scientist R.P. secretly takes photos of the designs for the company's groundbreaking new medical device, then offers to bring them to the company's rival for a higher paying position there.	●	●	●	●	●	●	●

The company threatened to sue if the woman did not take down the post, but when the blogging community learned of the threat, its members leaped into action. Within days, they posted multiple links to negative comments about the company, making sure that any keyword searches related to the company would turn up the unflattering results near the top. The strategy was so effective that the word "Kirk" morphed into a verb meaning to suffer a loss in reputation for trying to stifle free speech among bloggers.[5]

ICT also affects decision making, especially because of the way the online world can affect human behavior. As we discussed in Chapter 8, people often become disinhibited when they interact online and the psychological distance between them is greater. These features can cause people to underestimate the harm their actions might inflict—out of sight, out of mind. For instance, research shows that college students judge actions differently depending on whether ICT is involved. They consider cheating on tests, plagiarizing term papers, and illegal copying of intellectual property to be somehow more acceptable if they use the computer and the Internet to do it.[6] For the survey in Figure 10-2, add up your points for questions 2, 4 and 5, and compare that total to the sum of your points for 1, 3 and 6. If you tend to judge ethically questionable actions as less serious when they involve ICT, your total score for 2, 4, and 5 is lower.

Explain how intellectual property and plagiarism pose challenges for information ethics, and describe technologies that are used to deal with them.

2 Information Ethics

The ethical issues most important for managing information systems touch especially on the storage, transmission, and use of digitized data. As that mound of data grows, the scope of information ethics grows with it, and so do the controversies.

Figure 10-3 lists many dilemmas involving information ethics. Intellectual property (IP), which is now overwhelmingly digitized, is one example. Some consider IP protection to be a natural right. Others argue that the greater good is served when information is as widely distributed as possible.

FIGURE 10-3

Information ethics issues and the dilemmas they present.

Information Ethics Issue	Sample Dilemma
Intellectual property rights	Is it more important to protect intellectual property (IP) rights or to make information as widely available as possible? Will IP creators stop creating if there are fewer incentives?
Hacking	Is it ethical to break into the corporate network, not to do harm, but to demonstrate that the company needs better security?
Plagiarism	When a person gets an idea from reading another's work and then paraphrases it in a paper without crediting the source or even remembering where it came from, is that plagiarism? Or is it just forgetfulness?
Parasitic computing	Is it ethical to borrow a few CPU cycles from thousands of private computers without the owners' consent when they are not being used? What if the purpose is to do medical research?
Spam	Is it ethical to harvest millions of e-mail addresses from websites and send them unsolicited commercial messages?

INTELLECTUAL PROPERTY AND DIGITAL RIGHTS MANAGEMENT

Intellectual property (IP) includes intangible assets such as music, written works, software, art, designs, movies, creative ideas, discoveries, inventions, and other expressions of the human mind. Most societies have developed a maze of copyright laws, patents, and legal statutes to protect intellectual property rights. These give the creator of the property the right to its commercial value.

Enforcing all those laws is nearly impossible, however, when the IP is digitized. Media giant Viacom, for example, unsuccessfully tried to sue YouTube for $1 billion for allowing its copyrighted movies to play on the video site. But when more than 24 hours of video are uploaded to YouTube *every minute*, spotting one pirated clip is a formidable challenge.[7]

The Business Software Alliance reports alarming financial losses to businesses due to software piracy—more than $50 billion in 2009. For every $100 worth of software sold that year, the Alliance estimates $75 worth was installed illegally.[8] In some countries with weak enforcement, very little software used by consumers and businesses is purchased legally, and vendors openly sell pirated versions on street corners.

Yet efforts to fight piracy can lead to unfortunate results. The Recording Industry Association of America (RIAA) initially battled the music piracy problem by suing a few end users for up to $150,000 per downloaded song, targeting individuals such as Brianna, a 12-year-old child in New York. The litigation strategy was so unpopular that RIAA finally gave it up. Instead, the organization hopes to persuade Internet service providers to cut off service to repeat offenders.[9]

Most people conform to laws because they agree with the underlying ethical principle and because they fear punishment. Many think it is not a very serious ethical violation to break IP laws when the material is digitized. They see no victim and no harm to the IP owner—not even a lost sale if the violator had no intention of purchasing a legal copy. Unlike a DVD in a jewel case, a digital copy costs next to nothing, and violators may believe they are unlikely to get caught. Also, not everyone agrees that such extensive legal protection for all IP rights is the best ethical decision. The Free Software Foundation, for example, advocates for much less restrictive software copyright laws, insisting that users should have the freedom to run, copy, distribute, and improve software products. The foundation argues that access to the source code is essential, so independent developers can examine it, fix bugs, and add new features.

intellectual property (IP)
Intangible assets such as music, written works, software, art, designs, movies, creative ideas, discoveries, inventions, and other expressions of the human mind that may be legally protected by means of copyrights or patents.

FIGURE 10-4

Digital rights management scheme. Photos/Illustrations: iofoto/Shutterstock, Alex Kalmbach/Shutterstock, Psycho/Shutterstock.

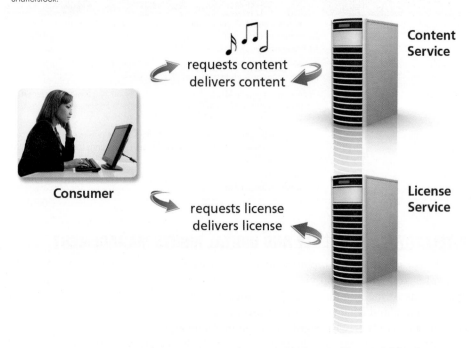

Nevertheless, intellectual property is a bedrock of an organization's intellectual capital and competitive advantage. Trade secrets, software, patents, and copyrighted works are all part of what creates that advantage, and many organizations use technology to protect it themselves rather than relying on law enforcement. **Digital rights management (DRM)** refers to technologies that software developers, publishers, media companies, and other intellectual property owners use to control access to their digital content. For example, one scheme requires end users to first connect to a content service to request the material, and then a request is sent to another server to obtain the license for actually viewing it (Figure 10-4).

Some cumbersome DRM schemes may be thwarting legitimate users more than pirates, though. For example, e-book distributor Fictionwise angered its clients when 300,000 purchases had to be invalidated because one of its publishers decided to stop supplying e-books. The customers who had already downloaded the e-books could continue to read them, but the DRM system would prevent them from downloading another copy if their computer crashed or if they wanted to put their purchase on another device. DRM often interferes with screen readers as well, frustrating the visually impaired who use them to turn on-screen text into speech. As the technologies mature, however, they will give IP holders some technological protection for their products without inconveniencing their customers.[10]

PRODUCTIVITY TIP

When you purchase digital content, keep copies of online receipts, serial numbers, and confirmation numbers, just in case you have to contact customer support to reinstall it over DRM schemes.

PLAGIARISM

A type of intellectual property theft that mushroomed with the easy cut-and-paste ability offered by word processors is plagiarism, which involves reproducing the words of another and passing them off as your own original work, without crediting the source.

Plagiarism scandals have tarnished some prominent authors and journalists, but technologies are also available to track this kind of activity. Ironically, just as

FIGURE 10-5

Checking written work for originality and possible plagiarism.

Source: Turnitin.com, accessed May 30, 2011. Used with permission.

the Internet made plagiarism easy, it also made it easy to track. Turnitin. com from iParadigms, for example, offers an "originality checking" service that color codes documents submitted to it, showing the sources of passages that match existing written work (Figure 10-5). The company's database includes the billions of pages on the public Internet and also term papers, journals, and books. Its software even applies automated translation technology to spot passages in foreign languages that appear to be translated directly from samples of English text without crediting the source.

PRODUCTIVITY TIP

Students can use free originality-checking software, such as www.writecheck.com, to examine their own work for unintentional plagiarism. The output will show which sections are not original and will need citations.

Privacy

3 Describe information privacy and strategies to protect it, and explain why organizations may implement surveillance.

> *" You have zero privacy anyway. Get over it."*
>
> –Scott McNealy, cofounder, Sun Microsystems

> *"If you have something that you don't want anyone to know, maybe you shouldn't be doing it in the first place."*
>
> –Eric Schmidt, former CEO, Google

Stern warnings like those—from technology leaders who should know—are stark reminders of how elusive privacy has become. On a typical day, you might visit hundreds of websites, enter dozens of search terms, download a free screen saver, collect dozens of cookies, bid in an auction, upload a batch of photos, and click on some ads. Your photo might be snapped repeatedly by security cameras, and your credit card is swiped for every transaction. Your corporate ID badge, your car's EZ pass, your mobile phone, your passport, and your GPS device track your whereabouts. Your profiles on social media show your profession, hobbies, friends, and family members. Information about many of your life events is publicly available online—

digital rights management (DRM)
Technologies that software developers, publishers, media companies, and other intellectual property owners use to control access to their digital content.

birth, marriage, home purchase, awards, criminal offenses, and death. And you never know whose cell phone is silently shooting an embarrassing video of you, to be uploaded to YouTube this evening.

The power to weave all these tidbits into a rich portrait is a marketer's dream, since it might point to the products you'll buy, the investments you might make, or the charities you choose to support. No wonder more than two-thirds of U.S. adults say they are seriously concerned about identity theft. The ease with which information systems can collect and interconnect data makes privacy a top ethical issue. But what exactly is privacy?

The United Nations identified privacy as a fundamental human right in 1999, but its definition remains hazy. Governments, legal bodies, and privacy advocates identify a number of features that might be included (Figure 10-6), though countries certainly vary in the degree to which they respect these elements. Nevertheless, societies from ancient history onward recognize the concept. The Qur'an, the Bible, and Jewish law all refer to elements of privacy, and legal protections against privacy violators—such as peeping toms and eavesdroppers—have existed for hundreds of years in many countries.

Information privacy, which refers to the protection of data about individuals, is a special concern for ICT. When all this data was on paper or in separate systems with clumsy interconnections, information privacy was easier to achieve. Now, it mainly rests on the decisions people, organizations, and governments make about what to collect, use, and distribute. Facial recognition software, for example, is a valuable tool for police officers, who can snap a photo using a smartphone, upload it, and check the image against the department's database of inmates, gang members, and suspects.[11] But the same kind of software can crawl the web to start automatically tagging faces.[12] Some will object to being publicly identified without their consent.

Did You Know?

European Union commissioners insist that Facebook comply with the EU's stringent privacy rules, one of which is the "right to be forgotten." The goal is to give each user the ability to withdraw consent to share data and photos, so digital footprints can be erased before a prospective employer sees those embarrassing photos.[13]

FIGURE 10-6

Elements of privacy.

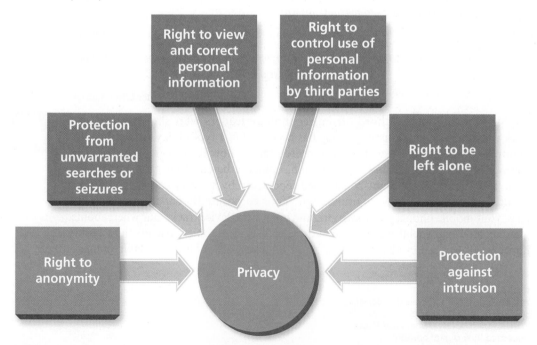

TRADING PRIVACY FOR CONVENIENCE AND FREEBIES

People are surprisingly willing to disclose personal data to marketers for a little convenience, a discount coupon, or a free digital sample. Allowing a site to leave cookies, for instance, means we experience a more compelling site on our next visit, one that features information, products, and promotions tailored to our interests. Grocery chains have no difficulty persuading patrons to attach bar-coded loyalty cards to their keychains for some small discounts, so the stores can collect voluminous data on individual buying patterns. Drivers also trade privacy for convenience when they purchase EZ passes so they can zip through tollgates.

To earn trust, organizations should clearly state in their privacy policies what they are collecting and why. They must also take great care to protect the data they do collect and adhere to their own policies. But unfortunately, blunders abound, and the technology's power can be quite hard to control. Besides taking street-view images, Google's camera-equipped cars were also identifying wifi hot spots. But Google's equipment was inadvertently intercepting data traffic from unsecured wireless networks, so the cars compiled mounds of web-surfing data from people using laptops in their homes or offices. Governments in the United States and Germany launched investigations, while Google argued that it never meant to harvest such data.[14] Oops.

ANONYMITY

Although it may seem obvious that "On the Internet, no one knows you're a dog,"[15] anonymity in the online world is actually more difficult to achieve than people assume. Furthermore, whether people's ability to remain anonymous online should be protected as a feature of privacy is a controversial issue. On the positive side, anonymity can be crucial for corporate whistleblowers, police tipsters, news sources, and political activists in oppressive regimes. It also protects people who participate in online support groups where they reveal personal details without fear of disclosure.

However, anonymity also protects criminals and spammers, as well as vengeful posters wreaking considerable harm or retaliation. A corporate recruiter, for instance, stumbled onto a blog whose author—possibly a jealous coworker—was impersonating her online and touting her love of micromanaging and throwing tantrums. The recruiter had little recourse and said, "I'm part of a global company where reputation is everything … this could be up there forever."[16] As we discussed in Chapter 8, anonymity can lead to disinhibition and bring out troubling behavior. It can remove the accountability that makes people feel responsible for their own actions.

Online identity can be obscured by using fake names, nicknames, free e-mail, and public computers. Erasing digital tracks entirely, however, is far more challenging. Any network connection requires a handshake between the device and the server, so that the device's IP address, along with its location, is exposed. Hiding that information usually requires handing off the transmission to a **proxy**, an intermediary server that receives and analyzes requests from clients and then directs them to their destinations. The transmission then appears to come from the proxy, not the actual sender (Figure 10-7).

A drawback to using the proxy server to ensure anonymity is the need to rely on the company that operates the proxy and its promise to protect its customers' identities. Another approach depends instead on a distributed network of servers. The encrypted transmission is relayed from one server to the next, and no single server has access to all the addresses that relayed any particular message (Figure 10-8).[17]

> **PRODUCTIVITY TIP**
> TOR is a free service operated by volunteers (www.torproject.org) that anonymizes web surfing. An add-on is available for some browsers so that users can enable it only when needed, since it can be quite slow.

---

information privacy
The protection of data about individuals.

proxy
An intermediary server that receives and analyzes requests from clients and then directs them to their destinations; sometimes used to protect privacy.

FIGURE 10-7

Proxy servers can be used to mask a web surfer's IP address. Photos/Illustrations: Luna Vandoome/Shutterstock, Psycho/Shutterstock, Sashkin/Shutterstock, vector-RGB/Shutterstock.

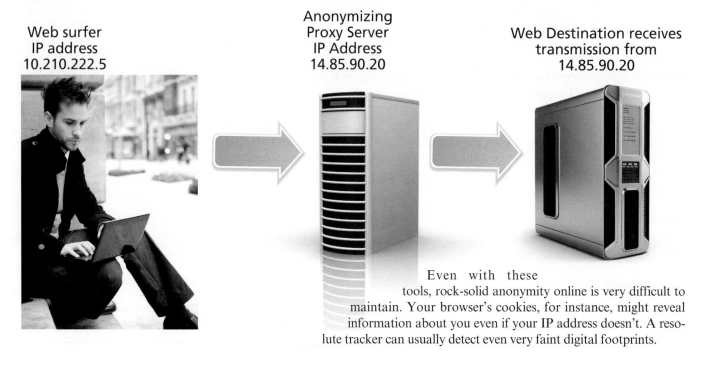

| Web surfer IP address 10.210.222.5 | Anonymizing Proxy Server IP Address 14.85.90.20 | Web Destination receives transmission from 14.85.90.20 |

Even with these tools, rock-solid anonymity online is very difficult to maintain. Your browser's cookies, for instance, might reveal information about you even if your IP address doesn't. A resolute tracker can usually detect even very faint digital footprints.

SURVEILLANCE

Surveillance technologies to monitor e-mail, web surfing, and other online communications are readily available to all organizations, and surveys show that many have already adopted them. Employers lean toward surveillance for several reasons:

► Concerns about employer liability for allowing harassment or hostile work environments
► Need to protect security and confidentiality
► Concerns about employee productivity and "cyberslacking"
► Concerns about bogging down corporate e-mail systems with personal e-mail

Liability is a powerful driver, given several legal findings that hold employers responsible for employees' offensive e-mails or web-surfing habits. Continental

FIGURE 10-8

A network of distributed servers can relay a transmission and hide its source. photos/Illustrations: iofoto/Shutterstock, Psycho/Shutterstock, Lana Rinck/Shutterstock, CLIPAREA/Custom media/Shutterstock, Alex Kalmbach/Shutterstock

Airlines was hit with a harassment suit when its first female pilot complained that male employees were posting harassing and insulting comments to an online discussion group called "Crew Members' Forum." Since the group was not hosted by the airline and no one was required to participate or subscribe, lower courts dismissed the case. But the New Jersey Supreme Court reversed the decision, insisting that employers have a duty to counteract harassment when they know or have reason to know it is taking place, not just in the workplace, but in related settings as well.[18]

Security concerns about trade secrets also prompt employers to keep tabs on communications. A pro football team, for instance, implemented software to track leaks of the team's playbook secrets. Any message that included the phrase "first 15," meaning the first 15 plays of the game, triggered an alarm. Employers sometimes step up surveillance on employees who will soon be gone due to layoffs or firings and who might decide to take confidential customer lists or other proprietary information with them.

Although sound reasons for surveillance exist, the downsides are not trivial. Despite concerns about "cyberslacking," surveillance itself can sometimes cause a drop in productivity. Some argue that it suggests that the employer does not trust them. Pitting management against staff, surveillance can undermine the bond of loyalty that might otherwise develop and that can help an organization succeed. Monitored employees may also suffer more stress, depression, and anxiety, resulting in increased absenteeism and lower productivity. Whatever policies the company chooses to implement, managers should make sure everyone understands what those policies are, and the reasons for adopting them.

Although security is one reason for surveillance, no surveillance system will stop someone from accidentally leaving a smartphone loaded with confidential data in a taxi. As the next section explains, information security must be a fundamental concern for every company, government agency, and nonprofit organization.

Information Security

> **4** Explain the steps that organizations use to manage security risks, identify threats, assess vulnerabilities, and develop administrative and technical controls.

Millionaires who stashed money in HSBC's bank branches in Switzerland are on edge as the details of a security breach unfold. A former tech employee filched information about thousands of clients, apparently intending to sell it to governments trying to crack down on people who use Swiss accounts to evade taxes.[19] Governments in France, the United Kingdom, Germany, and the United States may now have those files and may plan to use the information as evidence. French prosecutors offered the perpetrator a new identity for his own protection. (Government agents used a utilitarian ethical framework here, judging that protecting the thief would lead to the greater good.)

Information security broadly encompasses the protection of an organization's information assets against misuse, disclosure, unauthorized access, or destruction. Like most aspects of information systems, it draws on the four familiar pillars: technology, processes, people, and information. For the bank, the weakest link was the people, as it often is.

RISK MANAGEMENT

Banks spend millions on earthquake-proof vaults, surveillance cameras, secure access cards, and many other security precautions to protect their assets. But with countless threats and limited budgets, organizations can't eliminate all risks and must make careful assessments to manage them. Risk managers consider many issues, beginning with a clear

---

information security
A term that encompasses the protection of an organization's information assets against misuse, disclosure, unauthorized access, or destruction.

FIGURE 10-9

FIGURE 10-9

Issues for risk managers.

> ▶ What information needs protection?
>
> ▶ What are the major threats from inside or outside the organization?
>
> ▶ What are the organization's weaknesses, strengths, and vulnerabilities?
>
> ▶ What would be the impact of any particular risk?
>
> ▶ How likely are each of the risks?
>
> ▶ What controls can be used to mitigate risks?

understanding of what information assets need protection (Figure 10-9). Laws play a large role here, requiring organizations to safely secure medical records, financial information, Social Security numbers, academic records, and other sensitive data. Governments in turn must secure classified documents, and companies must protect their trade secrets.

IDENTIFYING THREATS

Figure 10-10 shows examples of the many threats to information security that arise both inside and outside the organization. They can be natural events or human-made, accidental or deliberate.

MALWARE AND BOTNETS   Human-made threats barrage servers and computers every day with automated attempts to install all types of **malware**—malicious software designed to attack computer systems (Figure 10-11). One computer security lab recorded more than 40 million malware samples in a single year, or about 50,000 per day.[20] Labs like this one often set up baits nicknamed "honeypots," which are computers configured with specific vulnerabilities so they can attract different varieties of malware in the wild, study their properties, and find out who started them.

Many attacks are launched by criminal gangs that build and manage thousands of **botnets**. The term combines "robot" and "network" and refers to a collection of computers that have been compromised by malware, often through some vulnerability in their software or operating system. The Conficker botnet, believed to have control over almost 7 million Windows computers, sneaks its malware in through a hole in the operating system. Although Microsoft offers a patch to remove and block the Conficker infection, the millions of systems running pirated copies of Windows don't have access to it, so the army remains very strong.

The gangs activate their botnets to capture user IDs, passwords, credit card numbers, Social Security numbers, and other sensitive information. They can then transfer funds, steal identities, and purchase products, or they might just sell the information to other criminals. They also rent out their zombie armies to various customers, such as spammers who use them to relay the millions of unsolicited messages that now comprise the vast majority of Internet e-mail traffic.

Malware might also be installed when an innocent user downloads a screen saver or other seemingly benign freebie. Without the user's knowledge, the infected computer

FIGURE 10-10

Types of information security threats.

Human Threats

Accidental misuse, loss, or destruction by employees, consultants, vendors, or suppliers

Actions by disgruntled employees, insider theft, sabotage, terrorism, hackers, spam

Information Assets

Environmental Threats

Fire
Floods
Earthquakes
Hurricanes
Industrial accidents
War
Power failures
Arson

FIGURE 10-11

Examples of malware.

Malware	Description
Computer virus	A malicious software program that can damage files or other programs. The virus can also reproduce itself and spread to other computers by e-mail, instant messaging, file transfer, or other means.
Spyware	Software that monitors a user's activity on the computer and on the Internet, often installed without the user's knowledge. Spyware may use the Internet connection to send the data it collects to third parties.
Keylogger	Monitoring software that records a user's keystrokes.
Worm	A self-replicating program that sends copies to other nodes on a computer network and may contain malicious code intended to cause damage.
Trojan horse	A seemingly useful, or at least harmless, program that installs malicious code to allow remote access to the computer, as for a botnet.

becomes a "zombie," added to the gang's growing botnet. Some analysts estimate that up to one-fourth of the world's computers contain botnet code that can be activated whenever the commander chooses. The Mariposa botnet, shut down by Spanish and U.S. law enforcement agencies in 2009, spanned more than 12 million computers in 190 countries.[21] The challenges of coordinating legal investigations across national boundaries can make these gangs especially difficult to prosecute.[22]

DISTRIBUTED DENIAL OF SERVICE Another grave threat posed by the botnets is the **distributed denial of service (DDoS)** attack, in which zombies are directed to flood a single website server with rapid-fire page requests, causing it to slow to a crawl or just crash.[23] Someone with a grudge can rent a botnet for a day to damage political enemies, corporations, government agencies, or universities. One massive attack targeted Twitter, Facebook, and several other sites, in an attempt to silence a single blogger posting about the conflict between Russia and Georgia. DDoS attacks cost organizations many millions of dollars in downtime, lost business, and lost client goodwill (Figure 10-12).

✸ THE ETHICAL FACTOR Ethical Dilemmas in a Distributed Denial of Service Attack

Scenario: *An elementary school librarian is trying to install some software to create avatars from students' photos so they won't be tempted to upload their own photos. The installation fails the first time, but rather than read the lengthy manual or phone the vendor, the librarian tries turning off the firewall and antivirus software. That works, and the librarian turns the security back on.*

Two weeks later, the school's whole network goes down. The school's IT technician can see that the server's CPU is overloaded with Internet traffic, but can't do anything. By noon, the harried principal is wondering whether to close the school since so much depends on computers, from bus scheduling and reporting to communications and academic records. At 1:30, the principal receives a call from the security officer of a government agency in Canada, who says the school's server was turned into a zombie by a botnet and used in a denial of service attack against the agency. The agency's minister insisted on stopping the attack at once, so the officer triggered a counterattack to target the zombies as quickly as possible. First embarrassed, then angry, the principal says, "But this is an elementary school! You can't just bring it down like that without telling us. It's not ethical. What if this were a hospital?!" The principal ponders suing someone, but isn't sure who to blame. The officer complains that no one can identify who created the botnet, or who paid to use it to launch this DDoS.

The well-intentioned librarian took a shortcut to install software and made the school's network vulnerable. Once the malware was installed and the DDoS against the government agency got underway, the security company in Canada used intrusion-detection techniques to identify the zombies by their IP addresses. That company was tasked with stopping the DDoS, so its staff quickly shut down the zombies with a counterattack, without taking time to learn who they were or what impact that decision might have. Recovering from this event will cost the school considerable time and money.

The scenario involves many players: the librarian, the principal, the school's IT technician, the security officer in Canada, the agency's minister, the botnet creator, and the one who purchased use of the botnet and set off the DDoS. How would you evaluate their ethical decision making?

malware
Malicious software designed to attack computer systems.

botnet
A combination of the terms "robot" and "network" referring to a collection of computers that have been compromised by malware, and used to attack other computers.

distributed denial of service (DDoS)
An attack in which computers in a botnet are directed to flood a single website server with rapid-fire page requests, causing it to slow down or crash.

FIGURE 10-12

Distributed denial of service attack (DDoS). Under the control of the botnet, the zombies send rapid-fire page requests to the targeted site, bringing down the server and blocking out regular customers. Photos/Illustrations: Psycho/Shutterstock, CLIPAREA/Custom media/Shutterstock, vector-RGB/Shutterstock, ArchMan/Shutterstock.

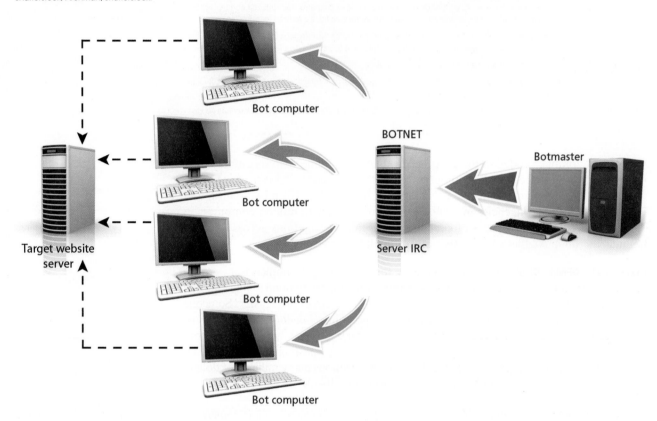

PHISHING   Since the botnets mask the actual source of the millions of incoming messages, they are often used for **phishing** attacks. These typically start with an e-mail such as the one in Figure 10-13, which cleverly lures taxpayers to click on a link. Recipients land on what appears to be a genuine website, where they innocently type in their Social Security number and other personal details. The lure can be anything that gets users to enter personal information, from e-mails offering employment to Twitter messages containing the phrase "This You????." A bank was victimized by the Twitter lure, and the attacker began sending out salacious tweets under the bank's name. Although no account information was stolen, the bank's reputation was tarnished.

INFORMATION LEAKAGE   The threat of information leaks comes not just from cyber-criminals. Employees can lose laptops and smartphones, mail containing backup media may go astray, and people may drop unshredded sensitive documents into the dumpster (Figure 10-14). These leaks are not uncommon, and governments have passed numerous laws imposing huge fines on organizations that lose customer data and requiring them to inform everyone whose information has been compromised. Although the laws may help stop identity theft, the sheer volume of leaked credit card and Social Security numbers has made this information rather cheap to obtain. In the underground market where it is bought and sold, oversupply drives down prices. Credit card numbers might fetch just a few dollars, and a full profile might go for under $10, complete with Social Security number, date of birth, driver's license number, mother's maiden name, and even an ATM PIN.[24, 25]

PRODUCTIVITY TIP

Check your credit card statements carefully for any unauthorized purchases, and get free credit reports from www.annualcreditreport.com. The three credit services will each provide one free report per year, so you can check for suspicious activity every 4 months.

FIGURE 10-13

Sample phishing e-mail.

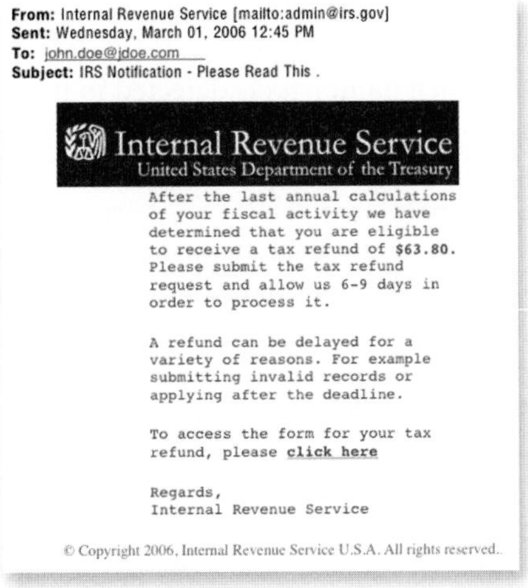

```
From: Internal Revenue Service [mailto:admin@irs.gov]
Sent: Wednesday, March 01, 2006 12:45 PM
To: john.doe@jdoe.com
Subject: IRS Notification - Please Read This .
```

Internal Revenue Service
United States Department of the Treasury

After the last annual calculations of your fiscal activity we have determined that you are eligible to receive a tax refund of **$63.80.** Please submit the tax refund request and allow us 6-9 days in order to process it.

A refund can be delayed for a variety of reasons. For example submitting invalid records or applying after the deadline.

To access the form for your tax refund, please **click here**

Regards,
Internal Revenue Service

© Copyright 2006, Internal Revenue Service U.S.A. All rights reserved.

Source: www.irs.gov/pub/irs-utl/phishing-email.pdf

Did You Know?

The 2011 Cybersecurity Watch Survey conducted by *CSO* magazine in cooperation with the U.S. Secret Service, the Software Engineering Institute Program at Carnegie Mellon University, and Deloitte found that insider attacks comprise 21 percent of the events. These are growing more sophisticated and costly compared to events caused by outside hackers. Nevertheless, the general public is not very aware of damage caused by insider attacks because 70 percent are handled privately, with no prosecution or legal action.[26]

FIGURE 10-14

Recent information leakage events.

Organization and Date	Event
Heartland Payment Systems, January 20, 2009	Malicious software attack compromised the security of 130,000,000 customer credit cards.
U.S. Army Reserve, May 13, 2010	Laptop stolen from a contractor contained media with 207,000 names, addresses, and social security numbers of Army reservists.
Her Majesty's Revenue Collection (HMRC), UK, May 27, 2010	Government agency mailed the wrong private information to taxpayers.
Alaska Department of Education and Early Development, March 6, 2011	A hard drive was stolen containing the names, birthdates, and other information about 89,519 students.
Shell, Chevron, Mountain View, CA March 8, 2011	Devices were attached to gas pumps that skimmed the credit card numbers from cards used at the pumps.
Se San Diego Hotel, CA, March 10, 2011	Malicious software uploaded to the hotel's computer system resulted in the loss of guests' credit card information.
Health Net, Inc., March 15, 2011	Nine data servers with 1.9 million records of current and former policy holders went missing from the data center.
Sony Pictures, Sony Corporation of America, June 6, 2011	A hacker gang called LulzSec stole over 1,000,000 customer records, including passwords.

Source: Chronology of data breaches—Security breaches 2005–Present. Privacy Rights Clearinghouse. www.privacyrights.org/data-breach, accessed May 29, 2011.

phishing
An attempt to steal passwords or other sensitive information by persuading the victim, often in an e-mail, to enter the information into a fraudulent website that masquerades as the authentic version.

ASSESSING VULNERABILITY

An organization's risk assessment must examine its vulnerabilities to determine how effective its existing security measures are. Are employees ignoring warnings not to share passwords? Does the information system maintain a log of every access attempt? Are administrators alerted when dampness is detected in the data center?

When an Apple employee left a prototype of the newest iPhone in a California bar, the vulnerability posed by the human element—in this case, accidental loss—became glaringly apparent. Apple is known for the impenetrable security surrounding its supersecret product development, but that single iPhone slipped through.

Once vulnerabilities have been analyzed, the organization can evaluate controls that fill in security gaps and protect against specific threats. Industry standards are often used for this step. Examples include the federal guidelines for information security in government agencies and the security self-assessment questionnaire developed by the Payment Card Industry Security Standards Council for companies that operate e-commerce sites and accept credit cards.[27] The questionnaire helps organizations identify measures required to achieve compliance.[28]

Vulnerability depends partly on how likely any particular event may be. A major earthquake in Mexico City rates as highly likely, but hurricanes in that region are very rare. Even very unlikely events might pose serious risks, however, when their impact would be immense if they did occur. Risks also differ depending on the threat. A major information leak would compromise confidentiality, for example, while a power outage would affect availability by bringing down the systems.

The **risk matrix** lists the vulnerabilities in a table, and managers rate the level of risk each one presents in areas such as confidentiality, company reputation, finances, system availability, and operations. The matrix also includes an estimate of how likely that event might be, and managers may add other metrics to further refine the analysis for their own organizations. The matrix helps focus attention on the vulnerabilities that pose the greatest potential dangers. Figure 10-15 shows a simplified example using rating scales of 1 (low risk) to 10 (high risk).

ADMINISTRATIVE SECURITY CONTROLS

Administrative security controls include all the processes, policies, and plans the organization creates to enhance information security and ensure it can recover if things go awry. Some controls may establish information security policies that restrict the Internet sites that employees can visit, or that deny Internet access altogether. Such policies might add protection by prohibiting employees from downloading data to smartphones or USB drives. Industries that routinely handle sensitive information will need to put very strict policies in place, and take measures to enforce them. Leaving a workstation without logging out, for example, may be trivial in some settings, but disastrous in others.

The processes and policies that control employee access to systems are some of the most sensitive. Knowing how angry some terminated employees might become, some employers cut off their access before they deliver the pink slip. Ex-IT employees, like the one who walked off with HSBC's account holder data, can pose greater threats because of their expertise and high-level access.

FIGURE 10-15

Simplified risk matrix.

Vulnerability	Leak of Confidential Data	Lost Integrity, Reputation	Systems Unavailable	Financial Risk	Likelihood That Event Will Happen	Total Impact Rating
No backup power for a workstation	1	2	8	2	4	4
Loss of unencrypted backup data	10	10	4	7	3	6.8

FIGURE 10-16

Steps in an incident response plan.

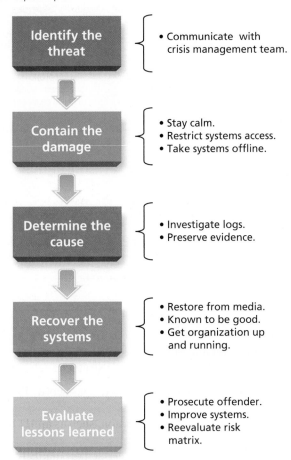

Identify the threat
- Communicate with crisis management team.

Contain the damage
- Stay calm.
- Restrict systems access.
- Take systems offline.

Determine the cause
- Investigate logs.
- Preserve evidence.

Recover the systems
- Restore from media.
- Known to be good.
- Get organization up and running.

Evaluate lessons learned
- Prosecute offender.
- Improve systems.
- Reevaluate risk matrix.

Administrative controls to enhance information security extend beyond the organization to its vendors, suppliers, and customers. For example, what background checks and due diligence should the organization do before signing an agreement with a cloud computing vendor? How should the organization monitor access to its systems by suppliers and customers?

To avoid chaos and missteps when something happens, the organization should also have a clear **incidence response plan** that staff use to categorize the threat, determine the cause, preserve any evidence, and also get the systems back online so the organization can resume business (Figure 10-16).

PRODUCTIVITY TIP

The administrative controls you establish for your own computer will help protect your information assets. Turning off the computer at night, for instance, will reduce your exposure to intrusion attempts, and save energy, too.

TECHNICAL SECURITY CONTROLS

The technologies available to protect information assets help with three important tasks: deterring attacks, preventing attacks, and detecting them after they occur. Surveillance cameras, for instance, can deter unauthorized entry. Even the automated message on a system's login screen, issuing dire warnings of criminal penalties for misuse, will deter most people from trying to break in. Figure 10-17 shows how technical and administrative controls work together for several security areas.

risk matrix
A matrix that lists an organization's vulnerabilities, with ratings that assess each one in terms of likelihood and impact on business operations, reputation, and other areas.

incidence response plan
A plan that an organization uses to categorize a security threat, determine the cause, preserve any evidence, and also get the systems back online so the organization can resume business.

FIGURE 10-17

Examples of administrative and technical controls.

Category	Administrative Control Examples	Technical Control Examples
Account management	The organization requires appropriate approvals for requests to establish accounts.	The information system automatically disables accounts after a time period defined by the organization.
	The organization monitors for atypical usage of information system accounts.	The information system automatically logs any account creations, modifications, or termination actions.
Access controls	The organization defines the information to be encrypted or stored offline in a secure location.	The information system enforces approved authorizations for access to the system.
	The organization defines the privileged commands for which dual authorization is to be enforced.	The information system prevents access to any security-relevant information contained within the system.
Information flow	The organization defines the security policy that determines what events require human review.	The information system enforces the organization's policy about human review.
Separation of duties	The organization separates duties of individuals as necessary to prevent malevolent activity without collusion.	The information system enforces separation of duties through access control.

AUTHENTICATION STRATEGIES   Technical controls for preventing unauthorized access draw on technologies that can authenticate people and determine what access privileges they should be granted. Most authentication strategies rely on:

▶ Something the user knows, such as a user ID, password, PIN, or answer to a security question;

▶ Something the user has in his or her possession, such as an ID badge, credit card, or RFID chip; or

▶ Something the user is—a biometric characteristic that uniquely identifies the user, such as a voice pattern, iris configuration, fingerprint, or face.

Reliance on user knowledge is the simplest strategy, although in many ways the weakest and easiest to crack. Financial institutions especially have expanded password security to require the user to have several pieces of knowledge or to link each login to a particular IP address. They also take the precaution of sending the PIN to account holders by mail in a letter separate from the user ID.

Biometric identifiers are also widely used, especially for physical security, since they are more difficult to crack, forge, or copy. Most computer vendors offer laptops equipped with fingerprint scanners, for example, and the technology is used for smartphones as well.

Multifactor authentication combines two or more authentication strategies, creating much stronger security against unauthorized access to sensitive information. For example, a user required to swipe an ID badge or use the fingerprint sensor must then also enter a password to gain access.

ENCRYPTION   A powerful technical control that protects sensitive data is **encryption**. This process transforms the data using mathematical formulas, so that no one can read it unless they know the key to unscrambling it. You can encrypt individual files on your computer, or the whole disk drive, by adding a password, but you will not be able to retrieve the information if you forget it. Encryption is so effective that if an organization loses sensitive information that was encrypted, the notification laws described earlier do not apply. If the backup tapes shown in the matrix in Figure 10-15 were encrypted, the risk assessments would be much lower.

For Internet transmission, a popular strategy is **public key encryption**, which uses a pair of keys, one to encrypt the data and the other to decrypt it. One key is public, widely shared with everyone, but the other is private, known only to the recipient. For example, when you want to communicate with a company's website securely, your browser uses the organization's public key to encrypt the data you send, and the organization uses its private key to read it. Though the keys are mathematically related, the formulas are too complex and the keys too long for anyone to decipher the private key from its paired public key.

PRODUCTIVITY TIP
Before entering sensitive data into a form on a website, check for the https:// in the address bar. The "s" indicates the transmission will be encrypted.

INTRUSION PREVENTION AND DETECTION SYSTEMS   Astronomer Clifford Stoll tells the riveting detective story of how, back in the days of the Cold War, he was asked to look into a 75-cent accounting error on a server in the Lawrence Berkeley National Lab. Checking the logs, Stoll discovered that an unknown user had usurped 9 seconds of computer time and hadn't paid for it. His curiosity piqued, Stoll began to track down the intruder. Few detection tools existed at the time, but Stoll attached some old teletype printers to incoming lines and began recording every step the hacker took. The months-long hunt led him to a dial-up connection in Berlin. Since the hacker had shown special interest in files about the military's Strategic Defense Initiative, Stoll set up a hoax, inventing a new computer account called "SDInet" and adding numerous large files with impressive-sounding military names. The sting worked. The hacker, who had been selling information to the Soviet KGB for years, fell for the bait and was caught at his home in Germany.[29]

Many more tools are available now to prevent unauthorized traffic from entering the network and to detect any intrusions that do make it through. But the attackers' tools improve, too, and criminals constantly test defenses and hunt for vulnerable points.

The most important defense is the **firewall**, a technical control that inspects incoming and outgoing traffic and either blocks or permits it according to rules the organization establishes. The firewall can be a hardware device or a software program, and its rules regulate traffic based on different levels of trust. The rules might state that any other server in the same domain is trustworthy, so traffic would pass easily between them. External traffic from the Internet, however, would need different rules. The firewall might prohibit any external Internet traffic from reaching its database servers, for instance, but allow incoming requests to its public web server.

Other rules might control which ports on the machine can accept traffic or which IP addresses or domain names should be blocked. Organizations that prohibit access to sites like YouTube or Facebook, for instance, can customize their firewalls to enforce such constraints.

Firewall systems also include features to detect suspicious events and alert managers immediately. For example, a failed attempt to log in as the computer administrator may trigger a text message to designated smartphones, so IT staff can investigate.

Spam constitutes an estimated 90 percent of e-mail traffic, and intrusion prevention systems are also needed to control this costly menace. Combating spam has become even more critical as messaging moves to mobile devices, where calling plans might charge users for every kilobyte received. Many organizations install special e-mail content-filtering appliances inside their firewalls, so that all messages are examined for telltale signs of spam before they are delivered to any employees (Figure 10-18). Cisco, for instance, offers the IronPort appliance, which

PRODUCTIVITY TIP
Your college or university probably has spam blocks in place, but no filter is perfect. Check your junk mail occasionally in case messages you want to receive were trapped by the filter. Identify any false positives as "not junk" so the senders' messages are not trapped again.

multifactor authentication
A combination of two or more authentications a user must pass to access an information system, such as a fingerprint scan combined with a password.

encryption
Technique that scrambles data using mathematical formulas, so that it cannot be read without applying the key to decrypt it.

public key encryption
A security measure that uses a pair of keys, one to encrypt the data and the other to decrypt it. One key is public, widely shared with everyone, but the other is private, known only to the recipient.

firewall
A defensive technical control that inspects incoming and outgoing traffic and either blocks or permits it according to rules the organization establishes. The firewall can be a hardware device or a software program.

FIGURE 10-18

Blocking spam. Photos/Illustrations: Fenton one/Shutterstock, Login/Shutterstock, Broukoid/Shutterstock, ArchMan/Shutterstock, TyBy/Shutterstock, Spectral-Design/Shutterstock, Alex Kalmbach/Shutterstock

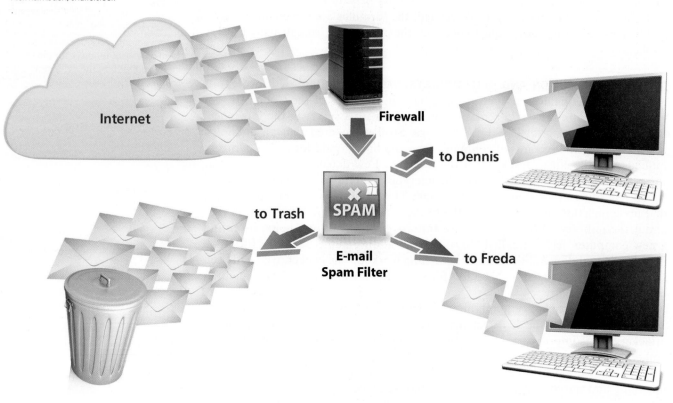

filters the content to block almost all spam from the network. Adjusting the filters is an ongoing challenge. The goal is to correctly trap, but avoid false positives in which important messages are blocked or labeled junk mail.

INFORMATION SECURITY AND CLOUD COMPUTING

The trend for businesses to move toward cloud computing, where their mission-critical applications and data are hosted by a service off-site and accessed via the Internet, is largely driven by cost savings and convenience. But what about security? A senior VP for a utilities company remarked, "Has everyone forgotten the dot.com meltdown? Whole websites, along with the companies that ran them, disappeared, never to be seen again. I want to control my own future."[30] IT managers worry about security for cloud computing and whether cloud providers can adequately protect the organization's most valuable assets. With countless information leaks and security breaches, they have cause for concern.

Nevertheless, most organizations are having their own struggles keeping track of data, as employees go mobile or take advantage of cloud services on their own. It takes considerable effort and resources for a company to continually upgrade security and meet compliance requirements. Budget pressures, along with the growing challenge of recruiting qualified information security staff, are leading even skeptical organizations to take a closer look at cloud computing.

A movement is underway to develop security standards and best practices for cloud computing, along with transparent auditing mechanisms that will help assure potential clients that their information will be safe. The Cloud Security Alliance is a nonprofit organization that brings experts together to develop standards and controls that parallel those already required for e-commerce and medical records. The IT community holds mixed views on how safe their data will be in the cloud, and the fate of this architectural trend may well depend on robust security.

The Human Element in Information Ethics, Security, and Privacy

5 Explain why human behavior is often the weakest link for ethics, privacy, and security, and provide examples of strategies that can be used to counteract the weaknesses.

Human behavior and decision making play a central role in almost any situation combining information ethics, privacy, and security. Indeed, human beings are very often the weakest link for a number of reasons.

COGNITIVE ISSUES AND PRODUCTIVITY

The sheer complexity of computers and information systems challenges even the brightest humans, and it is not surprising that people will turn off their security features for a few minutes to install software, as the librarian did in the DDoS scenario described earlier. We prefer to apply our cognitive skills to productive pursuits, and when security policies and procedures seem to get in the way, we may bypass them. In most cases nothing happens, but once in awhile, calamity results.

The limits of human memory (and patience) make the password the most widely used authentication strategy, a serious vulnerability. On their own, people tend to create very weak passwords that are easy to remember, but also easy to crack. A security breach at RockYou.com released 32 million passwords, and the data left no doubt about how feeble most passwords really are. Almost 300,000 people chose "123456," and thousands more chose a name, probably their own or a family member's. Pet names ranked high, along with the word "password" and "NCC1701" (the ID number of the starship *Enterprise*).

Although technical controls can force users to embed numbers and nonalphabetic characters and change them frequently, the results are still not promising. Users then tend to write passwords down and reuse them on multiple systems, even far less secure systems such as online games and news sites. Indeed, one way hackers break into corporate networks is to offer people free access to an enchanting service and allow them to create their own accounts. An alarming number will use their work e-mail address and their network password.

The cognitive obstacle for strong passwords is just the capacity of human memory.[31] Humans can't easily remember a long, meaningless string of letters and symbols, but we have no difficulty remembering such strings if they represent meaningful chunks of information. For example, you could create mhBs*124MTH as a very strong password, with 11 characters, mixed case, a special symbol, and no names or dictionary words. This string actually has far fewer meaningful chunks for an aspiring bowler to memorize: <u>m</u>y <u>h</u>ighest <u>B</u>owling <u>s</u>core <u>*</u> <u>124</u> <u>M</u>ust <u>T</u>ry <u>H</u>arder. Figure 10-19 offers tips on creating secure passwords.

To reduce the cognitive load associated with multiple passwords, many organizations implement the **single sign-on**, which is a gateway service that permits users to log in once with a single user ID and password to gain access to multiple software applications.

FIGURE 10-19

Creating secure passwords.

- ▶ Do not include personal information such as names, addresses, or phone numbers.
- ▶ Avoid real words.
- ▶ Mix different character types, including lowercase, uppercase, and special characters.
- ▶ To reduce the cognitive load of memorizing the password, create "pass phrases" with meaningful chunks and use the first letter of each word, such as "I love whitewater rafting_Done it 15 times" (Ilwwr_Di15t).
- ▶ Use different passwords for each login you want to secure, so loss of one does not compromise the others.
- ▶ Change your passwords every 30 to 60 days, or as required by the application.

single sign-on
A gateway service that permits users to log in once with a single user ID and password to gain access to multiple software applications.

Complexity hampers privacy decisions as well. Few people read the terms of service before they click "I agree," although those terms often contain troubling conditions that trade privacy away. Social networking sites balance users' privacy concerns against their own need to generate advertising revenue through targeted marketing that relies on information about each user and the user's friendship network. Facebook is often at the center of privacy debates, not just for its own policies, but for the terms users agree to when they play social games such as Cityville or Mafia Wars.[32] The case study at the end of this text explores how Facebook confronts privacy issues.

SOCIAL ENGINEERING AND INFORMATION SECURITY

At West Point, where cadets take a 4-hour course on information security, 80 percent of students still fell for a phishing scam that told recipients to click on a link to deal with a problem in their last grade report. The bogus e-mail, sent by a nonexistent colonel, was an experiment to test how well the training was working. It demonstrated the effectiveness of **social engineering**, which manipulates people into breaking normal security procedures or divulging confidential information. Humans are tempting targets for those with malicious intent who understand such behavior.

One weak spot is simply the human desire to help others. People routinely pass virus-laden hoaxes along to friends and neighbors, trying to be helpful. An employee who swipes his or her ID badge to open a secure door and then courteously holds it open for the person behind may be falling for a common social engineering trick to bypass physical security. The pressure to be helpful is even greater if the follower is holding packages or using crutches (Figure 10-20).

Respect for authority is another common human tendency that intruders exploit, relying on uniforms, titles, or just verbal hints that the company president wants something done. It is easy to obtain passwords from employees just by calling from the CEO's phone when the CEO steps out of the office. Wearing a tool belt is another social engineering trick that gives intruders easy access to office equipment.

FIGURE 10-20

Social engineering: Would you hold the door for these people so they don't have to search for their ID badges?

© Juice Images/Alamy

Humans are certainly not immune to greed, and scammers tap this human frailty routinely to persuade people to turn over confidential information or money. The so-called 419 scam, named after a section of Nigeria's criminal code, has conned many people out of thousands of dollars. Although many variations exist, the scam usually starts with an unsolicited e-mail inviting the recipient to participate in a scheme to gain large sums from a bank in Nigeria or other location, simply by allowing the sender to cleanse the funds through the target's bank account. The target is eventually asked to pay an advance fee of some kind, or a transfer tax, after which "complications" may require the payment of additional fees.

Ironically, another highly effective bit of social engineering relies on the human desire to *avoid* malware. When a pop-up appears that says your computer is infected and provides a link for you to buy a tool to remove the virus, you may have become a victim of "scareware." The virus didn't exist, and the tool to remove it may be harmless. It may even be malware itself. As real threats grow, more and more people fall for these scareware attacks (Figure 10-21).

FIGURE 10-21

Scareware persuades people that a computer is infected when it is not. The solution the victim pays for may be harmless or it may install its own malware.

SECURITY AWARENESS AND ETHICAL DECISION MAKING

Organizations should have robust security awareness programs to help educate and continually remind people about the risks that lax security presents. The program should cover the organization's own policies and procedures, as well as applicable laws and regulations about how information should be handled to ensure compliance. Figure 10-22 lists several relevant laws that touch on information security and privacy.

Beyond meeting legal compliance requirements, a security awareness program should also alert people to the many ways in which social engineering can exploit human tendencies toward kindness, helpfulness, greed, or just productivity. It should provide training in tools such as encryption and help people to spot areas in which breaches might occur.

Finally, it should reinforce the principle that the organization has an ethical responsibility to maintain information security.[33] Consider, for example, the extent of harm each of these actions might inflict on other people, from customers, employees, and students to stockholders and citizens.

▸ A sales rep copies customer data to her smartphone and quickly drops it into a jacket pocket. Corporate policy forbids taking confidential documents out of the building, but she just wants to work on them at home to catch up. She leaves her jacket on the subway, but says nothing to her supervisor about the incident.

▸ A sixth grader finds a USB drive in a school computer and sees the names and addresses of all the students and teachers. He uploads it to his social networking account so all his friends have contact information.

▸ A university employee looks up old academic records of political candidates and sends some provocative tidbits to the press.

▸ A coworker suspects an employee of accessing illicit websites at work, but hesitates to mention it because it might get the employee in big trouble, or even fired.

▸ Worried about some e-mail he exchanged with a supplier that might show a conflict of interest and get the company in legal trouble, the CFO asks someone in IT to delete his whole e-mail account from the server and backup media.

social engineering
The art of manipulating people into breaking normal information security procedures or divulging confidential information.

FIGURE 10-22

Examples of laws touching on information security and privacy.

Law/Regulation	Description
Privacy Act of 1974	Establishes requirements that govern how personally identifiable information on individuals is collected, used, and disseminated by federal agencies.
Health Insurance Portability and Accountability Act (HIPAA)	Includes provisions to protect the privacy and security of individually identifiable health information.
Family Educational Rights and Privacy Act (FERPA)	Establishes privacy rights over educational records. For example, federally funded educational institutions must provide students with access to their own educational records and some control over their disclosure.
CAN-SPAM Act	Prohibits businesses from sending misleading or deceptive commercial e-mails, but denies recipients any legal recourse on their own. The act also requires companies to maintain a do-not-spam list.
Gramm-Leach-Bliley Act	Stipulates how financial institutions are required to protect the privacy of consumers' personal financial information and notify them of their privacy policies annually.
Driver's Privacy Protection Act of 1994	Limits the disclosure of personally identifiable information that is maintained by state departments of motor vehicles.
State Security Breach Notification Laws	Require organizations to notify state residents if sensitive data are released. The wording varies by state.
European Union's Data Protection Directive	Establishes privacy as a fundamental human right for EU citizens. The law is more restrictive than U.S. laws. For example, it requires companies to provide "opt out" choices before transferring personal data to third parties.

How would you judge the actions of these people? These cases show how closely tied ethics, privacy, and security can be and how humans make decisions about small and large issues almost daily. Sometimes they are easy to make, but often they present dilemmas that challenge even people who understand security and who try hard to make ethical decisions. As information systems grow even more powerful and interconnected, the race to protect these valuable information assets will become ever more urgent.

MyMISLab | *Online Simulation*

Vampire Legends

A Role-Playing Simulation on Ethics, Privacy, and Security in the Muliplayer Online Game Business

The massively multiplayer online game business is lucrative, but very competitive. Your company has poured millions into the game, adding vivid graphics, tense storylines, and many features to support collaboration and team play, and the strategy is paying off. You are very proud of the way you were able to use social media to spread the word and persuade people to try it out. Most noticed right away that the avatars move very smoothly and they are much easier to configure and control compared to other games. That's thanks to the terrific IT staff, who also made programming breakthroughs so players could do more quests from their smartphones. A number of celebrities even play the game, although under false names and in disguise.

Now that the game's sequel is ready to release, you and the other senior execs must work out the strategy and budget. Everyone thinks Ancient Age of Vampires will be even more successful than the original game, and analysts project a significant revenue increase. Log in when you're ready to get to work...

KSPhotography/Shutterstock

Learning Objectives

1 Ethics is a system of moral principles used to judge right from wrong. One ethical framework focuses on natural laws and rights. A second, called utilitarianism, emphasizes the consequences of actions. Although many laws are grounded in ethical principles, actions can be legal but not ethical or ethical but not legal. Most people tend to judge unethical behavior, such as plagiarism or intelletual property theft, less harshly when the violator uses a computer and the Internet compared to similar acts committed in face-to-face settings.

2 Information ethics focuses on the storage and transmission of digitized data and raises both ethical and legal issues. Although most countries protect intellectual property (IP), digitized IP is extremely difficult to protect, and many companies use digital rights management technologies to safeguard their assets. Plagiarism has also become very difficult to prevent because of ICT, although it can also be much more easily detected with originality-checking tools.

3 Privacy is under considerable pressure because of the growing volume of personal information online, the complexity of privacy settings and privacy policies, and users' willingness to trade privacy for convenience. Services that use proxies can offer anonymity for online activity. Surveillance poses threats to privacy, but employers often choose to implement surveillance because of concerns about liability, security, confidentiality, and productivity.

4 Information security ensures the protection of an organization's information assets against misuse, disclosure, unauthorized access, or destruction. Organizations use risk management to identify assets needing protection, identify the threats, assess vulnerabilities, and determine the impact of each risk. Threats arise from both human and environmental sources and include accidental events, intentional attacks from insiders or external criminals, fires, floods, power failures, and many more. Distributed denial of service and phishing attacks are common threats that result in significant downtime and leakage of sensitive information. Administrative controls encompass the policies, procedures, and plans the organization creates and enforces to protect information assets and respond to incidents when they occur. Technical controls are implemented by the information systems and include strategies such as encryption and user authentication. Intrusion prevention and detection systems block traffic and activity based on the rules the organization develops and alert managers if suspicious activity occurs. The firewall is an important element for intrusion prevention. Standards for information security for cloud computing are under development but are critical to the future of this architectural trend.

5 Human beings prize productivity highly and may neglect security when it interferes. Social engineering tactics take advantage of human behavioral tendencies to manipulate people into disclosing sensitive information or bypassing security measures. Training in security awareness and the relationships between security, ethics, and privacy can help counteract these tendencies.

KEY TERMS AND CONCEPTS

- ethics
- natural laws and rights
- utilitarianism
- intellectual property (IP)
- digital rights management (DRM)

- information privacy
- proxy
- information security
- malware
- botnet

- distributed denial of service (DDoS)
- phishing
- risk matrix
- incidence response plan
- multifactor authentication

- encryption
- public key encryption
- firewall
- single sign-on
- social engineering

CHAPTER REVIEW QUESTIONS

1. What are ethics? What are two broad categories of ethics? What approach does each category take? What are examples of each category of ethics? What is the difference between ethics and the law?

2. What is intellectual property (IP)? What are the information ethics associated with IP? What is the impact of digital media on the information ethics of IP? What are examples of technologies used to control access to digitized intellectual property?

3. What is plagiarism? What are the information ethics associated with plagiarism? What is the impact of digital media on the information ethics of plagiarism? What are examples of technologies used to detect plagiarism?

4. What is information privacy? What is anonymity? What are strategies that may be used to achieve anonymity on the Internet?

5. Why do organizations implement surveillance? What are the advantages of surveillance? What are the disadvantages of surveillance?

6. What are the steps that organizations take in order to manage information security risks and build a risk matrix? What is involved in each step of this process?

7. What are the two types of threats to information security? What are examples of each type of threat?

8. What are information security vulnerabilities? How do organizations assess vulnerability?

9. What are examples of administrative controls that organizations implement to improve security?

10. What are examples of technical controls that organizations implement to improve security?

11. Why is human behavior often the weakest link for information ethics, information privacy, and information security? What are examples of strategies that organizations can implement to counteract the weaknesses in human behavior and decision making that have a negative impact on information security and privacy?

PROJECTS AND DISCUSSION QUESTIONS

1. According to Wikipedia.org, digital rights management is used by organizations such as Sony, Amazon, Apple, Microsoft, AOL, and the BBC. What is digital rights management? Why do organizations use technology to protect intellectual capital? Describe a typical DRM application that can be used to manage access to digital content. Are there disadvantages to using DRM?

2. Two dreaded "P" words for college students are procrastination and plagiarism. Does the first action necessarily lead to the second? Visit Plagiarism.org to learn more about the various forms of plagiarism. How are the different types of plagiarism similar? How are they different? What are the consequences of plagiarism at your university? Consult your student handbook to learn how plagiarism is defined by your school and how faculty members may respond to cases of plagiarism. What are the options for discipline in cases of plagiarism? Prepare a 5-minute presentation of your findings.

3. The Identity Theft Resource Center® is a nonprofit organization dedicated to helping users understand and prevent identity theft. Visit Google.com and search for "ITRC Fact Sheet 101" or visit www.idtheftcenter.org and select "Consumer Resources" and "ID Theft Test" to locate "ITRC Fact Sheet 101: Are You at Risk for Identity Theft." Answer 20 self-test questions relating to document disposal, Social Security number protection, information handling, and scams to determine your ID theft risk score. Are you savvy about identity theft risks or do you need to take some corrective actions? Prepare a 5-minute presentation to share with your classmates.

4. Do you trade privacy for convenience? Visit Google.com and select "About Google" to locate the privacy policy link located at the bottom of the page. Does Google place cookies on your computer or other devices? Why do they use cookies? What are location-enabled services? Does Google have information about your actual location? Under what circumstances does Google share personal information with other companies? How do you describe the information security measures that Google takes to safeguard access to personal information? Is there anything in the privacy policy that makes you uncomfortable? Are you likely to change your Google search habits as a result of reviewing its privacy policy?

5. Malware is malicious software that is developed for the purpose of causing harm. What are different types of malware? How does malware infiltrate a computer system? What is a botnet? Why do criminals use botnets? What is a distributed denial of service attack? What are three ways that DDoS attacks impact organizations? Visit Microsoft.com and search for "malicious software removal tool." How frequently does Microsoft release a new version of this tool? Search Microsoft.com to learn more about how to boost your malware defense and protect your PC. Prepare a brief summary of your findings.

6. Why is it important to verify the identity of computer users? What are three authentication strategies? Which is the strongest form of authentication? Which is the weakest? What credentials does your university use to verify your identity for access to e-mail and other web-based information such as personal financial aid information and

online course materials? Is this strong or weak authentication? What is a security token? Visit Wikipedia.org to learn how security tokens are used to authenticate users and prepare a brief report of your findings. Do you think it is a good idea to use security tokens to authenticate students? Why or why not?

7. Did you ever wonder why junk e-mail is called "spam"? The Monty Python sketch on spam has been viewed nearly 3 million times on YouTube. That's a lot of spam! Work in a small group with classmates to consider why spam is one of the biggest problems facing the Internet today. Approximately how much e-mail traffic is made up of spam? Is spam a problem on mobile devices? Why is spam a problem for consumers? Why is it a problem for organizations and Internet service providers? What types of technical controls do organizations use to combat spam? Prepare a brief report of your group discussion.

8. Recall from Chapter 3 how cloud computing generally requires leasing IT resources, depending on a third party to store data or depending on a third party to provide services. Work in a small group with classmates to consider the security risks associated with cloud computing. Why are IT managers concerned about protecting cloud-based information assets? What is the IT industry response to concerns about cloud computing? What is the Cloud Security Alliance? Consider the class registration application at your university. Does your group consider this a mission-critical application? Why or why not? Prepare a 5-minute presentation of your discussion that includes a recommendation for or against using cloud computing for critical applications at your university.

APPLICATION EXERCISES

EXCEL APPLICATION:
Citywide Community College

The IT Department at Citywide Community College developed a computer security incident response plan that requires users to provide information for each security incident. Louis Hermann, the IT manager, inventoried the major components of the college's computer systems and created a spreadsheet to track the equipment by manufacturer, model number, and serial number. He decided to confine the list to major computer components, and he does not try to track keyboards, mice, etc. Louis then created a spreadsheet to track systems security incident facts including information about the department reporting the incident, target-specific information (host machine name, etc.), source-specific information (source IP address), and information about the type of security incident or attack. Louis has asked you to use the data provided in the CCC Security spreadsheet, Ch10Ex01, to identify (1) the department reporting the highest number of security incidents and (2) the most prevalent type of intrusion. Use the "countif" function to count the number of security incidents in which the computer system was compromised. Use a memo format to submit a summary of your findings to Louis.

ACCESS APPLICATION:
Citywide Community College

Louis Hermann, IT manager at Citywide Community College, is working with two spreadsheets to manage computer security incident reporting. One spreadsheet tracks the major components of the college's computer systems, and the other spreadsheet tracks security incident facts. To provide for better reporting capabilities, Louis wants you to set up an Access database that tracks college departments, computer systems, and security incidents. Download the spreadsheet Ch10Ex02 and import the worksheets to create the database shown in Figure 10-23. Create a report that lists the number of security incidents reported by each department. Create a second report that lists the number of attacks in which the system was compromised for the department having the greatest number of security incidents. What other reports would Louis find useful?

FIGURE 10-23

Citywide Community College security database.

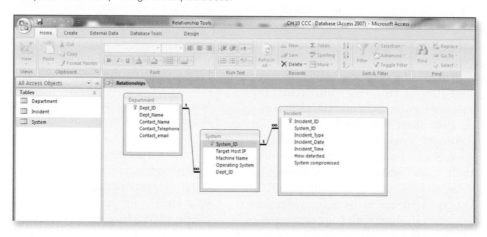

CASE STUDY #1

Online Behavioral Advertising: Criteo's Retargeting Strategy Pleases Clients but Spooks Privacy Advocates

Launched in 2005, Criteo helps e-commerce websites improve their return on marketing investments by turning visitors into profitable customers. As the world leader in personalized retargeting, the company focuses on visitors who browsed a client's site, but left without buying anything. Using third-party tracking cookies, Criteo's technology follows the visitor and displays a banner ad in real time that features whatever the visitor was viewing on the client's site earlier—or products that are very close.

Julie Matlin, for instance, clicked on shoes she thought were cute at Zappos.com, one of Criteo's clients. "For days or weeks, every site I went to seemed to be showing me ads for those shoes," said Matlin. "It's a pretty clever marketing tool. But it's a little creepy if you don't know what's going on."

Retargeting visitors with ultra-relevant display ads is very effective, according to industry research. In one study of 139 ad campaigns from 39 different advertisers, retargeting beat out several other strategies, such as those listed in Figure 10-24.

Privacy advocates, however, voice serious concerns about retargeting and other behavioral advertising strategies. Consumers don't understand how the technology works and may feel like they are being stalked. Governments are considering legal measures to control the practice, alarmed by the growing system of commercial surveillance and its escalating powers to personalize ad appeals. Calls for tighter regulation, including a "do not track" list that might resemble the "do not call" list in place for telephones, may be on the horizon.

Criteo CEO J. B. Rudelle recognizes the potential for consumer backlash and government regulation and knows his company is one of those at the center of the debate. But he argues that Criteo's technology addresses two very important trends in the media. "Less than 20 percent of people are willing to pay for their favorite news and information site online," he says. Also, "Seventy-nine percent of online news and information consumers had never or only rarely clicked an online ad." In other words, customers want free services, so advertisers have to find other ways to generate meaningful returns. Retargeting may seem spooky, but returns are very high.

Criteo also tries to alleviate consumer fears about tracking in an effort to build trust. Under each display ad it serves, the company adds the "I" symbol that links to text explaining why the ad is appearing, what information about the customer was used to generate the ad, and how to opt out. Rudelle also maintains that Criteo has one of the strictest privacy policies in the industry, and it operates in some of the most privacy-conscious countries in the world, such as Germany. "We believe that once consumers truly understand retargeting, the vast majority will see [it] as one of the most transparent, ethical, and valuable ad delivery methods in the industry."

While Criteo's approach emphasizes transparency, other online advertising networks resist sharing information with the consumer or making it easy to opt out of tracking. A rash of lawsuits against such networks and the websites that use them may help clarify the boundaries, and time will tell how consumers judge the pros and cons of behavioral targeting.

FIGURE 10-24

Relative effectiveness of online advertising strategies.

Online Advertising Strategy	Description	Lift*
Retargeting	Displays an ad after consumer has left the website, featuring a product the customer viewed.	1,046%
Audience targeting	Ads displayed are chosen based on online behavioral data.	514%
Contextual targeting	Ads served are related to the current page's content.	130%
Premium pricing	Ads are placed on high-volume sites with higher ad rates.	300%

*Lift refers to the average increase in search activity for the advertised brand within 4 weeks of exposure to the ad.

Source: comScore and ValueClick Media.

Discussion Questions

1. The Criteo CEO justifies the company's product based on the fact that consumers are not willing to pay for online content. Do you believe this is a valid justification?

2. What are the ethical and privacy considerations for online behavioral advertising?

3. How would a marketing executive respond to these ethical and privacy considerations?

4. Would a "Do Not Track" list be sufficient to address the ethical and privacy implications of online behavioral targeting?

SOURCES: Anonymous. (September 22, 2010). Press Release: comScore study with ValueClick Media shows ad retargeting generates strongest lift compared to other targeting strategies. *comScore.com.* www.comscore.com/Press_Events/ Press_Releases/2010/9/comScore_Study_with_ValueClick_Media_Shows_Ad_Retargeting_Generates_Strongest_Lift_Compared_ to_Other_Targeting_Strategies, accessed June 4, 2011. Blakeman, K. (September/October 2010). What search engines know about you. *Online.* 34(5), 46+. Ebbert, J. (September 14, 2010). Criteo CEO Rudelle responds to recent concerns over retargeting and consumer privacy. *AdExchanger.com.* www.adexchanger.com/online-advertising/criteo-ceo-rudelle, accessed January 10, 2011. Helft, M., & Vega, T. (August 29, 2010). Retargeting ads follow surfers to other sites. *New York Times.* www.nytimes.com/2010/08/30/ technology/30adstalk.html?sq=retargetingads&st=cse&adxnnl=1&scp=1&adxnnlx=1285340501-V925JwOdKeT6zySmG53JFA, accessed March 15, 2011. Hunt, A., Jacobsen, M., et al. (2010). When money moves digital, where should it go? Identifying the right media-placement strategies for digital display. *comScore* and *ValueClick Media.* www.comscore.com/Press_Events/ Presentations_Whitepapers/2010/When_Money_Moves_to_Digital_Where_Should_It_Go, accessed March 16, 2011. Valentino-DeVries, J., & Steel, E. (2010). "Cookies" cause bitter backlash. *Wall Street Journal.* September 20. pp. B1, B2.

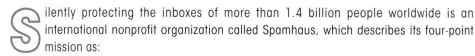

CASE STUDY #2

Community Policing on the Internet: Spamhaus Targets Worldwide Spammers

Silently protecting the inboxes of more than 1.4 billion people worldwide is an international nonprofit organization called Spamhaus, which describes its four-point mission as:

▶ Tracking the Internet's spam operations.
▶ Providing dependable real-time anti-spam protection for Internet networks.
▶ Working with law enforcement agencies to identify and pursue spammers worldwide.
▶ Lobbying governments for effective anti-spam legislation.

With headquarters in the United Kingdom and Switzerland, Spamhaus maintains a "block list" containing the IP addresses believed to originate spam. Many governments, corporations, universities, and other organizations check the list before delivering mail, blocking any messages whose senders match an entry on it.

Although the cause is noble, the stakes are extremely high, so the work itself can be both dangerous and secretive. Larry, Spamhaus' chief technical officer, who prefers not to reveal his last name, says, "We get threats every day. In the U.S., it is people bringing lawsuits against us. And then there are organized criminals in Russia and Ukraine, who use different methods." Police have advised Steve Linford, head of Spamhaus, to be suspicious of any unexpected packages delivered to his home.

How do senders wind up on the block list? Spamhaus defines spam as any mail that is both unsolicited and sent in bulk. Mail that meets this definition may not be illegal in many places, including the United States, so Spamhaus is the target of lawsuits claiming damages for lost business. A Chicago e-mail marketing firm called "e360" sued Spamhaus for more than $11 million in damages. Spamhaus argued that the United States has no jurisdiction over a British company and didn't bother to launch any defense. One U.S. judge awarded e360 the $11 million, but the award was reduced to $27,000 by an incredulous appeals judge who found e360's damage claims inflated and absurd.

Spamhaus refuses to pay even that amount, insisting that e360 is a spammer. "The Illinois ruling shows how spammers can game U.S. courts with ease," says Linford. Although e360 is now out of business, its main employee complains bitterly about this kind of community policing that works outside of traditional law enforcement. "Spamhaus.org is a fanatical, vigilante organization that operates in the United States with blatant disregard for U.S. law," he said.

Industry analysts know that community policing is not perfect and that block lists can contain false positives that harm legitimate businesses. It is time-consuming and expensive for companies to work through the process to get cleared. But as one analyst put it, "These [spammers] aren't just a nuisance. They're a cancer on society. And Linford has taken it upon himself to do something about them…. That these cops are self-appointed is troubling. But marketers would do well to understand that without Spamhaus, people's inboxes would be unusable."

Discussion Questions

1. How do the interests of computer users differ from the interests of spammers?

2. Do you agree with Spamhaus methodology to reduce spam?

3. What other approaches could be taken to reduce spam?

4. What are the relevant legal issues in this case?

SOURCES: Anderson, N. (June 16, 2010). Accused spammer demands $135M from Spamhaus; gets $27,002. *Ars Technica.* http://arstechnica.com/tech-policy/news/2010/06/accused-spammer-demands-135m-from-spamhaus-gets-27002.ars, accessed June 4, 2011. Magill, K. (September, 2008). In defense of blacklists. *Direct,* p. 47. Palmer, M. (2009). Secret war on web crooks revealed. *Financial Times* (London). June 15, p. 16.

E-PROJECT 1   Tracking the Trackers: Investigating How Third-Party Cookies Steer the Ads You See

This e-project will show how cookies read by a browser can shape the user's online browsing experience, particularly by targeting ads toward personal preferences.

To do this project, you will need to remove existing cookies so you can conduct the experiment with a clean slate, and then configure your browser to accept new third-party cookies. (If you prefer not to expose your usual browser to third-party cookies, you can download a different browser to do the experiment and then delete the browser when you are finished.)

To remove existing cookies in Firefox, click on Tools, then Options, and then choose the Privacy tab. Click on Show Cookies to see what cookies are there. Click on Remove All Cookies. Next configure the browser so that it accepts third-party cookies as well as cookies from the site you are visiting, and choose Keep until "they expire." For browsers other than Firefox, check the Help file to see how to remove cookies and then accept third-party cookies.

You want to target yourself as someone who wants a pair of unusual shoes. Choose to study Zappos.com, or visit www.criteo.com to identify a different client. Visit the site you choose, and look around the site for a product you would never actually buy.

Examine the product, clicking on features, and then add to your cart. Find a couple of similar products and examine them as well. The goal is to add cookies to your browser that will alert other sites that you have an interest in the product, the more unusual, at least for you, the better. Don't buy anything, of course.

To compare retargeting with Google's interest-based targeting strategies, described in the short video at google.com/ads/preferences, enter two unusual preferences that you don't actually have, so if ads for relevant products appear, they will stand out. The preferences should be totally unrelated to the product you examined at the Criteo client. Browse normally for three days. Once you have finished, uninstall the browser or reconfigure it to the trust settings you prefer.

1. Count ads that match the product you almost purchased on Zappos.com (or another site), and note the site(s) on which they appeared.
2. Also count ads that match your Google preferences, and note the site(s) on which they appeared.
3. How did the ad strategies compare?

E-PROJECT 2   Analyzing Spammers by Country, Using Excel Pivot Tables

In this e-project, you will explore Spamhaus' Registry of Known Spam Operators (ROKSO), a list the organization maintains and posts on its website.

Visit www.spamhaus.org and click on ROKSO. How does Spamhaus determine who or what should be in the registry?

Download the file Ch10_SpamHaus which contains a list of known spammers from 2011.

1. Sort the list by the TopTen column. Which entry is considered the #1 spammer?
2. Next, you will generate a pivot table and chart showing the list of countries, with the count of each country's known spammers. Select the data in all columns and then choose

Insert, Pivot Chart. Drag and drop Country to the Axis Fields, and Name to the Values box, so the chart shows the count of spammers by country.

a. Which country has the most known spammers?
b. Which country is second in terms of the number of known spammers on this list?

3. To view a chart containing just the Top Ten offenders by country, click on IsOnTopTen in the Field List, and then click the down arrow to the right. Uncheck "no" so the analysis will only include spammers who are on the top 10 list. Drag the IsOnTopTen field to the Report Filter box. Which countries have the most spammers in the top ten?

CHAPTER NOTES

1. King, L. (May 11, 2010). Wikimedia child porn row escalates. *PCWorld.*

2. Baase, S. (2008). *The gift of fire: Social, legal and ethical issues for computing and the internet (3rd ed.).* Upper Saddle River, NJ: Pearson Prentice Hall.

3. FTC files amicus brief opposing barriers to Internet casket sales. *FTC.gov.* www.ftc.gov/opa/2002/09/okcasketsales.shtm, accessed June 4, 2011.

4. Zimmerman, M. (2009). Judge overturns Lori Drew misdemeanor convictions. Electronic Frontier Foundation. www.eff.org/deeplinks/2009/07/judge-overturns-lori, accessed June 4, 2011.

5. O'Rourke, M. (2007). You've been "Kirked." *Risk Management.* 54, 7. DOI: ID Number: 1287557781. Retrieved March 4, 2010, from ABI/INFORM Global.

6. Molnar, K., Kletke, M., & Chongwatpol, J. (2008). Ethics vs. IT ethics: Do undergraduate students perceive a difference? *Journal of Business Ethics.* 83(4), 657–671.

7. Anonymous. (May 15, 2010). Science and technology: To catch a thief; spotting video piracy. *The Economist.* 395(8682), 88.

8. Business Software Alliance. (May 2010). BSA reports $51 billion worth of software theft in 2009. *Economics Week.* p. 111.

9. Coats, W. S., Lerner, J. L., & Krause, E. (2010). Preventing illegal sharing of music online: The DMCA, litigation, and a new, graduated approach. *Journal of Internet Law.* 13(7), 3–7.

10. Schiller, K. (2010). A happy medium: Ebooks, licensing, and DRM. *Information Today.* 27(2), 1–44.

11. (June 1, 2010). BI2 technologies awarded contract to implement statewide facial recognition system to identify inmates, suspects, and gang members. *Business Wire.*

12. Palmer, M. (May 20, 2010). Google debates face recognition technology after privacy blunders. *Financial Times.*

13. Dou, E. (March 17, 2011). Internet privacy and the "right to be forgotten." *Reuters.*

14. Bradshaw, T., Menn, J., & Schafer, D. (May 18, 2010). Google faces German and US probes over harvested wifi data. *Financial Times* (London).

15. Steiner, P. (July 5, 1993). On the Internet, no one knows you're a dog (cartoon). *The New Yorker.* p. 61.

16. Barret, V. M. (2007). Anonymity & the net. *Forbes.* 180(8), 74–81.

17. Edman, M., & Yener, B. (2009). On anonymity in an electronic society: A survey of anonymous communication systems. *ACM Computing Surveys.* 42(1), 5–5:35.

18. Supreme Court of New Jersey. (June 1, 2001). *Tammy S. Blakey vs. Continental Airlines, Inc.*, Rule Number 164, N.J. 38; 751 A. 2d 538; 2000 N.J. LEXIS 650.

19. Wolfe, D. (2010). Secret's out. *American Banker.* 175(41), 5.

20. Corrons, L. (March 2010). The rise and rise of NDR. *Network Security.* (3), 12–16.

21. Menn, J. (March 4, 2010). Investigators shut down Mariposa hacking network. *Financial Times.* p. 7.

22. Feigelson, J., & Calman, C. (2010). Liability for the costs of phishing and information theft. *Journal of Internet Law.* 13(10), 1–26.

23. Gupta, B. B., Joshi, R. C., & Misra, M. (2009). Defending against distributed denial of service attacks: Issues and challenges. *Information Security Journal: A Global Perspective.* 18, 224–247.

24. Buley, T. (2008). Hackonomics. *Forbes.com.*

25. *Chronology of data breaches—Security breaches 2005–Present.* Privacy Rights Clearinghouse. www.privacyrights.org/data-breach, accessed May 29, 2011.

26. (2011). U.S.S.S., Software Engineering Institute Program, Carnegie Mellon University, Deloitte, 2011 Cybersecurity Watch Survey Released. *CSO Magazine.*

27. Computer Security Division, Information Technology Laboratory. (2010). *Guide for assessing the security controls in federal information systems and organizations.* NIST Special Publication 800-53A. National Institute of Standards and Technology. U.S. Department of Commerce.

28. Payment Card Industry Security Standards Council. *PCI DSS new self-assessment questionnaire (SAQ) summary.* www.pcisecuritystandards.org/saq/index.shtml, accessed June 4, 2011.

29. Stoll, C. (1990). *The cuckoo's egg: Tracking a spy through the maze of computer espionage.* New York: Simon and Schuster.

30. Shipley, G. (2010). Cloud computing risks. *InformationWeek.* (1262), 20–24.

31. Carstens, D. S. (2009). Human and social aspects of password authentication. In Gupta, M., & Sharman, R. (Eds.). *Social and human elements of information security.* Hershey, NY: Information Science Reference.

32. Worthen, B. (May 27, 2010). Facebook settings don't quell critics. *Wall Street Journal* (Eastern Edition).

33. Matwyshyn, A. (2009). CSR and the corporate cyborg: Ethical corporate information security practices. *Journal of Business Ethics.* (88), 579–594.

Systems Development and *Procurement*

Chapter Preview

HOW DO INFORMATION SYSTEMS COME INTO BEING? SOME START OFF IN A PROGRAMMER'S BASEMENT, and a few of those burst out to earn billions for their creators. Most, however, are built or bought in response to a business need. The driver might be a core business function—accounting and general ledger perhaps. Or it might be an inventive idea that will attract loyal customers and stymie the competition. This chapter traces the life cycle of an information system, from the birth of the idea and the planning phase to the system's implementation and maintenance. We also examine how information systems age, and why they eventually must be replaced.

Systems can be custom-built in-house, and the chapter examines the different software development strategies that organizations use. But many systems are purchased from vendors who compete to offer the best products in the marketplace. The chapter also explores how organizations approach the "build or buy" decision, and how they can organize a systematic procurement process.

marco cappalunga/Shutterstock

11

Learning Objectives

1 Describe the seven phases of the systems development life cycle (SDLC).

2 Describe three major software development strategies.

3 Explain why organizations choose one software development strategy over another for particular projects.

4 Explain how organizations decide whether to build or buy, and the steps they use if they choose to buy an information system.

5 Identify several ways in which the human element is important for systems development and procurement.

Introduction

Bored at the thought of another frozen lasagna dinner, Lily looks closely at her refrigerator's shelves. Parmesan cheese, garlic, cream, oranges, anchovies, celery, mozzarella, and a jar of jalapeño peppers are all in there, along with eggs and other odds and ends. Thinking there must be something creative she can make, Lily rifles through the cabinets, searching for inspiration. Rice, spaghetti, chicken stock, tomato paste, olive oil, soy sauce, and other items hold promise, but she doesn't know what to do with them. Her few cookbooks have tempting recipes, but none match her supply. If only she could find one that uses what she has, not what she doesn't have. If a system had that information, could it do a matching process to recommend some dishes she hasn't considered?

Innovations often spring from frustrations like this one, and Lily starts mulling over a web application to fill this gap. As a senior manager for an online grocer that delivers to a 20-mile radius, she is also thinking about competitive advantage, and how this application, her "What to Make with What You Have" cookbook, might help the company. Lily is no stranger to web development; she was charged with implementing the company's main e-commerce website. She starts making notes, planning to bring the idea up at the next managers' meeting.

Information systems come to life in many different ways, and the process can be both exhilarating and aggravating. As a sophomore at Harvard, Mark Zuckerberg created Facebook in less than a month, attracting more than 1,000 members within the first 24 hours after launch. But other projects have less happy endings. The $170 million project to develop the virtual case file for the Federal Bureau of Investigation ran into one problem after another. The system was intended to replace the FBI's obsolete paper filing systems, but changing requirements and poorly managed contracts led to such buggy and unstable code that the whole system had to be scrapped.[1]

Describe the seven phases of the systems development life cycle (SDLC). **1**

Systems Development Life Cycle

The **systems development life cycle (SDLC)** is the process that begins with planning and goes through several phases until the system has been implemented and then enters its maintenance period. In theory, the process encompasses seven sequential steps (Figure 11-1), although, of course, the real world is often more unruly. The seven steps are planning, analysis, design, development, testing, implementation, and maintenance. Here we look at each.

PLANNING

The goal in this step is to define the business need for the project, assess its importance to the company, and determine whether the project is actually feasible. Most organizations are not short of ideas for information system projects, but they all have limited time and funding. Indeed, many have a long queue of ideas to enhance or replace existing systems or to implement brand new ones, all of which may seem worthwhile. Lily's cookbook project may face some tough competition for the company's resources. A steering committee with business stakeholders and IT staff often lead the planning phase and make the case for the new system.

ASSESSING BUSINESS NEED   Three major factors that bolster business need and determine where to allocate funding for systems development projects are:

▶ Return on investment (ROI)
▶ Competitive advantage
▶ Risk management

If the project will either save or earn more money than it will cost, the *return on investment* is positive. For some projects the ROI is relatively easy to calculate. For example, when two school districts in Canada merged into one, they struggled at first with separate and costly PBX phone systems. They then launched a project to replace the systems with unified communications and IP phones that rely on Internet connections, at a cost of $500,000. The savings of $200,000 a year returns the investment in just 2½ years, and the school benefits from many added features such as paging, public address system, videoconferencing, and free call forwarding.[2]

ROI can be much harder to estimate in other projects. Lily envisions that her website will promote online grocery sales by including a feature to suggest recipes that will also work well except for one or two items the customer

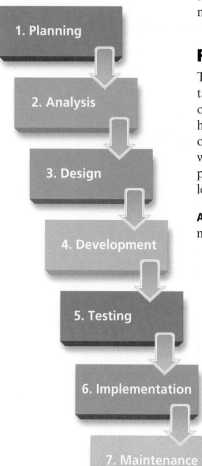

FIGURE 11-1

Systems development life cycle phases.

1. Planning
2. Analysis
3. Design
4. Development
5. Testing
6. Implementation
7. Maintenance

is missing and for which the grocer would offer a discount. For example, she had everything she needed to make spaghetti alfredo, except for garlic. The system could suggest that recipe, offer a coupon for garlic, and then—since she would already be paying the delivery charge—suggest some staples or other items to complement her pantry. The site would also have an RSS feed from the grocer's regular site, listing current promotions.

Leveraging information systems for *competitive advantage* is a powerful driver for systems development, and Lily thinks this aspect should be stressed in the proposal. Thinking about the site in those terms, she decides to add a loyalty feature for repeat customers who can earn points toward free deliveries. She also describes a commenting and reviewing function so that customers can rate the recipes and share their tips. That would help build a community of creative people who like to cook something fun on the spur of the moment, with little advance planning.

Risk management is a third driver of information systems development, one that usually touches on security, privacy, safety, and regulatory compliance. For example, the company's CIO might insist on new software development to better secure customer data collected during e-commerce transactions. The development effort won't increase sales, but it will protect the company from security threats. Lily's project doesn't mitigate risk, so it can't be justified on that basis. In fact, it may raise new privacy concerns. Customers might not be willing to divulge food preferences in connection with personally identifying information, since it might hint at medical problems or just abysmal eating habits. A strong privacy policy will be needed, and Lily will cover this in her proposal.

Did You Know?

MIT economist Alberto Cavallo developed software to gain competitive advantage, but not over other companies—over the Bureau of Labor Statistics (BLS). To obtain information on inflation, his software scours 300 retail websites to get current prices on more than 5 million goods. BLS canvasses businesses by phone, so its inflation estimates are weeks behind. Cavallo considers his software a public resource and hopes BLS will take advantage of it.[3]

FEASIBILITY STUDY The **feasibility study** is an important part of the planning process that examines whether the initiative is viable from technical, financial, and legal standpoints. It may not be technically feasible if the technologies either don't exist yet or are not mature enough to support the project's goals. Financially, the return on investment may be promising, but the organization may not have sufficient capital to fund it. A legal review may uncover grave risks that could expose the company to lawsuits. For instance, when RealNetworks developed DVD-copying software to bypass digital rights protection, the Motion Picture Association of America sued to block its sale to consumers. RealNetworks eventually had to settle lawsuits with many Hollywood studios and pay $4.5 million in legal costs as well.[4] A more thorough study of the legal feasibility might have prevented this costly blunder.

The feasibility of Lily's project depends partly on whether she can get access to recipes in a format that can be analyzed according to ingredients. Her company already has a huge database of grocery products, so that side of the matching is already in place.

systems development life cycle (SDLC)
The process that describes the seven steps in the life of an information system: planning, analysis, design, development, testing, implementation, and maintenance.

feasibility study
Part of the information system planning process that examines whether the initiative is viable from technical, financial, and legal standpoints.

ANALYSIS

Once the project has approval to proceed, the next step is to analyze and document what the system should actually do from the business (as opposed to the technical) perspective. During **requirements analysis**, stakeholders identify the features the system will need and then prioritize them as mandatory, preferred, or nonessential.

Gathering these requirements entails many meetings, interviews, and reviews of the way existing processes unfold. The person who leads this analysis needs a solid background in business management and information systems, but also outstanding listening and consensus-building skills. The stakeholders will have different views about how processes actually work and how they should be improved, especially when their own jobs are involved.

PROCESS DIAGRAMS AND BUSINESS PROCESS IMPROVEMENT   The analysis will develop a clear understanding of the processes the system will support, usually using **process diagrams**. These trace how each process operates from beginning to end in a way that is clear to all the stakeholders. Figure 11-2 shows an example.

A well-done requirements analysis should also uncover opportunities to optimize business processes and even eliminate some of them. As we described in Chapter 1, attention to how information systems can improve business process management (BPM) can yield rich dividends. For instance, a process that includes routing a supply purchase to a supervisor for approval might not be needed at all if the rules the supervisor uses to make decisions can be built into an expert system. Manual data entry from handwritten forms is a major target for elimination, drawing on intelligent character recognition, or customers who will happily input their own data on the web. When you buy an airline ticket on the carrier's website, you do all the data entry yourself, including your passport number if it is an international trip.

FIGURE 11-2

Sample process diagram.

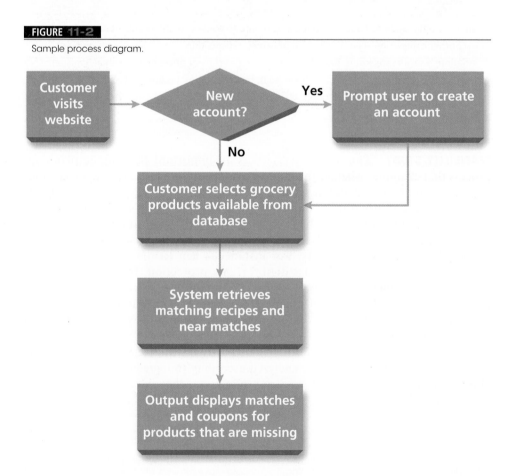

FIGURE 11-3

Types of requirements included in a requirements definition document.

Types of Requirements	Examples
Functional requirements	System features, prioritized by stakeholders; description of processes the system will support, and the system's input and output
Usability requirements	Ease of learning the software, task efficiency, screen attractiveness
Accessibility requirements	Accessibility for people with disabilities
Performance requirements	Response time, reliability, availability, scalability
Interface requirements	User navigation, data display
Security requirements	Authentication, privacy, encryption
Compliance requirements	Processes and reports required for compliance
Integration requirements	Interfaces with other systems
Language requirements	Support for English, Spanish, and/or other languages

Contrast that with a phone call to an airline reservation specialist, who will charge you a fee for making the arrangements and entering your data for you. As an added bonus, customers have a strong motivation to avoid errors in their own data, so accuracy improves.

An early form of BPM introduced in the 1990s was called **business process reengineering (BPR)**. In his article with the provocative subtitle "Don't Automate, Obliterate," Michael Hammer proposed BPR as a means to make sweeping changes that eliminated all processes that did not add value.[5] Following his advice, many companies went through wrenching, expensive, and ultimately unsuccessful projects led by consultants to redesign processes throughout the organization. It soon became clear that the human element is key to managing and improving business processes, and by 1995, BPR was criticized as a fad that forgot people. BPR's objectives are sound, though, if the techniques are used in a more focused way on smaller projects in the context of new system development and overall business process management.[6]

REQUIREMENTS DEFINITION DOCUMENT   The output of the analysis phase is the **requirements definition document (RDD)**, which specifies in detail what features the system should have, prioritized by the stakeholders. It also includes assumptions and constraints that affect the system, such as the need to migrate and possibly reformat data from an existing system. In addition to the system's actual features, the document should address the kinds of requirements listed in Figure 11-3. Stakeholders sign off on the document, confirming that this is indeed the system they need, specified as precisely as possible.

> **PRODUCTIVITY TIP**
> You can optimize one of your own processes by leveraging information systems. Before you run errands, make a checklist. Then use Google Maps or another navigational tool to find the most efficient order for your destinations and the best routes to take.

BUILD OR BUY?   Once the stakeholders agree on what is needed, a review of commercially available information systems may take place. The RDD is used as a feature guide to help compare the systems to see how well each one aligns to the organization's requirements. A general rule of thumb is that if an organization can buy or license software that meets at least 75 to 80 percent of its requirements, and costs are within reason, the "buy" option is probably a favorable approach.

requirements analysis
The process by which stakeholders identify the features a new information system will need and then prioritize them as mandatory, preferred, or nonessential.

process diagrams
Graphical representations that trace how each process that a new information system will support operates from beginning to end.

business process reengineering (BPR)
The design and analysis of workflows in an organization with the goal of eliminating processes that do not add value.

requirements definition document (RDD)
A document that specifies the features a new information system should have, prioritized by stakeholders. It also includes assumptions and constraints that affect the system, such as the need to migrate and possibly reformat data from an existing system.

"Buy" is also typically the best choice when the system supports common business functions, such as financial or human resource management. We will come back to the procurement process later in this chapter. For now, we continue with systems development when the choice is to build it from scratch. Design, development, testing, and implementation might proceed with in-house IT staff or it might be outsourced to a software development company. In either case, the RDD is the road map.

DESIGN PHASE

Translating the RDD into a workable technical design constitutes the design phase. Here, decisions have to be made about the system's architecture, and plans are drawn up that describe the technical details.

ARCHITECTURAL DESIGN   The choice of software development environments and hardware architecture is a critical one. As we discussed in Chapter 3, the organization has to consider the enterprise architecture as a whole. Although a particular software development environment might be marginally more efficient for a specific project, the disadvantages of a fragmented, poorly integrated architecture are too costly to ignore.

The choice will also be affected by the experience and capabilities of the IT staff. A company whose IT staff is very experienced with the Java programming language, Linux servers, and MySQL databases, for example, would lean in that direction for new projects to leverage its existing expertise. If the staff is experienced only in older technologies, however, the organization's chief architect will want to take this opportunity to train staff in new tools, ones that align with the enterprise's future architecture.

A growing trend in software design is **service-oriented architecture (SOA)**, in which systems are assembled from relatively independent software components, each of which handles a specific business service. For example, one chunk of code might "get the customer's credit rating," and different applications and business units could interface to this chunk to perform the same common task, rather than build it separately. The approach is especially useful in fast-moving, agile companies that need to make many changes to business rules and processes, and that also want to streamline common business services across the enterprise.

Verizon developers, for instance, built a service to "get the customer service record." The underlying software code was not pretty—it had to retrieve a complex jumble of data from 25 different systems. But other developers who needed that service for new web-based applications didn't have to worry about the innards—they only had to write a single link to interface with the service's outside wrapper. Without the service, those developers would have had to write interfaces to all those 25 systems independently, and the results that were returned for each customer may not have been consistent. Worse, when a 26th system is added, from a merger perhaps, every one of those systems would need changes, not just the one service.

Like many companies, the online grocer where Lily works has a mix of architectures, since some systems were purchased from software vendors and integrated with others that were custom-built. However, the grocery product database is in a MySQL database, and the web applications are all developed with the open-source programming language called "PHP." That architecture makes the most sense for the cookbook project.

Whatever architecture is selected, the organization must also consider size and capacity issues, since the application will put new pressures on it. Increased bandwidth may be needed to handle more website visits, and new hard drives might be required to handle storage.

FIGURE 11-4

Simplified use case diagram.

DATA MODELS AND DATABASE DESIGN   The design phase captures all aspects of how the system's components will function together to accomplish the goal, using descriptions, models, and diagrams. It is the technical blueprint for the whole system, with all the fine print and details. The analyst and IT staff will look this over very closely because fixing mistakes now helps avoid costly corrections later.

The database schema described in Chapter 4, for instance, will show all the details for the database's tables, the fields for each table, and the relationships between the tables. The **use case diagram** will show how different types of users will interact with the system (Figure 11-4). (They really do use those stick figures to represent users.) Other diagrams document specific business processes and rules, screen layouts, and navigation.

Many designers rely on standardized graphics symbols and notations to improve communication and clarity, often using the **unified modeling language (UML)**. Developed by a consortium of 11 companies, UML offers a standardized approach to modeling. Designers can use it to create visual models and blueprints that document the system's components, as well as the behaviors it is expected to perform.

The design phase also addresses usability and considers the needs of all the different end users who will interact with the system. For a customer website, for example, a positive user experience is essential. It will add business value and encourage visitors to come back. Eager buyers return again and again to Amazon because the developers have made it very usable, and customers can easily locate what they need, enter shipping information, and complete the purchase. Usability does not mean flashy graphics and slow-to-load animations, and such features can detract from a positive user experience.

End users with disabilities should also be considered in the design phase, and legal requirements to make systems accessible to them are growing. Target settled a lawsuit filed by the National Federation of the Blind, creating a $6 million fund to compensate visually impaired people who were unable to take advantage of the company's website using their screen readers.[7] Accessibility features will not just satisfy legal requirements; they will also broaden the customer base.

---

service-oriented architecture (SOA)
A set of design principles in which systems are assembled from relatively independent software components, each of which handles a specific business service.

use case diagram
Diagrams that show how different types of users will interact with the system.

unified modeling language (UML)
A standardized approach to modeling an information system using graphics, symbols, and notations to improve communication and clarity.

DEVELOPMENT PHASE

Converting the design into an operational information system is the goal of the development phase. Depending on the system's scope, this phase might require teams of developers to work for months or even years, each constructing one portion of the system.

Software developers use their own information systems to streamline work and keep one another informed about progress or challenges. For example, **version control software** tracks versions of the code, acting like a library with checkout procedures to prevent developers from writing over one another's files. To work on a program, the developer checks it out of the library. Other developers can still view it and see who has it, but they can't make their own changes. When the developer has finished, the code is checked back into the library as the latest version, and another developer can then check it out.

Project- and issue-tracking software offers useful features to help developers stay abreast of all aspects of their projects. Developers can upload diagrams and documentation, comment on activity, describe challenges, report bugs, and request assistance. The software maintains a complete history of project activity, including dates showing when each module was started and completed and who has been assigned each task. It also offers customizable dashboards so developers can see at a glance how the project is coming along and which activities they need to complete today (Figure 11-5). Software tools are available to facilitate **code review**, a peer review process in which programmers familiar with the project and the development environment check over one another's work to ensure it is well documented and properly written. The software can check for security vulnerabilities in the code so they can be fixed early and don't invite calamity later.

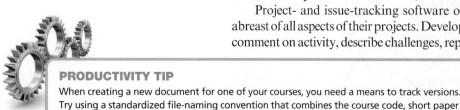

PRODUCTIVITY TIP

When creating a new document for one of your courses, you need a means to track versions. Try using a standardized file-naming convention that combines the course code, short paper title, and version number, such as BUS101_SDLC_v01. Don't fall into the trap of tacking the word "new" on to the filename for the latest version. "New" becomes old very quickly.

TESTING PHASE

Testing goes on during the development phase, as individual modules are completed. When the system has been completed, it undergoes much more rigorous testing

FIGURE 11-5

Project- and issue-tracking software.

Source: Jira, from Atlassian.

FIGURE 11-6
Types of testing for information systems.

Types of Testing for Information Systems	Description
Unit testing	Programmers can check the functionality of small modules of code during the development phase.
System testing	Both end users and IT staff test the functionality of the entire system.
Stress testing	Tests are conducted by IT staff to assess how well the system performs under peak loads.
Parallel testing	Using the same input, developers compare the new system's output to the output generated by the system it is replacing.
Integration testing	End users and IT staff test the new system's interfaces with other software components it links to.
Acceptance testing	End users perform final testing to determine whether the project is complete as specified.

to ensure that the whole system works smoothly together, not just its individual modules. Figure 11-6 lists several examples of the kinds of tests developers might perform.

Each test mimics events the system will handle when it goes live. The test cases are carefully documented so the developers can make corrections in case of any failures. Software tools help tremendously with this testing as well. For example, once developers have created a library of test cases, software tools can automatically run them against the system as it evolves to test for errors. The software can simulate an army of customers, simultaneously trying to complete a web-based form with different data, different input errors, different browsers, and different expected outcomes. For Lily's cookbook, the test cases would include a range of people, some whose cupboards are almost bare and others who have rare spices and specialty foods.

Other software tools can check for security holes, compliance with accessibility regulations, performance under loads, broken web links, and more (Figure 11-7). These tools, and also independent testers, are critical because programmers are notoriously inept at testing their own code. They know how the code actually works and unconsciously avoid the odd key presses and clicks that end users try.

Did You Know?

Kentico Software found a creative way to motivate end users to report bugs they spot in its web content management software. The company plants a tree in the bug finder's honor and maintains a Tree Gallery with photos of every tree planted by the developer responsible for fixing it, the name of the person who reported the bug, and the tree's location.[8]

IMPLEMENTATION

As the go-live date approaches, tasks shift to the needs of the end users who will be using and managing the system. They will need documentation and training to understand clearly how the new system works and how it differs from the old one, if there was one. Their tasks may change considerably and they must feel confident they can handle the new roles.

version control software
A type of software that tracks versions of the source code during development, enforcing checkout procedures to prevent developers from writing over one another's files.

code review
A peer review process in which programmers check over one another's work to ensure its quality.

FIGURE 11-7

Software testing tool to examine web applications for various types of problems, such as missing text descriptions for images.

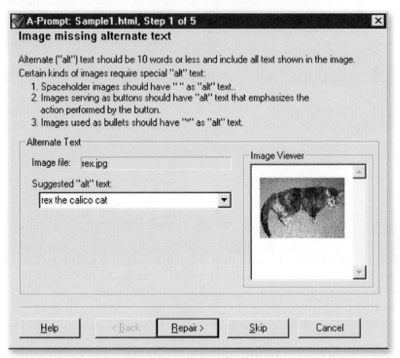

Source: From A-Prompt software, developed by the University of Toronto's Adaptive Technology Resource Center and the TRACE Center at the University of Wisconsin.

Organizations have several choices about how to implement a new system:

- ▶ Parallel implementation
- ▶ Phased implementation
- ▶ Direct implementation

A **parallel implementation** launches the new system while the old one is still running. Employees either do their jobs twice, once on each system, or two separate teams handle the same processes, one team on each system. An advantage to this approach is that both systems are processing the same cases, so if the new one is operating properly, the output should be the same. However, parallel implementation is very expensive and thus is usually in place for only a short period. Also, if the old system is being retired because it bungled some processes, the comparisons might not be valid.

A **phased implementation** launches modules in phases rather than all at once. For example, an ERP might start with human resources, then phase in components of the financial modules and supply chain. The implementation team and trainers can focus on one departmental group at a time, helping them become accustomed to the new software while the developers watch for glitches. A disadvantage is that the new system's modules may be tightly integrated, so implementing one without the others may create some confusion and require temporary interfaces to the old systems. For example, the human resources system will include payroll data that must be passed to the old general ledger if the new ledger isn't up and running yet. Consistency is also an issue if information is maintained in more than one place as the modules are phased in.

Direct implementation switches off the old system and launches all the modules of the new one on a single, very hectic go-live date, sometimes called the "big bang" (after the way astronomers describe the universe's explosive origin). Often employees go home at night and come back in the morning to find the new system all in place. A major advantage is that all those temporary bridges between old and new modules are unnecessary, and people whose roles span modules do not have to switch back and forth. The strategy works well for smaller systems and may be the only logical choice for them. But the risks can be high for large-scale implementations of complex software such as the ERP, involving thousands of employees.

Often the type of system determines which implementation plan is feasible. Lily's application, for instance, can easily be implemented in phases, with the matching feature that compares pantry contents to the recipe database launched first. Company staff will be trained to enter and maintain the grocery and recipe databases, with the IT staff prepared to respond to tech support questions. Customers can start populating the system with the contents of their larders and retrieve recipes immediately. The online grocer's marketing team will favor this sequence because it offers a quick win in terms of competitive advantage. The customers will be more likely to come back once they devote all that effort to enter their own data. Later phases can add user comments, reviews, and targeted promotions to further boost loyalty.

MAINTENANCE

During the first weeks, dedicated support people are usually on call to resolve technical glitches, train users, correct documentation, and make sure everyone has access to all the functionality they need to accomplish their jobs. As things settle down, the system moves into maintenance mode, in which the regular help-desk team can provide support. Maintenance does not mean changes are not being made to the system, however. Most information systems continue to evolve to fix bugs and respond to changing conditions.

BUG FIXES AND CHANGE REQUESTS Despite extensive testing, no system with any complexity is bug-free. The test cases used to pound the system into shape touch on only a small subset of all the possible events and combinations. Once the system has gone live, users introduce more cases and bugs surface.

Bugs also arise because the surrounding technologies evolve. For instance, Internet Explorer, Firefox, Safari, and other browsers are constantly being upgraded to new versions. Sometimes those upgrades cause trouble in systems that were tested with earlier browser versions, which is why you often see notices that say, "works best with [browser name, version number]." Databases such as Oracle or SQL Server also upgrade to new releases, and migrating to the latest version can cause some components of the software to break.

Maintenance encompasses the work needed to support changing business requirements. In a merger, for instance, changes will be needed to incorporate new data or build new interfaces between two information systems. Each company might have a comprehensive database of suppliers, but they can't just be consolidated. The fields may not match, and there are probably many duplicates that have to be weeded out. For example, the merger between United and Continental Airlines created a long list of systems maintenance issues. Frequent flyer account balances and reward rules had to be harmonized, along with records on the two companies' airplane fleets. Creating a single roster of employees with accurate human resource records is another challenge, complicated by different union seniority rules that govern work assignments for pilots and other positions.[9]

PRODUCTIVITY TIP
When you find a bug in one of your organization's systems, immediately take a screen shot, write down what you were doing at the time, and add any details that might help the IT staff replicate it, such as the browser you're using and the version number. Forwarding this information is much more productive for you, IT, and the whole organization compared to calling with the vague report that "it isn't working."

parallel implementation
A type of implementation in which the new system is launched while the old one it is replacing continues to run so output can be compared

phased implementation
A type of implementation in which the modules of a new information system are launched in phases rather than all at once.

direct implementation
A type of implementation in which all the modules of a new information system are launched at the same time, and the old system is turned off; also called the "big bang" approach.

Changes in government regulations also drive systems maintenance. For example, when states began passing legislation that required organizations to notify customers affected by a breach of their personal information, companies raced to encrypt the data, whether it resided on servers, laptops, smartphones, backup media, or other places that might leave data exposed. As long as the data files are encrypted, the notification requirements do not apply.

Most systems continue to evolve as new features and enhancements are added after the initial launch. Lily plans to collect feedback from everyone who uses the "What to Make with What You Have" website to help her decide which features to add to make the site more compelling and effective.

To manage all the bug fixes and change requests, organizations put into place a **change control process**. IT staff help clarify the change requests and estimate the resources required to accomplish them. They then work closely with business units and executive management to determine priorities. Backlogs of these fixes can grow very long, especially as the system gets older.

WHEN INFORMATION SYSTEMS GROW OLD Unlike mechanical gear, software doesn't wear out with use. Information systems do age, however, and eventually need replacement. Over time the maintenance burden may grow very heavy. All the changes pile up inside the code, adding patches and work-arounds that turn what started as a streamlined and elegant racehorse into a lumbering behemoth. Maintenance projects needed to keep a system secure and up-to-date with the latest versions of the underlying technology are often deferred, as business units devote resources to new features that offer competitive advantage. Like an old house whose owners add a lovely rose garden rather than replace the faulty copper wiring, information systems accumulate hidden signs of aging. The systems become harder to adapt to changing business needs, and they can also present risk of catastrophic failure.

For example, almost every system needed considerable maintenance work to dodge the inevitable breakdowns associated with Y2K, the computing problem that loomed in the late 1990s. Most systems had been designed to store the year as a 2-digit field rather than four digits to save space on hard disk drives. Thus, as December 31, 1999, neared, maintenance teams devised ways to avoid confusion by increasing the field size or adding rules that determined whether "00," for instance, meant 1900 or 2000. But many organizations used the imminent event to replace their **legacy systems**, older systems built on aging or obsolete architectures that continue in use because they still function reasonably well and replacing them is costly.

✳ THE ETHICAL FACTOR Developing Systems That Promote Ethical Decision Making and Social Responsibility

Just as organizations can develop innovative information systems that streamline operations and build competitive advantage, they can build in requirements for new systems that promote ethical decision making and social responsibility. For instance, software can promote the goal of "going green" by automatically reminding employees of the environmental cost each time they choose to print out a document. Systems that track each user's print usage and provide frequent reports also achieve that goal because they increase individual accountability.

To promote ethical decision making in procurement, the software can automatically compare current prices offered by qualified suppliers. When the buyer can see the comparison and knows that others can see them, too, he or she is more likely to make an objective choice rather than favor a supplier whose sales rep brought a nice gift on the last call. Ensuring transparency about the details of any decision is a powerful tool to promote ethical behavior.

Employees can also be alerted with pop-up boxes or color coding whenever they view confidential information about customers as a reminder to avoid privacy breaches. Systems can prevent employees from downloading such data as well.

When managers develop the requirements for new information systems, they should consider what features might facilitate ethical decision making. While the systems must meet minimum compliance requirements, they can do much more toward promoting high ethical standards and corporate social responsibility.

Software Development Strategies

2 Describe three major software development strategies.

The system development life cycle (SDLC) describes an orderly progression from planning to maintenance and eventual replacement, with discrete steps in between. However, actual projects may deviate from a straightforward step-by-step approach, using alternative development methods. The SDLC aligns closely with the waterfall method, which we discuss first.

WATERFALL SOFTWARE DEVELOPMENT

In the **waterfall method**, the SDLC tasks occur sequentially, with one activity starting only after the previous one has been completed (Figure 11-8). The analysis phase nails down the requirements, and at that point the developers estimate the time and resources needed to complete the project. Programmers don't start writing any code until all the previous phases have been completed, including the detailed design. Different people may be engaged in each task, and they hand off their work to the next team when their part is done.

In theory, the progression continues forward from one task to the next. In practice, though, requirements often change after later stages have already begun, forcing the waterfall to run back uphill. The design has to be changed, and then the programming must be changed as well. Although the waterfall method has been used for decades, success rates are often quite disappointing, especially for large projects that take a long time to complete. Over the year or more that design and development are underway,

FIGURE 11-8

Waterfall method of software development.

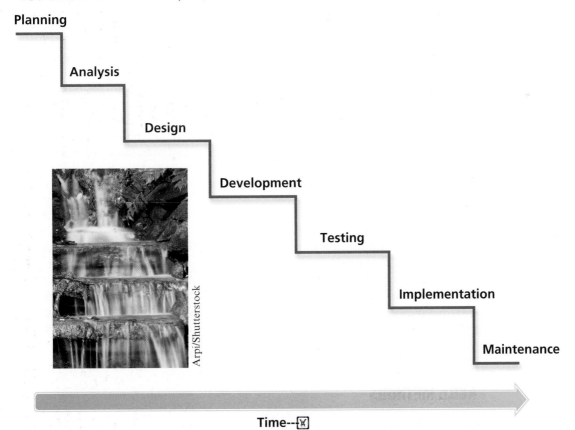

Planning

Analysis

Design

Development

Testing

Implementation

Maintenance

Arpi/Shutterstock

Time→

---

change control process
A process organizations use to manage and prioritize requests to make changes or add new features to an information system.

legacy systems
Older systems built on aging or obsolete architectures that continue in use because they still function reasonably well and replacing them is costly.

waterfall method
Method in which the systems development life cycle tasks occur sequentially, with one activity starting only after the previous one has been completed.

FIGURE 11-9

Task phases in an iterative software development approach, preparing for a release in six months.

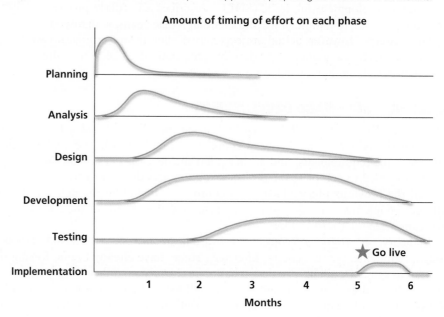

Amount of timing of effort on each phase

Planning

Analysis

Design

Development

Testing

Implementation

★ Go live

Months: 1 2 3 4 5 6

the organization's needs are quite likely to change, so the system the developers are building is already obsolete. The rework is costly and time-consuming, resulting in blown budgets and missed deadlines. These frustrations led to the development of alternative approaches that are better able to adapt to changes in the business landscape.

ITERATIVE METHODS

Iterative methods compress the time horizon for software development, partly to reduce the impact of changing business needs and the resulting rework. They focus on the time available until the next release, or iteration, and the development team determines how many of the requirements it can deliver in that timeframe. While the waterfall method estimates time and resources needed based on the analysis of requirements, the iterative methods do the reverse. Given available time and staffing, what features can we deliver?

Iterative approaches vary, but most incorporate the tasks in the SDLC rapidly, and they overlap. Figure 11-9 shows how the tasks might be undertaken for a project expected to release in six months. Notice how the tasks are sequenced, but they don't end before the next task begins. They extend for a longer period during the project compared to the waterfall approach.

A common approach used in iterative methods that helps software developers bring an application to life more quickly is called **rapid application development (RAD)**. Developers create a software prototype that they can share with users and get their feedback to make corrections and improvements before more time is spent building a fully functioning version. End users are much more helpful when they can see a prototype even if most of it doesn't actually work. The approach works well with the overlapping phases typical of iterative development, and it is often used in other software development approaches as well.

AGILE METHODS

Agile software development methods use a less structured approach in which tasks are not sequenced according to the SDLC. Instead, many activities occur simultaneously. The development team is typically very cohesive and usually collocated rather than geographically distributed as teams in a waterfall project might be. An agile team also includes one or more business users dedicated to the project. The duration for development, called the "time box," is quite short, often just two to six weeks.

FIGURE 11-10

The Agile Manifesto.

We value
▶ **Individuals and interactions** over processes and tools
▶ **Working software** over comprehensive documentation
▶ **Customer collaboration** over contract negotiation
▶ **Responding to change** over following a plan

In 2001, developers who were using various agile methods came up with a "manifesto" that clarifies how agile methods differ from more traditional approaches (Figure 11-10). Notice that key features include a very team-oriented approach that includes end users and an unconcern for strictly defined processes, written documentation, and contracts. Many different varieties of agile methods exist, but two that are widely used are Scrum and XP.

SCRUM   **Scrum** offers a framework for software development that relies on tightly knit, cohesive teams that do "sprints" of two to four weeks each. The customer's voice on the team is called the "product owner," and this person makes sure the project adds business value. He or she might be a marketing executive if the project involves customer relationships or a manager from finance if the new feature will improve the billing process. Lily would be the product owner for the "What to Make with What You Have" website. The project manager gets the colorful name of Scrum Master. The term "scrum" is actually a move in the sport of rugby, in which the team members pack together, acting in unison to get the ball down the field.

At the start of a sprint, the product owner describes and prioritizes the backlog of requirements for the software, and the team decides which ones are feasible for the next sprint. Once the team has confirmed the requirements, they are fixed for the sprint's duration so the team can get right to work. Short sprints, close collaboration, and daily meetings help ensure that developers don't work for months on a set of requirements only to face the waterfall problem: business needs have already changed. The goal is to have workable software with the new features at the end of each sprint.

EXTREME PROGRAMMING (XP)   **Extreme programming (XP)** is another team-based agile method that focuses on frequent releases of workable software and time boxes for development. The approach stresses four fundamental principles: coding, testing, listening, and designing, A project will start with user stories, often written on 3 × 5 index cards, and the team arranges these into a plan for the features that will be in the next software release.

A distinguishing feature of XP is that developers work in pairs, reviewing one another's work, providing each other with feedback and testing the code as it is written. The pair will sit side by side, viewing the same monitor and pushing the keyboard and mouse back and forth. As they apply their collective skills to the same code, they may come up with better programming approaches and also uncover bugs earlier. Paired programming is not a mentoring relationship, with one the teacher and the other the student. It is designed for equals who each bring well-developed skills to the task.

iterative methods
Strategies that compress the time horizon for software development, partly to reduce the impact of changing business needs and the resulting rework. They focus on the time available until the next release, or iteration, and the development team determines how many of the requirements it can deliver in that timeframe.

rapid application development (RAD)
A strategy in which developers quickly bring up prototypes to share with end users, get feedback, and make corrections before building the fully functional version.

agile software development
Development strategies involving cohesive teams that include end users, and in which many activities occur simultaneously rather than sequentially to accelerate delivery of usable software.

Scrum
An agile process for software development that relies on tightly knit, cohesive teams that do "sprints" of two to four weeks each.

extreme programming (XP)
A team-based agile method that features frequent releases of workable software, short time boxes, programmers who work in pairs, and a focus on testing.

XP's strong emphasis on testing is also an important feature, and one reason for its development was to improve software quality. Poor software quality costs the U.S. economy an estimated $59 billion annually, and more thorough testing can help reduce that waste.

Explain why organizations choose one software development strategy over another for particular projects. **3**

Comparing Software Development Approaches

How do organizations choose which method to use? While some developers are fanatical about one method or another, all can work well or poorly, depending on the situation and the people using them.

TYPE OF PROJECT

First, the choice of a development approach depends heavily on the type of project. For example, an iterative approach will work well for projects in which the requirements can be launched in discrete phases, as releases. The clarity of requirements can also affect the choice. A waterfall method can be used when the requirements are clear and stable and can be established in advance. When the end users aren't really sure about what they want, or the business is changing rapidly, an agile approach may well be best.

ORGANIZATIONAL CULTURE

The organization's culture is also an important element. Moving to an agile development approach means much more than programming in pairs or adopting the colorful Scrum vocabulary. It is a cultural shift that many development teams may find uncomfortable.[10] After years of using the waterfall method, for instance, developers are inclined to resist changes or additions to the requirements after the analysis phase has been done. They see it as rework, and they try to lock down the requirements through written documents, contracts, and user sign-offs. Agile methods need developers who welcome changes in requirements, because they understand that the ultimate goal is to develop software that users really want, not just to finish a project on time.

Another cultural shift is from the "me" mentality to "we." The waterfall method stresses sequenced tasks, so developers who complete their task on time consider themselves successful even if the project itself is falling behind. But agile teams are collectively responsible for delivery, and team members must help one another achieve the goal to be successful. The team must be cohesive and trusting, since each member's job and career may depend on the whole team's performance.

IS WATERFALL DEAD?

Excitement surrounding the nimble iterative and agile methods has led to predictions of doom for the traditional waterfall, but surveys show that the older approach is still widely used. Despite its spotty track record for delivering quality software on time and under budget, 75 percent of the respondents in one survey continue to use the waterfall method. Almost two-thirds indicate it is the approach they use most often.[11] One reason it persists is that business managers are comfortable with its logical and familiar structure. Developers are also adapting it to shorter time frames to better handle the inevitable changes in requirements that come late in the project. Those prolonged projects in which the software is delivered years after requirements were collected are, for the most part, a thing of the past.

The cultural challenges associated with agile methods are also larger than some organizations anticipate. They find that agile development needs more discipline, not less, especially for larger projects, and employees need coaching and time to adjust to a team-oriented approach. Some prefer not to make that switch.

The trend toward outsourcing development to external contractors keeps waterfall methodology in place as well. With a fixed-bid contract, the requirements phase determines the cost, and once contracts have been signed, the developers proceed with the remaining phases. Changes require negotiation over price increases.

Finally, organizations are increasingly adopting packaged solutions, especially for core business applications. The strengths that agile methods offer to respond to rapidly changing conditions are not needed for purchased software, but a structured approach is critical, as we discuss in the next section.

Software Procurement: The "Buy" Strategy

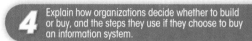

4 Explain how organizations decide whether to build or buy, and the steps they use if they choose to buy an information system.

As commercial software companies add more features and reduce licensing costs, organizations are increasingly considering the "buy" strategy, rather than custom development. Especially for business functions that don't offer very much competitive advantage, prepackaged software may be the best choice. The prepackaged options go beyond the commercial software products that an organization can license from the vendor and install on its own servers. They also include free, open-source software. The rapidly evolving software-as-a-service (SaaS) products described in previous chapters expand options still further. Organizations can lease just the subscriptions they need, and employees can access the cloud-based application with their web browsers or smartphone apps.

PROS AND CONS OF BUILD AND BUY

Figure 11-11 highlights the major pros and cons associated with custom systems development and prepackaged software. As mentioned earlier, prepackaged software that handles at least 75 percent of the organization's requirements could be an excellent choice. But the decision is really more complicated than that, and many factors should be considered. Strategic value, overall cost, time needed to deploy, the need for customization, and the availability of IT resources should all enter the equation.

THE PROCUREMENT PROCESS

Figure 11-12 shows the SDLC, including the steps organizations take when they decide to pursue a "buy" strategy.

RFI AND RFP During the early phases of the SDLC, IT staff and business users should be systematically exploring the landscape of prepackaged software that might fit the organization's needs. As the list of user requirements develops, they will send out a

---

FIGURE 11-11

Pros and cons of custom systems development and prepackaged software.

	Pros	Cons
Custom System Development	Is tailored closely to the organization's needs May offer strategic value that contributes to company's competitive advantage May not require employees to change their processes	Usually has higher overall cost Requires more time before going live Requires ongoing in-house maintenance, upgrades, and compliance
Prepackaged Software	Handles processes using industry best practices Requires shorter implementation time Usually carries lower cost Can include vendor's new features and maintains compliance requirements Works best for applications that offer few competitive advantages	Does not match all the organization's requirements Might overstate product's capabilities and vendor support Requires organization to change business processes and develop interfaces to other systems May not include new features needed by the organization May not fit enterprise architecture

FIGURE 11-12

SDLC including steps for the "buy" option.

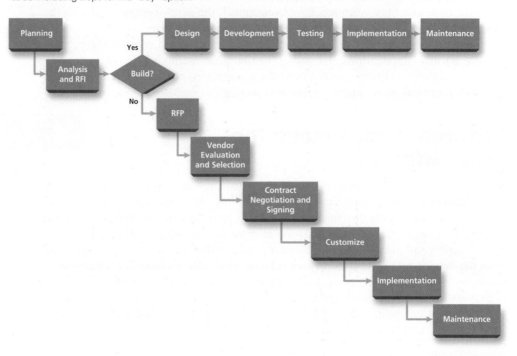

request for information (RFI) to a large number of potential vendors to serve as their initial market scan of the options. The RFI describes the new system in broad, high-level terms, and interested vendors send responses describing their products and services.

At this point, the steering committee decides whether to proceed with the design phase or buy. If the responses to the RFI and the committee's own research show some possible prepackaged options, the committee will develop a request for proposal (RFP), which is an invitation to software companies to submit a formal proposal, including a detailed description of their products, services, and costs. The RFP details the requirements that were developed in the analysis phase and also information about the organization's architecture, staffing, and other relevant details. This invitation is sent to the most promising commercial vendors and possibly also to companies that specialize in implementing open-source products.

Releasing an RFP does not commit the organization to the "buy" approach, and the steering committee may decide to custom-build the product after all. But the RFP provides the platform for vendors to compete fairly and present their best cases for meeting the organization's needs. The RFP process is also typically used to procure the services of a software development company to custom build the system, if the organization decides to outsource the project rather than build it in-house.

EVALUATING THE OPTIONS For large projects, especially ones that involve major systems for multinational corporations or large government agencies, the procurement process can be lengthy and complex. The bidders might offer many options with different prices, and as part of their bid they may include consulting companies that will serve as implementation partners.

The steering committee checks references, explores software demos, visits sites where the software products are in use, and narrows down the list. The finalists are invited to do presentations for the stakeholders, and the steering committee develops an evaluation strategy that prioritizes the criteria it will use to rate the solutions. For example, the spreadsheet in Figure 11-13 shows five weighted criteria. The stakeholders rate each vendor's responses on the criteria and start contract negotiations with the winning vendor.

The criterion "vendor architecture" deserves special attention because of the need to consider the overall enterprise architecture and the other systems the company is using. Some organizations choose a best of breed approach, in which they procure

FIGURE 11-13

Evaluating responses to an RFP on weighted criteria.

Weight	30%	20%	10%	20%	20%	100%
Scale (1=very poor to 5=very good)	Matches Requirements	Vendor Experience	Vendor References	Vendor Architecture	Cost	Totals
Commercial Software Vendor 1	5	3	2	1	1	2.7
Commercial Software Vendor 2	4	2	3	1	2	2.5
Open-Source Solution	2	1	4	2	4	2.4
SaaS	4	1	4	4	3	3.2

the best systems for each application regardless of the vendor. The CRM may be a cloud-computing solution, for instance, while the finance and human resources systems are on company premises and from a different vendor. With these different architectures, the firm must build interfaces that allow its systems to interact with one another and pass data back and forth.

Another approach is **unified procurement**, in which organizations strongly prefer systems that are offered by a single vendor, especially the one that supplies the ERP. Even if the ERP's customer relationship management system does not fit as well, the company chooses it over competitors to keep integration problems to a minimum and maintain a cohesive enterprise architecture.

ADAPTATION AND CUSTOMIZATION

When the packaged solution meets 75 percent or more of the organization's needs, what happens to the other 25 percent? One possibility is for the company to adapt its own processes to match what the software will support. Many vendors, especially the large ERP companies, strongly recommend this path, arguing that their software products build in the industry's best practices for standard processes, ones that stand the test of time and continue to evolve to meet changing needs. At Johns Hopkins, for example, employees in the medical institutions were paid every two weeks, which meant 26 paydays per year. But university employees were on a twice-monthly scheme, resulting in 24 pay periods. The ERP that was implemented to support the whole enterprise could not handle the two policies without customization, so a uniform payroll calendar was adopted.

Another possibility for that 25 percent is to customize the software, either by paying the software vendor or another company to do it or by making the code changes in-house. For processes that are not so easy for an organization to alter, or ones that support features that add strategic value and competitive advantage, customization may be the best approach.

The drawbacks to customization are not trivial, however, and managers should consider them carefully. Although tailoring some features to the organization's processes may make implementation easier, problems arise later. Adding customized code to a major software product can introduce errors that may not be discovered until well after going live, especially in large systems with tightly integrated modules.

request for information (RFI)
A request sent to software vendors containing a high level description of the information system an organization needs, so that vendors can describe their products that may fit.

request for proposal (RFP)
An invitation to software companies to submit a formal proposal, including a detailed description of their products, services, and costs. The RFP details the requirements developed in the analysis phase and also includes information about the organization's architecture, staffing, and other relevant details.

best of breed
An approach used by organizations in which they procure the best systems for each application, regardless of the vendor, and then build interfaces among them.

unified procurement
An approach used by organizations in which they prefer systems from a single vendor, especially to avoid the need to build interfaces.

The vendor may also refuse to support customized code it did not build. When bugs crop up, it is hard to tell whether the errors lie in the vendor's product, in the organization's custom-developed segments, or somewhere in between. Identifying just who is responsible for fixing the problem is important when support contracts are in place.

After implementation, the vendor will continue to upgrade the software with new releases to add features, correct bugs, improve security, and ensure compliance with current regulations. Organizations that add custom code have a major challenge with each new release, because they must add their customizations to the new version and test the whole system to make sure everything still works. In some cases, companies decide not to take advantage of a new release because of these headaches. Over time, the company's customized software drifts further and further behind the vendor's current offering, and the vendor may decide to drop support for the obsolete product. That leaves the organization entirely responsible. These lessons have been learned painfully over time, and most organizations wisely try to keep customization to a minimum.

Identify several ways in which the human element is important for systems development and procurement.	**5**

The Human Element in Systems Development and Procurement

The logical approaches to systems development and procurement described here do not always unfold quite so tidily. Communication on cross-functional teams, for instance, can be challenging.

CROSS-FUNCTIONAL TEAMS

Especially in the planning, analysis, and implementation phases, people who don't often work together will join cross-functional teams, and communication problems may arise. IT staff might not quite understand what the marketing team members mean when they talk about a system that will delight customers. And people in sales will scratch their heads when the IT person mentions RDDs or time boxes. Communication gaps and different priorities may also appear between different business units, such as marketing and accounting. The accounting people must ensure compliance, but marketing people may stress customer relationship management features. Whether the team decides to build or buy, the members will need to bridge the gaps to be successful.

During the planning and analysis phases, the cross-functional team members will try to describe how processes work and what the requirements for a new system should be. But most employees will only have a firm grasp on the part of a process that they deal with. They may find it challenging to design a system that can streamline the process from end to end and still satisfy all the requirements from accounting, finance, marketing, and sales. The exercise is often quite productive, though, as cross-functional teams with members from different parts of the company share knowledge and ideas. The analyst who leads this effort can promote this knowledge-sharing aspect of systems development, since it offers added benefits for the whole organization.

THE ROLE OF SENIOR MANAGEMENT

Senior managers play a key role in systems development and procurement, one that should stress the strategic value of the new information system to the organization. They can inspire employees to work together and ensure the resources the project team needs are available. Through their leadership, they can also prepare the organization for change.

However, senior managers can sometimes get involved in unproductive ways. For instance, the managing director of a an executive outplacement services company in the United Kingdom wound up influencing a purchasing decision by jumping into the process at the wrong time. The firm needed a client tracking system to help it deliver personalized service, and it started out with a dedicated project team tasked to gather requirements and investigate options. After several vendors showed ill-fitting products, the managers wanted to explore custom development. But when a very likable vendor rep presented his product, the managing director took control of the meeting and declared, "This system can do all we need…and more!" His decision had little to do with the project team's efforts or the company's needs and much more to do with outstanding salesmanship. Though the managers were far less impressed, they felt uncomfortable about expressing their views to a dictatorial boss. The software was not a good fit, and over a year later, the project was still stalled because the software needed so much customizing.[12]

The industry trend that promotes cloud computing and software as a service (SaaS) is affecting how decisions about systems development and procurement are actually made, and who makes them. Because IT support is not as much needed to manage servers or maintain software, some SaaS sales representatives bypass the CIO and make appointments with senior managers in finance, marketing, or other units. IT staff may have a long backlog of projects, so managers may decide to move ahead independently.

CIOs and senior managers in the business units must maintain close communication to implement cloud services wisely and securely, and to avoid the pitfalls of multiple independent systems that don't exchange data. Companies need master data management to deal with inevitable integration problems, as we described in Chapter 4. And they do need IT's help. For IT staff, the changes also take some adjustment. Mladen Vouk, head of IT at North Carolina State University, points out that for IT staff, letting go of tight control over corporate information systems "requires a cultural change that does not happen very easily."[13]

WORKING WITH CONSULTANTS

Implementing a new system, especially a large one from a commercial vendor, often means engaging consulting services to help configure, customize, and launch the software. The consultants might be employees of the software vendor or they might work for a separate company with expertise in that software product and a history of successful implementations in other organizations. The consultants can take on many roles to help make the project a success, such as those listed in Figure 11-14.

One advantage of engaging consultants is that it gives the organization access to experts who know the software well. Experienced consultants have seen how different companies implement the product most effectively, and they know where the trouble spots are. For example, some modules may need extra attention and training because the user interface is confusing, and others might have known bugs that require workarounds. The organization's own IT staff would not have this knowledge.

A special kind of consultant called a **systems integrator** has expertise in making the different hardware and software components of an information system work together. The components, such as scanners, servers, smartphones, software, and database, may all come from different vendors, and the systems integrator takes responsibility for making them function smoothly with one another.

Another advantage of consulting services is that the organization does not have to assign so many key people to the project full-time and then backfill their positions.

FIGURE 11-14

Common roles for information systems consultants.

- ▶ Requirements gathering and clarification
- ▶ Customization services
- ▶ Data cleansing and migration
- ▶ Software configuration
- ▶ Systems integration services
- ▶ Documentation
- ▶ User training
- ▶ Training of IT staff
- ▶ Project planning
- ▶ Communications
- ▶ Implementation support

systems integrator
A consultant who ensures that the hardware and software components of an information system work together when they come from different vendors.

The director of marketing, for example, can participate in a project to implement a CRM but still maintain oversight of the marketing unit.

Hiring consultants is not a cure-all, however, and disadvantages also exist. The organization's own employees will be less involved in many of the development and implementation tasks, so they will miss opportunities to learn the ins and outs of the software. They may also feel less ownership of the project and be less committed to all the changes that new processes will mean to their units.

Rancorous lawsuits are not uncommon when a project falters. For example, California's Marin County sued Deloitte Consulting for $30 million, accusing Deloitte of fraud when it claimed extensive knowledge of the ERP system the county was implementing. The county's suit states that the software was still not working four years after it went live and that Deloitte simply did not provide the skilled and knowledgeable people it claimed to have. Marin County insisted that Deloitte knew county employees had no expertise in this area and that Marin would be relying heavily on consultants to ensure the project's success. Deloitte countersued, filing a claim for an unpaid bill of more than $444,000, plus a hefty late fee. The consultants said the software was working fine when they left.[14]

The frequent need to engage consultants increases the value of an important skill information systems professionals need: contract management. The people who oversee such contracts will be negotiating terms and conditions, documenting any changes to the agreements, tracking progress, and ensuring that both the consulting company and the organization meet their obligations on time. The CIO and IT staff will help write the language for these contracts. They will also monitor the project and flag potential problems, since many IT-related tasks will not be familiar to business users. If the consultants are customizing the software and charging by the hour, the change control process will be especially important. Business managers will need a clear understanding of how changes in the requirements can escalate costs or delay the go-live date.

Regardless of whether the organization builds or buys the information system, successful implementation will depend heavily on effectively managing the project from start to finish. Dealing with budgets, timelines, escalating requirements, and the many "people" issues that go along with massive changes in the way the organization functions are all part of project management, and missteps are easy to make. The next chapter takes up this important topic, and how projects fit into the much larger picture of strategic planning.

MyMISLab | *Online Simulation*

Green Wheeling

A Role-Playing Simulation on Systems Development for a Fund-Raising Application

Green Wheeling! That's the campaign you're working on for a university, trying to raise funds from rich alums, donors, and corporate foundations. You get a list every week from the Development Office, and you try to contact each one to persuade them to help purchase a fleet of electric vehicles for student rentals so they don't need cars on campus.

The campaign is a mess. Your lists always have wrong numbers, or people who have never heard of the university. Yesterday, you visited a foundation that another rep had just contacted last week. The administration knows it needs an

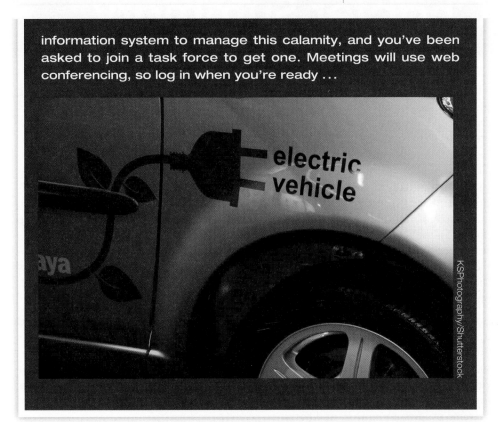

information system to manage this calamity, and you've been asked to join a task force to get one. Meetings will use web conferencing, so log in when you're ready …

KSPhotography/Shutterstock

Chapter Summary

Learning Objectives

1 The systems development life cycle (SDLC) includes seven steps. During the planning phase (1), the business need for the system is established and a feasibility study is conducted to ensure the project is feasible. In the analysis phase (2), the project team identifies the requirements for the system to create the requirements definition document (RDD), drawing process diagrams and listing features the system should support. The design phase (3) translates the RDD into a workable technical design, addressing issues such as data models, databases, usability, accessibility, and others. In the development phase (4), programmers translate the design into a working system, taking advantage of techniques such as version control and code review. During the testing phase (5), the unit modules are tested independently, and the whole system undergoes tests to ensure the units can work together properly. The system goes live in the implementation phase (6), which can be parallel, phased, or direct. Finally, the system enters the maintenance phase (7) in which bugs may continue to arise that need to be fixed, and the organization may choose to add enhancements.

2 Software development strategies include the waterfall method, iterative methods, and agile methods. In waterfall development, one phase of software development starts after the previous one has been completed. Iterative strategies compress the development process by focusing on the next release date and working only on features that can be included in that. The SDLC phases often overlap. Agile development methods are more unstructured, with activities occurring at the same time. Two examples are extreme programming (XP) and Scrum.

3 The choice of software development method depends on the type of project and the organizational culture. Agile methods require a team-oriented approach, for example. Waterfall methods are useful when organizations outsource development to external contractors.

4 The decision about whether to build or buy the system should consider whether a purchased system can handle at least 75 percent of the organization's requirements and whether the system is important for strategic reasons. Other factors include cost, time to market, architecture, and skill sets. Procurement usually starts with a request for information (RFI), followed by a request for proposal (RFP) to the leading candidates. The RFP process is also used to select a software development company to custom build the system, if the organization chooses to outsource the project.

5 The human element affects systems development and procurement, partly because people from different parts of the organization work together in cross-functional teams, and communication issues may arise. Senior managers should emphasize the system's strategic value and inspire employees to work together. Organizations are increasingly hiring consultants to assist with systems implementation, so information systems professionals need to develop effective contract management skills.

KEY TERMS AND CONCEPTS

systems development life cycle (SDLC)

feasibility study

requirements analysis

process diagrams

business process reengineering (BPR)

requirements definition document (RDD)

service-oriented architecture (SOA)

use case diagram

unified modeling language (UML)

version control software

code review

parallel implementation

phased implementation

direct implementation

change control process

legacy systems

waterfall method

iterative methods

rapid application development (RAD)

agile software development

Scrum

extreme programming (XP)

request for information (RFI)

request for proposal (RFP)

best of breed

unified procurement

systems integrator

CHAPTER REVIEW QUESTIONS

1. What are the seven phases of the systems development life cycle? What activities occur in each phase?

2. What is the waterfall method of software development? How do the SDLC tasks occur in this method of development? What are the success rates for systems developed using the waterfall method? Is the waterfall method dead? Why does the waterfall methodology persist despite its track record?

3. What is the iterative method of software development? How do the SDLC tasks occur in this method of development? What role does time play in this development methodology?

4. What is the agile method of software development? How do the SDLC tasks occur in this method of development? What role do teams play in agile software development? How does the time frame for agile development differ from that of iterative development?

5. Why do organizations choose one software development methodology over another? What are two factors that affect this decision? Why do organizations consider each of these factors when selecting a software development strategy?

6. What are the advantages and disadvantages of custom-building software?

7. What are the advantages and disadvantages of buying prepackaged software?

8. What rule of thumb do business analysts recommend for making the decision to buy or custom-build software? What other factors affect this decision?

9. What steps do organizations take when they decide to buy rather than build software? What activities occur in each step? How is an RFI different from an RFP? Does the logical approach to systems procurement always prevail? What are examples of ways in which the human element affects information systems procurement decisions?

10. Why are cross-functional teams needed for systems development and procurement? What kinds of problems might they experience?

11. What role should senior managers play in systems development and procurement?

12. What are the advantages and disadvantages of engaging consultants to assist with implementation? What kinds of skills do IS professionals need to work effectively with consultants?

PROJECTS AND DISCUSSION QUESTIONS

1. Lily's cookbook project faces some tough competition for the company's resources. She knows her coworkers, Stan and Rohit, are working on a proposal to incorporate a DVD rental feature on the company's website, and she needs to make a strong case for her "What to Make with What You Have" online cookbook if she wants approval for her project. You are on the steering committee that will help Lily in the planning phase, and your job is to help her identify and summarize the business need for the project. What are the major factors that support a business need and determine where to allocate funding for a systems development project? Which factors has Lily considered? Can you think of other potential benefits of this project? Are there any feasibility issues with this project? Prepare a brief summary of Lily's case that outlines the facts relating to the proposed online cookbook.

2. Consider Lily's online cookbook and describe the requirements for that system. Which requirements do you think are most important for Lily's website? Which are least important? Prepare a brief summary that prioritizes the requirements of Lily's online cookbook.

3. Recall from Chapter 3 that enterprise architecture describes the blueprint of the information technology

and organizational resources that are used to execute business processes. At what stage in the systems development life cycle do stakeholders determine the architecture they will use to build an information system? What is SOA? Visit YouTube.com and search for "infoclipz: service oriented architecture." View this 3-minute video and prepare a brief summary that includes a discussion of the benefits and challenges of SOA.

4. The first software bug was a moth. Really. Visit the Computer History Museum at www.computerhistory.org to learn how Grace Hopper, a rear admiral in the Navy, made history in the computer field with the first software bug. The rigorous testing that takes place during the development phase of the SDLC encompasses much more than looking for bugs. What are the six types of testing that may be performed in the development phase? What occurs in each test? How are scenarios used in the software testing process? How do software tools facilitate software testing? Is it a paradox to use software to test software?

5. If software doesn't wear out, which phase is generally the longest phase in the SDLC? Maintenance begins in the first few weeks of implementation and may last for many years until such time the system is

declared obsolete. For example, changes that occur at a university often require maintenance of the system. Describe the software modifications that might be needed if the university changed all the classes offered by a particular academic department to e-learning, so that no classrooms were needed. Describe the changes that might be needed to accommodate students who have more than one e-mail address.

6. Work with a small group of classmates to develop a process diagram that illustrates the steps necessary to register for a class at your university. Use standard flowchart notation to represent processing steps with rectangles, decisions with diamonds, and the ordering of steps (i.e., flow control) with arrows. Prepare a PowerPoint presentation of your process diagram to share with your class.

APPLICATION EXERCISES

EXCEL APPLICATION:
Jay's Bikes

Heather and Jay Madera started Jay's Bikes in the family garage. Cycling is their passion! They moved to their bicycle-friendly community because of its three great bike trails that were built by the city to promote tourism and strengthen the downtown area. Jay's Bikes' business is booming and now Heather and Jay are operating three retail stores with 18 full-time employees. The stores stock a wide range of bikes and apparel for both casual and professional riders, and they have become gathering points for local bike enthusiasts and tourists alike.

Jay is currently using an old version of point-of-sale (POS) software and he wants you to create the spreadsheet shown in Figure 11-15 to evaluate the alternatives for a new system. Jay has weighted the selection criteria according to his preferences. Create a formula to calculate the total weighted score for each

software alternative. Be sure to include a formula to calculate the total weight of all factors and use absolute cell references where appropriate. Based on the initial evaluation shown here, the best option for Jay's Bikes is SaaS for retail.

Questions

1. Which alternative scores highest if the "matches requirements" criterion is weighted at 50 percent and the "vendor architecture" is weighted at 0 percent?

2. Which alternative is best if the "matches requirements" criterion is weighted at 40 percent, "vendor architecture" is weighted at 0 percent, and "cost" is weighted at 30 percent?

3. Which alternative is best if the "matches requirements" criterion is weighted at 50 percent, "vendor architecture" is weighted at 0 percent, and "cost is weighted at 20 percent?

FIGURE 11-15

Vendor evaluation for Jay's Bikes POS system.

	A	B	C	D	E	F	G
1	Weight*	30%	20%	10%	20%	20%	100%
2	Alternatives	Matches Requirements	Vendor Experience	Vendor References	Vendor Architecture	Cost	Total
3	POS Vendor #1	5	3	2	1	1	2.7
4	POS Vendor #2	4	2	3	1	2	2.5
5	Open Source POS	2	1	4	2	4	2.4
6	SaaS for retail	4	1	4	4	3	3.2
7							
8	*Scale: 5 = very good, 1 = very poor						
9							

ACCESS APPLICATION:
Managing a Recipe Collection

Steve and Gail Horton are cooking enthusiasts who want to use a database to manage their collection of recipes. They have asked you to help them create the Access database shown in Figure 11-16. Use the information provided in the

Horton spreadsheet Ch11Ex02 to create and populate the tables. Create a report that lists the vegetarian recipes first, in descending order by the number of servings. Include the recipe ID number and the recipe name. Review the tables in the database and suggest other reports that Steve and Gail would find useful.

FIGURE 11-16

Managing a recipe collection with Access.

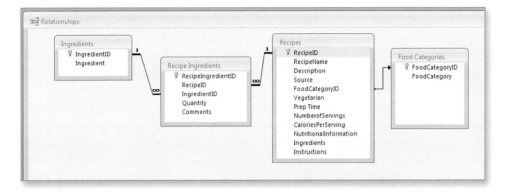

CASE STUDY #1

Baby Steps Toward Scrum: How Babycenter.com Made the Cultural Transition to Agile Software Development

Babycenter.com's website pioneers some of the most interactive and engaging tools for parents and parents-to-be, with birth announcements, customized pregnancy calendars, a baby names finder, e-mails timed to child development stages, and tips to help parents survive an 8-hour plane ride with children. Like many Internet companies, however, it started in a very fragile, understaffed, and chaotic development environment. Its network operations team consisted of just three people, and programming staff spent 85 percent of their time fighting fires and fixing bugs. Priorities for developing the site's new features kept changing, and attempts to use the waterfall method were frustrated by delays in nailing down requirements and delivering design specs.

Something had to change. While recovering from back surgery, the company's VP for engineering read about agile development, particularly Scrum. Intrigued, he handed out copies of *Agile Software Development with SCRUM*[15] and started a pilot project. The Scrum team held daily standup meetings, usually 15 minutes or less. The "product owner," who was the business manager from the department requesting the new features, collaborated closely with the developers to prioritize requirements. The pilot worked well, but the company's developers continued to struggle with competing priorities, complaining that they were splitting their time 50/50/50: "I'm spending 50% of my time on Project X, 50% on Project Y, and 50% on Project Z." Developers were still racing between projects and maintenance activities, and most were engaging in "cowboy coding," bypassing access controls and good programming practices to quickly fix bugs and get at least a few new features installed.

In the next phase, the VP demanded a more disciplined approach, blocking the developers out of the production system and drawing on Scrum principles. The most wrenching cultural change was management's drive to clear the company's backlog of requirements and establish priorities based on their strategic value or return on investment. Previously, business stakeholders would individually bring ideas to the developers, who did their best to decide which to work on first. The shift to using strategic value and ROI to prioritize projects dismayed managers whose requirements were pushed down the list, but it ensured that developers would work on high-value projects rather than managers' personal agendas. Now developers could say, "Sorry, that's not on my sprint. Go see the product owner."

More Scrum features were adopted, such as the full-time assignment of a product owner and at least two developers on every team. Product owners had to become accustomed to deeper involvement in the features they were requesting, attending the standup meetings and working much more closely with the software than before. Some of the developers had been used to the freedom of choosing which projects they thought were important, but they came to appreciate the value of Scrum's structure.

The Scrum sprints provided another way to add discipline to Babycenter's software development environment. Managers came to respect the planning meetings because they knew that requirements are fixed once the sprint starts. They also took more pains to review the software early, to avoid winding up with something that wasn't what hey wanted, but couldn't change for at least two weeks.

BabyCenter started with baby steps, but gradually it put into place a highly disciplined agile development environment that ensures its software projects align with business goals. The results speak for themselves. CEO Tina Sharkey says there "really isn't another parenting site…that thoroughly reaches this new generation of consumers." The site has registrations for more than 50 percent of babies born in the United States, and BabyCenter is launching a new voice messaging program for expectant mothers in India. "India's birthrate of 20 million babies a year made it a huge market for us," Sharkey said.

Discussion Questions

1. Describe the previous software development process at Babycenter.com.

2. Describe the new software development process at Babycenter.com. How has the software development process changed?

3. What cultural changes were required for Babycenter.com employees to adapt to the new software development process?

4. What might Babycenter.com business stakeholders and developers not like about the new software development process? How could Babycenter.com executives respond to these concerns?

SOURCES: Benton, E. (March 25, 2010). Tina Sharkey, CEO of BabyCenter. *Fast Company*. Nottonson, K., & DeLong, K. (2008). *Crawl, walk, run: 4 years of agile adoption at BabyCenter.com*. AGILE '08 Conference. Nottonson, K., & DeLong, K. (2008). Baby steps: Agile transformation at BabyCenter.com. *IT Professional*. 10(5), 59–62. Schwaber, K., & Beedle, M. (2004). *Agile software development with SCRUM*. Saddle River, NJ: Prentice Hall.

CASE STUDY #2

eXtreme Programming at the U.S. Strategic Command

The agile software development method called eXtreme Programming (XP) has its enthusiasts and detractors, and the jury is still out on when, or even whether, it is a better choice compared to other agile or traditional methods. Mindful of how important agility is for military software, the U.S. Strategic Command launched a pilot XP project.

XP shares many principles in common with Scrum and other agile methods, including the early and continuous delivery of functionality, close collaboration between developers and end users, and responsiveness to changing requirements. XP developers are less plan-driven and do much less documentation to define requirements. XP also features "pair programming," in which two developers work together on the same computer.

For the military project's pilot, the XP team's job was to add new search functionality to SKIWeb, the Command's strategic knowledge and information website used to share information about military operations and world events across the whole command and intelligence communities. All team members were contractors, except for the government functional manager who served as user collaborator. The two programmers sat next to one another in a cubicle, and the user collaborator's office was on the same floor. Other team members were either in the same building or nearby, so no one was participating in virtual mode.

The project got off to a rocky start when one of the two developers announced that she'd tried pair programming before and wasn't willing to do it again. The team didn't try to enforce it, but did encourage her to work closely with her programming partner to solve thorny logic problems together. Other agile practices were welcomed and adopted easily. For instance, the practice of delivering frequent small releases rather than infrequent major ones was already in place. Having the customer on-site is another critical element, and the user collaborator was right down the hall.

The daily meetings were very successful, but problems in work assignments and communications arose. XP team members are supposed to be fully assigned to the project to avoid distractions, but this project's team members were often pulled off for other assignments or emergencies. Midway through, they found they needed someone with expertise in interface design, but that person was skeptical about joining the XP project and communication suffered. One team member complained that there was resistance to change from a traditional hierarchy to the more collaborative XP style of communication.

Research with undergraduates suggests that paired programmers do about as well as the best performer of the pair, but no better, raising doubt about whether "two heads are better than one" for programming tasks. However, the students enjoyed the programming task more when working in pairs, and the weaker member gained some confidence. In the U.S. Strategic Command's pilot, the team members' perceptions about the project were also positive, despite the snags. They believed that the XP approach led to very good quality software, even better than the team might have produced using the old approach. Perhaps a boost to enjoyment and the value of training new programmers are important to XP's popularity, and to the overall enthusiasm of XP developers.

Discussion Questions

1. How did the U.S. Strategic Command adjust to unexpected issues as it implemented eXtreme programming?

2. What types of changes accompany the eXtreme programming methodology?

3. Why could a methodology such as eXtreme programming be good for a military project? What might be its disadvantages?

4. Does the research mentioned at the end of the case study influence your view of XP?

SOURCES: Balijepally, V., Mahapatra, R., et al. (2009). Are two heads better than one for software development? The productivity paradox of pair programming. *MIS Quarterly.* 33(1), 91–118. Fruhling, A., McDonald, P., et al. (2008). A case study: Introducing eXtreme programming in a U.S. government system development project. *Proceedings of the 41st Hawaii International Conference on Systems Science.* www.computer.org/portal/web/csdl/doi/10.1109/HICSS.2008.4, accessed June 11, 2011.

E-PROJECT 1   Watching Babycenter.com Change Over Time with the Internet Archive

The Internet archive (www.archive.org) is a nonprofit organization that builds the Internet's library, the "wayback machine." Copies of websites are archived at intervals for researchers, historians, and scholars. In this e-project you will take a look at Babycenter.com's website at different stages. (The archive doesn't maintain all the images and graphics, so often a page will not be displayed correctly; some links won't work.)

Visit www.archive.org and retrieve the historical files for www.babycenter.com.

Right-click on each of the following dates one at a time, and open each page in a new window to make it easier to compare.

February 8, 2004
February 4, 2006
February 2, 2008

(The archive sometimes removes pages, so if any date is not available, choose one that is reasonably close so you can see a sample every two years.)

Open another window with the current website for www. babycenter. com.

1. How has the website changed over this time period? What new features or services were added or removed?

2. What advantages does Scrum offer to the development of this website?

E-PROJECT 2   Analyzing Software Defect Rates Using Excel

Excel is a useful tool to analyze data from software development. In this e-project, you will analyze the pattern of software defects that are identified on each day of a 14-day programming project. Download the Excel file called Ch11_SoftwareDefects.

For each type of graph or chart you create, copy the image to the worksheet labeled Output, so you will be able to compare them at the end of the e-project.

1. Create a line graph that shows the number of severe defects on each day of the 14-day period. The x-axis should show the day number, and the y-axis should be labeled "Number of Severe Defects."

2. Now create another line graph that shows Minor Defects. One way to do this is to hide the "Severe" column by right-clicking at the top of the B column and click Hide.

(To unhide, select Columns A and B, right-click again, and choose Unhide.)

3. Next, create a stacked-column chart, and include Severe, Minor, and Total Defects.

4. Create another version of your stacked-column chart so that it only includes Severe and Minor Defects.

5. Create a clustered bar chart using Severe, Minor, and Total Defects columns.

6. Create a 100% stacked area chart using Severe, Minor, and Total Defects columns.

7. Compare the pros and cons of the different representations for this data set. Which representations do you think developers will find most useful? Which one do you think could be misleading to developers?

CHAPTER NOTES

1. Eggen, D., & Witte, G. (August 18, 2006). The FBI's upgrade that wasn't. *Washington Post*.

2. Duffy, J. (June 18, 2010). Unified communications saves Canadian school district $200K/year. *NetworkWorld*.

3. Sheridan, B. (February 14–20, 2011). Innovator Alberto Cavallo. *Bloomberg Businessweek*. p. 36.

4. Nuttall, C. (March 4, 2010). RealNetworks settles lawsuits. *Financial Times* (London).

5. Hammer, M. (July/August, 1990). Reengineering work: Don't automate, obliterate. *Harvard Business Review*. pp. 104–112.

6. Ozcelik, Y. (2010). Do business process reengineering projects payoff? Evidence from the United States. *International Journal of Project Management*. 28(1), 7–13.

7. Havenstein, H. (2008). Target pact won't lead to web access standards. *Computerworld*. 42(37), 18.

8. Kentico plants a tree for every bug found by their clients. *PRWeb.com*. www.prweb.com/releases/2011/03/prweb5194854.htm, accessed June 11, 2011.

9. Schlangenstein, M., et al. (2010). United and Continental reach for the sky. *Bloomberg Businessweek*. (4178), 19–20.

10. Hotle, M., & Norton, D. (2010). The cultural transition to agile methods: From "me" to "we." Gartner Research.

11. Light, M. (December 18, 2009). How the waterfall methodology adapted and whistled past the graveyard. Gartner Research.

12. Howcroft, D., & Light, B. (2010). The social shaping of packaged software selection. *Journal of the Association for Information Systems*. 11(3), 122–148.

13. How CIOs can manage cloud adoption outside the IT department. TechTargetNZ.com.au. http://searchcio.techtarget.com.au/articles/41111-How-CIOs-can-manage-cloud-adoption-outside-the-IT-department, accessed April 20, 2010.

14. Krigsman, M. (June 3, 2010). Marin County sues Deloitte: Alleges fraud on SAP project. *ZDNet*. http://www.zdnet.com/blog/projectfailures/marin-county-sues-deloitte-alleges-fraud-on-sap-project/9774, accessed June 11, 2011.

15. Schwaber, K., & Beedle, M. (2004). *Agile software development with SCRUM*. Upper Saddle River, NJ: Prentice Hall.

Project Management and *Strategic Planning*

Chapter Preview

PROJECTS THAT INVOLVE INFORMATION SYSTEMS NEED SKILLED OVERSIGHT, and poor project management is often the reason new information systems go awry. This chapter explores the phases of a project from the beginning, in which a plan is first developed, through the processes used during each phase. You will also learn about the project manager's role and the software tools that help track progress on tasks, work assignments, and expenses.

Strategic planning charts the course for all the organization's information system resources and all the people who will use them. It lays out the guiding principles and vision, showing how the organization's strategies align with its goals. The strategic plan is not just a list of projects or a tally of anticipated hardware expenses. It is the road map that clarifies how information systems contribute to the company's mission and strategy for the future, and what needs to be done to protect the organization's assets and ensure its success. The human element plays a large role in strategic planning, and the chapter includes examples of the human biases and tendencies that affect the process.

© Emmanuel LATTES / Alamy

Learning Objectives

1 Define a project, and explain how time, cost, and scope affect it.

2 Describe the five processes of project management.

3 Explain how project management software helps managers plan, track, and manage projects.

4 Identify the main factors that cause projects to succeed or fail.

5 Explain the importance of strategic planning for information systems, and provide examples.

6 Explain how the human element affects strategic planning.

Introduction

Reaction was mixed at the largest privately owned medical clinic in Georgia when the doctors, nurses, and staff learned of the project to implement electronic medical records (EMR). The CEO was solidly behind the project, seeing it as an important strategic initiative that would improve patient care and generate significant cost savings. But the $3 million effort dragged on, falling further and further behind. While primary care physicians embraced the new workflow that required them to key in patient information rather than write it by hand, others balked. Endocrinologists, cardiologists, and most top specialists found the system aggravating and unsuitable for their work, but their buy-in was essential for the project's success.[1] The CIO lamented that managing the project was more difficult than he imagined, and he is not alone.

Although this initiative eventually limped to a successful conclusion, projects that involve developing and implementing information systems are notoriously prone to delays, and even outright failure.[2] The root cause has less to do with software glitches, although bugs may certainly be hiding behind the user-friendly interfaces. Many projects intended to implement information systems struggle because of weak project management.

Define a project, and explain how time, cost, and scope affect it.

What Is a Project?

Successful project management starts with knowing what a project is and what it isn't. A **project** is a temporary activity that is launched for a specific purpose, to carry out a particular objective. Figure 12-1 lists common characteristics for most projects, from landing a spacecraft on Mars to running for political office. Launching virtually any new information system, whether it is EMR for a hospital or a web portal for customers, is a project.

PROJECTS VS. PROCESSES

Projects are temporary, with their own budgets, timelines, and sponsor. In contrast, a business process is a series of events designed to deliver a product or service that is repeated over and over. Projects are unique, but processes are recurring. For instance, publishing the next edition of a monthly magazine is not a project, even though all the stories are new, along with the cover photo, ads, images, and puzzles. It is a process in which the managing editors regularly repeat tasks such as assigning stories, proofreading copy, designing graphics, and scheduling print runs. Projects are one of a kind, and they involve uncertainty. People are doing things that are new to them, so their predictions about how long tasks will take may be well off the mark. In contrast, a process should be tweaked so that the underlying activities are streamlined, efficient, predictable, and cost effective. Figure 12-2 contrasts the tasks involved in a unique project to open a new restaurant and a frequently repeated procurement process.

Consider a wedding, and all the activities that go into organizing the flowers, refreshments, entertainment, invitations, seating plan, and other details. In some families, the bride's mother might be the project manager for the event, and she wisely treats it as a unique project. The wedding is a temporary endeavor with a unique purpose, and it meets all the other criteria for a project. Almost every task is new for mom. But to a professional wedding planner who handles dozens of events a year, the activities fall into several familiar processes—contracting with florists, hiring the photographer, renting the hall, and printing the invitations, for example. Without having to reinvent every wheel for each matrimonial, the planner develops standardized processes and can also take advantage of price discounts for larger volumes. A photographer, for example, would likely offer lower prices for the promise of steady work.

FIGURE 12-1

Common characteristics of a project.

A project

- ▶ is a temporary endeavor
- ▶ has a specific, unique purpose
- ▶ has a primary customer or sponsor, as well as stakeholders
- ▶ requires resources, staff time, and expertise from different areas
- ▶ includes an element of uncertainty
- ▶ has metrics for success

FIGURE 12-2

Projects vs. processes.

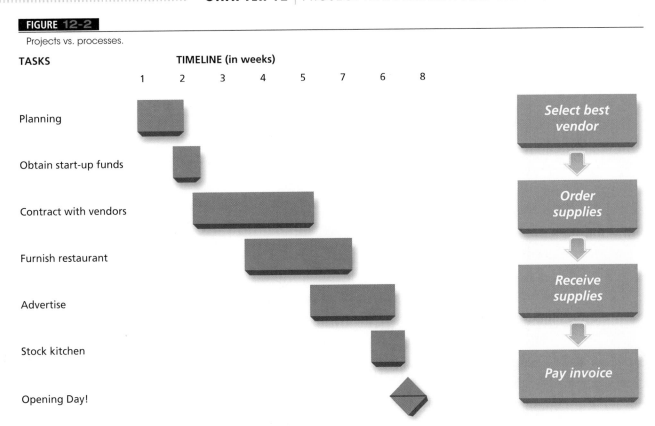

PROJECT: Opening a new restaurant

PROCESS: Procuring office supplies

Project management skills are essential for projects incorporating information systems. But many activities in IT are business processes that repeat, and they should be made as streamlined, routine, and cost-effective as possible. Help-desk support, information system maintenance, software updates and patch installation, user training, and backups are all processes, not projects.

THE TRIPLE CONSTRAINT: TIME, COST, AND SCOPE

Every project is constrained by three fundamental forces: time, cost, and scope. These three are interrelated, and if one changes, the others are affected (Figure 12-3). For example, when an electronic medical records project meets resistant physicians, the CEO may approve customizations for them, thus increasing the project's scope. This results in higher cost and longer time to deploy.

Often one of the constraints is fixed for a particular project, so the other two forces must be adjusted if change is needed. For a project proposal requesting $150,000, a manager might say $100,000 is the limit, not a penny more—thus fixing the costs. To stay within budget, the project's scope can be reduced. In some situations, the time constraint is critical. New financial information systems usually must launch at the beginning of the fiscal year. Though it isn't impossible to launch a financial system in midyear, it is far more complicated and costly, so managers face tough decisions when the go-live date nears. Costs may go up for more overtime and additional consultants. Training time may be cut to the bone, and any nonessential software features might be abandoned to avoid having to wait another year to go live. To implement its ERP on the cutover date, one state government agency went live with almost no accounting reports yet available.

PRODUCTIVITY TIP

You can improve your own productivity by distinguishing between projects and processes, and by better managing the projects using the information in this chapter. You can also find ways to streamline the processes. For term papers, for example, create templates with standard headers, footers, and naming conventions, and develop streamlined strategies for organizing your references. Don't treat everything as a unique project.

project
A temporary activity launched for a specific purpose, to carry out a particular objective.

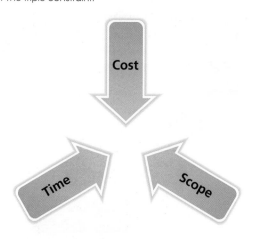

FIGURE 12-3

Time, cost, and scope: The triple constraint.

A frustrated budget analyst said, "With no reports, it's like driving wearing a blindfold." The alternative, though, might have been to spend another year using the legacy system.

Describe the five processes of project management. **2**

Project Management

As the theme park's newly hired assistant director for social media, Stan M. was eagerly anticipating his first assignment. The park's mammoth new waterslide, the largest in the region, is scheduled to open at the start of the summer, and the CEO wants a blockbuster social media campaign to promote it. With a background in business and information systems, Stan knows that managing a project like this without a plan is like launching a Broadway musical with no score and no script, so he gets to work.

Project management is a systematic approach to project planning, organizing, and managing resources, resulting in a project that successfully meets its objectives. It requires knowledge and skills in many areas, and a clear understanding of the processes that underlie a successful project.[3]

THE FIVE PROJECT MANAGEMENT PROCESSES

Every project has five underlying processes that require management, beginning with the very first stage in which the project is conceived. Each process becomes more intense at certain phases of the project, as shown in Figure 12-4.

▶ Initiating
▶ Planning
▶ Executing
▶ Monitoring and controlling
▶ Closing

INITIATING The **initiating processes** lay the groundwork for the project by clarifying the value it will bring to the organization, setting its objectives, and estimating the project's length, scope, and cost. Projects might be proposed by different people, but in this early phase managers should identify the major players in the project, including the sponsor, the project manager (PM), the team members, and other stakeholders.

A key document that authorizes the project is the **project charter**. The charter shows that the project has the commitment and support of senior management, an essential element for success. It should also include a clear statement of objectives, estimated start and end dates, the names of the relevant people and their

FIGURE 12-4

FIGURE 12-4

The five project management processes.

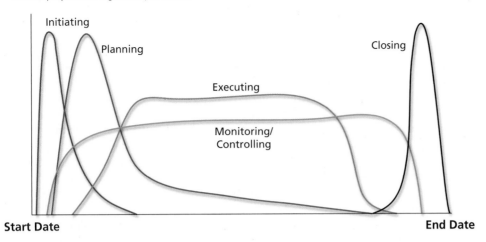

roles, a tentative budget, criteria for success, and any other pertinent information to get the project off to a good start. Although many managers might depend on less formal e-mails to authorize a project, or assume that some comments made at a meeting should get things rolling, those approaches put a fledgling project on shaky footing. If the manager leaves or decides to reassign a key team member, the project could be left hanging. The charter helps to avoid unexpected surprises later, but still leaves room for changes to best meet the organization's needs. Stan was burned in the past when he failed to get management's clear commitment and sign-off on a project, so he drafted the simple charter shown in Figure 12-5. More complex and costly projects will have charters with more detail that go through several versions before formal signoff.

FIGURE 12-5

Sample project charter.

Project: Social Media Campaign for The Wild River Waterslide Ride

Start and End Dates: April 2 – June 30

Key Participants:

▶ Project Manager: Stan M.
▶ Sponsor: Consuela T., Director of Marketing
▶ Estimated budget: $38,000 (includes personnel salaries)
▶ Team Members:
   ▶ Bailey L., Programmer/Analyst
   ▶ John C., Copywriter
   ▶ Lucinda V., IT Support

Project Objectives: Develop, launch, and track a social media campaign to promote the waterslide throughout the region. The goal is a 20% increase in number of park visitors from June 15 to July 15, compared to the same period last year. Additional metrics will include (1) web analytics on the blog and other online assets, such as percent change in the number of video views and unique visitors, and (2) survey of Wild River riders to determine how they learned about the ride.

Project Approach: With IT's support, launch a blog containing comments, images, and videos of employees and guests who experience the ride before opening. Post videos to YouTube and distribute links to popular bookmarking sites. Invite loyal customers who maintain their own blogs to a "Wild River Preview" day. Capture leads from the blog by offering discount coupons.

Signatures:

project management
A systematic approach to project planning, organizing, and managing resources, resulting in a project that successfully meets its objectives.

initiating processes
Processes that lay the groundwork for the project by clarifying its business value; setting its objectives; estimating the project's length, scope, and cost; identifying team members; and obtaining approval.

project charter
A document that authorizes a project that includes a clear statement of objectives, estimated start and end dates, the names of the relevant people and their roles, a tentative budget, criteria for success, and other pertinent information.

Another initiating process is the kickoff meeting, where the stakeholders meet one another, sometimes for the first and only time. Led by the project manager, the team reviews the charter and discusses next steps.

PLANNING The **planning processes** should start very early with the overarching **project management plan**. This will be the road map and guide for executing the project, and it describes the components needed to ensure success. The plan will include an organizational chart, a detailed description of the work to be performed, information about the schedule, details about meetings and reviews, success metrics, and notations about any information systems or project monitoring tools that will be used. It should also identify the **deliverables**, which are the products, documents, or services that will be delivered to the sponsor during the course of the project. For Stan's project, those will include the new blog and website, video clips, mass e-mails, a Facebook page, sample Twitter output, and reports showing the analytics on page views and other metrics. Given the uncertainty that is part of any project, the plan should include steps stakeholders take to make changes and get them approved.

The project management plan touches on several areas that affect all projects, and for larger ones, some of the areas need subplans of their own. For example, project scope always needs careful attention, so the project manager may create a separate scope management plan that explains how the scope will be clarified, approved, and changed to ensure all stakeholders have some input. Given their varying needs and requirements, stakeholders may quarrel over what is inside or outside the project scope, advocating for the features they prefer. A strategy that everyone agrees upon in advance will help resolve such disputes and avoid **scope creep**, in which features are added in an uncontrolled way, often without considering the impact on the budget or timeline.

The project management plan will also include strategies for managing time, quality, human resources, communications, cost, risk, and overall integration, as shown in Figure 12-6. The project manager might work with the project team to create separate documents for each of these, depending on the project's size and complexity.

Several documents are especially critical to the planning process, such as the scope statement, which clarifies the scope and provides a work breakdown structure (WBS). This is an orderly listing of actual tasks that the project team must complete to produce the project's deliverables. Another is the **Gantt chart**, which lists the tasks on the WBS along with each task's projected start and finish dates in graphical format (Figure 12-7). The bars graphically show the sequence of tasks and their duration. Diamonds indicate milestones for the project.

These documents, along with many other planning and tracking aids, are typically generated through project management software, described in a later section.

FIGURE 12-6

Project management planning areas with sample outputs.

Area	Description	Sample Outputs
Integration	Overall management of the project	Project charter; project management plan
Scope	Clarifying what work is part of the project, and what is not	Scope statement; work breakdown structure; scope management plan
Time	Ensuring the project meets its deadlines	Project schedule; Gantt chart; critical path analysis; time management plan
Cost	Determining the budget, analyzing any need for changes, and ensuring the project's costs are tracked and managed properly	Cost estimate; running expenses; net present value analysis; return on investment analysis; cost management plan
Quality	Ensuring the project deliverables meet quality standards for the project	Quality standards, project metrics; quality management plan
Human resources	Managing the people involved in the project, motivating stakeholders, allocating tasks, monitoring workloads	Project organizational chart; assignment matrix; human resources management plan
Communications	Providing updates and status reports to stakeholders; presenting project to sponsor(s)	Status reports; meetings; project dashboard; website; communications management plan
Risk	Managing risks that may impact the project; implementing mitigation strategies	Risk management plan; risk register

FIGURE 12-7

Gantt Chart for the Wild River Waterslide social media campaign.

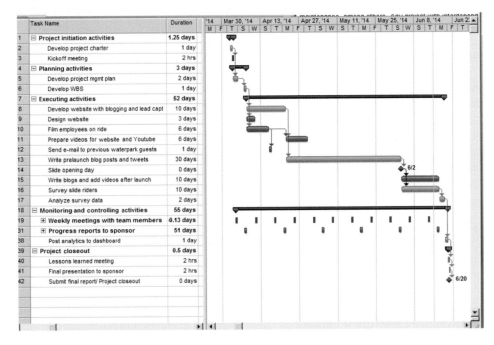

Key:

Bars show the projected start and end dates for tasks.

Red bars indicate tasks along the critical path.

Black diamonds indicate project milestones.

Connecting arrows indicate the sequence for tasks.

EXECUTING **Executing processes** include all the coordinating efforts that ensure the tasks on the WBS are carried out properly. For the project manager, tasks to execute include communicating with stakeholders, allocating work assignments, negotiating contracts, coaching team members, holding meetings, writing updates, doing presentations for the board, conducting research, and much more. The best project managers, however, spend a little more time on the other processes—especially planning—and a little less on executing. Inexperienced project managers often try to do everything themselves rather than learn how to manage the project by painstaking planning, delegating, and team building.

MONITORING AND CONTROLLING **Monitoring and controlling processes** track progress from start to finish, pinpointing any deviations from the plan. The project manager pays close attention to reports and dashboards that might show early warning signs that some tasks have fallen behind. If a team member is sick during a critical phase, the project manager must find a way to fill in or defend a delay in the schedule.

planning processes
The processes in project management that focus on planning how the project will be executed.

project management plan
The road map and guide for executing a project that includes information such as an organizational chart, a detailed description of the work to be performed, information about the schedule, details about meetings and reviews, success metrics, and notations about any information systems or project monitoring tools that will be used.

deliverables
The products, documents, or services that will be delivered to the sponsor during the course of a project.

scope creep
A term that refers to the way in which features are added in an uncontrolled way to a project, often without considering the impact on the budget or timeline.

Gantt chart
A graphic showing the tasks on the work breakdown structure along with each task's projected start and finish dates.

executing processes
All the coordinating efforts that ensure the tasks on the work breakdown structure are carried out properly.

monitoring and controlling processes
Processes that track a project's progress from start to finish, pinpointing any deviations from the plan that must be addressed.

Most tasks on the WBS have **predecessors**, which are the other tasks that must be completed before the particular task can begin. For example, Stan wants to have the project charter done before he holds the kickoff meeting, so the charter task is a predecessor of the meeting. In Figure 12-7, the connecting arrows show the predecessors. Other tasks are less dependent on previous activity, so they can be undertaken at various times throughout the project.

The **critical path**, shown in red in Figure 12-7, is the longest path through the project, and it identifies those tasks that can't be delayed without affecting the finish date. In Stan's project, the IT department has to build the website with blogging capabilities before the blog can launch, so the website is a predecessor of the blog. Both of these tasks are red, indicating that they are on the critical path. They both have to start and finish right on schedule if the project is to complete on time. In contrast, the task in which employees film themselves on the ride could slip a bit without affecting the schedule, so that task is in blue, indicating it is not on the critical path. Monitoring tasks that fall along the critical path is especially important.

CLOSING **Closing processes** will formally end the project in an orderly way. The sponsor may need to sign off that all deliverables have been received and accepted, and the team members may be reassigned to their regular jobs. Usually the project manager holds a final meeting with the team to celebrate (or mourn).

The closing phase should also include a process that documents the lessons learned from the project, so the experience can benefit other project teams and add to the organization's knowledge base. Stan and his team will have much to say about how to make social media work better the next time, and also how to better manage any project for the theme park. John might want to alert managers that plan approvals took so long the team couldn't start the project until its success was in jeopardy. Bailey may praise the CEO for rock-solid support, essential to the project's overall success.

Unfortunately, many organizations neglect the lessons-learned component of closing processes. One man who worked on a product development team at an auto company in the United Kingdom explains why:

> "Occasionally people will come by and they will ask for lessons learnt, but when you are struggling with a lot of issues, a high-level workload, and not a lot of resources, to be honest lessons learnt get prioritized at the bottom of the list, and if you do anything on lessons learnt it is really only five or ten minutes worth of effort."[4]

Team members have little incentive to spend more time documenting the lessons learned for the organization. They already know those lessons, after all, and will benefit from them when they participate on another project team. Time spent writing them all up is time away from their other priorities. As you may recall from Chapter 9, that lack of incentives plagues knowledge management initiatives in general. Reluctance to document lessons learned is especially acute for failed projects, where people don't want to admit mistakes or risk blame. Despite the challenges, smart managers in a high-performing organization will develop incentives to encourage team members to share what they learned about project management.[5]

PRODUCTIVITY TIP

Take time to document your own lessons after each project in which you're involved. You can use these to make recommendations to the next team or improve your own performance as project manager.

THE ROLE OF THE PROJECT MANAGER

In *The Apprentice* TV series, real estate mogul Donald Trump challenged the contestants to take on a business project each week, appointing one person on each team as project manager (PM). The tense competitions offered some useful lessons in what makes a good PM—and what can lead to failure. In one episode, each team was given

FIGURE 12-8

Characteristics of effective project managers.

> ▶ Strong leadership skills
> ▶ Excellent communication abilities
> ▶ Outstanding "people" skills
> ▶ Technical competence in project area
> ▶ Good listening skills
> ▶ Strong team-building skills
> ▶ Excellent presentation skills
> ▶ Good problem-solving and critical-thinking skills
> ▶ Ability to balance priorities, stay organized, and keep the team on track

a budget of $20,000 to renovate a Long Island home, and the team that increased its home's value the most was declared winner. Apex team was plagued by management failures that led to the team's loss and the PM's firing. The renovation decisions were questionable, the team didn't finish the project on time, and the PM tried to shift blame to his team members. Another episode allowed Trump to pinpoint a highly desirable trait for project managers: ethical behavior. Learning that a client's advertising sign had slipped off the rickshaw that was supposed to carry it through the streets of New York, the PM compensated the client, even though team members objected. That leader easily survived the round.

The PM needs leadership skills, excellent communication abilities, and strong team-building skills (Figure 12-8). Although technical competence in the task at hand is valuable, "people" skills are equally so. The PM will motivate the team members and rely on their capabilities and drive to carry out the project. This person must be an attentive listener to hear the views of all the stakeholders and also an effective speaker to present the project's status to sponsors and defend resource needs. The job is demanding, and project success can depend so heavily on the PM's skills that many organizations require professional certification, especially for those charged with managing large projects. The Project Management Institute (PMI) offers programs to certify project managers who can demonstrate their qualifications and agree to PMI's code of professional conduct and ethics.

Another knowledge area project managers must master is **change management**, which is a structured approach to the transition employees must make as they switch from their existing work processes to new ones. Much change accompanies the introduction of new information systems, particularly when some processes are drastically revised or eliminated through business process management efforts. Resistance to change can sink an entire project, as it nearly did for the electronic medical records project described earlier.

Stan confronted a change management issue because his project plan relied on employees to take the ride and then post blogs and tweets about their experience throughout the campaign and beyond. He also wanted them to video their death-defying descents along the Wild River's path with a head-mounted camera, so he could post them on the website and YouTube. This was obviously not part of the employees' job descriptions, and many were concerned that if they refused, their chances for promotion would be affected. After listening to their concerns, Stan skillfully presented the project at an all-staff meeting, showing the video of his own ride along with his earsplitting screams. Emphasizing carrots rather than sticks, Stan got approval to lend free smartphones to every rider who would blog and tweet for the next 2 months, to make their participation more convenient. Throughout the

predecessors
The tasks that must be completed in a project before a particular task can begin.

critical path
The longest path through the project which identifies those tasks that can't be delayed without affecting the finish date. Monitoring tasks that fall along the critical path is especially important.

closing processes
Processes that formally end the project in an orderly way; they include a signoff by the sponsor confirming that all deliverables have been received and accepted.

change management
A structured approach to the transition employees must make as they switch from their existing work processes to new ones, especially with the introduction of a new information system.

THE ETHICAL FACTOR Code of Ethics for Project Managers

Project managers adhere to a code of ethics, and one widely used in the field is from the Project Management Institute.[6] The values that form the foundation for this code emphasize responsibility, respect, fairness, and honesty.

For example, PMs are expected to make decisions and take actions based on the best interest of society, public safety, and the environment. They must also accept assignments only when the position matches their background, experience, skills, and qualifications. They can accept "stretch" assignments, provided they keep the key stakeholders informed about areas in which they have gaps.

The PMI code stresses that project managers have an obligation to avoid any conflicts of interest. Such conflicts are not uncommon, and they present a major challenge to the profession. For example, a PM employed by the company sponsoring the project should answer questions like these:

▶ Have you done any consulting work for any of the vendors who will be bidding on the project?

▶ Have any of your close relatives done such work?

▶ Do you own stock or have investments in any of the companies that might be hired for this project?

The prohibition against conflicts of interest extends to even the appearance of it, because that could compromise the PM's effectiveness. The code of ethics establishes a very high standard of ethical behavior for project managers that will serve them and their employers well.

campaign, Stan communicated with every poster individually to thank them and let them know how valuable their contribution was for the park's first foray into social media marketing. He expected many employees to start checking stats on their own videos, in a friendly competition to see who got the most views.

 Explain how project management software helps managers plan, track, and manage projects.

Project Management Software

The market for project management software is very strong, and project managers enjoy a broad range of tools that can help manage and track a project. Although it is possible to use Excel or even a word processor to create a work breakdown structure, fill in timelines and due dates, and assign people to tasks, specialty software offers far more capabilities.

MANAGING TIME

Project management software provides extensive tools to help the PM manage time, one of the three constraints in any project. For instance, the software automatically adjusts start and end dates as the PM creates the work breakdown structure. Stan enters the approximate duration for each task and then identifies each task's predecessors. For instance, he estimates that analyzing the survey data from customers who ride the waterslide will take two days, and the predecessor is the "Survey slide riders" task in which John will be collecting the data. If John needs a couple of extra days for the survey, Stan can increase the duration of that task and the dates for his analysis will automatically adjust.

The PM can also use the project plan as the baseline schedule. Once the project starts, the PM can enter actual completion dates for each task or percent completed, and the software can display two bars for each task, one for the baseline and one for the actual progress. Figure 12-9 shows that Stan took a bit longer to develop the project charter than he projected. The software adjusts the schedule for Stan's project, delaying the kickoff meeting and later tasks to compensate. Stan will have to find ways to tighten the schedule later to finish on time. It takes skill to balance resources and time constraints, especially to avoid burning out the team toward the end.

MANAGING PEOPLE AND RESOURCES

Another useful feature in project management software is the ability to assign people to tasks and then track their workloads and duties across the project. The PM can enter the people who will be working on the tasks, along with their working calendars

FIGURE 12-9

Comparing the project's baseline to actual progress. The gray bars under each subtask show the original baseline, and the blue bar indicates actual progress and schedule adjustments for future tasks.

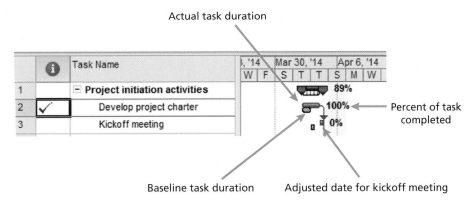

Actual task duration

Percent of task completed

Baseline task duration   Adjusted date for kickoff meeting

and planned vacations. Team members can each be assigned to the appropriate tasks in the work breakdown structure, and reports will show the level of effort required of each person each day. If someone is overloaded for a period of time, perhaps because the schedule calls for that person's skills on two overlapping tasks, the PM can use the software to test scenarios that stretch out some tasks or delay others so the project team doesn't have to put in so much overtime. Stan can see he is overloaded in the beginning of the project, but he decides to work on weekends rather than delay the slide's opening.

The reports showing everyone's schedule are especially useful because many projects include team members who work in other departments or projects, and their skills have to be shared. The smart PM will keep team members and their managers well informed about when tasks requiring them start and end, to avoid unpleasant surprises that affect work in their departments. Stan assigns Bailey to develop the website with blogging capability, and the duration estimate assumes that Bailey will work full-time on that. Bailey is also needed for the kickoff and various weekly meetings, and the software can generate a report showing Bailey's projected schedule. If the timing on tasks changes, Stan can send out updated schedules. The cooperation of Bailey's supervisor is essential, since the department's ongoing work has to adapt to her absence.

The project may also need other kinds of resources, such as equipment, conference rooms, software license fees, or postage. The use of the shared videocameras, for example, can be entered in the software. Stan can then schedule resources in conjunction with the task that needs them and track their costs.

MANAGING COSTS

Salaries, consulting fees, equipment, travel, rentals, and other expenses can all be estimated up front with project management software and then tracked against the baseline as the project progresses. The PM might enter team members' hourly rates for regular hours and for overtime if the rates are higher. Equipment costs can be added to the task that uses them as a one-time expense or be spread over the duration of the project. If the project is charged for the use of meeting rooms, those fees can be embedded in each meeting task.

The software calculates the baseline costs for the project and provides reports on variances as the project proceeds. Figure 12-10 shows a sample report that alerts the PM to cost variances by task. For example, the extra time Stan spent on the project charter affects not only the schedule for the project, but also its costs because of his salary. If the website takes longer to build, that will add to costs as well. Juggling the three constraints is a constant challenge for project managers, and Stan may need to check with the project sponsor about whether to reduce the scope so that the project comes closer to the original budget and timeline.

FIGURE 12-10

Tracking the Wild River Waterslide social media marketing budget.

Task	Baseline Cost	Actual Cost	Variance
Develop project charter	1,280.00	1,920.00	640.00
Kickoff meeting	670.00	670.00	0
Develop project management plan	1,280.00	1,280.00	0
Develop WBS	640.00	640.00	0
Develop website with blogging capability	8,800.00	11,440.00	2,640.00

Identify the main factors that cause projects to succeed or fail.

4

Why Projects Succeed, and Why They Fail

After investing more than $300 million in modernizing its financial information systems, the Veterans Administration (VA) has little to show for it. The first project failed, and the major components of the second were canceled over doubts that the project could ever be successfully executed within the budget.[7] The same year, the Department of Defense finally canceled a decade-long project to replace more than 90 legacy human resource management systems with an integrated application called DIMHRS. Robert Gates, the Defense Secretary at the time, commented, "I would say that what we've gotten for a half-billion dollars is an unpronounceable acronym."[8]

WHY DO PROJECTS FAIL?

Several critical factors contribute to failure:

- ▶ Lack of executive support
- ▶ Lack of stakeholder involvement
- ▶ Unclear requirements
- ▶ Technology problems
- ▶ Scope creep and excessive customization
- ▶ Unclear roles and responsibilities
- ▶ Unrealistic time frames
- ▶ Poor communications
- ▶ Poor change management

Although technical problems do contribute to failures and delays, most fail factors have more to do with the way projects are managed, monitored, communicated, and supported by senior execs. Some spectacular failures happen because of the **escalation of commitment** phenomenon. People are loathe to pull the plug on a project in which huge sums and organizational resources have already been invested. Instead of weighing the value of further investment, they forget that sunk costs are bygones and should not guide future decision making. The VA's $300 million investment was a sunk cost, and the project managers wisely decided not to escalate their commitment any further.

SUCCESS FACTORS FOR PROJECT MANAGEMENT

The success factors are almost the mirror image of those that contribute to failure. Figure 12-11 lists characteristics that describe projects that have the best chance of succeeding, grouped by category.[9] In the category called "People factors," executive support tops the list, just as lack of that support does for failed projects.

The RAND Corporation also stresses the need for clarity at the very start of the project, at the point when stakeholders, project manager, team members, and sponsor all must agree on the project's objectives, success criteria, scope, and other details. The project charter is an effective tool to achieve this clarity and ensure everyone is on the same page.

FIGURE 12-11

Success factors for projects.

	Does the project have...
People factors	Executive support and sufficient resources allocated? Talented and motivated personnel assigned to the project? Leaders with project management expertise? A strategy to manage conflicts among stakeholders?
Organizational factors	Involvement and buy-in from a broad range of end users? An objective that is perceived to be aligned with business goals?
Project factors	A clear objective and a well-defined scope? A design that will allow any new systems to interact with existing systems?
Project management factors	A well-defined system development methodology that is appropriate for the project? Appropriate project management software and other tools? A clear change control process for managing scope creep? A strategy for assessing quality? A clear process for monitoring and tracking progress?
External factors	Well-understood and binding agreements with vendors and consultants?

IT consultant Bronnie Brooks adds that project managers need to be willing to make unpopular decisions that might dismay the sponsor or clients. The PM has to clearly communicate the time, cost, and scope constraints as the project unfolds. Features that the stakeholders were expecting may have to be dropped if sticking to the budget and launching on time are judged more important.[10]

Another factor that should not be underestimated is the need for end-user training and hand-holding after launch. If help is readily available, employees will master the new processes and software much more quickly, and with much less frustration.

Most organizations have several projects underway simultaneously that incorporate information systems and technology, so strategic planning is essential for establishing priorities and resources for the project portfolio. For information systems, strategic planning also entails several other essential activities, discussed in the next section.

> **PRODUCTIVITY TIP**
>
> If you take on the role of project manager for a student team project or a project at work, pay close attention to the factors that contribute to success or failure. The project manager shoulders much of the blame for failures and delays, deserved or not. You should also use a team agreement, as described in Chapter 8.

Strategic Planning for Information Systems

> **5** Explain the importance of strategic planning for information systems, and provide examples.

Information systems are like the nervous system of an organization, with neurons that extend into and support every organ and muscle fiber. Because information systems are so central to success and strategic competitiveness, organizations create a strategic plan to provide a road map that charts the course. This road map should be aligned with the strategy the company establishes, as we described in Chapter 2. Whether that strategy is low cost leadership, product differentiation, or something else, the strategic plan for information systems should be closely aligned and used to guide decision making. While the CIO leads the effort, stakeholders from across the organization also participate. Some of the major areas the plan covers are:

▶ Vision, principles, and policies
▶ Project portfolio management
▶ Disaster recovery and business continuity

Let's take a closer look at each.

escalation of commitment
The tendency to continue investing in a project, despite mounting evidence that it is not succeeding; often comes about because people mistakenly let sunk costs affect decision making rather than weighing the value of further investment.

VISION, PRINCIPLES, AND POLICIES

Vermont's information technology strategic plan begins with a vision that "Vermonters are *the* one. We will think as one… act as one… and have one mission." The plan emphasizes that information systems projects must be aligned with the state's over-arching goals, which include bringing services to the citizens in very cost-effective and convenient ways, and adopting an enterprise-wide approach to guide information systems planning. This vision lays the groundwork for strategic decision making and indicates that integration and online customer service will be major themes.

The organization's vision, mission, and culture determine the principles that guide how its information systems are managed and used, and how resources are allocated. A risk-averse financial company will lean toward strategies that protect assets and ensure compliance with regulations. A high-energy start-up might stress innovation, establishing principles that promote individual creativity.

FUNDING MODELS The vision, and the principles that drive it, are translated into policies and procedures that reach down into business processes and workplace culture. For example, the procurement policy may require all technology purchases to be approved by the IT department to ensure compatibility and to help build a coherent enterprise architecture. If your company only supports Windows laptops, your plea for a MacBook will fall on deaf ears. A desktop printer request may be denied by an organization that lists "going green" as a fundamental principle.

The organization's guiding principles also influence how it allocates IT expenses and recovers costs. Some organizations develop charge-back strategies for various services, such as help-desk calls, hardware purchases, software development, website maintenance, server usage, or storage space. Each service carries a fee, charged directly to the department requesting it. Other companies treat these services as over-head and then allocate amounts to each department at the end of the fiscal year based on a formula, such as employee head count.

Funding models like these have effects on behavior, and they sometimes lead to unintended consequences. For example, a staff member in a charge-back setting may be prudent about requests for new software and would download a trial version first to make sure the software performs as advertised and will add value. But another employee who downloads some malware by accident may spend many wasted hours trying to remove it, rather than calling the help desk and incurring a charge that the manager will see. A manager trying to control expenses may unwisely leave workers struggling with unbearably slow and ancient computers, reducing their productivity. In organizations that don't charge costs back, department heads have less incentive to be frugal since the expenses they incur are not transparent to management. They will be spread around without regard for which department spent more per employee. Contentious battles may also erupt, when some departments are branded IT "hogs" that elevate everyone's share of costs.[11]

ACCEPTABLE-USE AND SECURITY POLICIES CIOs weigh all these factors when they work with other senior managers and determine how to pay for the information systems the organization needs. The organization's principles also guide the **acceptable-use policy**, which employees must agree to before accessing IT resources. The policy lays out the rules about what employees are allowed to do with IT resources and what activities are disallowed. These policies touch on the services each employee will be provided, whether and how much they can use company resources for personal use, and what kinds of surveillance are in place (Figure 12-12). Policies also reinforce legal require-ments, such as prohibitions against unauthorized copying, copyright infringement, or exporting encryption software. Harassment, fraudulent use, and any attempts to disrupt information systems or circumvent authentication are covered as well.

Acceptable-use policies should contain clear language describing the organiza-tion's security and confidentiality requirements. For instance, the policy might require all PCs and laptops to be secured with a password-protected screen saver. The feature might require users to re-enter their password if they don't touch the keyboard or move the mouse in 10 minutes or less. With the dramatic rise in lawsuits related to imprudent

FIGURE 12-12

Elements of an acceptable-use policy.

> ▶ What IT services are provided to each employee?
> ▶ Can employees access the Internet?
> ▶ Is access to certain websites prohibited?
> ▶ What kind of surveillance and monitoring is in place?
> ▶ Are employees permitted to use the company's IT resources for personal use? If so, what are the constraints?
> ▶ How does the organization respond to violations? What are the penalties?
> ▶ Can employees download and install software without IT approval?
> ▶ Can employees send mass e-mail to colleagues about personal issues, such as "kittens are ready to adopt" or "donuts available"?
> ▶ Can employees use IT resources for fund-raising or commercial ventures?
> ▶ Can employees use the company name when they post on blogs or other social media?
> ▶ Security requirements
> ▶ Password construction and change schedules
> ▶ Encryption requirements
> ▶ Prohibition against sharing accounts
> ▶ Confidentiality requirements

e-mail exchanges, many organizations establish specific e-mail policies. Some require employees to add disclaimers to their e-mail signatures designed to diminish legal threats to the company, such as those in Figure 12-13.

Acceptable-use policies are expanding to cover how employees use information and communications technologies (ICT) outside work as well. For example, IBM encourages employees to contribute to blogs, tweet, and join virtual worlds, but the company publishes social computing guidelines that let employees know what is and is not acceptable.[12] Some bullet points include:

> ▶ Don't cite or reference clients, partners, or suppliers without their approval. When you do make a reference, where possible, link back to the source.
> ▶ If you publish content to any website outside of IBM and it has something to do with work you do or subjects associated with IBM, use a disclaimer such as this: "The postings on this site are my own and don't necessarily represent IBM's positions, strategies, or opinions."

FIGURE 12-13

Why do companies require employees to add disclaimers to their e-mails?

Potential Threat	Purpose of Disclaimer
Breach of confidentiality	The disclaimer can warn recipients against disclosing information contained in the e-mail.
Accidental breach of confidentiality	If the e-mail contains confidential information intended only for the recipient, a third party (such as the postmaster) might receive it accidentally. Wording that the message is intended only for the addressee provides some protection.
Transmission of viruses	The disclaimer can warn recipients that they are responsible for checking the message for viruses.
Implied contractual obligations	An employee's e-mail might contain wording that implies a firm contract. The disclaimer can add that any contract must be confirmed by the employee's manager.
Negligent misstatements	The company may be liable if an employee provides advice that the recipient then relies on. The disclaimer can include wording to protect the company from this.
Employee misuse	Absent a disclaimer, the employer may be held responsible for an employee who misuses e-mail and violates the company's policies, for example by making libelous or defamatory statements in e-mail.

acceptable-use policy
An organizational policy that describes what employees are allowed to do with IT resources and what activities are disallowed; employees agree to the policy before gaining access to IT resources.

Did You Know?

With so many employees wanting to link their own smartphones to corporate systems, managers are struggling to develop practical policies for these personally owned mobile devices. For example, should the company insist that it can remotely wipe an employee's iPhone clean if it is misplaced, to protect any confidential data it might contain? The data would vanish, but so would all your personal photos, videos, and music.[13]

ENTERPRISE ARCHITECTURE   As we discussed in Chapter 3, the enterprise architecture is the organization's overarching ICT environment, and the plan for this architecture should address its current and target state. As new systems are added and old ones retired, the components of the architecture continue to change. Without a strategic plan to guide the architectural decisions, changes will be haphazard. Systems that don't talk to each other now could be replaced by new systems that still can't interface easily. Redundant and inconsistent data will persist, and fragmented hardware choices will lead to higher support costs. Strategic planning for a flexible and forward-looking enterprise architecture will ensure the organization can meet its current information systems needs, and be positioned for future success.

PROJECT PORTFOLIO MANAGEMENT

The strategic plan should outline how the organization will guide investments in new information systems projects, especially to show how they will support business goals. **Project portfolio management** is a continuous process that oversees all the projects for an organization, selecting which projects to pursue and then managing the whole portfolio. The process also includes culling those projects that have a poor prognosis, such as the Veterans Administration's troubled financial system.

DECIDING WHICH PROJECTS TO PURSUE   Most organizations are not short of project ideas that rely on technology. Almost every proposal for improving efficiencies, developing new products and services, reducing costs, or increasing revenue has some ICT-related element. Some projects are rejected early, perhaps after the feasibility study in the planning phase of the systems development life cycle. Managers may learn that the system they imagined is too expensive or that the technology is still too buggy.

   To choose among the rest, the organization must decide on selection criteria and a strategy to determine which projects will make the best contribution and which are worthy of investment and staff time. While some managers use gut instinct, a growing number recognize that a significant percentage of their information systems budgets are tied up in projects. Organizations can make important gains by strategically managing the project portfolio, and they can also avoid losses due to lack of oversight. Some typical criteria for selecting projects are shown in Figure 12-14.

   One important criterion is whether a project will contribute to competitive strategy and distinguish the company from rivals. Phil Libin, head of Evernote, bills

FIGURE 12-14

Criteria for comparing the value of projects.

Criterion	Example
Contribution to competitive strategy	Projects that advance the organization's competitive position should be rated highly. One example is Carfax.com's web-based software to access a used car's history of accidents or defects based on the vehicle identification number.
Return on investment	Projects that offer a substantial return on investment earn high ratings. For example, Oregon Corrections switched to Voice over IP for its call center, staffed by prison inmates, reducing monthly telecom charges by 40%.
Compliance and risk reduction	Reducing risk and ensuring proper compliance are especially important drivers in some industries. Companies in the financial services industry spend more than 8% of their net income on IT projects and services, much of it to ensure compliance and mitigate risk.

the company's custom-built web application as "your external brain." His unstructured document management site allows users to clip web articles, upload photos, add voice or text notes, and store it all for free in an organized and easily searchable online repository. Libin charges for premium services, and about six percent of his user base pays for more storage or offline access. He remarks, "The easiest way to get one million people paying is to get one billion people using." For him, projects that enhance the site, attract new users, or tempt them to pay for premium access will get highest priority.[14]

Return on investment (ROI) is another important criterion, one that may not be easy to estimate. Calculating the costs and savings for a project to replace individual servers with a smaller number of virtualized servers may be straightforward. But ROI can be a challenge to estimate when project costs are slippery, or revenue increases are hard to predict. For instance, managers often underestimate the cost of customizing prepackaged software, especially because of scope creep and the need to maintain the custom code throughout the system's life cycle. Those costs will continue to grow as long as the system stays in use.

Savings can be elusive, too. A supply chain management system might save considerable time for staff in the procurement office, and the original ROI projection included reduced personnel costs. But those workers might not be let go. Instead, they may be assigned to other duties, so personnel costs don't change. Nevertheless, organizations can reap very substantial returns on many of their information systems investments, even though the actual figures can be a challenge to predict.

Compliance and risk reduction are also important drivers for projects. This sentence belongs at the end of the preceding paragraph. One survey found that business owners invested an average of $225,000 in projects to achieve payment card industry compliance, necessary for companies that process online credit card transactions. Of course, the cost of noncompliance can be much higher. Fines for a single security breach are hefty, and restitution paid to customers whose data are compromised can reach into the millions of dollars.[15] The credit card issuers can also prevent a noncompliant merchant from accepting credit cards for online transactions, which is potentially devastating for retailers.

MANAGING THE PORTFOLIO By some estimates, *Fortune* 500 companies sink well over half their strategic initiatives into projects, but many executives do not have a clear picture of how they all are faring. To better manage the portfolio, some organizations have established a **program management office (PMO)** that oversees all the projects going on throughout the organization and provides project management training, software, and support. These offices also help resolve the conflicts that arise between project managers vying for the time of IT staff or other resources. With the organization's goals in mind, the PMO can make the tough decisions about how whole scarce resources are assigned and which projects will take precedence.

To track progress on all the projects, the PMO collects data from each one and aggregates it, building a larger picture of the overall health of the organization's project portfolio. On the dashboard, summary charts show how well all the projects are doing in terms of cost, schedule, or other metrics, and managers can drill down into specific projects to see where each one stands. Figure 12-15 shows a dashboard that summarizes progress on all IT projects at federal agencies. In the pie chart, almost 60 percent are showing green, meaning right on track. The graph on the right shows ratings on agencies' projects over time.

Collecting consistent data is a challenge for the PMO, since human beings will always judge things differently. What do green, yellow, and red really mean, for instance? Yellow is a warning sign that might mean that a few tasks are a little behind schedule. But it could also signal serious deficiencies. Another source of inconsistency occurs when people estimate the duration for tasks in the first place. One overconfident and optimistic programmer might estimate 10 days for a task, assuming full-time, top-speed work. A more cautious programmer might estimate 20 days for the same task, knowing that interruptions happen and that it's better to be safely in the green

project portfolio management
A continuous process that oversees all the projects for an organization, selecting which projects to pursue and which ones to terminate.

program management office (PMO)
The part of an organization that oversees all the projects going on throughout the organization and provides project management training, software, and support.

FIGURE 12-15

Dashboard used to manage the IT project portfolio of the U.S. federal government.

Source: http://it.usaspending.gov

rather than risk a yellow or red flag. Managers should stay alert to the human element that can lead to dramatically different reporting styles.[16]

DISASTER RECOVERY AND BUSINESS CONTINUITY

The CIO of Entergy, a New Orleans–based energy company, recalls the day Hurricane Katrina hit the city. "That was not a good day," said Ray Johnson. "But it is not a unique event for us. We've got our disaster plan nailed." Thanks to the frequent reviews and drills, Entergy was able to move its primary data center after the storm devastated the Louisiana facility. Employees brought the systems back online from backup tapes at the designated recovery site in Little Rock, Arkansas, well out of the storm's path.[17]

Disaster recovery refers to all the procedures, documentation, and resources the organization puts into place to prepare for a disaster and recover the technical infrastructure. The list of possible disasters is very long, from the hurricanes and snowstorms that damage facilities and knock out power grids, to security breaches, environmental hazards, pandemics, and terrorism (Figure 12-16). One study shows that as many as 60 percent of U.S. enterprises have not developed adequate disaster recovery plans, and few test their plans routinely.[18]

Recovery from disaster is not just about bringing the systems back online, however. It also means ensuring **business continuity**. Faced with many different kinds of disasters, the organization must develop plans for maintaining its business operations to avoid a devastating revenue loss and damaged reputation. How will employees communicate with each other, and where will they work? How will they access the information systems? When H1N1 flu began surfacing, for example, about 40 percent of companies prepared a "work at home" solution for employees, using virtual private networks to access the company network. The rest either had no plan in place or thought the flu would not affect their operations.[19]

FIGURE 12-16

Types of disasters and possible consequences to information systems.

Types of Disasters	Possible Consequences
Natural disasters (floods, fires, hurricanes, snowstorms, earthquakes, volcano eruptions)	Electrical outages, destruction of technology infrastructure; disruption of supply chains
Security breaches (unauthorized break-ins, employee theft, denial of service attacks, information leaks)	Release of confidential information, disabled servers, corruption or alteration of data, malware infections
Pandemics (H1N1 influenza)	Massive absenteeism
Environmental hazards (hazardous materials spills, radiation, letters containing white powder)	Evacuation; system disruptions; inability of staff to work in the company's facilities

Disaster recovery and business continuity planning start with an analysis of the impact various disasters might have on operations, and how the organization can compensate and recover. For instance, the analysis would prioritize the most critical and time-sensitive information systems, and explain how they would be brought back up. An online retailer should make recovering its e-commerce website a top priority. A utility company must focus on its power regulation and distribution systems. An airline will need its reservation and plane scheduling systems back online. Many organizations will need a plan to support system access for workers who can't get to the office. Other features of the analysis include:

▶ Data backup schedules
▶ Offsite storage locations for backup media
▶ Recovery sites where the data can be restored
▶ Procedures for restarting the systems

Creating a plan that gathers dust on a shelf is not an effective approach. The plan must be tested and then revised when flaws surface. Sometimes it's the details that cause the most trouble—the little things no one anticipated. When the insurance company USAA tested its plan to evacuate employees from one location to another building, it found that computer and phone setup at the new site took a surprisingly long time. Employees were quickly ushered out of the evacuation site, but then stood in the sweltering Texas sun for more than two hours, waiting to get into the alternate building. Many realized they had run out of the evacuation site without their car keys, so now had no way to get home without re-entering the evacuated building.[20] USAA managers learned from these slip-ups, and incorporated measures in the plan to deal with them.

Did You Know?

When the massive earthquake struck Japan in 2011, Otis Elevators was prepared. In regions with high earthquake risk, each elevator carries a seismic detector. If the device senses vibration, the elevator is programmed to return to the ground floor. Doors open so passengers can exit, but further use is blocked pending safety checks. All 80,000 elevators worked flawlessly during the quake, and no one was trapped inside any of them.[21]

Planning for the Future: The Human Element

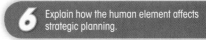
6 Explain how the human element affects strategic planning.

Every strategic planning effort calls for human judgment. Planners must assess the current environment, drawing on what they hope is reliable and up-to-date information about trends and patterns. Ideally, they have access to the rich analyses that business intelligence systems can provide to help them see a clear picture of strengths, weaknesses, opportunities, and threats—not just within the organization, but for suppliers, customers, and competitors as well.

CIOs and others engaged in planning then must make predictions about the future, stating what their assumptions are and how they arrived at them. Do they forecast a moderate pace of e-commerce sales growth? How difficult will it be to recruit the talent the company needs to develop the web portal? Will citizens take advantage of the new online government services? How reliable will the cloud-computing service be? Will that new technology explode in popularity or become just another flash in the pan? Will any of our software vendors go out of business?

disaster recovery
The procedures and documentation the organization puts into place to prepare for a disaster and recover the technical infrastructure.

business continuity
The maintenance of the organization's operations in the event of disaster or disruption.

FIGURE 12-17

Missing the mark: Some of the worst predictions about ICT.

> "There is no reason anyone would want a computer in their home."—*Ken Olson, president, chairman, and founder of Digital Equipment, mini and mainframe computer manufacturer, 1977.*
>
> "I have traveled the length and breadth of this country and talked with the best people, and I can assure you that data processing is a fad that won't last out the year." —*The editor in charge of business books for Prentice Hall, 1957.*
>
> "I think there is a world market for maybe five computers." —*Thomas Watson, chairman of IBM, 1943.*
>
> "The wireless music box has no imaginable commercial value. Who would pay for a message sent to no one in particular?" —*Associates of David Sarnoff responding to the latter's call for investment in radio in 1921.*
>
> "The Americans have need of the telephone, but we do not. We have plenty of messenger boys." —*Sir William Preece, chief engineer, British Post Office, 1878.*
>
> "This 'telephone' has too many shortcomings to be seriously considered as a means of communication. The device is inherently of no value to us." —*A memo at Western Union telegraph company, 1878.*
>
> "When the Paris Exhibition closes, electric light will close with it and no more will be heard of it." —*Oxford professor Erasmus Wilson, 1878.*

COGNITIVE BIASES AND STRATEGIC PLANNING

Crystal balls are in short supply, and making predictions about events that affect information systems planning is a considerable challenge. Although hard data and business intelligence can inform the plan and keep it grounded in reality, human beings are remarkably fallible. The quotes in Figure 12-17 show how far off the mark people can be. One reason for such mistakes is that humans show certain biases that can cloud how they interpret data and predict the future.

A **cognitive bias** is a common human tendency to make systematic mistakes when processing information or making judgments. Figure 12-18 lists some examples. For instance, people show **confirmation bias** by choosing information to examine that supports the view they already hold and ignoring data that might refute their hypothesis. A CIO who wants to include cloud-based services in the strategic plan might skip over white papers examining security flaws and point instead to case studies showing how other organizations have benefited. From the CIO's perspective, the reviewed data support the decision, but the choice the CIO made about which data to review was biased. Stan's confirmation bias might play out as he analyzes the survey data. He is convinced that social media are a powerful marketing tool, so he might give less weight to survey respondents who said they learned about the ride from the billboard in the park.

Another bias is overconfidence in the accuracy of our own estimates. In one study, students were asked to provide three predictions for how long it would take them to finish their senior thesis, one for which they were 99 percent certain they would meet, and two shorter estimates about which they were less confident.[22] Regardless of how certain they were about their estimates, the majority of students didn't meet any. Just 45 percent met the time estimate they said they were 99 percent certain they could meet. Not only do people underestimate how long tasks like this will take, but they also tend to be quite confident in their mistaken estimates. For project managers, this kind of overconfidence can lead to many adjustments in the schedule, as team members take longer than they thought they would take on their tasks.

FIGURE 12-18

Examples of cognitive biases that can affect strategic planning.

Cognitive Bias	Description
Confirmation bias	The tendency to choose information to review that supports our existing position and ignore conflicting evidence
Overconfidence	The act of having more faith in our own estimates than is realistically justified
Planning fallacy	The tendency to underestimate the time it will take to complete a task
Anchoring	Reliance on one piece of information, however irrelevant
Availability bias	The tendency to judge the probability of an event based on how easily examples come to mind
Hindsight bias	The belief that an actual event was predictable even if it was not

FIGURE 12-19

Which causes the most deaths—shark attacks or objects falling from planes?

People often rely too heavily on one piece of information to adjust their estimates, even if it is irrelevant. The phenomenon is called **anchoring**. For instance, suppose someone throws out a wild guess to estimate the costs for a future software project, say $100,000, but the requirements are extremely vague. Even if the CIO doubts its credibility, that one guess becomes the anchor. The CIO might adjust it up or down a little, but that first number has a powerful influence. If the guess had been $500,000, the adjusted estimate would have been far higher. For strategic planning, an anchoring bias can influence time estimates as well as budgets. If managers are asked to draw up a 3-year plan, that duration itself will be an anchor on their estimates about how long it will take to accomplish the plan's objectives. Chances are, you will find quite a few projects on the plan with 3-year timeframes.

Which causes more deaths, shark attacks or objects that fall from planes (Figure 12-19)? Most people choose the shark because such attacks get so much publicity in the news.[23] But deaths caused by falling plane parts, though still unusual, are actually 30 times more common. The example illustrates the **availability bias**, which is the tendency for people to judge the likelihood of events based on how readily they come to mind, and this bias can also distort strategic planning. It may affect how people develop disaster recovery plans, and especially what disasters they judge most likely. Major security break-ins by hackers get considerable media attention, but the financial costs from more common but less widely publicized threats, such as scareware and careless employees, can be far higher.

THE BLACK SWAN

FIGURE 12-20

The black swan.

Until the 18th century, people in Europe thought the black swan was either exceedingly rare or nonexistent, because they had seen only white ones. The bird actually thrives in Australia, but the term **black swan** became a symbol for those extremely rare events that are difficult or nearly impossible to predict. Though the odds of their occurrence might be less than one percent, these rare events have an immense impact in areas such as technology, finance, and science, and they pose enormous challenges for strategic planners. They also lead to many mistakes in judgment and prediction.[24] Examples of black swans include events such as World War I, the attack on September 11, 2001, or inventions such as the personal computer or the rise of the Internet.

---

cognitive bias
A common human tendency to make systematic mistakes when processing information or making judgments; cognitive biases can distort strategic planning.

confirmation bias
The human tendency to choose information to examine that supports the person's view, but ignore data that might refute that view.

anchoring
The tendency for people to rely too heavily on one piece of information to adjust their estimates, even if it is irrelevant.

availability bias
The tendency for people to judge the likelihood of events based on how readily they come to mind, rather than their actual likelihood.

black swan
Used to describe an extremely rare event that is difficult or nearly impossible to predict, but which can have an immense impact in areas such as technology, finance, and science; black swans pose enormous challenges for strategic planners.

How might black swan events affect strategic planning? A CIO who systematically rates potential threats according to their likelihood might judge a terrorist attack on the data center so unlikely as to make costly and controversial precautions unnecessary. Building cinderblock protective walls, adding bulletproof service windows, and even arming the staff are expensive measures that seem less important compared to intrusion-detection software or off-site backups. Unlike announcing new killer apps or brilliant marketing campaigns, preparing year after year for a highly unlikely disaster that never happens is a thankless task. Yet these improbable events do occur, however rarely, and they can cause enormous damage. Smart managers in every business unit will need to balance all the risks and rewards, and at least consider how to handle a highly unlikely black swan.

 Hindsight, they say, is 20/20. The **hindsight bias** refers to the human tendency to think an unusual event was (or should have been) predictable, once they know it actually happened. This tendency explains why people heap blame on strategic planners who are caught off guard by the black swan.[25] Bill Gates, for instance, was soundly criticized for not predicting the Internet's potential, and the 9/11 Commission dug deeply to find out why security agencies missed the signals that should have foretold the attack.

The disruptive technological innovations we discussed in Chapter 2 are black swans that reshape entire industries, and Bill Gates is not the only savvy technology leader who missed some. Those very smart people quoted in Figure 12-17 failed to predict the technology black swans that soon transformed much of the world. Their predictive powers may also have been hindered by simple wishful thinking. Ken Olson, for example, founded Digital Equipment Corporation (DEC), and his company's entire business model rested on larger mainframe and minicomputers with proprietary operating systems. Unlike IBM, whose leaders found ways to reinvent their company after the PC disrupted the mainframe and minicomputer industry, DEC foundered and eventually vanished.

What black swans are swimming in the marshes now? We may not be able to predict them, but given how suddenly black swans in ICT appear and how fast they spread, organizations will need strategic plans that are agile and responsive, not carved in stone. Like Stan and those waterslide riders in the social media project described in this chapter, we're in for a wild river ride.

MyMISLab | *Online Simulation*

eXtreme Virtual Reality

A Role-Playing Simulation on Managing a Project to Open a New Business

"Just try this on...see what you think," says Theo. You reluctantly put on the headgear and gloves, and then enter a dimly lit glass chamber in a room surrounded by computer gear. Theo helps you settle into the swing and clicks the seat belts, saying, we'll just do a short one. He signals to Trina, sitting at one of the terminals, and you hear the sound of rushing air. An explosion of bright light reaches your eyes, and you're now suspended far above the earth for a VR hot air balloon ride! You swoop down low over an orchard so you can reach out and grab what feels just like a real orange, and then climb high into the stratosphere, where you touch the icy cold metal of an orbiting satellite.

Exhilarating! Trina programs the balloon to land gently near the orchard, with a strong orange fragrance.

Theo and Trina are the founders of eXtreme Virtual Reality, a company with plenty of venture capital funding and about 30 employees—mostly programmers and graphic designers. It will open its first locations within a couple of months. Right now, they have several VR adventure scenarios programmed, including the hot air balloon ride, a breath-taking underwater adventure, and a planetary mission to Mars. They also have one VR training program for health workers in development, to practice suturing techniques on virtual patients.

You joined the company as a project manager, and the upcoming opening is your first assignment. Log in when you're ready to get started...

Scenic Shutterbug/Shutterstock

hindsight bias
The human tendency to think an unusual event was (or should have been) predictable, once they know it actually happened.

Learning Objectives

1 A project is a temporary endeavor with a unique purpose, primary customer or sponsor, and stakeholders. It also involves an element of uncertainty because the project team takes on tasks that may be unfamiliar. Projects differ from processes, which are repeated activities, and should be managed differently. All projects are subject to the triple constraints of cost, time, and scope.

2 Project management has five major processes: initiating, planning, executing, monitoring and controlling, and closing. The project usually begins with a project charter that authorizes it, and the project manager develops a comprehensive project management plan that includes a work breakdown structure, Gantt chart, and additional subplans as needed to explain how the project will manage scope, human resources, risk, and other areas. The closing processes include sharing lessons learned to document what went right and what could be improved. The project manager is responsible for coordinating the project and managing the triple constraints.

3 Project management software provides tools to help manage all aspects of a project and track its progress. The software can automatically adjust start or end dates for tasks and alert managers when team members are overloaded. It can also compare ongoing progress to a baseline established during the planning phase and provide reports on cost variances.

4 Primary reasons that projects fail include poor project management, lack of executive support, lack of stakeholder involvement, unclear requirements, and technology problems. The opposites of these, such as strong executive support and user involvement, contribute to success. Other success factors include clear objectives, well-defined scope, a team with some project management experience, and a strategy to manage conflicts.

5 Information systems are central to an organization's success, so strategic planning is needed to ensure they continue to align with and support the organization's vision, mission, and goals. The plan should clarify the underlying principles that guide policy development and include topics such as funding models, acceptable-use policies, security requirements, and enterprise architecture planning. The strategic plan should also cover the organization's approach to project portfolio management, explaining how projects are selected and managed. The disaster recovery and business continuity plan should clearly identify the time-sensitive and mission-critical systems that must be recovered first after a disaster and explain how the organization will handle the event. Business continuity issues also include how employees will communicate with one another and where they will work.

6 The human element plays out in strategic planning for information systems because cognitive biases systematically affect the way people process data and make predictions. For example, humans show a confirmation bias in which they tend to ignore or downplay information that doesn't agree with their position or prediction. Strategic planning must also encompass strategies to deal with black swans—events that may be extremely unlikely, but can have enormous impact if they do occur. Organizations should be prepared to respond in fleet-footed, agile ways when the unexpected happens.

KEY TERMS AND CONCEPTS

project	scope creep	change management	business continuity
project management	Gantt chart	escalation of commitment	cognitive bias
initiating processes	executing processes	acceptable-use policy	confirmation bias
project charter	monitoring and controlling processes	project portfolio management	anchoring
planning processes	predecessors	program management office (PMO)	availability bias
project management plan	critical path	disaster recovery	black swan
deliverables	closing processes		hindsight bias

CHAPTER REVIEW QUESTIONS

1. What is a project? How do projects differ from business processes? What three forces constrain every project? How does each constrain a project?

2. What are the five processes of project management? What are examples of activities that occur in each process of project management?

3. What role does a project manager play in overseeing a project? What skills do project managers need? What are the characteristics of effective project managers?

4. How does project management software help plan, track, and manage projects?

5. What is the purpose of a Gantt chart? How is it used in project management?

6. How is a work breakdown structure used in project management?

7. What are the main factors that cause projects to fail? What are the main factors that enable projects to succeed?

8. Why is it important for an organization to have a strategic plan for information systems? What major areas are covered in an organization's IT strategic plan?

9. What are two IT funding models that organizations use to determine how IT expenses are allocated and costs recovered? How are IT expenses charged in each model? How does each funding model affect human behavior?

10. What is an acceptable-use policy? What are example elements of an acceptable-use policy? Why do organizations implement an acceptable-use policy? How do acceptable-use policies affect human behavior?

11. What is project portfolio management? Why do organizations need project portfolio management?

12. What is the purpose of a program management office (PMO)? What are typical services provided by a program management office? How does a PMO use dashboards? Why is collecting consistent data a challenge for the PMO?

13. What is disaster recovery? What are the major tasks associated with disaster recovery?

14. What is business continuity? What are the major tasks associated with planning for business continuity?

15. What is a cognitive bias? What are examples of cognitive biases? What is a black swan phenomenon? How do cognitive biases and black swan phenomena affect strategic planning for information systems?

PROJECTS AND DISCUSSION QUESTIONS

1. Project management skills are at the top of the list of skills desired by employers, and those with project management credentials are sought by many organizations because they understand the role of the project management discipline in delivering successful projects. The Project Management Institute (PMI) is a leading nonprofit association that sets standards of good practice and certifies project management expertise. Visit www.pmi.org to learn more about the Project Management Professional (PMP) certification and code of ethics. What are the benefits of PMP or similar project management credentials? Click on Business Solutions to locate the Case Study Library, a collection of brief case studies that highlight the effective use of project management methods. Select and review a case study, and prepare a brief summary of a case that includes a discussion of at least one project management process presented in this chapter.

2. The Wild River Water Park is excited to open its new waterslide this summer. Following an established project management methodology, Stan drafted the project charter, illustrated in Figure 12-5, to launch the waterslide social media campaign project. What are the characteristics of Stan's charter that link to factors listed in Figure 12-11 to suggest his project will be successful? What factors do you think need more attention to ensure success of Stan's project?

3. Which project management phase has a component that is neglected in many organizations? Why is this process ignored? Is there one reason or many reasons why this process is ignored? What are the benefits of completing this phase in a thorough manner? Prepare a brief summary that highlights the challenges of this phase of project management.

4. In the planning phase, Stan identified the deliverables for his project: a new blog and website, video clips, mass e-mails, a Facebook page, sample Twitter output, and reports showing the analytics on page views and other metrics. Now he is concerned about scope creep. What is scope creep? How does scope creep affect a project? What steps can Stan take to manage scope creep? Describe three documents he can use to minimize scope creep.

5. Recall the characteristics of effective project managers listed in Figure 12-8. How do these characteristics relate to change management? What is change management? Briefly describe the skills that Stan used to resolve the change management issues on his social media campaign project.

6. Interview a friend or family member who works for a small to midsized company to learn whether they have a disaster recovery or business continuity plan. Does the plan include data backups or offsite storage of data? Does the plan include a designated recovery site? Prepare a brief summary of your interview to share with classmates.

7. Work in a small group with classmates to consider the work breakdown structure for Stan's project. (See Figure 12-7.) What is the purpose of a work breakdown structure? What activities did Stan schedule for the initiation phase? What is the purpose of a kickoff meeting? Describe the activities in the executing phase of the project. Identify which activities are likely to be concurrent and which have predecessor tasks. What is a critical path? Which tasks make up the critical path for Stan's project? Prepare a brief summary of your group discussion.

8. Most universities require faculty and students to be aware of and comply with an acceptable-use policy regarding the use of information technology and e-mail. Do you recall agreeing to abide by your school's acceptable-use policy? Work in a small group with classmates to find the policy on your school's website and review it. Does the policy address copyrighted computer software? Computer ethics? Game playing or electronic chatting? What are the consequences of failing to comply with the policy? Prepare a 5-minute presentation of your findings.

APPLICATION EXERCISES

EXCEL APPLICATION:
Creating a Gantt Chart with Excel

In 1920, Henry Gantt, a U.S. engineer, developed the scheduling and monitoring diagram that bears his name. At the time it was an innovation. Today, the Gantt chart is a standard management tool used by project managers around the world to chart the progress of their projects. Project managers likely use specialized software such as Microsoft Project to create Gantt charts. Another option is to use Excel.

You can create a Gantt Chart with Excel by customizing a stacked bar chart. Enter the data from Figure 12-21 into Excel.

▸ Select the headers and data for Tasks, Start Date, and Duration (Days) and create Stacked Bar Chart.
▸ Right-click on the chart and click Select Data.
▸ In Legend Entries (Series), remove Duration (Days).
▸ Click on Add to add a new series with Series Name "Start Date" and Series values B4:B11.

▸ Click on Add again to add another new series, with Series Name "Duration (Days)" and Series values C4:C11.
▸ Click on the y-axis, select Format Axis, and check the box "Categories in reverse order" to put the rows in order.
▸ Right-click on the first part of the first stacked bar and choose Format Data Series. Choose Fill, then click No Fill to make those parts of the stacked bar invisible.
▸ To start the chart at the project's start date, you need to correct that axis. Excel converts June 1, 2011, to 40695, which you can see for yourself if you change the format of the cell to numeric rather than date. Now click on the x-axis at the top of the chart, and select Format Axis. Change the Minimum to Fixed, and then enter 40695.
▸ Finally, delete the legend at the right. Your Gantt chart should look similar to the one in Figure 12-22.

If you need more help, you can find videos that walk you through the process on YouTube by using search terms "Excel Gantt Chart."

FIGURE 12-21

Data for Gantt chart.

	A	B	C	D
1	Project Management Gantt Chart			
2				
3	Tasks	Start Date	Duration (days)	End Date
4	Task 1	6/1/2011	7	6/8/2011
5	Task 2	6/2/2011	5	6/7/2011
6	Task 3	6/3/2011	9	6/12/2011
7	Task 4	6/8/2011	13	6/21/2011
8	Task 5	6/12/2011	22	7/4/2011
9	Task 6	6/13/2011	11	6/24/2011
10	Task 7	6/16/2011	24	7/10/2011
11	Task 8	6/29/2011	14	7/13/2011

FIGURE 12-22

Gantt chart created from Excel.

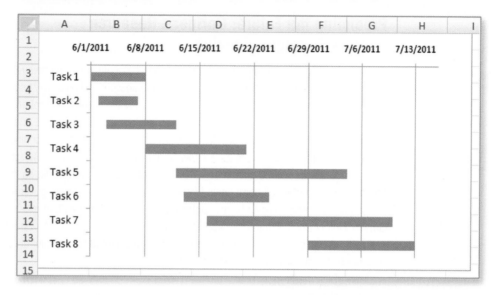

ACCESS APPLICATION:
Apprentice Project Managers

Donald Trump asked you to create a database to track the project management skills of the latest group of contestants vying to become his apprentice. Create a contestant database that includes two tables: the Contestant table to store contestant data, and the Skills table to store the characteristics of effective project managers listed in Figure 12-8. Use the Lookup Wizard to look up values from the Skills table and insert them into the Contestants table to identify each contestant's primary skill (PrimarySkill), secondary skill 1 (SS1), and secondary skill 2 (SS2).

Record the relevant data for the 16 contestants listed in Figure 12-23 that includes rating scores on three skills: leadership, communication, and people. Write a query that identifies the contestant(s) whose primary skill is leadership. Modify the query to identify the contestant(s) whose primary skill is leadership and SS1 is communication. Modify the query to identify the contestants whose critical thinking skills are rated primary, SS1 or SS2.

Create a calculated field in the query to calculate a weighted "Score" for each contestant wherein leadership is weighted highest, communication is weighted second highest, and people is weighted third highest. Use the following formula to calculate score. When you type the expression in the Field row, be sure to put the field names inside brackets.

$$Score = ([Leadership]*3) + ([Communication]*2) + ([People]*1)$$

Based on this weighted score, which candidate should Donald Trump hire to be his next apprentice?

FIGURE 12-23

Apprentice project management.

	A	B	C	D	E	F	G	H
1	Contestant_ID	Contestant_Name	PrimarySkill	SS1	SS2	Leadership	Communication	People
2	1	Tyana Alvarado	7	8	5	6	8	6
3	2	Kelly Smith Beaty	1	3	5	10	9	9
4	3	Poppy Carlig	3	5	6	7	8	10
5	4	Stephanie Castagnier	1	2	3	10	9	8
6	5	Nicole Chiu	3	5	2	7	6	10
7	6	Alex Delgado	3	2	6	6	9	10
8	7	Gene Folkes	1	3	5	10	8	9
9	8	Wade Hanson	6	3	2	6	7	9
10	9	David Johnson	1	8	9	10	7	6
11	10	Brandy Kuentzel	1	2	6	10	9	5
12	11	Steuart Martens	8	2	7	7	9	7
13	12	Lisa Mucheru-Wisner	2	1	3	9	10	8
14	13	Clint Robertson	6	5	7	6	8	6
15	14	Mahsa Saeidi-Azcuy	1	3	2	10	6	9
16	15	Anand Vasudev	3	5	8	7	7	10
17	16	James Weir	6	2	3	6	9	8

CASE STUDY #1

Predicting the Future: Gartner's Research Informs Strategic Planning

As the world's leading research and advisory company on all matters relating to information technology, Gartner, Inc., attempts to see far into what is often a hazy future. Its 1,200 analysts and consultants rely on in-depth research, surveys, interviews, and countless analytical studies to examine every aspect of ICT. CIOs, business leaders, government agencies, and professional organizations depend on Gartner's research to help them with their own strategic planning.

A major competitive advantage for this $1.1 billion company is simply size. Gartner analysts are in contact with 60,000 clients from 10,000 organizations worldwide, so they gather information from large and small companies in every industry, and also from government agencies and nonprofits. This breadth gives them insights into patterns and trends that others do not have. Chief Gartner Fellow Daryl Plummer remarked, "Thought leadership is mostly about insight—making connections that others have not yet made.... We have a lot of topics, a lot of customers, and a lot of analysts. Insight flows from those intersections."

One of Gartner's most useful planning tools is the legendary "hype cycle," which tracks the evolution of technologies or IT-related business trends. A cycle begins with a technology trigger, often a disruptive innovation or a start-up company that gains attention. The innovation's popularity rises quickly through the "Peak of Inflated Expectations." But then it promptly begins falling into the "Trough of Disillusionment," as organizations learn the pitfalls and real-world challenges. If it survives, the innovation starts coming out on the other side and eventually reaches the "Plateau of Productivity," becoming a standard technology or business practice that makes solid contributions.

The hype cycle researchers also estimate the time period for each prediction. Figure 12-24 shows Gartner's predictions about several innovations, including when (or whether) they will

FIGURE 12-24

The Gartner Hype Cycle.

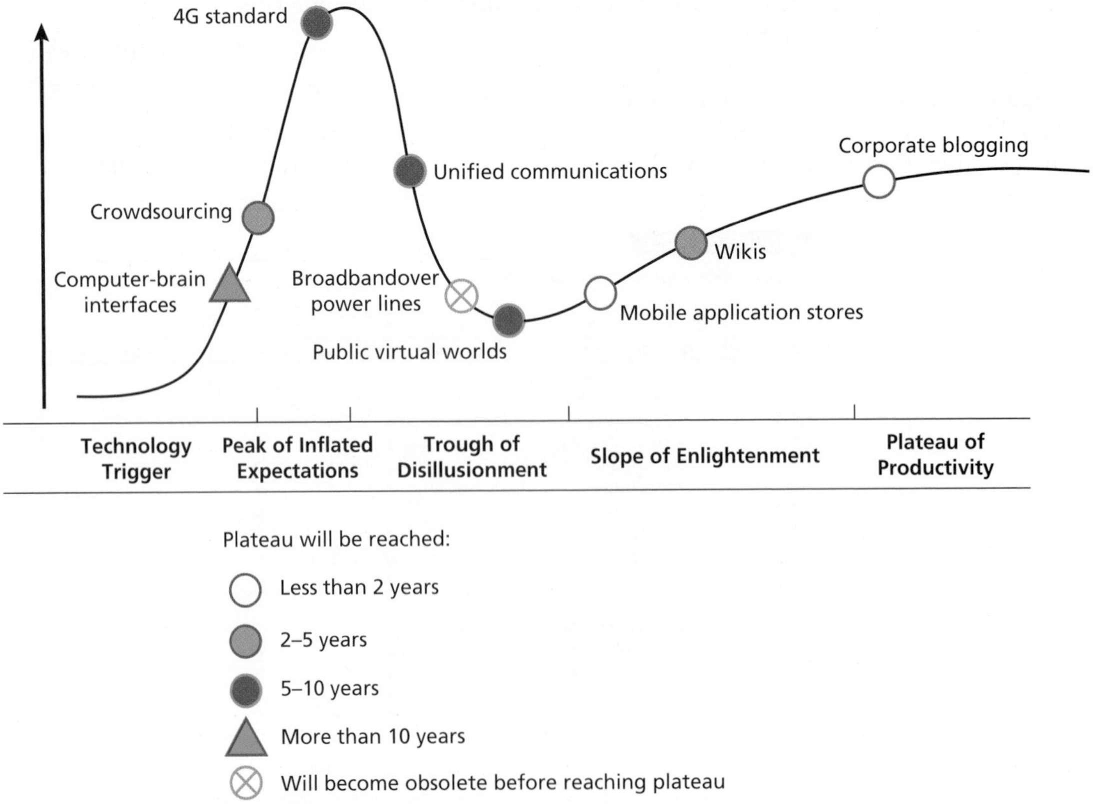

Source: Data include innovations drawn from several Gartner hype cycle charts from 2010.

reach the plateau. Corporate blogging is almost there, and wikis are not far behind. But the 4G standard (for smartphones) is teetering on the peak of inflated expectations. Based on analysis and research, Gartner predicts it will take 5–10 years for 4G to become standard. Broadband Internet access over power lines has a bleak future with its orange X. That means it is not likely to ever emerge from the trough of disillusionment and will probably vanish. The fate of computer-brain interfaces is still very uncertain, and its widespread appearance is not expected for at least 10 years. Crowdsourcing, while also still in its infancy, is likely to become widely accepted much sooner.

Gartner occasionally audits its own predictions, to see when they are off track. In 2005, for instance, Gartner predicted that organizations would routinely be using alternatives to Microsoft's Office suite by 2009. That didn't happen, but many other predictions were on target.

Strategic planning is fraught with pitfalls, but companies such as Gartner offer a window into the future that can help organizations move in the right directions. Arguably, they also play a role in shaping that future by influencing the choices organizations make.

Discussion Questions

1. What does this case tell us about the relationship between information systems and strategic planning?

2. What other information do company executives need to have beyond the type of information provided by Gartner?

3. How could organizations apply the Gartner life cycle to their strategies?

4. What is the value of having Gartner review its past predictions?

SOURCES: Anonymous. (August 16, 2010). Government should use cloud to reduce IT costs: Gartner. *CIO).* DOI: ID Number: 13284045, 4 Business Source Complete, EBSCOhost, accessed June 11, 2011. Landry, S. (August 4, 2010). Hype cycle for social software, 2010. Gartner Research. Otter, T., Hollincheck, J., et al. (July 24, 2009). Hype cycle for human capital managements How promissory organizations shape technology and innovation. *Social Studies of Science.* 40(525). Prentice, S., & Fenn, J. (August 4, 2010). Hype cycle for human-computer interaction, 2010. Gartner Research.

CASE STUDY #2

JetBlue and WestJet: A Tale of Two Software Implementations

The reservation system is more than just automated ticketing for an airline; it is the interface that customers come to know and love (or hate) as they find cheap flights, select seats, upgrade for more leg room, and cash in their frequent flyer points. Two discount airlines, JetBlue and WestJet, both chose to replace their aging systems with software from Sabre, the company that owns Travelocity and handles reservations for more than 300 other airlines. The similarity in their software implementation projects ends there, however, and the differences between them offer some important lessons.

WestJet, Canada's second-largest airline, was in the unfortunate position of going first. Company executives wisely decided to make the cutover during the winter, when passenger count was lower, but they didn't try to lower the volume further by limiting the number of tickets sold. They also decided against warning passengers that a change was coming until the go-live date. WestJet VP Bob Cummings commented, "We didn't want to telegraph dates so a competitor would put on a big fare sale."

For the cutover, WestJet had to transition 840,000 customer accounts to the new system for passengers who had already purchased tickets, migrating the data from WestJet's servers in Calgary to Sabre's servers in Tulsa. The migration suffered from glitches, and WestJet's website crashed. Customers suffered long waits and angry bloggers posted their complaints.

WestJet had kindly invited JetBlue staffers to observe the transition, and the visitors eagerly absorbed the lessons. First, they knew they could avoid the website crash by bringing up a backup site. They also learned to emphasize communications and they alerted customers and other stake-holders weeks ahead. The JetBlue blog was the platform they used to explain how the company was preparing for the software implementation. JetBlue wanted to keep the number of passengers low when the cutover occurred, giving employees more time to troubleshoot problems, so it pre-canceled 56 flights and restricted ticket sales on the remainder. To make sure customers didn't have to wait in long phone queues, the company hired 500 temporary reservation agents and kept them on board for two months. Rick Zeni, the JetBlue VP who led the project, said the extra agents were "one of the wisest investments we made."

Although glitches occurred and not all kiosks immediately functioned properly, observers gave JetBlue high marks. The whole company pitched in, and even executives were in the airport in shifts, solving problems and helping out. Changing an airline's reservation system is an enormous project with major risks, one that airlines do very rarely. JetBlue learned from WestJet's missteps, so its "brain transplant" caused minimal disruption.[26]

Discussion Questions

1. What are some key differences between the JetBlue and WestJet software implementations?

2. What are the advantages and disadvantages of communicating a major project in advance?

3. What are the advantages and disadvantages of adjusting business volume during a major business project?

4. Beyond not being the first firm to implement a particular piece of software, what other more general lessons apply for software implementation?

SOURCES: Canada, Y. F. (October 19, 2009). Westjet's "slick new reservation system." *The Wings of the Web, Airliners.net.* www.airliners.net/aviation-forums/general_aviation/read.main/4582650, accessed June 11, 2011. Carey, S. (2010). Two paths to software upgrade. *Wall Street Journal* (Eastern Edition). 255(85), B6. wolvie007. (October 18, 2009). Disgraceful. www.flyertalk. com/forum/westjet-frequent-guest/991443-westjet-switching-sabre-2.html, accessed June 11, 2011.

E-PROJECT 1   Checking on Gartner's Predictions

Gartner makes many very concrete predictions about how different technologies or business practices will fare in the future, and even how particular businesses will evolve. For this e-project, conduct an "audit" to determine whether Gartner's predictions panned out.

1. In 2009, Gartner analysts were very impressed by Amazon's strategic efforts to become customer-centric and predicted that by 2011 the company would have the highest customer-satisfaction score on the American Customer Satisfaction Index (ACSI). Visit www.theacsi.org and learn how this organization rates companies on customer satisfaction. Check out Amazon's performance during the last few years by going to Scores by Industry, and then selecting Internet

Retail. How did Amazon do this year? If it didn't earn the highest score, which Internet Retail companies did?

2. Gartner was not impressed with the Windows Vista operating system when it launched in 2006, especially because the software had limited application support. Analysts predicted it would take at least 18 months for Vista to be used on 10 percent of the computers in enterprises. In fact, they even recommended that companies not rush to adopt Vista. Was that prediction reasonably accurate? Use a search engine to find reports on Vista's market share in companies and also in general use during that period. The website e-janco.com offers helpful historical data on enterprise infrastructures. Use the Search feature to find market share information for Vista.

E-PROJECT 2   Analyzing Airline Performance with Excel Pivot Tables

In this project, you will download departure data for JetBlue and other airlines, using flights that depart from Los Angeles. The project will help you understand how Excel's Pivot Table function analyzes large data sets.

Download the Excel file Ch12_Airlines. Select all the columns containing data, and then choose Insert/Pivot Chart.

1. Drag Carrier Code to the Axis Fields (Categories) box, and drag Departure Delay to the Values box. The chart will default to the sum of departure times. Which airline had the highest number of delay minutes in this time period?

2. Since the airlines have a different number of departures, the average (mean) of delay minutes is a better metric than the

sum. Click on the Sum of Departure Delays and select Value Field Settings. Change the setting to average. Which airline has the shortest average departure delay?

3. Now let's examine the delays in terms of where planes are headed. Click on the black arrow inside the Carrier Code symbol in the Axis Fields box, and choose Remove Field. (You can also just drag the Carrier Code symbol out of the box to remove it, or just uncheck the box next to Carrier Code in the field list). Drag Destination airport to that location to break down the average delays by destination. Which destination experienced the largest average departure

delay for flights from Los Angeles, and what is the average departure delay for this destination?

4. That result could mean that Milwaukee's February weather is partly the cause. But now drag Carrier Code back into the Axis Fields Box, and place it just above Destination Airports. Which airline operates flights from Los Angeles to MKE?

5. The file also includes columns that break down the delays based on what caused them. What factor is causing most of the delays for the flights from Los Angeles to Milwaukee?

CHAPTER NOTES

1. Hoffman, T. (2007). What's plaguing e-health? *Computerworld.* 41(13), 21–24.

2. Preston, R. (March 14, 2011). Can the healthcare industry handle all this IT? *InformationWeek.* (1294).

3. (2008). *A guide to the project management body of knowledge (PMBOK guide),* (4th ed.). Newtown Square, PA: Project Management Institute.

4. Swan, J., Scarbrough, H., & Newell, S. (2010). Why don't (or do) organizations learn from projects? *Management Learning.* 41(3), 325–344.

5. Robertson, S., & Williams, T. (2006). Understanding project failure: Using cognitive mapping in an insurance project. *Project Management Journal.* 37(4), 55–71.

6. Project Management Institute code of ethics and professional conduct. 2006. www.pmi.org/About-Us/Ethics/~/media/PDF/Ethics/ap_pmicodeofethics.ashx, accessed September 12, 2010.

7. Censer, M. (July 26, 2010). VA cancels financial management system in wake of federal IT squeeze. *Washington Post.*

8. Philpott, T. (February 18, 2010). Combined pay, personnel system dumped as "a disaster." *Military.com.* www.military.com/features/0,15240,210873,00.html, accessed June 11, 2011.

9. Jones, C. G., et al. (2010). Strategies for improving systems development project success. *Issues in Information Systems.* XI(1), 164–173.

10. Levinson, M. (June 23, 2010). IT project management: 10 less considered keys to success. *CIO.com.*

11. Govekar, M. (July 6, 2010). Chargeback cost recovery: Moment of truth. Gartner Research.

12. IBM social computing guidelines: Blogs, wikis, social networks, virtual worlds, and social media. *IBM.* www.ibm.com/blogs/zz/en/guidelines.html, accessed June 11, 2011.

13. Connolly, P. J. (March 7, 2011). iPad, iPhone challenge management orthodoxy. *eWeek.* 28(5), 18–21.

14. Macsai, D. (July 2010). Remember the money. *Fast Company.* 147, 42.

15. Feigelson, J., & Calman, C. (2010). Liability for the costs of phishing and information theft. *Journal of Internet Law.* 13(10), 16–26.

16. Fragola, J. (2010). Know your portfolio. *Information Management.* 20(1), 22–25.

17. Overby, S. (September 16, 2005). Lessons from Hurricane Katrina: It pays to have a disaster recovery plan in place. *CIO.com.*

18. Kadlec, C., & Shropshire, J. (2010). Best practices in IT disaster recovery planning among U.S. banks. *Journal of Internet Banking & Commerce.* 15(1), 1–11.

19. (August 27, 2009). Poll results on business preparedness for H1N1. *H1N1 Business Continuity.*

20. Slater, D. (nd). Business continuity and disaster recovery planning: The basics. *CSO Security and Risk.*

21. Layne, R. (March 28–April 3, 2011). How Otis Elevator found the right floor. *Bloomberg Businessweek.* p. 20.

22. Buehler, R., Griffin, D., & Ross, M. (1994). Exploring the "planning fallacy": Why people underestimate their task completion times. *Journal of Personality and Social Psychology.* 67, 366–381.

23. Ruscio, J. (2002). *Clear thinking with psychology: Separating sense from nonsense.* Pacific Grove, CA: Wadsworth.

24. Taleb, N. (2005). *The black swan: Why don't we learn that we don't learn.* New York: Random House.

25. Yudkowsky, E. (2008). Cognitive biases potentially affecting judgement of global risks. In Bostrom, N., & Cirkovic, M. (Eds.). *Global catastrophic risks.* Oxford University Press: Oxford, UK. pp. 91–119.

26. Carey, S. (2010). Two paths to software upgrade. *Wall Street Journal* (Eastern Edition). 255(85), B6.

Case Studies

CASE STUDY #1
Facebook's Privacy Challenges

With more than 500 million people around the world posting personal data, photos, and videos (Figure 1-1), Facebook struggles with thorny privacy issues. The site's loyal users rely on it to share news and special moments with their friendship networks, but their personal information and preferences can leak out in ways they often don't understand. Over half the respondents in a 2011 *USA Today*/Gallup telephone survey of adults age 18 and older said they were "very or somewhat concerned" about invasion of privacy.

FACEBOOK'S PRIVACY POLICIES: A MOVING TARGET

Facebook frequently changes its privacy policies, and every tweak can either reassure users that their data are safe or cause further alarm. In 2005, when the site was called "Thefacebook," the policy was very simple: *No personal information that you submit will be available to any user of the web site who does not belong to at least one of the groups specified by you in your privacy settings.* Five years later, the privacy policy stretched to thousands of words in legalese. Lawyers write much of this text, using language they hope will satisfy regulators and privacy advocates, but that often confounds users.

One change that users called "creepy" happened in 2007, when Facebook launched a service that could track people's actions on third-party websites and broadcast that information to their Facebook friends. Users objected to this lack of control, and Facebook soon dropped the practice. In 2010, the company decided to have the user's privacy account settings default to "everyone," so that anyone could view the information unless the user proactively altered the privacy settings to limit access to friends. After privacy advocates protested, Facebook reversed course and changed the default to more restrictive settings.

The Facebook Places service, launched in 2010, raises additional concerns about privacy. This service allows you to "check in" so others can see your current location on a map. Facebook defaulted the setting to "friends only," having learned from experience that a default to "everyone" would trigger objections. The service also offers you the option to broadcast your location to other users who happen to be nearby who are not in your friends network, but prudently, that was disabled by default. One potential snag, though, is that your friends can check you into a location without your permission, even if you aren't actually at that location. Michael Zimmer of the School of Information Studies at the University of Wisconsin-Milwaukee tested this

FIGURE 1-1

Facebook statistics.

Number of accounts	500 million+, almost 8% of the world population
Friends	Average user has 130 friends
Minutes spent	In total, users spend 700 billion minutes per month on Facebook
Content creation	Average user creates 90 posts, photos, or other kinds of content each month
Applications	Users install 20 million applications every day

Source: www.facebook.com/press/info.php?statistics, accessed March 12, 2011.

feature by checking his wife into a local liquor store. The information appeared in his newsfeed and could have been viewed by any Facebook user if his privacy settings allowed it. His wife received an e-mail alert, but she didn't check it for days, so the bogus check-in remained viewable.

SOCIAL MARKETING

Facebook is in a unique position for marketing because the site has so much information about what you like, who your friends are, and what *they* like. While search engine marketing relies on the keywords you enter, social marketing can tap into a deeper understanding of your behavior patterns. It can also draw on whatever influence you have on your friends and turn products into overnight sensations through viral marketing. For instance, Facebook introduced "Sponsored Stories" as a way for paying advertisers to keep your friends informed whenever you click the "Like" button on their brand or check in at one of their stores. The action appears on the right side of the friends' home pages, along with events, questions, and other content. The entry suggests that you endorse the brand, and a logo with another "Like" button allows your friends to endorse it, too.

Privacy advocates argue that there should be some way for users to opt out of this feature so they can "like" things that won't be shared with their friends. But company representatives point out that Sponsored Stories will follow the same privacy settings as the original post.

FACEBOOK APPS

The third-party companies that develop applications for Facebook have also come under fire for privacy breaches. These companies make agreements with Facebook so that users can access social games and activities like Farmville, Texas HoldEm Poker, and Family Tree Builder. Some applications were collecting information about users in a way that violated Facebook's own privacy rules, all without the user's permission. In one case, the information was transmitted to a company that compiles dossiers on individuals to use for targeted advertising. Facebook disabled the applications involved in the scandal, and the company blocks apps it finds are violating its policies.

Social gaming and online marketing have become so complex, however, that it is possible some of the third-party game developers did not even know they were breaching privacy rules. Facebook's policies prohibit the third party apps from transferring personal information to marketers, but the technical challenges of complying are daunting.

CHALLENGES AHEAD

Managing privacy becomes more complicated for Facebook as the site's capabilities expand. The myriad privacy settings confuse users, although Facebook has made headway by revising its interface, trying to make each setting more comprehensible (Figure 1-2). The company's default and recommended settings may permit

FIGURE 1-2

Examples of Facebook information categories with customizable privacy settings.

▶ Posts by me

▶ Who is allowed to comment on my posts

▶ Relationships

▶ Religious and political views

▶ Places I check in

▶ Mobile phone number

▶ Photos and videos I'm tagged in (posted by others)

▶ Whether to be included in the listing of "People Here Now" on Facebook Places

more sharing than you prefer, but you can further restrict access to each category of information to just friends, specific friends, friends of friends, or just to yourself. Facebook also introduced a "hide" setting so you can identify certain friends in your network who should not be allowed to view photos or other categories.

The fact that users don't have much control over what other people upload is another challenge for privacy. Once a friend uploads a photo that tags your image with your name, the friend's privacy settings have control over who sees that photo on his or her page, and those settings might cause trouble. Facebook has generated some fascinating research on the technology needed to collaboratively manage privacy settings. For example, one system creates an alert when content with your name appears, and you can request to co-manage the privacy settings for that particular photo.

With a worldwide footprint, complying with privacy laws in all the countries in which users live is another immense challenge. European regulators, for example, insist that Facebook safeguard user data according to the EU's privacy rules. They also recognize, however, that laws vary from one country to the next in the European Union, so they are trying to harmonize the maze of privacy rules for online data. But even if that effort succeeds, the resulting privacy laws will probably not match those in the United States and other countries.

Finally, a nagging challenge is whether fickle fans will get "Facebook fatigue" and begin dropping Facebook in favor of other social networks, such as LinkedIn. When Facebook was first launched, an important competitive advantage was its exclusivity. The site targeted college students, first at Harvard, Stanford, Columbia, and Yale, and then at other colleges and universities. Users built their social networks from their college connections. As it expanded, Facebook opened its doors to everyone, and people over 50 now constitute the site's fastest-growing population. Adding grandparents to friendship networks originally meant for college buddies changes their character.

Whatever its demographics, concerns about privacy could well become a much bigger threat to Facebook's future. Despite all the tweaks to improve privacy controls and the reassurances about data protection, people may decide that liberal information sharing is just too risky, whether on Facebook or any other social network. But to earn revenue, Facebook has to find ways to monetize its most valuable asset: user data. When marketers can't access the data because of strict privacy settings, they won't pay for it. This puts Facebook in an awkward position.

Since its launch in 2004, Facebook has continually broken new ground. Perhaps it is not surprising that founder Mark Zuckerberg admitted candidly, "Basically, any mistake you think you can make, I've probably made it, or will make it in the next few years."

Discussion Questions

1. How might privacy and user considerations differ for an application such as Facebook, which is used primarily by individual users, compared with an application such as an ERP system that is used primarily by corporations?
2. How does the default selection of sharing versus not sharing information impact the subsequent choices of individual users?
3. What is the likely perspective of marketers on privacy issues at Facebook?
4. How do app developers fit into the social media industry?

Sources

Acohido, B. (February 9, 2011). Most Google, Facebook users fret over privacy. *USA Today*. www.usatoday. com/tech/news/2011-02-09-privacypoll09_ST_N.htm, accessed March 28, 2011.

EU clarifies proposed data-privacy rules. (March 16, 2011). *Wall Street Journal Online*. ABI/INFORM Global. (Document ID: 2294432821), March 23, 2011.

Fowler, Geoffrey A. (February 25, 2011). Facebook Tries to Simplify Privacy Policy. *Wall Street Journal Online*. ABI/INFORM Global. (Document ID: 2278461711), March 23, 2011.

Microsoft, Facebook offer new approaches to boost web privacy. (February 25, 2011). *Wall Street Journal Online*. ABI/INFORM Global. (Document ID: 2276507341), March 23, 2011.

Morales, L. (February 17, 2011). Google and Facebook users skew young, affluent, and educated. *Gallup Poll Briefing*, 2. http://www.gallup.com/poll/146159/facebook-google-users-skew-young-affluent-educated.aspx, accessed June 12, 2011.

Sorensen, C. (2010). The Anti-hero. *Maclean's*. 123(48/49), 120–122. EBSCOhost, accessed June 12, 2011.

Steel, Emily, & Fowler, Geoffrey. (October 18, 2010). What they know: A *Wall Street Journal* investigation: Facebook in privacy breach: Top-ranked applications transmit personal IDs, a *Journal* investigation finds. *Wall Street Journal* (Eastern Edition). p. A.1. ABI/INFORM Global. (Document ID: 2165042171), March 23, 2011.

When no patient privacy interests were implicated, court enjoined nursing college's suspension of student who posted medical photos on Facebook. (2011). *Computer & Internet Lawyer*. 28(4), 19–20. EBSCOhost, accessed June 12, 2011.

Zimmer, Michael. (August 25, 2010). Facebook places privacy falls short, part 2: Opting out. *Michael Zimmer.org*. http://michaelzimmer.org/2010/08/25/facebook-places-privacy-falls-short-part-2, accessed June 12, 2011.

CASE STUDY #2
A Humanitarian Supply Chain for the Red Cross

Humanitarian organizations such as the Red Cross face logistics challenges that would stump a Walmart or Dell. Up to 80 percent of their costs are in logistics, so it is not surprising that they should seek excellence in their supply chains. But their operations are fraught with uncertainties and urgency, so many of the principles that apply to business supply chains do not fit as readily.

Composed of 186 separate National Societies, the International Federation of Red Cross Red Crescent Societies (IFRC) is the largest humanitarian organization in the world. Coordinating such a dispersed organization is no easy feat, as was made clear when Hurricane Mitch struck Honduras in 1998. IFRC was embarrassingly slow to organize relief efforts. Its aid did not begin reaching victims until weeks after the event, long after other aid organizations were already on the ground. The lackluster performance caused donors to wonder whether their dollars were well spent and whether the IFRC was capable of managing a world-class supply chain that could respond to disasters in an efficient and cost-effective way.

THE IFRC'S EARLY SUPPLY CHAIN

IFRC's cumbersome supply chain was centrally managed in its headquarters in Geneva, Switzerland. Whenever disaster struck, a team from Geneva would go evaluate the damage and send back information to create the Relief Mobilization Table, which described what was needed and where. Tents, blankets, food, water, medical supplies, and thousands of other items might be on the table. Geneva then sent this data out to suppliers, the separate National Societies, and also to donors, letting them know where to send the relief supplies. These agents would then ship the goods to IFRC's emergency units near the disaster area, handling customs clearances, inventory, warehousing, and other logistics duties. Then the emergency units would distribute the supplies to local partners, who transported them to the beneficiaries.

That centralized supply chain model stumbled badly, especially because of poor information flow and a lack of transparency about who was sending what. The disaster site might be flooded with blankets and tents, yet never receive desperately needed telecom equipment. Many well-meaning organizations sent unsolicited goods, which often hindered rather than helped the IFRC's ability to obtain and distribute the needed relief supplies. Also, the failure to coordinate transportation led to unnecessarily high costs for multiple transatlantic flights and shipments. Unlike Walmart, whose supply chain managers know precisely where all the warehouses and supercenters are and what products they need, the IFRC lacked a supply chain that could handle uncertainty.

CREATING A DECENTRALIZED SUPPLY CHAIN

To improve its performance, IFRC began to transform its supply chain to a decentralized model, creating three regional logistics units in Dubai, Kuala Lumpur, and Panama. These units preposition supplies in warehouses for the most common disasters in their areas, so they can ramp up quickly (Figure 2-1).

For the information system, IFRC deployed the Humanitarian Logistics Systems (HLS), created especially for disaster recovery by the Fritz Institute. Although enterprise resource planning (ERP) vendors offer supply chain modules along with their core modules for finance and human resources, their products are not designed for situations with so much uncertainty. Instead, IFRC needed a relatively simple system with a single data repository that could handle rapid mobilization. It also needed a system that could be accessed in real time in the field by its regional units, emergency teams, and also the local National Societies.

FIGURE 2-1

Revamping the IFRC supply chain with Regional Logistics Units in Dubai, Kuala Lumpur, and Panama.

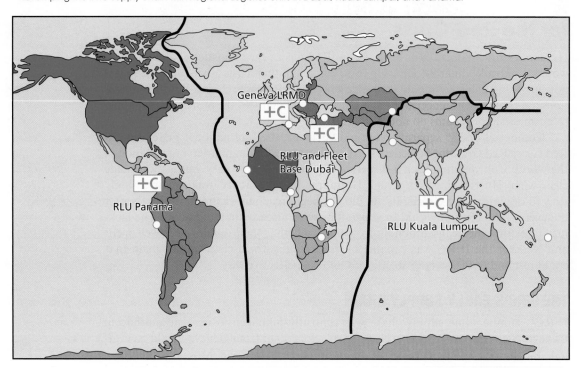

The web-based HLS software supports several essential functions that helped transform the IFRC supply chain. First, it maintains country and disaster data for the regional units, so they can intelligently pre-position supplies. Once disaster strikes, the system can aggregate the items needed and generate the mobilization table. The software also manages appeals to potential donors, helping to avoid the duplication that plagued earlier efforts.

For procurement, the software helps manage supplier relationships, tracking agreements and requests for bids, and generating standard purchase orders and invoices. HLS includes tables for tracking shipping information, and it can generate shipping documents, receipts for goods, and reports on where items in the pipeline are currently located and when they can be expected.

THE FIRST TEST

The IFRC's new supply chain was first tested when an earthquake struck Indonesia, and the just-opened Kuala Lumpur Regional Unit took the lead. Although glitches occurred, the supply chain was in motion in just three days, less than a third of the time it took IFRC to mobilize for the earthquake in Pakistan the previous year. The operation was also much more cost-effective. By one estimate, the new supply chain cut the cost of responding to Indonesia's earthquake in half (Figure 2-2).

IFRC won a coveted industry award for its efforts, beating out world-class competitors from both the public and the private sectors. The panel judges remarked that the IFRC's new supply chain was outstanding:

> "…all the more so when you realize that they exist to operate in precisely the places where normal supply chains have broken down; that they have only moral rather than legal charges over their sources of supply and funding, and that despite being a global brand with relatively little direct control over its local operations, it has successfully transformed its supply chain to meet even better the demands that the world places on it."

FIGURE 2-2

Comparison of supply chain metrics for disasters before and after IFRC's supply chain was decentralized.

Supply Chain Effectiveness Metric	Indian Ocean Tsunami	Pakistan Earthquake	Indonesia Earthquake
Supply chain organization	Centralized	Partially decentralized	Decentralized, with RLU in Kuala Lumpur
Families receiving at least a partial package by 2 months	26,021 (26% of families affected)	29,229 (31% of families affected)	53,112 (82% of families affected)
Average number of families served per day	445	555	613
% of goods delivered from the region	13%	68%	100%
Days to activate end-to-end supply chain	18	10	3
Cost to deliver relief package to families at 2 months	Not available	$824	$142

Discussion Questions

1. What were the deficiencies in the previous Red Cross supply chain?
2. What role did IT play in the new Red Cross supply chain?
3. What other elements are part of the new Red Cross supply chain?
4. What were the business results for the Red Cross?

Sources

Gatignon, A., Van Wassenhove, L. N., & Charles, A. (2010). The Yogyakarta earthquake: Humanitarian relief through IFRC's decentralized supply chain. *International Journal of Production Economics.* 126(1), 102–110.

International Federation of Red Cross Red Crescent Societies website. www.ifrc.org/index.asp, accessed June 12, 2011.

Stapleton, Orla, Martinez, Pedraza, Wassenhove, Alfonso, and Van, Luk N. (July 23, 2009). *Last mile vehicle supply chain in the International Federation of Red Cross and Red Crescent Societies.* INSEAD Working Paper No. 2009/40/TOM/INSEAD. SSRN: http://ssrn.com/abstract=1437978, accessed June 12, 2011.

CASE STUDY #3
Clearwire and the Race to 4G

The competition to win the hearts and minds of smartphone users seeking faster 4G Internet access wherever they roam started in a Maryland basement office in 2003. Billionaire Craig McCaw sent representatives to meet with the lawyer for a Spanish-language broadcaster who happened to control an important chunk of the electromagnetic spectrum. McCaw wanted that broadcaster's license, and hundreds of others, which would grant his company the rights to transmit in the 2.5 gigahertz frequency. Much of that spectrum had been handed out to schools and nonprofits around the country over the years, so they could broadcast educational TV. But because many of the licenses weren't being used anyway, McCaw was able to buy more than 1,000 of them.

Why did he want this spectrum? McCaw knew customers wanted faster mobile access to the Internet. At the time, they were paying hefty fees for small adapters they could use with their laptops when they traveled by train or car. The next generation of mobile broadband, called "4G," would be the solution; it would let users access the net with their mobile, wireless devices at speeds comparable to wired services from cable or phone companies.

McCaw was betting on WiMax wireless broadband technology, and he believed customers would rather pay monthly subscription fees for a service they could use anywhere—in their homes, in cars, on trains, and at the beach. He wanted the service to work for desktop computers, laptops, cell phones, tablets, and new devices that haven't yet been invented. He also thought he could offer better pricing than Verizon and other Internet service providers, since it's cheaper to construct cell towers to provide the signals than to build a traditional network.

CLEARWIRE'S STRATEGIC ADVANTAGES

Clearwire, the company McCaw launched to fulfill this vision, was the first mover in wireless broadband, and by 2011, its service was available in 71 U.S. markets. Its subscriber base grew at a very rapid pace, reaching 4.4 million subscribers by 2011. The company expects that number to more than double in 2011, partly because its 14,500+ cell sites cover an area in which approximately 119 million people reside.

The company's major competitive advantage is its wealth of spectrum compared with other wireless providers. On its website, the company touts this feature:

> "Think of it like the number of lanes on a freeway. We have more lanes, so we can move more traffic."

Clearwire acquired the spectrum licenses at bargain basement prices and will pay only about $5 billion for this "oceanfront property" over three decades. Compare that to the $16 billion Verizon and AT&T paid at a government auction to license the spectrum they want to use for 4G. Analysts project that Clearwire's spectrum holdings alone could be worth $50 billion.

Clearwire offers customers access to its network through its own brand, called "Clear," and also partners with Sprint, Comcast, Time Warner Cable, and other providers to offer mobile broadband service to their customers.

CLEARWIRE'S CHALLENGES

Alongside its competitive advantages, Clearwire faces major challenges. It has not yet turned a profit, mainly because of the cost of network expansion to serve more areas. The company received major investments from Intel, Comcast, Time Warner Cable, Google, and Bright House Networks. Sprint Nextel added $1.5 billion, making it the majority shareholder of the company. But cell sites are not cheap. In 2010, for instance, Clearwire put up about 5,000 cell towers and other cell sites, and each one cost from $130,000 to $150,000. The company wants to double that number for 2011 to reach more customers, at a cost of more than $3 billion.

Yuri Arcurs/Shutterstock

4G promises much faster transmission speeds that will improve Internet access from smartphones.

Clearwire's competitors are not standing still, of course. Although they got a later start, they are rolling out their own 4G capabilities using different technologies for their networks. Verizon and AT&T do not use WiMax and instead have adopted a technology called LTE, for long-term evolution. Analysts speculate that LTE has a good chance of becoming the industry standard for wireless broadband, especially because the companies that use it have such a large subscriber base. Verizon, for instance, has more than 90 million customers. Wireless providers in many other countries are adopting LTE, including NTT DoCoMo in Japan and Telstra in Australia.

If LTE becomes the dominant technology, Clearwire will be pressured to move its services in that direction as well. Companies that invent and manufacture mobile handsets and other devices will focus on LTE, so Clearwire's customers may wind up with fewer choices. In 2011, the company announced that LTE trials are underway in Phoenix, Arizona, hinting that a technology shift is coming. Clearwire's approach is called "LTE 2X," which takes advantage of the fact that it has more spectrum, so can use a wider range of channels at faster speeds. Technically, neither WiMax nor LTE is an "official" 4G technology; neither meets the industry standard. But both offer tremendous improvements over the 3G networks. Actual speed advantages depend on distance to the cell site and other factors.

Converting its WiMax network to LTE, though, is another very expensive proposition, and Clearwire is already heavily indebted. It had to lay off 15 percent of its workforce, and the company clearly needs more funding to continue. Sprint had been investing heavily in the past and depending on Clearwire to be able to offer 4G services to its own customers. But whether Sprint will continue to support Clearwire's rollouts and upgrades is not clear. To raise funds, Clearwire is even willing to sell some of its own spectrum, at least parts that it doesn't need. Its stock price soared in 2007, but has declined since then (Figure 3-1).

In a surprise move, Craig McCaw stepped down as chairman of the company in December 2010, and Clearwire's new leadership faces very difficult challenges. Whether this early frontrunner in the mobile broadband market will overcome its technical, financial, and strategic hurdles is an open question.

FIGURE 3-1

Clearwire closing stock prices from 2007 to 2011.

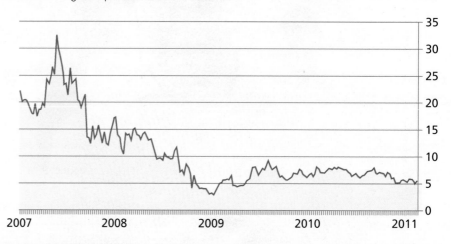

Discussion Questions

1. The case provides a list of investors in Clearwire. What does this list of investors tell us about the Clearwire company and the mobile phone service industry?
2. What does the case tell us about entrepreneurship and opportunities in technology industries?
3. What does the case tell us about cash flows in technology industries?
4. What role do standards play in the mobile phone service industry?

Sources

Clearwire website. www.clearwire.com, accessed June 11, 2011.

Dechter, G., & Kharif, O. (May 20, 2010). How Craig McCaw built a 4G network on the cheap. *Bloomberg Businessweek*. http://www.businessweek.com/magazine/content/10_22/b4180035396063_page_2.htm, accessed June 12, 2011.

Raice, S. (December 31, 2010). Craig McCaw to resign as Clearwire chairman. *Wall Street Journal Online*. http://online.wsj.com/article/SB10001424052748703909904576052413367715204.html, accessed June 12, 2011.

Raice, S., & Cheng, R. (2011). Corporate news: Sprint sees an end to Clearwire flap. *Wall Street Journal*. March 3, p. B4.

CASE STUDY #4
Managing the Federal Government's IT Project Portfolio

The Department of Veterans Affairs (VA) takes 160 days to process benefit applications, mainly because the process still requires moving manila folders from one staff member to the next. At the Patent Office, applications come in online, but then are printed out so clerks can rekey the information into an outdated legacy system. "This is not the way to run a modern government," said Vivek Kundra, the federal CIO at the time.

Governments have a long list of information systems projects underway and an even longer list of good ideas to deploy information systems to improve services, reduce costs, or engage citizens. However, managing this immense project portfolio is an overwhelming challenge.

DECIDING WHICH PROJECTS TO FUND

Some projects are clearly destined for failure and should have been scrapped long ago. The troubled financial system commissioned by Veterans Affairs suffered from escalation of commitment, and its expenses topped $500 million before Kundra announced that the project would be cut. Although its mounting costs and paltry progress made that project an obvious candidate for culling, other shaky projects are more difficult to evaluate.

To determine which projects should be terminated, Vivek Kundra initiated a major review of all the high-risk IT projects. The review focused on each project's potential return on investment and also ways to reduce the project's risk to an acceptable level. Strategies for reducing risk include:

▶ Setting project scope in a realistic way
▶ Clearly defining the deliverables
▶ Ensuring the project has strong executive support and a clear governance structure

Kundra's directive was a wake-up call to all the federal agencies, and their CIOs were asked to identify high-risk IT projects, develop improvement plans, and then present them at the CIO's "TechStat" Accountability Sessions. Many were already seriously behind schedule and over budget, and those that didn't pass muster would be candidates for termination. Kundra believes these meetings are essential to improve oversight of the government's unwieldy project portfolio. Agency staff spend months preparing for the review meetings, but the meetings themselves are time-boxed to 60 minutes, with no meandering or small talk (Figure 4-1). The reviews represent what Kundra calls "a very relentless pursuit of oversight."

One TechStat session in 2010 covered the Small Business Administration's (SBA) project to equip its employees with smart cards, which was far behind schedule and running up expenses. To prepare for the meeting, SBA staff had done their homework, looking into how other agencies handled these smart identity cards. While the SBA estimated it would spend more than $1,600 to implement each card, the General Services Administration (GSA) found ways to issue similar cards for just $250 per unit. During the session, the SBA head recommended that his agency's own smart card project be halted, and the SBA should obtain cards through the GSA. Eliminating this kind of duplication is an important goal of project portfolio management.

FIGURE 4-1

Schedule for a TechStat Accountability Session.

5 minutes	Overview of the IT project
10 minutes	Focus on problems identified by the agency
30–45 minutes	Discussion of possible solutions
5 minutes	Attendees create a list of corrective measures the agency must implement and report back on

FIGURE 4-2

Overall ratings for the IT projects at the Department of Veterans Affairs.

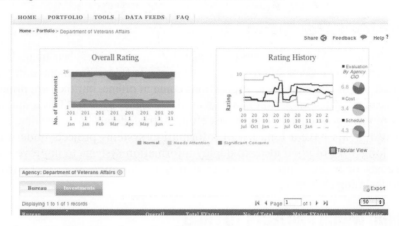

Source: http://it.usaspending.gov/portfolios

THE IT DASHBOARD

Another strategy the federal government uses to track its project portfolio is the publicly accessible IT dashboard (www.it.usaspending.gov). Agencies submit detailed information about their IT investments and the projects that make them up, and visitors to the website can slice and dice the data. They can drill down to individual investments in each agency, viewing charts and graphs of costs, schedules, and overall ratings of each project's status. Green means the project is on track, yellow indicates that it needs attention, and red points to significant concerns. The charts in Figure 4-2 vividly illustrate with hemorrhaging red paint the difficulties the Department of Veterans Affairs was having with its IT projects. With an agency budget over $3 billion, the cost overruns are very substantial. Roger Baker, the agency's CIO, said he planned to put dozens of projects on hold.

The dashboard also shows projects that are well on their way to a successful implementation, with no problems in terms of costs, schedule, or scope. The Smithsonian Institution, for example, launched a $1.2M project to implement ArtCIS, a state-of-the-art collections management system to track more than 600,000 objects that the museum holds in trust for the nation (Figure 4-3). The project was so successful that it was expanded to manage the collections held by NASA and the National Postal Museum.

Much of the data for the IT dashboards comes from standardized forms that each agency completes for IT projects. Figure 4-4 shows one example, called "Exhibit 300." These forms are also available online for the public to view.

Dashboards like this should make the organization's project portfolio more transparent, but they also have critics. Some project managers complain about the bureaucratic overhead and the time-consuming job of collecting data from every team leader to find out the status of each task. Managers know that people report differently, as well. Many want to avoid showing up as red, and they don't want to stay in the yellow for very long, so they can be reluctant to share bad news. Top-level management may not be aware that disaster looms until the deadline nears and there is no way to hide the problems.

Although Kundra resigned as federal CIO in August, 2011, his efforts led to significant improvements in the way the federal government manages the IT project portfolio. The TechStat accountability sessions, the IT dashboard, and the willingness to terminate failing projects are key examples that contribute to smarter decision making in the agencies, and wiser use of taxpayer dollars.

FIGURE 4-3

Smithsonian's collection management system.

Source: Smithsonian, http://www.si.edu. Reprinted with permission.

FIGURE 4-4

Sample data fields from Exhibit 300 submitted by the Federal Aviation Administration to the IT dashboard.

Investment Title	Total IT Spending FY 2011 (Budget) (in $ million)	Overall Rating	Cost Variance (in %)	Schedule Rating	Cost Rating	Schedule Rating	Evaluation by Agency CIO	CIO Evaluation Comments
FAAXX013: Aviation Surface Weather Observation Network (ASWON)	41.8	5	1.79	−10.9	9.46	6.82	3	Corrective actions for the Enhanced Precipitation Sensor are still under review. CAP being finalized.
FAAXX084: Instrument Flight Procedure Automation (IFPA)	7.571	5	−4.75	−1.83	8.58	9.45	3	Successful implementation of Release 1 in June 2010, as scheduled; satisfactory progress on EVM activities.
FAAXX084: Integrated Terminal Weather System (ITWS)	10.341	7.5	0.04	1.79	9.99	9.46	4	The program has been reviewed in the areas of Risk Management Requirements Management Contractor Oversight Historical Performance Human Capital and other factors including status of their strategic plan and has been assessed as Green overall.
FAAXX224: Terminal Radar Digitizing Replacement and Establishment (TRDRE)	16.235	7.5	0.61	−0.13	9.82	9.96	4	The last two ASR-11 systems achieved ORD last month (Green Bay was 6/8/10 and Peoria was 6/28/10). Tech Refresh work will continue. The program is assessed as Green overall.
FAAXX294: ATC Beacon Interrogator Replacement (ATCBI-6)	8.181	7.83	10.9	−2.77	6.82	9.17	4	Project management metrics indicate that the program is on track.
FAAXX456: ASR-9 Transmitter Modifications	1.871	7.39	-2.44	17.99	9.27	5.40	4	The program has been reviewed in the areas of Risk Management REquirements Management Contractor Oversight Historical Performance Human Capital and other factors including status of their strategic plan and has been assessed as Green overall.
FAAXX610: Aviation Safety Knowledge Management (ASKME/ AVS)	16.465	5.26	34.71	−15.07	2.29	5.99	4	CIO team is investing schedule slippage with the project team.
FAAXX705: Traffic Flow Management (TFM)	76.229	5	15.57	1.07	5.89	9.68	3	Existing contractor issues that are currently impacting schedule continue to be monitored against the Corrective Action Plan.

Discussion Questions

1. What unique challenges does the federal government face in managing its IT project portfolio?
2. The federal government CIO focused primarily on asking agencies to identify high-risk projects. What other information might be valuable for the CIO to receive from agencies?
3. The current communication effort is focused on identifying and managing high-risk projects across federal agencies. What are other ways in which the CIO could use communications across federal agencies to improve performance?
4. What are the relevant human considerations in reporting high-risk projects?

Sources

Douglas, M. (August 3, 2010). Federal CIOs TechStat initiative seeks to diagnose troubled IT initiatives and deliver quick treatment. *Public CIO*. www.govtech.com/gt/articles/767303?id=767303, accessed June 12, 2011.

Hasson, J. (June 21, 2009). VA CIO wants to end IT failures. *Fierce Government*. www.fiercegovernmentit.com/story/va-cio-wants-end-it-failures/2009-06-21, accessed June 12, 2011.

Kundra, V. (July 28, 2010). Memorandum for heads of executive departments and agencies. www.scribd.com/doc/35188288/Vivek-Kundra-IT-Failures-Memo, accessed June 12, 2011.

Miller, J. (June 4, 2009). CIOs cautiously optimistic about OMB's IT dashboard. *1500AM Federal News Radio*. www.federalnewsradio.com/?sid=1689099&nid=35, accessed June 12, 2011.

Montalbano, E. (September 13, 2010). Watchdogs blast fed IT execution. *InformationWeek*. 18.

Mulrain, M. (July 29, 2010). Kundra announces government-wide review of federal IT projects. *ExecutiveGov*. www.executivegov.com/2010/07/kundra-announces-government-wide-review-of-federal-it-projects, accessed June 12, 2011.

Glossary

A

acceptable-use policy An organizational policy that describes what employees are allowed to do with IT resources and what activities are disallowed; employees agree to the policy before gaining access to IT resources.

agile software development Development strategies involving cohesive teams that include end users, and in which many activities occur simultaneously rather than sequentially to accelerate delivery of usable software.

AJAX A mix of technologies that builds on Javascript and draws on live data to create interactive online displays.

anchoring The tendency for people to rely too heavily on one piece of information to adjust their estimates, even if it is irrelevant.

application software The type of software used to support a wide range of individual and business activities, such as transaction processing, payroll, word processing, and video editing.

artificial intelligence (AI) The capability of some machines to mimic aspects of human intelligence, such as learning, reasoning, judging, and drawing conclusions from incomplete information.

ASCII code A code that defines how keyboard characters are encoded intodigital strings of ones and zeros.

assistive technologies Devices and software that help people with disabilities, such as screen readers for the visually impaired.

autonumbering Process that assigns incremental numbers to records as they are created to ensure that each record has a unique primary key.

availability bias The tendency for people to judge the likelihood of events based on how readily they come to mind, rather than their actual likelihood.

B

bandwidth The maximum amount of information in bits per second that a particular channel can transmit.

batch processing The process of sequentially executing operations on each record in a large batch.

benchmark A reference point used as a baseline measurement.

best of breed An approach used by organizations in which they procure the best systems for each application, regardless of the vendor, and then build interfaces among them.

bits per second (bps) The measurement of transmission speed, defined as the number of bits transmitted each second; each bit is a single zero or one, and a string of eight bits makes up a byte.

black swan Used to describe an extremely rare event that is difficult or nearly impossible to predict, but which can have an immense impact in areas such as technology, finance, and science; black swans pose enormous challenges for strategic planners.

blog Short for "web log," and used to facilitate collaboration and knowledge sharing. Posts are displayed in reverse chronological order so that the most recent appears on top.

Bluetooth A technology that uses radio waves for connectivity, commonly used for wireless connections over very short distances.

botnet A combination of the terms "robot" and "network" referring to a collection of computers that have been compromised by malware, and used to attack other computers.

bullwhip effect Describes the distortions in a supply chain caused by changes in customer demand, resulting in large swings in inventory levels as the orders ripple upstream from the retailer to the distributor and manufacturer.

business continuity The maintenance of the organization's operations in the event of disaster or disruption.

business intelligence The information managers use to make decisions, drawn from the company's own information systems or external sources.

business process A set of activities designed to achieve a task; organizations implement information systems to support, streamline, and sometimes eliminate business processes.

business process management (BPM) Focuses on designing, optimizing, and streamlining business processes throughout the organization.

business process reengineering (BPR) The design and analysis of workflows in an organization with the goal of eliminating processes that do not add value.

business to business (B2B) E-commerce relationship in which businesses can buy and sell products or services online to one another.

business to consumer (B2C) E-commerce relationship in which businesses offer products for online sale to consumers.

byte Measurement unit for computer storage capacity; a byte holds eight zeros and ones and represents a single character.

C

CAPTCHA A test created by software developers that the visitor must pass before continuing to register or enter the site; designed to thwart software bots.

cascading style sheets (CSS) The part of a website template that controls the fonts and colors which appear when an editor identifies some text as a page heading, a paragraph title, or some other style.

central processing unit (CPU) The brain of a computer, which handles information processing, calculations, and control tasks.

change control process A process organizations use to manage and prioritize requests to make changes or add new features to an information system.

change management A structured approach to the transition employees must make as they switch from their existing work processes to new ones, especially with the introduction of a new information system.

chief information officer (CIO) The person who heads the department responsible for managing and maintaining information systems, and ensuring they support the organization's strategic goals.

circuit-switched network A type of network in which the nodes communicate by first establishing a dedicated channel between them.

click-through rate (CTR) A metric used to assess the impact of an online ad; computed as the number of visitors who click on the ad divided by the number of impressions.

clickstream data Business intelligence data that includes every click by every visitor on a website, along with associated data such as time spent on the page and the visitor's IP address.

client-server network A type of network in which the workload for running applications is shared between the server and the client devices, such as desktop computers, laptops, or smartphones.

closing processes Processes that formally end the project in an orderly way; they include a signoff by the sponsor confirming that all deliverables have been received and accepted.

cloud computing ICT architecture in which users access software applications and information systems remotely over the Internet, rather than locally on an individual PC or from servers in the organization's data center.

coaxial cables Wired medium, initially used for cable TV, consisting of a single inner conductor wire (typically copper) surrounded by insulation, which is then surrounded by a mesh-like conductor.

code review A peer review process in which programmers check over one another's work to ensure its quality.

cognitive bias A common human tendency to make systematic mistakes when processing information or making judgments; cognitive biases can distort strategic planning.

commercial off-the-shelf (COTS) Commercially available computer software that is ready to buy, install, and use.

communities of practice Groups of individuals who come together to learn from one another and share knowledge about their professions; they typically rely on online discussion forums, shared workspaces, wikis, blogs, and other social media.

competitive advantage Anything that gives a firm a lead over its rivals; it can be gained through the development and application of innovative information systems.

computer Any electronic device that can accept, manipulate, store, and output data, and whose instructions can be programmed.

confirmation bias The human tendency to choose information to examine that supports the person's view, but ignore data that might refute that view.

consumer to business (C2B) E-commerce relationship in which individual consumers can sell products or services to businesses.

consumer to consumer (C2C) E-commerce relationship in which individual consumers can buy and sell to one another over the Internet.

content management system Software used to manage digital content in collaborative environments. The web content management system supports teams that develop and maintain websites.

cookie A small text file left on a website visitor's hard drive that is used to personalize the site for the visitor, or track web activities.

creative destruction What happens in an industry when disruptive innovations threaten the established players.

crisis management team The team in an organization that is responsible for identifying, assessing, and addressing threats from unforeseen circumstances that can lead to crisis situations.

critical path The longest path through the project which identifies those tasks that can't be delayed without affecting the finish date. Monitoring tasks that fall along the critical path is especially important.

crowdsourcing Delegating tasks to large diffuse groups or communities, who often volunteer their contributions.

customer relationship management (CRM) system An information system used to build customer relationships, enhance loyalty, and manage interactions with customers.

D

dashboard A graphical user interface that organizes and summarizes information vital to the user's role and the decisions that user makes.

data The individual facts or pieces of information.

data definition Specifies the characteristics of a field, such as the type of data it will hold or the maximum number of characters it can contain.

data dictionary Documentation that contains the details of each field in every table, including user-friendly descriptions of the field's meaning.

data mining A type of intelligence gathering that uses statistical techniques to explore records in a data warehouse, hunting for hidden patterns and relationships that are undetectable in routine reports.

data model A model used for planning the organization's database that identifies what kind of information is needed, what entities will be created, and how they are related to one another.

data steward A combination of watchdog and bridge builder, a person who ensures that people adhere to the definitions for the master data in their organizational units.

data warehouse A central data repository containing information drawn from multiple sources that can be used for analysis, intelligence gathering, and strategic planning.

data-driven decision making Decision making that draws on the billions of pieces of data that can be aggregated to reveal important trends and patterns.

database An integrated collection of information that is logically related and stored in such a way as to minimize duplication and facilitate rapid retrieval.

database management software (DBMS) Software used to create and manage a database and that also provides tools for ensuring security, replication, retrieval, and other administrative and housekeeping tasks.

database schema A graphic that documents the data model and shows the tables, attributes, keys, and logical relationships for a database.

deliverables The products, documents, or services that will be delivered to the sponsor during the course of a project.

demand forecast accuracy (DFA) The difference between forecasted and actual demand.

digital rights management (DRM) Technologies that software developers, publishers, media companies, and other intellectual property owners use to control access to their digital content.

digital subscriber lines (DSL) Technology that supports high-speed two-way digital communication over twisted pair phone lines.

direct implementation A type of implementation in which the all the modules of a new information system are launched at the same time, and the old system is turned off; also called the "big bang" approach.

disaster recovery The procedures and documentation the organization puts into place to prepare for a disaster and recover the technical infrastructure.

disruptive innovation A new product or service, often springing from technological advances, that has the potential to reshape an industry.

distributed denial of service (DDoS) An attack in which computers in a botnet are directed to flood a single website server with rapid-fire page requests, causing it to slow down or crash.

document management systems Systems that manage electronic documents, often converted from paper sources, making them searchable and easily transmitted.

Domain Name System (DNS) The hierarchical naming system that maps a more memorable URL to the actual IP address.

E

e-commerce The buying and selling of goods and services over the Internet or other networks, encompassing financial transactions between businesses, consumers, governments, or nonprofits.

e-discovery The processes by which electronic data that might be used as legal evidence are requested, secured, and searched.

e-government The application of ICT to government activities, especially by posting information online and offering interactive services to citizens.

e-learning A varied set of instructional approaches that all depend on ICT, especially the Internet, to connect trainees with learning materials, and also with their instructors and other trainees.

e-marketplace A website that facilitates transactions by bringing together buyers and sellers from all over the world.

ecosystem An economic community that includes the related industries making complementary products and services, the competitors themselves, the suppliers, and also the consumers.

electronic data interchange (EDI) An electronic bridge between partner companies in a supply chain that is used to transmit real-time information about orders, inventories, invoices, and other data.

encryption Technique that scrambles data using mathematical formulas, so that it cannot be read without applying the key to decrypt it.

enterprise architecture (EA) A roadmap created by an organization to describe its current situation and where it should head to achieve its mission, focusing on business strategy and the technology infrastructure required to achieve it.

enterprise resource planning (ERP) Integrated application suite to support the whole enterprise that includes modules to manage financials, human resources, supply chain, customer relationships, and other business processes.

escalation of commitment The tendency to continue investing in a project, despite mounting evidence that it is not succeeding; often comes about because people mistakenly let sunk costs affect decision making rather than weighing the value of further investment.

ethernet   A communication protocol widely used for local area networks.

ethics   A system of moral principles that human beings use to judge right and wrong and to develop rules of conduct.

executing processes   All the coordinating efforts that ensure the tasks on the work breakdown structure are carried out properly.

executive information system   The software tools that support strategic-level decision making for senior managers.

expert location system   An information system that can find people in an organization with specific types of expertise based on their education, experience, and activities.

expert system   Software that mimics the reasoning and decision making of a human expert, drawing from a base of knowledge about a particular subject area developed with the expert's assistance.

explicit knowledge   Knowledge that can be documented and codified, often stored in information systems, on websites, in spreadsheets, or in handbooks and manuals.

eXtensible Business Reporting Language (XBRL)   Part of the XML family of standardized languages specialized for accounting and business reports; tags identify data elements to make them transparent, and also computer-readable.

extract, transform, and load (ETL)   A common strategy for drawing information from multiple sources by extracting data from its home database, transforming and cleansing it to adhere to common data definitions, and then loading it into the data warehouse.

extreme programming (XP)   A team-based agile method that features frequent releases of workable software, short time boxes, programmers who work in pairs, and a focus on testing.

F

feasibility study   Part of the information system planning process that examines whether the initiative is viable from technical, financial, and legal standpoints.

field   An attribute of an entity. A field can contain numeric data or text, or a combination of the two.

file transfer protocol (ftp://)   A URL component which indicates that the resource is a file to be transferred.

financial management system   Enterprise information system that supports financial accounts and processes, including accounts payable, accounts receivable, procurement, cash management, budget planning, assets, general ledger, and related activities.

firewall   A defensive technical control that inspects incoming and outgoing traffic and either blocks or permits it according to rules the organization establishes. The firewall can be a hardware device or a software program.

focused strategy   A company strategy that involves differentiating a product or service for a particular market niche.

forecasting   A statistical decision support tool used to analyze historical trends and other business intelligence to estimate some variable of interest, such as customer demand.

foreign key   A primary key that appears as an attribute in a different table is a foreign key in that table. They can be used to link the records in two tables together.

functionally dependent   For each value of the table's primary key, there should be just one value for each of the attributes in the record, and that the primary key determines that value; the attribute should be functionally dependent on the value of the primary key.

G

Gantt chart   A graphic showing the tasks on the work breakdown structure along with each task's projected start and finish dates.

global positioning systems (GPS)   Electronic devices that receive signals from orbiting satellites that transmit time and location data; GPS devices help drivers navigate and keep managers in touch with their transportation fleets.

goal seeking   A decision support tool, often based on an Excel model, in which the user sets a target value for a particular variable, such as profit/loss, and tells the program which variable to change to try to reach the goal.

group decision support system (GDSS)   Collaborative technology that helps groups brainstorm and make decisions in face-to-face meetings, led by facilitators. Participants can contribute anonymously via their computers.

H

hashtag   Microblogging tool invented by web users in which posts on a similar topic all include a keyword prefixed by a #.

hertz (Hz)   The number of cycles per second of a wave.

hierarchical database   An early database approach that linked records based on hierarchical relationships, such as those in the organizational chart.

hierarchical website architecture   Website structure in which the top-level home page contains links to second-level pages, which then link to further relevant pages.

hindsight bias   The human tendency to think an unusual event was (or should have been) predictable, once they know it actually happened.

human capital   The competencies and knowledge possessed by the organization's employees.

human capital management (HCM)   Encompasses all the activities and information systems related to effectively managing an organization's human capital. The HCM information system includes applications and modules with the employee as the central element.

human resources management system (HRM)   Typically the heart of the HCM system, the HRM system tracks each employee's demographic information, salary, tax data, benefits, titles, employment history, dependents, and dates of hire and termination.

hypertext markup language (HTML)   The original language used to create web pages; HTML specifies the web page's format using tags in angle brackets that browsers can interpret and put into reader-friendly output.

hypertext transfer protocol (http://)   A URL component which specifies that the resource is a web page containing code the browser can interpret and display.

I

IMAP (Internet mail access protocol)   A protocol for handling incoming e-mail.

incidence response plan   A plan that an organization uses to categorize a security threat, determine the cause, preserve any evidence, and also get the systems back online so the organization can resume business.

infomediary   Focuses on informing visitors and empowering them with aggregated information about products from different suppliers.

information   Data or facts that are assembled and analyzed to add meaning and usefulness.

information and communications technology (ICT)   The term encompasses the broad collection of information processing and communications technologies, emphasizing that telecommunication technology is a significant feature of information systems.

information privacy   The protection of data about individuals.

information security   A term that encompasses the protection of an organization's information assets against misuse, disclosure, unauthorized access, or destruction.

information system   A system that brings together four critical components to collect, process, manage, analyze, and distribute information; the four components are people, technology, processes, and data.

information technology (IT)   The hardware, software, and telecommunications that comprise the technology component of information systems; the term is often used more broadly, to refer to information systems.

initiating processes   Processes that lay the groundwork for the project by clarifying its business value, setting its objectives, estimating the project's length, scope, and cost, identifying team members, and obtaining approval.

instant messaging (IM)   Also called "chat." IM consists of real-time text-based interactions over a network.

instructional designer   The person on an e-learning development team who brings the knowledge and skills about what strategies work best for e-learning.

intellectual capital (IC)   All the intangible assets and resources of an enterprise that are not captured by conventional accounting reports, but still contribute to its value and help it achieve competitive advantage.

intellectual property (IP) Intangible assets such as music, written works, software, art, designs, movies, creative ideas, discoveries, inventions, and other expressions of the human mind, that may be legally protected by means of copyrights or patents.

intelligent agents Software programs or "bots" that are sent out to conduct a mission and collect data from web pages on behalf of a user.

intelligent character recognition (ICR) Software that can interpret hand printed text written on paper forms.

interactive voice response (IVR) A technology that facilitates access to the database from signals transmitted by telephone, to retrieve information, and enter data.

Internet Corporation for Assigned Names and Numbers (ICANN) The nonprofit organization charged with overseeing the Internet's naming system, establishing policies, and resolving disputes.

Internet Protocol Version 6 (IPv6) The next generation protocol for the Internet, which will support far more IP addresses compared to the current scheme.

intranet An organization's private web space. It relies on TCP/IP and web browsers, but it is password-protected and accessible only to authorized individuals through the organization's portal.

iterative methods Strategies that compress the time horizon for software development, partly to reduce the impact of changing business needs and the resulting rework. They focus on the time available until the next release, or iteration, and the development team determines how many of the requirements it can deliver in that timeframe.

J

Javascript A language used to add interactivity to web pages.

K

key performance indicators (KPI) The quantifiable metrics most important to the individual's role and the organization's success.

knowledge management (KM) A set of strategies and practices organizations use to become more systematic about managing intellectual capital. It is also a field of study in which researchers investigate all the roles these intangible assets play, how they contribute to competitive advantage and productivity, and how human behavior interacts with efforts to capture and share knowledge.

L

learning management system (LMS) An information system used to deliver e-learning courses, track student progress, and manage educational records. Such systems also support features such as online registration, assessments, collaborative technologies, payment processing, and content authoring.

learning object A self-contained digital resource embedded in an e-learning course that can be edited and reused for other purposes.

legacy systems Older information systems that remain in use because they still function and are costly to replace.

local area network (LAN) A network that connects devices such as computers, printers, and scanners in a single building or home.

low cost leadership strategy *A company strategy* that involves offering a similar product at a lower price compared to competitors.

M

malware Malicious software designed to attack computer systems.

management information systems (MIS) The study of information systems—how people, technology, processes, and data work together. Also used to describe a special type of information system that supports tactical decision making at the managerial level.

market basket analysis A statistical technique that reveals customer behavior patterns as they purchase multiple items.

mashup An approach to aggregating content from multiple internal and external sources on customizable web pages that relies on Web 2.0 technologies.

master data management An approach that addresses the underlying inconsistencies in the way employees use data by attempting to achieve consistent and uniform definitions for entities and their attributes across all business units.

media richness A measure of how well a communication medium can reproduce all the nuances and subtleties of the messages it transmits.

metadata Data about data that clarifies the nature of the information.

microblogging A form of blogging in which the posts are quite short, and especially suitable for mobile devices. As in a blog, the entries appear in reverse chronological order.

microformats A set of formats that rely on the XML family of standards to represent metadata in HTML code, and that support electronic exchange of business cards, calendar appointments, and other kinds of data.

microwave transmission The technology involving signals in the gigahertz range that are transmitted to relays in the line of sight.

middleware Software used as a bridge to integrate separate information systems and synchronize data across multiple systems.

monitoring and controlling processes Processes that track a project's progress from start to finish, pinpointing any deviations from the plan that must be addressed.

Moore's Law A principle named for computer executive Gordon Moore which states that advances in computer technology, such as processing speed or storage capabilities, double about every two years.

multi-dimensional cubes Data structures used for online analytical processing that permit very rapid analysis from different perspectives and groupings.

multi-dimensional website architecture Website structure with multiple links to pages at all levels, allowing visitors multiple paths through the site.

multifactor authentication A combination of two or more authentications a user must pass to access an information system, such as a fingerprint scan combined with a password.

N

n-tier Type of network architecture in which several servers, specialized for particular tasks, may be accessed by a client computer to perform some activity, such as retrieving a bank balance.

natural laws and rights An ethical system that judges the morality of an action based on how well it adheres to broadly accepted rules, regardless of the action's actual consequences.

network A group of interconnected devices, such as computers, phones, printers, or displays, that can share resources and communicate using standard protocols.

network database An early database approach that allowed flexible links to support M:M relationships.

network effects The increased value of a product or service that results simply because there are more people using it.

normalization A process that refines entities and their relationships to help minimize duplication of information in tables.

O

object-oriented programming A type of software programming that focuses on "objects" rather than lists of instructions and routines to manipulate data.

online analytical processing (OLAP) Software that allows users to "slice and dice" or drill down into massive amounts of data stored in data warehouses to reveal significant patterns and trends.

open source software A type of software whose licensing terms comply with criteria such as free distribution, so other people can access the source code to improve it, build upon it, or use it in new programs.

operating system (OS) The category of system software that performs a variety of critical basic tasks, such as handling device input and output, maintaining file structures, and allocating memory.

operations management The area of management concerned with the design, operation, and improvement of the systems and processes the organization uses to deliver its goods and services.

optical character recognition (OCR) The capability of specialized software to interpret the actual letters and numbers on a page to create a digital document that can be edited, rather than a flat picture.

optical fiber Cables that transmit bits by means of light pulses along a glass or plastic fiber instead of electrical signals over a conductor; ideally suited for long distances.

optical scanners Electronic devices that capture text or images and convert them to digital format.

optimization An extension of goal seeking in which the user can change many variables to reach some maximum or minimum target, as long as the changes stay within the constraints the user identifies.

P

packet switching A technology used by networks in which data is broken into segments called packets for transmission. The packets contain information about their destination and position in the whole message, and they are reassembled at the receiving end.

parallel implementation A type of implementation in which the new system is launched while the old one it is replacing continues to run so output can be compared.

payment gateway An e-commerce application that facilitates online shopping by mediating the interconnections to the merchant's bank, the bank or other entity that issued the card, and then back to the original website to approve or decline the purchase.

peer-to-peer network A type of network in which there is no central server and computers can share files, printers, and an Internet connection with one another.

phased implementation A type of implementation in which the modules of a new information system are launched in phases rather than all at once.

phishing An attempt to steal passwords or other sensitive information by persuading the victim, often in an email, to enter the information into a fraudulent website that masquerades as the authentic version.

planning processes The processes in project management that focus on planning how the project will be executed.

portal A gateway that provides access to a variety of relevant information from many different sources on one screen; for an enterprise, the portal provides a secure gateway to resources needed by employees, customers, and suppliers.

power of buyers The advantage buyers have when they have leverage over suppliers and can demand deep discounts and special services. This is one of Porter's five competitive forces.

power of suppliers The advantage sellers have when there is a lack of competition and they can charge more for their products and services. This is one of Porter's five competitive forces.

predecessors The tasks that must be completed in a project before a particular task can begin.

presence awareness IM software feature that allows users to display their current status to their contacts, colleagues, or buddy list.

primary activities Activities directly related to the value chain process by which products and services are created, marketed, sold, and delivered.

primary key A field, or a group of fields, that makes each record unique in a table.

private branch exchange (PBX) Technology that manages all the office phone lines, voice mail, internal billing, call transfers, forwarding, conferencing, and other voice services.

process diagrams Graphical representations that trace how each process that a new information system will support operates from beginning to end.

product differentiation strategy A company strategy that involves adding special features to a product or unique add-ons for which customers are willing to pay more.

program management office (PMO) The part of an organization that oversees all the projects going on throughout the organization and provides project management training, software, and support.

programming language An artificial language used to write software that provides the instructions for the computer about how to accept information, process it, and provide output.

project A temporary activity launched for a specific purpose, to carry out a particular objective.

project charter A document that authorizes a project that includes a clear statement of objectives, estimated start and end dates, the names of the relevant people and their roles, a tentative budget, criteria for success, and other pertinent information.

project management A systematic approach to project planning, organizing, and managing resources, resulting in a project that successfully meets its objectives.

project management plan The road map and guide for executing a project that includes information such as an organizational chart, a detailed description of the work to be performed, information about the schedule, details about meetings and reviews, success metrics, and notations about any information systems or project monitoring tools that will be used.

project portfolio management A continuous process that oversees all the projects for an organization, selecting which projects to pursue and which ones to terminate.

proxy An intermediary server that receives and analyzes requests from clients and then directs them to their destinations; sometimes used to protect privacy.

public key encryption A security measure that uses a pair of keys, one to encrypt the data and the other to decrypt it. One key is public, widely shared with everyone, but the other is private, known only to the recipient.

R

radio frequency identification (RFID) A technology placed on tags with small chips equipped with a microprocessor, a tiny antenna to receive and transmit data, and sometimes a battery, that stores information on the tagged object's history.

random access memory (RAM) A computer's primary temporary storage area accessed by the CPU to execute instructions.

rapid application development (RAD) A strategy in which developers quickly bring up prototypes to share with end users, get feedback, and make corrections before building the fully functional version.

record A means to represent an entity, which might be a person, a product, a purchase order, an event, a building, a vendor, a book, a video, or some other "thing" that has meaning to people. The record is made up of attributes of that thing.

referential integrity A rule enforced by the database management system that ensures that every foreign key entry actually exists as a primary key entry in its main table.

relational database The widely used database model that organizes information in tables of records that are related to one another by linking a field in one table to a field in another table with matching data.

request for information (RFI) A request sent to software vendors containing a high level description of the information system an organization needs, so that vendors can describe their products that may fit.

request for proposal (RFP) An invitation to software companies to submit a formal proposal, including a detailed description of their products, services, and costs. The RFP details the requirements developed in the analysis phase and also includes information about the organization's architecture, staffing, and other relevant details.

requirements analysis The process by which stakeholders identify the features a new information system will need and then prioritize them as mandatory, preferred, or nonessential.

requirements definition document (RDD) A document that specifies the features a new information system should have, prioritized by stakeholders. It also includes assumptions and constraints that affect the system, such as the need to migrate and possibly reformat data from an existing system.

resource description framework (RDF) Part of the XML family of standards, RDF is used to describe online resources and their properties for the semantic web.

risk matrix A matrix that lists an organization's vulnerabilities, with ratings that assess each one in terms of likelihood and impact on business operations, reputation, and other areas.

rivalry among existing competitors The intensity of competition within an industry. Intense rivalry can reduce profitability in the industry due to price cutting or other competitive pressures. This is one of Porter's five competitive forces.

S

scalability A system's ability to handle rapidly increasing demand.

scope creep A term that refers to the way in which features are added in an uncontrolled way to a project, often without considering the impact on the budget or timeline.

Scrum An agile process for software development that relies on tightly knit, cohesive teams that do "sprints" of two to four weeks each.

search engine optimization (SEO) An Internet marketing strategy used to increase the quantity and quality of traffic from search engines, often by improving the site's position in result lists.

semantic web A web with meaning, in which online resources and their relationships can be read and understood by computers as well as human beings.

semi-structured information Information category that falls between structured and unstructured information. It includes facts and data that show at least some structure, such as web pages and documents, which bear creation dates, titles, and authors.

sentiment analysis A capability of specialized software to scan text input surveys, blogs, or other user-generated content and classify the opinions as pro, con, or neutral towards the company or product.

sequential architecture Website structure that guides visitors step by step through a transaction, survey, or learning module.

service-oriented architecture (SOA) A set of design principles in which systems are assembled from relatively independent software components, each of which handles a specific business service.

shadow system Smaller databases developed by individuals outside of the IT department that focus on their creator's specific information requirements.

Sharable Content Object Reference Model (SCORM) A set of standards that govern how e-learning objects communicate with the LMS on a technical level, so a user can import a SCORM-compliant object to any LMS that supports the standard.

shared workspace An area on a server in which team members can post documents, maintain membership lists, feature news and announcements, and collaborate on edits and updates.

shopping cart software Computer software that tracks purchases as customers navigate an e-commerce site and click "add to cart" as they go. The software tallies the purchase, calculates taxes based on the customer's location, computes shipping costs, and also posts a discount if the customer enters a valid promotional code.

single sign-on A gateway service that permits users to log in once with a single user ID and password to gain access to multiple software applications.

SMTP server Mail server using the simple mail transfer protocol; handles outgoing e-mail.

social capital The number and quality of all the relationships an organization's employees maintain, not just with one another, but with clients, customers, suppliers, and prospective employees.

social engineering The art of manipulating people into breaking normal information security procedures or divulging confidential information.

social network analysis (SNA) A technique that maps and measures the strength of relationships between individuals and groups, represented as nodes in the network. The measures provide insights into network clusters and the roles different people play as leaders or connecting bridges to other networks.

social networking sites Online communities of people who create profiles for themselves, form ties with others with whom they share interests, and make new connections based on those ties.

software The computer component that contains the instructions that directs computer hardware to carry out tasks.

software as a service (SaaS) A type of commercially available software which is owned, hosted, and managed by a vendor, and accessed by customers remotely, usually via the Internet.

source code All the statements that programmers write in a particular programming language to create a functioning software program.

stickiness The measurement of how long visitors linger at a website.

strategic enabler The role information systems play as tools to grow or transform the business, or facilitate a whole new business model.

structural capital The knowledge stored as documentation, often electronically, about business processes, procedures, policies, contracts, transactions, patents, research, trade secrets, and other aspects of the organization's operations.

structured information Facts and data that are reasonably orderly, or that can be broken down into component parts and organized into hierarchies.

Structured Query Language (SQL) A standard query language, widely used to manipulate information in relational databases.

subject matter expert The person on an e-learning development team who knows what content should be included in the course and possesses the content expertise.

supply chain management (SCM) Strategies that optimize the flow of products and services from their source to the customer.

Supply Chain Operations Reference (SCOR) A model that illustrates five processes that underlie the supply chain: (1) plan, (2) source, (3) make, (4) deliver, and (5) return. The model standardizes terminology to improve communications among suppliers and customers, and also draws attention to the interrelationships and trade-offs among all the chain's elements.

support activities Activities performed as part of the value chain model that are not primary; support activities include administration and management, human resources, procurement, and technology support.

sustaining technologies Technologies that offer improvements to streamline existing processes and give companies marginal advantages.

switching costs Costs that customers incur when they change suppliers.

system software The type of software that controls basic computer operations such as file management, disk storage, hardware interfaces, and integration with the application software.

systems development life cycle (SDLC) The process that describes the seven steps in the life of an information system: planning, analysis, design, development, testing, implementation, and maintenance.

systems integrator A consultant who ensures that the hardware and software components of an information system work together when they come from different vendors.

T

table A group of records for the same entity, such as employees. Each row is one record, and the fields of each record are arranged in the table's columns.

tacit knowledge Knowledge that encompasses the insights, judgment, creative processes, and wisdom that come from learning and long experience in the field, and from many trials and errors.

tag cloud A visual depiction of key words related to the search, with font size and position indicating relevance.

talent management module As part of the HCM system, the talent management module focuses on the employee life cycle, including recruitment, performance evaluations, career development, compensation planning, e-learning, and succession planning after retirement or departure.

TCP/IP Abbreviation for Transmission Control Protocol and Internet Protocol; used for Internet communications.

telepresence The impression created when remote participants in an interactive video meeting are almost life-sized and vividly clear; useful for sensitive negotiations.

text mining A technique used to analyze unstructured text that examines keywords, semantic structures, linguistic relationships, emotion-laden words, and other characteristics to extract meaningful business intelligence.

third-party cookies Small text files which a website leaves on a visitor's computer that are not deposited by the site being visited; used by ad networks to track customer behavior across all their client websites.

threat of new entrants The threat new entrants into an industry pose to existing businesses; the threat is high when start-up costs are very low and newcomers can enter easily. This is one of Porter's five competitive forces.

threat of substitutes The threat posed to a company when buyers can choose alternatives that provide the same item or service, often at attractive savings. This is one of Porter's five competitive forces.

top-level domain   The last string of letters in a URL that indicates the type of organization or country code.

transistor   A small electrical circuit made from a semiconductor material such as silicon.

twisted pair wires   The most common form of wired media, these wires consist of thin, flexible copper wires used in ordinary phones.

U

unified communications (UC)   Technology that integrates multiple communications channels and applications into a single interface, accessible from many different devices.

unified modeling language (UML)   A standardized approach to modeling an information system using graphics, symbols, and notations to improve communication and clarity.

unified procurement   An approach used by organizations in which they prefer systems from a single vendor, especially to avoid the need to build interfaces.

uniform resource locator (URL)   The unique global address for a web page or other resource on the Internet.

unstructured information   *Information that* has no inherent structure or order, and the parts can't be easily linked together.

usability   Refers to the ease with which a person can accomplish a goal using some tool, such as a website, a mobile phone, or a kiosk.

use case diagram   Diagrams that show how different types of users will interact with the system.

user-generated content (UGC)   The content contributed to a system by its users.

utilitarianism   An ethical system that judges whether an act is right or wrong by considering the consequences of the action, weighing its positive effects against its harmful ones.

utility software   The category of system software that includes programs to perform specific tasks that help manage, tune, and protect the computer hardware and software.

V

value chain model   A model developed by Michael Porter that describes the activities a company performs to create value, as it brings in raw resources from suppliers, transforms them in some way, and then markets the product or service to buyers.

version control software   A type of software that tracks versions of the source code during development, enforcing checkout procedures to prevent developers from writing over one another's files.

virtual reality   Describes what people experience when some of their sensory input is not from the real world, but from a computer-generated one. Technologies such as stereoscopic goggles and specially wired gloves enhance the illusion of physical immersion.

virtual world   A graphical, often 3-D, environment in which users can immerse themselves, interacting with virtual objects and one another using avatars.

virtualization   Cost-cutting approach to servers in which multiple operating systems run concurrently on a single physical PC server.

visibility   Describes how easily managers can track timely and accurate supply chain metrics.

Voice over IP (VoIP)   The technologies that make voice communications across networks using packet switching feasible, including over the Internet.

W

war room   A large area in which team members on the same project work closely together, surrounded by whiteboards, large digital displays, and other tools to facilitate impromptu meetings and smooth collaboration.

waterfall method   Method in which the systems development life cycle tasks occur sequentially, with one activity starting only after the previous one has been completed.

wavelength   The distance between one peak of an electromagnetic wave to the next.

Web 2.0   The second generation of web development that facilitates far more interactivity, end-user contributions, collaboration, and information sharing compared to earlier models.

web accessibility   Refers to how easily people with disabilities can access and use web resources.

web beacon (or web bug)   A tiny, invisible image, typically a single pixel with a unique identifier, used on websites to track visitors.

web browser   The software application that retrieves, interprets, and displays web resources.

web conferencing   Technology that supports online meetings or "webinars" via the Internet. Participants join the meeting from their own computers or smartphones.

web feed   Standardized and regularly updated output from a publisher, such as CNN or Weather.com, that can be embedded in a customized mashup.

what-if analysis   A simulation model, often constructed using Excel, which calculates the relationships between many variables; users can change some variables to see how others are affected.

wifi   Short for wireless fidelity; refers to a computer network in which connections rely on radio waves at frequencies of 2.4 GHz or 5 GHz for transmission.

wiki   Web software frequently used to build knowledge bases that allows users to add and edit interlinked web pages.

WiMax   Technology that relies on microwave transmissions to blanket large metropolitan areas from microwave towers, usually on buildings.

wireless router   A device connected to a computer network that emits signals from its antenna and enables wireless connectivity to the network.

workforce management module   As part of the HCM system, the workforce management module helps track time and attendance, sick leave, vacation leave, and project assignments.

World Wide Web Consortium (W3C)   An international body that establishes and publishes standards for programming languages used to create software for the web.

Index

Note: Page numbers in **bold** indicate definitions.